*Internationally renowned anthropologist **Kathleen Gough Aberle** died September 8, 1990. Just prior to her death, she had been leading the planning for a linkage program between UBC and the Vietnam National Center for Social Sciences. She was a Senior Research Associate with the Centre for Human Settlements at UBC and an Honourary Research Associate in the Department of Anthropology and Sociology.*

*From her work on multi-national kinship in India in 1961 to her 1990 book, Political Economy in Vietnam, she has been a model and inspiration for two generations of social scientists. Gough Aberle will be remembered by her many friends and colleagues in Canada and abroad for her commitment to sound research in support of social justice.*

*While she was ill, Dr. Aberle received copies of her last book on rural India which she asked the Centre for Human Settlements to distribute on her behalf to yourself and a few others. We are pleased to fulfill her request.*

# DATE DUE

| | | |
|---|---|---|
| MAR - 5 1994 | | |
| | | |
| | | |
| | | |
| | | |
| | | |
| | | |
| | | |
| | | |
| | | |
| | | |
| | | |
| | | |
| | | |
| | | |
| | | |
| | | |

*Cambridge Studies in Social Anthropology*

Editor: Jack Goody

38

RURAL SOCIETY IN SOUTHEAST INDIA

*For other titles in this series turn to page 457*

# Rural Society in Southeast India

KATHLEEN GOUGH
*University of British Columbia*

**Cambridge University Press**

Cambridge
London New York New Rochelle
Melbourne Sydney

Published by the Press Syndicate of the University of Cambridge
The Pitt Building, Trumpington Street, Cambridge CB2 IRP
32 East 57th Street, New York, NY 10022, USA
296 Beaconsfield Parade, Middle Park, Melbourne 3206, Australia



First published 1981

Printed in the United States of America

*Library of Congress Cataloging in Publication Data*

Gough, Kathleen, 1925–

Rural society in southeast India.

(Cambridge studies in social anthropology; no. 38)

Bibliography: p.

1. India – Rural conditions. 2. Villages – India – History. 3. Social classes – India. 4. Sociology, Rural. I. Title. II. Series.
HN683.G68 307.7′2′0954 80–27499
ISBN 0 521 23889 7 AACR2

# *Contents*

# *Preface*

This book is about changes in the political and economic structures of two villages in Thanjāvūr district of Tamiḷ Nāḍu State in southeast India. It is an attempt to view the villagers' changing internal class relations in the context of change in the larger structures of the district, state, and nation, in which some members of each village participate and which affect all of them.

I use the term "class" in this book in the Marxian sense. Thus, to quote Lenin's formulation, "classes are large groups of people distinguished by the place they occupy in an historically defined system of production, by their relations . . . vis à vis the means of production, by their role in the social organization of labour, and by the modes of obtaining and the importance of the share of the social wealth of which they dispose."[1]

The present volume concerns the two villages as they were when I first studied them in 1951–3. At that time, shortly after the independence of India, the villagers' lives were much affected by the impact of one-and-a-half centuries of British rule. In Part I, I deal with this heritage as it affected Thanjāvūr district as a whole, especially with reference to the economic impact of colonial rule and the resultant changes in the class structure. This involves examining Thanjāvūr's transition from a relatively self-contained and prosperous small kingdom to an agrarian hinterland that exported rice and labor to British plantations in southwest India, Ceylon, and Malaya and to the modern cities in the southern part of the Madras Presidency, which now forms the state of Tamiḷ Nāḍu.

In Part II, I describe socioeconomic life and relations in Kumbapeṭṭai, a village of northwest Thanjāvūr near the district capital, where I lived and worked between October 1951 and August 1952. In Part III, I make a comparative analysis of social structure in Kirippūr, a village of similar size near the port of Nāgapaṭṭaṇam in east Thanjāvūr, about sixty miles from Kumbapeṭṭai, where I lived from October 1952 to April 1953.

In a subsequent volume I hope to analyze the major changes in these villages between 1953 and 1976. In particular, my second book will treat the effects of Tamiḷ Nāḍu's land reform acts and of the "green revolution," which has been sponsored by the government of India since the mid 1960s. This work will be based on a restudy of the two villages carried out in 1976.

The theoretical significance of the present volume lies chiefly in its attempt to define more clearly the characteristics of rural class relations. On the one hand, we have many studies – including a few from this region – that describe changes in political and economic relations inside individual villages. On the other hand, theoretical debates have occurred about whether Indian agrarian relations in general are still precapitalist or "semifeudal," or whether they have been so affected by the market that they are to be regarded as capitalist relations. I hope to bridge these two kinds of study by showing that both in Kumbapeṭṭai and in Kirippūr, although production relations retained certain characteristics from pre-British times, a large part of the surplus product was siphoned off to individual merchant capitalists, foreign or indigenous capitalist corporations, or absentee landlords, who were themselves sellers of produce in the market and also often merchants, moneylenders, industrialists, or bureaucrats. This meant that in most villages, apart from a very small number of big landlords, the people as a whole, including the former aristocrats, fell within the lower ranks of a class pyramid that incorporated both urban and rural inhabitants. At the same time, many individuals who were born in the villages and counted themselves residents also belonged to the petty bourgeoisie or the working classes of cities or plantations through migrant labor. The various forms of incorporation of villagers into the wider class structure affected their internal power relations, status rankings, conflicts of interest, judicial processes, political party affiliations, and general world views. In Parts II and III, I explore both the internal political economies of the two villages and also these external relations, which are often omitted from village studies.

I hope that this work and my later book may have practical value for labor organizers in south India. Thus, I explore the conditions in which villages retain traditional hierarchies of authority through caste assemblies, and those in which such hierarchies disappear. I discuss conditions favorable to the rise of unions among agricultural laborers and the effects of such unions on the political consciousness of workers. I also consider obstacles to union formation, especially among tenant cultivators and smallholders. Finally, I note reasons why many village people, despite their poverty, support extremely conservative political groups. These and similar questions relate, of course, to the revolutionary potential of various classes of villagers, a potential yet to be realized in India.

I first arrived in Thanjāvūr in September 1951 at the age of twenty-six. Having already done fieldwork in Kēraḷa in 1947–9, I was familiar with south India and had learned some Tamiḷ. I outlined my research to the district officer, who introduced me to Mr. N. Kandaswāmy Piḷḷai, a well-known Tamiḷ scholar and poet. This gentleman took me home to his family for a fortnight, gave me valuable information and warm hospitality, and helped me to find a village suitable for my research.

After riding about the countryside of Thanjāvūr *tālūk* (administrative subdivision) for several days, I chose Kumbapeṭṭai for my first village study. The reasons for my choice were that the village was beautiful, it had a convenient building for rent, and its *panchāyat* president[2] and village headman welcomed me and offered help with my research. With fewer than 1,000 inhabitants, Kumbapeṭṭai was small enough for me to visit and take a census of every household, yet large enough to contain a full complement of castes. Before settling there, I had decided to study one village owned largely by Brahmans in the highly fertile western delta and one village owned by Non-Brahmans near the eastern seaboard; Kumbapeṭṭai met the first of these conditions.

I was housed in a *taṇṇīr pandal,* or watershed, a building ordinarily set aside as a religious charity to distribute drinking water to passersby in the hot summer months. The house had a single room about thirteen by seven feet, a wooden loft for my luggage, and a flat concrete roof, which I ascended by a bamboo ladder and on which I slept in the summer. The building was fronted by a narrow verandah that served as the village bus stop and meant that I had frequent visits from passengers. At my request, two small bamboo and palm-leaf shelters were put up by Harijan laborers behind my house in the coconut garden, one containing a trench for my latrine and the other a water butt and dipper for bathing. The villagers found it odd that I carried on these functions in private and especially that I bathed naked, but they were tactfully discreet and only a few small children occasionally peeped at me.

My cook and his sixteen-year-old son (my companion and handyman) lived in a rented, thatch-roofed house two doors from mine. Coming from Malabār, they had some difficulty in adapting to the lack of privacy in Thanjāvūr's densely populated streets, but they quickly learned Tamiḷ and became friendly with our neighbors. I found it an advantage to have "foreign" servants because they were not led to take sides in village disputes between castes. At the same time, they were treated politely as strangers like myself, and remained to some extent unplaced in the village hierarchy.

My house in Kumbapeṭṭai was ideally situated for fieldwork. Living in the center of a middle-ranking, Non-Brahman street of tenant farmers and traders, I was able to associate freely with my Non-Brahman neighbors. At the same time I was close to the Brahman street. I received daily visits from one or another Brahman leader and occasional ones from Brahman women. I visited the Brahman street almost every day and received a great deal of hospitality there.

The village's Harijans ("untouchable" agricultural laborers) lived outside the main village site, as is usual in Tamiḷ Nāḍu. Many of them passed by my house on their way home from work and stopped to chat, although the Brahmans prevented them from entering, in accordance with caste customs. From the garden behind my house I had an excellent view of agricultural operations in the paddy fields and went there almost daily to see the progress of the crops. My greatest difficulty was in persuading the landlords to let me visit the Harijan streets, an act strictly forbidden to Brahmans and avoided by Non-Brahmans. After a few weeks, however, I did persuade them that these visits were essential to my work, and I was allowed to come and go freely provided that I took a purifying bath before reentering my house or the Brahman street.

I lived in Kumbapeṭṭai for eleven months, apart from two visits to Madras and one to Kōḍaikkāṉal to write up my field notes and receive medical treatment for amoebic dysentery. In September 1952 I chose my second village, Kirippūr in East Thanjāvūr, with the help of Mrs. P. Rājālakshmi Naidū, a landlord who befriended me and took an interest in my work. Having toured East Thanjāvūr, I chose Kirippūr because, again, it was of convenient size. In addition it had a wide range of Non-Brahman and Harijan castes and was in the heartland of the Communist movement in East Thanjāvūr.

I lived in Kirippūr for six months, renting a house among the middle-ranking Naidūs of Upper Street. This tile-roofed dwelling comprised a large inner courtyard with a central square open to the sky, a kitchen, a storeroom, and a verandah. I was comfortable in this spacious, pleasant place and learned to write notes while surrounded by visitors. In Kirippūr I had no difficulty in visiting the Harijan streets, for the landlords had ceased to govern the village collectively and the Communist movement had broken down some of the barriers between castes.

My daily life in the villages consisted of visiting homes in turn; talking informally to the residents and collecting census data; writing down information from friends who visited me; watching agricultural and craft work; attending temple festivals, agricultural and household ceremonies, weddings, initiation rites, and funerals; going out to lunch or coffee when I was invited (as frequently happened); and making trips to nearby villages. Perhaps thirty times, I went by bus, train, or bullock cart to more distant towns and villages to see famous temples or festivals, interview *sannyāsis,* magicians, politicians, or government servants, or visit relatives of the villagers.

It is hard to write of the emotional side of fieldwork and of my relations with the villagers, for these were complex and deep and engaged the most private parts of my personality. My main goal was always to understand the social structure and religious life of the people rather than to help them or to take sides in their conflicts. I found, however, that the more I worked the more I became attached to particular people, especially of course those who entered into my project, worked hard with me, and opened their homes and lives to me. In the end, there were twenty-four people in Thanjāvūr to whom I was deeply attached and whom I regarded as personal friends, twenty of them in the two villages and four in towns.[3] There were also some fifty other people whom I knew well and to whom I had reason to be grateful,[4] as well as a host of others who helped me occasionally and showed me kindness. I am glad that throughout my stay no one behaved more than momentarily in an unfriendly way, and that in spite of occasional impatience or even anger on my part, I think I made no enemies. It continually made me happy that people high and low accepted me warmly and showed pleasure in my intention to study (as they put it) their "manners and customs."

As well as making close friends, I formed political opinions in Thanjāvūr. Both there and in Kēraḷa, I came to feel that the ruling Congress Party woud not make the radical, let alone revolutionary, changes that were needed to improve the lot of the common people, and that the Communist Party had policies that were more likely to bring these changes about. I was not completely on the side of the Communists because I thought, and still think, that they admired the Soviet Union too uncritically and were oblivious to the crimes of Stalin. Nevertheless, especially after living in Kirippūr, I felt that the Communists were essentially correct in their analysis of agrarian problems and that they were the only party that truly sought the welfare of the most downtrodden. Therefore, although I did not meet Communist Party members for discussions, I wished them well and sometimes defended their policies.

I do not think that my personal friendships or political values harmed my work or my relations with the villagers. Although I tried not to favor particular people to the neglect of others, I found it more honest to give my views and express my feelings when I was asked for them than to hide behind professional neutrality. Occasionally, when I saw what seemed unkind or irritating behavior toward women, the lower castes, or myself, I am afraid I lost my temper and gave opinions unasked.

Regarding customs, I behaved in Thanjāvūr like a visiting Englishwoman, which of course I was, while trying to fit in and not seriously infringe local usages that were accepted by everyone. I wore English dresses and shoes most of the time because I found them more convenient than *sāris* when walking, especially across rough fields. The villagers found these acceptable and indeed expected me to wear my native dress, although they were pleased when I dressed up in a *sāri* for a wedding or festival. Even in Kumbapeṭṭai I found it possible to eat meat and fish in my home without offending the Brahmans. They simply regarded this as one of my "caste customs," although they made it clear that they thought vegetarianism ethically superior. Some local habits came easily and seemed suitable, such as doffing shoes and washing my feet before entering a house, or rinsing my mouth after meals. I also respected the high castes' customs by not visiting their streets or temples when I was menstruating, although I did not remain indoors.

A few Brahmans asked me why I visited their temples and even received *prasādham* (the offerings first made to the diety and then distributed to the worshippers) when I was not a Hindū. I told them that I respected all religions, wanted to learn about Hinduism, and had a feeling of reverence for creation. This seemed to satisfy them, although it did not entirely satisfy me.

Eleven men in Kumbapeṭṭai and six in Kirippūr spoke fluent English. I naturally spent considerable time with them, gained much information from them, and often used them as interpreters. This, together with the landlords' power, gave my work a middle-class and upper-caste bias; I have more field notes from Brahmans and Veḷḷāḷars, and from English speakers of middle castes, than from others. Toward the end of my stay in Kumbapeṭṭai, however, I spoke and understood Tamiḻ well enough to manage most subjects in the language. In Kirippūr, where my best friend did not speak English and only six men did, I used Tamiḻ most of the time.

My fieldwork was weakest with regard to women. As a scholar and perhaps especially as a "Britisher," I found that the men tended to disregard my gender, draw me into their company, and monopolize my time. In the beginning, too, my relations with women were slight because none in the two villages spoke English. Most important, I was more interested in predominantly male pursuits, such as politics, village religion, land tenure, inheritance, trade, judicial processes, lineages, and caste assemblies, than in the domestic sphere to which women were largely confined. Of my twenty-four close friends, only seven were women, and of my fifty less close respondents, only nine. I did, however, come to know a few women well in each of the Brahman, Non-Brahman, and Harijan groups.

In most respects my class position and social status were higher than those of the people of Kumbapeṭṭai and Kirippūr. My stipend was £400, or about 5,334 rupees (Rs.) a year. The wealthiest landlords in Kumbapeṭṭai had incomes of about Rs. 10,000 a year for a whole family, so that I was near the top of the income scale and could afford two manservants, a housemaid, and a research assistant. My university education and experience of travel gave me prestige in the eyes of the villagers. So, perhaps, did the fact that I was British, for some villagers still had some awe of the British left over from colonial times. Because doctors, politicians, authors, lawyers, rich landlords, and government servants sometimes called on me, the village people no doubt assumed that I had influence, if not power. It is possible that as a result some were more willing to oblige me than they might have been if I had been a poorer person with fewer influential friends. Certainly, my status commanded respect, and, except in the case of the wealthiest landlords, a degree of deference. Even so, I had very little actual power. In Kirippūr, for example, the village accountant refused me access to the land records, and I was never able to get permission to see them from a higher authority nor even to buy a copy of the register showing the size and quality of the fields. Instead, one friendly landlord gave me his private copy of the register, and another paced the fields with me and gave me the names of every owner and cultivating tenant. In Kumbapeṭṭai and the neighboring villages, however, the headmen and accountants took an interest in my work and helped me to copy the records. On the whole, I think that most people gave me information because they liked talking about their lives and took an interest in their village's organization.

When I had worked in Kumbapeṭṭai for several weeks, Srī M. Bālu Iyer, then aged nineteen, began to help me with translations from Tamiḷ literature and from written accounts of customs, myths, and festivals, and with seeking out useful books, collecting newspaper clippings, and doing census work. I engaged him as my research assistant, and he worked indefatigably for me in 1951–3 and 1975–80. During my early fieldwork in Kumbapeṭṭai, Srī T. P. Kandaswāmy Iyer gave me great help as an informant and interpreter without remuneration. He became my research assistant in 1976, and he and Srī Bālu have helped me from a distance in preparing this book. I am deeply grateful to these friends for their hard work and kindness over many years. In Kirippūr in the past four years I have received help from two other assistants, Srī K. Bragadeesan and Srī K. Manōharan, both of whom I wish to thank.

I have transliterated Tamiḻ words by the traditional method commonly used in south India.[5] In an effort to protect my informants' identity and privacy, I have used pseudonyms for all places and people except well-known towns and public figures.

Writing up a field study conducted more than two decades ago has both drawbacks and advantages. On the one hand, the data were collected with somewhat different theoretical concerns in mind than those that are prominent today, so that there are some factual gaps. On the other hand, several implications of my data that did not occur to me at the time have since become clear as a result of other studies and of my own intellectual history. I have tried to develop these insights, while at the same time omitting from this volume information on events since 1953. In this way I hope to compare and contrast quite clearly the relationships and circumstances of the early 1950s with those of the mid-1970s, to be described in my later work.

If this book has merit, credit must go to many people and influences. The late Professor J. H. Hutton, who first instructed me in the anthropology of India and whose interests were historical and evolutionary, encouraged in me a fascination with sociocultural origins that I have never been able to suppress, although I have tried not to let it run away with me in this study. Among modern social anthropologists, I owe to the late Professors E. E. Evans-Pritchard and Max Gluckman, and above all to Professor Meyer Fortes, my training in "structural-functional" analysis, the dominant influence on my Thanjāvūr fieldwork, and to Professors M. N. Srinivas, Louis Dumont, David Mandelbaum, and many others, basic insights into the Hindū caste system and Indian village structures.

The late Professor Leslie A. White and his successors in American cultural evolutionary and cultural ecological studies, especially my husband, David F. Aberle, gave me an understanding of major stages of cultural evolution and epochs of cultural history, and so helped me to put in perspective both Thanjāvūr's classical civilization and the modern period of colonial dominance and capitalist development. Since 1957, the works of Marx and of certain Marxist writers have especially influenced my approach to social science generally and to India in particular. For general orientation, I am especially indebted to the work of Paul Sweezy, Paul Baran, Harry Magdoff, Rāmkrishna Mukherjee, André Gunder Frank, A. R. Desai, E. M. S. Namboodiripāḍ, Hamza Alavi, Joan Mencher, Immanuel Wallerstein, the late Saghir Ahmad, Mohan Rām, and Mythily Shivarāman.

I owe my information to the people of Kumbapeṭṭai and Kirippūr and especially to personal friends in Thanjāvūr district, who gave me inestimable help. In addition to my research assistants, I am indebted to Srī T. S. Ananda Natēsha Iyer, Srī R. Bālaya Kurukkal, the late Srī C. Kalyānasundaram Mudaliar, Mrs. P.

Rājālakshmi Naidū, the late Thiru N. Kandaswāmy Piḷḷai, Srī T. Janaki Rāman, and the late Dr. E. K. Menon, then Civil Surgeon at the Thanjāvūr Hospital.

The field research on which my book is based was carried out with the aid of a British Treasury Studentship in Foreign Languages and Cultures. Funds for later fieldwork, library research, and writing were granted by the Canada Council, the Humanities and Social Sciences Research Council of Canada, and the Shāstri Indo-Canadian Institute. To all these bodies I wish to express my thanks.

I am grateful to Cambridge University Press and to the editors of *Review* and of *The Economic and Political Weekly* for permission to reprint sections of articles, which appear in Chapters 6, 15, and 17.

The manuscript was typed by Mrs. Hilary Blair and Mrs. Jean Webb and the maps made by Miss Deborah Yee and Srī K. Manōharan. I am indebted to Mr. Frank Flynn for statistical advice and computer work connected with Chapter 5, and to my husband for his patient advice and encouragement. I wish to thank all of them.

Most of all, I am grateful to my cook, the late Srī M. V. Rāman, and his son, Srī M. R. Velayudhan, whose care and kindness helped to make the years of my work in India among the happiest in my life.

K. G.

# PART I: THANJĀVŪR

# 1 The District

## Towns and Temples

Thanjāvūr district lies in the extreme southeast of India, jutting out into the Bay of Bengal. In 1951, three years after the independence of India, it was one of twenty-six districts of the state of Madras (see Map 1). The neighboring districts were South Ārcot to the north, Tiruchirappalli to the northwest and west, and Rāmanāthapuram in the extreme southwest. To the southwest, the small state of Pudukoṭṭai, formerly governed by a Rāja, had recently been incorporated into Tiruchirappalli district. In 1956 the eleven Tamiḷ-speaking southern districts of Madras were combined with Kānya Kumāri in the extreme southwest to form a new state, which in 1962 was given its ancient name of "Tamiḷ Country" or Tamiḷ Nāḍu.

Thanjāvūr's nearest large city was Madras, the state capital, as the crow flies 160 miles north-northwest of Thanjāvūr municipality, the district's capital town. Tiruchirappalli (population 218,921 in 1951), sixty-six miles west of Thanjāvūr, and Madurai (population 361,781 in 1951), one hundred miles southwest, were the two other large centers visited by the elite and the more adventurous working people. Tiruvannāmalai in North Ārcot, Tirupati in Chittur, Chidambaram in South Ārcot, Kānchipuram in Chingleput, Rāmēswaram in Rāmanāthapuram, and Tiruchendūr in Tirunelvēli were religious centers to which the devout of Thanjāvūr, especially Brahmans, made pilgrimages.

Thanjāvūr municipality, once a magnificent capital several times its modern size, had a population of 100,680 in 1951 (see Map 2). It was a sacred center at least 1,000 years old, renowned for its Brahadeeswara Temple, which was constructed by the Chōḷa King Rājarāja I in the tenth and eleventh centuries. Thanjāvūr's other main towns were Kumbakōnam (population 91,643 in 1951), a famed religious center twenty-two miles from Thanjāvūr city on the banks of the Kāvēri, and the port of Nāgapaṭṭaṇam (population 57,854 in 1951) seventy-five miles east of the capital. Other minor ports, from northeast to southwest, included Tirumullaivāsal, Tranquēbar (once a Danish possession), Nāgore, Vēlānganni, Point Calimere, and Adirāmpaṭṭaṇam. The larger port of Kāraikkal, in the center of the east coast, was still a colony of the French.

Like its major cities, Thanjāvūr's smaller towns and villages contained a number of ancient, famous, and wealthy religious centers, for the region had more Brahman priests and Hindū temples than any other district of south India.

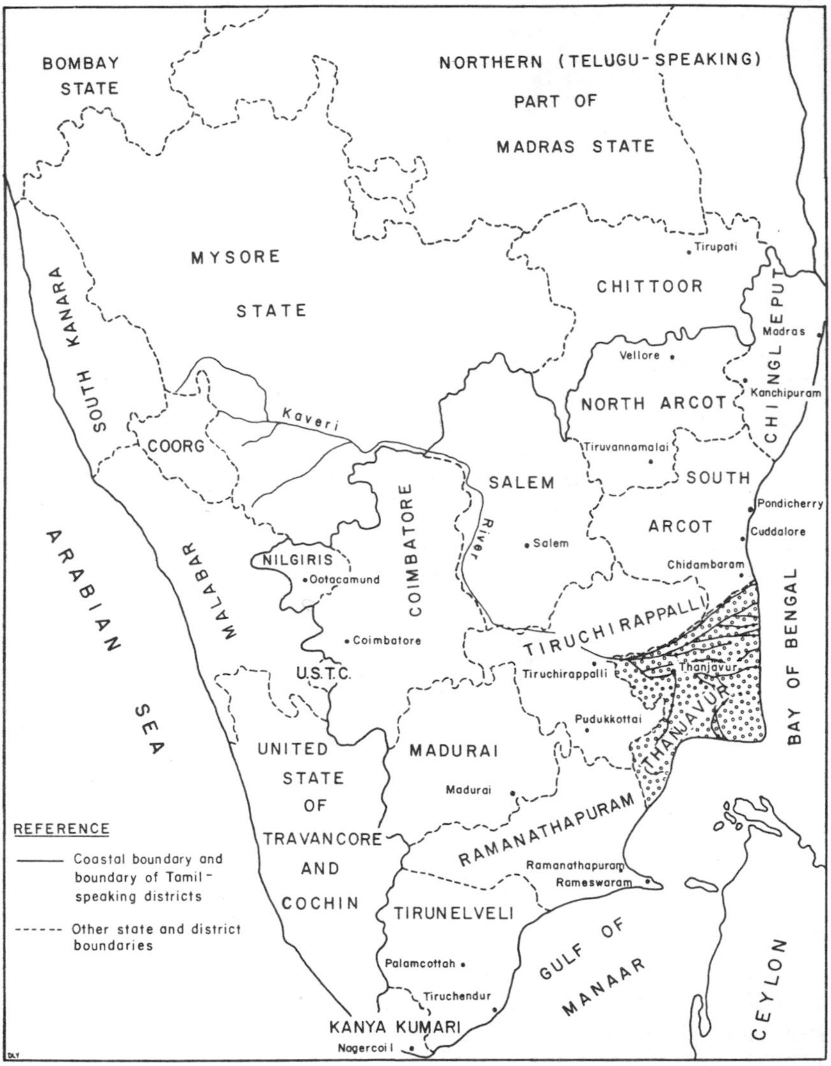


Map 1. Location of Tamiḻ Nāḍu area and Thanjāvūr district, 1952.

The Chōḷa temples (ninth to thirteenth centuries) of Tiruvaiyāru, Tiruvidaimarudūr, Vaideeswarankōvil, Tiruvārur, Āvadayarkōvil, and Dārāsuram, the Subramania temple at Swāmimalai, and the Vijayanagar and Nāyak temples (fifteenth to seventeenth centuries) of Maṉṉārguḍi, Tirukkaṇṇapuram, and Kumbakōṇam, were among the more impressive and drew thousands to their annual festivals.

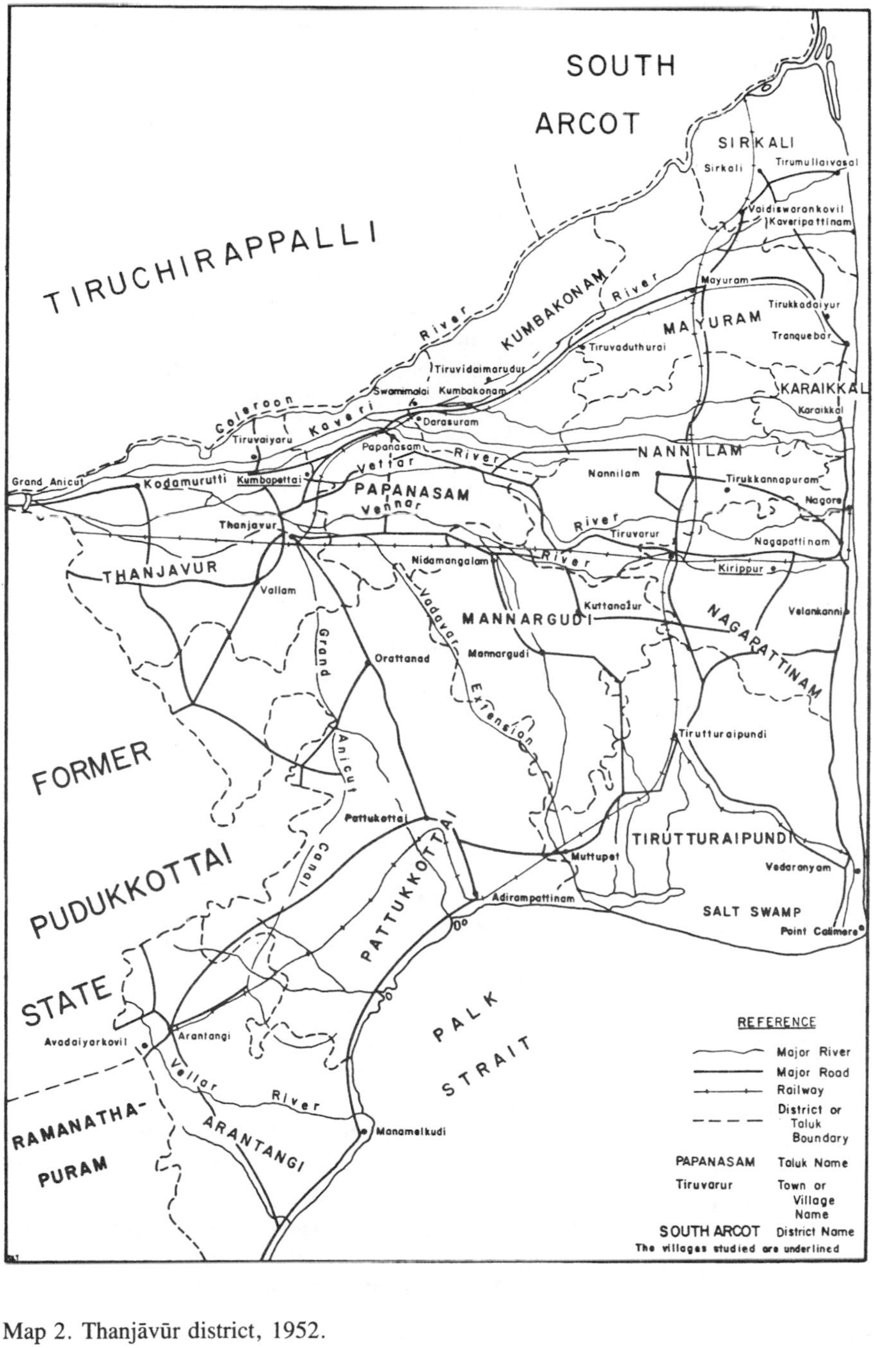


Map 2. Thanjāvūr district, 1952.

The massive, awe-inspiring stone towers of these numerous temples, intricately carved with mythological themes, and the beauty of the stone idols and art-metal figurines of the deities within them, lent grandeur and solemnity to Thanjāvūr's towns and countryside in spite of the district's modern poverty and partial desolation.

## Ecology, Density, and Productivity

With an area of 3,738 square miles and a population of 2,983,769, Thanjāvūr was the Tamiḻ Country's second most densely populated district in 1951. It had 798 people to the square mile.[1] The district's high density was even more remarkable considering that 81 percent of the people lived in villages and only 19 percent in towns of more than 5,000. Thanjāvūr's high density was attributable to its extensive irrigation and wet rice agriculture, more productive per acre than any other grain crop in south India. In what later became Tamiḻ Nāḍu as a whole, about 42 percent of the gross cultivated acreage was irrigated in the early and mid-1950s. About 31.5 percent of the gross sown area, including part of the unirrigated land, was used for rice, but rice constituted 67 percent of the area's food grains, the rest being chiefly millets. The greater part of the region's rice was grown in the four coastal districts of Chingleput, North and South Ārcot, and Thanjāvūr, together with the central part of Tiruchirappalli. In 1953 Thanjāvūr supplied 21 percent of the rice grown in Tamiḻ Nāḍu, while forming only 8 percent of its population and having only 6 percent of its area.[2] In addition, part of Thanjāvūr's rice crop was normally exported to the west coast Malayālam-speaking areas of Malabar (then a district of Madras Province) and the united state of Travancore and Cochin.

Most of Thanjāvūr lay in the delta of the Kāvēri, south India's most important and sacred river, often called the "southern Ganges." The river rose in the Western Ghāts and flowed through Mysore, Salem, and Tiruchirappalli, entering Thanjāvūr in the northwest of the district. Its major subsidiary, the Coleroon, then branched off to form the northern boundary between Thanjāvūr and the districts of Tiruchirappalli and South Ārcot (see Map 2). The main stream of the Kāvēri flowed a few miles south of the border and reached the ocean at Kāvēripaṭṭaṇam. This village was the Chōḷa kingdom's illustrious capital in the first centuries of the Christian era.

Between the northwest corner of the district and Kāvēripaṭṭaṇam, most of the Kāvēri's waters became dispersed into numerous branches and channels that irrigated the greater part of the district and finally reached the sea. In the northern part of the district the main irrigation channels dated from at least the ninth century, some of them, indeed, from the beginning of the Christian era in the period of the first Chōḷa kingdom.

The "old delta," which predated British rule, watered about half the district in 1951. This half formed a triangle running from the northwest corner of the district to the mouth of the Coleroon, southward down the coast to Point Calimere, and diagonally across the district to the northwest corner again. This half of Thanjāvūr was the more fertile, its most fecund and sacred area being near the banks of the Kāvēri in the northwestern *tālūks* of Thanjāvūr, Pāpaṉāsam, and Kumbakōṇam.

The southwestern half of the district was formerly a largely unirrigated region of dry cultivation, with a slightly elevated plateau in Paṭṭukkoṭṭai and the southern portions of Thanjāvūr and Maṉṉārguḍi *tālūks*. The southwestern half, however, was partly irrigated in 1934 by the completion of the Grand Anicut and Vadavar canals, and became known as the "new delta." Although improved, the new delta remained less fertile and densely populated than the old delta region. Irrigation in the old delta was also improved in the 1930s by the British government's construction of the Mēttūr dam in Salem, which regulated the river's flow. The extreme southeast of the district in Tirutturaipūndi *tālūk* was uncultivated and formed a salt swamp.

The greater part of the Thanjāvūr was almost completely flat, its monotony broken only by clumps of palm trees, by the brick or mud dwellings of its tightly settled, nucleated towns and villages, and by the massive stone structures of its great Hindū temples. For much of the year the villages emerged as small brown islands surrounded by oceans of green wet paddy fields. From early March to late June, however, the Kāvēri's water was conserved at the Mēttūr dam and the district's fields and river beds dried up. This was the hottest season, when the temperature might reach 116 to 120 degrees Fahrenheit. With little agricultural work and with brightly moonlit nights for half of each month, the people used this season for the grandest of their religious festivals. Some of them required the deities of seven or more temples in a region to be carried along the roads or the dry river beds from village to village in colorful processions, with music, dancing, and palanquins.

The temperature of Thanjāvūr ranges from an average maximum of eighty-one degrees in January and February to ninety-seven degrees in May and June, the average minimum ranging from seventy-one degrees in January to eighty degrees in May. The average rainfall is forty-six inches, most of it falling in the northeast monsoon in October and November, with lighter showers in July and August.[3]

Because the delta rises very little above sea level and the rivers and channels are heavily silted, floods are a major problem, especially during occasional cyclones in the coastal regions. On November 30, 1952, during my first fieldwork, for example, a cyclone hit the whole Madras coast and devastated trees, buildings, roads, and railroads. About 300,000 houses were destroyed, and ocean flooding ruined crops up to ten miles inland. Three hundred and forty-nine people were reported killed and thousands went hungry for several days until relief supplies arrived. Thirteen villages experienced a cholera epidemic in the breakdown of sanitation.[4] The district has since experienced devastating cyclones in 1961 and 1977, and a lesser one in 1978.

### Transport

Compared with south India as a whole, Thanjāvūr's transport and communications in 1951 were efficient. The railway connected Thanjāvūr city with the major towns and ports of south India and with all the *tālūk* capitals and other centers within the district (see Map 2). Bus services on paved roads linked the towns and the larger villages, and dirt roads, suitable for bullock carts, the smaller villages. Except for rare long journeys, most of the landlords and more prosperous peasants still traveled by bullock cart in 1951; most of the tenant farmers and laborers, on foot. Small trading boats plied often between Thanjāvūr and Ceylon, while European cargo ships visited Nāgapaṭṭaṇam and Kāraikkal.

### Historical Background

The Tamiḷ Chōḷa kingdom had arisen in Thanjāvūr's delta by the third century B.C. From about 100 to 250 A.D., the famous Sangam Age, it became a brilliant center of Hindū, Buddhist, and Jain civilization and literacy. During this period, the basic structure of royal government, the systems of irrigation and land tax, the multicaste settlement patterns of towns and villages, the religious supremacy of the Brahmans, and the presence of certain other castes such as the Paṟayars, were established much as in later centuries. So were many familiar cultural features, among them the Vēdic ceremonies of the Brahmans and the worship of Siva as the bisexual Ardanārīswara, of his son Murugan or Subramania, and of Vishnū as Rāma and Krishṇa. The kinship system of the dominant castes was already patrilineal. As in later centuries, aristocratic widows sometimes burned themselves on the husband's funeral pyre. Reincarnation, and the effects of *karma* in successive births, were established beliefs.[5]

This first heyday of the Chōḷas, however, was characterized by a joyous faith in good living and an enjoyment by all castes of such pleasures as meat, fish, and alcohol. The robust optimism of the period declined with the end of the Sangam Age, probably with the ascendence of Buddhism. Thanjāvūr's literature and culture thereafter acquired its characteristic pessimism and emphasis on the sin and sorrow of desire, the virtues of nonviolent submission, and the need to escape the chain of rebirths through repression of the will to live. Although Buddhism declined in the eighth century with the rise of the Advāita philosophy of the Hindū Sankarāchārya and the dominance of Saivism, Thanjāvūr's Brahmanical Hindūism itself became permeated with the Buddhist themes of nonviolence and elimination of desire.

The first Chōḷa kingdom fell into a dark age in the late third century A.D. In the sixth century it reemerged as a tributary province of the Tamiḷ Pallavas of Kānchipuram. The Chōḷas regained their independence about 850 A.D., and reached the height of their expansion in the tenth and eleventh centuries. For about two centuries they commanded tribute from all the kingdoms south of the Tungabhadra, and at times extended their sway north to the Ganges and south to Ceylon, to Burma and Indochina, and to the Srī Vijaya empire of Malaya and Indonesia. Thanjāvūr's Brahman and Veḷḷāḷar bureaucracy, many of its great temples, and most of its towns and villages, were established in this period.

The empire declined in the twelfth century and Thanjāvūr became tributary to the rising Tamiḷ Pāndhya kingdom of Madurai in the early thirteenth century. In the early fourteenth century, it was briefly conquered by Muslim invaders from the Delhi Sultanate, and later, in 1365, became feudatory to the Telugu empire of Vijayanagar. By 1534 the Chōḷa dynasty had disappeared. The kingdom, reduced to the limits of the present district, came under the rule of Nāyaks, Telugu governors appointed from Vijayanagar. The Nāyaks declared their independence of Vijayanagar in the 1620s, but Thanjāvūr was again conquered, this time by Maratha invaders from Bijapūr in 1674. Except for brief invasions by Muslims from South Ārcot (the southwesternmost extension of the Mōghul empire) in the 1690s and 1770s and from Mysore in 1781, the Maratha dynasty held Thanjāvūr until its annexation by the British East India Company in 1779.[6] The kingdom was, however, feudatory to the Nawāb of Ārcot from the 1690s and indirectly to the East India Company from 1771. After the annexation of 1799 the British pensioned the Maratha royal family, and arbitrarily declared it extinct in 1855.[7] Thanjāvūr or Tanjore became a revenue district of the Madras Presidency of British India. With India's independence in 1947 it remained part of the same multilingual region, named the Madras Province, until the separation of the smaller, Tamiḷ-speaking Madras state in 1956.

### Regional and Local Units

Thanjāvūr district was governed by a district Collector (of revenue) or district officer under the government of Madras, assisted by a district board. Thanjāvūr municipality, the largest town, was the focus of administration relating to such matters as revenue collection, the judiciary, the police, medical services and the government hospital, education, registration, transport, post and telegraph, and record keeping. Apart from the French port of Kāraikkal containing 110 villages, the district was divided into eleven administrative divisions called *tālūks*, – Thanjāvūr, Pāpaṉāsam, Kumbakōṇam, Māyuram, Sirkāli, Naṉṉilam, Nagapaṭṭaṇam, Tirutturaipūṇḍi, Maṉṉārguḍi, Paṭṭukkoṭṭai and Aranṭāngi (see Map 2) – each headed by a town of the same name as the *tālūk*. The *tālūks* were grouped into six revenue divisions. In each *tālūk*, a subordinate officer called a *tahsildar* was in charge of revenue collection and other matters.

Within the *tālūk* the basic social units were the towns (*paṭṭaṇam*) and villages (*ūr* or *grāmam*). In 1951, 34 percent of Thanjāvūr's 2,280 towns and villages contained fewer than 500 people, 24 percent between 500 and 1,000, 27 percent between 1,000 and 2,000, 13 percent between 2,000 and 5,000, and 1 percent between 5,000 and 10,000. Nine towns numbered 10,000 to 20,000 people, three (Māyuram, Tiruvārur, and Maṉṉārguḍi) 20,000 to 50,000, two (Kumbakōṇam and Nāgapaṭṭaṇam) 50,000 to 100,000; only Tanjore municipality had slightly more than 100,000.[8] Most of the villages under 500 were situated in the southwest upland tracts. Only the six largest towns were constituted as municipalities.

Each village was led by a village headman (locally called VHM), employed by the government under the authority of the Collector. The village headman was almost invariably of the dominant caste of landlords; his office tended to be hereditary. His duties included revenue collection, reporting of births, marriages, deaths, and serious crimes, and the settlement of minor disputes. He was attended by two servants or *veṭṭis*, usually of Non-Brahman caste, and commanded a *talayāri*, or village watchman, who might be a low-ranking Non-Brahman, Muslim, Christian, or Harijan. Second to the village headman ranked the *karṇam,* or village accountant, who kept the village map and land records, recorded the payment of revenue, surveyed fields in cases of boundary disputes, and recorded land sales. The *karṇam* was often appointed from another town or village, had stricter educational qualifications than the headman, and was usually a Brahman.

Beginning in the 1920s, a small number of the larger villages in South India were constituted as *panchāyats*, units of local government concerned with public works and economic development. Under the Madras Village Panchayats' Act of 1950, which went into effect in April 1951, all villages of over five hundred were in theory constituted as *panchāyats* and elected three-year boards composed of five to fifteen members, headed by a *panchāyat* president and vice-president. Each board had a reserved seat for a Harijan member. The elections were by universal adult franchise. The entire electorate voted for the president, while the vice-president was selected by the board. Whereas *panchāyats* had formerly come under the joint authority of district boards, local boards, and an inspector of municipal councils, they were now brought under the Inspector of Municipal Councils and the local boards without reference to the district board, and were responsible to the Collector only in emergencies. Throughout India, the modern *panchāyat* was a creation of the new Congress Government with its focus on community development projects as a means of "uplifting" the villages and of carrying out economic and social development.

The *panchāyat* board's duties included constructing and repairing roads, bridges, culverts, and drains, lighting public places, cleaning streets, and removing garbage. It was expected to construct public latrines, maintain cremation and burial grounds, sink and repair public wells, and take preventive and remedial measures in cases of epidemics. It was at liberty to plant trees, maintain a slaughterhouse or a village market, regulate village-owned buildings, open an elementary school or a library, run a dispensary or a maternity and child welfare center, provide veterinary aid, set up a public radio or a sports club, or build a playground. *Panchāyat* boards were given control of unreserved forests, village roads, minor irrigation works not controlled by the Public Works Department, watercourses, springs, ponds, or "tanks," and other communal property. The *panchāyat* was free to administer charitable endowments such as sheds (*chattrams*) to provide shelter or drinking water to passersby.

The work of the *panchāyat* board was financed by village taxes on houses, professions, vehicles, and transfers of property. The board was at liberty to levy a special additional land cess of 1.56 percent of the village's land revenue to be charged to the land owners, and to levy fees on sales of commercial crops, pilgrim taxes, fishery rents, ferry tolls, and market charges. Large *panchāyats*

Table 1.1. *Gross paddy and gross irrigated acreages as percentages of gross sown acreage, selected years, 1875–1954*

| Year | Gross sown acreage (1) | Gross paddy acreage (2) | (2) as % of (1) (3) | Gross irrigated acreage (4) | (4) as % of (1) (5) |
|---|---|---|---|---|---|
| 1875–6 | 1,264,965 | 946,647 | 74.8 | [a] | [a] |
| 1905–6 | 1,392,552 | 1,074,152 | 77.1 | 966,903 | 69.4 |
| 1910–11 | 1,437,358 | 1,087,618 | 75.7 | 990,308 | 68.9 |
| 1912–13 | 1,449,973 | 1,097,630 | 75.7 | 1,000,116 | 69.0 |
| 1920–1 | 1,472,792 | 1,133,301 | 76.9 | 993,231 | 67.4 |
| 1930–1 | 1,565,170 | 1,098,636 | 70.2 | 962,142 | 61.5 |
| 1940–1 | 1,531,484 | 1,229,172 | 80.3 | 1,084,851 | 70.8 |
| 1944–5 | 1,729,189 | 1,361,180 | 78.7 | 1,172,839 | 67.8 |
| 1946–7 | 1,668,818 | 1,326,302 | 79.5 | 1,157,268 | 69.3 |
| 1950–1 | 1,674,880 | 1,332,478 | 79.6 | 1,322,802 | 79.0 |
| 1951–2 | 1,643,529 | 1,336,493 | 81.3 | 1,336,628 | 81.3 |
| 1952–3 | 1,587,613 | 1,285,036 | 80.9 | 1,290,538 | 81.3 |
| 1953–4 | 1,678,246 | 1,353,790 | 80.7 | 1,364,613 | 81.3 |

[a]Not available.
*Source:* T. Venkasami Row, *A Manual of the District of Tanjore in the Madras Presidency*. Madras: Government Press, 1883, p. 648; F. R. Hemingway, *Gazetteer of the Tanjore District,* Vol. 2, pp. 10–11; Madras District Gazetteers, 1906. Madras: Government Press; P. K. Nambiar, *District Census Handbook, Thanjavur,* Vol. 1, pp. 556–8; *Census of India, 1961,* Vol. 9, Part 10–5, Director of Stationery and Printing, Madras, 1965.

with more than 5,000 members were entitled to 12.5 percent of the state land revenue and to contributions from the district board for elementary education.[9]

## Crops

In 1949–50 Thanjāvūr had a net field crop area of 1,376,325 acres, of which 1,173,925, or 85 percent was irrigated, making it suitable for wet rice fields. The acreage used to grow two or more crops a year was 289,932 (21 percent of the total), 157,237 acres (13 percent of the total area) being irrigated twice a year and therefore suitable for double cropping of paddy.[10] Altogether the district had a gross field crop acreage of about 1,554,400, that is, a total acreage for the cultivation and harvesting of one or another crop in the course of a year.

Paddy cultivation covered roughly 80 percent of Thanjāvūr's gross cultivated field acreage. About 95 percent of the gross paddy acreage was wet, the 5 percent of dry acreage being mainly in the upland tracts of south Maṉṉārguḍi and Paṭṭukkoṭṭai *tālūks* (see Table 1.1). Paddy had been Thanjāvūr's main crop

Table 1.2. *Net cropped and net irrigated acreages and paddy production, selected years, Thanjāvūr district, 1773–1954*

| Year | Net cropped acreage (1) | Net irrigated acreage (mainly paddy) (2) | (2) as % of (1) (3) | Gross paddy produce (metric tons)[a] (4) |
|---|---|---|---|---|
| 1773–4 | | 572,549 | | 281,919 |
| 1774–5 | | 579,332 | | 291,574 |
| 1775–6 | | 578,664 | | 230,969 |
| 1776–7 | | 585,454 | | 309,848 |
| 1777–8 | | 433,593 | | 308,226 |
| 1778–9 | | | | 289,308 |
| 1779–80 | | | | 301,526 |
| 1780–1 | | | | 45,594 |
| 1781–2 | | | | 39,576 |
| 1782–3 | | | | 110,413 |
| 1783–4 | | | | 154,128 |
| 1784–5 | | | | 188,737 |
| 1785–6 | | | | 174,734 |
| 1786–7 | | | | 190,599 |
| 1787–8 | | | | 189,805 |
| 1788–9 | | 337,302[b] | | 205,294 |
| 1789–90 | | | | 230,691 |
| 1790–1 | | | | 234,834 |
| 1792–3 | | | | 253,937 |
| 1793–4 | | | | 245,892 |
| 1794–5 | | | | 263,741 |
| 1795–6 | | | | 261,375 |
| 1800–1 | | 530,215 | | 308,441 |
| 1801–2 | | 542,185 | | 297,303 |
| 1802–3 | | 419,206 | | 167,364 |
| 1803–4 | | 429,317 | | 197,251 |
| 1804–5 | | 472,681 | | 262,197 |
| 1805–6 | | 552,807 | | 293,764 |
| 1806–7 | 649,534 | 451,561 | 69.5 | 291,572 |
| 1824–5 | | | | 371,170 |
| 1832–3 | | 515,499 | | 382,892 |
| 1833–4 | | 503,543 | | 371,045 |
| 1836–7 | | 491,276 | | 342,206 |
| 1852–3 | 937,000 | 708,000 | 75.6 | |
| 1857–8 | 835,032 | | | 402,936 |
| 1867–71 | | | | 531,322[c] |
| 1871–5 | | | | 606,144[c] |

Table 1.2 (*cont.*)

| Year | Net cropped acreage (1) | Net irrigated acreage (mainly paddy) (2) | (2) as % of (1) (3) | Gross paddy produce (metric tons)[a] (4) |
|---|---|---|---|---|
| 1875–6 | 1,042,061 | 745,151 | 71.5 | |
| 1893–4 | | | | 550,836 |
| 1905–6 | 1,282,142 | 572,549 | 75.4 | |
| 1910–11 | 1,331,941 | 990,308 | 74.4 | |
| 1950–1 | 1,403,183 | 1,207,214 | 86.0 | 812,698 |
| 1951–2 | 1,393,756 | 1,212,027 | 80.0 | 918,903 |
| 1952–3 | 1,361,120 | 1,134,677 | 83.4 | 826,551 |
| 1953–4 | 1,406,905 | 1,199,582 | 85.3 | 1,008,177 |

[a]Where necessary, Tanjorean *kalams* and British tons have been converted into metric tons.
[b]Average for 1788, 1789, 1793, and 1794.
[c]Average.
*Sources:* T. V. Row, *A Manual of the District,* pp. 45, 648; F. R. Hemingway, *Gazetteer,* 1, p. 190, 2, pp. 10–11; Census of India, 1891–1961, Madras Volumes, *passim; District Census Handbook, Thanjāvūr,* 1961, 1, pp. 556–8; *Technoeconomic Survey of Madras,* Government of Madras, 1960, p. 94; C.W.B. Zacharias, *Madras Agriculture,* Madras University, Economics Series, No. 6, 1950, Appendix 1.

from time immemorial; the channel irrigation of the delta with its rich silt was ideal for this high-calorie grain. In the early 1800s when British rule began, however, only 70 percent of Thanjāvūr's net cultivated acreage was irrigated. Wet paddy must therefore have covered a smaller proportion of the area. It is likely that although the total acreage was much smaller, a greater proportion of other field crops was grown, in addition to an undoubtedly greater extent of pasturage. The increase in irrigation, paddy acreage, and to a lesser extent, in double cropping, in the nineteenth and twentieth centuries, illustrated in Tables 1.1 and 1.2, was both cause and effect of Thanjāvūr's growing importance as an exporter of rice to the British plantation regions of Malaya and Ceylon (see Chapter 6).

During the Grow More Food campaign of World War II, the Madras government had introduced a small quantity of chemical fertilizers to supplement the traditional organic manures, and after independence it had begun to encourage the adoption of hybrid seeds, composting, and improved green manures. By 1951, however, their impact had been minimal and had been more than offset by drought in the previous four years.

In 1951 Thanjāvūr grew a variety of other crops in small acreages. The most important were maize (*chōlam*), and various kinds of millets (*kumbu, ragi,* and *varagu*) grown on about 47,370 acres, or about 3 percent of the gross acreage. Most of the millet crops replaced rice in the dry southwest uplands; some were grown in the paddy fields during the dry season in the delta. Legumes, chiefly greengram and blackgram, with small quantities or redgram and horsegram, occupied about 102,900 acres, or 6.6 percent of the total. They were grown almost entirely as "intercrops" in paddy fields in the dry season in the most fertile parts of the delta. Groundnut, chiefly for export to Europe and North America, occupied about 44,700 acres, or 2.8 percent of the gross acreage, mainly in the dryer southwest uplands. Small quantities of chillies, sugar cane, gingelly-oil seeds, cotton, and tobacco, amounting to less than 30,000 acres, or 1.9 percent of the gross acreage, completed the picture.[11]

In addition to its wet and dry field cultivation, Thanjāvūr had a relatively small area of garden and orchard crops. They were grown in fenced gardens (called *tōpes*), mainly behind the rows of densely packed houses of the village streets. Groves of coconut, palmyra, and other trees stood on slightly elevated patches of ground at intervals among the wet paddy fields. The garden acreage for 1951 is not available; it was reported as 49,364 acres, or 3.7 percent of the total cultivated acreage, in 1912–13,[12] and 85,829 acres, or 5.6 percent of the total, in 1960–1.[13] The sixty-year increase in garden lands had come about through expansion into land classified as "culturable waste" or as "not available for cultivation." These uncultivated lands declined from 638,363 to 578,322 acres during the period, probably mainly during the Grow More Food campaign. In 1951, Thanjāvūr's garden crops were chiefly coconut, palmyra, banana, chillies, betel vines, green beans, and a few other vegetables. Coconuts alone occupied 39,900 acres, or 46 percent of the garden lands. The fertile banks of the irrigation channels (*paḍukai*) were often used for bananas, which were grown on a total of 12,700 acres.[14] Small amounts of fresh fruit and vegetables were imported by rail from Tiruchirappalli and points westward and sold to the wealthy in stores or markets in the major towns.

### Stock Raising and Fishing

Thanjāvūr's domesticated stock comprised cattle, buffalos, goats, and chickens. Almost all stock were severely malnourished. Village people thought their condition had deteriorated within living memory because of the increase in the paddy-growing area and the decrease in pasture lands. Male buffalo were used for ploughing and to trample paddy in the second threshing; oxen for ploughing and to draw passenger and goods carts.

Seasonally, Thanjāvūr was invaded by large flocks of ducks and sheep. In the dry months from March to June, pastoralists from Rāmanāthapuram drove their sheep in flocks of a hundred to graze the grasses and paddy stalks of the district's wastelands and fields. In return for the valuable sheep manure, farmers paid the migrants in grain or money by the night to station flocks in their fields. By contrast, the villagers levied a charge on the owners of ducks driven into the delta from Tiruchirappalli in March to seek worms and grubs in the fields. In both cases the migrants set up camp on wastelands on the edge of villages. Apart from business arrangements, they had almost no social contact with the inhabitants, who regarded them as innocuous but culturally strange.

The meat of goats or chickens was eaten on market days and special occasions by most people in the nonvegetarian castes (roughly 84 percent of the population). Only the lowest Ādi Drāviḍa castes of Paṟayars (scavengers) and Chakkiliyars (leather workers), about 15 percent of the total, ate beef, and that carrion, because the slaughter of cows was forbidden in this strongly Brahmanical culture. The Ādi Drāviḍas in general could rarely afford the meat of domesticated animals. They obtained much of their protein by catching rats in the paddy fields or their homes and by fishing in the irrigation channels for minnows and small crabs.

The larger fish in the village bathing pools belonged to resident village landlords and were sold by them once a year to local or migrant fishermen. On the coast, fishing provided a livelihood for about 20,000 people in specialized Hindū, Muslim, and Christian fishing castes. Some of the coastal villagers bartered their fish for grain in villages up to about fifteen miles inland. Others worked for merchant boat owners who exported fish to markets in the larger villages and towns.

### Crafts and Industries

In 1951 Thanjāvūr's few machine industries were almost all for the processing or semiprocessing of agricultural produce. The district had about 700 rice mills, 158 of which were sizeable and employed 2,820 workers. At Nāgapaṭṭaṇam there was a steel-rolling mill for the railroad built in 1936 and employing over 500 workers. There were also thirty printing presses in the district, three mills for processing edible oils, and three bone-meal mills at Thanjāvūr.[15]

Thanjāvūr's famous hand industries had declined during British rule but at the end of it there was still considerable hand weaving and dyeing of silk *saris*, some combined silk and cotton weaving, and silk, cotton, and woolen carpet making for elite consumption. Thanjāvūr was also still famous for its gold jewelry and art-metal work, chiefly of idols and other ritual objects for temple and domestic use. Religious paintings, pith images and garlands, musical instruments, wood carvings, bell metal, brass and silver household vessels, wax prints, leather goods, mats, and rattan baskets, were among the other artistic and craft products. Altogether about 5.5 percent of the population was predominantly sustained by industrial and craft production.

### Trade

In 1951 Thanjāvūr was a classic example of a virtually monocrop food-producing region that exported grain to urban centers and to other districts heavily involved in the production of industrial or luxury crops. In 1951–2 the then Madras State as a whole had 27.4 percent of its cultivated area under such crops, 11.9 percent of it being under ground nuts and the rest under cotton, sugar cane, and tobacco. About 24 percent of the cultivated land in what later became Tamiḻ Nāḍu was devoted to such crops, and about 40 percent in what later became the west coast state of Kēraḷa.[16] Most of Tamiḻ Nāḍu's tobacco and ground nuts and most of Kēraḷa's tea, rubber, and coconut products were exported to Western nations. Until World War II, the food deficit of these areas and of the cities had been made up chiefly through imports of rice from Burma. With the conquest of Burma by Japan, Thanjāvūr became the largest single source of food for Tamiḻ Nāḍu and Kēraḷa. In the late 1940s and in 1950–2 it officially exported about 200,000 tons of paddy (or the equivalent in husked rice) per year under government procurement schemes, or about 34 percent of its normal output.[17] Unofficially, an unknown but substantial quantity was exported on the black market by private traders.

Thanjāvūr's minor exports in 1951 were silk and cotton hand-loomed textiles, art and household metalware, turmeric and other dyes, hides, sugar cane, palmyra jaggery, molasses, and ocean fish. Ground nuts, cashew nuts, onions, and tobacco brought by rail from other districts were also shipped out of Nāgapaṭṭaṇam, while Thanjāvūr itself exported small quantities of ground nuts and edible oils. Most of Thanjāvūr's minor exports went by sea to Malaya or Ceylon, as its grain had done in earlier decades. Thanjāvūr's chief imports were cotton textiles and other manufactures, both British and Indian, farinaceous foods, arecanuts for chewing with betel leaves, lac, gums, and resins from Malaya, timber from Burma, sea shells from Ceylon for making quicklime to whitewash buildings, and kerosene, coal for the railroad, tin and other unwrought metals, silk, cotton yarn, and jute sacks (for carting rice) from elsewhere in India or from Europe.

Unfortunately, we cannot estimate the real value in labor power of Thanjāvūr's exports and imports and so discover the extent to which it was involved in unequal exchange. We cannot even estimate the quantities or rupee values of exports and imports, for no records of inland trade are available for the period. As will be shown in Chapter 6, we do know that from 1840 to 1930 the rupee value of Thanjāvūr's ocean exports (the majority of its exports) greatly exceeded that of its imports. This was still true of Thanjāvūr's ocean trade in 1949–50: Total exports from Nāgapaṭṭaṇam were valued at Rs. 3,989,148, and total imports at Rs. 2,837,234, although the imbalance had been much greater in the nineteenth century.[18] It is likely from qualitative accounts that throughout the British period exports exceeded imports in Thanjāvūr's inland trade as well. All we can say with certainty for 1951, however, is that Thanjāvūr's exports came from a substantial part of the labor of its agricultural, craft, industrial, and transport workers. Apart from a limited quantity of cotton textiles, by contrast, its imports were luxuries that went almost entirely to the landlord, merchant, and rich farmer classes (at most, 20 percent of the people), to provide raw materials for craftsmen, or to service the district's machinery for processing and transporting its export goods.

**Education**

Twenty-three percent of Thanjāvūr's population were literate in Tamiḻ in 1951, whereas only 11 percent had been in 1881. In 1951 only 10 percent of the women were literate, but 36 percent of the men. About 3 percent of the people, or 12 percent of the literate, had attended middle school and spoke English, while about 4 percent of the literate had matriculated from high school. In addition to several hundred elementary schools and public and mission high schools, Thanjāvūr had a government college granting bachelor of arts degrees at Kumbakōṇam, a number of private colleges for advanced Sanskrit education, and Anglican and Methodist Arts' colleges in Thanjāvūr and Maṉṉārguḍi, respectively. Predictably, the largest percentages (37–44 percent) of literates were among the landlords and those engaged in commerce, transport, and urban service work; there were fewer (15–30 percent) among the peasants, artisans, and other producers, and fewest (7 percent) among the agricultural laborers.[19]

**Traditional and Popular Culture**

As the heartland of the ancient Chōḻa kingdom, Thanjāvūr had a brilliant heritage of classical dancing and music and of both Tamiḻ and Sanskrit literature, most of it religious.[20] Traditionally, this heritage had been mainly transmitted by the Brahmans. In pre-British times they were the kingdom's chief ruling caste of religiosi. They retained their preeminence in education and government service during British rule. Tamiḻ literature was enriched by a number of Non-Brahman Hindū saints and scholars, both aristocratic and commoner, and before the ninth century by Jain and Buddhist authors.

In 1951, only 23 percent of the population who were literate had some direct knowledge of Tamiḻ literature from home or elementary school. Tamiḻ proverbs and sayings from the classics, Tamiḻ hymns, and mythological stories usually derived from Sanskrit were, however, widely known by nonliterate people among the peasants, merchants, and artisans, who heard them from their elders or listened to public recitations at religious festivals.

In villages the best-known works included the *Tirukkural* of Tiruvaḷḷuvar, a manual of sayings, perhaps Jain in origin, about ethics, politics, and love, and the epic poems *Silappadikāram* and *Maṇimēkalai*. These all date from the close of the period of the first Chōḻa kingdom, which gave birth to the famous Sangam literature during the first to fifth centuries A.D.

From the sixth to ninth centuries came the devotional hymns of sixty-three Saivite saints, or *nāyanārs*, compiled by Nambi Āndar Nambi in the tenth century, and those of Vaishnavite devotees (*āḻvārs*) of the same period collected by Nāthāmuni. Appar, Sundaramūrti, and Tirugnānasambandar, authors of the *Dēvāram*, were the best loved of the Saivite hymnists, together with Mānikka Vāçagar, the somewhat later author of the *Tiruvāçagam*. Mythological stories, sometimes associated with the origins of temples, abounded concerning these saints, and groups of devotees walked from village to village singing their hymns in festival seasons. The favorite Vaishnavite hymns that corresponded to them were those of Periyāḷvār and his daughter Āndāl, drawn from the *Nālāyira Dīvyaprabandham*, or "Four Thousand Sacred Hymns."

Most of the hymns and myths of the great composers were recorded during the heyday of the second Chōḷa empire in the ninth to thirteenth centuries. To this period belong many other well-known works. In the 1950s, the more educated villagers' favorites were the epic poems *Jīvakaçintāmani* by the Jain poet Tiruttakkadēvar (tenth century), the Saivite *Periya Purāṇam* ("Great Epic") of Sēkkiḷār (twelfth century), and Kamban's Tamiḷ rendering of the Sanskrit epic *Rāmāyaṇa* of the late twelfth century. Among more recent compositions, the nineteenth century hymns of Tyāgarāja Bhāgavadar and the songs of Subramania Bhārathi, a famous nationalist poet who died in 1921, were the most popular.

In the early 1950s modern media had already made inroads into the village culture of Thanjāvūr. Tamiḷ films, chiefly concerned with love themes and mythological stories, were shown in cinemas in all the municipalities. Many of the larger villages enjoyed film shows in tents during the summer. Village people under forty flocked to these shows on foot, in buses, or by bullock cart, the popularity of the shows rivaled only by that of the great temple festivals. Even Harijans, the lowest "Untouchable" caste of landless laborers, used part of their meager earnings to visit local film shows. Among the upper ranks of the landlords and merchants, a few Tamiḷ and English newspapers could be found in most villages. Young, literate women in these groups, although still mainly confined to a patriarchal home life, occasionally read novels and romantic stories in such magazines as *Ānanta Vikaṭan*, and dreamed of a wider existence.

# 2 Castes and Religious Groups

## The Jāti

A word commonly on everyone's lips was *jāti*. In its widest sense it might mean almost any "type" or "kind." Villagers often referred to *jātis* of bicycles, cloth, goats, chickens, paddy, coconuts, or cattle. With respect to humans, *jāti* might refer to nationalities, religious communities, or preliterate "tribes" outside the regular society of Hindūs. To Hindūs of Thanjāvūr, for example, Christians, Muslims, Jains, Telugu speakers, the British, or the Koravar gypsies who wandered through their villages were all *jātis*. When speaking to Christians or Muslims, Hindūs themselves might say that they belonged to the "Hindū *jāti*."

In everyday life in Thanjāvūr, however, especially among the Hindūs who formed 90 percent of the population, *jāti* usually referred to the group that Europeans translate as "caste." In this sense, as is well known, *jātis* were ranked birth-status groups.[1] The caste or *jāti*, or a subsection of it, was endogamous in Thanjāvūr as in most of India. A caste was a named category usually extending over all or most of a linguistic region, and sometimes beyond it. Invariably, castes were segmentary units containing two or more levels of subdivisions or subcastes within them. The caste, or a subcaste within it, was usually associated with a traditional occupation, although many castes carried on agriculture in addition and some members of all castes had moved into noncaste occupations with the development of capitalism. The members of a caste, or in some cases of a subcaste within the caste, might eat together, enter each others' households, touch others of the same sex, and share a relatively egalitarian social life. Among castes, and to a lesser degree among those subcastes of a caste that were ranked in relation to one another, rules of ritual pollution obtained. A member of a lower caste might not eat with one of a higher caste, touch him, enter his family's kitchen, or in some cases even penetrate his house or his street. People of higher caste might give cooked food and water to those of lower caste but might not receive these from them. Members of much lower castes might not approach those of higher castes within designated distances, and must use humble, self-abasive language in addressing them. In theory, members of higher castes might not have sexual relations with persons of lower castes, although this rule was often broken in the case of high caste men and lower caste women. Many other prohibitions, too numerous to detail here, associated with pollution existed or had recently existed.[2] Some of them will be explored in later chapters. It is enough to note here that the ranking of castes and subcastes, as distinct from that of families or classes, was religious or ritual ranking associated with their relative pollution or purity. It was closely related to socioeconomic rank but was not coterminous with it.

Hindū castes have traditionally formed a hierarchy with the Brahman at the top and the lowest "Untouchable," or Scheduled Castes at the bottom. In Thanjāvūr as in other parts of India where the Hindūs are numerically dominant, Christians, Muslims, and members of other non-Hindū religions also formed castes that were ranked in relation to one another and to the major Hindū castes, although rules of ritual pollution were less strictly observed by non-Hindūs.

Villages and towns were multicaste communities, with each caste or each small group of similar castes occupying a separate street. Not all castes were found in every town or village. Distribution was discontinuous, and some of the smallest, highly specialized castes were found only in certain towns. Before and to some extent during British rule, the castes of a village had designated economic functions in the village establishment under the authority of the dominant caste. Correspondingly, they held hereditary, differential rights to shares from the produce from the village lands. Castes were thus firmly embedded in the pre-British mode of production, although their efflorescence was not strictly required by the society's economic system but in part had a dynamic of its own. During British rule with the gradual development of capitalist relations, castes lost their legal rights in village produce and some occupations slowly changed. By 1951 castes had become partly disembedded from the economic system and the ritual rules governing their relations were being challenged and had begun to atrophy. In some cases the caste remained chiefly significant as a kinship network. Even there, however, endogamy was beginning to crumble. A few marriages took place within the largest-named caste category rather than the traditionally endogamous subcaste, and even, very rarely, between members of different castes. In 1951 caste was still, however, the most salient organizing principle of which villagers were conscious in their daily lives, and endogamy was its most enduring characteristic.

Thanjāvūr contained at least sixty-six separate named castes, each divided into several, or many, endogamous subcastes. In 1951 a single village of 500 to 1,000 people normally contained groups from some fifteen to twenty castes and about thirty endogamous subcastes. Most of the castes of Thanjāvūr spread into other districts. Some of them, such as the Mūppaṉārs, Paḷḷis, and Vaṉṉiyars, spread north and east into Tiruchirappalli and South and North Ārcot. Others, such as the Iḍeiyars, Agambaḍiyars, Kaḷḷars, and Maṟavars, spread southeast into Pudukkoṭṭai, Rāmanāthapuram, and Madurai. Some castes, such as the Veḷḷāḷars and the Kammāḷars, were found throughout Tamiḷ Nāḍu. Several castes in Thanjāvūr of Telugu, Maratha, or Gujarāti origin came to the district in the wake of conquering armies in the fourteenth to seventeenth centuries. Some of these castes recognized corresponding groups in their former homelands and in a few cases, such as the Kamma Naidūs, occasionally intermarried with them. Alone of all the Thanjāvūr castes, the Brahmans extended throughout Hindū India and, throughout India, regarded themselves as a single *jāti*.

The men of a caste used a title associated with their caste, or in some cases with their subcaste, as a surname. Sometimes this name was the name of the caste (for example, Paḍaiyācchi, Poṟayar, or Vaṇṇāṉ). Sometimes it was a special title reserved for one or more castes or subcastes, as in the case of Iyer (Saivite Brahmans), Ayyangār (Vaishnavite Brahmans), Piḷḷai (most Veḷḷāḷar and Agambaḍiyar divisions), Mudaliar (used for the high-ranking subcaste of Toṇḍaimaṇḍalam Veḷḷāḷars, but also for the rather low caste of weavers or Kaikkiḷars), or Paṇikkar (Paḷḷars and Paṟayars). The Kaḷḷar, Maṟavar, and Ambalakkārar castes, however, who once formed semiindependent chiefdoms in Madurai and Rāmanāthapuram, used the titles of their patrilineal clans, such as Sērvai, Nandiār, Kaṇḍayār, or Nāttār.

The Hindū castes of Thanjāvūr divided themselves into three broad categories, Brahmans, Non-Brahmans, and Ādi Drāviḍas. The three groups ranked in that order and there was wide social and ritual distance between them, especially between the two upper groups and the Ādi Drāviḍas (also called Harijans, Scheduled Castes, or Panchamas). Brahmans formed roughly 6 percent of the population, Non-Brahmans 62 percent, and Ādi Drāviḍas 22 percent. Although their proportions varied, all three categories were present in virtually all towns and villages.

This three-fold division, found throughout Tamiḷ Nāḍu, was complicated by the fact that the Tamiḷ Hindūs also recognized the all-India classification of four *varṇas* (literally "colors"), Brahman, Kshattriya, Vaishya, and Sūdra, plus the "exterior" or "non-*varṇa*" population, historically called the "fifth group" or Panchamas. This division dated from the ancient north Indian society of about 1,200 to 1,000 B.C. In that society as in later periods, Brahmans were the priests, law givers, scholars, and literati; Kshattriyas the rulers and warriors; Vaishyas the traders, peasants, and artisans; Sūdras the servile manual workers; and Chandālas, later called Panchamas, members of the population who lived outside the villages and had been conquered, or not yet conquered, by the invading Āryans.[3] Originally, these divisions were socioeconomic orders that were not strictly hereditary; they became so in later centuries. Brahmans, Kshattriyas, and Vaishyas were "twice-born" groups whose male members underwent initiation around puberty, wore a sacred thread over one shoulder, and were evidently free citizens. Sūdras were of much lower rank, were forbidden literacy, and appear to have had a status similar to serfs or slaves. Panchamas were probably enslaved after conquest. By about the sixth century B.C. they were confined to the heaviest and most polluting occupations.

Although castes within the *varṇas* had proliferated and become numerous as early as the sixth century B.C., the ritual classification into four *varṇas* and one non-*varṇa*, or *avarṇa*, spread throughout Hindū India and has persisted to the present. In 1951 in Thanjāvūr, however, only the Brahmans and Panchamas fully occupied their traditional status. A few thousand Telugu and Maratha former royalty and aristocrats retained their high ritual rank of Kshattriyas, but most of them were impoverished and powerless, virtually disregarded by the population at large. Some of the artisan and trading castes, such as the various groups of Cheṭṭiars and the Kammāḷars, claimed to be Vaishyas, wore the sacred thread, and regarded themselves as of higher rank than the Sūdras. In most cases, however, their claim was not accepted by the higher-ranking Sudra castes such as Veḷḷāḷars, Kamma Naidūs, and even Kaḷḷars, who, although Sūdra, had occupied positions of authority as nobles, army officers, and land managers in the pre-British kingdom. The local and *varṇa* classifications corresponded thus:

| *All-India varṇas* | *Local categories* |
|---|---|
| Brahman | Brahman |
| Kshattriya<br>Vaishya<br>Sūdra | Non-Brahman |
| Avarṇa or Panchama | Ādi Drāvida or Panchama (Harijans) |

Among the Non-Brahmans, however, in most contexts, regardless of the *varṇa* classifications a local rank order of castes prevailed.

### Caste and Subcaste

Castes are segmented into several levels of subcastes that are usually named, and each of which is usually also called a *jāti* in relation to others of like order. The number of levels of subcastes varies, being usually greater in the case of the highest castes. In Thanjāvūr it appeared that most Non-Brahman and Harijan castes had four levels, a few small castes only three, some castes five. Most of the Brahmans apparently had six. The four most common levels were as follows:

#### *The Local Subcaste Community*

This was the group that Mayer calls the "kindred of cooperation"[4] and Yalman the "micro-caste."[5] It consisted of the members of a single endogamous subcaste located in a single town or village. Often, they lived contiguously on a single street. In large castes the group might number forty or more households. In small, specialized castes, such as Washermen, Barbers, or Village Temple Priests, they were usually only one to five households. (As is common in the literature on India, I have used capitalized words for the translations of caste names, but have used the lowercase for persons, such as goldsmiths, who actually follow the occupation. In modern times, many people belong to, and bear the title of, an occupational caste, but no longer follow its traditional occupation.)

All members of the local subcaste community were related to one another. The group was divided into small exogamous patrilineages (*kooṭṭams* or *kulams*), which were stronger and more ancient in the higher castes, weaker and shallower in the lower castes. Unless the local subcaste community formed a single patrilineage (which was rare), marriages took place either inside or outside the local community.

The subcaste community traditionally had an assembly of male heads of households who settled disputes, ratified marriages, and arranged religious ceremonies. Often, the group owned its own small shrine to some Hindū deity, usually Piḷḷaiyar, the eldest son of Siva, Vishnū as Lord Rāma, his servant Hanumān, the monkey god, or one of the non-Sanskritic village deities. The local subcaste community had no generic name. It was simply a local segment of the endogamous subcaste, the latter being located in several villages. Nevertheless, beyond the household it was the most significant corporate group in a villager's life. Its members might refer to themselves by the village name plus their caste name, as in "Kumbapeṭṭai Brahmans" or "Kirippūr Paṟayars."

### *The Endogamous Subcaste*

This group resembled Mayer's "kindred of recognition."[6] Its members regarded and referred to themselves as a *jāti* in relation to other *jātis* of their maximal *jāti* or caste; thus, this group might be termed a "minor caste." It consisted of the local subcaste communities dispersed in a number of villages and often in several towns as well, whose lineages had regularly intermarried over generations. Kinship and affinity could usually be traced within this group, although some members might be very distantly related. The members of the group often referred to themselves as *sondakkār* ("own people") or *orumuṟaiyar* ("one rule people"), both of which meant "relatives." Normally marriage did not occur outside this group. If a marriage did occur into another, similar subcaste of the same caste, and was accepted, the new family would gradually be regarded as belonging to the endogamous subcaste.

In most cases the endogamous subcaste did not meet as a corporate group and had no headman nor, in 1951, any assembly of elders. Formerly it had an assembly that met regularly to discuss breaches of caste law and to determine whether these merited excommunication. In 1951 some of the subcaste elders from several nearby villages might still gather to settle serious disputes within the subcaste, but this was becoming rare. In general, the endogamous subcaste was simply a group with a sense of solidarity, from which spouses were chosen and within which people might interdine freely and, when traveling, claim hospitality. Because marriage was predominantly patrilocal, women who had married outside their natal villages formed the chief links between communities of the endogamous subcaste. Some men, however, married and moved into communities other than their natal villages, and boys were sometimes adopted from other communities of the endogamous subcaste.

Among Brahmans and in some of the other castes, the endogamous subcaste was a clearly designated group with a name and sharp boundaries. In such cases it commonly comprised the subcaste members of some ten to thirty definitely known villages within a former *nāḍu* of the Chōḷa kingdom, plus those members who had fairly recently migrated to other places.

In other cases the endogamous subcaste was unnamed and was a rather vaguely bounded category. All members of a single subcaste community in one village would share the same circle of villages as their endogamous subcaste, but another, related community might count in its subcaste those of its caste in a somewhat different circle of villages. In some castes it appeared that endogamous subcastes joined by chains of marriages overlapped from the western to the eastern borders of Thanjāvūr. In some other castes such nearly endogamous circles overlapped with others in South Ārcot and Tiruchirappalli, and in some in Pudukkoṭṭai, Rāmanāthapuram, or Madurai. It seems probable that in Chōḷa times all or most of the castes of Thanjāvūr had definitely bounded endogamous subcastes, each confined within a *nāḍu* or district. Subsequently, with numerous migrations and conquests, the boundaries of many endogamous circles became blurred.

### *The Regional Subcaste*

This group, containing several endogamous or near-endogamous subcastes, was scattered over the district or some region of similar size. It was named, and its members regarded each other as of the same ritual rank. If they met they might eat together. Although the endogamous subcaste was the one in which the vast majority of marriages took place, no great harm was done if a marriage occurred outside the endogamous subcaste in the regional subcaste, for its members thought of themselves as the same kind of people, they had almost identical kinship and other customs, and they were likely to have a tradition of having once been related. Beyond this, the regional subcaste had little solidarity. Its members simply recognized one another as of the same rank and, if they traveled about the district, they could normally expect hospitality from one another. The regional subcaste was called a *jāti* in relation to others of like order.

Several regional subcastes together made up a still wider, named regional subcaste or else the caste as a whole. Often, however, the regional subcastes of a caste were ranked in relation to one another so that the lower-ranking ones might receive but not give food to the higher. This relationship obtained, for example, between certain subcastes of Kaḷḷars, Maṟavars, Iḍaiyars, Agambaḍiyars, and others living in Thanjāvūr, and others living in Rāmanāthapuram or Madurai. The latter were considered inferior, ostensibly because their widows remarried, whereas in the subcastes of Thanjāvūr they purported not to do so. In some cases regional subcastes within a caste disputed for precedence and would not accept food from one another.

In yet other cases, two or more subcastes of the same caste were found in the same region and were mutually ranked. Their ranking might be merely explained by a myth or by some vague belief in different places of origin. Alternatively, one subcaste might serve in a menial or polluting capacity yet be sufficiently closely related to another to be regarded as of the same broader caste.

In Thanjāvūr, for example, the regional subcaste of the Ādi Drāviḍa castes of Paḷḷars and Paṟayars each had small, lower-ranking regional subcastes of Barbers and Laundryworkers. The higher Brahman and Non-Brahman castes were served by a completely separate Barber caste called Ambaṭṭar. The Paḷḷars and Paṟayars were not permitted to employ this caste and, probably in imitation, had set aside

A wandering bard with *Kama Dhenu*, the Cow of Plenty.

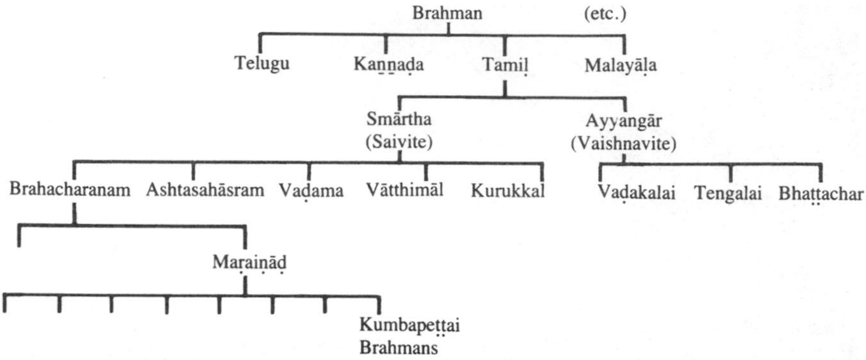


Figure 1. An example of segmentation in the Brahman caste

part-time barbers and washermen of their own. These small subcastes, however, were recognized to be respectively Pallars and Parayars, probably because, like the Pallars and Parayars and unlike the more specialized Ambattars, they were still primarily engaged in agricultural labor.

### *The Caste*

As I have mentioned, the caste was the largest-named category whose members regarded each other as of a single *jāti*. The caste almost invariably extended more widely than a single district. Its component subcastes were very loosely affiliated and often had no more binding tie than a sense of common origin.

Beginning in the late 1890s or early 1900s, however, some castes had formed voluntary caste associations for the education, mutual aid, and "uplift" of their members. Some of these associations built schools; some agitated for representation in government service. Some associations of relatively low castes, such as the Kammālars or the Vanniyars, followed the teachings of a *guru* and attempted to "purify" their customs by giving up widow marriage, alcohol, or meat. Some associations formed caste-based political parties. The Vanniyar association in North and South Ārcot named Vanniya Kula Kshattriya, for example, formed the Tamil Nādu Toilers and the Commonweal parties in the Madras assembly elections of 1951. In Thanjāvūr, however, single-caste associations were less active than in some other districts of Tamil Nādu, perhaps because broad-based political parties such as the Congress Party, the Drāvida Kazhakam, and the Communists were more prominent.

In some of the higher castes, one or two other layers of subcastes might exist between the regional subcaste and the caste. These might be still wider regional groups, relate to slight differences of occupation, or spring from differences of religious sect. In the latter two cases there would be rank ordering among the subcastes within each order.

An example of proliferation may be given from among the Brahmans (Figure 1).

Thus, most of the Brahmans living in Kumbapeṭṭai village in northwest Thanjāvūr formed a single local subcaste community. Together with the Brahmans of eighteen other villages in northwest Thanjāvūr and a small area of Tiruchirappalli, they formed the Maṛaināḍ (rain country) endogamous subcaste. This subcaste and several others formed the Brahacharaṇam regional subcaste located mainly in north and west Thanjāvūr. All Brahacharaṇams ranked equally. The Brahacharaṇams and several other subcastes formed the Smārtha or Saivite Brahman sect or subcaste of Tamiḷ Brahmans.

The regional subcastes within this sect were ranked: Of the "ordinary" scholar Brahmans, the Ashtasahāsrams ("8,000 houses") ranked highest and the Brahacharaṇams lowest. The Kurukkal subcaste occupied a different status from those of the other subcastes, for its members were priests in the temples of Siva, whereas the members of other subcastes were land managers and scholars. Whereas such subcastes as Ashtasahāsrams, Vaḍamas, and Vātthimāls lived mainly in different localities, one or two Kurukkal houses were found serving the temple in every village of Smārtha Brahmans. As specialist servants, Kurukkals ranked slightly lower than the regional subcastes they served.

The other main sect of Tamiḷ Brahmans was the Vaishnavite, or Ayyangār sect, which had its own subdivisions, including its own temple priestly subcaste, the Bhaṭṭachārs, who were comparable to the Kurukkals but who served only in temples of Vishnū. Ayyangārs ranked above Smārthas and would not receive food from them. They were divided into Vaḍakalai (northern) and Tengalai (southern) subcastes, Vaḍakalais ranking above Tengalais. Each of these subcastes was in turn divided into smaller regional and endogamous subcastes.

Finally, the Tamiḷ Brahmans were one of many linguistic regional subcastes of the Brahman caste, which was spread throughout India. Each of the linguistic regional subcastes had, of course, its own subdivisions.

As in other segmentary systems, people tended to identify with that layer of the *jāti* or still larger grouping that was distinguished from or stood opposed to the *jāti* of those to whom they were relating at any given time. Correspondingly, when considering others, they paid attention to the widest *jāti* that differentiated that group from their own. Moreover, although adults were usually fairly knowledgeable about the subdivisions within their own caste, they tended to be unsure or ignorant of those in other castes. A Veḷḷāḷar, for example, usually related to a Brahman simply as a Brahman, not as a Smārtha Brahman, a Brahacharaṇam Smārtha Brahman, or a Maṛaināḍ Brahacharaṇam Smārtha Brahman. If the same subject met a strange Veḷḷāḷar he was concerned to know whether he belonged to the Kāraikkāṭṭ, Toṇḍaimaṇḍalam, Chōḷiya, Koṇḍaikkaṭṭi, Koḍikkal, Kamāla, Poṉṉēri, or Pūndamalli regional subcastes. If the subject was himself a Toṇḍaimaṇḍalam Veḷḷāḷar (titled Mudaliar) and met another of that subcaste, he was concerned to know whether the other belonged to the higher endogamous group of Mēlnāḍu (higher country) Toṇḍaimaṇḍalam Mudaliars or to the slightly lower, Kīlnāḍu (lower country) group.

Until modern times different subcastes of the same caste were probably seldom found in the same village unless one served the other in a subordinate capacity. With the growth of modern occupations and transport, however, single households or small groups of "alien" subcastes often settled in a village. In these cases they usually lived near those of their caste most closely related to themselves, and maintained polite relations with their caste fellows. Other castes in the village regarded them as of the same *jāti* as their street mates without differentiating their subcaste. Over a generation or two they might begin to interdine with their hosts on equal terms, although intermarriage was unlikely except among the most "modern" Western-educated families.

### Foundations of the Caste System

Why do castes exist? It seems to me that three factors combine to explain them. First, India has experienced many waves of immigration, internal migration, and conquest. Throughout the country migrant, sometimes conquering, groups of different culture have piled up on top of each other. Many caste divisions derive from such migrations.

Second, although varying in their modes of production, from about the tenth century B.C. the kingdoms of India all possessed five main orders. These were the professional religiosi, the secular royalty and aristocracy, the merchants, the semiservile peasantry, and the menial slaves. Each of these orders had its own attached groups of specialized clients or servants. For three thousand years, these orders and their attached specialists formed the backbone of the caste system and underlay the basic principles of religious ranking. Only with the rise of capitalism are they being eroded.

Third, however, the system owes its enormous proliferation to the hegemony of the Brahmans as religious specialists. As the priests and the religious arm of government, their task was to explain and elaborate the social structure, to philosophize about it, to reconcile the lower orders to their lot, and (whether consciously or unconsciously) to assist the secular rulers in repressing the people and preventing rebellion.

The Brahmans *elaborated and codified* the social system with the aid of commonly held beliefs in ritual purity and pollution, carried in India to extraordinary lengths. In this respect the caste system has a certain dynamic of its own, not explicable in political or economic terms. Thus, for example, specialized castes and subcastes of funeral priests, providers of oil for temple lamps, garland makers for temples, or launderers of the cloths of birth and menstruation, are not required by the mode of production on economic grounds. Yet they exist in many parts of India, having been set apart by the Brahmans as an outgrowth of the purity–pollution theme.

In this society the social divisions were *explained* by the Brahmans through the belief that the four *varṇas* had sprung from different parts of the Primeval Being's body: The Brahmans from his head, the Kshattriyas from his shoulders, the Vaishyas from his thighs, and the Sūdras from his feet.

The system was *justified*, and attempts made to *reconcile the lower orders* to their lot, through belief in the transmigration of souls and in *karma* (lot or fate).

As is well known, this belief holds that souls are born into a higher or lower caste according to their good or evil deeds in a previous life. The goal of life is to carry out one's caste duty, or *dharma*, so that one is reborn next time in a higher estate, and eventually, through the accumulation of virtue in many lives, is released from the chain of rebirth and enabled to join with the divine. Although there is considerable evidence that the lower castes of Sūdras and Panchamas are, in fact, not persuaded of this belief, it has had a powerful effect in rationalizing the caste system through the ages.

Finally, the Brahmans helped to *repress* the common people and to prevent rebellion by separating them in each kingdom into almost innumerable tiny cells that were ranked in relation to one another or else encouraged to dispute for rank. Whether or not this procedure was deliberate, it is hard not to see in the caste system the familiar "divide and conquer" of dictatorial regimes. The vast number of castes and subcastes within each kingdom and each province and district of a kingdom, separated from each other by exclusive commensality, touch pollution, and endogamy, obscured the relatively simple class structure and must have discouraged both the aristocrats and the exploited from uniting against their rulers.

### The Castes

It remains to mention the main castes of Thanjāvūr as an introduction to subsequent chapters.[7] In what follows I shall refer almost exclusively to castes, mentioning subcastes only when their specialized occupations, languages, or bodies of belief make them noteworthy.

#### *The Brahmans*

The Brahmans regarded themselves as a single caste (*jāti*) as well as the first of India's four broad strata of *varṇas*. As a whole, they were 6.2 percent of the population in 1931, and were probably about the same proportion in 1951. Altogether, they had traditionally owned the land in some 900 out of 2,400 villages. In the 1950s in Thanjāvūr they were wealthier, more numerous, and more powerful than in any other south Indian district.

By far the most numerous were the indigenous, linguistic-regional subcaste of Tamiḷ Brahmans. They received grants of land (*brahmadeya*) from the Chōḷa and later kings and, as a result, in 1951 were still settled with their lower caste servants in separate "Brahman villages," or *grāmams*. Most of them lived in the *tālūks* of Thanjāvūr, Papaṉāsam, Kumbakōṇam, Māyuram, and Sīrkāli near the main branch of the sacred Kāvēri.

The majority of Tamiḷ Brahmans in Thanjāvūr were of the Saivite or Smārtha sect. They counted themselves followers of the eighth-century philosopher, Sankarāchārya, and professed Sankara's Advaita or monistic philosophy in which God (*paramātmā*) and the soul (*ātmā*) were viewed as one. Prayers, penances, and duty (*dharma*) in this life were seen as helping to liberate the soul from the chain of rebirths and allowing it to realize its union with *paramātmā* in a selfless state known as *mōksa*, or release. Smārtha Brahmans worshipped both Siva and Vishnū but regarded Siva as the supreme being. In their own streets, or *agrahārams*, their temple worship focused around Siva, his consort Parvati, and their sons Ganapati (also called Ganēsh or Piḷḷayar) and Subramania, or Murugan. As secondary deities they worshipped Vishnū and his consort Lakshmi, often represented in their incarnations of Krishṇa and Rādha or of Rāma and Seetha.

A smaller number of Tamiḷ Brahmans belonged to the Vaishnavite sect of Ayyangārs, originally converted mainly from the Vaḍama subcaste of Smārtha Brahmans. They professed to worship only Vishnū and his consort Lakshmi. They followed the teachings of Rāmānuja, the twelfth-century Vishishta Advaita philosopher who taught that the soul is a separable appendage of God as the branch is of the tree.[8] Smārthas and Ayyangārs were bitter enemies in the nineteenth century and earlier, but by 1951 they lived peaceably in neighboring villages.

In the pre-British period, these Tamiḷ Brahman communities provided the kingdom's scholars, judges, and ministers, the priests of the great *yāgams*, or goat sacrifices, for the welfare of the whole kingdom, the upper ranks of the bureaucracy, and in Chōḷa times even the chief army commanders. During British rule the Brahmans became private landlords, mostly of small or medium-sized holdings. Many of them acquired an English education and entered government service. Some became traders or private salary earners. By 1900 a majority of Thanjāvūr or Brahman families had members living away from the district in trade or service in Madras or other cities. A smaller number lived in or commuted to Thanjāvūr or Kumbakōṇam municipalities or to the district's lesser towns.

Kumbakōṇam, and the smaller town of Tiruvaiyāru, both on the Kāvēri,were prime centers of Brahmanical worship and religious learning. The monks of a seminary in Kumbakōṇam, drawn from the Smārtha Brahman community, managed their monastic lands and expounded the philosophy of Sankara. Each Tamiḷ Brahman village community had one or two families of household priests, or *sāstrigals*, learned in the Vēdas, who performed the life crisis rites of initiation, marriage, death, and ancestral worship in houses of the Brahman community.

In each Smārtha Brahman village, as in each Non-Brahman Saivite village, one or two households of an endogamous Brahman subcaste of temple priests called Kurukkals performed the daily and festival services in the Siva temple. A similar priestly caste called Bhaṭṭachārs carried out the same functions in Ayyangār and in Non-Brahman Vaishnavite villages. The Chōḷa kings, who were Saivites, built many of the great Siva temples and also several to Vishnū in the tenth to twelfth centuries. The Vijayanagar and Nāyak rulers, who were Vaishnavites, built most of those to Lord Vishnū in the fifteenth to seventeenth centuries.

A small group of Telugu Saivite Brahmans, whose ancestors followed the Vijayanagar conquerors, were scattered about the district and employed as household priests (*purōhits*) by Non-Brahmans. In Thanjāvūr they ranked below the Tamiḻ Brahmans. Still smaller groups of Maratha, Konkanese, and Gujarāti Brahmans whose ancestors had followed the Maratha conquerors were traders in the larger towns.

### *The Non-Brahmans*

The Non-Brahmans formed four major groupings.

***Aristocratic Castes or Subcastes of Traditional Land Managers and Village Administrators.*** These castes were or had been the dominant castes in separate so-called Non-Brahman villages (called *ūr*), where they had traditionally occupied positions of authority similar to those of Brahmans in *grāmam* villages.

The Veḷḷāḷars were the dominant secular aristocratic caste under the Chōḷa kings, providing the courtiers, most of the army officers, the lower ranks of the kingdom's bureaucracy, and the upper layer of the peasantry. A few Veḷḷāḷars were still great landlords, especially in east Thanjāvūr, and many owned small estates. The caste as a whole, however, declined in power during the Vijayanagar and Maratha periods and failed to keep pace educationally with the Brahmans in the nineteenth century. Veḷḷāḷars formed 9.5 percent of the population in 1931. The caste contained several endogamous subcastes, formerly regional: the Kāraikkāṭṭ (Pāndhya country), Toṇḍaimaṇḍalam (Pallava country), and Chōḷiya (Chōḷa country), being the most important in Thanjāvūr. In 1951 Veḷḷāḷars were mainly landlords, tenant or owner cultivators, or white-collar workers. True Veḷḷāḷars, who might be either Vaishnavite or Saivite, were usually vegetarians. There were, however, a number of nonvegetarian "Veḷḷāḷar" subcastes that actually derived from the lower-ranking peasant castes. A proverb described this common process: "Kaḷḷar, Maṟavar and Agambaḍiyar, becoming fat, turn into Veḷḷāḷar."

Also among the aristocrats was the high-ranking caste of Telugu-speaking Kamma Naidūs, who governed villages and supplied military officers under the Vijanayagar kings and the Nāyak viceroys. In 1951 the Kamma Naidūs lived chiefly in Nāgapaṭṭaṇam and Naṉṉilam *tālūks*, most of them as small landlords or white-collar workers; a few lived on great estates. The caste had only 2,484 members in 1921; the Telugu Non-Brahman castes as a whole, 63,387 members, or 2.7 percent of the people.[9]

Although not of very high ritual rank or ancient aristocracy, certain subcastes of Kaḷḷars, Maṟavars, and Mūppaṉārs must be counted among the secular aristocrats. The Kaḷḷars and Maṟavars originated in the Pallava kingdom but for several centuries had had semiindependent chiefdoms in south Thanjāvūr, Pudukkoṭṭai, Rāmanāthapuram, and Madurai. The Mūppaṉārs were cultivators and former soldiers of South Ārcot and north Thanjāvūr who often worked as tenant farmers under the Veḷḷāḷars. A few families of Mūppaṉārs and Kaḷḷars led armies for the Maratha kings and were made revenue farmers. In 1951 they were great landlords and formed the heads of certain villages in west Thanjāvūr. Smaller peasant landowners of the Kaḷḷar caste also dominated some of the villages of southern Thanjāvūr, Maṉṉārguḍi, and Paṭṭukoṭṭai *tālūks*, especially in the less irrigated area.

A small and impoverished Maratha aristocracy of ninety-six families, the Channangūlya, concentrated in Thanjāvūr town, completed the list of aristocratic Non-Brahman castes. The Marathas as a whole, including former military and servant castes, numbered only 5,371 or 0.2 percent of the people in 1921.

***Craftsmen, Traders, and Other Specialists of the Towns.*** These castes included Tamiḷ, Kaṉṉada, Telugu, and Gujarāti castes of weavers; highly skilled indigenous Tamiḷ castes of woodcarvers, stonecarvers, goldsmiths, silversmiths, and brass workers who had separated themselves from the village artisan castes; and several castes of Telugu and Tamiḷ traders in varying commodities. Also among the urban castes must be counted such groups as the Tamiḷ Mēlakkār, musicians and dancers attached to the great temples. Altogether these specialized urban castes numbered about 186,000 in 1931, or 8 percent of the people. The more prominent among them were the Gujarāti Paṭṭunoolkārars, or silk weavers of Thanjāvūr, Ayyampet, and Kumbakōṇam; the Tamiḷ Kaikkiḷars, indigenous weavers in cotton or mixed cotton and silk threads; the Telugu Kōmati Cheṭṭiar caste of traders; the Nāṭṭukkoṭṭai Cheṭṭiars, traders and bankers from Sivaganga in Madurai district; and among the artisans, the Sīlpis, makers of stone and metal idols, and the Veḷḷikkaṉṉar, makers of silver vessels and other objects. Although there were exceptions, the specialized urban castes tended to rank ritually between the aristocratic Non-Brahman village administrators and the peasant and artisan castes of the villages.

***The Farming Castes.*** The peasant castes included the Agambaḍiyars, small owner and tenant cultivators in the south and west of the district who were thought to have once been palace servants of the Chōḷa kings; the Mūppanārs, chiefly of Kumbakōṇam *tālūk*, some of whom were formerly shepherds; the Paḍaiyācchis of south and east Thanjāvūr; and the Paḷḷis and Vaṉṉiyars of north Thanjāvūr, who were often tenants of Veḷḷāḷar and Brahman landlords, and who were related to, but slightly lower than, the Paḍaiyācchis. The Paḍaiyācchis, Vaṉṉiyars, Paḷḷis, and Mūppanārs collectively numbered 249,751, or 10.8 percent of the people in 1931; the Agambaḍiyars, 117,696, or 5.5 percent. Large groups of Kaḷḷars in west and south Thanjāvūr (207,684, or 8.9 percent of the people in 1931) and smaller numbers of the related caste of Maṟavars (3,758 in 1931) completed the main Tamil peasant castes. Near Nāgapaṭṭaṇam, however, were several middle-ranking Telugu castes, collectively called Naidūs, some of whom were once soldiers, traders, or stonemasons, but who in 1951 were mainly cultivators. These castes, chief of whom were the Kavarai Naidūs, numbered 60,903, or 2.6 percent of the people in 1931.

Each of these castes formed several endogamous, formerly regional subdivisions. Most of them were known to havc provided foot soldiers for the kings in various periods; the Paḍaiyācchis for the Chōḷas, the Naidūs for the Nāyaks, and the Kaḷḷars, Maṟavars, and Mūppaṉars for the Marathas.

The Kaḷḷars, some of whom came from Madurai in the nineteenth century, had in the past often been highwaymen or thieves who stole cattle and booty from Thanjāvūr's more settled landlords and peasants, and sold them in the southern districts. This banditry, which gave rise to the Kaḷḷars' name and to their designation as a "criminal caste" by the British government, apparently arose in the eighteenth century when the British crushed the Kaḷḷars and partly drove them from their homelands in Madurai. In the nineteenth century the Kaḷḷars' pillage became so regularized that the villages of south and west Thanjāvūr each appointed a resident Kaḷḷar watchman as "protector" to negotiate an annual tribute to the southern bandits. The custom persisted in 1951. When the tribute was not paid, cattle were apt to disappear at night from village byres. Most of Thanjāvūr's Kaḷḷars, however, had settled down in the villages as tenant farmers, cartmen, or ordinary grain and cattle traders by the 1950s.

The Tamiḷ Nāḍārs and Telugu and Tūlū Nayakkars (37,535 in 1931), coconut growers and tappers of palm wine, should probably be included in the peasant castes. Most of them were tenant cultivators of dry garden lands. Under the British, a small number of Nāḍār families became wealthy owners of licensed liquor shops, bought land, and came to administer newly settled villages. In general, however, the Nāḍārs ranked ritually below the other peasant castes, because intoxicating liquor was regarded as polluting by Hindūs.

Of similarly low rank to the Nāḍārs were various castes of fishermen, such as the Ambalakkārars and Valaiyars inland, and the Karaiyars, Sembadavars, and Paṭṭanavars on the coast. Altogether, the fishing castes numbered 198,520, or 8.5 percent of the people in 1921.

The Iḍaiyars, usually called by the honorific title of Kōṉār, by 1951 were shepherds and cattle herders, more numerous in Rāmanāthapuram than in Thanjāvūr. By 1951 Kōṉārs permanently living in Thanjāvūr had mostly taken to tenant farming or to the care of landlords' cattle, for pasturage had decreased in Thanjāvūr with the expansion of wet paddy land in the nineteenth and twentieth centuries. Iḍaiyars who lived permanently in Thanjāvūr numbered 76,299, or 3.3 percent of the people in 1921.

In 1931 these peasant, herding, and fishing Non-Brahman castes collectively numbered 982,881, or 42.2 percent of the people. Many of the urban specialists and the village artisans, however, supplemented their incomes with land ownership or tenant farming. Others became cultivators with the loss, during British rule, of their means of production or of demand for their products.

***The Specialized Village Servants.*** The fourth category of Non-Brahmans were specialized artisans or service workers in the villages. In general they ranked ritually between the peasant castes and the Ādi Drāviḍas, with many minute gradations of rank amongst themselves. The Kammāḷars or Panchāḷars ("Five Castes"), the village wood, stone, and metal workers, were the largest of these castes, numbering 61,162, or 2.6 percent of the people in 1921. They included the Tacchars (Carpenters), the Koltacchars (Blacksmiths), the Patthars (village Goldsmiths), the Kaltacchars (Stonemasons), and the Kaṉṉārs (Brass and Copper workers). In 1951 Carpenters and Blacksmiths were present in most villages, but Brasssmiths, Stonemasons, and Goldsmiths tended to cluster near the towns or in bigger villages. The five Kammāḷar groups intermarried, and wore the sacred thread like Brahmans. As Vaishyas, they traditionally regarded themselves (but were not accepted) as higher in rank than the peasant castes.

Other important village service castes were the Vāṇiyars (Oilmongers), the Vaṇṇars (Laundryworkers, 16,251 in 1921), the Ambaṭṭars (Barbers, 24,352 in 21), the Paṇḍārams (Sacrificial Priests in village temples), the Kusavars (Potters, 11,610 in 1931), and the Kūtthāḍis (Village Dancers, Puppet Players, and Prostitutes). Altogether, the Non-Brahman village specialist castes numbered about 5.2 percent of the people (about 8 percent of the rural population) in 1921.

Thanjāvūr had other small castes who wandered about seeking a living from their specialties. They included the Kamblattars (Mendicants and Sorcerers of west Thanjāvūr), the Āndis and Tādans (Ballad singers with gongs and finger drums), the Nokkars (Ropemakers), the Oṭṭars (Tank diggers), the Tombars (Weavers of baskets and mats of Russian bamboo), and the Koravars (Basketmakers, who were actually sometimes beggars and petty thieves). These castes numbered about 16,000 in 1921, and had a gypsy character, half outside the system of village castes. By 1951, many of them had settled in village occupations. Some of the Āndis had become village temple priests like Paṇḍārams, and some of the Koravars were employed by the government as road sweepers for a small cash wage.

### *The Harijans or Ādi Drāviḍas*

The third great category of Hindū castes was the Harijans or "Untouchables," also called the Scheduled Castes. In the 1950s they were called Ādi Drāviḍas, or "Original Dravidians" in Thanjāvūr, a census classification that villagers shorted to "ADs." They lived in separate hamlets or ghettos called *chēris* set in the paddy fields at some distance from the villages to which they were attached. The largest caste, both among the Ādi Drāviḍas and in the whole population, was the Paṟayars who numbered 337,445, or 14.5 percent of the people in 1931. Slightly above them in rank were the Paḷḷars, numbering 157,798, or 6.8 percent of the people in 1931. Both Paḷḷars and Paṟayars were agricultural slaves before the 1860s. In 1951 almost all of them were agricultural laborers or poor tenant farmers. The Paṟayars, but not the Paḷḷars, had certain specially polluting tasks in the villages. They carried out dead cattle from the streets of landlords and removed the hides. Unless the animals were diseased, they ate the carrion, a custom forbidden to other Hindūs to whom the cow was sacred. Paṟayar men drummed and played pipes at Non-Brahman funerals and guarded the cremation and burial grounds of all the castes. Some Paṟayars made mats and baskets, and some were engaged as village watchmen in the paddy fields.

Chakkiliyars were a small Telugu caste of leatherworkers numbering 4,017 in 1921. They were found in only a few villages, where they tanned the hides supplied to them by the Paṟayars and made them into shoes. Like the Paṟayars, they were highly polluting because they dealt in the products of dead animals. By 1951 many Chakkiliyars worked in town shops repairing shoes and other imported leather goods.

Altogether the Ādi Drāviḍas were 21.5 percent of the people in 1931 and 22.8 percent in 1951. The Paṟayar and Chakkiliyar village servants were traditionally paid in grain from the threshing floors like their counterparts among the Non-Brahmans, but were socially segregated from the other village servants by reason of their "low" birth and highly polluting occupations.

### *The Muslims*

In addition to its large majority of Hindūs, Thanjāvūr had several different communities of Muslims and Christians. A still smaller group of Jains, numbering fewer than a thousand, lived and traded in Thanjāvūr and Maṉṉārguḍi towns.

The Muslims, 6.1 percent of the people, lived mainly on the east and south coasts and in some inland villages of Kumbakōṇam *tālūk*. They were concentrated in the ports of Nāgore, Topputturai, Muttupet, and Adirāmpaṭṭanam, and at Chakkrāpalli, Nachiyārkōvil, and Kūttānallūr inland. Most Muslims were believed to be descended either from Arab men and native women of the fourteenth and fifteenth centuries, or from Hindūs who were forcibly converted to Islam by Tipū Sultān of Mysore in the 1780s. They were divided into two endogamous castes, the higher-ranking Maraikkars and the Labbais. Most of the Muslims were traders, many of them plying by sea between Thanjāvūr and Malaya. Smaller numbers wove, or produced and sold mats or betel leaves.

Nāgore was the site of a famous, graceful mosque built over the tomb of Meeran Saheb, or "Nāgore Āṇḍavar," a Muslim saint of the early fifteenth century. His spirit was believed to grant cures, and his twelve-day festival in autumn attracted large numbers of pilgrims from many parts of India.

### *The Christians*

Thanjāvūr's Christians were 3.8 percent of the people in 1931. Portuguese Jesuits from the Missions of Madurai and Mylapore, among them Francis Xavier, converted the first Roman Catholics in the sixteenth century. About 1610, Goanese Catholics built a famous church at Vēlānganni that, like the Nāgore mosque, was believed to be the site of miraculous cures. Rebuilt, it was in 1951 the scene of a ten-day festival in September at which Hindū and Christian pilgrims arrived from all parts of south India. The Goanese founded another large church at Tranquēbar in 1660, and the Madurai Jesuits founded Saint Joseph's College at Nāgapaṭṭaṇam in 1846. In 1706 the King of Denmark sent two famous German pastors, Heinrick Plutschau and Bartholamaus Zeigenbalg, to Tranquēbar, where they founded a Lutheran community. The greatest of the Tranquēbar evangelists, Frederick Schwartz, joined the English Society for the Propagation of Christian Knowledge in 1768, founded a church in Thanjāvūr town, and became a tutor and advisor of the young Maratha Rāja Sarfōji. The SPCK gave over its work to the Society for the Propagation of the Gospel in 1826. The latter built churches at Thanjāvūr, Nāgapaṭṭaṇam, and Tranquēbar, where English services were conducted in 1951. Four other churches in east and south Thanjāvūr were owned by the Methodists, who reached the district in 1841. The Protestants, who merged into the United Church of South India in the 1950s, numbered about 25,000 in 1951, the majority of the Christians being Catholics.

Most of Thanjāvūr's Christians were converts from the Ādi Drāviḍas. They lived in towns or in separate *chēris* close by their Hindū caste fellows and were almost, although not quite, as severely ostracized by the higher castes. Thanjāvūr had, however, a considerable number of Christians converted from Veḷḷāḷars and Kaḷḷars in the time of Schwartz. These two castes of Christians maintained their separation and did not intermarry with each other nor, of course, with the Ādi Drāviḍa Christians. The latter were chiefly agricultural or urban laborers; the upper castes, traders or white-collar workers.

# 3 The Agriculturalists

## A Colonial Profile

Seventy percent of Thanjāvūr's population depended mainly on agriculture for their livelihood in 1951, by comparison with 65 percent in Madras State as a whole.[1] Eighty-one percent of the people lived in villages and the remaining 19 percent in towns of more than 5,000. The high proportion of the agricultural and the rural populations reflected Thanjāvūr's extreme dependence on paddy cultivation. A further 2.4 percent of the people, not counted in the census as "agricultural," depended on fishing, raising sheep, goats, or cattle, or worked in forests or on plantations with specialties such as ground nuts.

The towns were mainly administrative, religious, and marketing centers, heavily dependent on the land. Four percent of the population lived in towns but depended on agricultural work or incomes, while another 1 percent lived in towns but derived part of their income from agriculture. At least another 5 to 6 percent of the people lived from the trade, transport, storage, or processing of paddy, even omitting railroad and trucking workers, who were involved in paddy export or transport. About 4 percent depended on trade in or transport of commodities other than paddy, chiefly fish and livestock. Primary production, or trade in and processing of primary products, thus accounted for roughly 82 percent of Thanjāvūr's income earners, some 77 percent being involved with paddy, the dominant crop.

Of the roughly 18 percent of the people not directly concerned with these pursuits, 3.6 percent were in government and professional service mainly connected with education or the collection of revenue (itself chiefly from the proceeds of paddy lands). One percent were priests or other workers in religious institutions. More than 6 percent were in menial services, chiefly domestic and restaurant employment, followed by hairdressing and laundry work. About 5.5 percent depended mainly on craft production and 5.5 percent on building and stone quarrying.

Altogether, Thanjāvūr presented a classical "colonial" occupational profile, overwhelmingly weighted toward primary production and processing for export. Except for some processing mills and the steel-rolling mill, there was almost no modern industry. There was undoubtedly a smaller proportion of handicraft workers than in precolonial times, and there were relatively large numbers involved in wholesale and retail trade and in menial, personal, and public services. As in most colonial countries the workforce participation was low, only 30 percent of the total population being involved in gainful occupations.

## The Agricultural Strata

### *The Landlords*

In 1951 Thanjāvūr had greater inequality within its agrarian population than the other districts of Tamiḷ Nāḍu. Only 43.4 percent of Thanjāvūr's agriculturalists depended mainly on their own land, under the census classifications of "noncultivating landlords" or "owner cultivators." This was by far the lowest rate of ownership in Tamiḷ Nāḍu, in which 61 percent of agriculturalists owned their own land in the region as a whole. Of the total landowners, as many as 28 percent in Thanjāvūr owned less than one acre. This percentage was higher than any district of Tamiḷ Nāḍu except Madurai, where 29 percent owned less than one acre; in the other nine districts, the owners with less than one acre varied from 10.8 percent to 26.9 percent. At the other extreme, 4 percent of the landowners in Thanjāvūr had holdings above twenty-five acres. This figure was slightly higher than the average of 3.9 percent for the districts of Tamiḷ Nāḍu, although it was not the highest in the state. In Thanjāvūr, however, 25 acres denoted ample prosperity, for the district was the most intensively irrigated, and the most highly productive for wet-rice agriculture in the state. Only 38 percent of the owners held moderate-sized holdings of between three and twenty-five acres, whereas in most Tamiḷ districts (except Chingleput with 32 percent), this proportion was 45 percent to 60 percent of the owners. Again, 5.6 percent of Thanjāvūr's agriculturalists lived mainly from the rent of their lands as noncultivating landlords, whereas in the other Tamiḷ districts the percentage of landlords ranged from 2.1 percent to 4.9 percent. At the bottom of the scale, 34.4 percent of the agriculturalists were extremely poor agricultural laborers; this percentage varied from 10.3 percent to 33.7 percent in the other districts of Tamiḷ Nāḍu, the state as a whole having 25.5 percent. Sixty point seven percent of all the agricultural families of Thanjāvūr had very little or no land of their own, being either tenant farmers or agricultural laborers; this percentage varied from 30.5 percent to 52.8 percent in the other districts.

Thanjāvūr's agrarian inequality was in fact much greater than these figures suggest, for there were a few very large estates of extremely wealthy families, temples, and monasteries. In 1961, nineteen famous temples were reported to own between them 44,109 acres of land, and to receive a total annual income of more than Rs. 3,240,000 (at that date about U.S. $432,000).[2] Altogether, temple lands roughly comprised about 200,000 acres, or about one-sixth of the cultivated acreage in 1961.

Other large estates were held by four Hindū monasteries whose heads also managed the lands of several temples. These monasteries (called *mutts* or *ādhīnams*) were located at Tiruvāduthurai and Dharmapuram in Māyuram *tālūk* and at Tiruppaṉandhāl and Kumbakōṇam in Kumbakōṇam *tālūk*. Between them they owned about 7,000 acres within the district, in addition to several tens of thousands of acres in other districts. Eccesiastical land ownership thus had great significance in Thanjāvūr – more so than in any other district of Tamiḻ Nāḍu.

In 1951 Thanjāvūr had, in addition, several private, family estates of phenomenal size. The largest were those of the Vaḍapādimangalam Mudaliars of Nāgapaṭṭaṇam and Tirutturaipūṇḍi *tālūks*, locally estimated at about 8,004 acres, the Kabisthalam Mūppaṉārs of Pāpaṉāsam and Kumbakōṇam *tālūks*, the Pooṇḍi Vāndayars of Thanjāvūr and Pāpaṉāsam *tālūks*, the Thēvars of Ukkadai in Pāpaṉāsam *tālūk*, and the Iyers of Kunniūr in Maṉṉārguḍi *tālūk*, each with more than 6,000 acres; the family of Mārimuthu Piḷḷai of Paṭṭukkoṭṭai, the Dēsigars of Valivalam in Tirutturaipūṇḍi *tālūk*, and several others, each with somewhat smaller estates. All of these estates dated from Maratha or Vijayanagar times. Most of them appear to have been granted, or usurped, in return for military services or the collection of revenue.

Altogether, large temple, monastic, or private estates, each comprising several villages, were estimated to cover roughly half of Thanjāvūr district in the early 1950s. The other half was divided into villages each containing many smaller holdings that ranged from about one-third of an acre to a hundred acres each. In such villages a core of about one to three dozen related households of traditional owners from one of the higher castes usually retained about one-fifth to two-thirds of the land. The rest was owned by newer, often absentee owners, some of whom were of middle to low caste and many of whom were traders, government servants, industrialists, or independent professionals. Kumbapeṭṭai and Kirippūr, the two villages I studied, were both of this latter type.

In 1951 landownership in Thanjāvūr was called *mirāsi*; the landowner, a *mirāsdār*.[3] The term was a Persian one meaning "inheritance," introduced by officers of the Nawāb of Ārcot during his conquest of Thanjāvūr in 1773–4. The older Tamiḻ term was *kāṇiyācchi*. Before British rule began, a group of related *mirāsdār* households of one of the aristocratic Hindū castes jointly managed the village lands and received a share called the *kīlvāram*, or "lower share" of their produce. The *mēlvāram*, or "upper share," which traditionally varied from about 33 percent to 45 percent of the gross produce, belonged to the king or to some designated representative of the government. Out of their "lower share" the *mirāsdārs* maintained not only themselves and their families but also their tenant cultivators and agricultural slaves in accordance with customary laws. Specialized servants of the village, such as artisans, received separate shares that amounted to about 10 percent of the gross produce.

During the nineteenth century the British government progressively modified the *mirāsi* right in different parts of Thanjāvūr in the direction of capitalist private ownership. Between 1889 and 1893, *mirāsi* rights throughout Thanjāvūr were finally divided among individual families and made virtually equivalent to *ryotwāri* rights in the rest of India. By 1951 the two terms were interchangeable.

In 1951 the lands of *mirāsdārs*, including wet and dry fields and orchards, were owned privately by individuals or, in the case of ancestral lands, jointly by a man and his heirs in the patrilineal line. Only small areas of common land in each village, or in some villages the sites (*nattam*) on which houses were built, remained jointly owned by all the resident *mirāsdārs*. Common lands were used as pasture, to collect wood and cow dung for fuel, and to obtain mud, wood, and thatch for building. The main village bathing pools, cremation and burial grounds, threshing floors, and the fertile banks of irrigation channels, were also normally common lands, whereas roadsides, channels, and other pieces of wasteland called *purambōke* belonged to the government.

By 1951, and indeed in most villages for the previous fifty years, the private lands of *mirāsdārs* amounted to a form of bourgeois property. They could be bought, sold, mortgaged, or leased freely in market conditions. The sale of land had increased in the twentieth century, so that from about one- to two-thirds or even more of the land in most villages belonged to people other than the traditional owners. The traditional families had also bought and sold family fields amongst themselves with their heirs' consent; thus few plots remained as ancestral lands. *Mirāsdārs* could grow on their land whatever crops they wished, or could leave them fallow. The only restriction on their use or neglect of the land was that in the case of wet land, they must contribute money or provide labor for the upkeep of the smaller, village-managed irrigation channels.

In return for these rights, *mirāsdārs* paid a cash revenue to the government which, in the late 1940s and early 1950s, amounted to about 7 percent of the market value of its gross produce. This revenue, called *kist*, had grown out of the old *mēlvāram*, but as a percentage of the gross produce it had been reduced during and since the revenue settlement of 1889. In that year the revenue had been fixed at roughly half the net produce (after deducting the costs of labor, inputs, stock, tools, marketing charges, and seasonal vicissitudes), or roughly 29 percent of the gross outturn. This rate was further reduced in the Resettlement of 1922–24 as a result of the agitations of landlords in the Madras legislative assembly, and again in the depression of the 1930s.

In 1951 the large majority of *mirāsdārs* in Thanjāvūr were either rentier landlords or ''gentleman farmers'' who did not work on their own lands. The former leased out their land to cultivating tenants. The latter, although classified as ''cultivating'' owners in the Census of India, had their lands cultivated by agricultural laborers whose work was supervised by the owner or an agent. A smaller proportion of owners did work on their own lands, especially in the less fertile areas of the southwest uplands and the tail end of the delta near the coast. Such people, although *mirāsdārs* in law and subject to the same terms as noncultivating owners, were usually referred to as *payirchelavukkārars*, or ''cultivators,'' a term also applied to tenant farmers who cultivated their leased fields.

Many of the ecclesiastical and some of the family estates of Thanjāvūr were formerly held under a second type of ''ownership'' as *iṉam* lands. In pre-British times *iṉams* were prebendal estates of a kind that dates back at least 2,000 years in Tamiḷ Nāḍu and still earlier in north India. Those recently in existence in Thanjāvūr were granted or reaffirmed by the Maratha Rājās in the seventeenth and eighteenth centuries, or in a few cases by the British in the nineteenth century.

Properly speaking, *inam* estates were royal grants, not of land itself or of its "lower share," but of all or a portion of the *mēlvāram* or "upper share" (that is, the king's share or royal revenue) of the produce of a piece of land, which might comprise anything from a small plot to a number of villages.

*Inams* were traditionally of varying kinds and values. They included:

1. Ecclesiastical grants of all or part of the "upper share" of lands to Hindū temples and monasteries, and in a few cases to Christian churches or Muslim mosques, for the maintenance of their personnel and the performance of ceremonies;

2. Grants of all or part of the "upper share" to maintain public works or charities such as major irrigation works, hospitals, colleges, rest houses, drinking water for travelers, and feeding centers for pilgrims;

3. Service grants of all or part of the "upper share" for the maintenance of ministers and of military, revenue, police, and other officers of the Maratha government in pre-British times. Small *inams* were also sometimes granted to the families of soldiers who died in battle. In general, service grants might be made either for the duration of services or as rewards for past services.

4. Sinecure grants of part or all of the *mēlvāram* of designated lands were grants made to individuals or communities of religious scholars, priests, famous artists, poets, dancers, or musicians, or to members or connections of the royal family, either for a lifetime or in perpetuity. The great majority of these grants were to Brahman communities or individuals, but some were to Marathas or to artists or favorites of other castes.

5. Village-service *inams*, usually called *māṉyams*, were small plots of land inside *inam* and some *mirāsi* villages, set aside for village servants and laborers. In pre-British times small *māṉyams* of about one *kāṇi* (1.33 acres) were often assigned in *inam* villages to each of the families of the village temple priest, the village accountant, carpenter, blacksmith, goldsmith, washerman, barber, doctor (sometimes the same as the barber), supervisor of irrigation water, the village watchman who guarded the fields from marauders or stray cattle, and the scavenger and tender of cremation and burial grounds. Such *māṉyams* were held from the king free of *mēlvāram*. The servants cultivated them themselves and lived mainly from the produce. Smaller tribute-free *māṉyams* of about one *māh* (one-third of an acre) were held by each of the village's tenant cultivators, and still smaller ones of half a *māh* or fifty *kuris* (one-sixth of an acre) by each of the families of "Untouchable" village slaves.

In addition, all of the families of village servants and laborers had the right to bounties or *swatantrams*, varying portions of the paddy threshed at each harvest in the village's main fields.

Village *māṉyams* seem to have been especially common in villages that were themselves within the *inam* of some major functionary of the king. In *mirāsi* villages, which paid *mēlvāram* directly to the government, the whole payment of village servants and laborers appears to have been usually in portions of the village grain.

In the early decades of the nineteenth century, most of the village service *iñams* were cancelled by the British government. The village accountant and police began to be paid cash salaries by the government. The other servants and laborers were left to the mercies of the *mirāsdārs*, who became free to appoint, pay, or dismiss them as they pleased. In some villages the *mirāsdārs* maintained certain plots as *mānyams* for village servants and slaves while paying the government revenue on these plots themselves. In others, the *mirāsdārs* gradually usurped all their servants' and laborers' plots, and instead paid them a mixture of grain shares and cash. In *mirāsi* villages paying revenue directly to the government, most village *mānyams* had died out by the 1940s, but in *inam* villages, village *mānyams* were maintained until the abolition of *inams* in 1948.

Even before British rule some *inamdārs* of categories (1–4) had bought or usurped the *kīlvāram* as well as the *mēlvāram* rights in their lands. The British government "resettled" the major *inams* in 1861, cancelling some and changing others into ordinary *mirāsi* holdings. In *inam* villages that were confirmed, the *inamdārs* were given the option of buying the *kīlvāram* right in installments if they did not already own it. In many cases they were also charged a light revenue by the government. In these ways much former *inam* land was turned into something closely approaching capitalist property, for the *inamdār* had no hereditary *mirāsdār* beneath him and could appoint or evict his tenants and laborers as he pleased. In some cases he could even sell or mortgage the land. Inalienable *inams* did remain, however, in the possession of some of the larger temples and monasteries, the former royal family, and a few individuals.

In 1931, 528,599 acres out of 2,486,215 in the district (about 22 percent) remained in *inam* holdings. More than three-quarters of them lay in the dryer upland tracts of Arantāngi and Paṭṭukkoṭṭai *tālūks*, but in every *tālūk* there were a few *inams* comprising rich deltaic fields.

Pre-British *inam* lands were not, in my view, feudal estates, although they tended to become somewhat more "feudalistic" in the seventeenth and eighteenth centuries than they had been earlier. They were not feudal estates because first, in pre-British times they do not appear normally to have been hereditary in law but only to have become so in certain cases during periods of weak central rule. Second, the *inamdar* often did not live on his estate or have close contact with its inhabitants. Instead he might merely draw his income from it while carrying out military, bureaucratic, religious, or ministerial duties elsewhere. Third, *inam* estates came under strict royal supervision. Their accounts were audited and their inhabitants, including the *inamdar* himself, could be removed, promoted, or demoted at royal pleasure. The proportion of the estate's income accorded to the *inamdar* could also be changed by royal fiat at any time. Fourth, *inam* holders did not normally command local troops on their estates. Indeed, unless they were appointed by the government as military officers over government troops stationed elsewhere in barracks, they had no military function at all. The *iṉamdar* was indeed more similar to a rentier. He was often a town dweller and usually a servant of the government, who simply received his income in the form of crops or money obtained from a particular piece of land. In my view, *iṉams* were prebendal estates that derived from a social system (the Chōḷa kingdom) best regarded as a theocratic, bureaucratic, tributary irrigation state, although that state, and some *iṉams*, did acquire certain feudal features under the Telugu and Maratha rules. I return to this subject in Chapter 6.

Shortly before 1951, another type of landed estate in Thanjāvūr had been the *zamindāri* estate, of which there were thirteen during British rule. In 1931 they comprised 190,925 acres, or about 11.5 percent of the district's cultivated area, and lay mainly in the dryer, southwestern *tālūks* of Paṭṭukkoṭṭai and Arantāngi. They ranged from less than 1,000 to more than 54,000 acres. They appear to have been given by the Nāyak rulers of the early sixteenth century to border warlords, chiefly of the Kaḷḷar caste. The managers of these estates became relatively autonomous feudalistic nobles who commanded their own armies and governed their own subjects, but paid part of their *mēlvāram* to the rulers of Thanjāvūr. These estates persisted through the Maratha period and, although their armies were disbanded, throughout British rule.

A third type of large private estate formerly belonged to a set of officers called *pattakdārs*.[4] These were revenue farmers appointed by the Maratha Rājas in the late 1780s and 1790s. Their appointment was an emergency measure following the devastation and partial depopulation of Thanjāvūr by the Muslim general of Mysore, Haidar Āli, in 1782–5. In order to collect the land revenue for themselves and the English East India Company from a depleted countryside, the Rāja's administrators grouped villages under some of the existing, prominent landholders and gave them the right to collect the revenue under threat of military force. In the short period of their control the *pattakdārs* acquired large estates with private armed forces and ruled somewhat like *zamindārs*. The East India Company removed their revenue and military functions shortly after it assumed outright control of the district in 1799, but the former *pattakdārs* held on to much of their land under ordinary *mirāsi* right. Examples of great landlords who were former *pattakdārs* were the Vaḍapādimangalam Mudaliars, the Valivalam Dēsigars, the Pooṇḍi Vandayars, and the Kabistalam Mūppaṉārs.

Under British rule, government supervision of *iṉams*, and of all temple and monastic properties, ceased with Act XX of 1861. Thereafter, the temple estates became the private bailiwicks of their local trustees. In some cases the trustees were elected by a small number of local dignitaries. In many temples, trusteeships became or remained hereditary in the families of the district's biggest *mirāsdārs* and merchants, who were often accused of using part of their income privately. Monastic estates were ruled by their religious heads, who were named by their predecessors or elected for life by a small committee drawn from the *mutt's* members. The heads of the four great *mutts*, in turn, each held the right to appoint the trustees and priests of several temples.

Thus, for example, the *pandārasanidhi* (head) of the Veḷḷaḷar *mutt* at

Tiruvāduthurai in Māyuram *tālūk* controlled 3,000 acres in Thanjāvūr, 25,000 in Tinnevelly, 1,000 in Madurai, and smaller amounts elsewhere. In addition he had the right to appoint priests and trustees to fifteen temples, each with endowments. The *pandārasanidhi* of the Veḷḷāḷar *mutt* at Dharmapuram controlled some 2,500 acres in Thanjāvūr district, and appointed or helped to appoint the priests and trustees of one subordinate *mutt* and twenty-seven temples with estates totaling roughly 24,179 acres. The third large Veḷḷālar *mutt* at Tiruppanaṉdhāl in Kumbakōṇam *tālūk* was similarly well endowed, whereas the Brahman *mutt* of Sankarāchārya at Kumbakōṇam owned less valuable properties.

Among the great temples the Tyāgarājaswāmy temple of Tiruvārūr owned some 6,667 acres in Thanjāvūr district. The ownership included both the *mēlvāram* and *kīlvāram* rights, so that the management had no subordinate *mirāsdārs* to contend with, received the whole surplus of the lands, and could appoint or evict tenants as it pleased. The temple had 13 departments, or *kaṭṭalais*, each owning land and each under a hereditary trustee vested with supervision of the functions attached to his department. The best-endowed departments were those of *apishēka* (libation) and *annādāna* (rice offering) to the deity, which owned two-thirds of the property and were managed by the head of Vēlakuricchi *mutt* in Tinnevelly district. Most of the remaining property belonged to the Rājam (royal) department managed by the head of the Dharmapuram *mutt*. The internal management (*uḷ-thurai*) of the whole temple, concerned with appointing the personnel and organizing and financing the daily services and festivals, was shared by two local landlord houses of the Toṇḍaimaṇḍalam subcaste of the Veḷḷāḷar caste, the Bāvas of Kulikarai and the Mudaliars of Vaḍapādimangalam. Both houses had been military officers under the Maratha Rājas; both became revenue farmers (*pattakdārs*) in the late 1780s after the defeat of the Mysorean invaders. In the nineteenth and early twentieth centuries they were great private landlords, the Bāvas owning a fort and some 6,667 acres, and the Vaḍapādimangalam Mudaliars an estate of some 8,004 acres, both under *mirāsi* ownership. In the early 1920s the Bāvas' wealth dwindled after division of the family estate. In a series of lawsuits, the Mudaliars challenged their hereditary right to manage the temple. The Bāvas were finally deposed from the temple management by a Supreme Court decision of 1973 and the Mudaliars were left in virtual control of its income, but in 1951 the two houses jointly managed the day-to-day affairs and most of the income of the temple.

From the mid-nineteenth century, therefore, the great temple and monastic estates, like the great family estates with which they were linked through trusteeships, were managed somewhat like private feudal landed properties; they were, however, in a gradual process of transition to capitalist relations as they became ever more deeply involved in the export of paddy.

From 1908 the ecclesiastical estates became again subject to a certain degree of government intervention as a result of pressure by a group of High Court lawyers for their reform and as a result of changes in the Code of Civil Procedure.[5] Thereafter, numerous lawsuits took place among and against their trustees and various claimants to trusteeships. The government of Madras instituted the Hindū Religious and Charitable Endowments Board in the early 1930s to supervise temple and charitable trust properties. Control was subsequently shared between the trustees and executive officers of the board. In the 1950s, however, there was still much complaint of misappropriation of funds by temple trustees.

Temple and monastic lands were leased to tenants. In many cases the trustees themselves or their close relatives were noncultivating intermediary tenants, and paid a rent to the temple that was only one-third to one-half of the rent they themselves received from their subordinate cultivating tenants. The relationship was clearly one through which trustees and other dignitaries privately mulcted the temples of part of the surplus of lands originally designed to support their religious functions.

*Zamindāri* estates and private *i̱nam* estates were abolished shortly after the independence of India under the Madras Estates (Abolition and Conversion into Ryotwari) Act of 1948. The act became operative in Thanjāvūr in 1951, although it was several years before a settlement of every estate could be concluded by tribunals and law courts.

Under this act, *i̱nam* and *zamindāri* rights (that is, *mēlvāram* rights) held by individuals or families were confiscated by the Madras government in return for substantial compensation. *Ryots* holding *kīlvāram* rights who had hitherto paid revenue to an *i̱namdar* or *zamindār* became ordinary *mirāsdārs* paying revenue to the government. *I̱namdārs* and *zamindārs* were permitted to keep, as their *mirāsi* lands subject to normal government revenue, those lands on their estates of which they had previously owned both *mēlvāram* and *kīlvāram* rights. They were also allowed to keep lands that had been abandoned, relinquished, or never occupied by a *ryot*, and that were being cultivated by agricultural laborers as private farms. Finally, these estate owners also retained possession of any ordinary *mirāsi* lands, not in their prebends, that they had purchased previously.[6]

Personal *i̱namdārs* and *zamindārs* thus became private *mirāsdārs* like all other landlords, in most cases of very large although reduced estates. The still-existing service *i̱nams* or *mā̱nyams* of village servants were also made the *ryotwāri* property of the holders, their owners being freed from any legal obligation of service provided that they were not in the service of a religious, charitable, or educational institution. By all these means, roughly 20 percent of the land of Thanjāvūr ceased to be under *i̱nam* or *zamindāri* tenures and became ordinary taxable and marketable private property.

Temples, educational institutions, and charitable institutions that had previously owned *i̱nam* estates were separated from these estates unless they owned the *kīlvāram* or *ryotwāri* right, in which case they retained that right. Instead of a lump sum as compensation for their *i̱nam* rights, these institutions were allotted annual incomes from the government roughly equivalent to their former incomes from their *i̱nam* rights. Individuals or families holding minor service *i̱nams* under the authority of temples, *mutts*, or charitable establishments were also accorded annual incomes from the government provided that they continued their services.

Under this act, therefore, religious, educational, and charitable establishments and their servants, like private estate holders, lost their prebendary rights, but whereas private estate holders were compensated with lump sums, public establishments and their servants were given annual salaries by the government. In both cases, the holders were permitted to retain certain lands as their private property, subject to normal taxation by the government. The act of 1948 thus virtually completed the transformation of Thanjāvūr landholding into bourgeois property – a transformation that had been brought gradually underway by the British government in the course of the nineteenth and twentieth centuries. At the same time, many private estate owners and religious establishments remained as very large private landlords, although their newly confirmed estates were less extensive than their former prebendal holdings had been. The 200,000 acres recorded as owned by temples in 1961, for example, were *mirāsi* estates left to these temples *after* the abolition of *iṉam* rights in 1948.

### *Owner Cultivators*

In 1951, 6.2 percent of Thanjāvūr's agricultural population were recorded as mainly rent-receiving landlords and their dependents, and another 37.2 percent as depending on the cultivation of land mainly owned by themselves. These figures have the merit of separating the landlords whose fields were cultivated by tenants from all those who lived mainly by hiring agricultural labor or by working their farms themselves. The figures do not, however, give an accurate presentation of owner cultivators who worked on their own farms, for in Thanjāvūr it was very common for even small landowners to abstain from manual work and to hire laborers who were supervised by themselves or by an agent. Except on some of the dry land of the southwest uplands, families owning more than five acres (25.3 percent of the total landowners) did not regularly till the fields themselves. The actual figure for noncultivating owners was even higher, for large numbers of Brahman and Veḷḷāḷar families owned small holdings of less than five acres that were leased out or cultivated by laborers. In many cases the owners worked in towns or as schoolteachers, village accountants, priests, or other kinds of nonmanual workers in villages.

Thanjāvūr had by far the largest noncultivating class of landowners (whether rentiers or hirers of labor) in Tamiḻ Nāḍu. Indeed, the whole Brahman caste, which formed 6.2 percent of Thanjāvūr's population in 1931, was forbidden by religious laws even to touch the plough. But large numbers of other owners, especially among the upper ranks of Veḷḷāḷars and Naidūs, regarded it as beneath their dignity to cultivate their fields. Although an exact figure for the district is not available, I found that only seven men, or 3.8 percent of the agriculturalists in Kumbapeṭṭai in west Thanjāvūr, could be counted as working owner cultivators, and only 28.9 percent in Kirippūr in the east of the district. Even taking account of the southwest uplands, it is doubtful whether more than 20 percent of the total agriculturalists in Thanjāvūr were working owner cultivators or *payirchelavukkārars*. The remaining "owner cultivators," or about 17 percent of the agriculturalists, might be better described as "supervisory farmers" or in some cases as "absentee farmers."

These supervisory and absentee farmers overlapped with the category of rentier landlords. Indeed, both were called *mirāsdārs*. Especially among landowners possessing between ten and fifty acres, it was common for the owner to lease out part of his estate to tenants and to have part cultivated by attached or hired laborers. Some landowning families employed different methods in different years, depending on whether or not they had an able-bodied man at home to supervise the laborers, or whether the owner was busy with other work. Most rentier landlords of any size kept *some* land under "personal" cultivation, that is, they had it cultivated by laborers rather than by tenants. The two census categories of "landlord" and "cultivating owner" therefore merged into one another gradually. In later chapters I shall describe both the rentier landlords and the noncultivating farmers as landlords, because neither of them performed manual work.

This usage conforms to that of Mao Tse-tung, who wrote in 1933: "A landlord is a person who possesses land, who does not engage in labour himself or merely takes part in labor as a supplementary source of income, and who lives by exploiting the peasants. The landlord's exploitation chiefly assumes the form of collecting rent; besides that, he may also lend money, hire labour, or engage in industrial and commercial enterprise." Mao Tse-tung added of China in 1933, "But his exaction of land rent from the peasants is the principal form of his exploitation." This was not always the case in Thanjāvūr in 1951, for some landlords owning as much as thirty acres had most or all of their land cultivated by laborers, as did many owning ten to twenty acres. On the whole, however, the bulk of the lands of noncultivating landlords (certainly, more than half) was leased out to tenants.

Like Mao Tse-tung, I shall also consider as landlords noncultivating owners who lived from very small patches of land, and those who, "although having gone bankrupt, still do not engage in labour but live by swindling and plundering or on the assistance of relatives or friends, and are better off than the average middle peasant."[7]

Those classified in the census as "owner cultivators," whether working or landlord, belonged mainly to the Non-Brahman castes, who formed 63.5% of the total population in 1931. A very few Ādi Drāviḍas had become small "owner cultivators" in recent years. "Owner cultivators" were chiefly to be found among the lower-ranking subcastes of Veḷḷāḷars and Naidūs and among the Mūppaṉar, Agambaḍiyar, Vaṉṉiyar, Paḍaiyācchi, Paḷḷi, and Kaḷḷar castes. In the less fertile east and south of the district, village artisans such as weavers, goldsmiths, carpenters, and blacksmiths sometimes owned a few acres that they cultivated themselves, but in this case part of their income came from their craft. In some instances coconut gardens were owned by the more prosperous members of the Nāḍār and Nāyakkar castes, Thanjāvūr's coconut growers and tappers of palm wine or toddy. Most coconut gardens and orchards, like paddy fields, were however owned by people of the high landlord castes such as Brahmans, Veḷḷāḷars, and Naidūs, and were either leased to Nāḍār tenant cultivators or tended by laborers.

A characteristic of Thanjāvūr's rice farming in 1951 was that even small, working owner cultivators did not do all of their own agricultural work. At the peak seasons of transplanting and harvest, almost all of them hired casual laborers of the lowest Ādi Drāviḍa castes. One reason for this was that the tasks of transplanting seedlings into newly flooded fields and of harvesting the paddy must be done quickly. Transplanting had to be speedy because irrigation water might be available to each farmer only for a few hours at a time, and harvesting, because the crop might be spoiled by rain or by rats and birds. A holding of more than one acre thus required other than family labor at these seasons. In addition, however, the irksome work of transplanting seedlings in muddy water or of reaping and threshing in the hot sun were thought socially appropriate only to very poor people and especially to Ādi Drāviḍas. In 1883, indeed, Ādi Drāviḍa women were reported to do all of the work of paddy transplanting in Thanjāvūr.[8] And in 1951 the women of owner cultivator families in fact seldom worked in the fields, so that even the weeding and gram harvesting, as well as paddy transplanting, were done mainly by Ādi Drāviḍa women. For even the working owner cultivator, "cultivation" tended to mean that the owner or, more probably, his grown or growing sons, ploughed and manured the fields, sowed the paddy and gram seeds, helped the laborers with the harvest, and carted the crops to the family granary or to the nearest rice mill. For the rest, he engaged in garden work and was on hand to supervise the operations of laborers.

We can see, therefore, that most of Thanjāvūr's working owner cultivators were both exploited by others, in the sense that they paid high rents to landlords for land they leased in addition to their own holdings, and were also exploiters of others, in the sense that they hired laborers. Even so, it is possible to separate the owner cultivators into rich and middle peasants by using the criteria employed in the Maoist definitions of peasant classes, and I do this in later chapters.

By these criteria, "rich peasants own the better means of production and have some floating capital. They themselves work, but as a rule they depend on exploitation for most or a part of their living. This exploitation chiefly takes the form of hiring . . . long-term labourers."[9] Rich peasants in Thanjāvūr were thus working peasants who owned about five to seven acres of wet land and might lease in from three to fifteen acres more. The men, or some men, of the family did the lighter tasks of cultivation, but the family engaged one or more married pairs of regular laborers throughout the year in addition to hiring extra labor at peak seasons.

Middle peasants, by contrast, "depend wholly or mainly on their own work for their living. In general they do not exploit others, and many of them suffer exploitation on a small scale in the form of land rent and loan interest. Usually they do not sell their labour."[10] In Thanjāvūr, the cultivators whom I shall call middle peasants usually owned less than five acres of wet land and leased in about two to eight acres more. The men of the family worked harder and more regularly than the rich peasants. In some cases, the women, too, might do occasional light agricultural work such as weeding or gram harvesting. Middle peasants did not hire year-round laborers, but in Thanjāvūr they did hire Ādi Drāviḍa laborers at the peak seasons of harvest and transplanting.

Middle peasants were distinguishable from poor peasants, whom I also describe as "tenant cultivators" or "pure tenants" in later chapters. These cultivators leased all or almost all their land from landlords and so suffered exploitation in the form of rent and interest. In addition, some of them occasionally had to hire themselves out as laborers to eke out a livelihood.[11] In later chapters, however, I separate still further those cultivators who depended mainly on hiring themselves out as laborers and only subsidiarily on leasing land, and classify them as in the upper ranks of the agricultural laborers.[12]

### Tenant Farmers

In 1951 Thanjāvūr had two main forms of tenure under which people leased land from landlords. The older and, in 1951, the less common tenure was *vāram* (literally "share"), a sharecropping lease usually held by cultivators of middle- or low-ranking Non-Brahman peasant castes and occasionally by members of the lowest Ādi Drāviḍa castes. *Vāram* dates back at least to the Chōḷa empire of the ninth to thirteenth centuries and probably long before. In 1951 the *vāram* tenant, or *vāramdār*, usually paid between three-quarters and four-fifths of the net yield of wet paddy fields after the village servants and harvest laborers had been paid, and one-half to two-thirds the yield of dry lands or gardens as rent to his landlord. Out of his share the tenant paid his expenses for nonharvest laborers, seed, half his manure, and the cost of his oxen, keeping the rest of the crop (about 7 percent to 10 percent of the gross yield) for his family's maintenance. The landlord normally contributed half the green manure, ashes, and cowdung used to fertilize the fields, and paid the laborers who dug out the irrigation channels once a year. Some *vāram* leases were still being given by resident landlords in 1951 and were said to have been much commoner fifty to sixty years ago, but in many villages they had died out.

Tenants under the second lease, called *kuthakai*, were found in all or almost all Thanjāvūr's villages in 1951. *Kuthakai* tenants paid a fixed rent to the landlord that in an average year amounted to about 60 percent to 70 percent of the average gross produce of wet paddy lands and coconut gardens and one-half to two-thirds of that of dry lands. As in the case of *vāram*, the landlord usually gave the tenant half his requirements in fertilizer, and paid the costs of channel digging. The tenant paid the rest of his cultivation expenses, including all those for agricultural laborers, and the harvest and other payments due from his land to the village servants.

The term *kuthakai* was apparently introduced into Thanjāvūr by the Vijayanagar

A *kuthakai* tenant takes a break with his son in the sowing season.

rulers sometime between the mid-fourteenth and the mid-seventeenth centuries. It is not known whether its provisions in those days were similar to those found in 1951. In 1951 both *kuthakai* and *vāram* cultivating tenants were called *kuḍiyāṉavar* ("occupants") by the landowners.

In 1951 *kuthakai* tenures were usually preferred to *vāram* by both landlords and tenants. The tenant had the advantage of being able to count on retaining his whole surplus above the fixed rent. In an exceptionally good year this might amount to up to half the gross paddy crop. In any case its elasticity was an incentive to hard work and careful cultivation. In an exceptionally bad year (like all the years between 1947 and 1951) the landlord might make concessions that would leave the tenant a bare margin for seed and subsistence. Not all landlords did so, however, and in 1951, after a series of bad harvests, most tenants were deeply in debt to their landlords for their very subsistence. Even so, tenants said they preferred the possibility of achieving some extra gain in future good harvests and preferred to pay fixed rent rather than to have the landlord supervise and divide the harvest.

For the landlord, the advantage of *kuthakai* over *vāram* was that *he* was assured of a fairly high rent in good or bad seasons, if he cared to extract it. He was also saved the bother of supervising and dividing the harvest, an advantage to landlords who worked elsewhere by day or who lived in a nearby town or village. All that was necessary in such cases was for the landlord to appear once at harvest time and make sure the right amount of grain or money was delivered to his home.

*Kuthakai* tenures, in the sense of fixed-rent tenures, seem to have superseded *vāram* or sharecropping tenures in many villages from about 1870. I suspect that this change was especially determined by two other important changes in Thanjāvūr's economy.

One was the export of an ever-increasing proportion of Thanjāvūr's paddy crop during this period, in the nineteenth century especially to the plantations of Ceylon and Malaya, and in the twentieth century to plantation regions inside India. In these circumstances *kuthakai* had the advantage of allowing both the landlords and the government to estimate landlords' paddy income in advance, and thus the probable amount available for export. *Kuthakai* also gave the tenant a somewhat greater incentive to produce and to sell more than he would do under *vāram*, and so increased the district's exportable surplus; except in very bad years, most *kuthakai* tenants did in fact market a portion of their grain.

The other change in the same period was the departure to urban work of an ever-increasing number of Thanjāvūr's Brahman landlords and, in the second quarter of the twentieth century, of some of its Non-Brahman landlords as well. When they commuted to towns in Thanjāvūr or lived part-time in nearby cities such as Tiruchirappalli or Madurai, such landlords often gave their land on *kuthakai* and came home merely to collect their rents.

When *kuthakai* tenants were themselves cultivators, they usually belonged to the same range of middle or low-ranking Non-Brahman castes or Ādi Drāviḍa castes from which *vāram* tenants were drawn. Their *mirāsdārs* were normally Brahmans or middle- to high-caste Non-Brahmans.

There was, however, in addition a category of noncultivating, intermediary *kuthakai* tenants in 1951. These were called *uḷ-kuthakaikkār* ("inside tenants") or *ul-kuḍiyāṉavar*, whereas the ordinary cultivating tenant might be referred to as a *pora-kuḍiyānavar* ("outside tenant") to distinguish him. The *uḷ-kuthakai* tenant was usually, although not invariably, of the same caste as the owner and was often a kinsman or affine.

*Mirāsdārs* usually gave their lands on *uḷ-kuthakai* if they were chronically ill or old and unable to supervise the land, or (most commonly) were employed or otherwise engaged in a distant city and could not easily visit the village at harvest time.

The *uḷ-kuthakai* tenant paid a lower rent than the ordinary cultivator under *kuthakai*, which might vary from about two-fifths to one-half of the wet paddy crop. Often, he kept the whole of any dry intercrop and paid only a small cash rent for house gardens or orchard lands. In turn, the *uḷ-kuthakai* tenant had the land cultivated by agricultural laborers or gave it on *vāram* or *pora-kuthakai* to a lower-ranking cultivator.

*Uḷ-kuthakai* tenants were in general more prosperous than cultivating tenants and were usually themselves *mirāsdārs*. The advantage to the *uḷ-kuthakai* tenant was that he made a small income with relatively minor supervisory work, and to the *mirāsdār*, that he received some income without the responsibility of supervising laborers or pursuing cultivating tenants to make sure they paid their full rent. Some absent *mirāsdārs* simply drew their share of the rent in cash. Others had bags of paddy and other crops sent to them by rail for use in the city.

In 1951, 15.5 percent of Thanjāvūr's people, or 22.2 percent of its agricultural population, were recorded as chiefly tenant farmers or their dependants. As far as I could judge, the majority of the tenants cultivated on *kuthakai*; a smaller number, perhaps 10 percent of the total tenants, on *vāram*. The proportion of *uḷ-kuthakai* tenants, who did not themselves cultivate, reached 26 percent of the total tenants in some Brahman villages near the Kāvēri river, but because most of them also owned land of their own they were probably classified in the Census as mainly dependent on landownership. The percentage of persons predominantly occupied as tenants in the agricultural population was much higher in Thanjāvūr than in the other districts of Tamiḷ Nāḍu, where tenants ranged from 7.8 percent to 17.4 percent of the agricultural population. As we shall see in Chapter 5, the relatively high proportion of Thanjāvūr's tenants reflected its high level of productivity and of noncultivating landlords.

### *Agricultural Laborers*

In 1951, 34.4 percent of Thanjāvūr's agricultural population, and 24.1 percent of its total population, were reported in the Census as depending chiefly on agricultural labor for their livelihood. Most of these laborers belonged to the Ādi Drāviḍa castes of Paṟayars and Paḷḷars, who ranked markedly below the rest of the people and lived in separate hamlets on the outskirts of villages. Ādi Drāviḍas were 22.8 percent of the population of Thanjāvūr in 1951, the vast majority being agricultural laborers. Among Ādi Drāviḍa agricultural laborers, in contrast to owner cultivators or even tenant farmers, women worked in the fields in all seasons along with men.

In terms of production relations, I found three main types of agricultural laborers in 1951, each with some internal and regional variation.

Although declining each year in numbers, the commonest type was still the *paṇṇaiyāḷ* (literally "farm man," fem. *paṇṇaiyācchi*), or attached laborer. Although there were attached laborers among the Non-Brahmans who were sometimes called *paṇṇaiyāḷs*, the term usually referred to Ādi Drāviḍas, Non-Brahman attached laborers being more often called *vēlaikkārars* (literally "workmen").

*Paṇṇaiyāḷs* among the Ādi Drāviḍas occupied a similar status to indentured laborers on the plantations of South and Southeast Asia, the relationship being a modification of the open slavery (*aḍimai*) under which their ancestors had lived until the 1860s.

The *paṇṇaiyāḷ* and his family were tied to their landlord or peasant master by debt. Only by repaying the debt, having it paid by a new master, or being forgiven it, could they free themselves and move elsewhere. If they ran away, they could be returned by other landlords or the police.

In 1951 some *paṇṇaiyāḷs* served the same families of masters as their ancestors had for generations. A larger number had changed or been obliged to change masters at least once or twice in their working life, while some were engaged annually and were liable to be dismissed, with their small debts forgiven or deducted from their harvest earnings, in any given year.

By 1951, in fact, attached labor was already beginning to change from a form of semislavery to which landlords clung in conditions of labor shortage, to a form of relatively secure, albeit servile, employment to which the laborers clung, as being preferable to casual daily labor in which they might be unemployed and unpaid for large parts of the year. This change had evidently come about in the previous two decades as a result of increases in the number and percentage of agricultural laborers. Thus, according to the decennial Censuses, male agricultural workers were only 30.9 percent of the agricultural workforce in 1931 and only 17.7 percent of the total male workforce, whereas in 1951 they were 35.4 percent of the male agricultural workforce and 29.1 percent of the total male workforce. Their absolute increase had been from 123,114 to 171,300 (including earning dependants) during the twenty-year period.

In 1951 male *paṇṇaiyāḷs* were called to work about 180 to 300 days a year, women about 120 to 240 days, and boys aged eight to fourteen about 260 days. Between them Ādi Drāviḍa men, women, and children did most of the wet rice cultivation. Male *paṇṇaiyāḷs* had other, collective obligations to the village as a whole, such as digging out the irrigation channels and dragging the temple car in village festivals.

Although usually hired as married couples or in families, *paṇṇaiyāḷs* were mainly paid individually for each day they worked. Their payment was in paddy, sometimes with a little cash. In addition to their daily payments a *paṇṇaiyāḷ* family's master supplied clothing, a house site, and various gifts at life crises and festivals. *Paṇṇaiyāḷs* also had collective rights in the village's common land and produce in the form of mud and palmyra leaves to build their huts, fuel, small fish, crabs and rats from the fields and irrigation channels, carrion beef and the hides of dead cattle, and gifts of cooked food at village temple festivals.

A second type of attached laborer was the *vēlaikkāraṉ* (literally "workman"). A *vēlaikkāraṉ* was of higher rank than an ordinary *paṇṇaiyāḷ*, for he belonged to one of the middle- or low-ranking Non-Brahman rather than to the Ādi Drāviḍa castes. In Thanjāvūr the castes from which *vēlaikkārars* were drawn were usually Paḍaiyācchis, Iḍaiyars, Mūppaṉars, Vaṉṉiyars, Nāḍārs, Nāyakkars, Ambalakkārars, or Kaḷḷars.

A *velaikkāraṉ's* work overlapped with that of an Ādi Drāviḍa *paṇṇaiyāḷ*. He was often even called a *paṇṇaiyāḷ*, but the fact that he was of higher caste entitled him to special tasks and minor privileges. *Vēlaikkārars* were mostly involved in dairy farming, the care of oxen for ploughs and carts, and garden work; their wives, in domestic work in the landlords' homes. In a few villages in 1951, *vēlaikkārars* husked the paddy of their masters as well as their own families by pounding it with a pestle in a cylindrical wooden vessel. This work, however, had almost died out because of the prevalence of industrial rice mills.

*Vēlaikkārars* were often *kuthakai* or *vāram* tenants as well as laborers. Most of them leased, at a minimum, a house site and garden in which to keep goats and poultry and to grow vegetables, bananas, and occasionally, nut or fruit trees. Smaller numbers leased wet rice fields. In this case they did most of their own paddy cultivation in the late afternoon, hiring a few Ādi Drāviḍa casual laborers at the peak seasons of transplanting and harvest. The leased fields of *vēlaikkārars* seldom comprised more than one to three acres, whereas those of the better-off Non-Braham tenants who were not *vēlaikkārars* might be up to ten or twelve acres.

*Vēlaikkārars*, like *paṇṇaiyāḷs*, were hired or confirmed in their jobs by the year. Like *paṇṇaiyāḷs*, most were in debt to the landlord and unable to change jobs unless they repaid the debt or another master cleared it. Most *vēlaikkārars* were thus in effect attached laborers, but because they had more opportunity to lease land or engage in private trade they were sometimes able to clear their own debts, borrow from external moneylenders, and simply become tenant farmers or petty traders.

Before the 1860s some Non-Brahmans of low rank (whose descendents are *vēlaikkārars*) were *aḍimai āḷukaḷ* or slaves, as were the ancestors of all of today's Ādi Drāviḍa laborers. As slaves they might be sold, beaten, or even killed by their masters. Non-Brahman *aḍimai āḷukaḷ* seem, however, always to have enjoyed somewhat lighter work, better conditions, and greater intimacy with their masters.

*Vēlaikkārars* and their wives were paid in paddy by the month, in contrast to the paṇṇaiyāḷ's and *paṇṇaiyācchi's* daily payments. A small amount of cash was usually added to the male *vēlaikkāran's* pay. The master made the same kinds of gifts to the *vēlaikkāraṉ* as to the *paṇṇaiyāḷ* during festivals, life-crisis rites, and emergencies, except that he spent rather more for his marriage. In all, the total payments a *vēlaikkāraṉ* obtained in the course of a year might run to about one-fifth to one-half as much more than those of an average Ādi Drāviḍa *paṇṇaiyāḷ*.

In 1951 a third type of agricultural laborer was becoming more common, the daily wage worker ("coolie" or "*kooliyāḷ*"). Most agricultural coolies were Ādi Drāviḍas; a few, Non-Brahmans of low rank. The occasional hiring of day laborers had existed in Thanjāvūr since the Chōḷa period and had increased in the nineteenth century. The regular hiring of coolies had, however, apparently become more prevalent than ever before since the early 1930s with the growth of a permanent superfluity of agricultural labor.

The growing glut of agricultural labor resulted partly from an increase in the population, for which south India's sluggish industrial development offered no adequate means of employment. The problem was complicated by the return of many workers from abroad. Beginning in 1840 and increasing after 1860, substantial numbers of Thanjāvūr's tenant cultivators and agricultural laborers had emigrated to the tea and rubber plantations of Ceylon and Malaya, and smaller numbers to Fiji, Burma, and other countries. Thousands had returned during the depression of the 1930s or had fled home during or after World War II. Although their numbers cannot be estimated, they swelled the ranks of underemployed agricultural labor in 1951, especially in east Thanjāvūr.

Other circumstances, as well as numbers, fostered an increase in coolie labor. Fragmentation of small holdings resulted from general growth of the population and so of the landowning class. On small family estates of about half to four acres of wet land, it had become common for the owner to hire coolies for each job of work rather than maintaining one or more *paṇṇaiyāḷ* families throughout the year. Some noncultivating smallholders even hired a cart, oxen, and plough from a neighbor for use by their coolies and avoided the expense of maintaining a cowshed. A few coolies owned their own stock and equipment and earned higher wages for using them in the service of their employers.

Another circumstance was a probable increase in tenant cultivation in the twentieth century that resulted from the departure of many landlords to urban work. Tenant cultivators, like small owner cultivators of Non-Brahman caste, did much of their own agricultural work but needed coolies at peak seasons.

The food shortage in India during World War II and the postwar years increased the supply of coolie labor. With the Japanese conquest of Burma in 1941, Indian imports from that country, which had been massive, ceased. Famine ensued in parts of the country, especially in Bengal, where up to three million died in 1943. Madras Presidency, which had imported extensively from Burma, was hard hit. Thanjāvūr, the "rice bowl of south India," had been exporting most of its surplus to the British plantations of Ceylon and Malaya before the war, but with the conquest of Malaya and Burma its trade patterns shifted and it was required to provision deficit regions of south India. From 1941 the government of Madras introduced controls on the sale of food grains. In different years it requisitioned varying proportions of the crops of landlords and peasants or forbade the private trade of rice between districts, and fixed the wholesale prices of requisitioned grains and the retail prices of grains sold in ration shops. Controls were lifted by the newly independent government in December 1947, but reimposed from January 1949 to June 1952 because of poor harvests.

In these conditions of shortage and regulation, Thanjāvūr's landlords extracted as much grain rent as possible from their tenants in order to meet government requirements and also to sell part of their surplus privately on the black market. In 1948 when the grain trade was decontrolled, yet scarcity prevailed in south India because of drought, many landlords raised their tenants' rents still higher. At the same time landlords tended to reduce *paṇṇaiyāḷs'* grain payments to a minimum and in the nonharvest season to pay part of their daily payments in cash. Given the labor glut, a growing number of landlords dispensed with *paṇṇaiyāḷs* and hired coolies whom they paid solely in cash except at harvest time.

By 1952 a further impetus toward hiring coolies had come from postwar legislation. Tenants' and laborers' annual incomes had fallen to unusually low levels during the 1940s. This was especially ture in the east of Thanjāvūr. In 1937 it was reported that a *paṇṇaiyāḷ* married couple's maximum annual income was sixty *kalams* of paddy plus Rs. 8 in Palākuricchi, a village of east Thanjāvūr about three miles from Kirippūr, where I worked in 1952–3 and 1976. (One *kalam* equals half a bag, or 63.69 pounds of paddy.) I have calculated that in 1952 few *paṇṇaiyāḷs'* incomes in Kirippūr amounted to more than forty-five *kalams* per year, and some to as little as thirty-six. With regard to tenants, the rent payable to the landlord was fifteen to twenty-four *kalams* per acre per year in Kirippūr in 1951–2, roughly the same as in Palākuricchi (twenty-three to twenty-four *kalams*) in 1937. Landowners' records showed, however, that the yield in Kirippūr had been declining from thirty to forty-two *kalams* per crop acre in 1940 to an average of only eighteen to thirty in 1948–52. With only one-tenth of the land doublecropped, this left little margin or even a loss for the tenant.

North and west Thanjāvūr, the traditionally more fertile region, apparently fared less badly in the 1940s. In Kumbapeṭṭai in west Thanjāvūr, for example, where both the productivity and the laborers' incomes were traditionally higher than in Kirippūr, the *paṇṇaiyāḷ* couple's income in 1951 equaled about fifty to fifty-five *kalams*. The tenants and laborers of west and north Thanjāvūr paid an average paddy rent of forty-five *kalams* per acre per year. The gross yield per year in 1947–52, although poor for the area, reached about thirty-six to forty-five *kalams* per crop acre or, on average, seventy-two to ninety *kalams* per year. The tenants and laborers of north and west Thanjāvūr were therefore less hard hit than those of the east coast region, although their incomes, too, had perhaps declined in the war and postwar period.

In these circumstances, in the late 1940s, labor unions of agricultural workers and tenant cultivators, which had been formed by both the Communist Party and the Gandhian Kisan (peasant) movement from 1938, greatly increased their agitations. Unions were especially strong in Naṉṉilam, Nāgapaṭṭanam, and Maṉṉārguḍi *tālūks* of east Thanjāvūr. The year 1948 saw an intense, six-week strike of agricultural workers and tenants in east Thanjāvūr for better pay and working conditions. As a result of these and later agitations, officials of the Madras state government effected several local wage agreements, the best known being the Māyuram Agreement of 1948. In August 1952, the chief minister of Madras passed a special emergency ordinance, the Tanjore Tenants' and Paṇṇaiyāḷs' Ordinance, which applied to the district as a whole. With minor modifications this was passed into permanent law by the Madras Assembly in November 1952.

When fully implemented (which was seldom) the new act increased the annual incomes of *paṇṇaiyāḷs* by about one-third to one-half, regulated the rents of *kuthakai* and *vāram* tenants at no more than 60 percent of the average annual paddy yield, gave paṇṇaiyāḷs continuing employment from year to year unless they failed to fulfil their duties, and granted fixity of tenure for five years to cultivating tenants.

The act, like the earlier Māyuram Agreement, did not apply to tenants and laborers on estates with less than six and two-thirds acres in one village, nor to casual day laborers (coolies). The result was that whereas smallholders tended to keep their tenants or *paṇṇaiyāḷs*, many big landlords evicted their tenants in advance of the act, dismissed their *paṇṇaiyāḷs*, and hired coolie labor. Where labor unions were strong, they managed to compel the landlords to pay higher wages than previously, but landlords were not constrained by law and usually managed to pay less than had been stipulated in the act.

Coolies were in theory hired for each separate day of work. On big estates they actually worked regularly under an agent of the landlord in much the same way as they had done as *paṇṇaiyāḷs*, but on small farms they were summoned when required. The coolie's daily wage in nonharvest seasons was usually paid in cash. In 1951–52 it was Rs. 1–2–0 per day, or U.S. 14–16 cents. Women received Rs. 0–8 to Rs. 0–12; children were not usually employed as coolies. These cash wages were roughly twice the ordinary nonharvest paddy wages of *paṇṇaiyāḷs* before the 1952 act, if one calculated according to the paddy price at harvest time. From April to September, however, the price of paddy on the black market rose to twice that obtaining at harvest time, and the retail price of husked rice in food stores even higher. Thus, if he worked as many days, the coolie's real wages in paddy were only about 1.5 times those of the *paṇṇaiyāḷ*. On some estates, coolies like *paṇṇaiyāḷs* were paid mainly in grain. In that case, too, their daily nonharvest wages were about 1.5 times those of a *paṇṇaiyāḷ* before the act. In the harvest season, coolies usually received much the same, higher wages as *paṇṇaiyāḷs*, and were paid in paddy. The coolie's overall income and status were, however, often lower than the *paṇṇaiyāḷ*'s. The coolie had no employment security, even for a year. He had no access to loans from a landlord that he could later pay off by working. In many cases he worked fewer days than a *paṇṇaiyāḷ*. Some male coolies worked up to 270 days a year, but in the prevailing conditions of labor glut some worked as few as 180. Coolies had no customary rights to a house site, building materials, or fuel, although their masters usually provided these in fact. They had no rights to a small plot of paddy land, clothing, or gifts at life crises and festivals. Although they were free to leave the master, and usually worked more limited and regular hours than did *paṇṇaiyāḷs*, coolies had no one who accepted responsibility for their survival throughout the year. In short, they were casual laborers of the most depressed variety.

# 4 The Nonagriculturalists

In 1951 about 28 percent of Thanjāvūr's people depended mainly on occupations other than primary production in agriculture, fishing, or pastoralism. A total of 211,429 self-supporting persons in this category were distributed as shown in Table 4.1.

I have already noted some of the unbalanced and "colonial" features of Thanjāvūr's workforce, especially the fact that about 77 percent of the people were engaged in producing, storing, processing, trading, or transporting paddy. Other colonial features apparent in Table 4.1 are the fact that in spite of the low technological level and extreme poverty of most of the people, only 30 percent of those outside primary production, or about 8.4 percent of the total workforce, were adding to the society's wealth through material production. They were equaled by those in trade or transport, and outnumbered by those in public or private services. In all these areas, as in agriculture, unemployment and underemployment were prevalent and competition was acute.

Whereas the state provided a skeletal framework of public services, and whereas such employment was eagerly sought, the public sector engaged a relatively small percentage of the people in 1951. Exact figures are not available, but because most of the personnel engaged in health, education, and public administration and a few in other services worked for the government, we can assess government employees as roughly 12 percent of the nonprimary producing workforce, or about 3.4 percent of the total workforce.

The census figures obscure economic classes under occupational rubrics, so that their proportions cannot be accurately determined. We may, however, distinguish the following social strata not predominantly involved in primary production in 1951.

## The Big Bourgeoisie

This term is used here to designate foreign or Indian business corporations that possessed many different enterprises and monopolized certain fields of production or trade. The main owners and directors of all these corporations lived outside Thanjāvūr and were represented by agents or subsidiaries. These absentees must, however, be considered if we are to understand the district's economy, for they conditioned its relations with the outside world as well as its internal economy.

Table 4.1. *Nonagricultural occupations in Thanjāvūr district, 1951*

| | Number | Percent |
|---|---|---|
| *Production* | | |
| Mining and quarrying, chiefly salt making and stone quarrying | 1,219 | 0.6 |
| Processing and manufacture of textiles, grains and pulses, wearing apparel, tobacco, prepared foods, and leather | 25,778 | 12.2 |
| Processing and manufacture of metals, chemicals, and their products, chiefly transport equipment, iron and steel, and art-metal objects | 7,509 | 3.6 |
| Other processing and manufacture chiefly wood, printing, salt, and bricks and tiles | 19,672 | 9.3 |
| Construction and utilities | 10,618 | 5.0 |
| Subtotal | 64,796 | 30.7 |
| *Commerce* | | |
| 28,369 in grains and other foods, followed by textiles leather, money lending, real estate, and insurance | 51,758 | 24.5 |
| *Transport, storage, and communications* | | |
| In order, road, rail, and postal services | 12,381 | 5.8 |
| *Health, education, and public administration* | | |
| In order, education, village officers, state government civil servants, medical and health personnel, Union Government civil servants, police, and municipal and local board employees | 27,552 | 13.0 |
| *Other services* | | |
| In order, domestic service, hotels and restaurants, religious and charitable, laundries, barbers, recreation, legal and business, and arts and journalism | 54,942 | 26.0 |
| Total | 211,429 | 100.0 |

*Source: Census of India, 1951, Madras and Coorg,* Vol. 3, Part 1–Report, by S. Venkateswaran, ICS Madras: Government Press, 1953, pp. 109–57.

### *The Imperial Bourgeoisie*

The extent of foreign capital, mainly British, in Thanjāvūr could not be estimated, but although some interests had recently been bought out by Indian capitalists or the Indian government, it was still prominent if not predominant in 1951.

British, or in some cases, joint Anglo-American, capital was strongly entrenched in steam shipping, banking and insurance, the import and export trade, and the largest retail stores in Thanjāvūr and Nāgapaṭṭaṇam. It had earlier dominated the railways, but these were taken over by the state in April 1951. British export firms handled a large share of the overseas trade with Singapore, Malaya, Ceylon, Burma, and other countries. British firms imported a variety of consumer goods and most of the significant capital goods, almost all of which were manufactured or processed by British or American firms in Britain, the United States, or in India itself. Readily recognizable items produced and/or imported by British firms included: coal, petroleum, and kerosene; tea, coffee, rubber, and jute goods; machinery and parts for rice mills and printing works; trucks and automobiles; bicycles, electrical equipment, typewriters, and cameras; a limited quantity of chemical fertilizers; toilet articles, shoes, drugs, cigarettes, patent foods, ink, and fountain pens; paper, cardboard, newspapers, and magazines; agricultural tools such as axes, hoes, and mattocks; and household articles such as lamps, clocks, cooking utensils, cutlery, and furniture. British capital had earlier been involved in Thanjāvūr's rice mills and grain trade, but appeared to have left these fields by 1951.

British capital operated in Thanjāvūr through (*a*) branch firms of British monopolies that had Indian or (in a very few cases) British managers, (*b*) British managing agencies that managed many smaller, Indian firms in return for a share of the profits, (*c*) local Indian firms, many of them Muslim, that operated as commission agents for foreign monopolies in Thanjāvūr or Tamiḷ Nāḍu, and (*d*) British investments in partly or predominantly Indian firms. Although rivalrous in specific instances, the relations between British and Indian big business were by this date largely cooperative and there were multiple, complex links between them.

### *The Indian Big Bourgeoisie*

This group was involved in some of the same activities as the British – banking, insurance, light industry, and trade within India and with Southeast Asian countries. Like their British counterparts, Indian big business houses such as Tata, Birla, Walchand, and Dalmia operated in south India through small local firms serving as commission agents, or had their own enterprises such as the Dalmia cement factory at Dalmiapuram in Tiruchirappalli district. The extent of their activities is unknown, but they imported to Thanjāvūr jute goods, toilet goods, factory-made pottery, household utensils, furniture, paper, books, newspapers and magazines, chemical products, bicycles, movies, and photographic film. In the early 1950s Indian big business was buying out or buying into a number of formerly British enterprises in south India such as tea estates, banking, the export and import trade, transport, and sugar, cement, and textile plants. In Thanjāvūr as elsewhere in south India, opposition to "Marwāri" or "Bania" dominance, that is, to big business owned by firms of the traditional north Indian trading castes, was a significant factor in the Dravidian nationalist movement led by the Non-Brahman bourgeoisie.

Large Indian firms located mainly or solely in Tamiḷ Nāḍu imported machine-made textiles from Madurai, Madras, and Coimbatore, cotton and silk yarn for handicrafts, matches, cigarettes, rubber items, glass and enamelware, pencils, chemicals, cement, sugar, and fresh fruits and vegetables from other districts. Large Tamiḷ firms exported Thanjāvūr's high-quality silk and cotton textiles, carpets, and art-metal work to other parts of the country, although they were often represented by local dealers.

The export of paddy, Thanjāvūr's main wealth, was carried out mainly by Muslim or Nāḍar traders living in Thanjāvūr or by Nāṭṭukoṭṭai Cheṭṭiars. Most members of this wealthy trading and money-lending caste came from Rāmanāthapuram district, although the caste claims an early origin in Kāvēripaṭṭaṇam, the first-century Chōḷa capital on Thanjāvūr's northeast coast. Nāṭṭukoṭṭai Cheṭṭiars were the wealthiest of Tamiḷ Nāḍu's traders, having large holdings in banks, insurance, private money lending, and the export and import trade with Ceylon and Southeast Asia, as well as the inland grain trade.

More than 1,000 paddy traders lived in Thanjāvūr in the 1950s and early 1960s, but many, perhaps most, were commission agents for bigger merchants or mill owners, some of whom lived in Coimbatore and Tiruchirappalli. A prominent landlord told me that three merchants, with many agents, monopolized most of Thanjāvūr's grain trade in the early 1950s, but I was unable to discover their identities. Thanjāvūr landlords who owned more than about fifty acres of paddy land sold the greater part of their crops and had contracts or traditional arrangements to deliver directly to big or medium wholesalers at the nearest railhead assembly point. Small landowners and tenants sold their surplus to village brokers who collected their paddy from the threshing floor and delivered it for a commission to local mill owners or to wholesale merchants at nearby assembly points. In the 1920s and 1930s some of Thanjāvūr's landlords had invested in rice mills, and in textile mills and other light industries in neighboring districts.

### *The Medium Bourgeoisie*

Thanjāvūr's medium bourgeoisie is somewhat hard to separate from the firms I have designated big bourgeoisie at one extreme and petty bourgeoisie at the other. I include in this term Tamiḷ business families and small joint-stock companies engaged in only one or two types of enterprise, mainly or entirely within Thanjāvūr, employing a dozen or more workers, and earning more than Rs. 10,000 per year. Whereas the foreign and Indian monopolies with boards of directors located elsewhere were invisible and their existence unknown to most people, the medium bourgeoisie were influential in the district. They were locally considered fabulously wealthy, were usually locally born, and were involved in local networks of caste, kinship, and patronage. They were called *periya paṇakkar* ("big money men"); others envied, admired, and stood in awe of them. Many of them were linked to the big bourgeoisie as retail outlets for imported goods, as traders procuring grains, other agricultural produce, or handicraft goods locally and selling them to big wholesalers, as local moneylenders who borrowed from city banks, or as commission agents. Others had family firms or small joint-stock companies that operated more or less independently.

Inland, Thanjāvūr's medium bourgeoisie were often from the Cheṭṭiar trading castes, the Nāḍār coconut grower and toddy-tapping caste, or from Kaḷḷar or Naidū farming and trading groups. On the coast, business was dominated by Muslims. Throughout the district, however, landlords of Brahman, Veḷḷāḷar, Naidū, or other castes were often involved in rice mills, general merchandise, or the paddy trade. The modern industrial segment of the medium bourgeoisie was largely confined to the ownership of rice mills.

Also in the medium bourgeoisie were owners of craft shops that produced textiles, carpets, brass, gold, and silverware. Most of these crafts were in the hands of families from the castes traditionally associated with them.

In transport, the medium bourgeoisie owned locally operated trucks, buses, or taxis. The financial segment of the medium bourgeoisie was mainly composed of moneylenders who made loans for agricultural operations, small business ventures, marriages, or emergencies, to landlords, owner cultivators, the salaried middle class, or the petty bourgeoisie. Their security was usually land or the heavy gold jewelry worn by Thanjāvūr's middle- and upper-class women. Their rates of interest varied from 12 percent to 100 percent per annum.

The trading section of the middle bourgeoisie was chiefly involved in buying paddy or other agricultural produce for independent export, for sale to bigger merchants, or as commission agents.

Retail stores, cinemas, restaurants, and urban rental properties in stores and housing were also common enterprises of the medium bourgeoisie in Thanjāvūr's towns. Labor contractors for agricultural plantations outside the district and for government road and irrigation works were members of this class. So were the medium-sized export and import firms that dealt with Malaya, Burma, and Ceylon, and mostly served as commission agents for the big bourgeoisie.

Although not always qualifying for membership in the medium bourgeoisie in terms of employment of a number of wage workers, the independent professionals belonged in this class by virtue of their incomes, specialized training, social networks, and status. They included private physicians, lawyers and accountants, each employing a small number of assistants, clerical workers, and menial workers. The large majority of professionals were Brahmans; a smaller number, Veḷḷāḷars or Naidūs.

### *The Petty Bourgeoisie*

The petty bourgeoisie shaded into the medium bourgeoisie at one end and the simple commodity producers at the other. I have included in this class individual or family businesses confined to one town or village and having fewer than a dozen workers. In 1951 the income of such a petty entrepreneur was likely to be less than Rs. 10,000 a year and was often less than Rs. 3,000. The petty bourgeois was almost always born in Thanjāvūr and usually lived in his native town or village, although his work sometimes took him to other districts. In contrast to the big and most of the medium bourgeoisie he was unlikely to speak idiomatic English and might speak none at all. Whereas there were few medium bourgeoisie in villages, there were representatives of the petty bourgeoisie engaged in nonagricultural ventures in almost every village.

The industrial petty bourgeoisie in villages owned small mills that processed rice and oils for local consumption, and small "soda" factories that made and bottled soft drinks from purchased "essences." Also among the petty bourgeoisie were master weavers, brass smiths, goldsmiths, carpenters, and other craftsmen who worked out of small sheds adjacent to their homes and employed a few wage workers.

The trade, transport, and services of the petty bourgeoisie sometimes duplicated those of the medium bourgeoisie but on a much more modest scale. They owned one or two wagons for trading paddy, coconuts, grams, or orchard produce; served as cattle brokers; sold fish, agricultural products, toilet articles, or cheap jewelry in stores or markets; ran village dry-goods stores; were petty contractors of labor for local projects; or owned small rental properties in towns. The more successful petty traders loaned money at interest to the less successful or to tenant farmers, village servants, or workers with steady jobs. They ran small restaurants, rest houses, barbers' saloons, and laundries; managed small groups of musicians and dancers for marriages and festivals; or ran traveling troupes of actors, jugglers, or acrobats. A number of them owned cinemas housed in town buildings or in tents in the countryside. In towns, members of the petty bourgeoisie hired out bullock carts or horse-drawn carriages for the transport of passengers.

Near the coast, some of the petty bourgeoisie, as of the medium bourgeoisie, had formerly lived in Ceylon or Malaya as shopkeepers. Some still had family members there. Some went back and forth in small boats from time to time, making money by exporting and importing and sometimes by smuggling. The smuggling of alcohol, wrist watches, fountain pens, and other consumer goods from the French port of Kāraikkal provided some profits, or even a livelihood, for some of the petty bourgeoisie and independent salesmen of east Thanjāvūr.

### *The Salaried Upper Middle Class*

The upper middle class, mainly bureaucrats, included or roughly paralleled the "gazetted officers" in government service. They chiefly comprised administrative personnel in the Indian Civil Service, or highly specialized officers such as judges, civil surgeons in government hospitals, school inspectors, or heads of departments of colleges. The higher salaries of this class roughly paralleled the salaries of the medium bourgeoisie. At best its influence paralleled that of the lower strata of the big bourgeoisie. Members of parliament and the legislative assembly should probably be placed in this stratum by virtue of their power and influence, if not their salaries.

### *The Salaried Lower Middle Class*

The lower middle class of salaried workers, the large number, carried out subordinate work as clerks, schoolteachers, policemen, post and telegraph workers, hospital nurses and orderlies, and so on.

Although low in salary and subordinate in the district's administrative scheme, some positions carried considerable local power. These included the village headmen who collected land revenues and settled local disputes, and the village accountants who kept the land records. Almost all of these village officers came from the locally dominant landowning castes of Brahmans, Veḷḷāḷars, and Naidūs.

The salaried middle classes were in service either for the government or for private employers such as large foreign or Indian firms, lawyers, and accountants. In 1951 some bailiffs or other agents on large landed estates and some temple priests and other officers were beginning to receive monthly cash salaries from the government or from landlords instead of their former grain payments, as a result of the abolition of *iṉam* lands and the desire of landlords to export their paddy for profit.

Altogether, the salaried middle classes may have formed about 10 percent to 12 percent of the nonprimary producing workforce, or about 3 percent to 3.6 percent of the total workforce.

A larger number of salaried workers, born and educated in Thanjāvūr and hailing from almost every town and village, had emigrated from the district and were living in Madras or other cities in many parts of India, or even abroad. The majority of the émigrés were Brahmans, but increasing numbers of Non-Brahman salaried workers were departing in the 1950s. Together with their wives and absent children, the emigrant salaried workers may have exceeded 150,000 by 1951. Most of them shared or maintained a dwelling in Thanjāvūr and returned for festivals and life-crisis rites. Some sent remittances; many took away paddy or money rents. Some, perhaps the majority, would return to the district as pensioners after retirement.

### *Simple Commodity Producers, Service Vendors, and Traders*

This category, usually poorer than the petty bourgeoisie, comprised all those who sold something individually or in family units through market relations. In 1951 it included artisans such as weavers, carpenters, blacksmiths, brass workers, leatherworkers, and tailors, in both town and countryside, who worked alone or in family groups and sold their wares at market prices. Some of them bought their own raw materials and sold their products in fairs or bazaar streets, to local customers, or to bigger merchants. Some, especially tailors and goldsmiths, simply did jobs on request for private customers who provided their own raw or semifinished materials.

This category also included individual service vendors such as astrologers, magicians, musicians, snake charmers, private teachers of dance or music, owners of a single bullock cart for transport, and individual traders such as small teashop keepers, owners of dry-goods stalls, and peddlers on the roadside or in local fairs and markets. The more successful of this category became petty bourgeoisie; the less successful drifted into, or back into, the agricultural workforce or the nonagricultural proletariat. Most of them lived in towns, but a few were found in most villages.

### *The Nonagricultural Proletariat*

In this category are included all those who did nonagricultural manual work for cash wages paid by the day, week, or month. Those more regularly employed worked in craft shops, mills, and rail and bus services; on the docks, as "sweepers" in government services or private establishments; or for traders, retail shopkeepers, or hotels or restaurants.

The less regularly employed among the working class were casual workers hired daily, seasonally, or for a job. Some of them congregated in railway stations or outside the larger mills, hoping for odd jobs as porters, sweepers, or mill hands. Some were hired by labor contractors for a season to repair roads or irrigation works.

In 1951 many members born into this stratum or into those of the tenant cultivators or agricultural laborers lived and worked elsewhere in India or abroad, chiefly on the tea or rubber plantations of Assam, Burma, Ceylon, or Malaya. Smaller numbers had migrated to Fiji, Thailand, Singapore, or Indonesia. The forebears of these migrants had been indentured laborers recruited from Tamiḷ Nāḍu to work on British plantations between about 1840 and 1918, when indentured labor was legally abolished. Even after 1918, large numbers of laborers were recruited annually by labor contractors to work abroad for a period, chiefly on the plantations. In 1951 about 150,000 recent migrants or their descendents from the whole of Madras State remained in Burma, 582,625 in Malaya, about 70,000 in Singapore, 10,000 in Indonesia, and 905,200 in Ceylon. Although it is impossible to estimate accurately the number of Thanjāvūr emigrant workers and their families still abroad in 1951, a rough guess might place it in the neighborhood of 200,000. Others had returned home in middle or old age, with or without small savings.

Emigration to these regions, however, had greatly declined since 1930 when the world depression began. Recruitment for the tea and rubber estates in Ceylon and Malaya had ceased in 1930–2, and large numbers of south Indian laborers were repatriated. Other multitudes fled from Burma and Southeast Asia during World War II with the advance of the Japanese. After the war, the government of Burma restricted immigration under the Burma Immigration (Emergency Provisions) Act. Sailings to Malaya and Singapore were resumed in 1947, but further Indian emigration to Ceylon was discouraged by the Ceylon Immigrants and Emigrants Act of 1948, which required passports and residents' permits. Altogether, several thousand workers probably returned from abroad to Thanjāvūr in 1931–51, while the flow of new emigrants was reduced to a trickle.

This shift in migration patterns, together with population increase and a dearth of employment in industry, probably accounts for the fact that Thanjāvūr's

Table 4.2. *Nonagricultural self-supporting persons as percentages of the total self-supporting adults, Thanjāvūr, 1951*

| | Employers | Employees | Independent workers |
|---|---|---|---|
| Noncultivating producers (crafts, mills, etc.) | 0.94 | 2.61 | 5.34 |
| Transport | 0.06 | 0.94 | 0.40 |
| Commerce | 1.19 | 1.69 | 4.14 |
| All other services and miscellaneous | 0.76 | 6.80 | 4.40 |
| Total | 2.95 | 12.04 | 14.28 |

*Source: Census of India, 1951, Madras and Coorg,* Vol. 3, Part I–Report, by S. Venkateswaran, ICS Madras: Government Press, 1953, pp. 134–8.

agriculturally dependent population increased from 62 percent to 70 percent of the total between 1931 and 1951. Most of the returned workers resettled in their home villages as tenant cultivators or agricultural laborers. Some swelled the nonagricultural proletariat or moved back and forth between the two. Like the agricultural and the middle-class workforces, nonagricultural workers suffered from unemployment and underemployment in 1951.

I have so far mentioned the primarily nonagricultural categories whose members were involved solely or mainly in market transactions. Most of them were already absorbed into the expanding world capitalist economy, although some of the independent peddlers, involved in local and partly disconnected markets, might be hard to distinguish from their medieval forebears.

The census of 1951 gives us some clue to the relative proportions of these strata by listing the percentages of employers, employees, and independent workers in each of the major nonagricultural sectors (Table 4.2).

Table 4.2 suggests that self-supporting members of the nonagricultural big, medium, and petty bourgeoisie resident in Thanjāvūr altogether numbered no more than 3 percent of the total of self-supporting persons, whereas the combined salaried middle classes and nonagricultural wage workers amounted to about 12 percent. The figures in Table 4.2 are probably fairly accurate, although the percentage of wage and salary workers must be reduced somewhat, perhaps to no more than 10 percent for several reasons.

Almost half the nonagricultural workforce is represented as "independent workers," who at first glance might be expected to equal my category of "simple commodity producers, service vendors and traders." In fact, however, the Census category of "independent workers" conceals at least two types of workers: the independent commodity vendors working in market conditions and people who, although appearing "independent" in terms of the Census definition, participated in forms of nonagricultural labor for temples, landlords, owner cultivators, or merchants. I regard the latter as examples of what Marx called "formal" rather than "real" subsumption of labor under capital (see Chapters 6 and 23). In these relations, the worker produced for a capitalist or a capital-owning corporation, but used preindustrial tools and techniques, often had partial control over his means of production and conditions of work, and was usually paid, or obtained his own income, at least partly in kind. Such workers are described in the following section.

***Semiproletarian Nonagricultural Laborers***

This category includes first, a range of specialized village servants (*grāma thōṛiḷāḷikaḷ*) who in 1951 continued to work for a designated group of village landlords or owner cultivators in the familiar *jajmāni* relationships, partly in return for customary payments in kind. Many village carpenters, blacksmiths, washermen, barbers, goldsmiths, village temple priests, midwives, scavengers, watchmen, and guarders of cremation grounds were in this category, although probably all of them had moved out of it to a greater or lesser degree into part-time, independent commodity production or service vending for anyone who would buy their goods or services for cash at market rates. In 1951, even those village servants who retained *mānyam* lands and were paid in grain on the threshing floor also usually received part of their incomes in cash for specific jobs. Nevertheless, some precapitalist features remained in the relations of most village servants.

A second group included weavers and other artisans who worked at home with their own equipment but who were essentially in the service of a merchant. Some weavers bought their yarn independently but sold their product to a merchant who advanced them loans and operated as a buyer-up. Others were putting-out workers who received yarn from the merchant dealer and were paid at piece rates. Both relationships had been prevalent under the British East India Company and its native agents in the eighteenth and the first decade of the nineteenth centuries, when exports of native textiles were at their height. Such workers entered into market transactions through their reception of cash and their purchase of essential commodities for their livelihood, but their often lifelong indebtedness, like that of tenant cultivators or *paṇṇaiyāḷs,* gave their work the character of unfree labor service.

A third type of labor service was strictly comparable to that of the tenant cultivator. This was the small tenant salt farmer in the salt swamps of southeast Thanjāvūr. These men leased plots of the swamp from the government on *kuthakai* or *vāram* tenures, paying rent in salt and retaining a portion of the "crop," which they sold to licensed dealers for cash. These workers, too, were involved in the market through their sales of salt and their purchase of consumer goods. Like indebted weavers or tenant farmers, however, they retained some control of their equipment and work process, yet paid such high rents or interest on loans that the relationship resembled precapitalist tribute rather than capitalist rent. In other parts of the swamp, tenants growing tobacco, or reeds used to feed buffalo, had similar relationships with private landlords. Elsewhere in Thanjāvūr, one found seemingly "independent" fishermen, jaggery makers, and other specialists who in actuality were tied to a capitalist through loans and sales.

A fourth type of labor servant is concealed among "employees" in the Census data, being lumped with the true wage workers. In 1951 this group included such people as domestic servants, restaurant workers, craft apprentices, and menial workers in temples and monasteries who received food or grain, clothing, and shelter from their employers. In almost all these cases some cash payments or additional cash earnings characterized such work by 1951, but payments in kind remained prominent.

# 5 Variations in Ecology, Demography, and Social Structure

Both within Thanjāvūr and within Tamiḻ Nāḍu there are wide variations in ecology, demography, agrarian relations, and the distribution of castes. In this chapter I explore these differences and attempt to explain the relations among certain major variables, making use of statistical correlations. My data are chiefly derived from the Censuses of India of 1951, 1961, and 1971. Although my interpretations for 1961 and 1971 to some extent encroach on my discussion in Volume II of this work, the data for those decades sufficiently resemble those for 1951 to be discussed here rather than in Volume II.

I began this investigation with the following arguments and hypotheses. Leaving aside the Nilgiris district with its mountainous terrain and relatively cold climate, it was hypothesized that the other areas of Tamiḻ Nāḍu practiced intensive paddy cultivation in those regions where heavier rainfall made this favorable. Millets and other grain crops, by contrast, were thought to be grown mainly on dryer lands. Paddy cultivation provides more calories per acre than do millets; it was therefore hypothesized that it would be found with denser populations. The areas of higher rainfall, more paddy cultivation, and greater density were hypothesized to possess more pronounced social stratification; from observation and history, it was thought that these areas were initially the ones that gave rise to the state. Once states arose, in the centuries preceding the Christian era, their governments used their coercive powers to build large-scale irrigation works and to foster a more intensive development of local irrigation. The heartlands of the major kingdoms of Tamiḻ Nāḍu, such as the Pāndhyas, Chōḻas and Pallavas, have thus been located in areas of intensive irrigation, and it was hypothesized that these also tended in modern times to be the areas of heavier rainfall, which permitted more extensive tanks and wells. The connection between irrigation and high rainfall was not, however, hypothesized to hold true in every case, for in limited regions such as the Thanjāvūr delta, channel irrigation allowed rivers to be used that were in part fed from rains in more mountainous regions elsewhere.

Because of higher agricultural productivity from paddy cultivation, therefore, the areas that were the heartlands of the former empires were expected to be the most densely populated because they could feed more people per unit of cultivation. Because of their higher productivity, moreover, it was hypothesized that their crops would tend also in modern times to yield a higher monetary value per acre.

Because they possessed the productivity to maintain a large leisure class and were the centers of government, the heartlands were believed to have had the steepest social stratification in terms of the highest percentages of tenant serfs and agricultural slaves rather than of peasant owners at the base of the society, and the highest percentage of noncultivating land managers at the top. In modern times, these classes have evolved into poor tenant farmers and agricultural laborers on the one hand and noncultivating landlords on the other. With some exceptions resulting from modern export cropping in dryer regions, it was hypothesized that their proportions remained somewhat the same as in pre-British times, and that they would therefore be most prevalent in the regions of high irrigation, rainfall, density, and paddy cultivation. Having more landlords, cultivating tenants, and agricultural laborers, these areas were hypothesized to have fewer owner cultivators.

Because the division of functions, bureaucratization, and ceremonialism have historically been more pronounced in the heartlands, they were hypothesized to have more Brahmans than other regions. And because they had more agricultural slaves historically, they were hypothesized to have a higher percentage of members of the Scheduled Castes.

It was further hypothesized that because land was more valuable, intensively cultivated, and productive, the heavily irrigated heartland areas would have a smaller size of average land holdings, a larger percentage of small holdings both in the "under three acres" and in the "under one acre" sizes, and a smaller percentage of large estates of the "over ten acres" and "over twenty-five acres" sizes. Because productivity was higher and population density greater, I also hypothesized that the heartland regions might require fewer workers per average family, and might therefore have a smaller total workforce in relation to the total population. Finally, because of their high productivity, I expected the heartland regions to be able to support a higher percentage of nonagricultural workers. I therefore hypothesized that the agricultural workforce would form a lower percentage of the total workforce in highly irrigated regions of heavier rainfall than in the less irrigated regions of lower rainfall and lower productivity.[1]

To test these hypotheses, statistical data were compiled for each district of Tamiḻ Nāḍu, and, independently, for each *tālūk* of Thanjāvūr district for 1951, 1961, and 1971.[2] Because no figures were available for Brahmans for these decades, I used the percentages for Brahmans that were compiled in the 1931 Census of Madras, and compared them with other variables compiled for the decades 1951 and 1961. This seemed justified because the proportion of Brahmans in each region probably did not change very greatly between 1931 and 1961. During the 1960s, however, a number of new Brahmans migrated to the cities; the figure for 1931 has therefore not been used for 1971.

Pearsonian correlation coefficients were obtained among all the variables for 1951, 1961, and 1971, respectively for Thanjāvūr and for Tamiḻ Nāḍu, yielding six separate matrixes of correlation coefficients. Significance tests of all the correlations were also run, yielding six other matrixes. Because I developed the hypotheses before running the statistical correlations, I discuss them in turn in what follows, even though some of them were negated or were not fully borne out.

Because I used three time periods and two regions, I have tested most of my hypotheses six times; this could not be done for all of them as the data were not available in every case. Obviously, the hypotheses that were substantiated in all six cases have yielded the most convincing results.

**Tamiḻ Nāḍu**

The ten districts of Tamiḻ Nāḍu in 1951 (excluding the Nilgiris), shown with their abbreviations, were:

1 Thanjāvūr (TH)
2 Chingleput (CH)
3 South Ārcot (SA)
4 North Ārcot (NA)
5 Madurai (MA)
6 Tirunelvēli (TI)
7 Tiruchirappalli (TR)
8 Coimbatore (CO)
9 Salem (SM)
10 Rāmanāthapuram (RA)

Although a Tamiḻ district, Kānya Kumāri is not included for it was joined administratively to Tamiḻ Nāḍu only after 1951. The twenty-three variables relating to my hypotheses, together with their abbreviations measured in my study of Tamiḻ Nāḍu in 1951, were:

1 Average rainfall in inches (R)
2 Population density per square mile (D)
3 Rural population density (RD)
4 Gross irrigated acreage as percent of gross sown acreage (GI)
5 Gross paddy acreage as percent of gross sown acreage (GP)
6 Landlords and dependents as percent of total population (L/TP)
7 Owner cultivators and dependents as percent of total population (OC/TP)
8 Tenants and dependents as percent of total population (T/TP)
9 Agricultural laborers and dependents as percent of total population (AL/TP)
10 "Cultivators" as percent of total workforce (C/TP)
11 Agricultural laborers as percent of total workforce (AL/TW)
12 Landowners as percent of agricultural workforce (LA/AW)
13 Tenants as percent of agricultural workforce (T/AW)
14 Agricultural laborers as percent of agricultural workforce (AL/AW)
15 Brahmans as percent of total population, 1931 (B/TP)
16 Scheduled Castes as percent of total population (SC/TP)
17 Average gross land holding per landowner and dependent (H/O)
18 Percentage of holdings under 1 acre (H1–)
19 Percentage of holdings under 3 acres (H3–)
20 Percentage of holdings over 10 acres (H10+)
21 Percentage of holdings over 25 acres (H25+)

22 Workforce as percent of total population (W/TP)
23 Agricultural workforce as percent of total workforce (AW/TW)

Map 1 shows these ten districts of Tamiḷ Nāḍu.

Table 5.1 shows the abbreviations for these variables listed together with their numerical values for the ten districts of Tamiḷ Nāḍu (noted by their abbreviations) for 1951.

Table 5.2 shows the matrix of Pearsonian correlations coefficients among the variables, and Table 5.3, the matrix of significance tests of the correlations. In this study a result of 0.05 or better is judged to be significant.

The first five of the twenty-three variables are geographic, demographic, and ecological ones that were expected both to be highly correlated among themselves and to influence the remaining sixteen variables in varying degrees. "Rural population density" was included in addition to "population density" in case the existence of towns in some regions weakened the correlations of "population density" with variables for agrarian relations.

The variables for 1951 include landlords, "owner cultivators," tenant farmers, and agricultural laborers together with their dependents, as percentages of the total population.[3] These data were supplied in the 1951 census, whereas in 1961 and 1971 livelihood classes were omitted and only workforce participation was given. In 1961 and 1971, most of the landlords, the owner cultivators, and the tenant farmers were lumped together as "cultivators," although it is possible from certain other tables supplied in the Census to obtain estimates of the percentages of tenants and of landowners in 1961. In listing the variables for 1951 I have used the available information on the agricultural livelihood classes provided in the 1951 Census but have also computed "cultivators" (namely, landlords, owner cultivators, and tenants) as a percentage of the total workforce to provide some comparability with 1961 and 1971. The percentage of "cultivators" is given in variable 10. In addition, in variables 13 to 16 I have provided the percentages of "landowners," tenants, and agricultural laborers in the agricultural workforce, and in variable 11, that of agricultural laborers in the total workforce. "Landowners" in variable 12 (1951) and variable 9 (1961) includes both noncultivating landlords and owner cultivators, but excludes farmers who were predominantly tenants.

As I have noted, the percentage of Brahmans in the total population listed for 1951, as for 1961, is actually the percentage for 1931, the best estimate I can offer.

No variable for the monetary value of produce per acre is given for 1951 and 1971 for this information was available only in 1961.

The eighteen variables, with abbreviations, that were computed for the same districts of Tamiḷ Nāḍu for 1961, were:

1 Average rainfall in inches (R)
2 Population density per square mile (D)
3 Rural population density per square mile (RD)
4 Gross irrigated acreage as percent of gross sown area (GR)

Table 5.1. *Variables for districts of Tamiḷ Nāḍu, 1951*

| Districts | R | D | RD | GI | GP | L/ TP | OC/ TP | T/ TP | AL/ TP | C/ TW | AL/ TW | LA/ AW | T/ AW | AL/ AW | B/ TP | SC/ TP | H/O | Hl - | H3- | H 10+ | H 25+ | W/ TP | AW/ TW |
|---|---|---|---|---|---|---|---|---|---|---|---|---|---|---|---|---|---|---|---|---|---|---|---|
| TH | 45.2 | 798 | 663 | 79.8 | 81.6 | 4.3 | 26.0 | 15.5 | 24.1 | 43.0 | 29.1 | 39.3 | 13.3 | 40.4 | 5.6 | 22.0 | 1.84 | 28.1 | 58.2 | 11.2 | 4.0 | 30.3 | 72.1 |
| CH | 47.7 | 6077 | 520 | 64.9 | 65.2 | 1.5 | 32.2 | 10.7 | 22.7 | 40.4 | 23.2 | 47.1 | 9.8 | 36.5 | 2.3 | 28.4 | 1.33 | 26.9 | 65.7 | 6.0 | 2.3 | 29.0 | 63.6 |
| SA | 46.8 | 660 | 594 | 47.2 | 35.7 | 1.6 | 47.3 | 8.7 | 24.1 | 55.3 | 26.2 | 57.8 | 9.6 | 32.2 | 1.6 | 24.8 | 1.14 | 16.6 | 52.6 | 10.2 | 4.8 | 27.7 | 81.5 |
| NA | 38.3 | 612 | 507 | 42.6 | 32.4 | 2.1 | 41.9 | 8.7 | 24.1 | 53.1 | 19.1 | 61.9 | 7.3 | 27.2 | 1.7 | 17.6 | 1.22 | 12.8 | 52.6 | 20.5 | 0.8 | 28.1 | 70.2 |
| TR | 34.6 | 535 | 447 | 33.8 | 30.7 | 1.4 | 47.1 | 8.9 | 13.6 | 56.1 | 16.8 | 65.0 | 7.6 | 23.1 | 3.1 | 16.9 | 1.13 | 11.7 | 38.6 | 18.0 | 2.8 | 29.9 | 72.9 |
| MA | 33.7 | 589 | 447 | 43.5 | 21.9 | 1.5 | 35.9 | 7.8 | 17.9 | 39.8 | 21.9 | 54.2 | 8.2 | 35.5 | 1.7 | 15.1 | 1.27 | 29.1 | 63.0 | 7.9 | 0.0 | 30.0 | 61.7 |
| SM | 33.2 | 477 | 416 | 21.2 | 11.6 | 1.4 | 48.7 | 5.9 | 15.0 | 55.4 | 17.2 | 68.4 | 6.3 | 24.0 | 1.3 | 14.8 | 1.09 | 15.7 | 48.5 | 16.1 | 4.5 | 27.9 | 71.5 |
| RA | 33.1 | 429 | 327 | 40.6 | 47.0 | 1.2 | 45.2 | 5.6 | 11.8 | 48.7 | 14.6 | 69.5 | 8.2 | 23.1 | 2.5 | 14.3 | 1.08 | 12.8 | 36.4 | 24.0 | 7.5 | 30.5 | 63.3 |
| TI | 32.1 | 563 | 416 | 38.8 | 24.1 | 2.4 | 31.4 | 9.5 | 11.2 | 41.7 | 13.8 | 58.7 | 7.3 | 24.9 | 3.1 | 15.2 | 1.52 | 17.3 | 48.0 | 20.5 | 6.3 | 31.8 | 55.5 |
| CO | 28.3 | 464 | 380 | 32.4 | 5.8 | 1.2 | 28.4 | 6.4 | 17.5 | 31.2 | 19.7 | 50.8 | 7.5 | 38.8 | 1.7 | 14.1 | 2.12 | 12.5 | 34.1 | 27.2 | 6.8 | 31.4 | 50.9 |

*Source: Census of India, 1951, Madras and Coorg,* Vol. 3, Part 1–Report. Madras: Government Press, 1953.

Table 5.2. *Correlation coefficients among variables for Tamiḷ Nāḍu, 1951*

| | R | D | RD | GI | GP | L/ TP | OC/ TP | T/ TP | AL/ TP | C/ TW | AL/ TW | LA/ AW | T/ AW | AL/ AW | B/ TP | SC/ TP | H/ O | Hl- | H3- | H 10+ | H 25+ | W/ TP | AW/ TW |
|---|---|---|---|---|---|---|---|---|---|---|---|---|---|---|---|---|---|---|---|---|---|---|---|
| R | 0 | | | | | | | | | | | | | | | | | | | | | | |
| D | .76 | 0 | | | | | | | | | | | | | | | | | | | | | |
| RD | .85 | .96 | 0 | | | | | | | | | | | | | | | | | | | | |
| GI | .73 | .80 | .72 | 0 | | | | | | | | | | | | | | | | | | | |
| GP | .77 | .67 | .64 | .92 | 0 | | | | | | | | | | | | | | | | | | |
| L/TP | .41 | .82 | .70 | .73 | .63 | 0 | | | | | | | | | | | | | | | | | |
| OC/TP | –.49 | –.71 | –.24 | –.81 | –.54 | –.55 | 0 | | | | | | | | | | | | | | | | |
| T/TP | .67 | .91 | .84 | .88 | .71 | .88 | –.77 | 0 | | | | | | | | | | | | | | | |
| AL/TP | .78 | .74 | .83 | .60 | .47 | .40 | –.22 | .54 | 0 | | | | | | | | | | | | | | |
| C/TW | .23 | .03 | .16 | –.28 | .02 | –.11 | .87 | –.11 | .01 | 0 | | | | | | | | | | | | | |
| AL/TW | .76 | .82 | .88 | –.72 | .57 | .53 | –.77 | .67 | .86 | –.12 | 0 | | | | | | | | | | | | |
| LA/AW | –.49 | –.71 | –.65 | –.81 | –.54 | –.62 | .85 | –.77 | –.61 | .63 | –.77 | 0 | | | | | | | | | | | |
| T/AW | .73 | .82 | .79 | .92 | .87 | .74 | –.48 | .84 | .59 | –.17 | .83 | –.77 | 0 | | | | | | | | | | |
| AL/AW | .39 | .55 | .53 | .64 | .57 | .40 | –.74 | .51 | .65 | –.68 | .80 | –.92 | .83 | 0 | | | | | | | | | |
| B/TP | .29 | .60 | .48 | .71 | .71 | .84 | –.52 | .83 | .08 | –.12 | .33 | –.52 | .74 | .25 | 0 | | | | | | | | |
| SC/TP | .95 | .64 | .75 | –.68 | .68 | .26 | –.54 | .60 | .72 | –.08 | .70 | –.54 | .64 | .45 | .20 | 0 | | | | | | | |

| | | | | | | | | | | | | | | | | | | | | | | | |
|---|---|---|---|---|---|---|---|---|---|---|---|---|---|---|---|---|---|---|---|---|---|---|---|
| H/O | −.15 | .21 | .14 | .32 | .04 | .42 | −.71 | .35 | .16 | −.80 | .29 | −.71 | .33 | .70 | .39 | .06 | 0 | | | | | | |
| H1 | .50 | .63 | .52 | .72 | .54 | .47 | −.72 | .61 | .41 | −.41 | .64 | −.72 | .64 | .66 | .36 | .48 | .17 | 0 | | | | | |
| H3- | .68 | .68 | .64 | .61 | .47 | .38 | −.53 | .55 | .61 | −.09 | .61 | −.53 | .47 | .46 | .10 | .63 | −.12 | .86 | 0 | | | | |
| H10+ | −.74 | −.63 | −.66 | −.54 | −.48 | −.24 | .45 | −.50 | −.53 | −.08 | −.67 | .45 | −.52 | −.41 | −.11 | −.72 | .26 | −.81 | −.89 | 0 | | | |
| H25+ | −.32 | −.42 | −.39 | −.23 | −.12 | .18 | −.05 | −.26 | −.48 | −.16 | −.33 | .18 | −.07 | −.18 | .11 | −.26 | .29 | −.46 | −.68 | .61 | 0 | | |
| W/TP | −.53 | .20 | −.40 | .08 | −.05 | .16 | −.63 | .07 | −.55 | −.68 | −.32 | −.23 | .03 | .13 | .45 | −.44 | .61 | .02 | −.38 | .45 | .45 | 0 | |
| AW/TW | .63 | .46 | .62 | .14 | .33 | .18 | .61 | .26 | .45 | .84 | .44 | .15 | .31 | −.17 | .09 | .46 | −.56 | −.01 | .25 | −.46 | −.30 | −.78 | 0 |

Table 5.3. *Significance tests of correlations among variables for Tamiḷ Nāḍu, 1951*

| | R | D | RD | GI | GP | L/ TP | OC/ TP | T/ TP | AL/ TP | C/ TW | AL/ TW | LA/ AW | T/ AW | AL/ AW | B/ TP | SC/ TP | H/ O | H Hl- | H H3- | H 10+ | H 25+ | W/ TP | AW/ TW |
|---|---|---|---|---|---|---|---|---|---|---|---|---|---|---|---|---|---|---|---|---|---|---|---|
| R | 0 | | | | | | | | | | | | | | | | | | | | | | |
| D | .005 | 0 | | | | | | | | | | | | | | | | | | | | | |
| RD | .001 | .001 | 0 | | | | | | | | | | | | | | | | | | | | |
| GI | .008 | .003 | .009 | 0 | | | | | | | | | | | | | | | | | | | |
| GP | .005 | .017 | .023 | .001 | 0 | | | | | | | | | | | | | | | | | | |
| L/TP | .121 | .002 | .012 | .008 | .025 | 0 | | | | | | | | | | | | | | | | | |
| OC/TP | .076 | .011 | .253 | .002 | .054 | .051 | 0 | | | | | | | | | | | | | | | | |
| T/TP | .017 | .001 | .001 | .001 | .011 | .001 | .005 | 0 | | | | | | | | | | | | | | | |
| AL/TP | .004 | .007 | .001 | .033 | .086 | .127 | .274 | .054 | 0 | | | | | | | | | | | | | | |
| C/TW | .261 | .468 | .326 | .219 | .477 | .379 | .001 | .379 | .484 | 0 | | | | | | | | | | | | | |
| AL/TW | .005 | .002 | .001 | .009 | .042 | .058 | .005 | .017 | .001 | .373 | 0 | | | | | | | | | | | | |
| LA/AW | .076 | .011 | .021 | .002 | .054 | .027 | .001 | .005 | .030 | .025 | .005 | 0 | | | | | | | | | | | |
| T/AW | .008 | .002 | .003 | .001 | .001 | .007 | .080 | .001 | .036 | .315 | .001 | .005 | 0 | | | | | | | | | | |
| AL/AW | .132 | .050 | .058 | .023 | .042 | .135 | .007 | .067 | .021 | .014 | .003 | .001 | .001 | 0 | | | | | | | | | |
| B/TP | .213 | .033 | .080 | .011 | .011 | .001 | .063 | .001 | .418 | .373 | .176 | .063 | .007 | .246 | 0 | | | | | | | | |
| SC/TP | .001 | .023 | .006 | .014 | .014 | .014 | .054 | .054 | .033 | .009 | .418 | .012 | .054 | .097 | .293 | 0 | | | | | | | |

| | | | | | | | | | | | | | | | | | | | | | | | |
|---|---|---|---|---|---|---|---|---|---|---|---|---|---|---|---|---|---|---|---|---|---|---|---|
| H/O | .345 | .280 | .340 | .180 | .458 | .115 | .011 | .159 | .326 | .003 | .213 | .011 | .176 | .012 | .132 | .436 | 0 | | | | | | |
| H1 | .071 | .025 | .063 | .009 | .054 | .086 | .009 | .030 | .122 | .122 | .023 | .009 | .023 | .019 | .153 | .080 | .315 | 0 | | | | | |
| H3- | .015 | .015 | .023 | .030 | .086 | .138 | .058 | .050 | .030 | .397 | .030 | .058 | .086 | .089 | .392 | .025 | .373 | .001 | 0 | | | | |
| H10+ | .001 | .025 | .019 | .054 | .080 | .253 | .096 | .071 | .058 | .418 | .017 | .096 | .063 | .122 | .379 | .009 | .230 | .002 | .001 | 0 | | | |
| H25+ | .180 | .115 | .132 | .261 | .373 | .307 | .448 | .230 | .080 | .326 | .176 | .307 | .426 | .307 | .379 | .230 | .213 | .089 | .015 | .030 | 0 | | |
| W/TP | .058 | .288 | .126 | .418 | .448 | .326 | .025 | .426 | .050 | .015 | .180 | .261 | .468 | .365 | .108 | .102 | .030 | .477 | .138 | .096 | .096 | 0 | |
| AW/TW | .025 | .089 | .027 | .340 | .176 | .307 | .030 | .230 | .096 | .001 | .102 | .345 | .190 | .315 | .397 | .089 | .046 | .484 | .472 | .089 | .201 | .004 | 0 |

5 Gross paddy acreage as percent of gross sown area (GP)
6 Rupee value of crops per acre per annum (V/A)
7 "Cultivators" as percent of total workforce (C/TW)
8 Agricultural laborers as percent of total workforce (AL/TW)
9 Landowners as percent of agricultural workforce (LA/AW)
10 Tenants as percent of agricultural workforce (T/AW)
11 Agricultural laborers as percent of agricultural workforce (AL/AW)
12 Brahmans as percent of total population, 1931 (B/TP)
13 Scheduled Castes as percent of total population (SC/TP)
14 Scheduled Caste workers as percent of total workforce (SC/TW)
15 Percent of Scheduled Caste members who are agricultural laborers (AL/SC)
16 Average gross holding per landowner, in acres (H/LO)
17 Workforce as percent of total population (W/TP)
18 Agricultural workforce as percent of total workforce (AW/TP)

The first five are variables also computed for 1951, as are variables 7 to 12, 13, 17, and 18. Variable 16 resembles variable 17 for 1951, except that in 1961 the available figures for average land holdings referred to actual landowners rather than to landowners and their family members. No figures were available for 1961 on the percentage of land holdings under one acre, under three acres, and above fifteen acres. I have added variable 15 relating to the percentage of Scheduled Caste members who were agricultural laborers because this information was available for 1961 and seemed likely to be related to the ecological variables. It was hypothesized that more Scheduled Caste members would be agricultural laborers in the high rainfall, heavily irrigated areas of paddy cultivation because these areas had given rise to agricultural slaves in the past.

Tables 5.4, 5.5, and 5.6 provide the figures for these variables by districts, the correlation coefficients, and the significance tests among them.

The eleven variables that were computed for the districts of Tamiḷ Nāḍu for 1971 were:

1 Average rainfall in inches (R)
2 Population density per square mile (D)
3 Gross irrigated acreage as percent of gross sown acreage (GI)
4 Gross paddy acreage as percent of gross sown acreage (GP)
5 "Cultivators" as percent of total workforce (C/TW)
6 Agricultural laborers as percent of total workforce (AL/TW)
7 Agricultural laborers as percent of agricultural workforce (AL/AW)
8 Average gross land holding per "cultivator" (H/C)
9 Workforce as percent of total population (W/TP)
10 Agricultural workforce as percent of total workforce (AW/TW)

A new district, Dharmapuri, was carved out of Salem in the 1960s. Dharmapuri and Salem are combined as "Salem" in Table 5.7. "Rural density" was omitted because it was not available at the time of writing. Neither were separate figures for noncultivating landlords, owner cultivators, and tenant farmers, these being lumped together as "cultivators" (variable 5). No figures were available for the percentages of land holdings of various sizes. Variable 8, average gross land holding per "cultivator," is not strictly comparable to the figures for average

Table 5.4. *Variables for districts of Tamiḷ Nāḍu, 1961*

| Districts | R | D | RD | GI | GP | V/ A | C/ TW | AL/ TW | LA/ AW | T/ AW | AL/ AW | B/ TP | SC/ TP | SC/ TW | AL/ SC | H/ LO | W/ TP | AW/ TW |
|---|---|---|---|---|---|---|---|---|---|---|---|---|---|---|---|---|---|---|
| TH | 45.2 | 868 | 716 | 78.7 | 78.2 | 231 | 36.3 | 32.7 | 31.0 | 21.0 | 47.3 | 5.6 | 23.0 | 31.0 | 37.0 | 4.16 | 42.0 | 69.0 |
| CH | 47.7 | 696 | 574 | 56.1 | 74.9 | 203 | 35.1 | 25.3 | 47.0 | 11.0 | 42.1 | 2.3 | 28.0 | 33.0 | 23.0 | 3.93 | 43.0 | 60.5 |
| SA | 46.8 | 724 | 648 | 46.2 | 37.1 | 205 | 49.5 | 28.7 | 56.0 | 7.0 | 37.2 | 1.6 | 26.0 | 32.0 | 28.0 | 2.80 | 46.0 | 78.1 |
| NA | 38.3 | 671 | 549 | 47.6 | 31.5 | 201 | 54.1 | 17.1 | 65.0 | 10.0 | 25.0 | 1.7 | 20.0 | 24.0 | 18.0 | 2.33 | 47.0 | 68.5 |
| TR | 34.6 | 579 | 471 | 34.2 | 26.3 | 164 | 54.8 | 16.3 | 67.0 | 10.0 | 22.5 | 3.1 | 17.0 | 21.0 | 20.0 | 2.51 | 49.0 | 71.2 |
| MA | 33.7 | 660 | 466 | 41.0 | 23.4 | 179 | 38.8 | 20.0 | 56.0 | 10.0 | 33.9 | 1.7 | 15.0 | 18.0 | 21.0 | 3.17 | 45.0 | 58.7 |
| SM | 33.2 | 539 | 459 | 20.6 | 10.7 | 148 | 54.7 | 12.8 | 74.0 | 7.0 | 19.1 | 1.3 | 17.0 | 19.0 | 18.0 | 2.30 | 46.0 | 67.6 |
| RA | 33.1 | 502 | 388 | 43.3 | 33.7 | 144 | 53.0 | 14.4 | 68.0 | 11.0 | 20.9 | 2.5 | 15.0 | 18.0 | 16.0 | 2.72 | 48.0 | 67.5 |
| TI | 32.1 | 619 | 457 | 40.9 | 25.4 | 189 | 35.2 | 16.1 | 57.0 | 12.0 | 31.4 | 3.1 | 16.0 | 20.0 | 20.0 | 3.78 | 46.0 | 51.3 |
| CO | 28.3 | 590 | 445 | 37.7 | 12.1 | 150 | 30.3 | 15.7 | 55.0 | 10.0 | 34.8 | 1.7 | 16.0 | 17.0 | 20.0 | 4.71 | 48.0 | 46.1 |

*Source: Census of India, 1951,* Part I-A (ii). *General Report,* by P. K. Nambiar, ICS, Government of Madras, 1968.

Table 5.5. *Correlation coefficients among variables for Tamiḷ Nāḍu, 1961*

| | R | D | RD | GI | GP | V/ A | C/ TW | AL/ TW | LA/ AW | T/ AW | AL/ AW | B/ TP | SC/ TP | SC/ TW | AL/ SC | H/ LO | W/ TP | AW/ TW |
|---|---|---|---|---|---|---|---|---|---|---|---|---|---|---|---|---|---|---|
| R | 0 | | | | | | | | | | | | | | | | | |
| D | .75 | 0 | | | | | | | | | | | | | | | | |
| RD | .87 | .94 | 0 | | | | | | | | | | | | | | | |
| GI | .68 | .85 | .76 | 0 | | | | | | | | | | | | | | |
| GP | .83 | .75 | .74 | .89 | 0 | | | | | | | | | | | | | |
| V/A | .80 | .94 | .90 | .82 | .76 | 0 | | | | | | | | | | | | |
| C/TW | –.03 | –.42 | –.18 | –.44 | –.30 | –.32 | 0 | | | | | | | | | | | |
| AL/TW | .86 | .93 | .93 | .83 | .81 | .85 | –.34 | 0 | | | | | | | | | | |
| LA/AW | –.57 | .87 | –.73 | –.89 | –.78 | –.76 | .72 | –.85 | 0 | | | | | | | | | |
| T/AW | .28 | .65 | .49 | .84 | .68 | .56 | –.45 | .55 | –.79 | 0 | | | | | | | | |
| AL/AW | .62 | .86 | .74 | .80 | .72 | .76 | –.75 | .87 | –.97 | .60 | 0 | | | | | | | |
| B/TP | .29 | .58 | .48 | .73 | .64 | .52 | –.27 | .52 | –.68 | .93 | .49 | 0 | | | | | | |
| SC/TP | .95 | .67 | .82 | .58 | .76 | .72 | –.14 | .79 | –.54 | .15 | .63 | .15 | 0 | | | | | |
| SC/TW | .98 | .78 | .89 | .69 | .83 | .83 | –.13 | .87 | –.63 | .31 | .68 | .34 | .97 | 0 | | | | |
| AL/SC | .68 | .91 | .90 | .80 | .71 | .78 | .36 | .93 | –.86 | .69 | .83 | .69 | .60 | .72 | 0 | | | |
| H/LO | .03 | .38 | .20 | –.47 | .34 | .24 | –.95 | .36 | –.74 | .52 | .74 | .38 | .15 | .15 | .42 | 0 | | |
| W/TP | –.68 | –.78 | –.70 | –.70 | –.77 | –.74 | .49 | –.75 | .78 | –.58 | –.78 | –.45 | –.61 | –.67 | –.72 | –.41 | 0 | |
| AW/TW | .57 | .22 | .46 | .14 | .26 | .27 | .76 | .36 | .13 | –.07 | –.15 | .10 | .41 | .48 | .29 | –.69 | –.04 | 0 |

Table 5.6. *Significance tests of correlation among variables for Tamiḷ Nāḍu, 1961*

| | R | D | RD | GI | GP | V/A | C/TW | AL/TW | LA/AW | T/AW | AL/AW | B/TP | SC/TP | SC/TW | AL/SC | H/LO | W/TP | AW/TW |
|---|---|---|---|---|---|---|---|---|---|---|---|---|---|---|---|---|---|---|
| R | 0 | | | | | | | | | | | | | | | | | |
| D | .006 | 0 | | | | | | | | | | | | | | | | |
| RD | .001 | .001 | 0 | | | | | | | | | | | | | | | |
| GI | .016 | .001 | .005 | 0 | | | | | | | | | | | | | | |
| GP | .001 | .007 | .008 | .001 | 0 | | | | | | | | | | | | | |
| V/A | .003 | .001 | .001 | .002 | .005 | 0 | | | | | | | | | | | | |
| C/TW | .468 | .115 | .309 | .103 | .198 | .184 | 0 | | | | | | | | | | | |
| AL/TW | .001 | .001 | .001 | .001 | .002 | .001 | .172 | 0 | | | | | | | | | | |
| LA/AW | .043 | .001 | .008 | .001 | .004 | .005 | .009 | .001 | 0 | | | | | | | | | |
| T/AW | .220 | .021 | .074 | .001 | .015 | .047 | .098 | .051 | .003 | 0 | | | | | | | | |
| AL/AW | .027 | .001 | .007 | .003 | .009 | .006 | .006 | .001 | .001 | .033 | 0 | | | | | | | |
| B/TP | .207 | .041 | .078 | .008 | .023 | .062 | .228 | .060 | .015 | .001 | .076 | 0 | | | | | | |
| SC/TP | .001 | .016 | .002 | .041 | .006 | .009 | .355 | .004 | .054 | .338 | .025 | .335 | 0 | | | | | |
| SC/TW | .001 | .004 | .001 | .013 | .001 | .002 | .365 | .001 | .026 | .190 | .015 | .170 | .001 | 0 | | | | |
| AL/SC | .015 | .001 | .001 | .003 | .011 | .004 | .156 | .001 | .001 | .014 | .001 | .013 | .033 | .010 | 0 | | | |
| H/LO | .468 | .138 | .288 | .086 | .165 | .253 | .001 | .153 | .007 | .063 | .007 | .138 | .345 | .345 | .115 | 0 | | |
| W/TP | .016 | .004 | .012 | .012 | .004 | .007 | .076 | .006 | .004 | .039 | .004 | .095 | .030 | .018 | .010 | .122 | 0 | |
| AW/TW | .044 | .266 | .090 | .347 | .234 | .222 | .005 | .155 | .359 | .429 | .345 | .394 | .121 | .082 | .209 | .014 | .460 | 0 |

land holdings in 1951 and 1961 because tenants and tenants' holdings are included with those of landowners in variable 8, the only measure available. The figure for Brahmans for 1931 was omitted from this list because considerable new urban migration of Brahmans occurred in the 1960s and it was thought that the 1931 figures might no longer approximate the reality. The figures for Scheduled Castes for the districts were not available at the time of writing. Tables 5.7, 5.8, and 5.9 present the numerical values of the variables by districts, the correlation coefficients, and the significance tests of correlations.

### Thanjāvūr

The same types of data, where these were available, for the *tālūks* within Thanjāvūr district for 1951, 1961, and 1971 are shown in the tables and lists that follow.

The *tālūks* of Thanjāvūr in 1951, together with abbreviations, that are listed in the other tables were:

1 Sīrkāli (SI)
2 Naṉṉilam (NA)
3 Nāgapaṭṭaṇam (NG)
4 Māyuram (MY)
5 Tirutturaipooṇḍi (TP)
6 Maṉṉārgudi (MN)
7 Kumbakōṇam (KU)
8 Pāpaṉāsam (PN)
9 Paṭṭukkoṭṭai (PK)
10 Thanjāvūr (TH)
11 Arantāngi (AR)

By 1961 a new *tālūk*, Orathanāḍ, was carved out of southern Thanjāvūr *tālūk*; it is listed in Table 5.13 under the abbreviation "OR." By 1971 a further new *tālūk*, Pēravurani, had been carved out of southern Paṭṭukkoṭṭai. This *tālūk* is listed in Table 5.16 under the abbreviation "PE."

The variables measured for Thanjāvūr district in 1951 were:

1 Average rainfall in inches (R)
2 Population density per square mile (D)
3 Rural population density (RD)
4 Net irrigated area as percent of total area (IR)
5 Gross paddy acreage as percent of total area (GP)
6 Landlords and dependents as percent of total population (L/TP)
7 Owner cultivators and dependents as percent of total population (OC/TP)
8 Tenants and dependents as percent of total population (T/TP)
9 Agricultural laborers and dependents as percent of total population (AL/TP)
10 Brahmans as percent of total population, 1931 (B/TP)
11 Scheduled castes as percent of total population (SC/TP)
12 Average holding per landowner or dependent (H/O)

"Irrigation" is presented in the form of net irrigated acreage as a percentage of the total geographical area in each *tālūk*. This was found to be more revealing

Table 5.7. *Variables for districts of Tamiḻ Nāḍu, 1971*

| Districts | R | D | GI | GP | C/TW | AL/TW | AL/TW | H/C | W/TP | AW/TW |
|---|---|---|---|---|---|---|---|---|---|---|
| TH | 45.2 | 1022 | 76.0 | 75.0 | 29.0 | 41.0 | 58.6 | 4.00 | 34.0 | 70.0 |
| CH | 47.7 | 592 | 72.7 | 71.2 | 26.0 | 31.0 | 54.4 | 2.94 | 35.0 | 57.0 |
| SA | 46.8 | 861 | 57.4 | 43.1 | 40.0 | 35.0 | 46.7 | 2.74 | 36.0 | 75.0 |
| NA | 38.3 | 793 | 51.2 | 39.6 | 37.0 | 31.0 | 45.6 | 2.42 | 37.0 | 68.0 |
| TR | 34.6 | 698 | 36.0 | 27.2 | 44.0 | 25.0 | 36.2 | 2.97 | 38.0 | 69.0 |
| MA | 33.7 | 809 | 38.0 | 20.6 | 29.0 | 32.0 | 52.5 | 3.26 | 38.0 | 61.0 |
| SM | 33.2 | 662 | 22.8 | 11.9 | 42.0 | 26.0 | 38.4 | 2.65 | 39.3 | 68.0 |
| RA | 33.1 | 589 | 37.5 | 41.2 | 38.0 | 25.0 | 39.7 | 3.85 | 37.0 | 63.0 |
| TI | 32.1 | 726 | 41.4 | 25.2 | 24.0 | 30.0 | 46.9 | 3.85 | 38.0 | 54.0 |
| CO | 28.3 | 723 | 37.8 | 11.3 | 23.0 | 31.0 | 57.4 | 4.32 | 41.0 | 54.0 |

*Source: Statistical Handbook of Tamiḻ Nāḍu*, Department of Statistics, Madras: 1972.

Table 5.8. *Significance tests of correlations among variables for Tamiḷ Nāḍu, 1971*

| | R | D | GI | GP | C/TW | AL/TW | AL/AW | H/C | W/TP | AW/TW |
|---|---|---|---|---|---|---|---|---|---|---|
| R | 0 | | | | | | | | | |
| D | .010 | 0 | | | | | | | | |
| GI | .001 | .009 | 0 | | | | | | | |
| GP | .001 | .044 | .001 | 0 | | | | | | |
| C/TW | .350 | .234 | .290 | .484 | 0 | | | | | |
| AL/TW | .034 | .009 | .006 | .048 | .162 | 0 | | | | |
| AL/AW | .227 | .031 | .046 | .182 | .003 | .005 | 0 | | | |
| H/C | .167 | .231 | .480 | .490 | .048 | .280 | .110 | 0 | | |
| W/TP | .001 | .069 | .001 | .001 | .363 | .046 | .304 | .414 | 0 | |
| AW/TW | .053 | .268 | .198 | .156 | .004 | .186 | .206 | .113 | .068 | 0 |

Table 5.9. *Correlation coefficients of variables for Tamiḷ Nāḍu, 1971*

| | R | D | GI | GP | C/TW | AL/TW | AL/AW | H/C | W/TP | AW/TW |
|---|---|---|---|---|---|---|---|---|---|---|
| R | 0 | | | | | | | | | |
| D | .71 | 0 | | | | | | | | |
| GI | .89 | .72 | 0 | | | | | | | |
| GP | .86 | .57 | .93 | 0 | | | | | | |
| C/TW | .14 | –.26 | –.20 | –.01 | 0 | | | | | |
| AL/TW | .60 | .73 | .75 | .55 | –.35 | 0 | | | | |
| AL/AW | .27 | .61 | .56 | .32 | –.79 | .76 | 0 | | | |
| H/C | –.34 | –.26 | .02 | .01 | –.56 | .21 | .43 | 0 | | |
| W/TP | –.87 | –.50 | –.87 | –.95 | –.13 | –.56 | –.19 | .08 | 0 | |
| AW/TW | .54 | .22 | .30 | .36 | .78 | .32 | –.29 | –.42 | –.50 | 0 |

than gross irrigated acreage as a percentage of gross sown acreage, probably because such a high proportion of Thanjāvūr's sown acreage in most *tālūks* is irrigated, and because "sown acreage" does not take account of the inhabited salt swamp, fishing areas, and forest areas in the coastal *tālūks*. Variable 5 also lists the gross paddy acreage as a percentage of the total geographical area for 1951. No figures were available for Thanjāvūr on the percentage of landholdings of various sizes in 1951.

The seventeen variables for Thanjāvūr in 1961 were:

1 Average rainfall in inches (R)
2 Population density per square mile (D)
3 Rural population density (RD)
4 Net irrigated area as percent of total rural area (IR)
5 Landowners as percent of agricultural workforce (LA/AW)
6 Tenants as percent of agricultural workforce (T/AW)
7 Agricultural laborers as percent of agricultural workforce (AL/AW)
8 "Cultivators" as percent of total workforce (C/TW)
9 Agricultural laborers as percent of total workforce (AL/TW)
10 Brahmans as percent of total population, 1931 (B/TP)
11 Scheduled Castes as percent of total population (SC/TP)
12 Landowners owning holdings of less than 1 acre as percent of total rural landowners (H1–)
13 Landowners with holdings of less than 2.5 acres as percent of total rural landowners (H2.5–)
14 Landowners with holdings of more than 15 acres as percent of total rural landowners (H15+)
15 Average holding per landowning household (H/LH)
16 Agricultural workforce as percent of total workforce (AW/TW)
17 Total workforce as percent of total population (TW/TP)

As in the case of Tamiḷ Nāḍu, "landowners" in variable 5 refers to both noncultivating landlords and owner cultivators, whereas "cultivators" in variable 8 refers jointly to landlords, owner cultivators, and tenant farmers. No figures were available for paddy acreage in the *tālūks* in 1961. In 1961 figures were available on the distribution of small and large holdings. These are provided in variables 12 to 14.

The eleven variables for Thanjāvūr district for 1971 were:

1 Average rainfall in inches (R)
2 Population density per square mile (D)
3 Rural population density (RD)
4 Irrigation as percent of net sown area (IR)
5 "Cultivators" as percent of total workforce (C/TW)
6 Agricultural laborers as percent of total workforce (AL/TW)
7 Agricultural laborers as percent of agricultural workforce (AL/AW)
8 Scheduled Castes as percent of total population (SC/TP)
9 Average land holding per "cultivator" (H/C)
10 Agricultural workforce as percent of total workforce (AW/TW)
11 Total workforce as percent of total population (TW/TP)

Table 5.10. *Variables for* Tālūks *of Thanjāvūr, 1951*

| *Tālūks* | R | D | RD | IR | GP | L/ TP | OC/ TP | T/ TP | AL/ TP | B/ TP | SC/ TP | H/ O |
|---|---|---|---|---|---|---|---|---|---|---|---|---|
| SI | 53.8 | 958 | 865 | 68.2 | 62.4 | 4.6 | 13.0 | 24.0 | 29.0 | 5.1 | 33.4 | 3.1 |
| NA | 48.2 | 854 | 818 | 76.4 | 76.4 | 8.0 | 15.4 | 16.5 | 34.3 | 7.2 | 27.9 | 2.9 |
| NG | 55.4 | 1088 | 762 | 62.8 | 54.2 | 4.5 | 16.1 | 6.0 | 28.4 | 5.3 | 26.3 | 1.9 |
| MY | 50.8 | 1140 | 953 | 75.9 | 72.6 | 7.1 | 12.3 | 21.3 | 26.0 | 7.3 | 24.6 | 2.4 |
| TP | 50.1 | 502 | 442 | 26.6 | 46.2 | 2.2 | 36.3 | 13.9 | 13.2 | 2.0 | 25.3 | 1.6 |
| MN | 44.9 | 827 | 703 | 67.8 | 75.2 | 4.2 | 32.0 | 14.8 | 28.3 | 6.1 | 24.6 | 1.9 |
| KU | 42.9 | 1642 | 1187 | 56.2 | 82.6 | 5.7 | 8.6 | 18.3 | 20.5 | 10.0 | 17.7 | 2.9 |
| PN | 42.2 | 950 | 855 | 82.2 | 82.5 | 6.3 | 16.1 | 20.8 | 31.3 | 5.2 | 24.4 | 2.9 |
| PK | 40.1 | 576 | 532 | 29.3 | 40.2 | 1.4 | 58.8 | 8.5 | 16.3 | 1.6 | 12.4 | 0.9 |
| TH | 36.8 | 798 | 663 | 38.5 | 52.0 | 3.4 | 30.3 | 13.5 | 20.0 | 7.2 | 16.4 | 1.5 |
| AR | 35.3 | 355 | 336 | 13.9 | 24.8 | 1.2 | 41.1 | 32.2 | 7.9 | 2.0 | 13.0 | 1.2 |

*Source: The 1951 Census Handbook, Thanjāvūr District,* Madras: Government Press, 1953.

Table 5.11. *Correlation coefficients among variables for Thanjāvūr, 1951*

| | R | D | RD | IR | GP | L/TP | OC/TP | T/TP | AL/TP | B/TP | SC/TP | H/O |
|---|---|---|---|---|---|---|---|---|---|---|---|---|
| R | 0 | | | | | | | | | | | |
| D | .34 | 0 | | | | | | | | | | |
| RD | .35 | .96 | 0 | | | | | | | | | |
| IR | .53 | .63 | .76 | 0 | | | | | | | | |
| GP | .32 | .76 | .86 | .89 | 0 | | | | | | | |
| L/TP | .43 | .68 | .80 | .90 | .87 | 0 | | | | | | |
| OC/TP | –.54 | –.78 | –.83 | –.77 | –.74 | –.84 | 0 | | | | | |
| T/TP | –.27 | –.13 | –.03 | –.06 | –.07 | .04 | –.18 | 0 | | | | |
| AL/TP | .54 | .50 | .63 | .95 | .79 | .83 | –.67 | –.21 | 0 | | | |
| B/TP | .15 | .86 | .87 | .63 | .78 | .76 | –.77 | –.03 | .54 | 0 | | |
| SC/TP | .89 | .26 | .37 | .70 | .48 | .52 | –.66 | –.20 | .68 | .32 | 0 | |
| H/O | .48 | .68 | .81 | .82 | .81 | .84 | –.89 | .26 | .74 | .65 | .62 | 0 |

Table 5.12. *Significance tests of correlations among variables for Thanjāvūr, 1951*

| | R | D | RD | IR | GP | L/TP | OC/TP | T/TP | AL/TP | B/TP | SC/TP | H/O |
|---|---|---|---|---|---|---|---|---|---|---|---|---|
| R | 0 | | | | | | | | | | | |
| D | .154 | 0 | | | | | | | | | | |
| RD | .144 | .001 | 0 | | | | | | | | | |
| IR | .047 | .020 | .003 | 0 | | | | | | | | |
| GP | .167 | .003 | .001 | .001 | 0 | | | | | | | |
| L/TP | .093 | .011 | .001 | .001 | .001 | 0 | | | | | | |
| OC/TP | .043 | .002 | .001 | .003 | .004 | .001 | 0 | | | | | |
| T/TP | .211 | .355 | .460 | .432 | .422 | .456 | .301 | 0 | | | | |
| AL/TP | .044 | .061 | .018 | .001 | .002 | .001 | .013 | .269 | 0 | | | |
| B/TP | .335 | .001 | .001 | .019 | .002 | .003 | .003 | .465 | .041 | 0 | | |
| SC/TP | .001 | .143 | .105 | .017 | .066 | .049 | .014 | .273 | .011 | .174 | 0 | |
| H/O | .070 | .011 | .001 | .001 | .001 | .001 | .001 | .220 | .005 | .018 | .021 | 0 |

Table 5.13. *Variables for* Tālūks *of Thanjāvūr, 1961*

| *Tālūks* | R | D | RD | IR | LA/ AW | T/ AW | AL/ AW | C/ TW | AL/ TW | B/ TP | SC/ TP | HI - | H 2.5- | H 15+ | H/ O | AW/ TW | TW/ TP |
|---|---|---|---|---|---|---|---|---|---|---|---|---|---|---|---|---|---|
| SI | 53.8 | 1089 | 978 | 72.8 | 18.9 | 20.4 | 60.8 | 27.8 | 43.1 | 5.1 | 34.5 | 17.3 | 56.9 | 1.9 | 5.4 | 70.9 | 39.8 |
| NA | 48.2 | 919 | 897 | 85.7 | 17.9 | 15.6 | 66.6 | 25.0 | 49.8 | 7.2 | 30.8 | 14.2 | 45.7 | 3.7 | 6.4 | 74.8 | 41.2 |
| NG | 55.4 | 1164 | 825 | 63.7 | 15.9 | 14.8 | 69.3 | 17.7 | 39.9 | 5.3 | 28.3 | 19.1 | 57.3 | 5.2 | 6.5 | 57.6 | 39.5 |
| MY | 50.8 | 1289 | 1081 | 65.8 | 20.0 | 20.5 | 59.5 | 26.1 | 38.3 | 7.3 | 26.3 | 14.6 | 47.4 | 3.1 | 3.2 | 64.4 | 37.8 |
| TP | 50.1 | 554 | 486 | 25.8 | 24.3 | 25.5 | 50.3 | 36.9 | 37.3 | 2.0 | 27.4 | 18.4 | 60.5 | 3.5 | 4.0 | 74.1 | 44.2 |
| MN | 44.9 | 902 | 753 | 73.1 | 26.2 | 25.3 | 48.5 | 38.0 | 35.8 | 6.1 | 26.2 | 23.0 | 59.0 | 2.2 | 4.8 | 73.8 | 42.1 |
| KU | 42.9 | 1737 | 1240 | 59.1 | 23.2 | 23.8 | 53.0 | 22.9 | 25.9 | 10.1 | 19.7 | 24.1 | 65.7 | 1.8 | 5.5 | 48.8 | 38.1 |
| PN | 42.2 | 1021 | 889 | 84.4 | 21.7 | 21.9 | 56.5 | 30.1 | 39.1 | 5.2 | 26.6 | 26.4 | 62.3 | 3.1 | 5.5 | 69.2 | 41.4 |
| PK | 40.1 | 714 | 638 | 48.8 | 31.3 | 35.1 | 33.5 | 51.6 | 26.0 | 1.6 | 11.0 | 19.8 | 57.8 | 2.6 | 5.3 | 77.6 | 48.6 |
| TH | 39.8 | 1001 | 642 | 28.1 | 26.9 | 28.2 | 44.9 | 32.3 | 26.3 | 7.2 | 17.8 | 21.3 | 59.6 | 3.6 | 2.9 | 58.6 | 39.7 |
| OR | 35.4 | 558 | 539 | 64.5 | 69.3 | 7.9 | 22.9 | 68.6 | 20.4 | 1.6 | 16.7 | 16.5 | 54.7 | 2.6 | 1.5 | 88.9 | 50.0 |
| AR | 35.3 | 389 | 366 | 25.3 | 53.9 | 33.6 | 12.5 | 72.5 | 10.4 | 2.0 | 12.8 | 13.8 | 52.1 | 3.2 | 1.9 | 82.9 | 49.3 |

*Source: Census of India, 1961. District Census Handbooks, Tanjore.* Madras: Government Press, 1965.

Table 5.14. *Correlation coefficients among variables for Thanjāvūr, 1961*

| | R | D | RD | IR | LA/ AW | T/ AW | AL/ AW | C/ TW | AL/ TW | B/ TP | SC/ TP | H1- | H2.5- | H15+ | H/ LH | AW/ TW | TW/ TP |
|---|---|---|---|---|---|---|---|---|---|---|---|---|---|---|---|---|---|
| R | 0 | | | | | | | | | | | | | | | | |
| D | .42 | 0 | | | | | | | | | | | | | | | |
| RD | .49 | .94 | 0 | | | | | | | | | | | | | | |
| IR | .33 | .41 | .63 | 0 | | | | | | | | | | | | | |
| LA/AW | –.77 | –.62 | –.63 | –.31 | 0 | | | | | | | | | | | | |
| T/AW | –.32 | –.19 | –.28 | –.60 | –.08 | 0 | | | | | | | | | | | |
| AL/AW | .86 | .66 | .71 | .56 | –.79 | –.38 | 0 | | | | | | | | | | |
| C/TW | –.78 | –.78 | –.76 | –.42 | .93 | .23 | –.96 | 0 | | | | | | | | | |
| AL/TW | .53 | .36 | .52 | .64 | –.89 | –.41 | .91 | –.79 | 0 | | | | | | | | |
| B/TP | .33 | .88 | .83 | .38 | –.61 | –.15 | .63 | –.33 | .39 | 0 | | | | | | | |
| SC/TP | .85 | .34 | .48 | .57 | –.66 | –.50 | .84 | –.71 | .90 | .38 | 0 | | | | | | |
| H1- | –.10 | .42 | .29 | .17 | –.30 | .17 | .20 | –.33 | .05 | .31 | –.01 | 0 | | | | | |
| H2.5- | –.12 | .27 | .09 | –.19 | –.12 | .25 | .00 | –.15 | –.19 | .09 | –.14 | .86 | 0 | | | | |
| H15+ | .31 | –.16 | –.27 | –.15 | –.20 | .20 | .27 | –.22 | .21 | –.11 | .14 | –.23 | –.27 | 0 | | | |
| H/LH | .33 | .51 | .58 | .56 | –.79 | –.09 | .78 | –.42 | .64 | .38 | .57 | .17 | –.19 | .15 | 0 | | |
| AW/TW | –.43 | –.88 | –.69 | –.04 | .69 | –.04 | –.62 | .80 | –.26 | –.81 | –.24 | –.47 | –.42 | –.13 | –.36 | 0 | |
| TW/TP | –.67 | –.85 | –.81 | –.36 | .83 | .19 | –.85 | .93 | –.63 | –.88 | –65 | –.29 | –.12 | –.09 | –.04 | .85 | 0 |

Table 5.15. *Significance tests of correlations among variables for Thanjāvūr, 1961*

| | R | D | RD | IR | GP | LA/ AW | T/ AW | AL/ AW | C/ TW | AL/ TW | B/ TP | SC/ TP | H1- | H2.5- | H15+ | H/LH | TW/ TP |
|---|---|---|---|---|---|---|---|---|---|---|---|---|---|---|---|---|---|
| R | 0 | | | | | | | | | | | | | | | | |
| D | .085 | 0 | | | | | | | | | | | | | | | |
| RD | .054 | .001 | 0 | | | | | | | | | | | | | | |
| IR | .144 | .091 | .014 | 0 | | | | | | | | | | | | | |
| LA/AW | .002 | .016 | .014 | .160 | 0 | | | | | | | | | | | | |
| T/AW | .159 | .279 | .185 | .019 | .408 | 0 | | | | | | | | | | | |
| AL/AW | .001 | .010 | .005 | .030 | .001 | .112 | 0 | | | | | | | | | | |
| C/TW | .001 | .001 | .002 | .085 | .001 | .235 | .001 | 0 | | | | | | | | | |
| AL/TW | .001 | .125 | .041 | .013 | .001 | .093 | .001 | .001 | 0 | | | | | | | | |
| B/TP | .150 | .001 | .001 | .111 | .018 | .316 | .014 | .002 | .106 | 0 | | | | | | | |
| SC/TP | .001 | .140 | .055 | .027 | .010 | .050 | .001 | .005 | .001 | .113 | 0 | | | | | | |
| H1- | .373 | .089 | .181 | .300 | .171 | .299 | .263 | .147 | .439 | .161 | .485 | 0 | | | | | |
| H2.5- | .351 | .194 | .395 | .281 | .359 | .219 | .497 | .323 | .280 | .396 | .338 | .001 | 0 | | | | |
| H15+ | .161 | .305 | .202 | .318 | .271 | .270 | .198 | .249 | .253 | .372 | .332 | .239 | .202 | 0 | | | |
| H/LH | .017 | .144 | .025 | .029 | .001 | .395 | .001 | .085 | .004 | .087 | .033 | .122 | .286 | .326 | 0 | | |
| AW/TW | .084 | .001 | .006 | .448 | .007 | .454 | .016 | .001 | .205 | .001 | .223 | .001 | .061 | .090 | .064 | 0 | |
| TW/TP | .008 | .001 | .001 | .129 | .001 | .273 | .001 | .001 | .014 | .001 | .011 | .177 | .360 | .392 | .040 | .001 | 0 |

No figures were available for the paddy acreage in each *tāluk* at the time of writing, nor were separate figures available for landlords, owner cultivators, and tenant farmers, but only for these categories jointly as "cultivators" (Variable 5). No figures were available for the distribution of holdings of various sizes.

Tables 5.16, 5.17, and 5.18 respectively list the numerical values of the variables for Thanjāvūr *tālūks* in 1971, the Pearsonian correlation coefficients, and the significance tests among them.

**Results**

Most of the relationships that I had hypothesized among the variables were borne out remarkably. Not all of the expected correlations were significant, however, and in a small number of cases the results caused me to modify my hypotheses. The most salient results are as follows.

***Rainfall, Density, Irrigation, Paddy, and Crop Value***

As predicted, these major variables are positively correlated in all cases where they are present. Value per acre is available only for Tamiḷ Nāḍu for 1961 (Tables 5.4, 5.5, and 5.6). It correlates very strongly and significantly with rainfall, density, irrigation, and paddy. Rainfall, density, irrigation, and paddy all correlate strongly and significantly with each other in Tamiḷ Nāḍu for 1951, 1961, and 1971. Although positive, however, some of these correlations are less strong and significant for Thanjāvūr. Paddy acreage was unfortunately not available for the Thanjāvūr *tālūks* in 1961 and 1971, but in 1951 it correlated strongly and significantly with density and irrigation. The main difference between Thanjāvūr and Tamiḷ Nāḍu as a whole is that in Thanjāvūr, rainfall was either not significantly or less significantly correlated with density, irrigation, or paddy in 1951 and 1961. The reason for these discrepancies in certain decades is already mentioned in my hypothesis. In the Thanjāvūr delta, density, irrigation, and paddy cultivation are less closely associated with rainfall than in the districts of Tamiḷ Nāḍu irrigated mainly by tanks and wells because water comes mainly from branches of the Kāvēri, which is replenished from rainfall in the Western Ghāts. Even the dryer *tālūks* of Paṭṭukkoṭṭai and Arantāngi are partly irrigated from the Grand Anicut Canal, which was built in the 1930s to branch off from the Kāvēri. Irrigation was, however, highly and significantly correlated with rainfall in Thanjāvūr in 1971. Conceivably, this was because many new irrigation projects were undertaken in the late 1960s that relied heavily on filter points (shallow tube wells), for which rainfall was relevant. In all decades, however, the correlations among these variables were positive.

***Landlords***

Separate figures for noncultivating landlords are available only for 1951 (Tables 5.1, 5.2, 5.3, 5.10, 5.11, and 5.12). Both in Tamiḷ Nāḍu and in Thanjāvūr the percentage of landlords in the population is strongly and significantly correlated with density, irrigation, and paddy, bearing out my hypothesis. In

Table 5.16. *Variables for* Tālūks *of Thanjāvūr, 1971*

| *Tālūks* | R | D | RD | IR | C/TW | AL/TW | AL/AW | SC/TP | H/C | AW/TW | TW/TP |
|---|---|---|---|---|---|---|---|---|---|---|---|
| SI | 53.8 | 1250 | 1132 | 97.8 | 24.5 | 50.0 | 67.3 | 33.4 | 1.8 | 74.5 | 32.3 |
| NA | 53.3 | 1044 | 1044 | 97.8 | 22.5 | 55.4 | 71.1 | 29.2 | 2.5 | 77.9 | 33.2 |
| NG | 53.3 | 1345 | 935 | 84.7 | 14.4 | 45.9 | 76.1 | 26.8 | 2.7 | 60.4 | 33.6 |
| MY | 51.9 | 1473 | 1217 | 99.1 | 21.2 | 46.5 | 68.6 | 26.2 | 2.0 | 67.7 | 31.2 |
| TP | 48.4 | 647 | 556 | 72.8 | 31.7 | 48.5 | 60.5 | 27.1 | 1.3 | 80.2 | 35.1 |
| MN | 46.7 | 1062 | 883 | 88.0 | 28.5 | 47.9 | 62.7 | 26.0 | 2.0 | 76.4 | 35.2 |
| KU | 43.5 | 2034 | 1422 | 87.9 | 19.0 | 36.0 | 65.5 | 18.9 | 1.5 | 55.0 | 32.0 |
| PN | 43.3 | 1155 | 1012 | 94.1 | 26.0 | 50.0 | 65.8 | 25.4 | 2.0 | 76.0 | 43.2 |
| PK | 42.9 | 958 | 784 | 83.1 | 36.6 | 39.4 | 51.8 | 10.9 | 1.4 | 75.9 | 35.6 |
| TH | 39.8 | 1215 | 791 | 61.5 | 25.8 | 35.4 | 57.8 | 16.9 | 1.8 | 61.2 | 31.7 |
| PE | 37.4 | 791 | 791 | 70.1 | 50.9 | 28.9 | 36.2 | 9.7 | 1.1 | 79.7 | 35.3 |
| OR | 35.4 | 691 | 667 | 66.6 | 56.3 | 31.1 | 35.6 | 16.4 | 1.1 | 87.5 | 35.0 |
| AR | 33.0 | 505 | 468 | 72.8 | 55.9 | 23.1 | 29.2 | 12.2 | 1.0 | 79.0 | 33.6 |

*Source: Census of India, 1971. District Census Handbooks, Thanjāvūr*. Vols. 1 and 2. Madras: Government Press, 1972.

Table 5.17. *Correlation coefficients among variables for Thanjāvūr, 1971*

| | R | D | RD | IR | C/TW | AL/TW | AL/AW | SC/TP | H/C | AW/TW | TW/TP |
|---|---|---|---|---|---|---|---|---|---|---|---|
| R | 0 | | | | | | | | | | |
| D | .45 | 0 | | | | | | | | | |
| RD | .56 | .92 | 0 | | | | | | | | |
| IR | .74 | .51 | .73 | 0 | | | | | | | |
| C/TW | –.79 | –.76 | –.72 | –.64 | 0 | | | | | | |
| AL/TW | .94 | .28 | .41 | .64 | –.68 | 0 | | | | | |
| AL/AW | .90 | .68 | .69 | .69 | –.97 | .81 | 0 | | | | |
| SC/TP | .86 | .31 | .44 | .67 | –.70 | .84 | .80 | 0 | | | |
| H/C | .79 | .46 | .49 | .61 | –.81 | .73 | .85 | .71 | 0 | | |
| AW/TW | –.30 | –.85 | –.62 | –.18 | .69 | –.12 | –.57 | –.13 | –.42 | 0 | |
| TW/TP | –.33 | –.67 | –.62 | –.33 | .52 | –.18 | –.47 | –.34 | –.34 | 69 | 0 |

Table 5.18. *Significance tests of correlations among variables for Thanjāvūr, 1971*

| | R | D | RD | IR | C/TW | AL/TW | AL/AW | SC/TP | H/C | AW/TW | TW/TP |
|---|---|---|---|---|---|---|---|---|---|---|---|
| R | 0 | | | | | | | | | | |
| D | .062 | 0 | | | | | | | | | |
| RD | .024 | .001 | 0 | | | | | | | | |
| IR | .002 | .038 | .002 | 0 | | | | | | | |
| C/TW | .001 | .001 | .003 | .009 | 0 | | | | | | |
| AL/TW | .001 | .173 | .083 | .009 | .005 | 0 | | | | | |
| AL/AW | .001 | .005 | .005 | .005 | .001 | .001 | 0 | | | | |
| SC/TP | .001 | .148 | .065 | .006 | .004 | .001 | .001 | 0 | | | |
| H/C | .001 | .058 | .044 | .014 | .001 | .002 | .001 | .003 | 0 | | |
| AW/TW | .157 | .001 | .013 | .280 | .005 | .352 | .021 | .341 | .079 | 0 | |
| TW/TP | .132 | .006 | .013 | .135 | .033 | .280 | .054 | .131 | .129 | .005 | 0 |

both regions it is positively, although not strongly or significantly, correlated with rainfall. Landlords are evidently most heavily concentrated in the intensely irrigated districts and *tālūks*, where high productivity permits a larger leisured population.

### *Owner Cultivators*

This category includes all landowners predominantly engaged personally in cultivation, with or without agricultural laborers. It roughly covers the commonly used category of rich peasants and the middle peasants who mainly cultivate their own land rather than land leased from landlords. The category was separately reported only in 1951. As I predicted, it was strongly negatively and significantly correlated with density, irrigation, and paddy cultivation in both Tamiḷ Nāḍu and Thanjāvūr. It was also negatively correlated with rainfall, although not quite significantly. Owner cultivators were strongly negatively and significantly correlated with the prevalence of Brahmans, noncultivating landlords, Scheduled Castes, agricultural laborers, and the average size of landholdings, and in Tamiḷ Nāḍu with small holdings of less than one or three acres. In Tamiḷ Nāḍu owner cultivators were positively correlated with the percentage of agriculturalists in the total workforce; the latter variable was not available for Thanjāvūr. All of these findings are in accordance with my hypothesis: Owner cultivators tend to predominate in the dryer and less irrigated areas of lower productivity, where there is a lower population density, less social stratification, less specialization of the workforce, and less expenditure on ceremonies and the priesthood. In Tamiḷ Nāḍu in 1951, owner cultivators were also strongly negatively and significantly correlated with the percentage of tenants in the total population, again in accordance with my prediction. In Thanjāvūr, however, owner cultivators, like most other variables, bore no relationship to tenants; this will be discussed in the section on "Tenant Farmers."

One surprising finding is that in Tamiḷ Nāḍu in 1951, owner cultivators were negatively and significantly correlated with the percentage of the workforce in the total population, the opposite of my prediction. (The latter variable was not available for Thanjāvūr in 1951.) No records of owner cultivators are available for 1961 and 1971, but in 1961, both in Tamiḷ Nāḍu and in Thanjāvūr, "landowners" and "cultivators," which are similar variables to "owner cultivators," correlated positively and in most cases significantly with the percentage of the workforce in the total population. This was also true of Thanjāvūr in 1971, whereas in Tamiḷ Nāḍu in 1971, "cultivators as percent of total workforce" (C/TW) and "workforce as percent of total population" (W/TP) were in no way significantly related. Although these correlations for Tamiḷ Nāḍu in 1961 and for Thanjāvūr in both 1961 and 1971 are in the direction of my prediction, I am unable to explain the negative correlation for Tamiḷ Nāḍu in 1951. It is consistent with the fact that in Tamiḷ Nāḍu in 1951, "total workforce as percent of total population" (TW/TP) and "agricultural workforce as percent of total population'' (AW/TP) were negatively and significantly correlated, whereas in 1961 and 1971 the correlation, although negative, was insignificant, and in Thanjāvūr in 1961 and 1971 it was positive and significant. Thanjāvūr thus bears out my predictions regarding owner cultivators, the total workforce, and the agricultural workforce, but Tamiḷ Nāḍu does not.

### *Tenant Farmers*

In Tamiḷ Nāḍu tenant farmers were strongly and significantly correlated with rainfall, density, irrigation, paddy, landlords, and agricultural laborers, both in 1951 and in 1961, the two periods for which they are listed separately (Tables 5.1, 5.2, 5.3, 5.4, 5.5, and 5.6). This is in accordance with my hypothesis, which states that cultivating tenants, like agricultural laborers, will be most prevalent in areas of high irrigation and productivity. In Tamiḷ Nāḍu, tenants were also strongly and significantly correlated with Brahmans, a high proportion of whom come from landlord families. In 1951 in Tamiḷ Nāḍu tenants were also highly and significantly correlated with Scheduled Castes in the total workforce. This association, although positive, was much weaker in 1961 than in 1951. This may have been because more Scheduled Caste members had become agricultural laborers rather than tenants, for the correlations between agricultural laborers and Scheduled Castes were higher in 1961 than in 1951.

In Thanjāvūr the variable ''tenants as a percentage of the agricultural workforce'' (T/AW) did not behave predictably in either 1951 or 1961. The variable was not strongly or significantly correlated with anything in 1951, whereas in 1961 it was negatively and significantly correlated with irrigation (IR) and Scheduled Castes. In 1961, tenants also had a fairly strong, although not significant, negative correlation with agricultural laborers, and a negative, although insignificant, correlation with rainfall and density. Surprisingly, tenants were not at all closely correlated with Brahmans, even though many of the latter were landlords.

I am unable to explain these unpredictable showings of Thanjāvūr tenants and can only offer guesses. One is that ''tenants'' may have meant different things to the enumerators in different parts of Thanjāvūr district. In Arantāngi, for example, 73 percent of the cultivated land was former *iṉam* land, by comparison with 21 percent in the district as a whole. It is possible that the occupants of these lands were recorded as tenants, even though some of them had a status similar to that of owner cultivators. Again, by 1961, it may be that some landlords had evicted cultivating tenants from their highly valuable, irrigated land in order to avoid granting them fixity of tenure. These lands would tend to be in *tālūks* where Scheduled Castes were most prominent. A comparison of the actual percentages of tenants in the different *tālūks* in the two decades seems to bear out this hypothesis, for the proportions of tenants in the total population declined in the highly irrigated areas of Sīrkāli, Naṉṉilam, Māyuram, and Pāpaṉāsam. Tenants were, however, still sufficiently numerous in Thanjāvūr in 1961 to uphold the correlations mentioned earlier for Tamiḷ Nāḍu as a whole.

***Agricultural Laborers***

As was predicted, one or another measure of agricultural laborers was strongly and significantly correlated with the major variables of rainfall, density, irrigation, paddy, and value per acre, in almost every case in both Tamiḻ Nāḍu and Thanjāvūr where these variables were tabulated. The conclusion is clear that both in Tamiḻ Nāḍu and among the *tālūks* of Thanjāvūr, agricultural laborers tended to be most prevalent where the land was most fertile from rainfall, irrigation was most developed, rural density was highest, and paddy was cultivated most intensively.

Among the other variables, agricultural laborers correlated rather highly and in most cases significantly with the prevalence of Brahmans and Scheduled Caste members both in Thanjāvūr and in Tamiḻ Nāḍu. These correlations were predicted because of the fact that Brahmans were usually noncultivating landowners, many of whom employed hired labor, whereas Scheduled Caste members were former agricultural slaves and are usually agricultural laborers today. Agricultural laborers correlated strongly with tenants in Tamiḻ Nāḍu as a whole, both laborers and cultivating tenants being most prevalent in areas of high productivity. As was noted, however, agricultural laborers had a rather weak but negative correlation with tenants in Thanjāvūr in 1961.

Both in Thanjāvūr and in Tamiḻ Nāḍu, agricultural laborers tended to be more numerous where the average holding per landowner or per "cultivator" was larger, although the association was not significant in every case where these variables occurred. This finding goes contrary to my hypothesis and is discussed later in the section on "Average land holding." In Tamiḻ Nāḍu in 1951, however, agricultural laborers were strongly and significantly correlated with the presence of a large proportion of smallholdings of less than one acre, and only slightly less strongly, and still significantly, with the prevalence of holdings of less than three acres. They were negatively, although not significantly, correlated with the prevalence of large estates of more than twenty-five acres. In Thanjāvūr in 1961, the other occasion for which the size distribution of holdings was recorded, the prevalence of agricultural laborers bore no relationship either to very small or to large landholdings.

The prevalence of agricultural laborers bore no noteworthy positive or negative relationship to the percentage of the agricultural to the total workforce in Tamiḻ Nāḍu as a whole in any decade. In Thanjāvūr, however, one or another measure of agricultural laborers had a strong and significant negative correlation with the percentage of the agricultural to the total workforce both in 1961 and in 1971, the two decades for which these variables were recorded. This finding bears out my hypothesis that in areas of high productivity resulting from either irrigation or rainfall, social stratification will be marked and a large percentage of the people will be relieved from agricultural work. These circumstances may then result in a high proportion both of agricultural laborers and also of nonagricultural workers relative to owner cultivators.

The prevalence of agricultural laborers was not significantly correlated with the percentage of the workforce in the total population in Tamiḷ Nāḍu in 1951. In 1961 and 1971, however, one or another measure of agricultural laborers was negatively and significantly correlated with the percentage of the workforce in the total population both in Thanjāvūr and in Tamiḷ Nāḍu. These latter findings bear out my hypothesis that high agricultural productivity tends to produce both a high percentage of agricultural laborers and a low workforce participation because a smaller proportion of the people need engage in gainful work. They probably also reflect the fact that in postcolonial India, as unemployment increased in the late 1950s to 1970s, surplus workers either became agricultural laborers or dropped out of the workforce, so that both the unemployed and the agricultural laborers increased together.

***Landowners***

This is an omnibus category that includes both noncultivating landlords and owner cultivators. Because it spans more than one class I did not expect it to correlate significantly with other variables, but I included it along with the still broader category of "cultivators" (that is, owners plus tenants) because these were the only measures of landowners available for 1961. In fact, as I should have expected from the small percentages of landlords, this category turned out to be closely similar to that of owner cultivators in 1951, correlating at 0.85. In these circumstances we may take "landowners" to refer predominantly to owner cultivators. Like owner cultivators in Tamiḷ Nāḍu both in 1951 and in 1961, landowners correlated negatively and significantly with density, irrigation, paddy cultivation, agricultural laborers, tenants, Brahmans, Scheduled Castes, the size of the average landholding, and the prevalence of small estates of less than one and three acres. In 1961, as might have been expected, landowners were strongly positively and significantly correlated with the percentage of the workforce in the total population. They bore no relationship, however, to the percentage of the agricultural workforce in the total workforce. Except for this last one, these findings merely reinforce the findings for owner cultivators in 1951, and suggest that the same results would have been found for owner cultivators in 1961 and 1971 had that variable been independently reported.

***Cultivators***

This omnibus variable includes landlords, owner cultivators, and tenants, in fact, all people deriving an income from agriculture who are not predominantly agricultural laborers. In 1961 and 1971 it was the only measure available for the whole population that included landowners, although it was possible to obtain separate rough estimates of landowners and tenants from sample surveys in 1961. Cultivators correlated positively and significantly with both owner cultivators and landowners where these latter categories were available. Cultivators correlated especially strongly with landowners (0.93) in Thanjāvūr in 1961, and statistically evidently acted as a fairly close approximation to owner cultivators in Thanjāvūr. As such they were, predictably, negatively and significantly correlated in Thanjāvūr with rainfall, density, agricultural laborers, and Scheduled Castes and were positively and significantly correlated with the percentage of the agricultural in the total workforce, and with the percentage of the workforce in the total population. They were also negatively correlated with irrigation, although significantly so only in 1971.

In Tamiḷ Nāḍu the measures for "cultivators" had less relevance because they evidently covered too wide a spectrum of classes. As might be expected, they correlated negatively and significantly with agricultural laborers in the total workforce and with the average size of the agricultural holding. Cultivators also correlated positively with the percentage of the agricultural workforce in the total workforce in 1961 and 1971, although the correlation was not significant in 1961. Other correlations of "cultivators as percent of total workforce" (C/TW) in Tamiḷ Nāḍu were insignificant; in terms of social class, the measure was evidently too ambiguous to have much value.

***Brahmans***

The variable "Brahmans as percentage of the total population" correlated with other variables almost entirely in the directions I had predicted, although the correlations were not always significant. Both in Tamiḷ Nāḍu and Thanjāvūr, the prevalence of Brahmans correlated strongly and significantly with density, landlords, and agricultural laborers. It also correlated strongly and significantly with irrigation, except in Thanjāvūr in 1961, where the correlation, although positive, was weak and not significant. Brahmans correlated positively with value per acre in Tamiḷ Nāḍu in 1961, although the correlation was not quite significant at the 0.05 level, being 0.062. As was predicted, Brahmans correlated negatively and significantly with owner cultivators and with landowners (primarily owner cultivators). The correlations between Brahmans and rainfall, although positive, were weak and insignificant, suggesting that it is not rainfall per se that provides the conditions for a large proportion of Brahmans, but a generally high level of productivity and population density. In Tamiḷ Nāḍu, the prevalence of Brahmans correlated strongly and significantly with that of tenants; this was predicted, because many Brahmans were landlords. The correlation with tenants was, however, completely insignificant in Thanjāvūr, as has been noted earlier. In Thanjāvūr the percentage of Brahmans correlated very strongly negatively, and predictably, with the percentage of the agricultural in the total workforce, and with the percentage of the workforce in the total population. These correlations, however, although negative, were not significant in Tamiḷ Nāḍu. In Thanjāvūr in 1951 Brahmans correlated positively and significantly with the average size of landholdings. This was the reverse of my prediction and will be dealt with in the section on "Average land holding."

In each case, Brahmans had a low positive correlation with the percentage of Scheduled Caste members in the total population. Although somewhat lower than I expected, and not significant, this finding tends to support my belief that the proportions of Brahmans and Harijans both issue mainly from the level of productivity rather than being directly related to each other.

### *Scheduled Castes*

The percentage of Scheduled Caste members in the population and the workforce correlated with almost all other variables in the directions that I had predicted, but the correlations were not always significant. Strong and significant correlations occurred in all cases with measures for rainfall, irrigation, and agricultural laborers, and significant negative correlations with owner cultivators, landowners, and cultivators. Scheduled Castes were strongly and significantly correlated with density, value per acre, and paddy cultivation in Tamiḷ Nāḍu and positively but not quite significantly with density and paddy in Thanjāvūr in 1951, the only date when both measures were available. Scheduled Castes were positively but not significantly correlated with Brahmans, as I have noted. As predicted, Scheduled Castes were positively but not significantly correlated with tenants in Tamiḷ Nāḍu in 1951; in 1961 the relationship was positive but weak and insignificant. Scheduled Castes were not significantly correlated with tenants in Thanjāvūr, but this was expectable because the measures for tenants did not behave predictably. In Tamiḷ Nāḍu, Scheduled Castes were not at all correlated with the size of the average landholding. In Thanjāvūr in 1951 and 1961, however, Scheduled Caste members increased significantly with the size of the average holding, a finding that contradicted my hypothesis but was in harmony with various other correlations with the average size of holdings in Thanjāvūr. In harmony with my hypothesis, in Thanjāvūr the incidence of Scheduled Castes was significantly negatively correlated with the percentage of the agricultural workforce in the total workforce and of the total workforce in the total population. In Tamiḷ Nāḍu, the latter of these correlations was found only in 1961; the rest were insignificant.

The percentage of Scheduled Caste members was in all cases most strongly correlated with rainfall. I am unable definitely to explain the particular strength of this connection as against irrigation, paddy cultivation, value per acre, or density. It may be that both rainfall and Scheduled Castes are measures that have not changed much over many centuries, whereas irrigation, paddy cultivation, value per acre, and density have been more subject to modern change. If this is true, the high correlation of Scheduled Castes with rainfall may reflect the fact that for hundreds of years, higher rainfall areas in Tamiḷ Nāḍu tended to be the areas of highest food productivity, and thus the ones where social stratification was most marked and agricultural slaves most prevalent.

### *Average Landholding*

My hypothesis predicted that the average landholding per landowner would be lower in areas of high rainfall, irrigation, density, value per acre, and paddy cultivation, because those areas were the most productive and the most intensively cultivated and therefore smaller holdings were able to furnish a family's subsistence. This also meant that average holdings would tend to be lower in areas having larger proportions of Brahmans, Scheduled Castes, agricultural laborers, landlords, and tenant farmers, and where there were higher percentages of holdings of less than one acre and less than three acres. The average holding was also expected to correlate positively with "agricultural workforce as percent of total workforce" (AW/TW) and "total workforce as percent of total population" (TW/TP).

In fact, where they were significant at all, the actual correlations were the opposite of this hypothesis. In Tamiḷ Nāḍu in 1951 and 1961 the average holding size was positively and significantly correlated with the percentage of agricultural laborers, and negatively and significantly with those of owner cultivators, cultivators, landowners, and the proportion of AW/TW; other correlations were insignificant, although the correlations respecting average holding and density, irrigation, paddy, value per acre, agricultural laborers, tenants, and Brahmans also ran counter to my hypothesis. In Thanjāvūr in 1961 the findings were even more strongly contrary to my hypothesis: Average holding size was strongly positively and significantly correlated with density, irrigation, paddy, landlords, agricultural laborers, Scheduled Castes, and Brahmans, and strongly negatively and significantly with owner cultivators and landowners. Average holding size was also positively correlated with rainfall, although not quite significantly. The fact therefore seems to be that social stratification determines the size of holdings more directly than does ecology; the richer the land, the more stratified the agricultural population, the larger the average holding, and the greater the percentage of the landless.

### *The Distribution of Various Sizes of Holdings*

It was hypothesized that because of the greater intensity of cultivation, there would be more small holdings of less than one acre and less than three acres in areas of high productivity, and more large holdings of more than ten acres, more than fifteen acres, or more than twenty-five acres, in areas of lower productivity.

This hypothesis was strongly upheld in Tamiḷ Nāḍu in 1951, the only date for the region for which I had data on the distribution of holdings of various sizes. Small holdings were positively, and large holdings negatively, correlated with rainfall, density, irrigation, paddy, tenants, and agricultural laborers, the correlations being significant in almost very case. My hypothesis was not, however, strongly upheld in Thanjāvūr in 1961, the only date for which holding size was available. There, the distribution of holdings of various sizes bore no significant relation to any of the other variables, although there were positive correlations between small holdings and both density and Brahmans, and negative correlations between large holdings and both rural density and small holdings, as well as between small holdings and both landowners and cultivators – findings in the direction of my hypothesis. Unfortunately the data did not bear on Thanjāvūr's very large holdings of more than 1,000 or more than 5,000 acres.

Insofar as the data are available, therefore, they tend to uphold my hypothesis with respect to the relation between productivity and its various correlates on the one hand, and the size distribution of holdings on the other hand, even though they contradict my hypothesis regarding the relation between productivity and the size of the average holding. These findings, although logically possible, are unexpected.

### *Workforce as a Percentage of the Population*

It was hypothesized that the workforce would be lower in regions of high rainfall, irrigation, density, paddy cultivation, and value per acre, because fewer people would need to be employed in order for families to earn a living, and perhaps because agricultural unemployment would be greater with higher density.

This hypothesis was generally borne out in both Tamiḷ Nāḍu and Thanjāvūr in 1961 and 1971. "Workforce in the total population" was negatively and for the most part significantly correlated with rainfall, density, and irrigation, with value per acre, to some extent with paddy cultivation, and also with agricultural laborers, Scheduled Castes, and Brahmans. It was positively and significantly correlated with landowners, and in Thanjāvūr with cultivators (the approximate measures of owner cultivators) and with the percentage of the agricultural workforce in the total population. The hypothesis, however, was not borne out in Tamiḷ Nāḍu in 1951 (Thanjāvūr for 1951 was not recorded). In Tamiḷ Nāḍu in 1951, TW/TP was negatively and significantly correlated with rainfall and agricultural labor, but also with owner cultivators and cultivators, and was not strongly correlated with any other variables. It seems likely that the lowering of the workforce in highly productive areas became more marked with the increasing density and unemployment of the 1950s, 1960s, and 1970s.

### *The Percentage of the Agricultural Workforce in the Total Workforce*

This variable, the last to be considered, was expected to be higher in the dryer areas of lower productivity and lower in the more productive regions of heavier rainfall and irrigation, on the theory that these latter areas would maintain a higher proportion of nonagricultural workers. This hypothesis was to some extent borne out in Thanjāvūr in 1961 and 1971 (1951 was not recorded). There, AW/TW was negatively and significantly correlated with density, agricultural labor, and Brahmans; positively and significantly, with cultivators and with TW/TP. The associations with rainfall, irrigation, Scheduled Castes, and small holdings were negative but weak. In Tamiḷ Nāḍu, by contrast, the hypothesis was not borne out. There, AW/TW was positively and significantly correlated with rainfall, and with rural density in 1951, but was also strongly and significantly correlated with owner cultivators and cultivators. It was negatively and significantly correlated with the average size of holdings, and negatively or not at all, with TW/TP. In Tamiḷ Nāḍu as a whole, ecology does not appear to have any marked effect on the size of the agricultural workforce, perhaps because industries have been developed without reference to agricultural productivity.

**Summary**

My statistical findings confirm the hypothesis that certain features of ecology and social structure tend to be found together both in Tamiḻ Nāḍu as a whole and among the *tālūks* of Thanjāvūr. Higher rainfall tends to be accompanied by more intensive irrigation, more wet paddy cultivation, a higher population density, and in Tamiḻ Nāḍu, a greater money value of crops per acre. These in turn tend to produce a social structure having relatively high proportions of noncultivating landlords, agricultural laborers, Brahmans, Scheduled Caste members, and Scheduled Caste members who are agricultural laborers. On the whole these regions tend to have a lower workforce in the total population, a tendency that increased in the 1960s and 1970s with the growth of unemployment.

Of the Tamiḻ districts studied, Thanjāvūr itself is the most striking example of this complex of variables, with Chingleput running next in most of them. Kānya Kumāri, which was not included in the tables, also provides a prime example of this complex of variables. In Thanjāvūr district, the eastern *tālūks* of Sīrkali, Naṉṉilam, Nāgapaṭṭanam, Māyuram, and northern Maṉṉārgudi, together with Pāpaṉāsam, are the most generally characteristic, although productivity is highest and Brahmans congregate most along the main branch of the Kāvēri and especially in Kumbakōnam.

In Tamiḻ Nāḍu as a whole, such regions have also produced a high proportion of cultivating tenants. Within Thanjāvūr, however, the proportion of tenants recorded was not closely related to the other variables in 1951, and may perhaps have been influenced by the distribution of former *iṉam* and/or *zamindāri* estates. In 1961 tenants in Thanjāvūr were negatively, although not very significantly, correlated with irrigation and Scheduled Castes, perhaps because some tenants had been evicted from the most fertile irrigated areas.

The dryer areas of Tamiḻ Nāḍu and Thanjāvūr tend to be less heavily irrigated and to depend more on millets for their staple food crops. On the whole they have lower population densities, higher proportions of owner cultivators, a higher workforce in the total population, and lower proportions of agricultural laborers, Brahmans, and members of the Scheduled Castes. In Tamiḻ Nāḍu as a whole, although not within Thanjāvūr, the dryer and less fertile areas tend to have fewer holdings of less than one acre and less than three acres and more holdings of more than ten acres. This does not mean, however, that the average size of the agricultural holding is larger in the dryer areas. In Tamiḻ Nāḍu the average size of the holding tends if anything to be larger in the more irrigated areas having more agricultural laborers. In Thanjāvūr this tendency is still more marked: It is definitely the most heavily irrigated areas with the highest proportion of agricultural laborers that have the largest average holdings. In Tamiḻ Nāḍu, Salem and Coimbatore best illustrate the dry region complex, with the other districts intermediate. In Thanjāvūr, the dryer and less fertile areas having this complex include the southwest upland tracts of Paṭṭukkoṭṭai, Arantāngi, the south of Thanjāvūr *tālūk*, and the southern salt swamp of Tirutturaipūṇḍi.

These findings suggest two general conclusions. One is that inequality is certainly greater, and poverty in the lower reaches of the society probably more accentuated, in the wealthier, more productive areas of Tamiḷ Nāḍu. The farmers of Rāmanāthapuram may have to leave their fields altogether and migrate periodically in seasons of drought, but it is in Thanjāvūr that one finds the most wretched conditions for landless laborers, and the highest proportion of this class.

The second conclusion is that struggle between the locally resident classes of the agrarian society is likely to be most acute in the well-watered and heavily irrigated regions of wet paddy cultivation, especially the struggles of agricultural laborers and poor tenants against local landlords. It is not surprising, therefore, that in south India the Communist movement has its deepest roots in the agrarian society of Thanjāvūr and Kēraḷa, areas of high irrigation and rainfall and of very high proportions of agricultural laborers. The Communist struggles of the late 1940s and late 1960s over wages and crop shares in these regions are prime examples. Political struggles in the dryer areas, by contrast, are more likely to find owner cultivators pitted against the state on such questions as crop procurement, debt relief, the costs of electricity and fertilizers, and the price of grain. In Tamiḷ Nāḍu, the violent demonstrations of small holders, led by landlords, against the government over these issues in Coimbatore, Salem, North Ārcot, Madurai, and Rāmanāthapuram in 1972 and again in 1978 were instances of this latter type of confrontation.

# 6 The Colonial Background and the Sources of Poverty

In 1951, the cultivating tenants and agricultural laborers in Thanjāvūr, as in India generally, lived in direst poverty, while the small holders and artisans were little better off. This poverty was not endemic to Thanjāvūr, but resulted from two centuries of colonial exploitation and distortion of the economy. In this chapter[1] I will trace the growth and entrenchment of poverty in Thanjāvūr up to 1951–3, and in so doing describe the changing class structure of the region. To understand Thanjāvūr's poverty we must go back at least to the 1770s, when the British effected a *de facto* conquest of the district. Before probing the changes of the colonial period, however, I shall first sketch the pre-British social system.

## Chōḷa Society

The Chōḷa kingdom of about 850–1290 A.D. appears to have been a complex variant of what Marx called the "Asiatic mode of production."[2] This type of state has more recently been described by Darcy Ribeiro as a "theocratic irrigation state," and by Samir Amin as a "tributary system" combined with "patriarchal slavery."[3]

Thanjāvūr in this period formed the heartland of a major kingdom, drawing booty and captured slaves from other regions. Its economy rested mainly on the government's maintenance of irrigation works, which made possible the intensive cultivation of wet rice, the staple crop. The major dams began to be constructed as early as the first century A.D., but irrigation was greatly expanded in the ninth to twelfth centuries. Sometime during this latter period, it seems probable that the transplanting of paddy from seedbeds into flooded fields became prevalent, for the technique appeared in South China in the ninth century and may have reached south India about the same time. In Thanjāvūr the communally owned agricultural slaves were the class especially set aside for building and digging out the irrigation channels and cultivating the wet rice. Irrigation, bureaucratization, military and commercial expansion, and agricultural slavery appear to have developed *pari passu* under the Chōḷas.[4]

Whereas the king was primarily a military and civic leader, his bureaucracy was drawn largely from religiosi of the Brahman caste. The bureaucracy included departments for the administration of land revenue, customs and other taxes, irrigation, construction, roads, justice, and the affairs of temples, monasteries, and royal palaces.

To maintain his government and armies, the king held a customary right to extract land revenue or tribute (*mēlvāram*, literally "upper share") that amounted to about 30–40 percent of the gross produce of the wet lands and 14–20 percent of the dry.[5] Varying portions of the revenue, together with the management of particular villages, were delegated by kings for indefinite periods to the great Hindū temples, monasteries, colleges, hospitals, ministers of state, and military officers. Part of the revenue of other villages was granted to communities of interrelated families of Brahman scholars from whom the bureaucracy, the priesthood, and even some of the army officers were recruited. As local land managers, all of these bodies were required to expand irrigation works, increase the cultivated area, and patronize crafts and trade. They formed a theocratic ruling caste, directly administering about a third of the villages.

Communities of the high-ranking Veḷḷāḷar caste of noncultivating land managers and rich peasants administered the other villages (the majority) and paid a revenue that was higher than that paid by Brahmans. They leased some lands collectively to sharecroppers or herders of lower peasant castes and cultivated others with the help of the village's slaves. Some Veḷḷāḷars did their own cultivation; others were soldiers or scribes. Sharecroppers appear to have lived in conditions similar to European serfdom. What distinguished the Thanjāvūr village, however, was its *joint* management by elders of a kinship community of scholars, military or official gentry, or peasants, comprising about twenty to forty households, and the cooperative character of most of the agricultural work done by sharecropping tenants and slaves. There was little or no private property in land,[6] the village's managerial caste being jointly responsible for production, revenue, and keeping order among the tenants and slaves. The managerial caste also supervised the smaller kinship communities of village servants such as Blacksmiths, Goldsmiths, Braziers, Carpenters, Leatherworkers, Policemen, Laundryworkers, Barbers, Physicians, Palm wine tappers, Accountants, Musicians, Dancers, Watchers of irrigation water, and Village Priests. After each harvest the grain was divided into heaps on the village threshing floors in customary amounts and distributed to the several castes. Although governed in daily matters by the managerial caste, the village servants and tenants were also supervised by the central government, whose officers regulated their payments and had the power to move them from place to place.

Either directly or through its great temples and other beneficiaries the government used the revenue to pay for its army, navy, urban artisans, traders, priests, scholars, artists, hetaerae, courtiers, servants, and all the paraphernalia of city life.

Slaves (*aḍimai āḷukaḷ*) produced most of the kingdom's rice, the staple food. It seems likely that most of them were conquered tribespeople from the jungles out of which the irrigation state was carved. The rulers strictly segregated the slaves from the rest of the commoners. They regarded both categories as ritually defiling and forbade contact with them, but kept the slaves altogether outside the village settlement in separate kinship communities. In addition to cultivation, slaves were conscripted by the state to construct irrigation works, quarry stone and transport it for building temples, and carry heavy goods and palanquins. In medieval theory, slaves received one-tenth of the gross produce for their sustenance.

The Chōḷa kingdom seems therefore to have comprised five main classes.

### *The State Class, or Ruling Class*

This was composed of the king, royalty, the ministers and upper ranks of administrators of departments, the highest religious officials in temples and monasteries, and officers of the army and navy. As I have noted, such officials normally lived from the state revenue (*mēlvāram*) of various ranks of prebendal estates. The state class appears to have been drawn entirely from Brahmans, the royal family, and the higher subcastes of Veḷḷāḷars. There were two grades of government officials, one higher and one lower.[7]

### *The State Servants*

These were mainly urban, and included Brahman temple priests, certain classes of urban artisans, scribes, soldiers, palace, temple and monastic servants, the lower ranks of monks, hetaerae, and artists, all serving the ruling class. They were paid from the *mēlvāram* of small prebendal estates or from cash stipends paid out of war booty, from the special royal estates, or out of the king's "upper share" of ordinary, nonprebendal land. The joint kinship communities from which the state servants were drawn appear to have been cultivators or noncultivating land managers.

### *The Commodity Producers and Merchants*

This prosperous class thrived during the Chōḷa period both from inland and overseas trade. Its different branches formed artisans' and trading groups (perhaps guilds, or kinship communities) that sometimes governed towns or sections of cities, and sometimes built or managed temples. Some merchant guilds that traveled to foreign lands or through forest areas not fully pacified by the state had their own troops to protect themselves and their merchandise. The merchant class appears to have been generally wealthy, but under strict control by the government. Large portions of its wealth were taken by the state as taxes and also in the form of donations of gold, cattle, and food to Brahmans and temples that merchants were induced to make in return for dignities and the assurance of religious merit.

The exact relations of the merchants and artisans are unclear, but it appears that some merchants and artisans were directly attached to the state class and were paid at fixed rates in kind or cash from the surplus product (the state taxes) or from the "upper share" of prebendal lands. These groups were evidently congregated around the royal palaces, forts, temples, and monasteries. Other artisans, however, evidently lived in a separate section of the city and engaged in commodity production on behalf of private merchants involved in market trade with the state class and state servants and with foreign lands. This division among the merchants and artisans seems to have been already established in the Chōḷa capital of Kāvēripaṭṭanam in the Sangam period,[8] but it seems probable that as the surplus product increased in the ninth to thirteenth centuries, commodity production must also have increased. Evidently, however, although they traded privately, leading merchants and master craftsmen could obtain rights of administration over settlements and temples only by grant from the king, undoubtedly in return for substantial gifts. The fact that as the Chōḷa period wore on, various artisan and merchant groups struggled to obtain honors, privileges, and sumptuary goods beyond those enjoyed by the peasants suggests the growing wealth and power of those producing and trading in commodities.[9]

### *The Peasants and Their Artisan and Service Attachés in Villages*

This class included the free Veḷḷāḷar peasants, who lived in self-governing villages and cultivated their lands in a form of ownership called *veḷḷāṉ vagai*. These peasants retained the *kīlvāram*, or lower share, and paid the revenue, or upper share, in cash or kind to the royal revenue officials. The class also included serflike tenants (*kuḍiyar*) who held lands communally on *vāram* ("share") tenure from Brahmans and high-ranking Veḷḷāḷars of the state class who had obtained rights in the *kīlvāram* as well as the *mēlvāram*. In the same class were the village servants described earlier, who lived partly from small service tenures and partly from shares in the total harvests of the village grain. Like the state class, the peasants had their own joint kinship communities in villages and their own regional assemblies to settle disputes and administer their affairs.

It is probable that as the Chōḷa period wore on, more and more free peasants became serflike, sharecropping tenants under resident noncultivating land managers of the state class. As irrigation expanded, more and more land came under the control of temples, Brahman communities, and bureaucrats, who appear to have often ousted the former peasants. In some cases individuals or communities of the state class lived solely from the *mēlvāram* of the land, but in other cases they appear to have acquired the *kīlvāram* rights in addition, and to have reduced the cultivators to the level of sharecroppers. In famines or other crises cultivators and artisans might even sell themselves, and sometimes their descendants, as slaves (*aḍimai āḷukaḷ*) to members of the state class.

### *The Slaves*

These apparently fell into three categories with different ranks and functions:

1. War captives, at least some of whom became servants in the royal palaces;

2. A wide variety of indigenous slaves of different grades and occupations, including menial servants; singers and dancers in temples, palaces, monasteries, and aristocratic households; cultivators; weavers; and fishermen. The slavery of such people, presumably of middle rank and ancestral to many of today's

Non-Brahmans, seems to have increased as the Choḷa period progressed. Sāstri speaks of its "general prevalence" in the twelfth century and of there being several grades of slaves. Slaves could be bought and sold between palaces, monasteries, temples, and communities. At least some of the slaves in this category were evidently owned individually, for aristocratic women were often given slaves on marriage as dowry by their fathers. Many people sold themselves, and sometimes their unborn offspring, into slavery in famines to avoid starvation. Most of the records of slaves come from monasteries, temples, and palaces. Slaves were branded with the inscription of their owners, the brand being changed if they were sold. Although the data are unclear, they suggest a constant transfer of people from peasantry to slavery in the course of the period, as more and more land became irrigated and organized with gang labor consisting of hereditary slaves and as more and more free peasants and artisans lost their land.

3. The lowest Panchama castes, at least some of whom were already called Paṟayars, were composed entirely of hereditary agricultural slaves. This class (or subclass) comprised the ancestors of today's Harijans or Scheduled Castes, its members being mainly engaged in wet rice cultivation and in building or providing the materials for temples, roads, and irrigation works. These agricultural slaves were owned and controlled jointly by the state and the local communities of land managers who provided its officers. Communities of slaves were attached on a hereditary basis to villages, as were the village cattle. When a village was sold or given with royal approval to a peasant, merchant, or prebendal community, its sharecropping tenants, slaves, and cattle were automatically sold with it unless they were expressly removed and placed elsewhere by the state. The local communities of slaves, like those of sharecroppers, merchants, rich peasants, artisans, and Brahman scholars, were kinship communities composed of small patrilineages whose members intermarried in perpetuity through bilateral cross-cousin marriage.

The poet Sēkkiḻar's *Periya Purāṇam* (ca. twelfth century) indicates that the lives of Paṟayar slaves were similar to those of their descendants in the 1950s. Already the lowest caste, they lived in hamlets of small thatched huts outside the villages and were agricultural laborers. As in modern times, they tanned the hides of cattle. They supplied leather to the temples for making drums and the strings of lutes, and were themselves drummers, probably at funerals as they are today. They used pieces of leather to hang in their doorways or to lay their children on to sleep. (In modern times, gunny sacks are used instead, for hides are usually sold.) The Paṟayars kept dogs and chickens, and their children wore black iron bracelets and waist bells. The men went to work at sunrise; the women sang as they husked the paddy. Both men and women drank alcohol, and danced communally while intoxicated. The slaves gave communal service in the nearby village or township, and lived partly by cultivating their caste's share of the communal land.

The Paṟayar slaves differed from the sharecroppers and the cultivating slaves in being especially responsible for irrigation and wet rice cultivation. Moreover, the Paṟayars did not control their own conditions of labor, but worked in gangs under the supervision of state agents or village managers. The sharecroppers, by contrast, worked on leased lands that they cultivated either in separate households or in joint village communities. Both the slaves and the sharecroppers appear to have used implements and oxen allotted to them by the village managers from the village's common stock.[10]

From the scant information available, the main conflict in this period appears to have been between the monarch, Brahmans, and Veḷḷāḷars (the state class) on the one hand, and the peasantry and artisans, some of whom were in the process of becoming sharecroppers or slaves. Inscriptions record refusals on the part of assemblies of peasants to pay excessive exactions of land revenue, and in some cases their armed revolt against Brahman and Veḷḷāḷar officials or their flight to some other place. If my interpretation is correct, these struggles were mainly rearguard actions in a process of increasing bondage of the peasantry and craftsmen. There were also revolts by Paṟayar slaves over paddy payments by their Brahman and Veḷḷāḷar masters.[11]

The bondage or outright slavery of large segments of the peasantry was evidently related to the availability of land. Until the late nineteenth century, not all of Thanjāvūr was cultivated. There were wastelands and considerable forest. The problem for the Chōḷas was to induce peasants to take up land irrigated under the sponsorship of organs of the state, cultivate it, and render all or most of their surplus as *mēlvāram*, or revenue. Free peasants could, and sometimes did, take flight to other places when the revenue became too heavy, sometimes to cultivate dry or forest lands. The later Chōḷa period appears to have been one in which, as irrigation expanded, the bureaucracy increased in size, and the *mēlvāram* grew heavier, more and more peasants were prevented from fleeing. Instead they were forced to enter bondage as payment for arrears of revenue. In this way control of most of the *kīlvāram* as well as the *mēlvāram* often passed to the temples or other noncultivating land managers, with the peasants on such estates joining categories 2 and 3. Whether category 3 was itself partly recruited from ruined, enslaved Veḷḷāḷar peasants is unclear, but the possibility exists.

I have mentioned that Thanjāvūr under the Chōḷas approximated Marx's model of the Asiatic mode of production. It seems to have been much closer to that model than, for example, either the feudal system prevalent on the southwest coast in Kēraḷa, or the Mōghul empire. Although it is impossible to examine this controversial question in detail here, I shall state briefly the ways in which Thanjāvūr resembled Marx's Asiatic mode and those in which it differed from it.

First, Thanjāvūr approximated the Asiatic mode of production in the crucial role assigned to the state in building and maintaining irrigation works, and thus in keeping the agrarian economy in motion. The state also built and maintained roads, and expended a large part of its surplus in the construction of vast temples. Marx did not regard government-controlled irrigation as essential to the Asiatic mode, but he thought it a common feature and important in the development of this mode of production.

Second, the village formed a rural commune controlled jointly by a kinship community of peasants, or of land managers who themselves formed a joint kinship community and governed joint communities of peasants and slaves.

Third, there was either a near or total absence of private property in land. There were individual prebends, some of which could be sold or given to others and that were partly or totally free of taxes. The transmission of such prebendal estates, however, could occur only with royal consent, under state supervision, and to one of a designated class of recipients, usually belonging to the ruling class. The "owner" of a prebend, moreover, was not free to change the crops or abstain from cultivation, and the tenants and slaves on his estate could not be evicted without the state's direction. In most cases the prebendary "owned" only the *mēlvāram*, and that often only for his lifetime.

Fourth, there was no class of private landlords apart from the state class, which itself removed the bulk of the surplus. In general in this society, most or all surplus labor went to provide state taxes rather than private rents or profits. Land tax and rent were thus virtually or entirely the same.

Fifth, the state was a theocratic state governed by religiosi and resting on religious law together with the oral commands of the monarch. The temples, monasteries, and kingship (which was itself divine), and perhaps also the great merchant associations, were arms of the state, which handled the society's surplus.

Sixth, there was a marked unity in each village of agriculture and crafts, in which peasants, artisans, and the village's slaves were together virtually self-sufficient. They provided a large surplus for the state class, its servants, and the merchants. They received in return such intangibles as religious services, the settlement of disputes, and the organization of public labor, especially irrigation.

Seventh, commodity production and exchange were largely restricted to the surplus product and confined to the state class, the state servants, and the urban artisans and merchants.

Eighth, the cities were primarily religious, royal, and military encampments in which commodity production and trade played a subordinate part, rather than being primarily settlements of merchants and artisans in opposition to the government of the countryside.

Ninth, the monarch was in theory a despot, but in fact exercised power mainly within the state class. As Marx recognized, the villages (and we may add, the temples, monasteries, and provincial assemblies of land managers) had a high degree of autonomy in local government, reflecting their relative self-sufficiency.

Tenth, the village structure was remarkably stable over many centuries. Although divided by caste and containing slaves, it had a simple division of labor among the working population that apparently changed little through the centuries.

Finally, the government was primarily a bureaucracy maintained from prebends, rather than a structure of fief-holding military nobles. It was guarded by a professional army located at the central points in barracks rather than being housed and trained privately in the villages.

The Thanjāvūr state differed profoundly from the Kēraḷa feudal states of the fourteenth to eighteenth centuries.[12] In the latter, the heavy rainfall and numerous rivers made irrigation and drainage unnecessary above the level of small blocks of fields. In Kēraḷa's mountainous terrain, there were virtually no roads. Although the houses of royalty and of nobles were imposing, there were few or no large temples. There was almost no state management of the economy, and almost no bureaucracy.

Instead, there were hereditary noble households of Brahmans, Kshattriyas, or Nāyars, each privately owning the land of one or several villages. These nobles were bound by ties of vassalhood between the smaller and the greater, such ties culminating in the king himself or in one of the two heads of the Brahman caste. Soldiers in Kēraḷa were quartered and trained in their own villages, not in barracks, each the vassal of his village lord or of some higher lord. Slaves were owned outright individually by households of the aristocratic landowning castes. Although normally attached to the soil, they could be leased, sold, given away, or even killed by the heads of their masters' households. There was no communal management or redistribution of lands, cattle, or slaves. As in Thanjāvūr, the peasants, artisans, and slaves of a village were largely self-sufficient and there was an interdependence of crafts and agriculture in each village. The village surplus, however, went to its private landlord who used it for village ceremonies, ostentation, or to pay his vassals when on military service, and who rendered only a small portion of it in feudal dues to his own lord. The wealth of the king came from his private estates and, importantly, from taxes on overseas merchandise; until the 1760s there was no land survey and no government land revenue. The dozen or so Kēraḷa feudal states were, of course, much smaller than the Chōḷa kingdom in its heyday. The Kēraḷa military were mainly mobile foot soldiers, whereas the Chōḷa kingdom had war chariots, elephants, cavalry, and large specialized military camps, with standing armies of infantry.

In addition to its differences from the Kēraḷa feudal state, the Chōḷa kingdom in Thanjāvūr differed in important respects from the Mōghul empire. In large parts of the Mōghul empire, rural communes were broken up and land came to be managed by individual families of landlords or state functionaries and cultivated by independent tenant or peasant households. In the Chōḷa kingdom, in contrast to the Mōghul empire, the religiosi, rather than the military, dominated the bureaucracy. In Thanjāvūr there were apparently no slaves in the administration itself, as there were under the Mōghuls; slaves were merely palace servants. In the Chōḷa kingdom revenue areas were not regularly allotted to military nobles, but were supervised by a revenue department of the government. Finally, in the Chōḷa village there was no government-appointed village headman, but only the joint assembly of household heads of the local managerial caste, directly responsible to traveling officers of the state.

Thanjāvūr under the Chōḷas did not, however, entirely fit Marx's model of the Asiatic mode of production. Although primarily royal and military settlements, in Thanjāvūr under the Chōḷas the cities had great significance. They contained separate sections for the merchants and artisan guilds and conducted a flourishing internal and overseas trade. Their size, and the prominence of the merchant class and, evidently, of commodity production deriving from part of the state's substantial surplus, contradict Marx's view that city development is necessarily more limited and artificial under the Asiatic than under other precapitalist modes of production, even though Marx was correct in emphasizing the state's control of the merchants.

Third, representatives of the state class actually resided in many of the villages of the Chōḷa kingdom and sometimes governed them as joint land managers, whereas Marx pictures the state class as outside and remote from the villages. This process of village government by local prebendaries seems to have increased as the Chōḷa period went on, the size of the surplus product increased, more and more prebends were granted to state officials, and control of part of the *kīlvāram* passed to these governors. Although the peasants, artisans, and slaves of each village were virtually self-sufficient, the land managers sold part of their surplus, had a "gold committee," and bought various commodities from the merchants. Among the state class, the merchants, and even the upper ranks of free peasants and artisans, sumptuary laws detailed the exact types of consumer goods to be enjoyed by each class and caste.

Fourth, the "peasants" were not egalitarian in their state servitude, as Marx tends to depict them. Instead, as Garaudy points out, the Asiatic mode characteristically includes a relatively free peasantry, serfs, slaves, and a small number of hired laborers. All of these were present in the Chōḷa villages of Thanjāvūr, the rift between slaves on the one hand and free peasants and middle-ranking serfs on the other being especially deep.

Finally, the Chōḷa state was not as unchanging as Marx tends to describe the Asiatic mode of production. Although the division of labor in villages was largely stable, land relations changed in different periods as a result of conquests or state edicts. New castes were formed, and new groups of slaves or specialists instituted. As I have suggested, the Chōḷa kingdom probably saw the gradual "enserfment" of a large part of the middle-ranking peasant class, and perhaps a great increase in the agricultural slave class concerned with irrigation and wet paddy cultivation, in the course of its development of the productive forces and of the size of the surplus product. Eventually, it was conquered from without, and a military government partly displaced its theocracy – as Ribeiro and Amin suggest may be the usual course of the tributary mode in its later phases.[13]

### Thanjāvūr from 1290 to 1749

When the Chōḷa empire declined, Thanjāvūr was conquered by the Pāndhya kingdom of Madurai in 1290, and after various vicissitudes, by the Vijayanagar empire in about 1340. The kingdom became independent under the Nāyaks, Telugu viceroys of Vijayanagar, in 1642. It was reconquered by Maratha armies from Bijapūr in 1674, and a Maratha ruler was installed. In 1680 the Maratha king declared his independence of Bijapūr. Thanjāvūr was invaded by

Mōghul armies in 1691, and its Maratha king became a tributary of the Mōghul empire. Thanjāvūr was thus a small, dependent kingdom surrendering booty and tribute to larger powers for most of this period.

The Vijayanagar and Maratha governments, perhaps influenced by the North Indian Muslim empires against which they were reacting, introduced some political and military relations of what have been called a tributary-feudal kind.[14] With the growing importance of cavalry and the introduction of gunpowder in the fourteenth century, forts became centers of local government. The conquering dynasties appointed secular nobles to patrol the countryside and maintain troops of cavalry and infantry in return for revenue allotments. Such nobles became particularly strong and independent in the dry upland tracts of southwest Thanjāvūr where the boundary was uncertain. Brahmanical government continued in the kingdom at large, however, and under the military magnates, as under the temples and monasteries, the joint village persisted in a modified form until British times.

The native fleets had given place to Arab traders in the fourteenth century. From the sixteenth century, the external trade passed to Europeans. They reorganized the villages surrounding their forest and began to grow export crops such as tobacco and indigo. They compelled communities of weavers to produce textiles for export in return for subsistence payments.[15] As European control over Thanjāvūr and its revenues tightened, native traders tended to become company agents earning commissions independent of royal patronage. Some of them bought individual shares in the produce of village lands.[16] As private commercial transactions increasingly penetrated the villages, the managerial households' shares in the produce became more unequal and fields, like slaves, tended to be parceled out for several years to individual families both of managing owners and of sharecroppers. By 1749, therefore, some institutions resembling feudal vassalage, and others influenced by capitalist markets and concepts of private ownership of the means of production, had already begun to penetrate the theocratic irrigation state.

During this period the five classes listed for the Chōḷa empire appear to have continued in existence but to have been joined by two new classes in some of the larger ports. The class structure was thus as follows.

### *The State Class*

This was now composed of the monarch, vassal nobles of certain provinces and districts combining civil and military roles, temples and monasteries under the nobles' supervision, a curtailed bureaucracy, and the village land managers, both religious and secular, from which these officers were drawn. Although village assemblies of leading land managers remained, the larger assemblies of the *nāḍu* ("province"), which had been prominent in Chōḷa times, declined as the powers of individual nobles increased. Officials of the state class held the *mēlvāram* and sometimes the *kīlvāram*, or part of the *kīlvāram*, of village produce, and there appears to have been a further enslavement of the peasantry. The villages remained organized as jointly managed village communes, but by the eighteenth century the land shares in some villages were being distributed for long periods to individual households and were becoming unequal.

***The State Servants***

These were almost certainly fewer than in the Chōḷa period. They apparently lived from the same sources of income as previously, except that booty became scarce and Thanjāvūr was itself often plundered from outside.

***European Capitalist Merchant Companies***

These settled with royal permission in self-governing ports. The Danes arrived in 1620, the Dutch in 1660, the French in 1739, and the British in 1749. They were sustained by the *mēlvāram* of lands granted to them and by their profits. They imported horses, weapons, ammunition, gold and silver, and baser metals, for the monarchs and the state class, and exported textiles, spices, drugs, pearls, art-metalware, and precious stones.

***The Native Commodity Producers and Merchants***

These appear to have declined in prosperity, their overseas trade and their guilds being virtually extinguished. In the seventeenth and eighteenth centuries many of them became agents, servants, or bondsmen of European companies.

***The Free Peasants and Their Attachés***

These appear to have decreased as the period progressed. In the delta region the large majority of peasants and village servants were evidently either sharecroppers (*vāramdar*) or slaves (*aḍimai āḷukaḷ*) of varying grades by the 1740s in villages governed by Brahmans, temples, monasteries, military nobles, or other members of the state class. Some free peasants probably remained prominent in the southwest uplands.

***Semiproletarian Workers***

This class was largely created by the European merchant companies from the sixteenth century and existed mainly in and near the ports. It consisted of such categories as "putting-out" weavers and indigo plantation workers. Although possessing a semiservile character, its members were paid in shares of their produce or in daily wages in cash or kind.

***The Slaves***

By the eighteenth century the slaves seem all to have been of categories 2 and 3 described earlier. Agricultural slaves of the Panchama castes were sometimes owned individually by families of the state class, the state servants, and the free peasants, although most of them remained communally owned by village communities of land managers. The slaves, some 20 percent of the people in the mid-nineteenth century, may have been a much larger proportion before Haidar Ali's invasion of 1781, for most of them fled, were kidnapped by the invaders, or starved in the famine of 1781–2.

As tribute and booty were drained from Thanjāvūr, public works diminished. The Vijayanagar rulers patronized Vaishnavism and built some magnificent temples, but there was little new irrigation and few new temples were built after about the mid-seventeenth century. To meet the demands of external tribute, land revenue increased to about 50 percent of the crop by the mid-eighteenth century. The actual cultivators of village lands often obtained little more than one-fifth of paddy crops and one-third of garden crops, more and more of the *kīlvāram* passing to the class of land managers. There were severe famines in the seventeenth and eighteenth centuries, and frequent invasions and wars.

Two modes of production seem to have coexisted in this period, with the newer one gradually encroaching upon the old. The new mode was merchant capitalist, represented by the European merchant companies and the semiproletarian workers. The old mode was the tributary or Asiatic, with certain "feudal" features resulting from the military conquests of alien rulers. The dominant class in the new mode of production increasingly preyed upon that of the old.

Along with these two linked modes of production went two forms of class struggle. In the older mode, class struggle chiefly took the form of peasants resisting taxation by the state class and also resisting the process of enslavement as they became indebted and were ousted from their lands. In the new mode, the chief conflicts occurred between the new semiproletarians and the European merchant companies. As the latter increased their exploitation, the former fought back or tried to run away. Struggles were also endemic between the rulers and state class of Thanjāvūr and the various external powers who tried to conquer them and make them tributary, including, in the eighteenth century, the Europeans who supported various external Indian powers.

## "Company" Conquests: 1770 to 1858

Thanjāvūr declined between 1749 and 1799, when the British annexed the district as part of their empire in India. The period was one of war and destitution as the British and French companies fought for commercial and territorial hegemony throughout the subcontinent. Through their subjugation of the native rulers, they squeezed revenue from the villagers to pay for ever more destructive military campaigns, company profits, and the salaries and remittances of their employees.[17]

The British first actually invaded Thanjāvur in 1771 along with the Nawāb of Ārcot, in order to compel its Rāja to pay 70 percent of his revenue as tribute to finance recent and future British wars. In 1773 the Nawāb invaded again and conquered the kingdom with British help. The modern fall of Thanjāvūr seems to have dated decisively from this experience. Its cities were plundered, its villages ravaged by revenue collections that amounted to 59 percent of the gross produce.

Thanjāvūr's peasants and slaves were made destitute and its leisure classes, artisans, government servants, and traders reduced to penury as the district's surplus product became diverted into British fortunes and wars.

The testimony of Mr. Petrie, a servant of the British East India Company, to a select committee of the company at Madras in 1782, graphically describes Thanjāvūr's downfall:

> Before I speak of the present stage of Tanjore country, it will be necessary to inform the Committee that not many years ago that province was considered as one of the most flourishing, best cultivated, populous districts of Hindustan. I first saw this country in 1768, when it presented a very different picture from its present situation. Tanjore was formerly a place of great foreign and inland trade; it imported cotton from Bombay and Surat, raw and worked silks from Bengal, sugar, spices, etc., from Sumatra, Malacca, and the eastern islands; gold, horses, elephants, and timber from Pegu, and various articles of trade from China. It was by means of Tanjore that a great part of Haidar Ali's dominions and the north-western parts of the Mahratta empire were supplied with many European commodities, and with a species of silk manufacture from Bengal, which is almost universally worn as a part of the dress by the natives of Hindustan. The exports of Tanjore were muslins, chintz, handkerchiefs, ginghams, various sorts of longcloths, and a coarse printed cloth, which last constitutes a material article in the investments of the Dutch and the Danes, being in great demand for the African, West Indian, and South American markets. Few countries have more natural advantages than Tanjore; it possesses a rich and fertile soil, singularly well supplied with water from the two great rivers Cauvery and Coleroon, which, by means of reservoirs, sluices, and canals are made to disperse their waters through almost every field in the country; to this latter cause we may chiefly attribute the uncommon fertility of Tanjore. The face of the country is beautifully diversified, and its appearance approaches nearer to England than any other part of India that I have seen. Such was Tanjore not many years ago, but its decline has been so rapid, that in many districts it would be difficult to trace the remains of its former opulence.
>
> At this period (1771) . . . the manufactures flourished, the country was populous and well cultivated, the inhabitants wealthy and industrious. Since the year 1771, the era of the first seige, until the restoration of the Raja (1776), the country having been during that period twice the seat of war, and having undergone revolutions in the government, trade, manufactures, and agriculture were neglected, and many thousands of inhabitants went in quest of a more secure abode.[18]

The British restored the Thanjāvūr Rāja as their puppet in 1776, but a worse fate befell the kingdom in 1781–5. Haidar Āli, the Muslim governor and general of Mysore, assisted by the French and the Dutch, made a thrust to oust the British from south India. In his sweep toward Madras, Haidar's armies devastated northern Thanjāvūr. Twelve thousand children were deported to Mysore and tens of thousands of Tanjoreans were massacred. Most of the remainder fled into jungles in nearby districts. Thanjāvūr's gross paddy output fell from 301,526 metric tons in 1780–1 to 45,594 tons in 1781–2 and 39,576 tons in 1782–3.[19] For those who remained in Thanjāvūr, the destruction of irrigation channels and agriculture brought about a severe famine in 1783–4; even so, Haidar's government reportedly collected 62 percent of what crops there were during his four-year visitation. The British reconquered Thanjāvūr in 1785, but normal production was not restored until the end of the century (see Table 1.2).[20] Indeed, even apart from the four years of Haidar's occupation, from 1776 until 1799, the Rāja's puppet government collected as revenue the equivalent in cash or kind of 54 percent to 62 percent of the gross produce of paddy lands. Seventy percent of this (amounting to Rs. 2,450,000 in 1776) went to the East India Company as "peace contributions," tribute, and liquidation of the Nāwab's private debts to company servants.[21]

The last quarter of the eighteenth century saw a steep decline in Thanjāvūr's population. Thanjāvūr city was reported to have 100,000 people in the late 1770s,[22] even after the Nāwab's invasion – a figure it did not reach again until 1951. Kumbakōṇam, the main center of religious learning, and Nāgapaṭṭaṇam, the major port, were towns of similar size. Judging from the grain output and the size of cities, the district's population may have been about 1.75 to 2 million. With Haidar's invasion it dropped phenomenally. Although some people returned afterwards from exile, the district was reported to have only 83,753 households (perhaps about 500,000 people) in 1802, and only 901,333 people at the first census of 1823. It reached 2,245,029 by 1901 and 2,983,761 by 1951, but because agriculture was developed at the expense of industries, Thanjāvūr's towns did not recover their size until British rule had ended. Thanjāvūr municipality, indeed, had only 57,870 as late as 1901, although, under the patronage of the pensioned Rāja, it had had 80,000 in 1838.[23]

The East India Company governed Thanjāvūr as a district of Madras Presidency from 1799 to 1858. In 1857–8, the "Mutiny" swept through northern and central India, almost ending British rule. Having crushed it, the British government assumed direct control of India.

The period of government by the East India Company saw a fundamental change from a relatively self-sufficient, still prosperous small kingdom with significant manufacturing exports, to a virtual monocrop region within a worldwide colonial system, exporting rice and labor.

In the first decade of the nineteenth century the East India Company restored the export of textiles that had been disrupted by its wars. Britain's rising industrialists had begun to exclude Indian textiles from the British market as early as 1720, but until 1812 the East India Company reexported them to Europe.

In 1813, however, the industrial bourgeoisie was strong enough in parliament to remove the East India Company's monopoly trading rights and, by the use of tariffs, virtually to end its imports of Indian manufactures to Europe. As a result, the Abbé Dubois reported in 1823 that misery and death prevailed in all the districts of the Madras Presidency and hundreds of thousands of weavers were dying of hunger.[24]

Concomitantly, British industrial commodities began to invade the Indian market. In 1820 Hamilton found India's larger villages, as well as its cities, "abundantly supplied with European manufactures of every sort," including woolens, textiles, scissors, knives, glasses, and hardware. By 1840, Britain supplied 42 percent of Madras's manufactured imports. Thanjāvūr's textile exports were ruined, as were the exports of steel and other manufactures from other regions of Madras.[25]

To pay for its imports, Madras gradually exported more raw materials, in the early decades, chiefly cotton, indigo, pepper, and tobacco. Thanjāvūr's contribution was paddy, together with small quantities of salt, indigo, hides, fruits, and coconuts. In 1799 Thanjāvūr was reported by an investigating commission never to have exported "any considerable grain at any period." By 1817 it monopolized the Madras grain market, which had previously received supplies from Bengal.[26]

These developments, however, did not compensate for the loss of European markets for textiles. After 1812 Thanjāvūr's export earnings fell drastically and the district, like the rest of India, entered a long period of deflation until the 1850s, the lowest year being 1843.[27] The same period saw deflation throughout the Western industrializing world as competitive free enterprise replaced the earlier government-sponsored monopolies. In Thanjāvūr, however, as in India generally, in contrast to Britain, deflation was accompanied by a dismantling rather than an increase of industrial production.

The collapse of Thanjāvūr's export trade in manufactures meant that large quantities of gold and silver were no longer imported from Europe. At the same time, the government continued to extract high land revenues, which were mainly spent by the company on external wars, salaries, private fortunes, pensions, or government "home charges." The revenue, which was 53 percent of the gross produce in 1800–1, in theory dropped to 45 percent in 1804–5 and 42 percent in 1805–6. Whereas, however, earlier rulers had collected the revenue sometimes in kind and sometimes in cash, the British demanded cash payments, sometimes in advance of the harvest. But cash was hard to come by – so hard that the torture of small landlords who refused to pay became standard practice in Madras until 1855. In some years, especially after 1815, the current grain price was so far below the government's commutation rate that landlords were in fact paying 60 percent of the gross produce as revenue.[28]

Revenue exactions thus mulcted the bigger landed estates of their accumulated treasures, while smaller landlords and peasants became irrevocably indebted to the big owners and to the more prosperous merchants, who themselves received credit from British banks and firms. Usurers, who in the eighteenth century had been permitted only jewels, houses, or standing crops as security, fastened on the land, which was increasingly sold to absentee creditors. Within the villages, cultivators and village servants became perpetually indebted to their landlords. This chronic indebtedness of all ordinary villagers to land magnates and city usurers has persisted to the present.

Except for substantial landlords and merchants, Thanjāvūr's villagers lived in acute distress from 1812 to 1850. Even before the decline of textiles, revenue demands combined with bad weather caused a severe famine in 1803–6 (see Table 1.2), worse than any of the eighteenth century. Famines recurred in 1811–12 and throughout the Presidency in 1823–6. Indeed, as Dharma Kumar notes, "Except in the 1880s there was (in south India) no decade of the nineteenth century which was untouched by famines or scarcity, and there was no district unaffected."[29] Moreover, whereas in 1807 the Collector of Thanjāvūr bought and distributed grains at fixed prices, after that date the Board of Revenue of the East India Company became converted to free trade and forbade interference with market forces, so that fewer deaths were averted by government distribution.

In the Presidency as a whole, Thackeray's report of 1819 declared that the country was worse off in many respects than in 1807, and in some, than in 1801. In 1830 Dalzell wrote that the condition of the poor had deteriorated everywhere except in the cotton-growing villages of Madras. Thousands of weavers were obliged to seek a living from agriculture, thus depressing the condition of the cultivating classes. In Thanjāvūr the southwest of the district, where wet paddy crops were traditionally poor, fared especially badly during 1845–54, when revenue charges were severely pressed. In 1854 Forbes, the Collector, reported that the able-bodied had fled to Mauritius or Ceylon while the aged and young were being fed at public expense. Because of the overassessment of the villagers' lands there were no gold ornaments or brass pots remaining among them.[30]

Until 1836 the company neglected Thanjāvūr's irrigation works. By the 1830s the main bed of the Kāvēri was so badly silted that it threatened to overflow its dam and flood its major tributary, the Coleroon, which marks Thanjāvūr's northern border with Tiruchirappalli and South Ārcot. Government works were then started in 1836, which saved and expanded the area of delta irrigation. Because of the increased yield, the government raised Thanjāvūr's revenue demand by Rs. 177,981 a year, affording a high profit on its total outlay of Rs. 200,000.[31]

Whether or not this was intended, Thanjāvūr's improved irrigation coincided with the early development of European plantation agriculture. By 1841 Thanjāvūr was exporting 23,918 tons of paddy and 44,533 of husked rice by sea to the plantations of Ceylon, Pegu, Mauritius, and Travancore and to the cotton-growing Madras villages of Madurai and Tinnevelly districts – about 27 percent of its total crop (see Table 1.2).[32] A further unknown quantity was exported in oxcarts to villagers growing export crops in nearby districts. For the rest of the century seaborne rice exports, chiefly to Ceylon and Malaya, remained high even in years of flood or drought. In the scarcity of 1857–8, for example, Thanjāvūr exported by sea the equivalent of 128,735 tons of paddy, 32 percent of the estimated total yield, leaving about 274,200 tons. With a population of 1,657,285 and an adult requirement of at least twenty ounces of husked rice per day, this would be barely enough to feed the people, even discounting exports by land.[33]

Paddy and rice formed 69 percent of the value of Thanjāvūr's seaborne exports in 1841–2, 79 percent in 1867–8, and 83 percent in 1868–9. By 1853, wet paddy covered 77 percent of the cultivated area, the earlier indigo plantations having been discontinued.

Thanjāvūr's paddy and rice exports in 1857–8 were worth Rs. 5,987,770 at current prices, while its total land revenue was Rs. 5,164,076, and its total revenue from all sources, Rs. 6,342,722.[34] From 1841 to 1887, total revenue ate up between 75 percent and 100 percent of the district's total seaborne export earnings, while the land revenue consumed between 70 percent and 96 percent of the value of grain exports. Because the major part of the revenue was spent outside Thanjāvūr or on British incomes and profits within the district, this means that at least half, and probably much more, of Thanjāvūr's exports represented surplus value paid gratis to the conquerors.

If seaborne exports went mainly to pay the revenue, we may ask who paid for seaborne imports. First, during colonial rule the value of Thanjāvūr's seaborne imports was always less than that of its exports, especially in this period. In 1841, for example, seaborne imports were only 18 percent of the value of seaborne exports. Forty-one percent of these imports comprised arecanuts for chewing, a luxury chiefly of landlords and merchants. Ten percent comprised British machine textiles, which were gradually ousting the local handwoven varieties, while another 30 percent comprised chinaware, luxury foods, timber, and raw tin and iron. Thanjāvūr's imports were thus mainly destined for the rich or the government, whereas its much larger volume of exports came from the labor of poor peasants and slaves.

In the hundred years from 1830 to 1930, Thanjāvūr was one of the main districts supplying labor to the plantations of south India, Ceylon, Burma, Malaya, Mauritius, and (in smaller numbers) the West Indies. Because these laborers were paid only trivial pocket money in addition to their sustenance, and because the money from Thanjāvūr's grain exports was used mainly to pay the revenue, Thanjāvūr was in effect raising laborers free of charge for the plantations and, by its exports, feeding them for little or no return. One hundred and fifty indentured laborers, the innocent victims of what Hugh Tinker calls "a new system of slavery," were first taken from Thanjāvūr in 1828 to the new British coffee plantations in Ceylon. All of them, however, deserted. Systematic recruitment to Ceylon started in the 1830s coupled with criminal laws prohibiting desertion, and in 1839, 2,432 Tanjoreans were sent there. Emigration increased thereafter and reached its peak in 1900. The legal freeing of India's slaves beginning in 1843 facilitated the export of indentured labor, for it allowed agents to beguile or kidnap indigent landless laborers.[35] At the same time it allowed south Indian landlords to retain a sufficient labor force through debt bondage while relieving them of the encumbrance of a growing slave population.

The British gradually transformed land ownership into private property and established the legal bases for capitalist production relations among landlords, tenants, village servants, and agricultural laborers. After various experiments, the government made households of the managerial castes separately responsible for specific amounts of revenue in 1822–3. In 1865 it issued individual title deeds of varying sizes in the village lands, although actual fields were not permanently parceled out until 1891–2.[36] In the first half of the century, however, it became common for separate households of the managerial group to sell all or part of their shares in the village produce to other households of their caste within or outside the village, or even to people of other castes, and for fields to be permanently allotted by the village council.

As we saw in Chapter 3, households of the managerial class also became landlords in another sense. Previously, the native government had allocated fixed shares in the village grain produce to itself, its beneficiaries, the village managerial group, the cultivating tenants, the village servants, and the village slaves. After 1807 landlords were made privately responsible for their cultivating tenants and for most of the village servants, and could evict them or raise their rents. After 1843 they could dismiss unwanted slaves and hire new laborers as they pleased. In practice, customary allotments of village grain shares to cultivating tenants, attached laborers, and some of the traditional village servants continued to be made in most villages until the 1950s, and are still made to the village temple priest and a few other officiants in some villages today. From the early nineteenth century, however, these villagers' shares could be adjusted, and they themselves could be evicted, at the landlords' discretion.

The government conferred "landlordship" on a variety of people, great and small. They included households of peasant managers and Brahman scholars who had previously administered villages, as well as the big temples, monasteries, royal households, nobles, ministers, and revenue officers to whom portions of the king's share of produce had been granted in Maratha times. Under the new system the former found themselves the owners of one to forty acres, while the latter might hold estates of several hundred to 7,000 acres. Twelve of these large owners, or 0.01 percent of the total, paid almost five percent of the revenue in 1857.[37] Others, especially temples and monasteries, who had held *iṉams* under the Marathas, paid no revenue under the British or else paid a lower revenue than the ordinary landlords. Thirteen families of former military nobles who had been appointed in Vijayanager times were settled by the British on *zamindāri* estates of 2,500 to 54,500 acres in the southwest upland area.[38] Provided they paid their allotted revenues, these princelings could govern their territories much as they pleased.

After the initial period of plunder, the British favored the great landlord at the expense of the small owner. The one lived luxuriously even in hard times, whereas the other was always hard pressed and indebted, little better off than his tenants and village servants. Harris, Thanjāvūr's first Collector, wrote in 1800, "One inhabitant has all the enjoyments to be procured from a fertile country, while another cultivating the same soil obtains little more than he would if he were cultivating a desert."[39] Harris wished to equalize the landlords' incomes, secure the tenants' holdings, and reduce the revenue. He was dismissed as incompetent and the situation has persisted with little change until the present. With the price rise of the 1860s the great landlords became rich bulwarks of British rule. But the small owners, too, did not oppose it, for their positions as employers and village managers set them in opposition to their tenants and laborers.

During this period it seems that from having an Asiatic mode of production, somewhat modified by its tributary relationship to larger empires, Thanjāvūr became gradually incorporated as a small colonial segment of the world capitalist socioeconomy that, as a whole, was evolving a single social formation and was also the sole worldwide example of a single mode of production.

My chief reason for arguing this lies in the changed utilization of Thanjāvūr's surplus during the period. Instead of being used, as under native rule, chiefly to pay for the indigenous system of government and the consumption of its state class, a large part of the surplus was now deflected in taxes to a colonial government that was itself, in the early decades of British rule, a capitalist merchant company. This surplus was used only in small part for local administration. Most of it went to pay for the conquest of other areas of India, to enrich British shareholders, and to finance British industry.

After about 1813, a further portion of Thanjāvūr's surplus went as profits to newly arising British firms and their agents, which exported Thanjāvūr's paddy (and from 1828, its indentured laborers), or imported manufactured goods. Toward the end of the period, yet another portion of the surplus was generated by the indentured laborers themselves, whose work on plantations outside Thanjāvūr provided profits for British plantation owners, but part of whose lifetime sustenance was provided in Thanjāvūr.

A portion of the surplus was, finally, retained by Thanjāvūr's new class of landlords. As the old state class, the *mirāsdārs* bitterly opposed the conquest. In the late eighteenth and early nineteenth centuries they suffered much as their treasures were plundered and their surplus relentlessly removed by the company's agents. By the 1830s however, the new bourgeoisie in Britain engaged in free enterprise and industry began to seek in the *mirāsdārs* reliable allies who would uphold British rule in the villages and form a class of private landlords furnishing paddy and laborers for the export trade and a market for British manufactured goods. With the expansion of irrigation works in the 1830s, their prosperity increased and by the late 1850s they were enjoying a minor share in the profits of colonial trade.

With respect to production relations, the new landed gentry maintained certain traditional features of labor relations in the villages, yet these, too, were gradually changed in the direction of peripheral capitalism. During the first half of the century, as we have seen, shares in village lands became freely marketable until eventually, in 1891–2, the outright title to the fields was allotted to private landowners. The rural commune was thus gradually broken up, and tenants and village servants became contractual laborers who could be evicted. Already in 1805, only 31 percent of the villages, or 1,774 out of 5,783, were found by the

British Collector to be held jointly by a village community of land managers. Some of these villages were held and cultivated collectively in *samudāyam* ("joint") tenure, others in *karaiyidu* tenure, in which shares in the village lands were distributable to owning households every one, three, or five years. Another 31 percent, or 1,807 villages, in *ēkabhōgam* tenure, were each under a single manager, either as *mirāsdār* or as *iṉam* or *zamindāri* holder. Such managers possessed either the *mēlvāram* or the *kīlvāram* rights or both. Some of them became private landlords who owned their estates outright, whereas others were confirmed in their *iṉams*, which they held privately and from which they obtained all or a portion of the revenue. Beneath these individual land managers were, however, joint village communities of free peasants, sharecroppers, or slaves, so that the joint village was probably preserved in some of its aspects in at least 62 percent of the villages. The other 38 percent, or 2,202 of the villages, were already in 1805 held in severalty, called *palabhōgam* (Sanskrit) or *arudikkarai* (Tamiḷ), with the lands permanently divided among the village shareholders, although the landowners of a village often continued to be collectively assessed for revenue.[40] During the nineteenth century, such villages' shareholders became private landlords, while the joint villages were also gradually divided among their owners.

As private landlords, the *mirāsdārs* themselves became involved in commodity production, being obliged to sell about one- to two-thirds of their paddy and other crops in the market in order to pay their revenue and buy imported commodities. As the export trade in paddy burgeoned after about 1840, more and more village produce was marketed. The *mirāsdārs* thus themselves became in part merchant capitalists similar to the merchants who engaged weavers or dyemakers in putting-out relations as bonded debt laborers or in small manufactories. With the gradual freeing of the slaves between 1843 and 1861, the *paṇṇaiyāḷ* relationship evolved as one of annual debt service, while some casual labor grew up alongside of it. At the same time, tenant farming became individual and contractual rather than communal and hereditary as previously. The tenant was engaged annually or every three years, and could be evicted, although he was often kept in a relationship of debt service as part sharecropper, part *vēlaikkāraṉ*. The tenant's relationship thus resembled that of a putting-out worker, for he controlled his own tools of production but was provided with natural resources or raw materials from which he produced commodities for his employer. Tenant farmers were, indeed, often also part-time putting-out workers in handicrafts or other forms of production. Some of them, for example, worked as spinners and weavers for a local merchant who supplied them with yarn and bought back their products. Others worked part time husking paddy for merchants or landlords, which was then sold to British firms for the export trade.

Most of the relationships of production that developed in the early part of the colonial period were not, therefore, fully developed proletarian relations. Nevertheless, such relations as those of the *paṇṇaiyāḷ*, the sharecropper, the putting-out worker, the indentured laborer, and the casual laborer were not precapitalist either. They were transitional or hybrid relations similar to those that existed in the core capitalist areas in the early decades of capitalist development. In Marx's terms the tenant or smallholder who produced commodities for a capitalist landlord or merchant was engaged in "formal subsumption" under capital although not yet in "real subsumption" as a wage laborer in a large-scale organization with modern, high-energy technology.[41]

The difference between the core and the periphery of the capitalist world was that in the periphery, most of the surplus that accrued from such primitive accumulation of capital was drained off to the core area as revenue, profits, or the private incomes of the British government's servants and their locally operating agents. In the periphery, therefore, although expanded reproduction occurred, it did not give rise, or gave rise only very slowly and patchily, to technological improvements and industrial development. Some capital investment did occur in the colonial region – for example in the new irrigation works and the expansion, first of indigo and tobacco and later of paddy lands – but it was small in relation to the profits reaped and exported. In such conditions of distortion and stunting of development in the colony, relations of production tended to remain hybrid for over a century, and only very gradually gave place to wage labor proper.

In this early period of transition to a capitalist hinterland, the chief emerging classes seem to have been as follows.

### The Nascent Bourgeoisie

These included:

1. British merchant and later industrial capitalists, their bourgeois colonial government, and their agents and government servants, chiefly tax collectors.

2. Thanjāvūr's bigger *mirāsdārs* and more fortunate merchants, who were gradually evolving into a dependent, compradore bourgeoisie. The latter became agents in the British export and import trade; the former, producers of export crops using sharecroppers, slaves, and later, debt peons or casual wage labor.

### The Nascent Petty Bourgeoisie

These included a new class of salary workers for the state and for private British firms, drawn mainly from the village landlords. They also included the smaller merchants and craftshop owners who employed laborers of various kinds and who were linked to the nascent bourgeoisie. This class, finally, included the smaller landlords and owner cultivators who were forced into mixed commodity and subsistence farming by the government's demand for a high cash revenue. They operated at first with subsidiary slave labor and later with *paṇṇaiyāḷs*, tenant cultivators, or casual wage laborers.

### Individual Petty Commodity Producers and Traders

These included independent craftsmen, various sellers of services, traders, peddlers, and middle peasants who did most of their own work but sold a large part of their grain. Unlike the petty bourgeoisie, this class mainly used family labor.

***The Semiproletarians***

These included all those who produced commodities for the bourgeoisie but who were not regular wage laborers; those engaged in "formal subsumption under capital." They were the sharecropping tenants, the *vēlaikkārars* and *paṇṇaiyāḷs*, the emigrant indentured laborers, the "putting-out" craftsmen and semiprocessors, and the casual laborers in the service of the bourgeoisie. Their relations were transitional between precapitalist and capitalist relations and were those most typical of a colonial, peripheral capitalist socioeconomy. Characteristically, members of this class had sources of livelihood other than their wages or crop shares, which allowed their employers to exploit them more mercilessly than they could have exploited a pure proletariat. Such resources included a patch of garden, goats and chickens, a small allotment of paddy land.

***The Slaves***

In the late eighteenth and early nineteenth centuries some slaves came to be owned by individuals in a relationship called *kaṭṭu adimai*, or "tied slavery."[42] Such slaves were auctionable and were sometimes sold between villages or between villages and the ports. Other slaves remained in a modified form of village communal slavery until the mid-century. The slaves were decimated in the conquests of the 1770s and 1780s, and were evidently fewer in the nineteenth century than in the early eighteenth.[43] Some, however, returned to Thanjāvūr from other districts to which they had fled or had been deported. As they were legally freed between 1843 and 1862, the slaves became semiproletarians. Some former slaves, together with some former sharecroppers, ruined artisans, and smallholders, emigrated either freely or under coercion as indentured laborers.

It is doubtful whether Thanjāvūr had any sizeable proletariat proper or free wage laborers in this period, for labor was scarce and unattached laborers were likely to be kidnapped and deported as indentured laborers. In the villages there was a small number of free coolies or casual laborers as early as 1807, and probably much earlier, but it seems likely that they worked only part time and had other sources of livelihood in smallholdings or rented lands.

Thanjāvūr's main class struggles apparently changed with the evolving class structure between the late eighteenth and mid-nineteenth centuries. From the conquest itself until about the 1830s, the main conflict appears to have been between the population as a whole, led by the old state class, and the new British government and its agents. In the nineteenth century this conflict centered mainly around the British exactions of land revenue and the new kinds of land survey and revenue settlement they effected periodically. In 1819–20, for example, *mirāsdārs* in Sīrkāli *tālūk* refused to harvest the second crop in order to prevent a field assessment of the produce under the *olangu* settlement. In Thanjāvūr *tālūk* in the same year, the *mirāsdārs* forbade their *porakuḍis*, or sharecroppers, to cultivate dry grains and indigo in protest against the new settlement. In 1827, *mirāsdārs* in Sīrkāli neglected the cultivation of the first crop in order to lower the produce to be collected by the government; when that failed, they refused to repair a breach in the dam that supplied water to the *tālūk*. In the same period the Collector uncovered a conspiracy among the *mirāsdārs* of Kumbakōṇam, Papaṉāsam, Sīrkāli, and Naṉṉilam, to avoid a reassessment of the revenue. The *mirāsdārs* hired a lawyer in Madras who had charges brought against the Collector, including a charge of murder.

The *mirāsdārs*' attempts to reduce the revenue exactions continued throughout the nineteenth century, but as time went on they resorted more frequently to bribery of the revenue officials, litigation, and appeals to the Board of Revenue, which sometimes favored them. As their prosperity increased with the export trade from the 1840s the bigger *mirāsdārs*, although jealous of their privileges, became reliable allies of the colonial government.

Class conflict occurred meanwhile between at least some of the semiproletarians and the *mirāsdārs*. After the depredations of Haidar Āli in the 1780s, a new category of sharecroppers of Kaḷḷar, Maravar, Mūppaṉār, and Vaṉṉiyar castes was imported by the Thanjāvūr Rāja partly to replace the slaves who had been deported or decimated in the war. These new tenants-at-will appear to have been the ones who, in the literature of the period, were known as *porakuḍis* or "outside tenants." They were distinguished from *uḷ-kuḍis* or "inside tenants," who appear to have been indigenous; such tenants had longer-term rights and paid lower rents.[44] Under the heavy revenue revenue exactions of the early nineteenth century, *porakuḍis* struggled against the *mirāsdārs* over their share of the crop, and sometimes appealed to the government against them. As I have mentioned, Thanjāvūr's first Collector was dismissed by the Board of Revenue in 1800 for trying to increase the tenants' shares and secure their tenures. In 1827, the Collector reported being "surrounded by crowds of *porakuḍis*" complaining of their landlords' exactions.[45] Such struggles apparently achieved little, for the tenants' crop shares remained virtually stationary throughout the century.

## Imperialism: 1858–1947

The colonial economy that had been established in 1840–57 flowered in the century that followed the mutiny. Four main technological changes helped this process: the opening of the Suez Canal in 1869, which facilitated the import of British manufactures to India and the export of cotton, tobacco, leather, groundnuts, and other raw materials from Madras Presidency to Britain; the repair and extension of roads and bridges, allowing extensive oxcart traffic and the export of grain by land from Thanjāvūr to other districts; the building of the railroad, which reached Thanjāvūr between 1873 and 1877 and linked Thanjāvūr town with the ports of Madras and Tuticorin and with Nāgapaṭṭanam, Thanjāvūr's own main port; and the construction of the Mēttūr dam higher up the Kāvēri in Salem district in 1930–4, which allowed wet paddy production in the delta to be expanded and intensified. In the industrial sphere, in the twentieth century a factory that produced parts for the railroad and several hundred small mills for processing rice and vegetable oils were built, and bus and truck transport eventually developed. Some of these industrial and transport outfits were owned by British firms; others by local merchants and land magnates.

Thanjāvūr's seaborne rice exports, chiefly to the plantations of Malaya and Ceylon, reached their height in 1850–1900. In 1866–77 they averaged 78.3 percent of the value of the district's seaborne exported commodities, in some years reaching 83 percent. Between 1849 and 1877, paddy and rice exports by sea averaged the equivalent of 108,179 metric tons of paddy annually or between 18 percent and 32 percent of the gross produce. Meanwhile, increasing amounts were being exported by land to neighboring Madras districts, especially Rāmanāthapuram, Tiruchirappalli, and Madurai, which were deficit in food grains but were expanding their production of raw cotton, tobacco, and later groundnuts for the European market.[46]

Thanjāvūr's export of handmade textiles also revived modestly in this period, as British manufacturing exports became diversified and textiles were no longer paramount among them.[47] From 1867 to 1930 "piece goods" formed from 3 percent to 17 percent of the value of Thanjāvūr's annual commodity exports. Like paddy, these exports went chiefly to Malaya and Ceylon. They were mostly coarse cloths made from British twists, and in any given year one-tenth to one-fifth of them were actually British machine cloths that had merely been dyed in Thanjāvūr. Thanjāvūr's high-class silk and cotton textiles continued to supply only a small elite.

British textile imports outweighed Thanjāvūr's handwoven exports. From 1867 to 1877 they averaged the value of 44 percent of seaborne imported commodities and 137 percent of the value of seaborne textile exports. British manufactured goods of all kinds averaged 76 percent of the value of sea-imported commodities in that decade. The other significant import commodities continued to be arecanuts and spices, which averaged 17 percent of the value of imported commodities in 1867–77.[48]

In 1873–7 the railroad linked Thanjāvūr with Madras to the north and Tuticorin to the south. Separate figures are not available for the district's rail trade after 1877. It involved large imports of British manufactures and exports of paddy and rice to other districts of Tamiḷ Nāḍu and to southwest India (modern Kēraḷa), where there were British tea and rubber plantations and where industrial export crops occupied at least 40 percent of the cultivated area. Thanjāvūr's sea trade became complicated by the fact that neighboring districts traded by rail to and from Thanjāvūr's main port of Nāgapaṭṭaṇam. Thus from 1902 to 1930 groundnuts destined for Europe, chiefly from Tiruchirappalli, averaged 32 percent of Thanjāvūr's seaborne exported commodities, rising to 61 percent by 1930. Similarly, rice imports from Burma, destined mainly for Rāmanāthapuram, averaged 23 percent of Thanjāvūr's imports in the same period. Something can, however, be said about the district's external trade in the later nineteenth and twentieth centuries. First, Thanjāvūr's rice exports to Ceylon and Malaya fell off in the 1890s as Burma became the chief supplier of the plantation regions as well as of parts of south India. By 1902–3 they were the equivalent of only 80,325 tons of paddy, 40 percent of the value of all exports excluding groundnuts. Thereafter, Thanjāvūr's seaborne rice exports were never more than the equivalent of 46,000 tons of paddy per year and were usually less than half that amount.

Instead, in the twentieth century Thanjāvūr's rice went by land to other districts of Tamiḻ Nāḍu and to Kēraḷa. It became increasingly important after Burmese exports to south India stopped during the Japanese invasion of World War II.

Ironically, however, until World War II the "rice bowl of south India" did *not* feed all of its own people. After 1872 Thanjāvūr imported up to 7,000 metric tons a year of coarse rice from Burma, with which many landlords fed the Untouchable (former slave) castes who did most of their rice cultivation. Presumably this was more profitable for both landlords and merchants. Burmese rice imports were 4,000 to 20,000 tons a year in the interwar years, part going by rail to inland districts.

Throughout the British period the value of Thanjāvūr's seaborne exports exceeded that of its imports. In 1867–77 the total value of imports reached 62 percent of that of exports. Thirty-two percent of these imports, however, was in "treasure," or gold and silver, whereas only 4.5 percent of exports was in treasure, so that the value of the actual commodities imported was only 37 percent of that of export commodities. Of this 37 percent, almost one-sixth represented arecanuts and spices for comparatively wealthy people, and more than three-quarters British manufactured goods that, although no longer confined to the very wealthy, were mainly bought by the top one-quarter of the population. The huge amounts of "treasure" imported to Thanjāvūr in the nineteenth century must have gone mainly into gold and silver idols and ornaments for the great temples, gold and silver threads woven into luxury silk clothing, and above all into the massive gold jewelry worn by women of the landed and merchant classes. It was into this jewelry that Thanjāvūr families put almost all their savings. Valued by the sovereign weight, it was given as dowry, worn for ostentation, inherited, hoarded, pawned in crises, or cashed at propitious times to buy new land, or to pay debts or revenue. From 1898 to 1918 total seaborne imports were 52 percent of the value of seaborne exports, or 49 percent excluding treasure. From 1919 to 1930 seaborne imports dropped again to 35 percent of the value of exports, with treasure negligible. The latter two sets of figures are not conclusive, for rail trade began in 1873. Qualitative accounts in general, however, and tonnage figures for rail trade in 1873–77, indicate that Thanjāvūr's rail exports, too, greatly exceeded its imports.

Throughout British rule, therefore, it seems certain that Thanjāvūr had a large export surplus, part of the value of which went to pay its revenue, while the much smaller quantity of imports still went mainly as luxuries or clothing to the wealthier classes. The total revenue increased from Rs. 6,340,000 in 1857–8 to more than Rs. 10,000,000 in 1912–13, and went on increasing thereafter. Because about two-thirds of the Madras Presidency's revenue was remitted to the Imperial Treasury, and much of the rest spent on British incomes in Madras, it continued to be a means of extracting surplus value from the district largely for the benefit of the colonial power.[49]

From the mid-nineteenth century, however, land revenue tended to become a smaller percentage of the gross agricultural output. It was about 32 percent in 1859–60, about 23 percent in 1880, about 16 percent in 1917, up to 32 percent again by 1937 during the world depression and fall in prices, but down to about 7–11 percent, depending on crop size, in 1947–53.[50] As trade increased, and perhaps also as the landed aristocracy became stronger in relation to the colonial power, more of the revenue was derived from sales taxes, duties, and professional taxes. In the villages this meant that more was collected indirectly from cultivating tenants and wage laborers and less from landlords, although the shares and wages of the former did not increase substantially. With the growth of productivity and mercantile capitalist relations, moreover, government revenue as a whole became a smaller proportion of surplus value than in all previous ages. Instead, a greater proportion went into landlords' rents, interest on loans due to landlords and merchants, and private profits on trade, transport, and industry. Because British monopolies controlled the export and import trades, shipping, banks, railroads, imported industrial commodities, a considerable proportion of motor transport, food industries, and grain trade, a large although unknown part of Thanjāvūr's surplus value went via private enterprise to British shareholders and their salaried representatives in India. Although to the sharecropper or landless laborer his immediate oppressor was the landlord or the local moneylender, behind these, often as their creditors, stood the British banks, trading companies, and agents of government.

By 1853, 76 percent of Thanjāvūr's net cultivated land was irrigated, mainly for wet rice cultivation, the total cultivated acreage having expanded by 44 percent and the wet acreage by 57 percent since 1807 (see Table 1.2). In the next hundred years the net cultivated acreage increased by 45 percent, the irrigated acreage by 60 percent, the population by about 80 percent, and the production of paddy by about 152 percent. By 1951, three years after independence, wet lands devoted almost entirely to paddy comprised 86 percent of Thanjāvūr's net sown acreage.[51] As we have seen, about 77 percent of the population depended mainly on the production, processing, or export of rice for their livelihood. With an import trade geared mainly to British manufactured goods, timber, arecanuts, spices, and only small quantities of pulses, this agricultural pattern created acute shortages of dairy products, fruits, vegetables, fuel, fodder, and meat for most of the people, while the depletion of forests contributed to seasonal flooding.

In addition to its paddy, Thanjāvūr exported perhaps a million people in the last century of British rule. Most went as indentured laborers to the plantations of Ceylon and Malaya; some as "free" laborers, whose conditions were, however, little better. A total of 622,543 emigrated by sea between 1881 and 1931, the peak year being 1900.[52] Smaller numbers went by land to plantations in the Western Ghats and Assam. In addition, several tens of thousands of professional, clerical, and service workers migrated to Madras and other cities, especially in the twentieth century.[53] Most of the indentured laborers were Harijans or from the lower castes of Non-Brahman peasants; most of the professional and clerical workers, Brahmans. About three-quarters of the indentured laborers were men; most of the rest, young women. About 12 percent of Thanjāvūr's population lived abroad in 1931. A minority of the emigrants returned, often in old age, while between 1881 and 1931 about half as many people immigrated to Thanjāvūr from other districts of Tamiḷ Nāḍu in seasons of famine, as the number who emigrated. Over the century, Madras as a whole shipped large numbers to foreign plantations, but of all the Madras districts Thanjāvūr became the most specialized, and the most intensively exploited, as a human and nutritional service station for British plantations.

Apart from the horrors of life and the frequency of death among the plantation workers,[54] emigration imposed extra burdens on Thanjāvūr. At its height, it removed perhaps 20 percent of the male able-bodied workers. These men and a smaller number of women lived off Thanjāvūr in their childhood and sometimes their old age, but gave most of their working lives in foreign estate service for contemptible wages. Some sent minute cash remittances, but plantation workers earned too little to maintain their families and some had children in both regions. Women and children left behind in Thanjāvūr had to work harder to maintain themselves and their aged dependents. The immigrants could not substitute for those who left because most of them arrived in families with their own dependents.

The clerical and professional workers who left for cities also took more from Thanjāvūr than they contributed. Like the unskilled laborers, they were maintained by the village in childhood and old age but gave their working years elsewhere. Some sent remittances, but most were small absentee landlords who took their rents to the cities either in cash or grain.

Despite its trade and emigration patterns, Thanjāvūr's agrarian relations show an extraordinary continuity during British rule. Landlords, *kuthakai* and *vāram* tenants, *paṇṇaiyāḷs*, and coolies were present under the same names in 1800 as in 1947. Customary economic and cultural rights and obligations among them changed only slowly. In 1921, for example, a census commissioner found that in some villages tenant cultivators had received exactly the same share of the gross produce for a century.[55] Throughout the district cultivating tenants, who received between 22 percent and 30 percent of the gross produce in 1805 and between 18 percent and 35 percent in 1881, still received between 20 percent and 33 percent in 1951.[56] In spite of the legal abolition of slavery in 1843, the actual conditions of Harijan laborers changed little throughout British rule.[57] In the 1870s, a decade of famine, a *paṇṇaiyāḷ*, his wife, and his working children earned about forty *kalams* of paddy a year, the equivalent of about 1,681 pounds of husked rice. They also received minimum clothing, small change, and space for a mud shack and sometimes, a vegetable plot and a small paddy field.[58] In 1885 such a family earned about fifty *kalams*, and in 1951–3 about forty to fifty-five *kalams* plus some of the same perquisites.

There was also a striking continuity in the distribution of holdings among the landowners. In 1876–7, the owners of fifty-seven percent of the holdings paid less than Rs. 10 a year in revenue, which meant that they were likely to own less than 2.65 acres. In 1950–1, 58 percent owned less than three acres. Similarly, in 1876–7 only 5.6 percent of holdings paid more than Rs. 100 in revenue, which meant that they probably comprised more than twenty-six acres of land. In 1951, 4 percent of holdings were above twenty-five acres.[59]

At first sight it seems, therefore, that the most serious charge that we can bring against British imperialism is that apart from railroads and processing plants it failed to industrialize Thanjāvūr and kept the population in much the same conditions and relationships as in 1800. The overall results of British rule seem, however, to have been worse than this, although they are hard to assess precisely.

On the credit side, the colonial period ended the wars, social disruption, and population decline of the late eighteenth century – that is, of the conquest itself. Villages and towns were rebuilt and in time, roads and irrigation works expanded. Modern transport, and in towns, electricity, eventually made their appearance. Epidemics declined after 1921. Literacy increased from 11.7 percent to 23.2 percent of the total population between 1881 and 1951.[60] For a small elite, Thanjāvūr was opened up to world communications and modern scientific knowledge.

Overall, however, deterioration seems to have occurred in the living standards of the majority, undoubtedly because while the population was increasing quite rapidly, part of the district's surplus value and labor power were siphoned off in the form of migrant labor for British plantations, revenue for the British government, and profits for British companies.

The most striking sign of deterioration was the fact that despite emigration and at least two major famines,[61] the ratio of agricultural laborers increased in relation both to the agricultural and to the total workforce. In 1871, male agricultural laborers, chiefly Harijans of the former slave castes, were 16.12 percent of the total male workforce and 22.62 percent of the agricultural male workforce. In 1911, they were 17.61 percent of the total male workforce and 28.91 percent of the male agricultural workforce. By 1951 male agricultural laborers were 26.01 percent of the total male workforce and 35.37 percent of the male agricultural workforce.[62] The increase came mainly after 1930 when the demand for plantation labor declined. Moreover, even though the workers themselves preferred to remain as indebted tied laborers assured of a regular income in paddy (that is, in relations similar to their former slavery), more and more of them were forced to work for very low cash wages as day laborers.

The real value of these wages also fell toward the end of British rule. In 1937 a survey of eight south Indian villages, including one in Thanjāvūr, recorded an increase in the proportion of agricultural day laborers for cash wages since an earlier survey of 1917. The wages of such laborers had risen slightly in the 1920s, but had slumped in the depression to lower than they had been before the boom, so that farm servants were unable to maintain their families and preferred their traditional roles as *paṇṇaiyāḷs*.[63] Yet the real wages of these laborers were to fall still lower during World War II. In 1939, male agricultural laborers earned four to six annas (As. 4 to As. 6 or Rs. 0.25 to Rs. 0.37) per day, and in 1945, As. 13 to As. 16, an increase of three times. In the same period, the price of rice in Thanjāvūr rose 3.38 times, that of other foods 4.95 times, and the rural price index 4.67 times.[64] It is clear, therefore, that although a minority of landlords, rich peasants, and merchants profited, Thanjāvūr's agricultural workforce became increasingly pauperized toward the end of British rule.

## The Class Structure in 1951

In Chapters 3 and 4 I have described the agricultural and the nonagricultural strata of Thanjāvūr separately and empirically in order to make clear the relations of production in each category. It is now necessary to ask what were the main classes in the population as a whole at the end of British rule. Although I realize that mine is not a conventionally accepted classification, I would argue that the urban and rural populations are not separable in class terms into "peasants" and others, but form segments of the same class structure.[65] In my view, the main classes at the end of the colonial period and shortly after independence were as follows.

### *The Bourgeoisie*

This included:

1. The colonial or imperialist bourgeoisie. This comprised chiefly British mill owners, trading and transport firms, banks, and the members of the colonial government.

2. The Indian big bourgeoisie. This was absent but operative within the district.

3. The local or medium bourgeoisie, mainly resident within the district. This included: (*a*) the industrial, financial, and merchant capitalists, and also, in my view, (*b*) the larger landowners owning more than about thirty acres and engaging more than about a dozen workers. The biggest of these landlords, owning from 1,000 to 7,500 acres, ranked in wealth along with lesser members of the Indian big bourgeoisie, and in some cases had shares in large industrial or trading concerns outside the district.

It is true that the landowners were not strictly capitalists, in the sense that some were rentiers, leasing out a part of their lands, whereas others used mainly attached labor. Nevertheless, because they were largely involved in commodity production for the local and export trades, I include them in the bourgeoisie. The landed bourgeoisie were also themselves often involved in the ownership of rice and oil mills or in the paddy trade.

Thanjāvūr's bourgeoisie may also be taken to include: (*c*) the independent professionals, and (*d*) the salaried upper middle class, or "bureaucrat capitalists." Their incomes were similar to those of the medium-sized capitalists and they usually owned land in addition to their salaried professions.

***The Petty Bourgeoisie***

This class included:

1. The industrial, merchant, and financial petty bourgeoisie.
2. The salaried lower middle class.
3. The noncultivating landlords and the rich peasants, having less than about thirty acres and engaging fewer than about a dozen workers or tenants, but regularly engaging some tenants or laborers. The largest *kuthakai* tenants, especially the noncultivators, who often also owned some land, fell into this class.

As in the case of the bourgeoisie, two or more of these categories often merged in individual families. Small noncultivating rentier landlord families usually had some of their members employed in the lower ranks of government service or private salary work for business firms, often in cities outside Thanjāvūr. Small rentiers and owner cultivators often owned a village store or rice mill, or carried on trade in paddy, cattle, or other commodities.

***The Simple Commodity Producers, Service Vendors, and Traders***

This group includes the weavers, carvers, carpenters, potters, laundry-workers, and smiths described in Chapter 2. I would also include in this class, however, Thanjāvūr's "middle peasants," few in the western delta but more prevalent on the east coast and in the southwest uplands. Like landlords and rich peasants, middle peasants often had another occupation in their own class, as independent weavers, teashop keepers, and so on. Like the rest of the class the middle peasants were an unstable category, the more successful becoming rich farmers and the less successful, proletarians or semiproletarians.

***The Semiproletariat***

This class included all those engaged in manual or service work for the bourgeoisie and petty bourgeoisie in intermediate labor relations, that is, those who were not strictly speaking wage laborers. It includes the ordinary *kuthakai* and *vāram* tenants or poor peasants and the *vēlaikkarars, paṇṇaiyāḷs*, and nonagricultural labor servants in transitional relations. Agricultural coolies are also included in the semiproletariat, although their relations were closer to capitalist wage work than those of *paṇṇaiyāḷs*.

The largest category of Thanjāvūr's workers in 1951, the semiproletariat, formed the backbone of this colonial-style economy, although it was gradually losing members to the proletarians. Although most of the semiproletariat produced commodities on behalf of their masters, the members of this class were not fully proletarians. In some cases, such as the tenant cultivators, village servants, and village craftworkers, they controlled their own tools and conditions of work and retained, or sold privately, part of their produce. In other cases such as the *paṇṇaiyāḷs, vēlaikkārars*, and agricultural coolies, they were paid at least partly in kind. Usually, they had some source of livelihood other than their wages: a plot of leased land, a small allotment, a kitchen garden, or rights to hunt, fish, and forage in the village's wasteland. Perhaps most important, the semiproletarians were often in fact (though not in law) subjected to extra-economic forms of coercion such as beating or confiscation of their property.

### *The Proletarians*

This class, much smaller than the semiproletariat class, comprised the nonagricultural manual wage workers. Its members were often closely allied with the petty bourgeois, the producers, vendors, and traders, or the semiproletariat, in that they came from families of smallholders, tenant cultivators, artisans, or *paṇṇaiyāḷs*. Some of them were not lifetime proletarians, but the younger generation of the petty bourgeois or semiproletarians who in time might become tenant cultivators or shopkeepers. Nevertheless, the regular wage workers were sufficiently distinctive to be counted separately, for they worked in true capitalist relations and were gradually evolving as a class solely reliant on wage work.

The class struggles in the last century of the colonial period were mainly: (*1*) those of the noncompradore medium bourgeoisie and the petty bourgeoisie against the imperial bourgeoisie and its colonial government in the course of the nationalist struggle, and (*2*) those of the semiproletariat and the proletariat against the petty bourgeoisie and bourgeoisie, as in the Communist-led struggles of the 1920s to 1950s of urban workers, tenants, and agricultural laborers against employers and landlords.

These struggles were to some extent cross-cut by those between castes – for example, by Non-Brahman against Brahman bourgeoisie and petty bourgeoisie, or in villages, by Ādi Drāviḍa against Non-Brahman semiproletarians. In the chapters that follow I shall try to show how these struggles were carried out in two villages in 1951–3: Kumbapeṭṭai in the northwest of the delta and Kirippūr near the eastern coast.

### A Note on the Mode of Production

My characterization of the Thanjāvūr socioeconomy as a peripheral segment of the world capitalist mode of production and social formation owes much to the work of André G. Frank[66] and Immanuel Wallerstein.[67] I realize that it runs counter to the formulations of all of the Communist parties of India and also of most independent South Asian Marxists. Of those writing on South Asia, my position is closest to those of A. R. Desai,[68] Hamza Alavi,[69] Doug McEachern,[70] Jairus Banaji,[71] Gail Omvedt and Bharat Patankar,[72] and Ashok Rudra,[73] although these authors do not precisely agree with one another and none of them is responsible for my views. The subject is difficult and complicated and I am aware that I do not have all the answers.

Four main positions seem to be found in the current debate on the mode of production in India:

1. The Indian rural economy, if not the urban, is still mainly feudal or semifeudal *and* semicolonial, although "pockets" of capitalist development may be developing in the course of the "green revolution." This view is held by the

two parliamentary Communist parties, the Communist Party of India and the Communist Party of India (Marxist), as well as by the self-styled Marxist-Leninist groups.

2. India contains one or more precapitalist modes of production (tributary, feudal, or independent commodity production) but they are dominated by peripheral capitalism. This view is held by Samir Amin with reference to the capitalist periphery as a whole.[74]

3. Until 1947, India exemplified a separate "colonial mode of production," which was in the service of the capitalist mode. This is the view held by Alavi.

4. My own view that India is a peripheral segment of the (changing) world capitalist system, which is characterized by a single, although changing, mode of production and forms a single, although changing, social formation, there being only one of it in the world.

The first view seems to rest mainly on the fact that the Indian rural economy is characterized by palaeotechnology, tenancies with very high rents, perpetual indebtedness of tenants and smallholders to landlords and moneylenders, peasants with incomplete access to the market, village servants paid partly in kind, and laborers working in debt service. Colonialism and postcolonial neoimperialism are seen as having perpetuated such relations and blocked India from becoming fully capitalist. The short-term goal of revolutionaries is seen as one of developing truly capitalist relations, prior to the advance to socialism, or else of proceeding to a "people's democracy" or a "noncapitalist" (but nonsocialist) society that will substitute for the capitalist phase and precede socialism.

My objections to this view are, first, that although the production relations referred to are not those of industrial capitalism, neither are they precapitalist, but are hybrid or intermediate. This view seems to underplay the fact that the colonialists *brought* capitalism to India and established a bourgeois state with bourgeois institutions and property relations, even though, by draining off much of the surplus to the "core" area, it hindered industrial development and the overall development of wage labor. It neglects to see the world economy as the interdependent unity that it is, and the essential and specific role of peripheral regions in the development of capitalism as a whole. This view treats India as a separate social formation, and thus sees it caught somewhere in a unilineal progression from feudalism to capitalism rather than as integral to the world capitalist system, whose parts change while in a state of interdependence. Although, in the course of world capitalist development, wage labor may become the predominant production relation in India (if it is not so already), in my view India cannot achieve independent industrial capitalism and can probably move out of its peripheral status only through a socialist revolution.

The second view seems more realistic, but open to two main criticisms. One is that production relations in the supposedly subordinate mode or modes of production do not in fact remain precapitalist but change their character in order to serve capitalism in the core areas.[75] The other objection, as Alavi has pointed out, is that if there are more than one mode of production, one would expect struggle between their dominant classes. No such struggle is, in fact, evident. Although there are struggles over shares in the surplus, the supposedly "feudal" landlords cooperate with the Indian agricultural merchant and industrial bourgeois and invest in their undertakings.

The third view is the closest to my own and has much to recommend it. My criticism is that, as Alavi himself recognizes, neither the "colonial mode of production" nor the "social formations" (colonies and spheres of influence?) that supposedly characterize it are independent. They cannot therefore be classed along with feudal or tributary modes or social formations. To comprehend the totality it is necessary to see it as part of the world capitalist, imperialist mode of production, which Alavi recognizes as a possibility. Alavi's objection, "Would such a unity be premised on a conception of its homogeneity, or do we assume a hierarchy of imperialist countries?" seems to me irrelevant, for the world system is obviously *not* homogeneous. Although it is a difficult and complex task to sort out the hierarchy and the interlocking of its component imperialisms, it is necessary to try. My second objection to the "colonial mode of production" is that at least some of its production relations (such as debt service, sharecropping, or "putting-out" relations) are similar to some of those that obtained in the early phases of capitalism in the core areas. They were simply more prolonged and more permanently poverty stricken in the periphery, presumably because of the drain of capital to the core. Neither in its production relations nor in its disposal of the surplus, therefore, is the "colonial mode" separable from the capitalist mode as a whole. Indeed, as Alavi says, "The colonial mode of production *is a capitalist mode*" (his italics). It is hard to see on what grounds it can be separated from capitalism as a total system.

# 7 Political Parties

In 1951 Thanjāvūr's politics were dominated by three political parties: the Indian National Congress, the Drāviḍa Kazhakam, and the Communist Party of India.

### The Congress Party

The Indian nationalist movement, spearheaded by the Congress Party, became active in Thanjāvūr about 1900.[1] In Tamiḷ Nāḍu it was perhaps inevitable that Brahmans should lead it, for they had provided the ministers, the bureaucracy, and the religious leadership of the Tamiḷ Hindū kingdoms in pre-British times and had not forgotten their loyalty to the native Rājas. At the same time, it was chiefly Brahmans who acquired English education and flocked into the learned professions and government service in the late nineteenth and twentieth centuries. This gave them expertise in modern education and government and strengthened their desire for an independent India. As carriers of the Sanskrit tradition, Brahmans had an all-India consciousness that tended to be lacking in the other castes. As the plan for national freedom unfolded in the 1930s, some Brahmans learned Hindi in preparation for an independent government with an all-India national language.

Thanjāvūr journalists were especially active in the nationalist movement. G. Subramania Iyer edited both the English nationalist paper *The Hindū* and the Tamiḷ *Swadēsamitran* in the early 1900s. He was followed by Kastūri Ranga Iyengar, who hailed from a Brahman village close to Kumbapeṭṭai. In addition to the Brahman professionals, the Congress Party gradually gathered strength among Veḷḷāḷar and other white-collar workers and among rich farmers, traders, industrialists, and other businessmen of Thanjāvūr's towns and its larger villages. Many government servants and most of the bigger landlords, however, including many Brahmans, remained loyal to the British until the eve of independence.

In the first three decades of the century, the Congress Party agitated for such programs as boycotts of British manufacture; the revival of Indian crafts and industries, especially handmade textiles; the boycott of alcohol, which corrupted the poor and afforded revenue to the British; the establishment of cooperative societies and elected village *panchāyats*, or councils, for public works; the gradual widening of the franchise; the reform of municipal, *tālūk*, and district administrations; and the institution of compulsory elementary education.

A populist movement, the Congress Party succeeded to some extent in uniting all classes against a British government that was seriously impeding the economic and social development of the country. Thus, in 1924 the Congress Party supported the landlords' boycott of land revenue payments in protest against the higher settlement recently imposed by the British. In 1926 it organized workers against the British government's removal of the railway workshop from Nāgapaṭṭaṇam to Tiruchirappalli and encouraged them to strike for higher wages. In the countryside the Congress demanded improved conditions for tenants and laborers and an end to religious discrimination against Harijans; yet, it drew its strongest support from small landlords and rich peasants who, at best, were lukewarm toward these causes.

The movement for total independence from Britain gained strength in the 1920s. It caught fire in Thanjāvūr with the "salt *satyāgraha*" of 1929, which was vividly recalled to me by older villagers in 1951.[2] Throughout India, Mahātma Gāndhi and his Congress followers organized marches to the ocean where the activists made salt in defiance of the British salt monopoly and the revenue it afforded. In south India the well-known Brahman Congress leader, C. Rājagopālachāri, led a march from Tiruchirappalli via the Grand Anicut Dam through Tiruvaiyāru in west Thanjāvūr to Kumbakōnam, Maṉṉārgudi, and Tirutturaipūṇḍi. The salt march terminated in the government-managed salt swamps of Vēdāranyam on the southeast coastal tip, where the marchers made salt illegally on the seashore. The vast crowds that assembled, the numerous arrests, and the subsequent arrest of 375 people in Thanjāvūr during a general boycott in October 1930, for a time made Thanjāvūr the center of the independence struggle in Tamiḻ Nāḍu.

A Congress Party government under Rājagopālachāri came to power on a limited franchise in the Madras Presidency in 1937–9. It clashed with the Tamiḻ Nationalist Self-Respect Party, the Justice Party, and the Scheduled Caste Federation over its program for compulsory Hindi in schools. One thousand protestors against the program were arrested in Madras. The agitation spread to Thanjāvūr, where a number of Non-Brahman supporters of Tamiḻ nationalism were arrested. By this date the lines were drawn both between Tamiḻ nationalism and all-India centralism and between Brahman and rising Non-Brahman power in Thanjāvūr.

The Congress Party resigned from the Madras Government in 1939 as part of its national boycott of India's participation in World War II. Thereafter, the movement against the war and for total independence gathered strength in Thanjāvūr, with occasional violent outbursts. When the "Quit-India" movement was launched in May 1942, repeated marches, strikes, and closures of stores followed in Thanjāvūr, Kumbakōṇam, Arantāngi, Tiruvaiyāru, and Nāgapaṭṭaṇam towns. The activists stopped traffic and cut telegraph wires, uprooted telegraph poles, removed railroad tracks, and set fire to railway stations. Three hundred people were arrested at Tiruvaiyāru, a few miles from Kumbapeṭṭai, on August 13, 1942. In the same period, 10,000 met in Thanjāvūr municipality, closed the stores, barricaded the streets, and pelted the houses of the British district magistrate and police inspector, provoking a *lathi* charge and numerous arrests.[3] After these events Congress agitation died down in Thanjāvūr but the party had won large support among the common people for independence.

With the end of the war and the transition to independence, successive Congress governments came to power in Madras in 1946, 1947, and 1949. In Thanjāvūr as elsewhere, independence brought a change in the Congress Party's responsibilities, character, and supporters. When the party had led moderate reforms and a fierce anti-British struggle, its spirit was typified by the *khādi*-clad Congress worker of modest means who courted arrest on behalf of his country's freedom. But when the Congress became the ruling party of India, most of the landlords, big businessmen, and religious reactionaries flocked to its side. In Thanjāvūr the Communist opposition, grown strong during the war, provoked violent assaults by the landlords and businessmen, most of whom now financed the Congress Party and looked to it to protect their property rights.

The first general elections to state and national legislatures with full adult franchise took place on January 16, 1952, arousing great interest and a large voter turnout in the towns and villages of Thanjāvūr. Already by that date, the Congress Party was a relatively conservative force, but with a platform of seemingly radical demands, a posture it was to maintain and perfect in the following thirty years. In Thanjāvūr, Congress Party candidates campaigned for "a good life in the future," fulfillment of the central government's first Five-Year Plan, solution of the current food shortage, a continuance of the Grow More Food campaign begun by the British, the expansion of electricity and industry, and the furtherance of scientific and industrial research. Adequate supplies of cotton yarn were promised to handloom weavers, and cooperative societies were proposed for farmers and cottage industries. Proposed changes in the social structure were confined to the final abolition of *zamindāri* estates (already decreed in the Act of 1948), "other land reforms" and "help" to tenants, "moderate rents, moderate wages and moderate prices," better housing for laborers, and financial and educational aid to Harijans. The party promised a reorganization of states along linguistic lines if this proved necessary in the future – a cautious response to agitations that were reaching white heat in the Telugu-speaking areas.

The Congress Party was flanked on the right in the election campaign by the right wing, religion-oriented Hindū Mahāsabha, which ran independent candidates in a few areas and had some support from among Thanjāvūr's more conservative village Brahmans and other high-caste religious devotees. The Mahāsabha called for the abolition of Pakistan and the reunification of the country. It promised the protection of Hindū religious culture and the departure of India from the Commonwealth. The property rights of landlords were to be guaranteed; landlords were to be permitted to engage and dismiss tenants and laborers as they pleased. The Congress Party's land reforms and its continued rationing of rice, sugar, and other commodities were blamed for the food shortages; decontrol of all commodities and an end to land reforms were promised. Free enterprise, it was argued, would end black market corruption and increase production. Although these sentiments echoed those among some of the landlords and many of the Brahmans, the Mahāsabha won few votes. In most cases its supporters felt that because the Mahāsabha could not win the election, Drāviḍa Kazhakam and Communist candidates should be kept out by voting for the next best option, the Congress Party.

In Tamiḷ Nāḍu the Congress Party won the 1952 elections with 133 seats out of a total of 190. Madras State as a whole had a total of 375 seats. The Congress Party came to power with 152. Fifteen seats in Tamiḷ Nāḍu were won by the Communist Party, thirteen of them with Drāviḍa Kazhakam support. In Thanjāvūr district, twenty-one Madras Assembly seats were contested in fifteen constituencies, six extra seats being reserved for Scheduled Caste (Ādi Drāviḍa) candidates.[4]

The Congress Party appeared to be supported mainly by Brahmans; a majority of big, and many small, landlords regardless of caste; government servants, especially Brahman and Veḷḷāḷar; and (as a result of the influence of their masters) some of the lower-caste tenants and laborers on Congress-supporting landlords' estates. Women showed a strong tendency to vote for the same party as their husbands. When they had no husbands, they usually voted with their fathers or brothers.

Congress Party candidates won only eight of the twenty-one seats, located in north and west Thanjāvūr. Five of the Congress seats (Thanjāvūr, Kumbakōṇam, Āduthurai, Sīrkāḷi, and Naṉṉilam) were won in areas where Brahman landlords had strength in the villages and could influence the votes of many of their tenants and laborers. Three seats (Arantāngi, Adirāmpaṭṭaṇam, and Paṭṭukkoṭṭai) were won by the Congress Party in the southwestern *tālūks* where agricultural laborers, and also Ādi Drāviḍas, were relatively few and owner cultivators numerous, and where, perhaps because of this, the rural class struggle had developed less forcefully (see Tables 5.10 and 5.13).

Although the Congress Party gained a plurality of seats in Thanjāvūr, the election results showed a decisive decline in the power of big landlords. Several ran for office but almost all were defeated, among them the Vandayār of Pooṇḍi, the Iyer (Brahman) of Kuṇṇiyūr, and the Mudaliar of Neḍumbalam.

Communists won six assembly seats in Thanjāvūr district, partly with the support of the Drāviḍa Kazhakam, which did not contest the elections independently. Five of the Communist successes (Niḍāmangalam, two in Maṉṉārguḍi, and two in Nāgapaṭṭaṇam) were in east Thanjāvūr, the Communist party's stronghold. These constituencies fell in the *tālūks* of Maṉṉārguḍi, Nāgapaṭṭaṇam, and Tirutturaipuṇḍi. In these *tālūks*, especially in Nāgapaṭṭaṇam and the northern parts of Maṉṉārguḍi and Tirutturaipūṇḍi, agricultural laborers formed a relatively high proportion of the agricultural population, and Ādi Drāviḍas were especially prominent among the agricultural laborers. In addition, the Communists won one reserved Harijan seat in Thanjāvūr *tālūk*, perhaps because the Drāviḍa Kazhakam organization and the Communist labor unions were strong in Thanjāvūr town.

Thanjāvūr's voters also sent four members of Parliament to the Lok Sabha in

Delhi in 1952 from the parliamentary constituencies of Kumbakōṇam, Māyuram, and Thanjāvūr (two seats). Congress candidates won in the Kumbakōṇam and Thanjāvūr constituencies and the well-known Communist candidate, K. Āṇanda Nambiar, in the Māyuram parliamentary constituency that included the Nāgapaṭṭaṇam and Maṉṉārguḍi Communist strongholds.

In all, in the parliamentary elections of 1952, Congress Party candidates won 545,348 votes in Thanjāvūr district, or 41.5 percent of the valid votes. Communist candidates with Drāviḍa Kazhakam support won 282,183 votes (21.5 percent of the total). The Communists declined to field candidates in the Thanjāvūr and Kumbakōṇam parliamentary constituencies, instead supporting independents. Altogether, independent candidates of various hues won 465,465 votes, or 35.4 percent of the total, and the Independent Scheduled Caste Federation, 21,950, or 1.7 percent. The large number of candidates run and votes won by independents suggested that the party system had not fully taken hold in Madras in 1951. It also reflected the fact that the Drāviḍa Kazhakam and its offshoot, the Drāviḍa Muṉṉētra Kazhakam, were in the process of organizing themselves and for this election had opted to support independents (or, in the case of the Drāviḍa Kazhakam, certain Communist candidates), rather than fielding their own men. The Congress plurality with 41 percent showed that the Congress Party, with its achievement of national independence and its nationwide reputation, was the strongest party in the district, but that it did not command the allegiance of the majority. Finally, the fact that every candidate in Thanjāvūr was a man reflected the strongly patriarchal character of this district.

### The Drāviḍa Kazhakam

In 1952 the Drāviḍa Kazhakam (DK), or "Dravidian Association," represented the strongest commitment to south Indian nationalism.[5] It operated in all four major Dravidian language areas (Telugu, Tamiḻ, Kaṉṉada, and Malayālam) but was most prominent in Tamiḻ Nāḍu. In Thanjāvūr its support came mainly from bourgeois and petty bourgeois urban Non-Brahmans, some Non-Brahman cultivators, especially in east Thanjāvūr, and a small number of Non-Brahman landlords.

In 1952 this party stood for an independent Dravidian state (Drāviḍastān) in southern India. In the short run it was opposed to Brahman dominance in education, government service, and the professions, the imposition of Hindi as a national language for India, and dominance of the south Indian economy by north Indian and British big business. It viewed the Congress Party as the preserve of Hindi speakers in north India, and the Brahmans in south India. It saw this control as stifling the development of the economy, culture, and arts of Dravidian India.

In the 1930s and 1940s the party and its predecessor, the Self-Respect Movement, had been militantly atheist and rationalist, calling for the closing of temples and monasteries and the destruction of idols. As the first general elections approached, it somewhat modified its stand on atheism, this being unpopular among most of the people. In their election campaigning some individual party members said that they personally believed in God, but were opposed to idols, polytheism, and the intercession of Brahmans. They called for the confiscation of temple and monastic lands and wealth and their distribution to landless people, or their use to create jobs for the unemployed. In line with its anti-Brahman stance, the party opposed the ban on widow remarriage and called for freedom of individuals to contract civil marriages without restrictions of caste or creed. In general the DK opposed caste divisions, the belief in *karma* and reincarnation, the laws of the Shāstras, and the inheritance of occupations in castes and families – provisions that had been upheld by Mahātma Gāndhi and were still favored by strict Gāndhians within the Congress Party.

In 1952 the DK supported the proposed Hindū Code Bill then being discussed in parliament, and castigated the Congress Party for not promptly introducing all of its provisions into law. DK leaders had supported temple entry for Harijans, along with Congressmen, and professed a more radical stance toward Harijan rights than did the Congress Party.

Politically, the DK's program was vague, although its leader, E. V. Rāmaswāmy Naicker, had visited the Soviet Union in 1931 and professed allegiance to socialism. The party had a radical bent that was underlined by its support for individual Communist candidates in 1952. Although it was not itself a south Indian nationalist party, contained many Brahmans, and was, indeed, headed by a Brahman, the Communist Party justified this alliance on the grounds that the DK stood for replacing the Congress, fought for civil liberties, supported workers' and peasants' struggles and was a friend of the USSR, People's China, and liberation movements in Asia. Perhaps more candidly, E. V. Ramaswāmy Naicker, the DK leader, stated that his electoral alliance with the Communists represented a railway compartment friendship: "My enemy's enemy is my friend."[6] Individual DK campaigners told me that they hoped to use the Communists to oust the Congress before eventually ousting the Communists. A year after the elections the DK indeed rejected the Communists, complaining that they were trying to change DK local units into Communist Party cells.[7]

The DK had its roots in an early Dravidian Association founded in 1916.[8] This group was the first to assert the demand for a Dravidian state to be governed by and for Non-Brahmans. The state was to remain under the British Raj, which the association thought essential to hold the scales against Brahman and north Indian dominance. This first Dravidian Association gathered few supporters, but in 1917 Sir P. Theagarāja Cheṭṭiar founded the South Indian Liberal Federation, later called the Justice Party. This party, at first an elitist group led by Rājas, landlords, and highly placed professionals, won elections on a limited franchise and governed Madras under British aegis in 1920–3 and 1930–7. The party became radicalized from 1935 when E. V. Rāmaswāmy Naicker, leader of the atheist and rationalist Self-Respect Movement, agreed to head it. In 1944 it split into conservative and radical wings, with the conservatives losing any popular base shortly after and the radicals reorganizing themselves under Naicker as the DK.

Some authors have stressed the British inspiration behind the Justice Party and its forebears and offshoots.[9] Certainly, the party's formation was in part a response to the British creation in 1917 of "communal representation," including separate Non-Brahman representation in government service, education, and elected bodies. British policymakers surely sought to pit castes and religions against one another in order to prolong their rule. British census classifications and proportional representation also did much to organize the population into separate blocks of Brahmans, Non-Brahmans, Ādi Drāviḍas, Muslims, and Christians. British inspiration could, however, be shown to have lain behind the rise of the Muslim League in 1906, a host of lesser caste organizations, and the Congress Party itself. Although initially encouraged by the British as a counterweight to the Congress Party in its demand for independence, the Dravidian movement had deeper roots in the changing society and mode of production in south India.

Undoubtedly because of their scholarly and governmental tradition under the pre-British rulers, Brahmans monopolized English education, government service, and the modern professions in Madras Presidency in the nineteenth and early twentieth centuries. In 1890–1 Brahmans provided 69 percent of the students in the Madras Presidency arts colleges, while forming 2 percent of the population in the Presidency. Non-Brahmans, more than 60 percent of the people, had only 20 percent of the students in arts colleges. As late as 1917, Brahmans formed 95 percent of the provincial civil service and 72 percent of all graduates in the Presidency.[10]

In the nineteenth and early twentieth centuries, Brahman lawyers and other agents represented the interests of the great Non-Brahman landlords to the British government in Madras. By 1912, however, a small English-educated Non-Brahman elite had emerged, composed of doctors, lawyers, and industrialists who pressed for reforms within their castes, improved education, and a place in government service. It is true that Brahmans continued to serve Non-Brahman magnates in many capacities, and that powerful Non-Brahmans often switched sides between the Congress and the Justice Parties according to their personal interest. Nevertheless, it seems clear that the rise of a mainly vernacular-speaking, literate Non-Brahman bourgeoisie and petty bourgeoisie whose interests were often genuinely opposed to north Indian and Brahman dominance lay behind the Dravidian nationalist movement of the 1910s to 1950s.

As time went on and more lower-caste Non-Brahmans became literate, the movement gained size and momentum. Having earlier underestimated the anti-imperialist aspirations of the common people, the movement recognized these during the nationalist struggle of the 1940s. In 1944 the newly formed DK finally asserted an anticolonial stance with its slogan "Wreck the Triple Alliance of the British, Brahman and Bania (north Indian trader)."[11] It thus offered an antiimperialist alternative to that of the Congress Party in the shape of an independent south India, although too late to gather massive popular support by the time of the first general elections of 1952. The DK Communist alliance was a temporary expedient designed by each to further its own ends.

In 1949 the Drāviḍa Kazhakam split into two parties, the DK and the Drāvida Munnētra (Progressive) Kazhakam (DMK). The source of the split was largely personal and factional. The DMK breakaway was led by C. N. Aṇṇāthurai, a veteran leader, in opposition to Rāmaswāmy Naicker's marriage to his secretary, a woman some forty-five years younger than himself. In 1952 the DMK's policies were virtually indistinguishable from those of the DK, although it purported to be democratic and have rejected the dictatorial procedures said to be characteristic of E. V. Rāmaswāmy Naicker. It was less adamantly opposed to religion and to Brahmans, and perhaps more cogent in its opposition to north Indian business firms. Support for the DMK came chiefly from students in peasant families and urban petty bourgeois youth, many of whom were attracted by the film stars who had joined it. Like the DK, the DMK declined to contest the elections of 1952 independently. Instead it supported two Vanniyar-based parties in Chingleput, South and North Ārcot, and Salem districts, and five independents, thus helping to elect thirty candidates to the Madras Assembly. In Thanjāvūr the DMK had gained little independent support by 1952. Many older villagers, less in touch than the youth with towns, newspapers, and cinemas, were unaware of the split.

The rise of the Congress Party, the DK, and the DMK reflected the growing dominance of peripheral capitalism in India. Each stood for a secular state, a national culture and inspiration, the preservation of private property and a market economy subject to certain restrictions by the government, limited land reforms, industrialization partly through state and partly through private enterprise, universal education and franchise, the political and to a limited extent the familial emancipation of women, and the transition from attached labor to free wage labor with wage guidelines by the state in both rural and industrial enterprises. With its earlier start, its attempt to win support in all classes throughout India, and the recency of its leadership by Gāndhi, the Congress Party in 1952 embodied more precapitalist features than did the DK and DMK. In practice, for example, the Congress Party compromised more seriously with landlordism, Hindū dominance, casteism, and the religious hegemony of the Brahmans. The Congress Party was associated with such high-caste Hindū mores as the ban on cow killing and the sale of alcohol. The Congress was also, of course, determined to bring about a more centralized and unified India, and to that end was prepared to impose Hindi as a national language and to tolerate the dominance of the Hindi region and north Indian capital. By contrast, the DK and DMK stood for south Indian and especially Tamiḷ nationalism, and in 1952 represented the aspirations of the regional bourgeoisie and petty bourgeoisie as against the north Indian and all-Indian bourgeoisie.

The DK's atheism was more than a cultural quirk. As mentioned in Chapter 6, the theocratic irrigation state had persisted in Tamiḷ Nāḍu and especially in Thanjāvūr with less modification than in most of India until the eve of British rule. It was an essentially religious state, coterminous with and governed through the regional caste system, and under the hegemony of the Brahman. Despite colonial rule, together with development of secular law and some growth of capitalist enterprise, orthodox Hindūism, the traditional caste system, and Brahman dominance continued to pervade the culture and social structure of Tamiḷ Nāḍu throughout British rule. This was most notably true in Thanjāvūr, where Mōghul dominance was never firmly established, Hindū royal influence persisted into the mid-nineteenth century, Brahmans were the most numerous, and industrialization had made little headway. When E. V. Rāmaswāmy Naicker rode in a cart through the streets of Thanjāvūr flogging wooden images of Rāma and Seetha, he was symbolically revealing the powerlessness of the gods and of their precapitalist theocratic state.

To some extent, history was rewritten to suit the needs of the Dravidian movement. In particular, an artificial separation was made between Tamiḷ and Sanskrit culture and literature, whereas these had in fact been interwoven, usually under Brahman leadership, for the past two thousand years. At the same time, the Dravidian movement, like the caste system itself with its major cleavages among Brahmans, Non-Brahmans, and Ādi Drāviḍas, did reflect certain apparent facts of history. The Brahmans did descend from the main thrust of Āryan and north Indian penetration of south India, traditionally believed to have begun with the migration of Agastya about 1,000 B.C. The Non-Brahmans probably did derive mainly from the Dravidian people, who may have conquered and settled south India as early as 2,000 B.C. The Ādi Drāviḍa castes had in recent times claimed to be the ''Original Dravidians'' and were in theory incorporated into the Dravidian movement. In fact, however, they remained largely outside it, for the Non-Brahman dominance of these castes was as onerous as the Brahman, and local Non-Brahman landlords and farmers proved unwilling to grant them either political power or social equality. It may be that the enslavement and domination of the so-called Ādi Drāviḍa castes was in fact originally Dravidian and pre-Āryan, and that they descend mainly from the pre-Dravidian, proto-Australoid population of south India.

Whether or not this was so, until the mid-nineteenth century the Ādi Drāviḍas had been agricultural slaves in Tamiḷ Nāḍu for at least 1,000 years. The Non-Brahmans had occupied more diverse positions in the traditional class structure, for their upper ranks had participated in government and local administration whereas their lower ranks were in serflike relationships. They were, however, intermediate between the dominant state-class of Brahmans and the agricultural slaves. In 1952 the Dravidian movement was making a bid to unite the Non-Brahman bourgeoisie and petty bourgeoisie against the erstwhile state-class of the Brahmans. Without Communist help, however, it was unable to penetrate the ranks of the laborers whose forebears had been slaves.

Although predominantly bourgeois and petty bourgeois in character, neither the Congress Party nor the Dravidian movement could ignore the socialist tradition. Both made rhetorical concessions to ''socialism'' and spoke of expropriating landlords, planning the national economy, and establishing a viable cooperative movement. Peripheral capitalism was too weak and poverty stricken to ignore the challenges of the Indian Communist movement, economic development in the Soviet Union, or the revolutionary developments in China. The outcome was dependent state capitalism with the rhetoric of socialism and, in the Congress Party case, with the retention of some precapitalist ideas and elements.

**The Communist Party**

The Communist Party of India, founded in 1923, conducted struggles in Tamil̤ Nāḍu from its earliest days.[12] Already in 1918, men influenced by the Russian revolution were organizing labor unions in Madras, Coimbatore, and Thanjāvūr district's Nāgapaṭṭaṇam. In 1919, Pakkiriswamy Piḷḷai, a retired station master, became president of the Nāgapaṭṭaṇam Railway Workers' Union, organized from the British-owned railway workshop in Nāgapaṭṭaṇam. In view of the workers' militancy, the British government moved the workshop to Goldenrock near Tiruchirappalli in 1919 and discharged 4,500 railway employees. About 10,000 workers went on Thanjāvūr's first strike for ten days in protest against this action. The colonial government severely penalized them and eighteen were deported to the Andaman Islands.

By 1935, thirty-six south Indian railway union branches had been established at Thanjāvūr, Māyuram, Tiruvārur, and Paṭṭukkoṭṭai, and in the late 1930s unions were founded in various cities among weavers, scavengers, steel-rolling mill workers, small merchants, and motor workers. Although not all of this organizing was done by Communists, the Communist Party, then active within the Congress Party, played a major role. *Janasakthi* (''People's Power''), the first Communist newspaper in Tamil̤, appeared in Thanjāvūr in 1937. A Communist Students' Union was formed in 1942.

Communist organizing among poor tenants and agricultural laborers began with conferences at Kīlvelūr and Nāgapaṭṭaṇam in east Thanjāvūr in 1938. Agricultural workers' unions were first established among poor tenants on the estate of the Utthirāpadi *mutt* in Themparai village near Maṉṉārguḍi in March 1943. Despite severe punishments by the government and the *mutt* authorities, 400 men and 150 women organized a procession in Maṉṉārguḍi demanding reductions of rent and security of tenure. In July, after the union had sent a delegation to the government of Madras, the Thanjāvūr deputy collector arbitrated the case. The Communists achieved their first victory when union members were granted a reduction in the rents of wet lands, cancellation of rent arrears, half the annual produce of coconut groves, the reinstatement of recently dismissed tenants, and compensation for future evictions. Following this victory, the Communist Party's Tamil̤ Nāḍu Agricultural Committee was formed in 1944. A conference of agriculturalists at Maṉṉārguḍi in May, 1944, drew 10,000 people including several hundred women, and was followed by the formation of the Tanjore District Agriculturalists' Association.

The years of the Second World War gave the Communists an advantage in organizing, for with the German invasion of the USSR, the Communist Party of India opted to support the Allied war effort in defense of the Soviet Union and in opposition to the world spread of fascism. From 1942 onwards, by contrast, most active members of the Congress Party were in jail for noncooperation in the war and for participating in the "Quit-India" movement against the British. While collaborating with the British war effort, the Communists used this period to extend their influence in both urban and agricultural unions.

In 1944, the first large-scale struggle of agricultural laborers as distinct from tenants took place on the 6,000-acre estate of the Brahman landlord of Kunniyūr in Maṉṉārguḍi *tālūk*. The *paṇṇaiyāḷs* on this estate joined the Communist agriculturalists' union and refused to leave it or give up their demands in the face of police harassment and torture by the landlords' agents. Twenty-three people were arrested for unlawful assembly. The union endured, although no immediate benefits resulted from the agitation. In 1945 an injunction was passed forbidding Communist meetings in Maṉṉārguḍi *tālūk*, but the movement continued to spread. By the time of independence in 1947 it had branches in every *tālūk* of the district. Its following was especially large in Nāgapaṭṭaṇam, northern Maṉṉārguḍi, northern Tirutturaipūṇḍi, and Naṉṉilam *tālūks* in east Thanjāvūr. There, Brahman influence was less prominent than in the northern *tālūks*, large estates were prevalent, and there were relatively large numbers of Ādi Drāviḍas and agricultural laborers. By 1947, the Communist Party had its strongest following among Ādi Drāviḍas and was often contemptuously dubbed "Paḷḷaṉ-Paṟayaṉ *katchi*" (Party of Paḷḷars and Paṟayars), although it also had support from some Non-Brahman poor tenants and urban trade unionists.

The first formal district conference of Communist Party members in Thanjāvūr was held in December 1947. Perhaps partly as a result of the planning at this conference, the year 1948 was a period of intense class struggle between landlords on the one hand and cultivating tenants and agricultural laborers on the other, in Thanjāvūr as elsewhere in India.

The militant struggles of this period may have sprung from three underlying conditions. First, as I have mentioned, the standard of living of Thanjāvūr's poor tenants and laborers appears to have fallen during the depression of the 1930s and the years of World War II. Moreover, the four years following independence – years of drought in south India – saw bad harvests and acute food shortages. Under these conditions, with a decade of union organizing behind them, the cultivators were ready for revolt, especially in east Thanjāvūr where the Communist movement was strongest and where the poverty of laborers appears to have been most acute.

Second, the revolt in Thanjāvūr was probably in part influenced by a Communist peasant war being waged in Telengāna, the largely tribal, Telugu-speaking area of the native state of Hyderabad, as well as by the recent success of peasant revolutionary warfare in China. Following the precepts of Mao Tse-Tung's *New Democracy*, the Telengāna Communists tried to combine rich, middle, and poor peasants and landless laborers in a partisan war that lasted from 1946 to 1951 and temporarily liberated some 3,000 villages from landlord and governmental control.[13] Knowledge of the Telengāna struggle must have encouraged the Thanjāvūr Communists. The Telengāna program of distribution of fallow land to agricultural laborers, withholding of rent from landlords who opposed the movement, reductions of rent paid to "loyal" landlords, prohibition against evicting tenants, stoppage of extra levies on cultivators, and guarantee of minimum wages to agricultural laborers, must have evoked a particularly warm response in Thanjāvūr's Communists and cultivators. It is possible that their own demands were based partly on this program.

Third, although differing from the Maoist line of the Telengāna Communists, the policy of the all-India Communist Party Polit Bureau changed at the Calcutta Party Congress of December 1947 from one of partial collaboration with the Nehru government to uncompromising attacks on it and attempts to produce a revolutionary situation throughout India. Under the leadership of the newly appointed Party Secretary, B. T. Ranadive, the Congress Party was declared to be the organ of the Indian bourgeoisie. India's independence from Britain was reinterpreted as a sham, and the bourgeoisie and the Congress Government were seen as tools of western imperialism. An all-out struggle led by the urban trade unions against the whole of the bourgeoisie was called for.

The Maoist line being followed in Telengāna called for a "four class alliance" (workers, peasants, petty bourgeoisie, and patriotic national bourgeoisie) against imperialism, feudalism, and the monopoly bourgeoisie, leading to a New Democratic Revolution that would precede the transition to socialism. By contrast, Ranadive's new line called for an "intertwining" of the democratic and socialist revolutions in an attack on the whole bourgeoisie as well as landlords. In theory Ranadive's thesis required the struggle to be led by the urban proletariat rather than by agricultural laborers and peasants. Nevertheless, Ranadive's policy gave temporary support to the Telengāna peasant war and, throughout the country, fostered attacks on government, landlords, and capitalists through strikes and sabotage. The militant Communist actions in Thanjāvūr in 1948–9 were undoubtedly influenced by this all-India policy.

The central event for Thanjāvūr's villagers was a six-week strike of cultivating tenants and agricultural laborers during the harvest season of January–February 1948.[14] About 100,000 tenants and laborers went on strike, especially in the east coast *tāluk* of Nāgapaṭṭaṇam. The strike was chiefly organized by the Communist-sponsored peasant unions, in cooperation with Gāndhian peasant leaders who had formed unions in some parts of west and north Thanjāvūr. The strikers' main demands were for a reduction of tenant cultivators' rents from the prevailing three-fifths or four-fifths to half the paddy crop, and for a doubling of agricultural wages. The poor harvests of 1948 were acknowledged to have impelled the strike. Most landlords succumbed to the strikers' control of their villages, but some hired thugs to beat up the striking unionists; two such landlords were reportedly killed. A small proportion of the strikers carried guns. Others beat off the landlords' gangs with picks and spades. In east Thanjāvūr a number of landlords were driven from their villages, and in the best-organized Communist communities, peasant militias cordoned off the areas they controlled. Support for the strike was widespread beyond its immediate locales, and peasants from neighboring districts smuggled food to the strikers. To prevent this and to localize the disturbance, police were ordered to blockade the district; within the best-organized Communist communities, however, the local police allowed the strike organizers to come and go. In those villages of east Thanjāvūr where the landlords' power was broken, the cultivators harvested the crop on their own behalf, in some cases paying one-quarter of it as rent to the landlords. In at least some villages, the Communists' confidence of their control was so high that they looked forward to the gradual capture of the countryside by peasant unions in south India, leading to eventual capitulation of the cities.[15]

The Thanjāvūr strike was eventually crushed by armed special police and many hundreds were jailed. The Madras Maintenance of Public Order Act of 1848, reenacted in 1949, provided for preventive detention, collective fines, censorship, the control or banning of public meetings or processions, the requisitioning of property, and the control of essential services. Most Communist leaders in Thanjāvūr remained in jail until shortly before the general elections of early 1952. Small strikes continued at intervals, especially at harvest time when the demand for labor was highest. These Communist agitations were the main force propelling the government toward instituting first, the Māyuram Agreement on tenants' crop shares and agricultural wages in October 1948, and later, the Tanjore Tenants' and Pannaiyals' Ordinance of August 1952, which passed into law in November 1952.

In 1951 the government of the Soviet Union reappraised its policy toward the Nehru government in the light of its opposition to the American intervention in Korea and its support for the People's Republic of China's admission to the United Nations. Moscow's previous intransigeance toward such Third World governments was now replaced by approval of their policy of nonalignment. The Soviet Union's line that India and comparable Third World countries could achieve socialism by peaceful transition was openly announced in 1951. In its own program of 1951, the Communist Party of India did not accept the idea that armed struggle could be abandoned in India indefinitely but, partly influenced by advice from the Communist Party of Great Britain, it did abandon the militant struggles of the previous four years and decided to enter the first general elections. In Thanjāvūr, party members released from jail held conferences in Nāgapaṭṭaṇam and Dārāsuram in 1951 and planned their election strategy. With support from the Drāviḍa Kazhakam, the Communist Party won five seats in the Madras Assembly and one in the Lok Sabha in Thanjāvūr, out of a total of twelve Communist Assembly seats and one Lok Sabha seat won in Tamiḻ Nāḍu as a whole. The Communist Party thus embarked on a long period of parliamentary democracy and peaceful trade union struggles.

# PART II: KUMBAPEṬṬAI

# 8 The Face of the Village

In Part I, I analyzed the political economy and historical background of Thanjāvūr district as a whole. In Part II, I turn to the microlevel and describe Kumbapeṭṭai, a village in northwest Thanjāvūr, as it was in 1951–2. My focus is on the political economy of the village, especially the changing structures of caste and class.

## The External Setting

Kumbapeṭṭai lay on a main bus route a few miles from the town of Thanjāvūr, slightly south of the main branch of the River Kāvēri. Its chief trading and shopping center was Āriyūr, a market town of about 9,000, three miles to the northeast. In August 1952, Kumbapeṭṭai's population was 817. The total acreage of the main socioeconomic unit was about 522 acres, some 90 percent of it being wet paddy land. Kumbapeṭṭai was a *grāmam*, that is, a village traditionally owned and governed by Brahmans.

Kumbapeṭṭai had two hamlets, or "side-villages," attached to it, whose populations and areas are not included in these figures (see Map 3). The houses in Veḷiyūr lay about half a mile to the north and those in Sheṭṭiyūr about three-quarters of a mile to the west. In 1952, Veḷiyūr, with 117 acres, had about 110 people, mainly Roman Catholic Paḷḷars on one street and Hindu Paḷḷars on another. Both served an absent Veḷḷāḷar landlord. Sheṭṭiyūr, with about eighty-four acres, had about 125 people, mainly Veḷḷāḷar owner cultivators and Mūppaṉār tenants. Sheṭṭiyūr drew its Harijan laborers from Kandipeṭṭai, a village to the northwest.

These hamlets belonged to the revenue village and *panchāyat* of Kumbapeṭṭai. They looked to the village headman of Kumbapeṭṭai for such matters as tax collection, police powers, and the registration of documents, births, and deaths. Similarly, they looked to the village's *panchāyat* board, especially its president, for such projects as new footpaths and public wells. The people of Veḷiyūr and Sheṭṭiyūr played some role in the annual temple festival of Kumbapeṭṭai's village goddess; they came to propitiate her during pregnancies or in times of drought, epidemics, or cattle disease. Some of Kumbapeṭṭai's landlords owned land in Sheṭṭiyūr, although not in Veḷiyūr. They went to Sheṭṭiyūr to collect their rents if their tenants failed to bring in their dues.

In general, however, the people of Veḷiyūr and Sheṭṭiyūr lived their own lives unhindered by Kumbapeṭṭai or by each other. Each hamlet had its own complement of village servants. Historically, they were separate entities. In addition, most of the lands in Sheṭṭiyūr and Veḷiyūr were owned by Veḷḷāḷars. Kumbapeṭṭai's Brahman landlords, although jealous of their rights over part of the village lands and population, did not interfere with them.

The villages surrounding Kumbapeṭṭai reflected the traditional diversity of landholding and caste dominance in the area, as well as some modern changes (see Map 3). Nallūr, about a mile to the east, had, like Kumbapeṭṭai, traditionally been owned on *mirāsi* tenure by Smartha Brahmans of the same subcaste as, and closely related to, those of Kumbapeṭṭai. As in Kumbapeṭṭai, the *mirāsdārs* of Nallūr had paid full land revenue to the government for at least two hundred years. By 1951 the lands of Nallūr had mainly been bought by Hindū and Muslim traders of Āriyūr and by Kaḷḷar and Paḍaiyācchi tenants of Nallūr. The Brahmans there were impoverished small rentiers and salary workers, many of whom had left for the cities and came home only for festivals, marriages, and funerals. Nallūr was an old village, its Vishnū temple dating from Vijayanagar times.

North of Kumbapeṭṭai's small hamlet, Veḷiyur, lay Periyūr, a large village that in 1951 was chiefly occupied by Veḷḷāḷar, Mūppaṉar, and Vaṉṉiyar landlords and cultivators and their Harijan laborers. Together with Veḷiyūr, this village formed one of 190 villages in Thanjāvūr district that the British government left in the private, tax-free *iṉam* estate of the Thanjāvūr Mahārājas and their descendents during most of the British rule. The Mahārājas had given the lands of Periyūr as prebends to Brahman scholars, Nāyakkar (Telugu) cavalry and stable managers, and families of temple dancing girls of the Mēlakkār caste. These minor prebendaries or *iṉamdārs* lived from part of the land revenue, or "upper share," of the produce (*mēlvāram*), paid part of the revenue for the upkeep of the main temple in Thanjāvūr, and had the lands cultivated by Vaṉṉiyar tenants and Ādi Drāviḍa slaves. In the course of time, as was common throughout Thanjāvūr, they acquired rights in the "lower," or local land managers' share of the produce (the *kīlvāram*) as well and so held the rights of both *mirāsdārs* and *iṉamdārs*. In the late nineteenth and early twentieth centuries, they sold most of their land to Veḷḷāḷar and Mūppaṉār landlords and cultivators from other villages. In 1934, the British government converted this and several other *iṉam* villages into ordinary *mirāsi* villages. Thereafter, the landowners had to pay full revenue to the government, a small portion of which continued to be paid over by the government for the upkeep of the Brahadeeswara temple in Thanjāvūr.

To the north-northwest of Kumbapeṭṭai lay Kalyānamangalam, a village mainly owned and managed by Vaishnavite Ayyangār Brahmans. Like Periyūr, it had been part of the Mahārājas' estate. Part of the *mēlvāram* had been granted as *iṉam* to the Brahmans, who acquired the *kīlvāram* rights as well. Like Periyūr, it became a *mirāsi* village in 1934. The Brahmans there fought a bitter suit against the government to prevent the conversion, but lost the suit and were obliged to pay full revenue from 1941.

West of Sheṭṭiyūr, Kumbapeṭṭai's other small hamlet, lay Kaṇḍipeṭṭai. It was

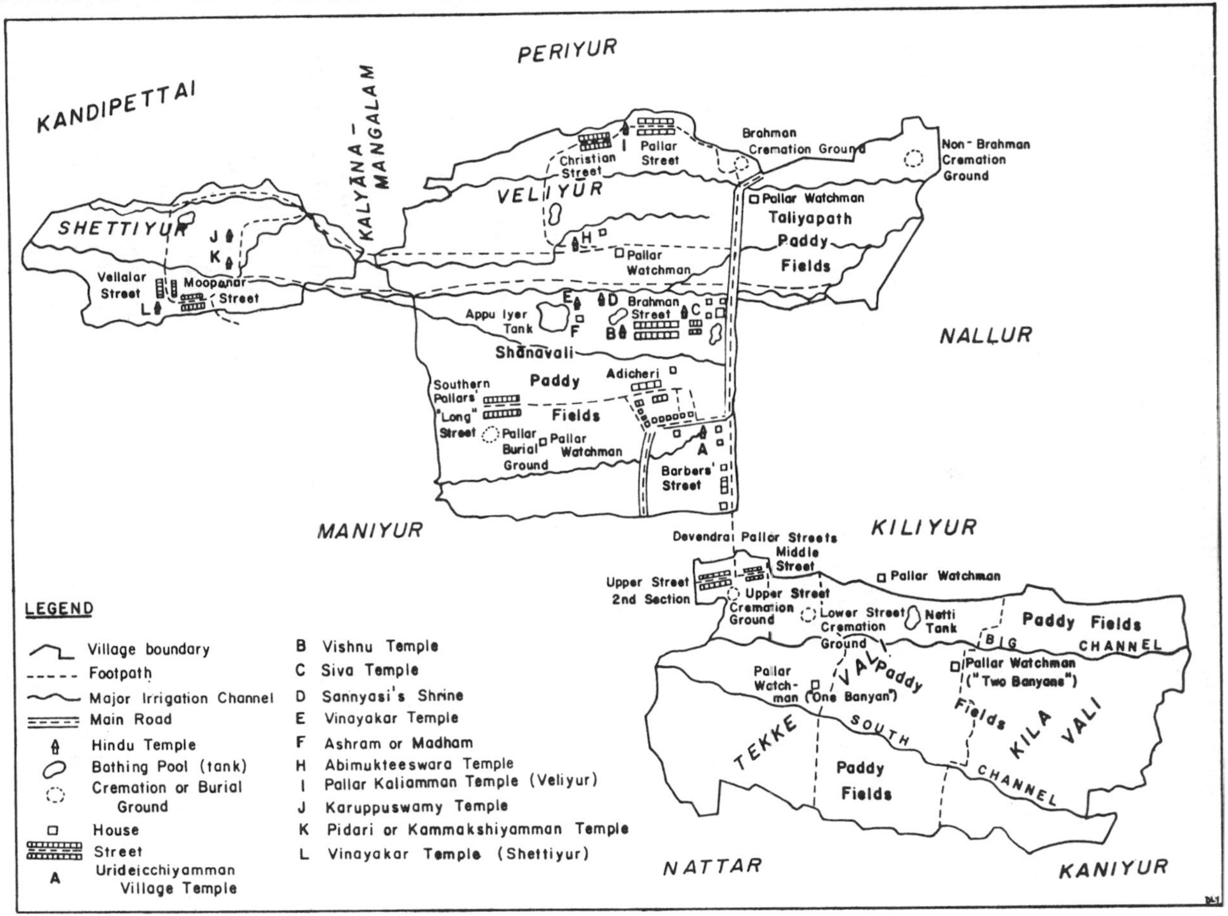


Map 3. Kumbapeṭṭai revenue village, 1952.

owned chiefly by Tamiḻ Smārtha Brahmans closely related to those of Kumbapeṭṭai and Nallūr. Like Periyūr and Kalyānamangalam, it had been given to the Brahmans as *iṉam* by the Mahārājas but was converted into a *mirāsi* village in 1934.

Southwest and south of Kumbapeṭṭai lay Māniyūr, a village whose lands were mainly owned by owner cultivators of the peasant caste of Agambaḍiyars, once palace servants of the Rājas. Part of this village, too, once fell in the Mahārājas' private estate and, like Veḷiyur, was allotted as *iṉam* to retainers of Sarfōji Mahārāja II in the early nineteenth century. It was eventually sold to the Agambaḍiyars' ancestors, probably its former tenants, and became a *mirāsi* village in 1934. The Agambaḍiyars had meanwhile occupied and cultivated another portion of Māniyūr that was formerly wasteland.

To the southeast of Kumbapeṭṭai lay Nāṭṭār, once the *iṉam* estate of a prominent Smārtha Brahman family who were astrologers for the king in Maratha times. During British rule they declined, and sold their estate to a rising family of the low-ranking Nāḍār caste who had made money from licensed palm-wine shops during British rule. In 1951 Nāṭṭār was owned chiefly by Nāḍār and Kaḷḷar cultivators. It has been a *mirāsi* village since 1934.

Further southeast lay Kāniyūr, a Smartha Brahman *mirāsi* village similar to Nallūr and Kumbapeṭṭai. The Brahmans in Kāniyūr, Nallūr, Kumbapeṭṭai, and Kaṇḍipeṭṭai had intermarried from time immemorial, being part of a larger subcaste traditionally drawn from eighteen villages. In Kāniyūr, as in Nallūr, most of the Brahmans had sold their land and many had emigrated by 1952. Part of the land had been bought by resident Mūppaṉār tenants and part by Agambaḍiyars related to those of Māniyūr.

East-southeast of Kumbapeṭṭai lay Kiḷiyur, a small hamlet owned by an absent Ayyangār family of Thanjāvūr. It was occupied by only one street of Harijan laborers. Kiḷiyūr was once the home of Kumbapeṭṭai's Brahmans, who moved to their present site after the devastation of the area during Haidar Āli's invasion of 1780–2. In 1952 a stretch of dry wasteland with ruined buildings still marked the site of the original Brahman street.

Beyond Kāniyūr, finally, lay Kaḷḷūr, four miles southeast of Kumbapeṭṭai. This village was given as *iṉam* by the Mahārāja in the 1780s to a Kaḷḷar military officer and revenue collector. Such officers, called *pattakdārs*, were appointed after the invasion and expulsion of Haidar Āli to collect the revenue, police the country, and restore cultivation. They tended to become minor princelings who usurped large estates and used their private armies to squeeze extra revenue from the villagers in the guise of ''protectors'' against invaders and cattle thieves. The Kaḷḷūr family, which had once managed three hundred acres, remained private landlords owning seventy acres in 1952.

Two Harijan (Paḷḷar) families of Lower Paḷḷar Street in Kumbapeṭṭai lived on house sites owned by the Kaḷḷūr landlord and maintained a ritual link with his family that dated back to Maratha times. In the late eighteenth century the Kaḷḷūr *pattakdār* engaged these two families as police to report to them any crimes in the area. In modern times these families had worked for the Brahmans of Kumbapeṭṭai along with others of their street. Even so, they still helped to drag the deities' chariot in the annual temple festival at Tiruvaiyāru, a famous religious center, on behalf of their Kaḷḷūr landlord. As late as 1979, one of these families retained unofficial police functions. If a crime was committed in the Harijan streets of Kumbapeṭṭai, the village headman would send a man of this family to arrest the accused on behalf of the government-paid village policeman, and only then would hand the case over to the police station four miles away.

This brief survey illustrates the fact that large areas of northwest Thanjāvūr were devastated and then repopulated after the invasion of Haidar Āli in 1780–2. After the reconquest some ancient villages of high-caste land managers were either confirmed in their lands (like Nallūr) or, like Kumbapeṭṭai, were moved to new sites nearby. Other areas like Periyūr, Veḷiyūr, and Maniyūr remained parceled out to connections of the royal family. Yet other areas like Kaḷḷūr were given to families of middle-ranking military officers, such as Kaḷḷars and Mūppaṉārs, sometimes from outside Thanjāvūr, who had come to the aid of the East India Company and the Thanjāvūr Mahārāja as mercenaries in the war. Groups of Agambaḍiyar, Paḍaiyācchi, Mūppaṉār, and Kaḷḷar tenants (*porakuḍis*) were also brought in from other districts to cultivate the land.

Second, our survey shows how in the nineteenth century, as the population increased, more and more wastelands were brought under cultivation until scarcely any forest or pasture remained. Some of these lands became owned, and their new village sites dominated, by cultivating castes such as Agambaḍiyars, Kaḷḷars, and Paḍaiyācchis, who either came from areas south or north of the delta or who had earlier been servants of Brahmans and Veḷḷāḷars. Parts of Māniyūr and Kāniyūr were examples of such modern, middle-caste settlements. As we shall see, Sheṭṭiyūr had a similar origin.

Third, some of the villages around Kumbapeṭṭai illustrate the purchase of some lands in the market during British rule by people, some of whom had not formerly been land managers but who were able to accumulate capital through private enterprise in colonial times. They included Nāḍār liquor merchants, Cheṭṭiar and Muslim traders and agents of British firms, and some enterprising tenant farmers who were able to buy their holdings from bankrupt rentiers or former holders of *iṉam* estates.

## The Village

The main village of Kumbapeṭṭai, shown on Map 4, had eleven streets in 1951. The castes, households, and population of the village are listed in Table 8.1. The wealthiest and most prominent street was the *agrahāram*, or Brahman street, which occupied the best garden land between two main irrigation channels in the northern part of the village. In 1952 it contained thirty-five occupied and fourteen unoccupied houses, all of the Brahman caste, together with seven abandoned house sites where the buildings had fallen down or had been converted into cart sheds or paddy barns.

Table 8.1. *The castes and subcastes of Kumbapeṭṭai, 1952*[a]

| Major group | Caste | Subcaste | Traditional occupation | House-holds | People |
|---|---|---|---|---|---|
| *Brahman* | 1. *Brahman* | (a) Ayyangār | Landlord, scholar priest | 1 | 11 |
| | | (b) Vaḍama Smārtha | " " " | 1 | 7 |
| | | (c) *Bṛahacharaṇam Smārtha* | " " " | 32 | 141 |
| | | (d) *Kurukkal* | Saivite temple priests | 1 | 15 |
| | | (e) Telugu Brahman | Household priests for Non-Brahmans | 1 | 4 |
| | | | Total Brahmans | 36 | 178 |
| *Non-Brahman* | 2. Veḷḷāḷar | | Landlord, rich peasant | 1 | 3 |
| | 3. Maratha | | Courtier, palace servant | 2 | 6 |
| | 4. Agambaḍiyar | (2 subcastes) | Palace servant, peasant | 4 | 13 |
| | 5. Kaḷḷar | | Peasant, cattle thief | 8 | 39 |
| | 6. Paḍaiyācchi | | Peasant, tenant farmer, soldier | 1 | 8 |
| | 7. Muslim | | Native doctor | 1 | 3 |
| | 8. *Kōnār* | | Cowherd | 20 | 74 |
| | 9. *Poōsāri* | (2 subcastes) | Village temple priest | 4 | 16 |
| | 10. *Kusavar* | | Potter | 3 | 19 |
| | 11. *Kammālar* | | Carpenter, brazier, blacksmith, goldsmith | 3 | 7 |
| | 12. Tōṛuvar Nāyakkar | | Toddy tapper, tenant farmer | 1 | 3 |
| | 13. Tamiḷ Nāyakkar | | " " " " | 8 | 39 |
| | 14. Nāḍar (Shanar) | | " " " " | 3 | 13 |
| | 15. Ambalakkārar | | Inland fisherman | 5 | 20 |
| | 16. Vaṇṇār | | Laundryworker | 1 | 4 |
| | 17. *Ambaṭṭār* | | Barber, midwife | 2 | 8 |

| | | | | | |
|---|---|---|---|---|---|
| | 18. Kūtthāḍi | | Puppet player, village temple dancer | 1 | 8 |
| | 19. Koravar | | Basketmaker, gypsy | 1 | 2 |
| | | | Total Non-Brahmans | 69 | 285 |
| *Ādi Drāvida* | 20. Paḷḷar | (a) Christian | Agricultural laborer | 1 | 4 |
| | | (b) Dēvendra | " " | 75 | 303 |
| | | (c) Parayāri | Barber, agricultural laborer | 1 | 4 |
| | | (d) Tekkaṭṭi | Agricultural laborer | 12 | 43 |
| | | | Total Ādi Drāviḍas | 89 | 354 |
| | | | Total village | 194 | 817 |

[a]The rank ordering of castes is slightly different in this table from that I provided earlier (see Gough, ''Caste in a Tanjore Village,'' in *Aspects of Caste in South India, Ceylon and Northwest Pakistan,* ed. E. R. Leach, p. 18. Cambridge University Press, 1962). I went over the list with Brahmans in 1976 and was persuaded that the rank order in Table 1 was closer to their conceptions. Table 1 also omits Brahmans who were absent from the village but considered it their home and owned a house or other property there, whereas such Brahams were included in my earlier table. Numbers in the table refer to households on Map 4. The castes and subcastes that are in italics are believed to have been present from the founding of the village.

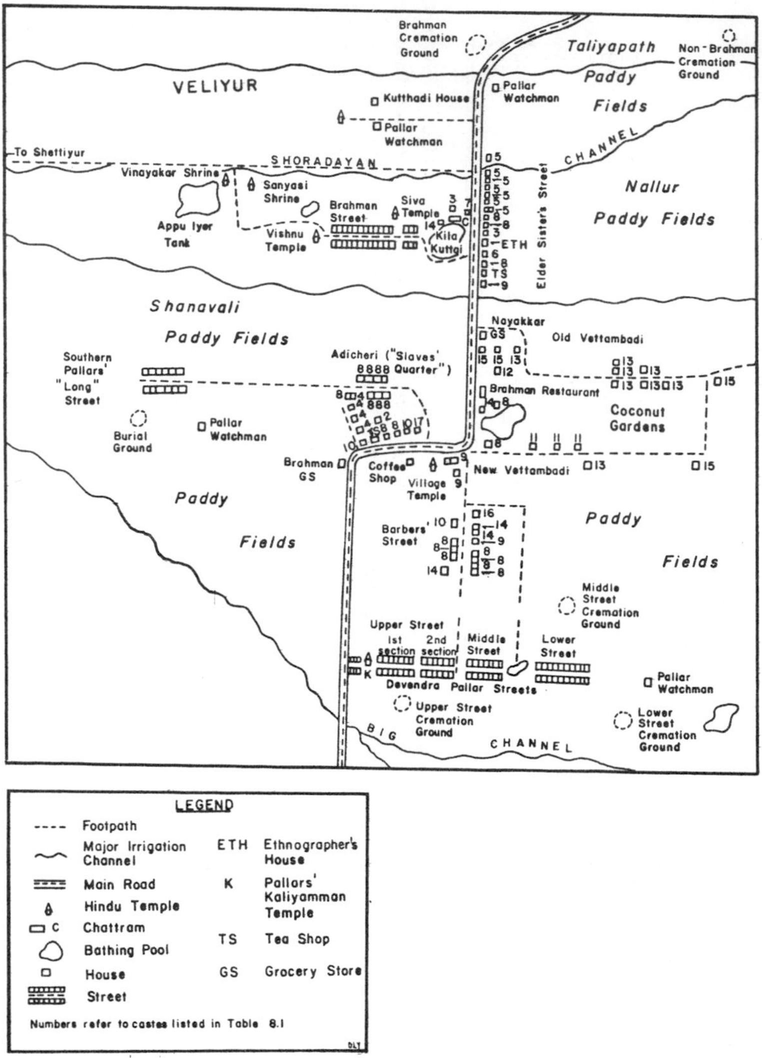


Map 4. Kumbapeṭṭai socioeconomic and residential unit, 1952.

To a Western eye these houses were small and unostentatious, but they were tile-roofed and spacious by comparison with those of the lower castes. Some of them had two stories. In 1951–2 most of them were in good repair and some were neatly painted.

Like high-caste houses everywhere, each house in the *agrahāram* had a spacious living room with a small, lowered yard (*muṯtam*) of stone a few feet square set at one side or in the center. The house roof sloped toward this yard, which was open to the sky. The yard, which had a drain, was used to wash hands and feet before eating, bathe babies, spit when rinsing the mouth after meals, and wash small articles of clothing. A sacred plant, *tulassi*, grew from a small brick platform (*tara*) set in the yard. Other rooms opened off from the main living room. Behind it was the kitchen and beyond that, a cow shed attached to the house.

In 1952, Kumbapeṭṭai's Brahman landlords included twenty-four households living in the village, and nine who lived away from it but counted it their home.

Each of these households owned between about one and sixty acres of land. The biggest landowner living in the village owned thirty acres, whereas nine others owned or managed more than ten acres each. The men of these ten houses who lived in Kumbapeṭṭai were the village leaders who managed most of the village's affairs. Altogether, 178 Brahmans lived in Kumbapeṭṭai, while fifty-eight absent men came home sufficiently regularly to consider it their home.

Most of the Brahmans' houses and gardens, like those of Aḍichēri and Barbers' Street, were the revenue free, common property (*nattam*) of their community, a relic of the old village commune. Only four houses at the ends of the *agrahāram* lived on ordinary land and paid full revenue; the rest paid small taxes on any coconut trees they had planted. Some Brahman families had exchanged houses for convenience within their owners' lifetime, whereas others were living rent free in an absent family's home. The houses faced each other in two rows across a narrow dusty street. Most of them were joined together with their neighbors. In the dividing walls of the living rooms, small circular peep holes allowed women to converse and older women to keep watch on their younger neighbors. Each house had a raised veranda outside its front door where men visited and sat to talk, and young men often slept at night. Married women visited other houses infrequently, although almost all in the street were kin. Children, however, dashed in and out of the homes and there was little privacy. To a large extent, the street was still a single community with a common patrimony, reminiscent of the village commune of pre-British times.

In 1952, apart from four households of other endogamous Brahman subcastes, the *agrahāram* contained four dominant, exogamous patrilineal lineages of the Maṛaināḍ Brahacharaṇam subcaste, together with a few related households that had arrived from other villages within the past 100 years (see Table 8.1). Although the presence of a few "alien" Brahmans had come to be accepted, any effort to sell an *agrahāram* house to Non-Brahmans would have been strenuously resisted in 1952; this, however, had already happened in Nallūr and some neighboring villages.

Kumbapeṭṭai's Brahmans owned certain other property in common, symbols of their communal life and religious concerns (see Map 4). A temple dedicated to the god Vishnū in the form of Rāma and his consort Seetha stood at the western end of the street, facing east. Another temple of the god Siva and his consort Pārvati lay toward the northeast end, facing south. Immediately northwest of the street, a small bathing pool was used exclusively by Brahman women during their menstrual and birth pollutions. Further west, across a stretch of dry wasteland, stood a large, beautiful pool bordered on the south by coconut trees. It was called "Appū Iyer tank," after the founder of the most prominent Brahman lineage. All Brahmans in good health who were not in a state of birth, death, or menstrual pollution, bathed in it daily.

At the northeast end of Appū Iyer tank near the irrigation channel stood a small shrine to Vināyakar or Ganapathi, built and given to the village by a Brahman in the 1870s. The eldest son of Siva and Pārvati, Vināyakar is the elephant-headed god of good luck, who waits eternally near streams and pools to watch women go to bathe, seeking a wife who will be as beautiful as his mother. Adjoining the Vināyakar shrine was a small room, or *madam*, fronted by an iron grill. It was built by the same Brahman and was visited by older Brahmans who wished to meditate, or simply to enjoy the cool breeze from the pool in an evening.

To the east and west of these buildings, three large, eagle-shaped stone platforms (*garuḍa chāyaṉams*) commemorated Vēdic public sacrifices of goats, or *yāgams*, carried out with much ceremony by famous priests of the Brahman street in the late nineteenth and early twentieth centuries.

A few yards further east, beside the stream, was a small shrine (*samādi*) built over the grave of a Brahman *sannyāsi* who lived for some years in Kumbapeṭṭai and departed this life in 1936. Having predicted the hour of his passing, he is believed not to have died as do ordinary mortals, but to have "attained *samādi,*" or joined with the divine, while in a state of meditation. As is usual with *sannyāsis*, he was buried in a grave of salt, sitting in the posture of meditation, and a commemorative shrine was built over him.

The dead bodies of ordinary Brahmans, as of most Non-Brahmans in Thanjāvūr, were cremated. A small patch of ground reserved for Brahman cremations lay near a bend in the road in the north of the village, surrounded by wet paddy fields. This cremation ground, actually located in Veḷiyūr, was built there early in the present century with the consent of Veḷiyūr's Veḷḷāḷar landlords. An earlier Brahman cremation ground had been located beside the Kuḍamuruṭṭi River, a branch of the sacred Kāvēri, about three miles away, for it was traditionally customary for Brahmans to cremate their dead beside a river and deposit the ashes in it. In modern times the Brahmans had preferred the more convenient method of cremating in the village and carrying the ashes later to the Kāvēri.

In 1952 five streets in the main village of Kumbapeṭṭai were occupied by Non-Brahmans (see Table 8.1). The sole exception was a restaurant on the roadside east of the main road (see Map 4). This was a shed with tables and benches owned by an impoverished Brahman family from Nallūr where Brahman and Non-Brahman bus passengers or pedestrians might stop for coffee and midday meals. The owners lived in a shack at the rear of their restaurant, somewhat to the disgust of the *agrahāram* Brahmans who were related to them.

The Non-Brahman castes, mainly tenant farmers and specialized village servants, occupied a middle position in the village, spatially and socially, between the Brahmans in their central street and the Ādi Drāviḍas who lived outside the main village site. Most of the Non-Brahman houses were single-storied dwellings of mud and thatch comprising a narrow veranda fronting the street, one to three rooms within, and a kitchen at the rear. Most stood separately but very close to their neighbors' homes; a few, housing the families of close patrilineal kin, formed groups of two to four adjoining dwellings.

The poorest Non-Brahman homes were low, windowless, one-room shacks, similar to those of the Ādi Drāviḍas, in which it was impossible to stand upright, and into which one crawled through a doorway hung with a grass mat or a gunny sack. Four Non-Brahman homes, however, had tile roofs and double stories like the Brahmans'. All four were the fruits of merchant enterprise. Two in Vēṭṭāmbāḍi had been built in 1906 and 1936 by a Nāḍār who had made money by selling toddy in British licensed liquor stores. A third, in Akkāchāvaḍy, had been built about the same period by a Kaḷḷar paddy merchant, and a fourth, in Aḍichēri, by an Agambaḍiyar, also a paddy merchant.

In 1952 the Non-Brahman streets were partly, but not entirely, segregated by caste. Kōṉars or cowherds, mainly tenants and *vēlaikkārars* of the Brahmans, predominated in Aḍichēri ("slave quarter") and Ambaṭṭān Teru ("Barbers' Street"). The latter street formerly contained only village servants: Barbers, Potters, Smiths, and the Village Temple Priests. Kōṉars had moved into it during this century, and the Smiths had recently occupied the new small street in New Vēṭṭāmbādi.

Old Vēṭṭāmbāḍi was occupied by the lower castes of Tamiḷ and Tūlū (or Tōṛuvar) Toddy Tappers, called Nāḍārs and Nāyakkars, together with five similarly low-ranking houses of Ambalakkārars or Fishermen.

Akkāchāvaḍy, or Elder Sister's Street, on the main road east of the *agrahāram*, was peopled mainly by eight households of the Kaḷḷar caste. A few Kōṉars and others had arrived within the past fifty years, and the Maratha household had been there for several generations. At intervals along the main road further south were a few scattered Non-Brahman houses, three Non-Brahman tea and coffee shacks, one Brahman and one Non-Brahman grocery store, and the Brahman-owned restaurant.

Across the main road from Akkāchāvaḍy lay a large pool, Kīla Kuṭṭai, or "lower tank." In 1952 it was used by the Non-Brahmans of Akkāchāvaḍy for bathing, obtaining drinking water, and washing the cattle and the household dishes of their own and their Brahman masters' families. Immediately north of this tank was a patch of dry land on which lay a ruined *chattram*, or guest house, together with a few small, thatched Non-Brahman shacks. Kīla Kuṭṭai tank and this piece of land belonged to a Muslim landlord who lived in Thanjāvūr. In 1952, a Muslim watchman and his family lived in part of the ruined *chattram*. He collected rents from the Non-Brahman tenants living on the site, and in summer sold the fish in the tank to professional fishermen on behalf of his master.

The *chattram* and tank, together with Akkāchāvaḍy, were once royal property like Veḷiyūr, Māniyūr, Periyūr, Nāṭṭār, Kaṇḍipeṭṭai, and four other nearby villages. All of these areas had originally been granted as *iṉam* estates to various retainers of Sarfōji Mahārāja I (1712–28). In the early nineteenth century the *chattram* remained as a Maratha guest house famed for the charitable feeding of local and itinerant Brahmans. After the termination of royal power and hospitality in 1855 the *chattram* declined, and in 1906 it was sold to the Muslim landlord. In 1952 the *chattram*, once a splendid edifice, was a mass of brick ruins in which children played and old people sat chatting in the shade. The resident Muslim family were social anomalies who were tolerated with good humor, wore the dress of Non-Brahmans, and lived among the Non-Brahmans as unobtrusively as possible; the father attracted some attention as a native doctor. The absent Muslim owners sold the fish in the bathing pool once a year and used the income to provide drinking water to passersby in the dry season and finance feeding of the poor in a mosque a few miles south of Thanjāvūr.

In the paddy fields of Veḷiyūr near the border of Kumbapeṭṭai proper stood the house and garden of a lone family of Kūtthāḍis, Non-Brahman village temple dancers, musicians, and prostitutes. Although living in Veḷiyūr, this family was socially part of Kumbapeṭṭai. The male ancestor of the family was brought early this century as a watchman and overseer by the Veḷḷāḷar landlord of Veḷiyūr. His daughter became the concubine of a village Brahman for about twenty years. Three of the other women became prostitutes for the Brahmans and Non-Brahmans of Kumbapeṭṭai. Because they lived in Veḷiyūr and not in Kumbapeṭṭai proper, the Kūtthāḍis had their own small cremation ground in the fields some distance from their home.

Although of nineteen separate endogamous castes, in 1952 Kumbapeṭṭai's 285 Non-Brahmans, living in sixty-nine households, to some extent shared a common social life. All of them, but no other castes, were free to bathe and wash bullocks or dishes in the large Akkāchāvaḍy and Vēṭṭāmbāḍi roadside bathing pools or tanks. The Non-Brahman castes joined to share a cremation ground set some distance from the village site in the northeast across paddy fields.

The village temple, dedicated to the goddess Uriḍeichiyamman (''Kōṉār Mother of the Village'') lay near the main road in the center of the village. It was managed by the Brahmans but, unlike those of the private Brahman temples, its deity was a *grāma dēvatai*, or village deity, worshipped by all the castes. Indeed, the complex rituals of this goddess's twelve-day annual festival in May provided a striking dramatization of the castes' separateness, their interdependence, and their dominance by the Brahmans. At the same time, the village temple was considered in some ways the special preserve of the Non-Brahmans. Its priests were of the Non-Brahman caste of Āndis, and its deity was believed to be a maiden of the Non-Brahman Oṭṭar (Roadmakers) caste. Some Non-Brahmans worshipped there daily, and Non-Brahmans had a special separate festival there on the first Tuesday in January–February, the month of Thai. Both the Brahmans and the Dēvendra Paḷḷars had their separate private shrines. As is often the case in other villages, the village temple was the Non-Brahmans' own special shrine as well as the common village deity.

Urịdeichiyamman was generally responsible for good and ill fortune in the village. She was capable of bringing or withholding epidemics, floods, crop failures, illnesses, the deaths of children and cattle, accidents, village fires, death in childbirth, madness, sudden misfortune, and formerly, invading armies. Her regular propitiation was necessary to ward off these disasters, which were especially caused by violating the village's moral laws.

The shrine and courtyard of the village goddess formed the home of several other minor godlings who obeyed the goddess and brought particular good fortune or maladies. In the inner shrine next to Uriḍeichiyamman stood a second, smaller idol of Nārāyaniyamman, the goddess's younger sister, wrapped in a fold of her sāri. Nārāyaniyamman was believed to have been the village goddess of Kiḷiyūr two hundred years ago when the Brahmans lived there. She was brought to live with Uriḍeichiyamman during the 1890s after pleading with one of the Brahman leaders in a dream.

Vināyakar, the elephant god, stood on the west side of the veranda of Uriḍeichiyamman's temple. On either side of its entry was the image of a female guardian, or *dōrasakthi*, one red, one yellow. Each held a spear, a drum, and a war club in three of her four hands, with a finger of the fourth hand held up in warning. Each had a snake as her necklace, a terrifying facc, and a grin showing bloody fangs. Whereas Vināyakar, a gentle and humorous figure, offered good luck to the worshippers who entered, the *dōrasakthis* warned them of the deity's terrible powers.

Outside in the courtyard of the temple were idols or roughhewn stones that represented the godlings Miniyāṇḍavar, Madurai Veeran, and Kārtha Varāyan, and the goddesses Kāmakshi, Uttira Kāṭṭēri, and Pēchiyāyi. Pēchiyāyi was represented by a clay idol with a hideous grin. She sat cross-legged with the broken body of a woman on her lap, holding aloft a fetus she had torn from it. Pēchiyāyi was responsible for sickness and death in childbirth, Uttira Kāṭṭēri for menstrual disorders, and Kāmakshi for accidents and for anything that caused people to fall down suddenly. Kārtha Varāyan was a policeman protecting Uriḍeichiyamman; Madurai Veeran, believed by some to have been a seventeenth century hero, was a warrior. In ancient belief, if a horseman rode through the village, Madurai Veeran would cause him to fall from his mount. The temple yard also contained a shrine for the warrior god, Karuppuswāmy (literally, "Black God"). Believed to be from Kēraḷa, he was depicted as a black demon with a knife in his hand, standing beside a lion.

Kumbapeṭṭai's Ādi Drāviḍas or Harijans lived in five streets across paddy fields, at some distance from the village proper. All were of the Paḷḷar caste. A single Paḷḷar family of Lower Street had been Roman Catholics for at least two generations. They attended church in Āriyūr, had their relatives in Periyūr and Veḷiyūr, and used a separate small burial ground near their street. They were treated like Hindu Paḷḷars by the Brahmans, being engaged as agricultural laborers.

Kumbapeṭṭai's "own" Paḷḷars, the Dēvendra Paḷḷars, occupied four streets across paddy fields about a quarter of a mile south of the main village (see Map

4). Almost all of their seventy-five households were related, and it is likely that they had occupied their site longer than had any other caste. Tradition had it that the Paḷḷars were already located in their streets before the invasion of Haidar Āli in 1780, when the Brahmans occupied a street about half a mile east of them in what is now Kiḷiyūr Revenue Village. A strip of Kiḷiyūr paddy fields, together with a strip of Māniyūr fields, in fact lay between the Dēvendra Paḷḷar streets of Kumbapeṭṭai and the main village lands (see Map 3).

In 1952 the Dēvendra Paḷḷar streets were called the First and Second Sections (*Shēttis*) of Upper Street, followed in the east by Middle and Lower Streets. Strictly speaking, the first section of Upper Street fell in Māniyūr revenue village, while Lower Street fell in Kiḷiyūr. Because the four streets were closely related and had all been slaves of Kumbapeṭṭai's Brahmans in the past, they were thought of as belonging in Kumbapeṭṭai and shared its social, economic, and ceremonial life.

These four streets shared a small shrine dedicated to the goddess Kāliyamman, believed to be a slave of Uriḍeichiyamman, goddess of the central village temple. This shrine lay west of the first section of Upper Street. Legally, it too lay in Māniyūr, but it was socially entirely in Kumbapeṭṭai.

The two sections of Upper Street had their own cremation grounds south of their streets; Middle and Lower streets, theirs, respectively to the north and south of their residential sites. The Paḷḷar streets shared a small bathing pool near their site, and a large one, Neṭṭi Kuṭṭai, to the east near the border of Kiḷiyūr.

In the southeast of the village, across paddy fields, lay Neḍum Paḷḷar Teru, or Long Paḷḷar Street, belonging to the Tekkaṭṭi or Southern Paḷḷars, who were of a separate, lower subcaste than the Dēvendra Paḷḷars. Tradition had it that the dominant Brahman lineage had brought them there some ninety years previously.

The Tekkaṭṭi Paḷḷars' twelve households, all related, were still rather segregated from the rest of the village. They were in some respects discriminated against as foreigners and were marginal to village life. Unlike the Dēvendra Paḷḷars, they had no caste shrine but only the lineage god of their dominant patrilineal group, housed behind one of their homes. Their role in the annual village temple festival was less ceremonialized than the Dēvendra Paḷḷars'. In recent years, however, they had begun to offer goats to Ūriḍeichiyamman on Thai Poojai Day, the day of the Non-Brahman festival, in an effort to ensure their health and safety and to merge in village life.

In village eyes, the Tekkaṭṭi Paḷḷars' low status was in part associated with the fact that they still buried their dead instead of burning them. The latter was the more favored, Brahman-influenced Thanjāvūr custom, and the former more characteristic of the less Brahmanical districts of Rāmanāthapuram and Madurai from which the Southern Paḷḷars came. The Southern Paḷḷars had their own small burial ground a little south of their residential site. When water was available they bathed and drew drinking water from the nearby irrigation channels, and in summer, from a well they dug in the paddy fields.

Kumbapeṭṭai's village organization required year-round watchmen who lived in shacks in the paddy fields. They checked the flow of the irrigation water, protected the crops from thieves, captured and impounded stray goats and cattle, guarded newly threshed straw and paddy on the threshing floors, and scared away birds. Watchmen were appointed by the Brahman landlords and were changed from time to time if they grew old or their work was unsatisfactory. In 1952, five of them lived in the five main blocks of paddy fields in Kumbapeṭṭai Grāmam (see Map 3), while Veḷiyūr and Sheṭṭiyūr had their separate watchmen.

Kumbapeṭṭai's dry lands were chiefly small gardens behind the houses, containing coconut trees, a vegetable plot, and sometimes a clump of bamboos or a teak, mango, or castor-oil tree. The Brahmans' gardens were larger and more varied than those of the Non-Brahmans, most of whom rented their sites from the Brahmans. The Paḷḷars had tiny sites, almost all of which belonged to the Brahmans in 1952. Twenty-seven Brahman, twenty-two Non-Brahman, and eighteen Paḷḷar households, kept cattle in 1952. Many Non-Brahmans kept goats, and some low ranking Non-Brahmans and Paḷḷars had poultry. A few other gardens with coconut, banyan, or palmyra trees lay at intervals on raised patches among the paddy fields. Coconut groves were found especially south of Vēṭṭāmbāḍi Street where the Nāyakkars owned or rented gardens from which they had tapped toddy before the Congress Government introduced prohibition in 1947. Sweet toddy was still tapped for legal sale and some fermented liquor was still made illicitly.

The wet paddy fields that beonged to Kumbapeṭṭai Grāmam proper fell into four blocks, or *kaṭṭalais* (Map 3): Taliyapath in the northeast of the village north of the Shōradayan ("rice") Channel; Shānavaṛi, south and east of the *agrahāram* between the Shānavaḷi and Periya ("Big") channels; Tekke Vaḷi (South Way) southeast of the Dēvenḍra Paḷḷar streets; and Kīla Vaḷi ("Lower Way") southeast of Tekke Vaḷi. Taliyapath and Shānavaḷi each had their separate watchmen. The whole block of fields southeast of the main village was divided into three (Map 3). The western portion, called "One Banyan Tree," had one watchman and threshing floor, and the eastern part, called "Two Banyan Trees," had another, while the Kiḷiyūr fields (largely owned by Kumbapeṭṭai landlords) had a third. "One Banyan Tree" had a single banyan growing on its threshing ground, whereas "Two Banyan Trees" had two. The quality of the land varied in the *kaṭṭalais* and they were differently assessed for revenue. Tekke Vaḷi and Kīla Vaḷi were the most low lying and fertile, followed by Taliyapath and Shānavaḷi. Although richly fertile, Kīla Vaḷi often flooded in October and November. About thirty acres of it were usually sown with only one long-season crop, harvested in February. The other fields in the village were normally sown with two crops a year. The fields in the four *kaṭṭalais* amounted to about 354 acres of wet paddy land, whereas the cultivated dry lands associated with them, including both dry fields and gardens, were fifty-six acres.

Three other large blocks of land had become associated with Kumbapeṭṭai in modern times. One was Veḷiyūr hamlet (117 acres, 100 of which were wet), which became joined to the village administratively in 1898. Most of it belonged to an absent Veḷḷāḷar family. The fields there were cultivated by Paḷḷars of Veḷiyūr who are not included in my census. The second block was Sheṭṭiyūr hamlet with eighty-four acres, seventy-nine of them wet. It lay east of Kumbapeṭṭai proper and was joined to the revenue village in 1898, although part of it had been counted inside the *grāmam* since at least 1828. In 1952 Sheṭṭiyūr lands were mainly cultivated by Veḷḷāḷars and Mūppaṉārs of Sheṭṭiyūr and by Paṟayar laborers from Kandipeṭṭai, none of whom are included in my census. Kumbapeṭṭai Brahmans owned some fields in Sheṭṭiyūr but had less attachment to them than to the main village site. The third block was composed of Akkāchāvady, Vēṭṭāmbaḍi, the east side of Barbers' Street, and the wet lands east of these streets that are included in Map 4. This area contained about thirty-six cultivated acres, twenty-four of them wet paddy fields. It belonged in fact to the revenue village of Nallūr, whose main residential site lay a mile away to the east.

The streets of Akkāchāvaḍy and Vēṭṭāmbāḍi had grown up in the past 100 years. They were less firmly integrated into the Kumbapeṭṭai Brahmans' establishment than were Aḍichēri, the west side of Barbers' Street, and the Paḷḷar Streets. Unlike the castes in those streets, their members were never *aḍimai āḷukal* (slaves) of the Brahmans. Nevertheless, these streets lay so close to Kumbapeṭṭai that their residents had become deeply involved in its socioreligious life. Their members were therefore included in my census. In 1952 the fields in this block belonged partly to households of these streets, partly to Kumbapeṭṭai Brahmans, partly to owners living in Nallūr proper, and partly to outsiders from Āriyūr.

In 1952 the name "Kumbapeṭṭai" therefore referred contextually to three different entities. One was the socioeconomic unit of everyday life, comprising the people I have described and enumerated in my census and the lands of Kumbapeṭṭai proper plus an adjacent section of Nallūr (Map 4). This was the most common usage, although everyone knew that Akkāchāvaḍy, Veṭṭāmbāḍi, and East Barbers' Street were "really" in Nallūr.

The second usage referred to the original Kumbapeṭṭai Grāmam founded in 1784 (Map 5). It excluded most of Sheṭṭiyūr, all of Veḷiyūr, and the newer streets of Akkāchāvaḍy, Vēṭṭāmbāḍi and east Barbers' Street. Strictly speaking, it was this area that in 1952 was considered to be protected by the village goddess and that was called Kumbapeṭṭai Grāmam. Its bounds were beaten at the start of the annual festival. No one living within them might leave the area or have sexual relations within it until the festival had ended. The newer, adjacent streets were invited to the festival "for companionship" and the idol was taken through them in procession, but their lands were, strictly speaking, outside the deity's blessing and her jurisdiction.

The third entity was the revenue village of Kumbapeṭṭai (Map 3), which was also the modern *panchāyat*. Since 1898 it had included Veḷiyūr and Sheṭṭiyūr, but it excluded the streets legally located in Nallūr village. In everyday life in 1952 this did not matter much. Sheṭṭiyūr and Veḷiyūr were too far away, and too independent, to feel the weight of the Brahmans' authority. On the other hand,

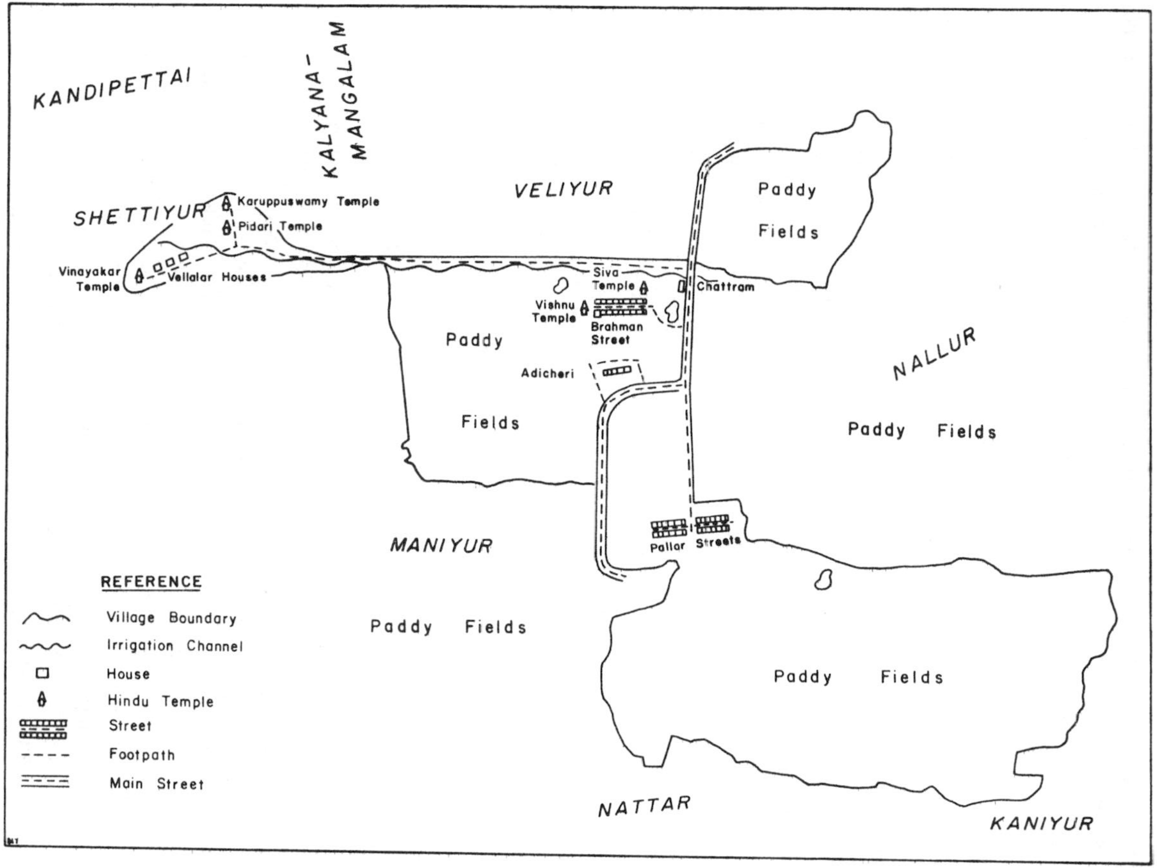


Map 5. Rough sketch of old Kumbapeṭṭai Grāmam, 1827.

Akkāchāvaḍy, Vēṭṭāmbāḍi, and Barbers' Street were too near, and too dependent on the Brahmans, to disobey them. Only their land revenue payments, registrations, and road repairs caused them to look to Nallūr as their other, less significant, village community.

I have mentioned the village temple goddess, Ūriḍeichiyamman, as being a *grāma dēvatai*. As is customary, her temple was located near a boundary of the *grāmam* proper, Vēṭṭāmbāḍi and the east side of Barbers' Street being in Nallūr Grāmam. Thanjāvūr had a number of popular *grāma dēvatais*, both male and female, who protected or threatened the villagers in various ways. Village goddesses were usually housed in covered shrines, whereas village gods usually sat in the open or in shrines that were open to the sky. In the west of the *grāmam*, bordering Sheṭṭiyūr, were boundary shrines to the male gods Ayyaṉār and Karuppayyan and the goddess Kāmakshiyamman. In the southwest, bordering Kiḷiyūr, a sacred spear stuck out of a dry patch of ground near a tree, representing the godling Miniyāṇḍavar. Further west, again bordering Nallūr, were two black stone idols on a patch of dry waste ground named Pachaikuṭṭy ("Green Child") Ayyaṉar and his wife Pachaiyammaṉ ("Green Mother"). On the northern boundary of the *grāmam*, bordering Veḷiyūr, was an image of the military god Madurai Veeran, riding a lion. Offerings were made to all these godlings by the village priest (Poosāri) to ward off such disasters as crop blight, flood, theft, cattle disease, epidemics, and mental illness.

These village deities, with their rich mythology and imagery and numerous ceremonies, must be treated in another context, that of village religion. Here it is enough to note that they controlled evils that had traditionally threatened the villagers as a community or as common mortals, from epidemics to crop failure and external invasion.

In 1952 Kumbapeṭṭai Grāmam proper had twenty-two threshing grounds. These were flat, open spaces of dry land amid the paddy fields with their floors stamped hard from beating and trampling the paddy, sometimes with a banyan tree for shade. In pre-British times all threshing floors were *grāma samudāyam*, or village common property, used by anyone to whom fields had temporarily been distributed nearby. In 1952 threshing grounds were of three types. Six were owned by the government as *purambōke*, or public land managed by the *panchāyat* board. Seven belonged each to a group of landowners, mostly from a single Brahman lineage. They were relics of village common lands, which had been distributed to separate lineages when shares began to be permanently parceled out in the mid-nineteenth century. Nine threshing grounds belonged to individual men who had built them on parts of dry land that they had bought for their own convenience. All the threshing of paddy crops, whether manually with sticks or by oxen, took place on the threshing floors, and paddy and straw were briefly stored there before being removed to separate landlords' homes. It was on the threshing floor that the threshed paddy was measured and their shares were given to the landlord, the village servants, the laborers who threshed the paddy, and the tenant cultivator, if any. Before British rule, the *mēlvāram* was separated from the *kīlvāram* on the threshing floor under the inspection of royal officers, and either sold locally by them at fixed prices or removed to storehouses of the king or of the local prebendary. Under the British, however, paddy came to be marketed privately and the revenue paid in cash.

Kumbapeṭṭai's main irrigation channels flowed from west to east. All main channels were branches of the Kuḍamuruṭṭi River, itself a branch of the Kāvēri. Each watered smaller streams that irrigated the paddy fields. The larger channels were classified as *purambōke* lands. They belonged to the government, and were repaired when necessary by the Department of Public Works. The smaller streams fell under the *panchāyat* board's jurisdiction. Formerly, they were managed jointly by the Brahman elders. In 1952 the annual digging out of the beds of these streams was still financed jointly by the elders under the leadership of the *panchāyat* president.

The fertile banks of the channels, privately owned, were often used to grow bananas. Cattle and goats grazed on the fresh grass or thistles on other banks. The fields themselves were divided by raised mud paths or bunds about one foot wide. In 1952 the paths formed the main pedestrian routes between the hamlets and villages, there being no roads into the paddy fields. During the dry summer months the channel beds were also used as footpaths and cart roads.

Kumbapeṭṭai's other *purambōke* lands were the sides of the main road. In the south of the village they were planted at intervals with coconut trees. The government revenue department auctioned the nuts once a year to the villagers.

In 1952 Kumbapeṭṭai had no government elementary school. Brahman children, both girls and boys, were tutored privately by a matriculate in his home in the *agrahāram* before attending the high school in Āriyūr. About a dozen Non-Brahman children from Kumbapeṭṭai and Sheṭṭiyūr attended the government elementary school in Māniyūr. About half a dozen Paḷḷar children went to a school in Nāṭṭār, and two Paḷḷar boys and one Non-Brahman boy attended the high school in Āriyūr. Most Brahman women under thirty were literate in Tamiḷ, but no Non-Brahman or Ādi Drāviḍa women, and no Ādi Drāviḍa men, could read or write. All of the Brahman men were literate; nine Brahman men and two Non-Brahmans spoke English, having passed or failed the secondary school leaving certificate in Āriyūr or Thanjāvūr.

The village had a post office, kept in the home of a Brahman small holder, toward the western end of the *agrahāram*. It had been there since 1901. Although used mainly by Brahmans, its location had disturbed intercaste relations. Non-Brahman tenants and laborers had long had the right to walk down the *agrahāram* and into the homes of their Brahman masters, but they were expected to appear with clothes only to their knees and were forbidden to wear shoes. Recently, a few Non-Brahman literates had begun to march up the street dressed in shirts and long lower cloths to post their mail. My elderly Brahman landlady complained bitterly that one of them, a high school student, had even dared to wear leather shoes.

In 1952, three buses a day plied each way through Kumbapeṭṭai between

Thanjāvūr and Kumbakōnam. The bus service first began in 1929 with one bus each way per day; the number increased in the 1940s. Buses were used mainly by Brahmans and Non-Brahmans, but even Ādi Drāviḍas had recently begun to ride them. For the most part, Brahmans still rode in covered passenger oxcarts between the villages. They were called *vil-vanḍies*, or "bow-carts," because of their bow-shaped roofs. Two Non-Brahman merchants owned freight carts with oxen to transport paddy to the mill in Āriyūr, but most Non-Brahmans and Ādi Drāviḍas walked. On holidays or festival nights, a round trip of sixteen or more miles to Thanjāvūr or other centers was considered a normal outing. Four Brahmans and two Non-Brahmans owned bicycles. Women, however, were not permitted to ride them on the grounds that this might damage their reproductive organs. I occasionally rebelled and rode into Āriyūr, to the Brahmans' evident dismay.

Kumbapeṭṭai's people regarded their village with a mixture of affection, reverence, and humor. In 1952 the village site was sacred. It was under the protection of the *grāma dēvatais*, who might strike the village with disease or disaster if one of them broke any of the thousand-and-one religious rules of the village or the caste. Myths and legends of ghosts or gods were associated with the trees and coconut groves, as well as the shrines, the castes, and the component patrilineages. The River Kāvēri and its irrigation channels were thought of as the villagers' mother. The muddy water in mid-July was her menstruation, the flood tide in early August her pregnancy, and the harvest her children. The earth itself was a goddess, while the god of good luck, Vināyakar, protected all agricultural undertakings.

Each of the three hundred-odd major paddy fields had a name, often derived from some deity. Examples were Bhūma Dēvi (Goddess of the Earth), Shakkarapāni, Ulahalangāḷ, or Tambi Nārāyanan (names of Lord Vishnū), Ummayāḷ and Thāmaṛaiyāḷ (names of Pārvati and Saraswathi), or descriptive terms such as Kāḍu Veṭṭi ("forest cutting"). Everyone in the village, including absent Muslim landlords, used these names to identify the fields, designating their modern subdivisions as "upper" or "lower," "west" or "east," or "north" or "south."

The Brahmans had humorous nicknames or tags for their villages by which they ticked off the supposed characteristics of their inhabitants. Kumbapeṭṭai was "eating and defecating Kumbapeṭṭai," because its people supposedly did little else. "Night-fasting Nallūr" suggested that Nallūr Brahmans were so excessively pious and niggardly that they never ate after sundown. "Karuppūr Justice" meant no justice at all; it referred to a village where the powerful were supposed to be notoriously unfair to the poor. "Tirupooṇḍuruṭṭi hospitality" referred to any house where guests remained unfed. It was said that if you visited Tirupooṇḍuruṭṭi at midday, your host would say, "What an unfriendly person you are! You have come here after taking food in such and such a village; you never eat with us" – and then you knew there would be no lunch. A "Mānguḍi Mundan" or "Mānguḍi Bully" was any quarrelsome fellow, for the people of Mānguḍi were believed to trade blows often. "Vanḍi-driving Varahūr," or "manure vaṇḍi Varahūr" described the Brahmans of Varahūr village, who were said to be so mean spirited that they saved money by driving their own manure carts to the paddy fields.

Like all of Thanjāvūr, Kumbapeṭṭai was very beautiful, and most, if not all of its people, appreciated its natural setting. For about six months of the year green paddy surrounding the village site waved softly in the breeze, and water gurgled gently through the canals and brooks. Coconut and palmyra trees formed majestic avenues against the sky. In the summer months of February to June, large herds of cattle were gathered to browse in the dry fields at eventide, their bells softly tinkling. Kids skipped about in the yards, and sheep, visiting from Rāmanāthapuram, moved sleepily in flocks, or baaed gently as they settled in the fields at night. The cool evenings from five to seven were especially memorable. Small gray squirrels dashed about excitedly in the groves. Blue jays, bright green and pink parakeets, and sparrows flitted to and fro. Large flocks of crows gathered for their nightly flight to outlying clumps of trees, and kites soared overhead. Spectacular, fiery sunsets lit up the sky, followed quickly by the dark. On full moon nights in summer, flat white moonlight flooded the village site.

Amid all this beauty the human scene was one of much poverty, exploitation, and suffering. In 1952 almost all the Brahmans themselves were poor. With their numbers increased, their fields divided and subdivided, and many fields sold to outsiders, most Brahmans felt pauperized by comparison with their forefathers. Most of the tenant farmers, artisans, and laborers reflected a much more grinding poverty, their bodies emaciated, their faces careworn, their clothing shabby and tattered. In the "dead" season of March to June when work was scarce, few tenant and laboring families ate more than once a day; some occasionally ate not at all. Carts were sometimes held up on the roadside by desperate men seeking grain or money, and night thefts of coconuts and paddy from the backyards of landlords and smallholders were common.

In the village at large illness and malnutrition were widespread. Two lepers, male and female, lived in the *agrahāram* with their families although their diseases were far advanced. Several villagers were diabetic. Many children showed the swollen bellies, sticklike limbs, and running sores of malnutrition. Babies died often of dysentery, and deaths in childbirth were not rare. In Thanjāvūr the civil surgeon told me about three-quarters of the patients in the government hospital were routinely found to have amoebic dysentery. By 1952 smallpox had been virtually eliminated through vaccination. Bites from snakes, rats, and rabid dogs, although dangerous, could usually be treated in time at the clinic at Āriyūr or the hospital in Thanjāvūr. Sudden severe illnesses from dysentery or viruses were, however, common, and in August 1952 an outbreak of cholera affected east Thanjāvūr and threatened the whole district. Hysterical outbursts among women, and occasional psychotic breaks in both sexes, were well-known illnesses.

To these hardships were added considerable cruelty on the part of some landlords to their tenants and laborers, of most men to their wives, and of some parents, to their children and daughters-in-law. In 1952 this was a strictly hierarchical, patriarchal society, with severe repression carried out indirectly through religious observances or directly through force and violence. Landlords frequently gave blows to their tenants and laborers. Only two Brahmans, and very few Non-Brahmans, did not beat their wives. Non-Brahmans and Ādi Drāviḍas often beat their children, although Brahmans seldom did so. In the district at large insane people were sometimes flogged mercilessly to drive out evil spirits. In Kumbapeṭṭai and nearby villages, several men had hanged themselves to avoid shame or poverty; several women had thrown themselves into wells to escape unhappy marriages. At least four times in the previous ten years, Brahman widows who bore illegitimate babies had thrown them into the Appū Iyer bathing pool.

Poverty necessarily imposed further cruelties. In the tenant and laboring groups old people were sometimes refused food or kept on short rations, to "encourage" them to die. When twins were born, it was expected or perhaps half consciously arranged that the weaker one would die of illness or malnutrition.

In this society it seemed that women bore the worst burdens of exploitation, ignominy, and cruelty. Ādi Drāviḍa women had greater freedom and equality with their menfolk than did women in the higher castes. They were sometimes beaten, but could give back blow for blow, and they were free to divorce a cruel husband. At the same time, they bore the triple burden of housework, childcare, and heavy agricultural labor. Non-Brahman women had less arduous agricultural tasks, but their lives combined hard work in their own and the landlords' homes with a high degree of patriarchal domination by their own husbands and by the landlords. Non-Brahman women were secluded in their homes between puberty and marriage, were not normally permitted to divorce or remarry in widowhood, and were often beaten by their husbands. At the same time, it was tacitly understood that they would submit to sexual advances by their landlords, or indeed, by any Brahman. Only two Non-Brahman women of childbearing age were said to be "moral," that is, to have evaded advances by the landlord or adultery with their neighbors.

Surprisingly, in view of their patriarchal morality, unmarried Brahman girls in 1952 were less cloistered than Non-Brahmans. In the previous twenty years child marriage, once obligatory, had virtually died out among them. Until their marriages, at fifteen to seventeen, girls were free to move about in the *agrahāram*. After marriage, however, a Brahman girl's life was usually hard. She was seldom allowed out of doors, had to work hard and obediently in the home, and was often ill treated by her husband and mother-in-law.

Amid such frequent misfortunes, the prevailing good humor and resilience of the villagers were little short of amazing. Confined in their numerous religious restrictions, and fearful of ritual pollution, or of rebellion from the lower orders, it seemed to me that most, although not all, of the Brahmans were more suspicious, more arrogant, and less outgoing than the lower castes. Most of them seemed more rigid in their personalities, although subtler and wittier, than the lower castes. Yet Brahmans, too, loved a joke or bizarre occurrence, showed exceptional hospitality to visitors, and were capable of deep emotions and attachment. More openly aggressive in their relations with one another, the Non-Brahmans and Ādi Drāviḍas tended toward greater directness, with occasional hot-tempered quarrels, great warmth, and a love of slapstick humor. In all the castes, kindness and fortitude were perhaps the highest virtues. ''He is a good man'' or ''She is a good woman,'' meant that one had these qualities. This was high praise, accorded regardless of rank.

# 9 Kumbapeṭṭai before 1855

In writing of the village's appearance and spatial relations, I have referred at times to the past. In this and the following chapter I discuss more systematically what is known or believed about the socioeconomic history of Kumbapeṭṭai. My sources are oral traditions and family documents of the Brahmans, and the government land records of 1827, 1897, and 1951. I have divided the two chapters at 1855, when the royal family was deposed by the British, because this was seen as a significant event by the villagers. As we saw in Chapter 6, the late 1850s and early 1860s were also in several other ways a significant watershed in Thanjāvūr's history.

## The Founding of the Village

As I have mentioned, Kumbapeṭṭai's Brahman ancestors once lived in an *agrahāram* in Kiḷiyūr, where they were served by the Dēvendra Paḷḷar slaves who lived on their present site. The Brahmans were (and are) Smārtha or Saivite Tamiḷ Brahmans of the Maṛainad subdivision of the Brahacharaṇam subcaste. They intermarried with other Maṛainad Brahacharaṇams who lived in eighteen villages in northwest Thanjāvūr and a small neighboring region in Tiruchirappalli district.

During the invasion of Thanjāvūr by Haidar Āli and his French allies in 1780–2, the *agrahāram* in Kiḷiyūr was believed to have been destroyed by Muslim armies and the surrounding fields laid waste. A large stretch of wasteland with a few ruined brick structures remained on this site half a mile east of the Paḷḷar streets in 1952. After the reconquest by the Thanjāvūr Mahārāja and the British East India Company in late 1782 the Brahmans moved to their present site in Kumbapeṭṭai with royal permission. The Brahmans believe that this site was then forest and pastureland, and that their slaves cleared it and irrigated the fields. They believe that all the present *agrahāram* houses except four were built in the 1780s, some of them being later subdivided. The other four houses were supposedly built about the 1860s. Soon after settling in Kumbapeṭṭai, the Brahmans built the Siva and Vishnū temples at either end of their street.

The lands then granted to the Brahmans comprised the area (about 485 acres, including the Paḷḷar streets) that they now regard as the *grāmam* proper. Vēṭṭāmbaḍi and the east side of Ambaṭṭān Teru, or Barbers' Street, were then unoccupied waste and, together with the paddy lands east of them, belonged to the Brahman *grāmam* of Nallūr, a mile to the east.

The area of Akkāchāvady, the *chattram*, and Kīla Kuṭṭai tank, together with Veḷiyūr hamlet, formed part of the estate of the Maratha Mahārāja of Thanjāvūr, as I have noted. It had been granted to retainers of the royal house in the early eighteenth century. In the early nineteenth century part of the *mēlvāram* and the *kīlvāram* of Veḷiyūr's lands belonged as *iṉam* to goldsmiths of Periyūr who served the royal house. Veḷiyūr itself was occupied by one street each of Paḷḷar and Paṟayar laborers. Before Haidar Āli's invasion there had been a temple dedicated to Ābimukthīswara (Siva) and, tradition had it, a few Brahman houses. During the invasion the temple was destroyed and the Brahmans evidently decamped. The idol, however, was hidden in a hut. About a hundred years later, the Veḷḷāḷar purchasers of Veḷiyūr built a new temple and placed the idol in its shrine (see Map 3).

Kumbapeṭṭai's *chattram* was built before the Brahmans moved to their present site, probably in the early eighteenth century. It had been held at one time by a famous Maratha Brahman, Donai Rao, an emissary of the king. Early in the nineteenth century, it is believed to have been occupied by a Non-Brahman Maratha woman, one of sixty-four concubines of the then Mahārāja, perhaps Sarfōji II. In 1952 the villagers thought that from the earliest years of Kumbapeṭṭai, the *chattram* fell in Kumbapeṭṭai *grāmam* while Veḷiyūr was a separate hamlet and Akkāchāvaḍy fell in Nallūr. Akkāchāvaḍy ("Elder Sister's Street") was named after an elder sister and attendant of the Maratha concubine, who lived there with various servants and tradespeople attached to the *chattram*. The two Maratha households living in Akkāchāvaḍy in 1952 were descended from this "elder sister."

Early in the nineteenth century, the *chattram* was reputed to have been a wealthy, flourishing guest house holding up to 500 visitors. To obtain religious merit, the Maratha occupants often served meals and made other gifts to Brahmans from the Kumbapeṭṭai *agrahāram* and from Kandipeṭṭai, the village to the northeast. After the concubine's death, the *chattram* remained occupied by her Maratha family for three generations. They continued to supply food to seven or eight Brahmans on auspicious days twice a month. This religious charity, and royal patronage of the Brahmans, seems to have come to an end soon after the British government deposed the royal family when its male heirs died out in 1855. Until 1906, however, the Maratha occupants collected rents on behalf of the royal descendants from their nearby estates.

The Brahmans of Nallūr and Kumbapeṭṭai still mourn the passing of the Mahārājas, who favored them as the former state class. They deeply resent the British government's having deposed the royal family and reduced the Brahmans to the status of ordinary colonial citizens. Unhappily, most local Brahmans regard the postcolonial governments of India and Tamiḻ Nāḍu as still worse. In 1976 a Brahman of Nallūr complained to me of preventive arrests and repression carried out under the Emergency of Prime Minister Indira Gandhi. I asked him what kind of government he would like to see. "To tell the truth," he replied, "things have never been right since Sarfōji."

### The Village Officers

By 1800, the Brahmans had established in Kumbapeṭṭai a *mirāsi* village of the *karaiyiḍu* type, in which the lands were held communally by the Brahmans and were redistributed among them every five years. The details of redistribution are unclear. The Brahmans believed, however, that they had five main lineages (*kooṭṭams*) in the early decades of the village's history, one of which had died out by 1952 except for a single widow. Each lineage had a headman whom the lineage's households annually selected or confirmed. The five headmen, called *panchāyattār* or *grāmapravartikkār*, divided the village land among the lineages every five years. Each lineage in turn distributed fields to its several households. Members of the same lineage were, and still are, called *pangālis* or shareholders, from *pangu*-share.

From an early date, however, perhaps even from the founding of Kumbapeṭṭai, the Brahman householders' shares were unequal and amounted to a form of private property, even though they could not lay permanent claim to particular fields. This inequality in land shares appeared to have come about as a result of trade in crops, and perhaps of individual employment, which allowed some households to buy larger shares of land. It must also have been the case that once privately owned shares had become established, they were inherited patrilineally. Given unequal family sizes, this would quickly lead to unequal shares. The present-day Brahmans do not know when their ancestors began to own unequal shares. They think that it was sometime in the Maratha period. As late as 1799, however, there were still some villages where there were no shares, and where all the land was held jointly and equally by the *mirāsi* community.

The *panchāyattars* were jointly responsible for paying the land revenue (*mēlvāram*, now called *kist*) to the Maratha government and the British East India Company. In the early years from 1784 to 1800, the local *pattakdār* or revenue farmer from Kaḷḷūr and his officers visited the village at harvest time and supervised the separation of the government's grain share on the village's threshing floors. The government share, amounting to about 50 to 60 percent, was then either removed in carts or sold locally at fixed prices and a money revenue obtained.

The *panchāyattārs* were responsible for maintaining order and settling all civil disputes in the village, and for reporting murders or suicides to government officials. They appointed their own *kaṇakku piḷḷai*, or Brahman recordkeeper, within the village. The *panchāyattārs* had the fields measured with a twelve-foot pole and the recordkeeper recorded the land shares and supervised the boundaries. The *panchāyattārs* also appointed a *nīrānyakkāran* to regulate the irrigation water in each block of fields, four Paḷḷar watchmen (*kāvalkkārars*) to guard the fields, a Non-Brahman *talayāri*, or policeman, to arrest criminals, and two Paṟayar *veṭṭiyars* from Māniyūr. All of these servants, like the village barber, washerman, potter, carpenter, and village temple priest, were paid twice annually in grain shares from the village threshing floors. In those days no government officer lived within the village.

The *veṭṭiyars* had the task of guarding cremation grounds, providing cow dung and coconut husks for cremation, and removing dead cattle after the Brahman's own, Non-Brahman cowherds had taken them from the Brahman cowshed to the yard behind the house. The *veṭṭiyars* also beat a *taṇḍōra*, or skin drum, to inform villagers to assemble when the revenue officers were arriving to collect the revenue, a new law had been passed that affected the village, or high officials were visiting the village in order to hear any grievances of the villagers. The *veṭṭiyars'* duties, finally, included beating a larger drum called *tampaṭṭam* for Non-Brahman funerals, and warning villagers not to release cattle into the fields during the growing and harvesting seasons.

Government-appointed headmen were first instituted by the British in Thanjāvūr in 1816 with police and judicial functions, and in 1836 they were ordered to collect the revenue. Given the existence of the village commune, the institution of a single, externally appointed headman appears to have been resisted by villagers. Kumbapeṭṭai's Brahmans did not know that it had even existed before the royal line died out in 1855. In 1865, however, individual *mirāsdārs* were given documents recording their shares in the village land and were made solely responsible in law for the payment of revenue via the village headman. The village headman's or *munsīff's* office then became a powerful post, and has been a subject of competition among the Brahman lineages and village factions ever since.

With the institution of the village headman came a government-appointed village accountant (*karṇam*), policeman (*talayāri*), and two peons or servants (*veṭṭis*),[1] all of whom still exist today. The *karṇam* maintains the village land records for government inspection.

The government-appointed *veṭṭis* are servants who assist the *karṇam* in surveying the fields, and in March to June help the village headman collect the revenue in cash from landowners. The government-appointed *veṭṭis* are no longer scavengers, may be either Non-Brahmans or Harijans, and are distinct from the Parayar *veṭṭiyars* who still attend at funerals and dispose of dead animals. "Government *veṭṭis*'" duties include reporting to the *karṇam* anyone who cuts a tree illegally or drains irrigation water into or out of his field at a time when he is not permitted. A government *veṭṭi* must also beat a *taṇḍōra* to summon villagers to any auction sale. When, however, the government *veṭṭi* is a Non-Brahman, he summons the old-style Paṟayar *veṭṭiyaṉ* to carry out this task.

Since the establishment of the often inherited position, the village headman has been selected by the district collector from a leading, indigenous Brahman family. The *karṇam*, who undergoes special training, is usually brought by the government from another village. In Kumbapeṭṭai he has always been a Brahman, and in 1952 was an Ayyangār who had come to live in the village in the 1940s. In 1952 the *talayāri* was an Agambaḍiyar of Māniyūr village to the south. The two *veṭṭis* were an Agambaḍiyar of Aḍichēri and a Maratha descendent of the "elder sister," who lived on the *chattram* site. This indigenous Maratha family had supplied the village's *veṭṭis* since at least the mid-1800s. In 1952, the village headman received a small government salary of Rs. 20 per month; the *karṇam* Rs. 23, and the three minor servants, Rs. 18. The village headman, however, had powers far beyond his income, and his post was much sought after.

### The Revenue

In return for their maintenance and their rights of land management, the Brahmans paid about 50 to 60 percent of the value of the village's grain, and a smaller proportion of its dry crops and tree crops, twice annually after each harvest as revenue to the government. Under the Mahārājas, the Brahmans' work was to administer their lands and the lower castes, perform religious rites in their homes, conduct agricultural and temple festivals, and periodically perform public sacrifices of goats, called *yāgams,* on behalf of the kingdom at large. As religious specialists, they regarded intimate participation in worldly affairs as harmful to their spiritual welfare. Although they supervised, they did no cultivation, and their religious rules forbade them to touch the plough.

### The Temple Lands

From very early days, paddy fields were set aside for the upkeep of the two Brahman temples dedicated to Siva and to Vishnū. A Brahman trustee appointed by the Brahman villagers managed these lands, which in 1952 amounted to about thirty acres. Their produce was used to pay a biennial stipend to the two temple priests. One household of the Brahman subcaste of Kurukkals, resident in the *agrahāram* and believed originally to have come with the other Brahmans from Kiḷiyūr, served the Siva temple and those of Veḷiyūr and Sheṭṭiyūr by hereditary right. Kumbapeṭṭai's Kurukkals also made the offerings in a Vināyakar temple in Sheṭṭiyur whose existence was already recorded in 1828, and in the Vināyakar shrine northwest of the Kumbapeṭṭai *agrahāram*, built in the 1890s. The village Kurukkal took charge of the annual festivals in the multicaste village temples of Uriḍeichiyamman in Kumbapeṭṭai and Kāmakshiyamman in Veḷiyūr, although a Non-Brahman priest performed the sacrifices and officiated normally. One household of the Brahman Bhaṭṭāchār subcaste, resident in Nallūr, served the Vishnū temple and those of several neighboring villages.

### The Other Early Settlers

The Brahmans believe that they brought with them from Kiḷiyūr, or attracted to Kumbapeṭṭai soon after, representatives of six other castes: Kōṉārs, Poosāris, Kusavars, Thacchars, Ambaṭṭārs, and Paḷḷars. As supposed indigenes, these castes are printed in italics in Table 8.1

The Kōṉār, or Iḍaiyar, are independent sheep and cattle herders in the upland areas of southeast Thanjāvūr, Pudukkoṭṭai, Rāmanāthapuram, and Madurai, where grazing grounds are extensive. In the Thanjāvūr delta, where grazing is confined to canal banks, small patches of dry land, and the stubble of paddy fields, Kōṉārs entered serflike relations with landlords of higher caste.

The Kumbapeṭṭai Kōṉārs' origins are uncertain except that they came at some period from Pudukkoṭṭai, where they still have relatives. The chief village goddess, Ūriḍeichiyamman, or "Iḍaiyar Mother of the Village," is especially associated with the Kōṉārs. Legend has it that an unmarried girl, age thirteen, of the Non-Brahman Oṭṭar, or Roadmakers' caste, died of smallpox in Kumbapeṭṭai while the main road was being built or repaired. Her spirit revealed itself to a leading Kōṉār one day as he was cracking a coconut against a stone. He noticed that the stone had the face of a goddess, and summoned leading Brahmans, to whom a voice spoke from the stone, asking them to build a temple to Ūriḍeichiyamman. They did so, and she became the village goddess of all the castes. In 1952 it was believed that although not herself the goddess of smallpox, Ūriḍeichiyamman had the power to keep Māriyamman, the smallpox goddess, outside the village, or to summon her if she was angry with the villagers. The date of the village temple is unclear; all we can say with certainty is that it was built after 1827, for it is not mentioned in the land records of that date.

Whatever their origins, four Kōṉār brothers, or patrilineal kinsmen, great-grandfathers of the elders of 1952, were settled at an early date in Aḍichēri as *aḍimai* (serfs or slaves) of the Brahmans. By 1952 the Kōṉārs had expanded to twenty households, comprising four small patrilineal groups with six unrelated households, some of whom had come more recently from Pudukkoṭṭai. Each of the Brahman lineages is said to have controlled one or more Kōṉār households and distributed their services among the households of the lineage. In the early nineteenth century the right of service of a Brahman lineage was normally inherited patrilineally; in 1952 some Kōṉārs still knew to which lineage their ancestors belonged. A slave might be transferred from one lineage to another if rearrangement of numbers became desirable. The Brahmans believed, however, that at a still earlier period *aḍimai*, like land and cattle, belonged to the Brahman community jointly and were redistributed to the Brahman lineages and households every five years along with the land.

Kōṉār men did garden work; milked, washed, and tended the Brahmans' cattle; drove their oxcarts; and helped to supervise their Paḷḷar slaves. Some cattle were kept in the Brahmans' own cowsheds. Others were farmed out to "their" Kōṉārs by the Brahmans and tended in the Kōṉārs' cowsheds. The Kōṉārs appear to have had the right to use the milk and labor of these cattle for their own purposes, but they were obliged to bring milk, curds, or buttermilk to the Brahman house whenever these were requested. Kōṉār women did light agricultural work; their children grazed and sometimes washed their masters' cattle. Each Kōṉār family received palm fronds; mud and wood for house building; the use of a garden in Aḍichēri; the right to fish in the irrigation channels; new clothing once a year; and gifts, including cash and clothing, at births, deaths, marriages, funerals, and festivals. Men were paid a fixed quantity of paddy each month by their masters; women and boys received separate smaller amounts. Like the other Non-Brahmans, the Kōṉārs also kept goats.

The garden land in Aḍichēri, like that of the *agrahāram*, was *nattam*, or common residential land, set aside tax free by the native and British governments. It remained so in 1952, as did the Dēvendra Paḷḷars' residential sites. By village custom the residents had the use of the land for vegetables, stock, fruit, and nut trees, but the Brahmans managed it and could summon their servants to bring them produce when they desired it.

In 1952 the Brahmans thought that in the early decades of their village there had been no *kuthakai*, or fixed-rent tenants, on their paddy lands, and that this custom had grown up in Kumbapeṭṭai in the late nineteenth century when land became private property and many Brahmans left the villages for urban work. They thought that from early times, however, a Kōṉār or group of Kōṉārs might occasionally be allotted certain paddy fields on *vāram*, usually receiving one-fifth of the harvest. Sometimes the land was leased only for the black and green gram season in March and April between the two paddy harvests. Sometimes only the second paddy threshing process, which consists of trampling by bullocks (*pōraḍi*), was farmed out in this way. The details are unclear, but it seems certain that from early times Kōṉār men occasionally ploughed the paddy fields, sometimes grew black and green gram, sometimes assisted with the paddy harvest and the first threshing by beating with sticks, and sometimes managed the second threshing by using bullocks to trample the grain. Kōṉārs were, however, always concerned mainly with garden and dairy work, and Paḷḷars with paddy cultivation.

The Dēvendra Paḷḷars, whose ancestors had served the Brahmans in Kiḷiyūr, were *aḍimai ālukal* in a stricter sense than the Kōṉārs. The Kōṉārs appear to have accepted serfdom from choice as an assurance of livelihood. Some of their relatives in other areas were independent herders, and if a suitable opportunity arose they appear to have been free to leave Kumbapeṭṭai for work elsewhere.

Paṟayars and Paḷḷars, however, were by law everywhere the slaves or *aḍimai aḷukaḷ* of *mirāsdārs* in a relationship that seems best designated as slavery. Until 1843 a truant Paḷḷar could be returned to his master by the police. Except by arrangement between two landlord communities, he could not change the village of his residence. In Kumbapeṭṭai as elsewhere, Paḷḷars and Paṟayars were and are regarded as Panchamas ("fifth caste") people, that is, exterior castes who were highly polluting and must live in separate hamlets outside the village settlement.

In the early decades of the village, the Paḷḷars were attached to the Brahman community collectively. Along with the land and cattle, they were redistributed to Brahman lineages and households every five years. As the sense of private property increased, however, some Paḷḷar families evidently became more permanently attached to particular Brahman lineages and households and were inherited in the male line. Such families were called *kaṭṭu aḍimai āḷukaḷ* ("tied" slaves) and worked for other masters only when their owners gave permission. The *kaṭṭu aḍimai āḷ* became bound to a particular master through acceptance of a loan, and could be sold by him to another owner.

The Paḷḷars had the right to smaller house sites than the Kōṉārs, to building materials from the village's wasteland to build tiny shacks, and to similar gifts at life-crisis rites and festivals. They were paid daily in grain when they were working and were given a portion, usually one-thirteenth, of the paddy they harvested and threshed. A small amount of wet paddy land, called *paṭṭakkāl*, amounting to about fifty *kuṛis*, or one-sixth of an acre per family, was set aside for use by each Paḷḷar family. Altogether, the Paḷḷars' total annual pay was less than the Kōṉārs', and their work more arduous, for between them the Paḷḷar men, women, and children did almost the whole work of paddy cultivation. Paḷḷars, like Paṟayars in those villages where they were found, were summoned to drag the heavy chariots (*thērs*) of the gods in temple festivals of the village or of nearby larger temples during the summer season of March to June. They were also required to dig out the irrigation channels once a year in the same dry season. Their own *mirāsdārs* organized them to dig the smaller village channels. As in Maratha times, the colonial government corvéed the Panchama slaves from villages to build roads and carry out repairs to major irrigation works, a form of labor known as *kuḍimarāmatt*.

From the founding of Kumbapeṭṭai, four groups of village servants (*grāma tōṟiḷāḷikaḷ*) served the village at large. They were the Barbers, or Ambaṭṭārs; Carpenters, or Thacchars; Potters, or Kusavars; and the Village Temple Priests. The Village Temple Priests came from the Āndi caste but were usually referred to as the Poosāri *jāti* (those who perform *poosai* or offerings to the deity). For most of the nineteenth century each of these castes seems to have been represented by a single household. These families lived on tax free village house sites (*nattam*) owned jointly by the Brahmans on the west side of Barbers' Street; in addition, they had between them the use of one *māh*, or one-third of an acre of wet paddy land in Kīla Vaḷi. In 1952 only one village priest's house remained on Barbers' Street, but the street was still named after the Barbers who were its earliest occupants.

The Āndis, or Village Temple Priests, were mainly engaged in serving the village temple, which had been built by the Brahmans. In the land records of 1828, no shrine to Ūriḍeichiyamman is mentioned. Instead, it is recorded that there were shrines dedicated to a village goddess, Piḍāri, and to two village godlings, Karuppuswāmy and Ayyanār. In 1952, Karuppuswāmy and Ayyanār were still worshipped in shrines just west of the border of Kumbapeṭṭai and Sheṭṭiyur. It is possible that Piḍāri, commonly regarded as the goddess of epidemics, was an earlier version of Kāmakshiyamman, who has a shrine near the border of Kumbapeṭṭai and Sheṭṭiyūr and is considered to be the consort of Karuppuswāmy. The Āndis believe that they propitiated all these village deities from the earliest years of the village. They offered palm wine to Karuppuswāmy and sacrificed goats to the village goddess and to Ayyanār. In addition, they had traditionally tended a flower garden near their home, belonging to the *agrahāram*, and made garlands and decorated palanquins and cars for the Brahman temple deities. In 1952, the Āndis of Kumbapeṭṭai comprised one patrilineal group distributed in three households, together with a recently arrived, unrelated house of refugees from the drought in Rāmanāthapuram.

The Carpenters, or Thacchars, made wooden ploughs, oxcarts, massive paddy storage chests for the landlords, small boxes to hold betel leaves and arecanuts for chewing, various other wooden utensils, and doors, pillars, and window frames for the Brahmans' houses. They also made rope beds, benches, tables, and stools. Although they did some jobs for all the castes, their work was chiefly for Brahmans, for in the early decades only Brahmans owned ploughs, oxcarts, and furniture, and only Brahman houses had pillars, staircases, and window frames.

The Kusavars were mainly employed in making unglazed household pots on a simple wheel. From time immemorial, they had made pots for all the castes, including Ādi Drāviḍas, in the villages of both Nallūr and Kumbapeṭṭai. In addition to kitchenware, the potters made large vessels (*kūjas*) for carrying water, containers to store palm wine and arack, and earthenware drums (*kuḍirs*) about six feet high to store paddy in the houses of all the castes. They made lime from seashells and used it to whitewash temples and houses, and in the nineteenth century they learned to work with cement. In 1952, the potters comprised one patrilineal group in two households together with one house of affines.

Perhaps because they frequently made pots for the Ādi Drāviḍas and had more contact with them than most of the Non-Brahman castes, the potters traditionally provided priests for Kāḷiyamman, the street goddess of the Paḷḷars. It was not known when this deity was installed, but it was certainly far back into the nineteenth century. In 1952, a priest drawn from the Potter caste propitiated Kāḷiyamman each evening with burning camphor, sacred water, and flowers, and sacrificed goats to her on behalf of the Paḷḷars at the Pongal Festival in January and after the main village festival in May. Kāḷiyamman was especially believed to bring cholera to the village. She did so with the consent of Ūriḍeichiyamman when that goddess was angry with the villagers. When cholera struck, it was said that "Kāḷi was playing."

In 1952 the Potter priest also propitiated a small idol of Ayyaṉār, known as Shātayappa Ayyaṉār, on the southeast boundary of the village, which belonged exclusively to the Paḷḷars. It is not known whether this idol existed in the nineteenth century, but it appeared, and was said to be, very ancient.

Men of the Barber caste were required to shave the body hair and part of the front of the head hair of Brahman and Non-Brahman men, twice a month. Brahmans had the fronts of their heads shaved in a half moon shape; Non-Brahmans, in a square. Ambaṭṭars manicured the fingernails of Brahman men, and shaved the heads of Brahman widows. Barber men were also village doctors. They knew herbal remedies for illnesses, set broken bones, did simple surgery, applied leeches for blood letting in case of fever, and extracted teeth. When a death occurred in a Brahman or a Non-Brahman house, the Barber came to shave the heads of the chief male mourners – the eldest son among Brahmans and all the sons among Non-Brahmans. The Barber helped the washerman to make a bier to carry the corpse to the cremation ground; among the Non-Brahmans this was a palanquin decorated with flowers. The Barber also carried a lit lamp before the mourners when they went to the cremation ground on the *sanchayaṉam*, the third day after the death, and instructed the mourners how to collect the bones and ashes in a mud pot, perform an offering to them, and dispose of them in a sacred river or beneath a sacred tree. Ambaṭṭār women served as midwives for all the castes above Ādi Drāviḍas. In 1952, the Barbers comprised a single small patrilineal group divided between two households, both of whom lived in Aḍichēri.

As their main source of livelihood, the servant groups received shares from the total grain harvest of the village in February–March and September–October. These shares are described in Chapter 12.

**Specialists from Outside the Village**

Throughout the nineteenth century, Kumbapeṭṭai drew upon the services of Laundryworkers, Blacksmiths, Goldsmiths, and Paṟayar scavengers *(veṭṭiyars)* from Māniyūr, the village to the south. These families received twice-annual grain payments on the threshing floors in much the same way as the local Barbers, Poosāris, Carpenters, Potters, and Paḷḷar watchmen.

Washermen and women washed clothing for Brahmans and Non-Brahmans for occasions such as marriage, and also the especially polluted cloths used during menstruation, death, and childbirth. The Washerman provided lamps for temple festivals, decorated marriage booths, helped the Barber make funeral biers, and strewed cloths before funeral processions. He carried rice in a cloth to the cremation ground so that some of it could be placed in the mouth of the corpse as a last offering before the burning, and a mud pot of water, which the chief mourner broke against the funeral pyre.

In 1952, the Paḷḷars of Kumbapeṭṭai and the Paṟayars of Māniyūr each had two small, lower-ranking subcastes of their own castes serving as Barbers and Laundrymen. Those of the Paḷḷars came from Nāṭṭār, a mile away. Barbers cut the hair of Paḷḷar men; Barber women were midwives. Laundryworkers washed the clothes of people in birth or death pollution. Clearly, these groups were created because the Non-Brahman village Barbers and Washermen traditionally refused to handle the personal refuse of Ādi Drāviḍas. I was, however, unable to discover how long the Ādi Drāviḍas had had their own servant castes.

Goldsmiths, or Pattars, made the heavy gold necklace, earrings, nose studs, and bangles worn by women of the Brahman and Non-Brahman *mirāsdārs* and trading classes; the much more modest pieces of jewelry worn by the lower-ranking Non-Brahmans; and the silver anklets, toe rings, and waist bands worn by children in those houses that could afford them. The metal was provided by the local patrons and was sometimes remelted to provide new jewelry in each generation. Blacksmiths, or Kol-Thacchars, made plough points, iron vessels, door bolts and hinges, bullock shoes, cart axles, chains for household swings, and iron tips for ox whips. Goldsmiths, Blacksmiths, Carpenters, Stonemasons, and Braziers formed a single endogamous caste called Kammāḷar. Kumbapeṭṭai's Carpenters traditionally married with Māniyūr's Blacksmiths, and in 1949, a Kol-Thacchar brother-in-law of the current Carpenter finally moved to Kumbapeṭṭai and took charge of the village's blacksmithing. Similarly, in 1941, the patronage of Māniyūr and Kumbapeṭṭai was divided between two branches of the Māniyūr Vaṇṇārs' patrilineage, one household of which moved to Kumbapeṭṭai as the village's Launderers.

From far back into the nineteenth century, two other specialist castes served Kumbapeṭṭai by hereditary right. I have already mentioned the Paṟayars of Māniyūr, two of whose families were and still are Kumbapeṭṭai's scavengers, funeral drummers, and tenders of cremation grounds. The other specialist caste was the Non-Brahman Mēḷakkārs, whose men were musicians in Brahmanical and village temples. Some of the women were ceremonially married to the deities of famous temples. They were expert temple dancers, and incidentally became concubines or prostitutes for Brahmans and the higher Non-Brahman castes. A community of Mēḷakkārs lived in Āriyūr three miles from Kumbapeṭṭai. They comprised seven patrilineages of musicians and dancers, each group holding the right of service in three neighboring villages. Kumbapeṭṭai's group had long visited the village for Brahman marriages and temple festivals, and still did so in 1952. At festivals, the players were traditionally paid in grain from the Brahman temple lands; at marriages, in grain, fruits, coconuts, and other items supplied by the hosts.

## The Character of the Village Economy

I have so far described the traditional occupations of the castes in which they once had the legal right and obligation to engage when they were required. It seems clear, however, that even a stable village economy could not function entirely through hereditary occupational groups, and one would guess that Kumbapeṭṭai's economy has never been stable since the founding of the village. In particular, a given village could not guarantee to require the full-time services of all the specialists traditionally attached to it. Three main forms of flexibility seem to have existed. First, although village service rights were normally patrilineally inherited, considerable movement of specialists was arranged by the land managers of nearby, and sometimes quite distant, villages. Second, whole caste communities might migrate and change their occupations and production relations over time. The Kōṉārs arrival from Pudukkoṭṭai and their change from independent pastoralism to a serfdom based on mixed gardening and dairy work is an example. Third, agriculture seems always to have provided a secondary source of livelihood for the Non-Brahman specialist castes. Although *kuthakai* tenures were reported not to have existed in Kumbapeṭṭai until the late nineteenth century, they did exist to some extent elsewhere. Especially after the invasion of Haidar Āli and the partial depopulation of Thanjāvūr, there was a demand for migratory tenants, or *porakuḍis*, from other districts. In the district at large, many Agambaḍiyars, Kaḷḷars, Mūppaṉars, and Paḍaiyācchis who had formerly been soldiers became tenant farmers, and so did some weavers, braziers, and other artisans whose crafts declined with the deindustrialization brought about by colonial rule. In addition, ordinary Non-Brahman village specialists such as Barbers, Potters, and Washermen, who might be temporarily unemployed, seem always to have had the option of cultivating paddy lands on *vāram* tenure, while Paṟayars who lost their roles as village scavengers and funeral workers simply joined the rest of their caste as communally owned agricultural slaves.

The economic relations of the castes that I have so far mentioned had the following characteristics. Each caste community seems to have been relatively homogeneous in occupation and wealth, Brahmans being considerably wealthier than their Non-Brahman servants, and Non-Brahmans slightly better off than the Ādi Drāviḍa slaves. As late as the early nineteenth century, it appears that in this village the overwhelming majority of economic relationships were hereditary and caste determined. In spite of the large number of castes, economic specialization was relatively simple. Few specialists cooperated in the production of a single object; exceptions included the Brahman house, the plough, and the oxcart. It is significant that carpenters, stonemasons, and ironworkers, whose tasks were most often complementary, formed a single endogamous caste. Otherwise, specialization within the caste, except on the basis of sex and age, was almost unknown. A single household, and in some cases a single worker, could control each of such skills as cultivation, cattle tending, pottery making, laundry work, and barbering. When a group of workers was required, as in digging channels, transplanting paddy, harvesting, or threshing, they did identical or similar tasks.

Within Kumbapeṭṭai itself in this period, there was apparently less scope for middlemen traders and for the market than in later decades. Almost all economic relations among the village castes and among the villagers and the other specialists I have mentioned appear to have involved the provision of goods or services in direct exchange for paddy, the chief source of livelihood, and in some cases for other foodstuffs such as coconuts and bananas. Although there was some exchange among the lower castes, most goods and services were rendered upwards to the *mirāsdārs* in return for bare subsistence. The village economy was, in short, a matter of redistribution of necessities by the Brahmans to their servants, and of mobilization by the Brahmans of the total surplus. The *mirāsdārs* in turn gave a very high proportion of the surplus, indeed the value of half or more of the total produce, as revenue to the colonial state. They received back very little except some road building and some improvements in irrigation during the 1830s. The repressive and exploitative character of the state in this period is reflected in that the externally appointed village officers were solely engaged in revenue collection and policing the villages. The charities maintained by the Marathas for at least a portion of the people, such as the Kumbapeṭṭai *chattram*, were kept alive to some extent in the early nineteenth century, but tended to abate after the monarchy was abolished in 1855.

Another feature of this period was that apart from the Brahmans, the village's caste groups were apparently all or almost all in a state of bondage. The Kōṉārs came from Pudukkoṭṭai and perhaps could have returned there, but the price of living in Aḍichēri was *aḍimai*. The Kōṉārs and village servants' hereditary work was lighter, their pay somewhat larger, and their housing and clothing slightly better than the Paḷḷars' and Paṟayars', but like them they could be called to work at any time and could be flogged, fined, or in other ways treated harshly by the *mirāsdārs*. The members of all these castes owned no property that was not also their *mirāsdārs'*. Land, stock, and implements belonged to the village establishment and were merely loaned to its servants. The *mirāsdārs* could, moreover, at any time commandeer the produce of their servants for their own use.

The village servants, like the Paḷḷars, were clearly not free to move from village to village without the consent of both sets of landlords. It is true that the members of each caste, including the Panchamas, regarded their hereditary work as a right and a privilege. They referred to it, and to the area they served, as their *mirāsi*, as did the *mirāsdārs* or landlords with respect to their own status and the area they managed. Nevertheless, *aḍimai* was a condition of bondage and forced labor quite different from the rights of land management, village government, and religious pursuits of the Brahmans.

Because the Brahmans' livelihood depended on village lands, one might ask whether they were "free" to leave the village. It may be significant that the Brahman and Veḷḷāḷar land managers, traders, and others not in the state of *aḍimai were* free – to go on extensive pilgrimages to distant temples, or permanently to become wandering religious ascetics, or *sannyāsis*. It is true that in the latter case they gave up all claim to land, property, or family, and set forth with a begging bowl. Nevertheless, others of this society were obliged by religious sanctions to feed them, and they could be sure of hospitality at charitable resthouses such as the Kumbapeṭṭai *chattram*. Village servants and workers in *aḍimai* apparently did not have the right to become *sannyāsis*. Neither, significantly, did women of the upper castes. In some respects like the lower castes, they were in perpetual bondage to and dependent on their male guardians, at first the father and later the husband, his father, and his brothers.

### Trade

During the early nineteenth century the Brahmans carried on two forms of exchange with people from outside the village: barter and market trade. A number of itinerant castes visited the village occasionally to barter their wares or services. They included Basketmakers, Puppet players, and Acrobats, all of whom were paid in grain. Seasonally, Paḍaiyācchis would arrive from Tiruchirappalli and South Ārcot, north of the Coleroon, bringing cartloads of dhāl, ginger, tamarind, mustard seed, chillies, and other products, which they exchanged in Kumbapeṭṭai for paddy. From the dry tracts of south Thanjāvūr and Pudukkoṭṭai would come Kaḷḷars and others bringing dhāl, mangoes, and millets, which they, too, exchanged for paddy.

Beginning in 1804, the Brahmans were obliged to sell much of their produce for money in order to pay their land revenue in cash as the British demanded. It is not clear how they managed to sell one-half or more of their paddy in the first half of the nineteenth century, or where they sold it. It seems probable that for some years after 1804 government agents bought it as they had sometimes done in Maratha times, and transported part of it by sea to Madras and other parts of India where paddy was less readily available. The Brahmans do know, however, that from as far back as they have records or legends, until government rationing came in World War II, men of the *agrahāram* would load carts with paddy after the harvest and drive them south to Pudukkoṭṭai where they could sell the paddy in a market at up to twice the price it would fetch in Thanjāvūr. In Pudukkoṭṭai they would use part of the money they obtained to buy gingelly seeds, mangoes, dhāl, tamarind, millets, and marble tiles for houses. They would sell the tiles, and some of the produce, to wealthy people in Thanjāvūr town for twice what they had paid in Pudukkoṭṭai, keep the rest of the produce for their use, and use the profits they had made to pay their revenue. In the later nineteenth century some Brahmans became still more ambitious traders who borrowed from money lenders in Thanjāvūr, bought paddy in the *agrahāram* or other villages, sold it in Pudukkoṭṭai, and brought back quantities of merchandise to Thanjāvūr town. As we shall see, some Non-Brahmans also began this trade in the second half of the nineteenth century. It is not known how much of their crop the Brahmans sold in the early nineteenth century or whether they were already borrowing from money lenders to carry on their trade.

Young, able-bodied Brahmans also traded by oxcart westward for cash in villages all the way to Tiruchirappalli, some thirty-five miles to the west. They would go on one-week expeditions, living and trading with their relatives in the villages west of Kumbapeṭṭai. In Tiruchirappalli they ate steamed and fried rice powder cakes brought from home. They carried cooked rice mixed with tamarind, which stays fresh for a week. Although of a traditionally non-violent caste, these young Brahmans knew *kutchiveḷiyāṭṭam* (stick play) and carried heavy staffs and swords. At Shukkambāl near Kōviladi they were sometimes waylaid by Kaḷḷar highwaymen and forced to fight for their goods or even their lives.

From Kumbapeṭṭai the Brahmans carried paddy and a black root vegetable, *kaṛunaikirangu*, somewhat like a potato, grown on the fertile channel banks. They sold these in Brahman and Veḷḷāḷar streets, and brought back cash, jaggery made from sugar cane, a black, intoxicating, puddinglike substance made from vegetables called *rēka*, and sometimes, special potions made in Tiruchirappalli, which ''caused'' women to love the donor. In turn, Brahmans from Vishnampet, Varahūr, and western villages would arrive in December and January with four or five carts of jaggery, which they sold for money in Kumbapeṭṭai, Nallūr, and neighboring villages. Some Kumbapeṭṭai Brahmans used cash to buy jaggery for trade as well as household purposes, and sold it at a profit as far east as Naṉṉilam *tālūk*.

The Brahmans believed that in this period their ancestors bought few articles in stores. As late as 1900, Āriyūr had only three sizeable shops, selling dry goods, betel, arecanuts, and *sāris*. In the nineteenth century the Brahmans bought their own and their servants' clothing from itinerant Cheṭṭiyar traders, or in the case of silk *sāris*, directly from weavers of Āriyūr. Akkāchāvaḍy was reported to have contained a few shops selling dry goods, buttermilk, curds, and betel and arecanuts to the *chattram*.

**The Land Records**

The land records of 1828, compiled in 1827, provide a fascinating glimpse of Kumbapeṭṭai's early history, and confirm some of the Brahmans' beliefs about its past. Map 5 gives a rough sketch of Kumbapeṭṭai in 1827 as nearly as I can reconstruct it from the records.

The village at that date comprised 485.13 acres and covered roughly the area that the Brahmans recognize as their traditional *grāmam*. The village included fifteen acres of what is now Sheṭṭiyūr, but excluded Veḷiyūr. The main road already ran through Kumbapeṭṭai, and the Maratha *chattram*, called Vēngakkā *chattram*, was included in it. The village contained eight streets. Although it is not clear where they were located, they probably included the Brahman *agrahāram*, Aḍichēri, the west side of Barber Street, and the four Dēvendra Paḷḷar streets in the south of the village. The eighth street may have been near the chattram, where there appear to have been ten acres of dry *iṉam* land, probably belonging to Marathas. Alternatively, the eighth street may have comprised three Veḷḷāḷar houses in Sheṭṭiyūr. The most likely possibility seems to be that the eighth street was on the main road near the *chattram*, for it is recorded that the village contained six shops. Kumbapeṭṭai's people believe that there were no shops in the *grāmam* proper until the twentieth century, but that there were several in Akkāchāvady at an early date to serve the *chattram*. It is possible that some of them were across the road north of the *chattram*.

The population comprised thirty-three *mirāsdārs*' houses, fifty-two *aḍimai ālukaḷs*', and six "new houses." It is not clear whose the "new houses" were. At least three probably belonged to early Veḷḷāḷar peasant settlers in Sheṭṭiyūr, for the Brahmans believed that three Veḷḷāḷar households arrived in the 1820s, and the land records contain the names of two Veḷḷāḷar owners. The other new houses may have contained shopkeepers, or village servants living on Barber Street. The fifty-two *aḍimai aḷukaḷs*' were presumably those of the Dēvendra Paḷḷars of south Kumbapeṭṭai and perhaps (if they had already arrived) the Kōṉārs of Aḍichēri. The proportions are interesting because in 1952 the Brahmans, Kōṉārs, and Paḷḷars together formed 151 households, of which the Brahmans occupied forty-two, or 28 percent. In 1827 they comprised thirty-three out of eighty-five *mirāsdār* and *aḍimai* houses, or 39 percent. In 1827, moreover, the Brahman *mirāsdārs* were 36 percent of the total households in the village, whereas they were only 21 percent in 1952. It is possible, however, that the fifty-two *aḍimai* houses of 1827 were all Dēvendra Paḷḷars, and that the six "new houses" were either Kōṉārs or village servants. In this case, the Brahmans in 1827 formed 39 percent of the total Brahman and Dēvendra Paḷḷar households, whereas they formed 35 percent of them in 1952. This suggestion would fit the probable rate at which the Brahman and the Dēvendra Paḷḷar populations expanded over the 125 years, while allowing for the fact that after about 1890 a number of Brahmans emigrated to the city. The record suggests that in 1827 there was still a labor shortage left over from the depopulation of Haidar Āli's invasion. Later in the century, the Dēvendra Paḷḷars expanded, the Tekkaṭṭi Paḷḷars were brought in, and many new castes of workers and traders entered the village, some of them from other districts.

In 1827 the village contained six temples. The Brahman temples of Gōthandarāmaswāmy (Lord Vishnū) and Kailāsanātharswāmy (Lord Siva) were already there, as were the shrines of Ayyanār, Karuppuswāmy, and Vināyakar near the western boundary of the *grāmam* in Sheṭṭiyūr. As I have mentioned, Piḍāri, a common village goddess, may have been the predecessor of Kāmakshiyamman whose shrine is now situated on the boundary with Sheṭṭiyūr. The village had seven threshing floors and three tanks "fit for bathing."

The village land was divided as follows:

| | *Acres* |
|---|---|
| 37 irrigation and drainage channels | 15.02 |
| 1 road and 8 streets | 3.07 |
| 3 bathing pools | 4.19 |
| 8 paths | 0.13 |
| 7 threshing floors | 4.12 |
| 6 shop sites | 1.00 |
| 6 temple sites | 0.17 |
| 33 *mirāsdār* (landlord) house sites and yards | 5.06 |
| 52 *aḍimai* (slave) house sites and yards | 5.41 |
| 6 new house sites and yards | 0.11 |
| 1 Maratha *chattram* site and garden | 0.07 |
| Grant of *inam* land | 10.05 |
| Land set aside for use by *aḍimai ālukaḷ* (slaves): wet | 11.23 |
| Land set aside for use by *aḍimai ālukaḷ*: dry | 3.00 |
| Wasteland | 10.94 |
| Channel bank growing bananas | 0.29 |
| Dry land growing *ragi* (millet) | 13.10 |
| Dry waste, sometimes cultivated | 7.07 |
| *Purambōke* (government) land on road side | 12.03 |
| Wet lands | 379.07 |
| Total | 485.13 |

The village contained fifty-two ploughs, the same number as the *aḍimai* households, and so must have had a minimum of 104 oxen to draw them. It also contained 388 trees, probably coconut, palmyra, tamarind and mango, yielding nuts or fruits, and 283 "unyielding" trees.

It is noteworthy that wet paddy lands already comprised 86 percent of the total cultivable lands in 1827. Only 87.1 acres, however, or 22 percent of it, yielded two crops, for the irrigation improvements of the 1830s and 1930s had not occurred. In 1952, 87 percent of the cultivable area in the old *grāmam* was wet land, but 91.5 percent of it grew two crops. In 1827 the village still had twenty acres of dry land capable of being used to grow millets and eleven acres of wasteland usable as pasture. Most of these areas were used as coconut gardens by 1952.

The records of 1827 provide valuable information on land holding. Although there were thirty-three *mirāsdārs*' houses, there were only thirty-two *mirāsdārs*, all of them men. One Brahman woman did own half a share of land in Nallūr in 1827, but none did in Kumbapeṭṭai. Evidently, childless widows were not yet allowed to inherit independently of their husbands' patrilineal kin, and daughters could not own land given by their fathers, independently of their husbands. Both of these had become possible by 1898.

The village land was still jointly owned as a commune. According to the records, the wet paddy lands were redistributed on *karaiyiḍu* tenure every five years. The wet land was reported to be divided into 100 shares (*pangus*); however, when we total the shares recorded, they amount to 110. Four of the thirty-two village shareholders were reported to be "*paṭṭā* (document) holding *mirāsdārs*"; perhaps they were the heads of four Brahman lineages. Two of them witnessed the record. A fifth Brahman, described as the village *karṇam*, or record keeper, signed the record as "Documentary Authority and Signatory"; like the land owners, he was a Smārtha Brahman with the title "Iyyan" or "Iyer." Twenty-seven other shareholders are listed. The total list is as follows:

| | *Paṭṭā holding mirāsdārs* | *Shares (Pangus)* |
|---|---|---|
| 1 | Rāma Iyyan | 8 |
| 2 | Parasurāma Subbayyan | 7¼ & 1/16 |
| 3 | Ānanṭa Subbayyan | 9 |
| 4 | Dēvanātha Ayyan | 8⅛ |
| | *Documentary authority and signatory* | |
| 5 | Ayyāsāmy Iyyan | 6¾ |
| | *Other shareholders* | |
| 6 | Vēngappāyyan | 1¼ |
| 7 | Ayyāvayyan | 1½ |
| 8 | Ayyāthurai Ayyan | ½ |
| 9 | Annāthurai Ayyan | 2¼ |
| 10 | Ramaiyyan | 8 |
| 11 | Ānanṭa Rāmaiyyan | 10 |
| 12 | Visvanātha Ayyan | 7¾ |
| 13 | Venkata Subbayyan | 2½ |
| 14 | Pichalai Subbu Iyyan | 5 |
| 15 | Ānanta Nārayanappaiyyan | 1 1/16 & 1/32 |
| 16 | Subbarāma Siva Ayyan | 1 1/16 |
| 17 | Appū Siva Ayyan | ¼ & 1/16 & 1/32 |
| 18 | Panchanāthayyan | 4¼ |
| 19 | Harihara Iyyan | ¾ & 3/16 |
| 20 | Appū Iyyan | 3 |
| 21 | Sivarāma Iyyan | 4¼ |
| 22 | Kāsi Siva Ayyan | 1½ & 3/16 & 1/64 |
| 23 | Appādurai Iyyan | ¼ & 1/32 |
| 24 | Sēvandiyyan | ½ |

| | | |
|---|---|---|
| 25 | Panju Siva Iyyan | 1 |
| 26 | Kāḷiyayyan | 3¼ |
| 27 | Kuppēriyyan | ½ |
| 28 | Vishnū Iyyan | ¾ |
| 29 | Subbū Iyyan | 1 1/16 & 1/32 |
| 30 | Ayyā Iyyan | 1¼ |
| 31 | Peṟiya Thambi Piḷḷai | 1 |
| 32 | Seeniya Piḷḷai | ¾ |

It seems clear that over the years, the shares had been divided and subdivided into multiples of two, and that in some way – either through inheritance among different numbers of sons in different households, or through sale – the portions held by different landlords had become unequal. In British law, moreover, each share was by 1827 viewed as private, marketable property similar to the shares in a joint stock company. The biggest owner with ten shares owned twenty times as much as the smallest owner, with half a share. The eight biggest owners, or 25 percent of the total, owned 60 percent of the wet paddy land. If we regard the village's wet acres as being of equal value, the biggest owner owned the equivalent of 34.5 acres of wet paddy land, and the three smallest owners, the equivalent of 1.72 each.

The inequality in shares may have related at least partly to kinship status. If the four "*pattā* holding *mirāsdārs*" and the "documentary signatories" were really the heads of the lineages, they may have been *allotted* more land by the villagers in keeping with their status. This would allow them to finance temple ceremonies, which even today are vested in the heads of lineage segments. Similarly, some of the small shares may have belonged to sons or younger brothers who headed their own households but whose fathers or elder brothers were still living and who had not yet inherited or divided their full shares of ancestral land. Even so, the differential shares of the household heads suggest a degree of inequality over and above their kinship status.

Thirty of the thirty-two owners were Smārtha Brahmans, as the suffixes "ayyan" and "Iyyan" indicate. The last two, having the suffix "Piḷḷai" (literally "child"), are known to be ancestors of the present Veḷḷāḷars of Sheṭṭiyūr. Between them they owned 1.6 percent of the village's wet land, the Brahmans owning 98.4 percent. Although they believe that they owned the whole *grāmam* apart from the dry area of the *chattram* when they moved from Kiḷiyūr to Kumbapeṭṭai, the Brahmans had evidently parted with the equivalent of about six acres of wet land to Veḷḷāḷar settlers by 1827. In 1952 the Brahmans said that their ancestors had brought three such families as tenants in the 1820s to cultivate land belonging to their temples that was distant from the main village site. It is possible that the Veḷḷāḷars had newly irrigated their own fields with the consent of the colonial government, for the British were encouraging settlers to cultivate unused land between village settlements when the local *mirāsdārs* failed to do so.

The Brahmans were in far more complete control of their *grāmam* in 1827 than they were by the end of the century. The same was even more true of Nallūr, a mile to the east. The Nallūr Brahmans owned 94.5 percent of their village land in 1827, whereas they owned only 69.8 percent of it in 1898, and only 23.2 percent in 1952.

# 10 Kumbapeṭṭai from 1855 to 1952

The century after about 1855 was one of momentous change in Kumbapeṭṭai as in all of Thanjāvūr. Merchant capitalism made much deeper inroads, and the colonial economy of crop and labor exports and manufactured imports was firmly established.

## Labor Migration Abroad

As we saw in Chapter 6, Thanjāvūr became "hooked" to the new plantations of Ceylon, Malaya, the Western Ghāts, and other regions, as early as 1840, supplying both indentured laborers and the paddy to feed them. Perhaps associated with the need for plantation labor and for greater mobility of labor in India in general, slavery was gradually abolished in law between 1843 and 1861.[1] Act V of 1843 forbade masters to beat their slaves, allowed slaves to own property, and, although it did not forbid slave owning, made it impossible to uphold the claims of slave owners in law. In 1861, slave owning was forbidden under the penal code.

Perhaps about forty of Kumbapeṭṭai's Paḷḷars migrated to the plantations of Ceylon, Malaya, Burma, and Mauritius in the second half of the nineteenth and the early twentieth centuries, as did several hundred Paḷḷar, Paṟayar, Kaḷḷar, and Paḍaiyācchi laborers from adjacent villages. Until 1918 they went as indentured laborers; thereafter, as free wage laborers who, however, had to pay off the price of their passage through work on arrival. A small proportion of these laborers returned after ten to twenty years, some of them having fled before the Japanese advance in World War II. Three former plantation workers lived in Kumbapeṭṭai's Paḷḷar streets in 1952.

## Changes in Agricultural Labor

West Thanjāvūr being remote from the coast, however, most of Kumbapeṭṭai's Paḷḷar and Kōṉār *aḍimai āḷukaḷ* stayed on as debt peons or *paṇṇaiyāḷs* with the end of slavery. Such servants accepted loans from their masters in cash or kind in order to tide them over the lean months of April to June and to meet the expenses of marriages, births, and funerals. Once tied by debt, the *paṇṇaiyāḷ* relationship appears to have been only a little better than that of the former *kaṭṭu aḍimai āḷ*, or individually owned slave. In 1952, for example, a male *paṇṇaiyāḷ* in Kumbapeṭṭai received the equivalent in cash and kind of about twenty-six *kalams* paddy per year as wages. In addition, he and his wife and working children received a harvest bonus of about sixteen *kalams*, so that the man's own total annual earnings might be reckoned at about thirty-four *kalams*. In 1819, C. M. Lushington, then Collector of Tiruchirappalli, reported that a male slave's annual wages, including his harvest wages, totaled about twenty-seven *kalams*.[2] If this included the bonus, it was about seven *kalams* lower than the 1952 scale in Thanjāvūr, but if it excluded the bonus, it was about the same. Working conditions also remained similar. Male *paṇṇaiyāḷs,* for example, were required to work when necessary from sunrise to sunset with about half an hour's break for the midday meal. Moreover, although not in law, as late as 1952 *paṇṇaiyāḷs* could be beaten or otherwise physically abused much as in the days of slavery.

The *proportions* of the Paḷḷars and Kōṉārs engaged as *paṇṇaiyāḷs*, and the duration of the *paṇṇaiyāḷ* relationship, changed in the late nineteenth and early twentieth centuries. In the days of slavery, even though some slaves might be or become the personal, *kaṭṭu aḍimai āḷukaḷ* of particular masters, all *aḍimai āḷukaḷ* belonged as slaves to the *mirāsdār* community collectively throughout their lives. Under pre-British law, all of them had to be employed by the village and maintained from its threshing floors. Although this condition was in theory relaxed by the British legal view that the *mirāsdārs* were private landlords who could hire or fire their servants at will, it seems in fact to have been observed in the first half of the nineteenth century. But after slavery was abolished in 1861, and after the *mirāsdārs* became individually responsible for their land shares and revenue in 1865, Paḷḷar servants were engaged privately in separate households of *paṇṇaiyāḷs*. Not all of them, however, were so engaged. A number of Paḷḷars remained on the fringes as *kooliyāḷukaḷ* ("coolies"), or marginal wage laborers who were hired chiefly at the peak seasons of channel digging, transplanting, and harvesting. As the population increased, so did the proportion of coolies. Their numbers may also have increased with the expansion of *kuthakai* tenures among incoming Non-Brahmans, for many of these used family labor, kept only one or no *paṇṇaiyāḷ* families, and hired coolies at peak seasons. By 1952, fifty-four out of 112 of Kumbapeṭṭai's male agricultural laborers (almost 50 percent) were casual coolies, thirty-seven of them being Paḷḷars and seventeen, Non-Brahmans.

The growth of a pool of marginal, coolie labor meant that landowners could pick and choose their *paṇṇaiyāḷs*, and that they could, and often did, dismiss them. Although the *paṇṇaiyāḷ*'s debt prevented *him* from leaving his landlord unless he could find a new master to repay it, a master could withhold all or part of his loan from a *paṇṇaiyāḷ*'s harvest wages and get rid of him. Some masters even occasionally dismissed a *paṇṇaiyāḷ* in midyear if his work was poor, sometimes after withholding his wages for several days or weeks. As the population increased, the element of debt in the *paṇṇaiyāḷ* relation in fact became less significant, for laborers were so plentiful that *mirāsdārs* scarcely needed to make loans to them. Most laborers, especially men with families, preferred *paṇṇai* to coolie work and were willing to enter it for a small loan each New Year in mid-April to tide them over the lean months until June. *Mirāsdārs* hired their *paṇṇaiyāḷs* on New Year's Day and some of them changed hands every few years or even every year.

Although the details are unclear, some of Kumbapeṭṭai's Paḷḷars seem to have rebelled against their masters and tried to improve their conditions shortly after the abolition of slavery. During the 1860s the Paḷḷars of Upper Street, who served the largest and most powerful Brahman lineage, are believed to have struck against their masters, demanding higher rates of pay. The head of the Brahman lineage reportedly broke the strike by bringing in a dozen households of Tekkaṭṭi, or Southern Paḷḷars, from Pāpāṉasam, a few miles east, by agreement with landlords there. Thereafter, the Tekkaṭṭi Paḷḷars became the main *paṇṇaiyāḷs* of that Brahman lineage. Tradition had it that the Dēvendra Paḷḷars, "realizing their mistake," prostrated themselves before the Brahman elders and were received back into service by various masters from the five lineages.

## Sales of Land and Colonization

The British government's deposition of the Thanjāvūr royal family on the absence of a male heir in 1855 affected the composition of Kumbapeṭṭai and speeded up the sale of land in the neighborhood. Although the former royalty retained certain rights in the revenues of most of their estates, their income was reduced and they no longer governed the area of the Fort in Thanjāvūr City. With the drying up of royal expenditures, groomsmen, dancing girls, Brahman priests, and other retainers and beneficiaries lost their work and gradually sold their *iṉam* rights in part of the land revenue of the royal estates on which they lived. In Veḷiyūr these rights were first bought by a Smartha Brahman in about 1855 and later by a Veḷḷāḷar landlord from Tiruchirappalli in about 1875. This family rebuilt the Siva temple, reinstalled the idol, and engaged Kumbapeṭṭai's Kurukkals to propitiate it. Veḷiyūr was joined to Kumbapeṭṭai as a "side hamlet" in the 1890s, and became a *mirāsi* settlement in 1934.

Kumbapeṭṭai's *chattram* ceased to be a place of charity sometime after the mid-nineteenth century, although it remained occupied until 1906 by a Maratha Brahman family who collected revenue on the royal estate of Kandipeṭṭai. At that point the *chattram* and its tank were bought by a Muslim trader and landlord, as I have mentioned. Some of the land west of the *chattram* had meanwhile been sold to Brahmans of Kumbapeṭṭai for new house sites and gardens.

With the collapse of the *chattram* as a center of royal patronage in the 1850s, most of Akkāchāvaḍy's shopkeepers and other retainers moved away. Two families remained who had earlier served the Mahārāja's concubine as male body guards and women sweepers: one Kaḷḷar and one Maratha. The men of the Maratha house came to provide one of the government-paid village *veṭṭis*, or messengers, on a hereditary basis for Kumbapeṭṭai, a job they had held earlier on behalf of the royal family on its nearby estates. The Kaḷḷar family expanded and by 1952 comprised seven households in one patrilineal group together with one house of affines. Some of them became paddy traders while others leased paddy land from Nallūr's and Kumbapeṭṭai's landlords. Other gardens in Akkāchāvaḍy were bought and sold several times between 1855 and 1952, chiefly among Kumbapeṭṭai Brahmans. By 1952 my own rented house was a Brahman water *pandal*, as I have mentioned. Other small house sites had been bought by two Kōṉārs from Barber Street in the early 1900s and by a Telugu Nāyakkar arrack shopkeeper from Vēṭṭāmbāḍi in the 1920s. The arrack shop was closed by prohibition in 1947, and in 1952 was rented by my cook. A Paḍaiyācchi laborer who had fled from Rāmanāthapuram in the drought of 1949, and a Poosāri tea-shop keeper, rented small shacks on the Nāyakkar's site. In these ways Akkāchāvaḍy, once a royal preserve, had been bought up by "bloody Nāyakkars and Kaḷḷars and other nonsense people" – as the *panchāyat* president disgustedly observed to me.

The colonial economy of the "British century" brought new sources of wealth to other new kinds of people through both land and trade. Because of the demand for paddy as an export crop, the government encouraged cultivators of middle rank to occupy fallow land on the outskirts of villages. After the improvements in Thanjāvūr's irrigation works in the 1830s, moreover, some formerly wasteland became irrigable. By the late nineteenth century, population pressure was probably also a factor in the expansion of village sites. Sheṭṭiyūr hamlet was colonized as a result of these developments. In the early nineteenth century, about eighty-six acres of mainly waste and fallow land lay west of Kumbapeṭṭai *grāmam*, in which the Brahmans of Kumbapeṭṭai held nominal rights. Part of it had been bequeathed by them to Siva and Vishnū, the deities of their two temples, but because of their distance from the village the fields were only sporadically cultivated. As early as the 1820s, the Brahmans invited three households of Veḷḷāḷar cultivators of a nearby village to irrigate and cultivate part of the land as *kuthakai* tenants paying rent to the temples. A group of Mūppaṉār tenants followed in the 1830s and cultivated more of Kumbapeṭṭai's temple lands. Meanwhile, the Veḷḷāḷars had increased in numbers and established a street with coconut gardens behind their houses. When the Brahmans asked them to pay rent for these gardens or vacate the land they argued that their house sites were their own, as they had occupied them unmolested for more than twelve years. Through their temple trustee, the Brahmans contested this claim in a bitter lawsuit in 1919, arguing that temple deities are legal minors and are therefore incapable of giving their lands away. The Sheṭṭiyūr villagers lost the case in the Madras High Court. The Brahmans then descended one night on Sheṭṭiyūr with a party of Non-Brahman and Harijan servants, fought the Veḷḷāḷars with staffs and ransacked their homes in an effort to evict them. Having lost the case and the battle, the Sheṭṭiyūr villagers begged to be allowed to buy their house sites. The Brahmans sold their gardens to them for the then outrageous sum of Rs. 3,000 and used the money to buy eight acres of wet land from individual Brahmans in south Kumbapeṭṭai for the upkeep of their temples. Both before and after this incident, several impoverished Brahmans sold considerable wet land in addition.

By 1897 Veḷḷāḷar houscholds owned fifty-two acres of wet land in Sheṭṭiyūr. Twenty-two acres were retained by the Brahmans collectively for their temples, and ten acres remained in the private possession of several Brahman individuals. In 1952 Mūppaṉār tenants were still paying rent to the temples or to individual Brahmans for these thirty-two acres on the border of Kumbapeṭṭai and Sheṭṭiyūr.

Vēṭṭāmbāḍi, an outpost of Nallūr, was similarly colonized by even lower-ranking Non-Brahmans in the teeth of Brahman opposition. Until about 1890 this land, being in Nallūr, was owned by Brahmans of that village. Part of it was wasteland and part, coconut groves. Traditionally, each village tended to have one or more families of the low-ranking Non-Brahman caste of Nāḍār, some subcastes of whom called themselves Nāyakkar in this part of Thanjāvūr. Such families lived in coconut groves on the outskirts of village sites, for their work of tapping palm wine (toddy) was considered highly polluting by the upper castes, whose religious laws forbid intoxicating liquor. In each village the Nāḍārs paid *vāram*, or crop shares, in coconuts and paddy to the village landlords. They kept a toddy shop at which they served toddy, and sometimes arrack, to the village slave population in exchange for paddy, at midday and in the evenings. Vēṭṭāmbāḍi had one such family, called Nāyakkars, from time immemorial. This family tapped the coconut and palmyra trees of the Nallūr Brahmans. They kept a toddy shop in the paddy fields to barter liquor to the Ādi Drāviḍas and low-caste Non-Brahmans of Nallūr, Kumbapeṭṭai, and Kiḷiyūr.

During the nineteenth century, the British prohibited the free sale of alcohol and set up licensed toddy shops at intervals of two to three miles among the villages. Some Nāḍārs, fortunate enough to obtain licenses for a string of shops, became extremely wealthy. One such man bought up most of Nāṭṭār village southeast of Kumbapeṭṭai in the 1880s and obtained the lease of coconut groves in Māniyur, Kumbapeṭṭai, and Nallūr. One of his agents, Pēchi Nāyakkar, arrived in the neighborhood from Naṉṉilam, married the daughter of Vēṭṭāmbāḍi's Nāyakkar family in 1895, and obtained the license to run a toddy shop of his own in Vēṭṭāmbāḍi. Growing prosperous, he eventually bought most of Vēṭṭāmbāḍi, the adjacent coconut groves, and some paddy fields, a total of nine acres, from declining Nallūr residents, and populated a street of six households with his children and affines. This enterprising businessman built his family a large, tile-roofed house in Vēṭṭāmbāḍi in 1906, a second such house in 1930, and a grocery shop on the main roadside in 1935. In 1937 he also built a shrine dedicated to the spirit of a dead Veḷḷāḷar holy man who had once helped him find a purse of money that he had lost while bathing in a strange village on his way between Naṉṉilam and Kumbapeṭṭai. This shrine became Vēṭṭāmbāḍi's street shrine and was tended by Pēchi's eldest son, Karthān, in 1952, Pēchi having died in 1941.

Kumbapeṭṭai's Brahmans put up the most strenuous opposition to this settlement by low-ranking, but prosperous and influential Nāyakkars on the outskirts of their village. In 1925 a wealthy Brahman landlord, Chidambara Iyer, owned a garden that blocked Vēṭṭāmbāḍi street from the main road. Previously, toddy tappers, like Paḷḷars, had approached their houses by narrow footpaths through the paddy fields, avoiding the main roads because of caste pollution. Having built a business, Pēchi needed a right-of-way to drive his carts of paddy and toddy from the new Vēṭṭāmbāḍi street to the main road. The Brahman fenced his land and forbade Pēchi access by either footpath or cart road. In fury, Pēchi one day ripped up the fence and drove his vandy through. The village headman brought the police. They were divided in their allegiance to the local Brahmans and to the rich Nāḍār of Nāṭṭār and counselled a court case. Pēchi filed a suit for access, lost in the local court, but won on appeal in the Thanjāvūr subcourt. Chidambara Iyer carried the case to the high court of Madras. Believing that he would lose, two prominent Brahman elders summoned the disputants and effected a compromise. Chidambara Iyer agreed to sell his garden to Pēchi for a right-of-way, in return for Rs. 1,000 or ten times its market value. Pēchi agreed, wanting to carry on his business and perhaps fearing the Brahmans' control of force in the village.

Chidambara Iyer had other troubles with headstrong toddy tappers. In 1910 a Brahman landlord brought a poor Telugu Nāyakkar, Ārumugam, from Thanjāvūr to work as his servant and settled him in a garden north of Vēṭṭāmbāḍi tank. In time, the Nāyakkar managed to obtain the license for an arrack shop, which he built in Akkāchāvaḍy on land owned by Chidambara Iyer. The roadside shop prospered, partly from a few Kumbapeṭṭai Brahmans who broke their religious vows and became secret visitors. In 1928, Chidambara Iyer tried to evict Ārumugam, it was said out of jealousy "because he was growing rich." Like the Sheṭṭiyūr villagers, Ārumugam claimed that he owned the land through *anubōga bādyam* or "right of time" as he had been there for twenty years. Chidambara Iyer filed a suit against him, but was again persuaded by Brahman leaders to compromise and sell his garden. To avoid fuss, Ārumugam bought it for Rs. 1,000, its market value being Rs. 400.

The licensed trade in alcohol was just one major source of disturbance of the traditional order in the late nineteenth and early twentieth centuries. Another was, of course, the paddy trade. The building of the railroad in the 1860s and 1870s vastly increased the export of paddy from west Thanjāvūr via the east and south coast ports. In the early nineteenth century, as I have noted, the Brahmans seem to have traded their own surplus paddy by cart to Pudukkoṭṭai and Tiruchirappalli. Some of this trade continued until the late 1950s, when motor trucks plying from Thanjāvūr largely replaced the local oxcarts. Already in the 1870s, however, specialized traders began to buy paddy from landlords and cultivators and deliver it by cart to railheads. In the 1930s, a mechanized rice mill was built by a Cheṭṭiār trader in Āriyūr. Kumbapeṭṭai's paddy traders then became agents who delivered paddy to this mill owner on behalf of the local land owners, receiving a commission on each bag from the miller.

In villages like Kumbapeṭṭai, composed of small holders, the paddy trade for small family traders seems to have been most lucrative from about 1880 to about 1930. After that date, a few big merchants monopolized the district's trade and small traders, by then grown numerous, were forced to compete as agents for the low commission fees. Between 1880 and 1930 two or three Brahman families who specialized in the paddy trade temporarily increased their wealth and expanded their land holdings at the expense of their neighbors. So did three Non-Brahmans who managed to break free from their traditional servitude and borrowed money to start family businesses. These families were the leading Kaḷḷar of Akkāchāvaḍy, a Kōn̲ār of Aḍichēri, and an Agambaḍiyar whose father had been brought to Aḍichēri as a Brahman's workman in the 1860s. Each of these men made modest fortunes in the early 1900s and built tile-roofed houses that rivaled those of the Brahmans. In his heyday the Agambaḍiyar owned seven acres of wet land and two of dry; the Kōn̲ār, six acres of wet land and 200 cows; and the Kaḷḷar family, less prosperous, a small amount of dry land and about Rs. 5,000.

After about 1930, however, it seems that these families' prosperity declined. To some extent this resulted from the increase in their members. On the deaths of the Agambaḍiyar and Kōn̲ār fathers, their households each divided into two; that of the Kaḷḷar, eventually into six. Probably more important were the world depression and the slackening and increasing monopolization of the paddy trade. By 1952, two houses of the Kaḷḷars remained as impoverished agents for the Āriyūr rice mill. The Kōn̲ār and Agambaḍiyar houses had almost ceased trading and reverted, in the one case to tenant farming, and in the other to bonded labor for Brahman landlords.

The toddy tappers' prosperity continued longer than the paddy traders', for they were assured of licenses for particular areas. They were, however, hard hit by prohibition under the Congress Government in 1947. Some tapping continued illicitly, and some toddy, arrack, and other fermented liquor was sold in the tea shop in Akkāchāvaḍy. For the most part, however, the Nāyakkars in 1952 were forced to live from a few leased paddy fields, a small dry goods store, and the sale of coconuts.

Among the Brahmans, individual family fortunes waxed and waned greatly during the century between 1850 and 1950. In 1865 *mirāsdārs* were made individually responsible for their land revenue. It seems to have been about that date, or soon after, that Kumbapeṭṭai's fields were permanently divided among the *mirāsdār* households according to their shares, even though fields were not registered in individual names until 1887–91. Certainly, the second half of the nineteenth century saw a great deal of selling and buying of paddy land and a further polarization of the Brahmans' holdings. In the 1870s one Kumbapeṭṭai Brahman who had prospered through the paddy trade owned seventy acres of land and an elephant, which he kept in his backyard to ride upon. This seems to have been the peak of wealth in Kumbapeṭṭai, but in the 1920s one Brahman possessed forty acres and Rs. 200,000. This man gave Rs. 15,000 in jewels, clothing, and vessels to dower each of his two daughters, a record in the village at that period. In the 1890s, one Brahman family began to make milk sweets in their home and sell them to the Maratha royalty and aristocracy in Thanjāvūr.

From being paupers, they earned forty acres of land. Later a son of the family became a commercial tax officer of the government in Madurai. Having moved to Thanjāvūr, the women of his family continued to organize trade in rice and milk and in cow-dung cakes to fuel urban homes. This family also lent out money at 6 percent per annum to needy Brahmans in Kumbapeṭṭai. By 1952 they owned 67 acres in Kumbapeṭṭai and Nallūr, and were the richest absentee landlords connected with the village.

**The Village's Impoverishment**

As a whole, however, the Brahman community lost wealth and land in the late nineteenth century and still more in the twentieth century. By 1952, nine out of thirty-six resident Brahman households owned no land at all apart from house sites, and four of the nine did not own those. Population increase, unaccompanied by adequate new forms of wealth, was partly responsible. It is true that the resident Brahmans had only thirty-six households in 1952, whereas they already had thirty-three in 1827. In the intervening period, however, large numbers of Brahmans left the village and many of these retained fields or shares in their families' lands. Whereas there were thirty registered Brahman landowners in the *grāmam* in 1827, there were sixty-six in the same area in 1897, probably belonging to some fifty-one families, and seventy-one in 1952. By 1952 most fields had been divided into several subsections. Those Brahmans who remained in Kumbapeṭṭai owned only 41 percent of the *grāmam* land that their forefathers had owned almost entirely in 1827.

A more significant cause of impoverishment, however, was the loss of land to enterprising peasants, merchants, moneylenders, and more prosperous landlords from outside the village who were not related to the Brahman community. Of the total *grāmam* land, 15 percent had been sold to such people by 1897; 27.3 percent by 1952. The sale of this land was more harmful to the resident Brahmans than was the ownership of fields by absent members of their own community. The latter usually gave their fields on a favorable *uḷ-kuthakai* or "inside tenure" to one or another of their relatives remaining in the village. Such men reaped a profit by subletting the land to a lower-caste man on *pora-kuthakai* ("outside lease") for a higher rent or by cultivating through laborers. When traders and landlords from outside the village bought land, they leased it directly to lower-caste tenants within the village. When peasants bought it, they cultivated it themselves with the aid of laborers.

The sale of land to external merchants and money lenders occurred, it seems, because Brahmans began to buy an increasingly wide range of manufactured goods, often British-made, in urban stores. Some of these goods were necessities that, as a result of colonial tariff policies, were no longer made in Thanjāvūr. Others were luxuries that the small *mirāsdār* found it hard to resist. Yet other articles, made by native craftsmen, were traditional luxuries appropriate to the Brahmans' caste status. In the new, competitive economy of private enterprise, the Brahmans had to spend more than they could afford on such items in order to attract "suitable" husbands of appropriate education and wealth for their daughters. The payment of heavy dowries of jewels, clothing, vessels, and other personal property became the chief cause of indebtedness in the late nineteenth and twentieth centuries, so that Brahmans with many daughters to marry were often bankrupted.

Some Brahmans also lost wealth through gambling, drinking, prostitution, or going off on pilgrimages or binges to various cities. Brahmans usually blamed such vices for the loss of wealth in their community, sometimes with justice. The main point, however, is that no matter how dissolute they were the Brahmans could not have lost their land in such ways until shortly before British rule, for land was vested in the village commune and could not be sold by individuals. It was bourgeois property rights and merchant capitalism that brought about the downfall of the less enterprising and produced a polarization of wealth in the community. Most important, it was the operation of the colonial economy, with its heavy land revenues and commercial taxes, its British corporations' profits, and its favoring of big landlords, compradore merchants, and money lenders, that led to the universal impoverishment of small-holding communities such as Kumbapeṭṭai.

**Migration to Urban Work**

It was no doubt largely because they were losing wealth to merchants, money lenders, and British tax collectors, that so many Brahmans left the village for urban work. I do not know how early in the nineteenth century this process became significant. Certainly some Brahmans found work in trade or under the British government from the beginning of colonial rule, for the Brahmans were the traditional state class, and their members had always served as bureaucrats, ministers, and priests under the native rulers. The major exodus from Kumbapeṭṭai seems to have begun about 1870, as the railroads speeded up trade and travel and the lower echelons of government service expanded. By 1900, a large proportion of Thanjāvūr's Brahmans lived and worked in Madras and other cities of the Presidency, returning home for temple festivals, funerals, and marriages, and to collect their rent in paddy after the harvest season.

By 1952 fifty-eight Brahman men of Kumbapeṭṭai, many of them with wives and children, lived and worked outside the village but still viewed it as in some respects their home. Thirty-six of these men retained ownership rights in village fields, most of them drawing rents in cash or kind. Nine of these thirty-six men lived entirely from their rents, while four sent regular remittances to their village relatives. Twenty-four of the thirty-six men were salary or wage workers, chiefly in lower-grade government service. Two drew pensions after a lifetime in government service; four were university students; one was a doctor; one a university professor; and five ran businesses. Most of the salary workers and businessmen made contributions to village festivals, helped finance household ceremonies, and made occasional loans or gifts to their village relatives. On average, however, they received more from the village than they contributed to it.

Twenty-two other absent men owned no land in the village and came home only for occasional visits. Seventeen of these men were salary workers; three were in business; one worked as a household priest; and one was a devotee in a religious *āshram*. These men had severed most of their economic links with the village, and to all intents and purposes lived independently of it.

### The Growth of Tenant Farming

The departure of many Brahman *mirāsdārs* to urban work, and the sale of some land to external merchants and landlords, probably accounts for the growth of *kuthakai* tenures in the late nineteenth and the twentieth century. The term *kuthakai* is Telugu and dates from the Vijayanagar period. *Kuthakai* tenures with fixed rent in cash or kind, however, apparently became common in Thanjāvūr only after about 1860.

It seems probable that tenant cultivation in general was rare before the invasion of Haidar Āli in 1780–2, for before that date the majority of village cultivators, usually Paḷḷars or Paṟayars, were evidently slaves.[3] After the partial depopulation of Thanjāvūr during Haidar's invasion and in view of the shortage of Panchama slaves, large numbers of Paḍaiyācchis, Mūppaṉārs, Kōṉārs, and Kaḷḷars were encouraged to settle in the district and rehabilitate the land. Because of the labor shortage and the death or dispersal of many *mirāsdārs*, these cultivators were settled as tenants-at-will rather than being enslaved. Cultivating tenants of this kind were called *porakuḍis*, or "outside (foreign) tenants" as distinct from *uḷ-kudis* or "inside tenants." The latter came mainly from inside the village and held hereditary rights. *Porakuḍis* were numerous when the British took over Thanjāvūr in 1799. Most of them appear to have cultivated on *vāram* or sharecropping tenures and to have paid about 70 to 78 percent of their crop to the landlord in addition to providing seed, cattle, and implements. It is possible that the Kōṉārs and the early Veḷḷāḷars who settled in Kumbapeṭṭai were initially *porakuḍis*, but the Kōṉārs became virtually enslaved in the nineteenth century, and were allowed to take land on *vāram* tenure only occasionally. Although the data are unclear, I suspect that the reenslavement of *porakuḍis* may have been common in the district between about 1790 and 1830 as the returning *mirāsdārs* regained control of their land. Neither Kumbapeṭṭai nor Nallūr were recorded as having *porakuḍis* in 1828.

The situation appears to have changed from about the mid-nineteenth century, as absentee landlords became common and paddy exports increased. In Kumbapeṭṭai merchants and other external landlords who lacked kinsfolk in the village began to give their land regularly on *kuthakai* to Non-Brahman cultivating tenants from whom they could be assured of a fixed rent, with minimal supervision, after every harvest. Most absent Brahmans preferred to give their land on *uḷ-kuthakai* for a lower rent to a relative within the village in order to retain the goodwill of their community. Some absent Brahmans, however, who lived nearby, chose to engage *pora-kuthakai* tenants of lower caste directly. Some Brahmans who held land on *uḷ-kuthakai* leased it out again on *porakuthakai* if they already had enough lands of their own to supervise. By 1952, therefore, about 44 percent of Kumbapeṭṭai's total wet land was under *kuthakai* cultivating tenures. With the further growth of absentee landlordism in the 1930s and the 1940s, some Ādi Drāviḍas had been given *kuthakai* tenures for the first time, although usually for a somewhat higher rent than the Non-Brahman tenants.

Although heavily exploitative, *kuthakai* tenures allowed some Non-Brahmans in Kumbapeṭṭai to save a little money and buy their own house sites. Most of the residents of Akkāchāvaḍy and the east side of Babger Street who had bought their own gardens had done so from *kuthakai* profits or from the profits of paddy trade. In a few cases the tenant was even able to buy a little paddy land or to start an independent business as a paddy trader, a milk vendor, or a cattle broker. The Kōṉār and the Agambaḍiyar paddy traders of Aḍichēri whom I mentioned earlier made their first savings from *kuthakai*. Most *kuthakai* tenants, however, were little better off than the *paṇṇaiyāḷs*, and in a lean year might lose all or be in debt when their rents were paid. In 1952, indeed, twenty out of Kumbapeṭṭai's fifty-one Non-Brahmans and Ādi Drāviḍa *kuthakai* tenants were in fact either *paṇṇaiyāḷs* or casual coolies in addition to their tenant cultivation.

Like *paṇṇaiyāḷs*, *kuthakai* tenants were engaged by the year. In 1952, some Non-Brahman families had leased the same fields for twenty to thirty years. Others had had them for much shorter periods, for the owners often changed their arrangements, bought or sold land, or dismissed tenants if they were dissatisfied. Some tenants were never sure whether they would receive land on a given New Year's Day or whether they would have to work simply as *paṇṇaiyāḷs* or as casual coolies. Although the Tenants' and Pannaiyals' Act gave permanency to the tenants of landlords owning more than 6.67 acres, Kumbapeṭṭai's *mirāsdārs* acted on the principle that the landowner had the right to hire and fire tenants and laborers as he pleased.

**Movement Between Villages**

The growth of coolie labor and the increasingly short-term contracts of *kuthakai* tenants and *paṇṇaiyāḷs* meant that more and more workers wandered about and entered new villages in the late nineteenth and twentieth centuries. I have already mentioned Kumbapeṭṭai's Agambaḍiyars, Nāyakkars, Paḍaiyācchis, and Kūtthāḍis who came or were brought to the village, in some cases from places up to fifty miles away, to do agricultural work. In the same category were the Ambalakkārars, the Nāḍār family, and a single Veḷḷāḷar widow and her children. The Ambalakkārars, formerly inland fishermen, arrived from Pudukkoṭṭai during a drought in the 1880s and settled in Kumbapeṭṭai as coolies and *paṇṇaiyāḷs*. The Nāḍārs arrived a little later from the same area. The Veḷḷāḷar widow, also from Pudukkoṭṭai, wandered in with her children during the drought of 1952. She was given a shack in Aḍichēri by the Agambaḍiyars, who came originally from the same area and were acquainted with some of her relatives. Although of high caste, she began to eke out a living through casual agricultural labor and housework for the Brahmans.

Some families came and went. An impoverished Veḷḷāḷar household arrived from Koḷḷiḍam, the area between the Kāvēri and the Coleroon Rivers, in about 1880. They lived in Aḍichēri and worked for the Brahmans as tenant farmers and *paṇṇaiyāḷs*, eventually expanding to four families. About 1930, they moved south to Pudukkoṭṭai. As late as 1978, these families sent representatives each year to offer goat sacrifices to the village goddess, who remains their lineage deity *(kuḷa dēvan).*

Village servants, too, had lost their legal service rights and become more mobile. In the Maratha period village servants were part of the kingdom's economic system. Their conditions and payments were supervised by revenue officers of the state. When the harvest grain was divided on the village threshing floors these officers were present. They witnessed the payment of grain shares to the village servants and the Ādi Drāviḍa laborers who had harvested the crop. Only after these payments were made was the grain divided into *mēlvāram* and *kīlvāram* between the king or the *iṉam* holder on the one hand and the *mirāsdārs* on the other. In the early nineteenth century, however, the British made most village servants the private responsibility of the landlords and calculated the *mēlvāram* amount in advance of their payment, thus robbing the village of part of its grain share. In 1836, the village accountant, messenger, and policemen were separated from the other village servants and given state-paid salaries as subordinates of the newly created village headman. Other village servants became workers whom the *mirāsdārs*, as private landlords, could hire and fire as they pleased.

In fact, most of Kumbapeṭṭai's village servants had stable employment from the various times that they were brought to the village. A test case did, however, occur in 1925. The village Barbers and Potters lived on the common land set aside by the Brahmans for village servants on the west side of Barber Street. During the 1920s the Barbers waxed prosperous through funds sent to them by kin in Malaya, and bought about five acres of wet land in south Kumbapeṭṭai. In 1925 the Potters and Barbers decided to cut down a large flowering tree on their site and use it for firewood. The Brahmans forbade this on the grounds that the land belonged to the Brahman community collectively and not to their servants. The Barbers and Potters went ahead, claiming the land as their own. The Brahmans then tried to evict them, but they refused to move. A court case ensued in which the village servants won in the lower courts, but the Brahmans, led by Chidambara Iyer, won on appeal in the Madras High Court. The Brahmans then evicted all four brothers in the Barber family as the ringleaders. The Barbers moved to Thanjāvūr, set up a modern saloon, made money, and still own land in Kumbapeṭṭai and elsewhere. The Brahmans invited a new Barber to come to Kumbapeṭṭai from a village between the Kāvēri and the Coleroon. Having just returned from Rangoon, he was anxious for work and his family settled down as village servants. The village Potters asked pardon of the Brahmans, prostrating themselves on the ground before them. They were received back as dependents of the *agrahāram*.

In 1952 Kumbapeṭṭai's Barbers, Launderers, Village Priests, Potters, Carpenters, and Paḷḷar watchmen all worked most of the time for their traditional local patrons and were paid partly in traditional ways in kind. The Goldsmiths had broken with custom, however. Having lost their service right in a village in Tiruchirappalli, they wandered to Kumbapeṭṭai in 1952 and began to do small cash jobs for Brahmans and Non-Brahmans. The Māniyur Goldsmith, whose hereditary service right extended to Kumbapeṭṭai, was unable to prevent this encroachment. State law no longer upheld his right, and the new Goldsmith, being of a different regional subcaste, could not be disciplined by the local community of artisans.

Kumbapeṭṭai's Telugu Brahman was a fascinating example of a man torn between traditional service obligations and modern strivings. Telugu Brahmans traditionally held service rights as household priests (*purōhits*) and astrologers of Naidū and Maratha aristocrats. With the extinction of the royal family and the loss of wealth of its retainers, some Telugu Brahmans began to work for the lower Non-Brahman castes. In their efforts to rise in the ritual hierarchy, these castes were glad to employ impoverished Brahmans as astrologers and household priests. Sometime in the late nineteenth or the early twentieth century, Kumbapeṭṭai's Non-Brahmans began to call a Telugu Brahman from Nāṭṭār to make horoscopes for their infants and to do Sanskrit ceremonies for them at marriages, on the sixteenth day after a death, on the death anniversaries of their parents, on the sixteenth day after a birth, and at the ear-boring of their children at the age of one or three years. In 1947 the Nāṭṭār *purōhit* died without a son. His sister's son, an unemployed film director from Madras, came to live in a borrowed house in Kumbapeṭṭai's *agrahāram* and inherited the post.

The new *purōhit*, however, was a hot-tempered man who found it irksome to work for the illiterate lower castes and to be treated with patronage in the *agrahāram* as a Brahman of lower rank. One hot night in April 1952, having gone to bed on his roof, he awoke and surprised a group of thieves trying to break into a neighbor's house. The thieves ran away. Next day the *purōhit* saw three strange Koravar (gypsy) men lounging on the bridge in Nāṭṭār. He decided that they were the thieves, called the police, and had them arrested. In fact, they came from Periyūr, where they had settled down and become agricultural laborers. After several days their Veḷḷāḷar masters managed to bribe the police to release them. The Veḷḷāḷars of Periyūr came to complain to Kumbapeṭṭai's Brahman elders, who scolded the *purōhit*. Infuriated because "no one appreciated him" the *purōhit* tore off his Brahmanical sacred thread, shouting that he would no longer be a Brahman and try to please foolish villagers. At the First Ploughing ceremonies a few days later, he persuaded me to photograph him in the field of a local Brahman as he made the traditional offerings to Vināyakar and the sacred cattle, hoping to sell the photographs to the *Illustrated Weekly of India*. Having done the ceremony (a Brahman prerogative), he seized hold of the plough from the Non-Brahman and began to guide it through the earth to show his disregard of caste restrictions. This act of touching the plough, which flagrantly broke the Brahmans' religious law, aroused still further anger and contempt in the *agrahāram*.

Disgusted, the *purōhit* flung off to Thanjāvūr, where he lived for several days as a guest in a Maratha house of charity for Brahmans. Kumbapeṭṭai's Non-Brahmans were consternated. The *purōhit* had taken with him a notebook containing the dates of their parents' death ceremonies, of which, being mostly illiterate, they had no record. The Non-Brahmans approached the local Kurukkal of the Siva temple, Kumbapeṭṭai's other Brahman officiant of relatively low social rank. They begged him to get back the book for them so that they could give it to another *purōhit*. The Kurukkal refused, saying that the book was valuable evidence of the *purōhit's* neighborhood right and should either go to his heir or be sold to a new incumbent. After two months, the erring *purōhit* returned, for he had a family to maintain but no job and no money. Two prominent Brahmans persuaded him to take a purifying bath, restore his sacred thread, make offerings, and pay an expiatory fine (*prāyaschittam*) for the Siva temple. He returned to his work, a sadder and wiser Brahman.

Kumbapeṭṭai's final category of immigrants was government servants who had been posted to the village. They included the village clerk (*karṇam*); an Ayyangār Brahman; a former village clerk; a Smārtha Brahman of the Vaḍama subcaste who had retired on a pension; and one household of the low Non-Brahman caste of Koravars, formerly wandering gypsies engaged in basket making, palmistry, and theft. In an effort to rehabilitate this caste, the Congress Government had settled several families as road sweepers in villages.

All of these families received their maintenance in cash from government sources outside the village. They had no kin there, and were partly excluded from its social life. The village clerks, however, had been drawn into the structure of power and patronage by their close working relation with the village headman and their control of the land records. On the one hand, the clerk could extract small bribes and favors from the poorer *mirāsdārs* whose fields were recorded at lower than the current revenue value. On the other hand, the village clerk himself had to please the richest landlords and shield them from excessive revenue exactions, for they had the power to complain of his work to higher authorities and to have him transferred. The Koravars did their lowly work under the eagle eye of the *panchāyat* president, and had come to be regarded as little different from the lowliest village servants.

## The Land Records as Historical Documents

The village land records of 1897–8 and 1952 cast an interesting light on certain changes when compared with records of 1827. Considering first the area of the traditional *grāmam* (about 485 acres), we may note the following developments:

1. In 1897, actual fields were registered for the first time with individual owners, rather than the owners being allotted varying shares in the village at large. Although many fields had in fact been allocated permanently some years previously, the village commune may be said to have come to an end legally in 1897.

Table 10.1. *Percentages of land owned in Kumbapeṭṭai Grāmam by ethnic groups and by residents inside and outside the village, 1827, 1897, and 1952*

| | Inside | | | Outside | | |
|---|---|---|---|---|---|---|
| | 1827 | 1897 | 1952 | 1827 | 1897 | 1952 |
| Temples | — | 2.5 | 2.5 | — | — | — |
| Brahmans | 98.4 | 80.5 | 41.2 | — | — | 28.1 |
| Veḷḷālars | — | — | — | 1.6 | | 5.7 |
| Middle and Lower Non-Brahmans | — | 2.0 | 0.5 | — | 9.8 | 17.3 |
| Muslims | — | — | — | — | 5.2 | 4.3 |
| Harijans | — | — | 0.4 | — | — | — |
| Total | 98.4 | 85.0 | 44.6 | 1.6 | 15.0 | 55.4 |

*Source: Paimash* land records of 1828, Government Archives, Thanjāvūr; Land registers for Thanjāvūr district, 1898. Tamiḻ Nāḍu Archives, Madras; Land register maintained locally in the village I have called Kumbapeṭṭai, 1952.

2. In 1897 and 1952 the house sites in the *agrahāram*, Aḍichēri, the west side of Barbers' Street and the Dēvendra Paḷḷar Streets were still regarded as *nattam*, or tax-free residential land, but the fourteen acres of wet and dry fields that had been formerly set aside as service tenures (*paṭṭakkāl*) for the village slaves had been divided among the private *mirāsdārs*. One *māh* (0.33 acres) did, however, remain as a minute service tenure for the village Barbers, Potters, and Temple Priests.

3. Whereas 86 percent of the cultivable land was wet paddy land in 1827, 93 percent was wet land in 1898. Only 87 percent, however, was wet land in 1952, some land having been turned into coconut gardens.

4. Whereas only 22 percent of the net paddy land was growing two wet paddy crops in 1827, 76 percent grew two paddy crops in 1897, and 93 percent in 1952. This means that the gross paddy cultivation increased in Kumbapeṭṭai Grāmam by about twenty-one acres between 1897 and 1952, as part of the increase in double cropping and the intensification of paddy cultivation in the district as a whole. In 1952 as in 1897, moreover, no land was recorded as waste or fallow dry land. This meant that the cultivation of marketable crops had virtually abolished the twenty acres of pasture, millets, and scrub found in 1827.

5. As nearly as I can estimate, landownership was distributed among the major ethnic groups in the three periods, and among internal and external owners, as shown in Table 10.1.

Table 10.1 is probably inaccurate with respect to the percentages of land owned by Brahmans living inside the village in 1827 and 1897; some of the owners may have been absentees. There is no doubt, however, the absentee Brahman land ownership increased greatly between 1897 and 1952. Similarly, I have no way of knowing whether some of the land owned by ''external Non-Brahmans'' in 1827 and 1897 was owned by Veḷḷāḷars or by Agambaḍiyars, so I have bracketed the two together.

We should note that the temple lands were managed by the Brahmans in these periods, and that Brahmans living in Kumbapeṭṭai managed almost all the land of the absentee Brahmans, their relatives. This means that resident Brahmans actually controlled 98.4 percent of the land in 1827, 83 percent in 1897, and 71.8 percent in 1952.

The land records do not allow us to judge accurately the occupations and socioeconomic classes of the owners in every case. ''Lower-caste Non-Brahmans inside Kumbapeṭṭai'' refers, however, to Kōṉārs and Agambaḍiyars of Aḍichēri. It is interesting that having gained 2 percent of the *grāmam* land through trade by 1897, they had lost almost all of it again by 1952.

The ''external Veḷḷāḷars'' listed for 1952 were an enterprising family of owner cultivators of Periyūr who took advantage of the sale of royal lands and earned money in the paddy trade. They expanded their estate and eventually became landlords. Among the external ''middle and lower-caste Non-Brahmans'' in 1952, 4.3 percent of the total land was owned by Hindū traders of Āriyūr, some of them Gujarāti weavers in the textile trade. Thirteen percent was owned by Agambaḍiyars, Vaṉṉiyars, and other owner cultivators of Periyūr and Māniyur, who saved and prospered through the paddy trade in the same way as the Veḷḷāḷars. The ''external Muslims'' were all traders of Āriyūr and Thanjāvūr, some of whom served as agents for British firms trading in paddy and manufactures in Malaya and Singapore.

In the late nineteenth and twentieth centuries, therefore, the Brahman landlords, salary workers, and noncultivating land managers lost 27 percent of their land in the *grāmam* to lower-ranking owner cultivators and traders of nearby towns and villages whose traditional occupations and ways of life helped them to take advantage of the colonial trade. Most of this land transfer went on during world depressions, especially that of the 1930s, when the prices of land and paddy fell, those of imported manufactures remained high, and several Brahmans became too indebted to keep their land.

6. Whereas there were no women owners registered in 1827, eleven out of the ninety registered landowners were women in 1897, and twenty-seven out of the 139 landowners in 1952. This change occurred because of the breakdown of the village commune, and to some extent, of the extended family. When land was owned jointly by the Brahman community, the male heads of lineages and households redistributed and managed it. Women had rights only to maintenance from the land. Unmarried girls lived under the guardianship of their fathers; married women, of their husbands and fathers; and widows of their sons, or if there were no sons, their husbands' closest *dāyādis,* or patrilineal kin. In the nineteenth century, indeed, it still happened that a few widows burned themselves on their husbands' funeral pyres, even though this custom was forbidden by law in 1825. The last *sati* took place in a village near Kumbapeṭṭai as late as 1906.

When shares in the land became unequal, a man's land shares, like his personal property, were inherited equally by his sons, by a chosen daughter's son if he had no son, or by an adopted son if he had neither daughters nor sons. Land shares came to be divided among sons within a few years of the father's death, and brothers moved into separate houses when their land shares had been divided. If a man who had separated his property died without children, his ancestral land share passed to his widow for the duration of her life, and then back to his brothers and their descendents. Self-acquired land, like other property, might however be willed entirely to a childless widow, or to the widow and daughters if there were daughters and no sons. Similarly, when land shares (and later, actual fields), became individual property, men sometimes gave small pieces of land to their daughters as dowry along with jewels, vessels, and other movables. In these ways both married women and widows frequently became landowners. If a childless widow inherited land from her father or from her husband's self-acquired property, she was free to adopt a son as her heir after her husband's death.

Disputes sometimes arose over control of the property between such widows and their adopted sons, in which case the court would usually decide in favor of the adopted son. Sometimes, however, the dispute was settled out of court by the woman's agreeing to pay income to her adopted son, or the land being divided between them. A man was at liberty to will his self-acquired property to his widow, sons, daughters, or adopted son in any manner he chose, although he usually left it to his sons or adopted son, if any, in preference to his widow or his daughters. In general, the turning of land shares into private property, and the great increase in self-acquired property, meant that as the nineteenth century wore on, several widows in *mirāsi* families became heads of households managing their own property alone or through a chosen kinsman. Six such widows lived in the *agrahāram* in 1952, while several other married women or widows owned land in Kumbapeṭṭai but lived in other towns or villages.

7. Kumbapeṭṭai *grāmam* had thirty-two registered landowners in 1827, ninety in 1897, and 139 in 1952. It had thirty Brahman owners in 1827, sixty in 1898, and seventy-one in 1952. This increase partly reflected the growth in population in the region, and partly, the earlier division of land among brothers after the father's death. Most of the Brahmans' land holdings were correspondingly smaller, as is shown in Table 10.2

Some Kumbapeṭṭai Brahmans also owned land in other villages, so that Table 10.2 does not record all the total holdings but only the distribution within the *grāmam*. Table 12.1 lists the distribution of the holdings of all Kumbapeṭṭai's landowners in 1952.

These figures are not a completely adequate reflection of the Brahmans' wealth in the three periods, for more of the land produced two crops in the later decades, and many Brahmans had urban jobs. Nevertheless, the figures do give some idea of the gradual impoverishment of the Brahmans as a community. Double cropping did not make up for their average loss of land per family, and most urban jobs were not very lucrative; had they been, their holders would have

Table 10.2. *Distribution of landed estates within the grāmam by size among Kumbapeṭṭai Brahmans, present and absent, in 1827, 1897, and 1952*

| | 1827 | | 1897 | | 1952 | |
|---|---|---|---|---|---|---|
| | No. | % | No. | % | No. | % |
| 20 + acres | 9 | 30 | 3 | 5 | 1 | 1 |
| 15–19.9 acres | 3 | 10 | 1 | 2 | 3 | 4 |
| 10–14.9 acres | 2 | 7 | 4 | 7 | 4 | 6 |
| 5–9.9 acres | 6 | 20 | 10 | 17 | 8 | 12 |
| 2–4.9 acres | 9 | 30 | 21 | 35 | 23 | 34 |
| 1–1.9 acres | 1 | 3 | 8 | 13 | 12 | 18 |
| Under 1 acre | — | — | 13 | 21 | 16 | 25 |
| Total | 30 | 100 | 60 | 100 | 67 | 100 |

Table 10.3. *Distribution of land holdings in greater Kumbapeṭṭai by ethnic group and by internal and external owners in percentages, 1897 and 1952*

| | Inside | | Outside | |
|---|---|---|---|---|
| | 1897 | 1952 | 1897 | 1952 |
| Temples | 2.6 | 2.6 | — | 0.3 |
| Brahmans | 61.1 | 32.2 | 2.7 | 24.5 |
| Veḷḷāḷars | 7.3 | 7.3 | | 13.4 |
| Middle and Lower Non-Brahmans | 1.9 | 2.6 | 20.8 | 12.5 |
| Muslims | — | — | 3.6 | 4.3 |
| Harijans | — | 0.2 | — | — |
| Total | 72.9 | 44.9 | 27.1 | 55.0 |

bought more land. By 1952, 41 percent of the resident Brahman owners owned less than five acres, the lowest amount regarded as adequate for a decent livelihood without other earnings, while nine of the thirty-six resident families had virtually no land. When we consider that the village's Non-Brahmans and Harijans had gained very little over the whole period, and that seven of the sixteen Brahmans owning more than five acres within the *grāmam* were absentees in 1952, it is clear that the village as a whole had been impoverished.

8. Sheṭṭiyūr and Veḷiyūr were joined to Kumbapeṭṭai in 1898, and Akkāchāvaḍy and the east side of Barbers' Street became socially part of the village. Table 10.3 gives data on ownership by ethnic group and by external and internal owners in the larger village, including these three areas, in 1897 and 1952.

As in Table 10.1, the percentage recorded as owned by Brahmans living in Kumbapeṭṭai in 1897 is probably overrepresented, for only those living in Nallūr are recorded as "external" to the village. Even so, Brahmans as a whole lost some land in the larger village between the two periods, and Brahman residents lost considerably. By 1952 the Brahmans were trying to maintain dominance in a village in which, even counting their absent kinsmen, they and their temples owned only 60 percent of the land. They were able to do so to a large extent because they did control the land of the absent Brahmans. Even so, the Veḷḷāḷars of Sheṭṭiyūr ("internal" Veḷḷāḷars in Table 10.3) had largely broken away from the Brahmans' control in the 1890s and acknowledged their dominance only with respect to the *panchāyat* board and the village headship. The Veḷiyūr Harijans, too, mostly ignored village politics and confined their allegiance to their own, absent Veḷḷāḷar landlords. Table 10.3, finally, reflects the fact that between 1897 and 1952, in the larger village as in the *grāmam*, more land had been bought by Non-Brahman cultivators from outside the village and by traders of Āriyūr.

**Conclusions**

To summarize, in the hundred years between the 1850s and the 1950s, Kumbapeṭṭai, like other villages of Thanjāvūr, moved much farther away from being a precapitalist closed corporate community to being an open one penetrated by colonial capitalism. Slavery came to an end and was replaced by debt peonage and casual wage labor. The village commune was finally abolished in favor of private, marketable property, and landed estates, including those of the royal family, were turned into personal property. The service tenures of village servants and former slaves virtually disappeared, becoming the private plots of landlords who used the land for their own purposes or allowed their servants to live on it while retaining the power of eviction.

Both the debt peons and the village servants continued to be paid largely in kind for judicial services, but commodity production and work for cash wages were increasing in these relationships, and were general among about 40 percent of the population engaged primarily in trade, salary work, or casual labor by 1952.

The Brahmans, once communally organized, land-managing slave owners and religiosi, had become petty bourgeois, living from subsistence crops grown on their own holdings; the marketing of export crops; trading grain, cattle, foodstuffs, and other commodities; and mostly low-paid salary work. Although forced to become trading and farm-managing entrepreneurs, their religious ban upon themselves engaging in plough cultivation and their aristocratic patterns of consumption put them at a disadvantage in the colonial mercantile economy. They lost land through indebtedness to more enterprising farmers, merchants, and bigger landlords. The growth of population, unaccompanied by new forms of production, and the removal of surplus by merchants, absentee landowners, moneylenders, the colonial government, and indirectly by British manufacturing and trading companies, impoverished the village.

Meanwhile, new lower-caste groups of petty bourgeois and of independent commodity producers and traders (middle and rich peasants in Sheṭṭiyūr, small family traders in grain and alcohol on the borders of Nallūr) occupied some of the land between adjacent villages and challenged the Brahmans' dominance. For a while in the early 1900s they prospered in the face of bitter resistance from the Brahmans, but eventually the independent traders sank back into poverty, their enterprises curtailed by new laws or by the growth of quasimonopoly traders in the town of Thanjāvūr.

Absentee landownership, and the departure of many Brahmans to urban work, allowed scope for contractual, fixed-rent tenant farming on almost half of the village land by some of descendants of its former slaves. Some descendants of former slaves, too, prospered modestly in the early 1900s, but the growing competition for land permitted rack renting and kept most of them in conditions little better than those of the landless laborers. The competition for land among tenants and laborers was increased by the loss of their former occupations among pastoralists, fishermen, foot soldiers, cavalry, groomsmen, toddy traders, puppet players, and some of the village priests and potters, and their reversion to agriculture. In general, except in the case of the Ādi Drāviḍas, caste membership became a limiting rather than a determining factor in class relations and the choice of occupations.

# 11 The Annual Round

Eighty-three percent of Kumbapeṭṭai's men gained their livelihood directly from agriculture as rentiers, managers, or workers, whereas 52 percent of the women were actively engaged at least part time in agricultural work or management. The annual cycle of agricultural activities and festivals is therefore essential for an understanding of the villagers' lives and production relations. In this chapter I describe the main events of this cycle. In order to place the yearly round in perspective, I shall also mention major nonagricultural, especially religious, events.

Table 11.1 gives the Tamiḷ months, seasons, and major agricultural events and festivals.

## New Year

The agricultural year began on New Year's Day (*Varusha Pirappu*) on Chittrai 1. On that date *mirāsdārs* finally selected their *kuthakai* tenants and *paṇṇaiyals* for the coming year and made them loans of about Rs. 50 per *paṇṇaiyāḷ* and Rs. 100 per tenant. This sum tided the servant over the lean months of Chittrai, Vaigāsi, and Āṉi when rivers and channels were dry and there was little agricultural work. It allowed the tenant to begin ploughing and to buy cow dung and pay for sheep from Rāmanāthapuram to fertilize his fields. On New Year's morning, the *mirāsdār* received a promissory note from the tenant or the *paṇṇaiyāḷ* for the amount forwarded. He reclaimed it from the man's wages or harvest shares in the course of the year, sometimes at 6 percent interest and sometimes interest free. Even in the case of interest-free payments, however, the *mirāsdār* gained much if he took the amount from the harvest payments in paddy, for paddy might be worth only half as much in the harvest seasons as it was in Chittrai to Āvaṉi, the season of scarcity. In 1952, for example, paddy sold for Rs. 24 per bag on the black market from Chittrai to Āvaṉi, but was worth only Rs. 12 during the two harvests of Purattāsi–Aippasi and Thai–Māsi months. *Mirāsdārs* had the advantage of being able to store surplus paddy and sell it in seasons of scarcity, but small owners, tenants, and laborers had to pay their debts in paddy or money during the harvest seasons, the only times when they had surplus.

On the evening of New Year's Day all the *mirāsdārs* assembled outside the temple of Srī Rama at the head of the Brahman street. This event was paid for each year in turn by one of two branches of one of the four Brahman lineages, all

Table 11.1. *The agricultural year in northwest Thanjāvūr, 1951–2*

| English month | Tamiḻ month | Season | Weather | Agricultural activities and festivals |
|---|---|---|---|---|
| April–May | Chittrai | Vasantha | Very hot (79°–97°). Dry. Rivers dry. | New Year, Chittrai 1. First Ploughing. Cattle grazing. Sheep arrive from Rāmanāthapuram. |
| May–June | Vaigāsi | Rathu | Hot winds, late Vaigāsi. | Sheep grazing. Cattle grazing. Ploughing. |
| June–July | Āṉi | Grishma | Hot (78°–95°). Winds. Water arrives mid–late Āṉi. | *Kuruvai* seed sown. Ploughing. Channel digging. Ceremony for arrival of water. *Kuruvai* transplanting. |
| July–Aug. | Āḍi | Rathu | Fresher breezes, some showers. | Āḍi 18 or Āḍi Flood. *Kuruvai* transplanting. Ploughing *sambā* seedbeds. |
| Aug.–Sept. | Āvaṉi | Varasha | Rather hot (76°–93°). | Weeding *kuruvai* fields. Final *kuruvai* transplanting, early Āvaṉi. Single crop *sambā* sowing. No transplanting, Āvaṉi 15–25. |
| Sept.–Oct. | Purattāsi | Rathu | Occasional thunder storms and showers. | *Kuruvai* harvest and threshing. *Sambā* ploughing. *Sambā* sowing. *Sambā* transplanting. |
| Oct.–Nov. | Aippasi | Shārad | Rather cool (72°–84°). Rain begins. | *Kuruvai* harvest and threshing, early Aippasi. Ploughing. Deepāvaḷi. *Sambā* transplanting. |

| | | | | |
|---|---|---|---|---|
| Nov.–Dec. | Kārthikai | Rathu | Frequent, heavy rain (N.E. Monsoon). | *Sambā* transplanting. |
| Dec.–Jan. | Māṛgaṛi | Hementha | Cool (70°–82°). Some showers. | *Sambā* weeding. Black and green gram sown, late Māṛgaṛi. |
| Jan.–Feb. | Thai | Rathu | Heavy dew. | Black and green gram sown, early Thai. *Sambā* harvest and threshing from mid-Thai. Pongal, Thai 1st. |
| Feb.–March | Māsi | Shishira | Warm (72°–88°). Dry. Leaves fall. | *Sambā* harvest and threshing. |
| March–April | Panguni | Rathu | Hotter. Rivers dry up. | End of *sambā* harvest. Black and green gram harvest. Cowdung put on fields. Ducks arrive from Tiruchirappalli. |

members of that branch being expected to come home for it. Non-Brahman tenants and *vēlaikkārars* of that branch were also invited and stood outside the gate of the temple, the Brahmans assembling inside. Ādi Drāviḍas were not invited, for they were forbidden to enter the Brahman street.

The Bhaṭṭachār Brahman priest from Nallūr performed a *poojai* to the deity, that is, a service with chanting in Sanskrit and offerings of incense, flowers, cooked food, sacred water, a burning lamp, and libations on the central stone idol. Small brass images (*vigrahams*) of the god Rāma and his consort Seetha were then taken down the street and back again in procession in a decorated palanquin with music. The women of each Brahman house made offerings of a coconut, banana, and burning camphor on the way, while Brahman children followed the procession noisily and excitedly. When the gods had been replaced in the temple and a second *poojai* with loud bell ringing performed, Kumbapeṭṭai's most senior *sāstrigal*, or household priest, one of the Brahacharaṇam Brahmans and himself a landlord, read the almanac for the year in Sanskrit and Tamiḻ to the assembled company. His discourse included information on the weather, eclipses, and the auspicious day for the First Ploughing festival. In 1952, for example, the *sāstrigal* told us that there would be an eclipse of the moon, plenty of cow's milk, moderate paddy crops, not much rain, and good green and black gram crops. He then forecast the personal fortunes of people whose birthdays fell on various stars. One friend, for example, was told that if he gained fourteen of anything, he must lose seven. The *sāstrigal* ended with a *poojai* to Vināyakar, the elephant god of good luck. The Bhaṭṭachār concluded the proceedings with final *poojais* to Rama and Seetha, ending by distributing *prasādham*, or sacrificial materials, to all men, women, and children present in order of rank. Gifts of Rs. 1 were made by the hosts to the Bhaṭṭachār and the *sāstrigal*, after which the company went home to a special feast in those houses that could afford it. The *mirāsdārs* later sent messages to all their servants to tell them on which day to assemble for First Ploughing.

At 9:00 P.M. in 1952, a small function for Brahmans and Non-Brahmans took place in the village temple of Ūriḍeichiyamman. Interestingly, this event had been created by the *panchāyat* president seven years previously. It involved a special *poojai* to the goddess and the lesser godlings by the village Poosāri and the waving before each of them of the large candelabra brought from the Vishnū temple by the Brahman Kurukkal. Some leading Brahmans and their wives and children sat nearest the inner shrine at these proceedings, while leading Non-Brahman men, their wives, and some children of the Non-Brahman streets stood at the rear. After the *poojai* the Poosāri distributed sacred cow dung ash and the auspicious red powder, *kungumam*, to those present in order of caste, gender, and age. As was customary, each worshipper placed some of the appropriate powder on his or her forehead, with widows using only ash and married women, *kungumam*. The Kōṉār headman of the village, who had been persuaded to pay for the festival each year as his *maṇḍahappaḍi*, or privilege, then gave out fried chickpeas, bananas, and pieces of coconut. Most of this food went to the

Brahmans, the remainder going to the Non-Brahmans, especially children, when the Brahmans had left. At this function it was noticeable that the Non-Brahman children were much quieter than the Brahman, the former being hit on the head by their elders if they misbehaved. When the last food was distributed the Non-Brahman children stretched out their hands, obviously hungry. Yet two of them insisted on giving me the two bananas they received, in exchange for some chickpeas I had given them earlier. "Eat it, mother, simply eat it!" they cried. This sad experience seemed even sadder when one thought of the Paḷḷar children who were not invited at all.

New Year's Day was chiefly a family and business festival, not traditionally a ceremonial event uniting all the castes. Within each street, relatives and neighbors wished each other, "May this year go well." Ideally, all debts should be repaid on New Year's Day. In 1952 merchants in Āriyūr sent printed invitations to their debtors to come and visit them. Kumbapeṭṭai's *mirāsdārs* did so and tried to pay off the whole, a half, or at least a quarter of the debt. The debts of *paṇṇaiyāḷs*, *vēlaikkārars*, and tenants to their *mirāsdārs* had to be repaid by New Year's Day, or else carried forward in a new promissory note for another year. The houses were cleaned and decorated in the early morning, fresh cow dung being plastered on the floor and walls and a design of colored rice powders (*kōḷam*) made before the entry by the women and little girls. Those who could afford it made a feast including jaggery, sweetmeats, buttermilk, and a curry containing margosa leaves to honor the goddess Māriyamman and fend off smallpox, formerly rampant in this season.

### First Ploughing

First Ploughing followed on an auspicious day in Chittrai. It was called *Nalla Yēr Kattravadu* or *Nallēr* ("Good Plough" or "Making a Good Plough"). The day was selected by the *sāstrigal* according to the village's star. In 1952, each *mirāsdār* assembled with his male Non-Brahman *vēlaikkārars* and Ādi Drāviḍas *paṇṇaiyāḷs* in one of his paddy fields at about 9:00 A.M. The Brahmans and Non-Brahmans had already taken their morning baths and prostrated themselves before Lord Siva. The *paṇṇaiyāḷ* men and boys had washed the landlord's bullocks in the tank and adorned them with flower garlands around their necks and saffron paste and red powder on their foreheads. In this season the fields were dry and hard, the river and channel water having been turned off at the Mēttur Dam in Māsi (February–March). The *paṇṇaiyāḷs* harnessed the bullocks and ploughed furrows round the fields three times, cutting the first sods of the year. One of the Non-Brahman servants brought a brass tray with two small saffron *lingams* (phallic symbols) on it representing Vināyakkar, the deity of good luck. He offered a *poojai* to them using incense (*sāmbrāni*) burning on a cake of cow dung, coconuts, bananas, betel leaves, arecanuts, and flowers. He waved a camphor flame to the earth goddess, Bhūmā Dēvi, and to the oxen. The Non-Brahman and Paḷḷar servants then prostrated themselves on the ground before the earth goddess, the oxen, their *mirāsdārs*, and any other visiting

Brahmans. The Non-Brahman "priest" gave materials from the offerings, called *prasādham*, to each Brahman in order of age, to the Non-Brahmans, and finally to the Paḷḷars, who stood some nine feet away from the Brahmans according to custom. The *mirāsdār* gave half to three annas to each boy and one *marakkāḷ* of paddy to each man. He gave these to a Non-Brahman servant without touching him, and asked him to hand their shares to the Paḷḷar men and boys individually. The ceremony ended, the *mirāsdār* went home to prostrate himself before the elders of his family and offer them the *prasādham* of the ritual as a blessing. In some houses the Non-Brahman servants assembled at the front of the Brahman house and the Paḷḷars at the back to receive their gifts.

Non-Brahman and Paḷḷar *kuthakai* tenants held Nallēr independently in their leased fields. No Non-Brahman owners or tenants of Kumbapeṭṭai engaged *paṇṇaiyāḷs*; instead they used family labor and hired coolies at peak seasons. For Nallēr the tenants washed their own oxen and did the ceremony in small male family groups. Non-Brahmans were forbidden to do Nallēr in their leased fields before the Brahmans had finished theirs, and Ādi Drāviḍas, before the Non-Brahmans. Anyone who broke this rule was fined by the *mirāsdārs*, all such fines going to the village temple funds.

Between Nallēr and mid-Āṉi, the farmer had to see that his paddy fields were ploughed four times to ensure that the soil was friable before transplanting. A little of this ploughing was done in Vaigāsi if light rains fell for two or three days, but most of it took place in Āṉi shortly before and after the water was released to Thanjāvūr's rivers from the Mēttur Dam.

Nallēr, like the other major agricultural festivals of Pongal and Āḍi Perukku, in fact occurred about a month earlier than was appropriate according to the agricultural schedule in the 1950s. The reason was that the building of the Mēttur Dam in the mid 1930s had delayed Thanjāvūr's year-round agricultural operations because it meant that no water was released to the rivers and channels between mid-February and late June or even July or early August. Before the dam was built, Thanjāvūr's rivers were usually full by Vaigāsi and often earlier. Correspondingly, the first, or *kuruvai* crop was sown in early Vaigāsi and harvested in Āvaṉi, while the later, *sambā* crop (sometimes a second crop and sometimes the only crop of the year) was ready for harvesting in early Thai. The use of the dam delayed most operations by a month or more. Its disadvantage was that if the dam filled slowly and the water was released late, it might cause the *kuruvai* harvest to fail during the rains and floods of Kārthikai. Its advantage was that it prevented periodic flooding of the Kāvēri in Panguni to Āḍi and made it possible to grow the first, or *kuruvai*, crop in much larger areas.

## The Seasons

### *The Dry Season*

Dry ploughing became common in Thanjāvūr only after the Mēttur Dam was built and the rivers and channels were kept dry for four months. After the dam was built, Kumbapeṭṭai's farmers began to prefer dry to wet ploughing and by 1952, almost all ploughing in Kumbapeṭṭai was dry. Even after the water arrived, most people preferred to plough without releasing water to their fields.

Between early Māsi and mid-Āṉi, landlords and tenants hired sheep from the visiting shepherds from Rāmanāthapuram to fertilize their fields. Some twenty shepherd families camped in Kumbapeṭṭai from early Māsi to early Āṉi. In the daytime they grazed their sheep freely from stubble and weeds in the dry fields once the gram crops had been harvested. At night they leased out the sheep at three to four *marakkāḷs* of paddy per 100 sheep in Māsi-Panguni and at six *marakkāḷs* (half a *kalam*) in Chittrai-Vaigāsi, when fresh manuring just prior to transplanting was most valuable.

In the same season, some of the Kōṉār cowherds of Kumbapeṭṭai assembled cattle from the landlords and grazed them in the paddy fields of landlords and tenants for a fee. This grazing began in Panguni after the black and green gram harvest and continued into Āṉi. During the rest of the year the cattle were grazed by boys or old men of *paṇṇaiyāḷ* families on the channel banks or were fed straw or oil-seed cake in their sheds. The oil cake was made partly in Kumbapeṭṭai from gingelly, castor, and other oil seeds, and was partly purchased in stores. In Panguni to Āṉi, paddy stubble and weeds were available in the dry fields.

Both *mirāsdārs* and tenants had to see that their fields were properly manured before the ploughing season. Shortly before the fields were ploughed by Paḷḷar servants or Non-Brahman tenants, extra carts of cow dung, dust, and ashes were driven from the cowsheds and unloaded in small compost pits at the corner of each field. Non-Brahman servants usually drove the carts for *mirāsdārs,* the manure being spread before ploughing by the Paḷḷar workmen. Paḷḷar and Non-Brahman tenants borrowed their *mirāsdārs'* carts to drive to their leased fields. *Kuthakai* leases usually provided that the *mirāsdār* should supply, or pay for, half the total manure each year and the tenant the other half.

Agriculturally, the period from Panguni to Āṉi was the slackest season, especially for the landlords. The weather was intensely hot, the full moon nights exceedingly bright. Most of the village festivals of *grāma dēvatais* and of the great temples dedicated to Siva, Vishnū, or Subramania took place in this period. Kumbapeṭṭai's own festival to Ūriḍeichiyamman occupied twelve days of Chittrai or Vaigāsi, with several earlier, preliminary ceremonies. The twelfth night was a time of great rejoicing. After the final ceremony, Non-Brahmans and Ādi Drāviḍas feasted on sacrificial meat and toddy, and married couples were reunited after forty days of celibacy.

Most of the Brahmans and some Non-Brahmans walked, drove by oxcart, or went by bus to other festivals in the neighborhood, notably at Tiruvaiyāru, Chakkrāpalli, and Thanjāvūr. Pilgrimages by train or bus to more distant temples in east Thanjāvūr or other districts were especially favored from Panguni to Āṉi, and in Kumbapeṭṭai were chiefly undertaken by the Brahmans. Until 1947 the Paḷḷars had been excluded from the temples of the higher castes, but even they had a role in the village festival and the smaller festival to their own goddess,

Kāḷiyamman. For the Paḷḷars, this season as a whole was mainly one of underemployment, hardship, and hunger. Occasionally, however, even Paḷḷar men went by bus or walked to Thanjāvūr to visit a cinema. In 1952, Kumbapeṭṭai's own village festivals did not occur because of disunity in the *agrahāram* and class struggle in the village. Many villagers did attend the festivals of Periyūr and other nearby villages.

### *Arrival of the Water*

Water normally arrived in Thanjāvūr's rivers and channels during Āṉi, the date depending on rainfall in the Western Ghāts and the height of water in the Mēttur Dam. In wet years it arrived in the last week of June; in dry years it might be withheld until mid-August (late Āḍi). This delay caused hardship to the cultivators, whose crop was late and had to be harvested during the rains in November or December. In 1952 the water reached Kumbapeṭṭai on July 12, an average date, arriving in east Thanjāvūr one week later.

The arrival of the water was a momentous, ceremonialized event. For a day or two in advance, word was passed on from upstream in Tiruchirappalli district that the water was coming. A species of crow called *kākkā kuruvai* began to call out a few hours before its arrival. Brahman men assembled on the western boundary of the *grāmam* near Sheṭṭiyūr, where the Shōradayan and Periya channels divided. As the water rushed into these channels at 2:00 P.M., the *sāstrigals* offered *poojais* with coconuts and camphor flames to Vināyakar. The Brahmans then ate gram and rice flour cakes and drank coffee while standing in the water, rejoicing. Lower down the channels Non-Brahmans and Paḷḷars waited to cut their own coconuts and wave camphor flames as the water arrived. In this ceremony as in all others connected with the river, and in daily bathing, Non-Brahmans entered the water of each village downstream from the Brahmans because of their lower caste rank, and Ādi Drāviḍas downstream from the Non-Brahmans. In this way it was believed that the lower castes would be prevented from polluting the higher. Presumably, the water purified itself while running through the paddy fields between the villages.

### *Channel Digging*

One day during Chittrai or Vaigāsi, the *mirāsdārs* gathered in one of the Brahmans' homes. The Brahman trustee of the village temple collected money from each Brahman landowner to pay for digging out the village channels before the water came, the amounts varying according to the land that was owned. Wherever possible, money was obtained from the absentee owners, for this responsibility rested with *mirāsdārs* and not with *kuthakai* tenants. A day was fixed for channel digging and the Paṟayar messenger from Māniyūr was sent to the streets to summon all the Paḷḷar men. The Shōradayan Channel, Kumbapeṭṭai's main channel, had already been dug out by coolies sent by the Public Works Department of the government, while each *mirāsdār* had his own small channels dug privately. Ideally, 340 Paḷḷar men were needed to dig out the remaining channels. Traditionally, due warning was given and all Paḷḷar men and boys were required to arrive on the appointed day at dawn. Other Paḷḷars and Paṟayars from other villages, and the poorer Non-Brahmans of Kumbapeṭṭai, were also welcomed to make up the numbers, but were not obliged to come.

Kumbapeṭṭai's Paḷḷars were summoned by the Paṟayar's drumbeat, street by street. Men of the First Section of Upper Paḷḷar Street began the work after the Brahmans had measured twelve feet of channel for each Paḷḷar with a measuring rod. Each Paḷḷar dug out his segment quickly while the Paṟayar beat his drum and the landlords stood by, urging on their servants. Meanwhile, Paḷḷars of the Second Section of Upper Paḷḷar Street began work on a second series of twelve-foot lengths in each of the main channels in turn, and finally all the Non-Brahmans and "outside people" joined in the process. In this way the channels were dug out in two to three days. Each workman was paid one *marakkāḷ* of paddy and As. 2 per day from the common fund.

If any Brahman failed to pay, the others prevented him from receiving water in his fields. In 1948, for example, the *agrahāram's* religious healer, an eccentric oldster, failed to pay his dues. On sowing day when he told his Paḷḷars to let in water from the main channel to his field, the *panchāyat* president arrived on behalf of the community and ordered them not to do so. The erring Brahman promptly paid his Rs. 10, and the sluice was opened.

In 1952 disunity in the *agrahāram* was so great that the digging was not organized until the morning of the day the water arrived. The *panchāyat* president, usurping the temple trustee's function, then sent the Paṟayars at dawn to summon the Paḷḷars by drum and himself took up a collection among the Brahmans. At such short notice, only forty Paḷḷars at first arrived from the five streets, others following later. The Paḷḷars dug hard for ten hours with little pause until the water came, with each man cutting several lengths as best he could. The Paṟayars drummed to stimulate them, and the Brahmans shouted encouragement from the bunds. Some of the private digging of smaller channels and mending of bunds took place after the water had come.

### *Sowing the Paddy Crop*

The sowing of the first, or *kuruvai*, crop began a few days before the water arrived. Kumbapeṭṭai's farmers knew ten varieties of *luruvai*, but regularly used only three, with growing seasons of ninety to 110 days. Those farmers whose fields lay near a well, a tank, or a river containing a little water sowed early to ensure an early harvest and ample time to sow a second crop. Others, the majority, waited until immediately after the water arrived. Each farmer set aside one-fifteenth of his land near a channel as seed beds (*nāṯṯangāl*).

Two to three days before the sowing, enough bags of seed were brought from the landlord's house and soaked in a tank or a channel to effect germination. They were removed at night, then resoaked the following day. Seeds sown in dry-ploughed beds were soaked for two days; those sown in wet beds for three.

On the day of sowing, the landlord and his male and female *paṇṇaiyāḷs* arrived soon after dawn. The Brahman, or his household priest, first made the usual *poojai* to a saffron *lingam* of Vināyakar at an auspicious time with coconuts, incense, and a camphor flame. Some Non-Brahman tenants did their own *poojai* in their leased fields; others hired the Telugu Brahman household priest. Paḷḷar tenants, of only ten years' standing, sowed their leased fields without benefit of *poojai*.

If the ploughing had been dry, the men broke up the clods in the seed bed field with wooden hammers until the soil was soft and smooth, then divided the field into small beds of about one-hundredth of an acre (one cent) each. The beds were separated latitudinally by small ridges of earth two to three inches high, and longitudinally by narrow, shallow furrows to let the water in. Male *paṇṇaiyāḷs* prepared the beds, built the ridges and channels and then carefully scattered seed on the beds, using one bag for each cent of land.[1] Meanwhile, a Non-Brahman servant drove a cart of cow dung ash as near as possible, and women *paṇṇaiyāḷs* carried the ash in baskets to the fields. After the sowing, men or women laborers opened the channels slightly to each plot in turn and allowed a little water to seep in and soak the plot before closing the channel again with earth. If the sowing took place before the river water arrived, bamboo baskets made by Koravars were used to ladle and carry water to the fields. When each bed was soaked, women sprinkled cow dung ash from baskets, lightly covering the seed.

### *Transplanting*

*Kuruvai* shoots appeared about three days after sowing and were transplanted on the eighteenth to twenty-seventh day depending on the seed.

*Kuruvai* transplanting began at the end of Āṉi and went on through Āḍi and into Āvaṉi. The first transplanting, or *mudal naḍavu*, was an important, ceremonious event in the landlord's or tenant's year. Those with most land and power tried to hold their first transplanting early and to call many laborers. In 1952 the *panchāyat* president kicked off with the biggest crowd of 100 Paḷḷar women, all in the village plus some of their relatives from outside. He was closely followed by the lesser cultivating landlords and a little later, the Non-Brahman owners and tenants, each man summoning about twenty to fifty Paḷḷathis according to his means. Sometimes more women would arrive than had been summoned, for women's work was scarce and there were special small gifts on the first transplanting day. Occasionally, if several men had planned their first transplanting on the same day, there was a shortage of labor and relatives of Kumbapeṭṭai's Paḷḷar women were quickly summoned from nearby villages. In one case Non-Brahman women of the Ambalakkārar caste came to substitute for Paḷḷathis, but usually Non-Brahman women would not take part in the hard work of transplanting except in their own families' leased fields.

Male *paṇṇaiyāḷs* arrived at dawn for first transplanting and collected the seedlings in large clumps from the seed bed to carry to the fields. A few days before transplanting, the fields had received their fourth ploughing. Cow dung, and sometimes potash bought by the landlords in Āriyūr, had been ploughed in. After ploughing, mattocks and hammers had been used to break up clods in the flooded fields, and a wooden board had been dragged across them to smooth the

First transplanting, Kumbapeṭṭai. A Harijan woman bows before her Brahman landlord before starting to work.

soil. On the appointed day the fields were flooded so that they appeared as small lakes of liquid mud. On arrival at about 10:00 A.M. the landlord stood on a bund near the fields. Each Paḷḷar woman approached him with a small bundle of seedlings in each hand and bowed three times, touching the ground with her seedlings about six feet away from him. At the *panchāyat* president's first transplanting he held a cane with which he lightly hit the women's heads when they bumped into each other or scrambled before him, as he shouted at them to be respectful and orderly.

The women then assembled in rows across the fields to be planted and pushed the seedlings haphazardly about three inches into the mud, roughly four inches apart. Male *paṇṇaiyāḷs* or Non-Brahman servants, about one to every fifteen women, brought the clumps to the fields and broke them into smaller bunches, which they dropped beside each woman. The women moved forward briskly, singing folk songs, or laughing and chattering as they worked. Later in the broiling sun, the work grew harder, and by 2:00 P.M. when they had finished, they were exhausted. On the few occasions when I tried it I found transplanting the hardest work women did apart from carrying slabs of stone on their heads for building. The bent posture was back breaking, the warm muddy water was slimy, and leeches all too often attached themselves to the women's legs. A large crowd of women usually could complete the first day's work in four hours, but

Transplanting, Kumbapeṭṭai, 1951.

with only a few minutes' rest for rice gruel drunk in the field, even four hours seemed arduous. At the end of the work day, the women assembled at the back door of their landlord's house to sing final songs blessing his family. Through his Non-Brahman servant the landlord paid them their wages of cash or paddy, together with small quantities of betel and arecanuts for chewing, rice, tamarind, chillies, salt, and sometimes dhāl for their families' evening meal. These materials had been prepared by the landlord's wife. A senior Paḷḷathi gave one bundle of seedlings to the oldest woman of the landlord's household through the Non-Brahman servant and the landlord. This woman placed the bundle inside her house before the *tulassi* plant in the courtyard as an offering to Lord Vishnū.

Some Non-Brahman owner cultivators and tenants served their coolies cooked instead of raw food in the backyards of their houses on the first-transplanting and cattle-driving days. Brahmans did not practice this custom, probably feeling themselves to be of too high rank to serve food to their former slaves.

*Kuruvai* transplanting might continue as late as mid-Āvaṉi, although most of the work was usually completed by the end of Āḍi. On regular days the women planted from 6:00 A.M. until 2:00 P.M. with a short break for gruel at noon. Twelve women were normally needed for an acre of planting; if fewer came, they worked longer, and if more came, they shared the wages of twelve. Some landlords were "cruel" in the eyes of both the lower castes and the other Brahmans, turning away all women except their own servants and others they really needed.

During ploughing, sowing, and transplanting, quarrels over irrigation water were frequent between landlords with adjacent fields sharing a common water supply. A state law held that as the water flowed from west to east those in the west had priority over those in the east and could block the flow in order to flood their fields for sowing, transplanting, or wet ploughing. Village convention, however, allowed a man to the east to release the flow if his western neighbor's fields were very full or if he arrived first in the morning intent on sowing or transplanting. Friendly neighbors asked each other politely for water or sent a servant to remonstrate, but spiteful men or neighbors with a long-standing dispute often used irrigation water to pay off an old grudge.

Transplanting was forbidden between Āvaṉi 15 and 25, for the earth goddess was said to be menstruating. The period afforded a ten-day respite to women between the latest *kuruvai* and the earliest *sambā* planting. Meanwhile, Paḷḷar women weeded each *kuruvai* field twice between transplanting and harvesting. Other than to confirm that women went to the fields and to pay them at the end of each day, the landlords took little interest in this work.

***Āḍi Flood***

At the height of the *kuruvai* transplanting the festival of Āḍi Flood took place. By this time the rivers were in full spate and the main channel was at a depth of about three feet. The festival was said to celebrate the pregnancy of Mother Kāvēri, perhaps leading to the *kuruvai* harvest as a season of birth. It was a joyful festival especially important for women, as Nallēr was for men. Non-Brahmans and Ādi Drāviḍas ate goatsmeat on this day, with four or five houses of relatives sharing one animal.

The day before, each servant family had received a loan of three *marakkāḷs* of paddy and Rs. 2 in order to celebrate the festival. In the morning Non-Brahman servants and Paḷḷar *paṇṇaiyāḷs* came to the front and back doors respectively of their masters' homes. The Paḷḷar men were each given one *marakkāḷ* of paddy and As. 8 or Re. 1 in cash; the women As. 4. In some houses, Non-Brahman male servants received up to Rs. 5 and one *kalam* of paddy; in others, less.

About 4:00 P.M., Brahman women assembled on the bank of the Shōradayan Channel behind their homes, Non-Brahmans of Akkāchāvaḍy and Vēṭṭāmbāḍi near the road bridge further east, and Paḷḷar women at Neṭṭi Kuṭṭai Tank in the southeast of the village. In 1952, the Non-Brahman women of Aḍichēri and Barber Street actually assembled earlier than the Brahmans higher up the channel above the Vināyakar shrine in the northwest of the village. No objection was made although there were a few older people who mentioned that this was against caste custom.

The women brought with them covered vessels of rice cooked with curds, lime fruits, coconut and gingilly seeds, and materials for *poojai*. After bathing in the channel and dressing, each group of Non-Brahman and Paḷḷar women made three small saffron *lingams* representing Vināyakar and placed them by the river bank. The married women took off the *tālis,* or marriage badges, that hung round their necks on strings, put on new strings, and placed these necklaces around the *lingams*. Before the *lingams* they arranged the *poojai* objects of coconut, lime fruits, betel leaves and arecanuts, and walked round them, sprinkling them with water from the channel. They burned incense before the *lingams*, sang and danced around them, then removed the *tālis* and replaced them round their necks. All the women then tied thin strings of cotton, colored with saffron, several times round each others' necks and wrists, signifying a sacred, auspicious occasion from which harmful influences were excluded. The married women and unmarried girls put spots of *kungumam*, the red powder signifying fertility and happy marriage, on each others' foreheads. They threw the lime fruits and a little cooked food into the water as an offering to Mother Kāvēri, and added to them bangles and ear plugs made from leaves to decorate the goddess. Then they waded into the water and standing in it, ate their own food with merriment. Small boys and old men gathered on the bridges to watch and applaud, and in the *agrahāram* young Brahman men and boys brought gaily decorated palanquins to carry pictures of the deities Subramania, Rāma, and their wives up and down the street.

As it happened, in 1952 an old Kaḷḷar man got drunk on French polish. He came roaring up Akkāchāvaḍy and routed the women from the channel with his stick in the middle of their picnic, shouting that they were doing everything wrong. The women scattered and ran home, screaming with laughter. This festival was particularly important for Paḷḷar and Non-Brahman women, for they (especially the Paḷḷathis) had done the agricultural work. The Brahman women held a quieter picnic later in the afternoon without a *poojai* and without changing their *tāli* strings.

Āḍi Flood was important to Brahman men as a day for fulfilling vows. Men of substance were in the habit of making offerings to deities, especially Vināyakar, if they succeeded in marrying off a daughter or buying a piece of land. Because both these events usually occurred in the dry season, several Brahmans were likely to offer sweetmeats or other delicacies at the shrine of Vināyakar on the evening of this day. The offerings were later distributed to the assembled Brahmans.

### *Harvest*

The harvest of the first, or *kuruvai*, crop took place in Purattāsi and Aippasi, occasionally being delayed into Karthikai if the water had arrived very late. Both men and women cut the ripe stalks with semicircular sickles, about twelve people being required per acre. If more came, they divided the same wages; if fewer, they worked harder and might reveive more. As in the case of transplanting, each farmer employed his own *paṇṇaiyāḷs* and *vēlaikkārars* first, adding men and women from the village's pool of casual coolies as they were needed. Usually, a landlord or tenant had about one to two acres cut per day. As usual, Paḷḷars did most of the work, but Non-Brahman male servants helped with their masters' harvest, and Non-Brahmans of both sexes harvested their own families' leased fields. Each field was harvested and threshed in a single day. The work began at 6:00 A.M. and ended about dusk at 6:00 to 7:00 P.M. From 10:00 to 2:00 P.M. the laborers usually rested under the trees in the fields and ate rice gruel or cooked rice brought to them by old women or by children. The laborers were divided into groups of three or four, each group being given designated areas to harvest.

The cut paddy was collected into hand bundles (*kōṭṭus*) and then into headloads of twenty bundles (*kaṭṭus*), each bundle and headload being tied with straw. Having cut the paddy in the morning, the laborers carried the loads on their heads to the nearest threshing floor in the early afternoon. They then lined up in three rows. One row of men or women (or both) stood in front of the row of newly cut paddy loads and carried bundles of it about six yards forward to a second row of men. The men beat each bundle on the ground about four times to release the grain, then handed over the straw to three or four men behind them who were stacking it. When the threshing was completed, the chaff was winnowed from the grain by both men and women. Each winnower filled a flat basket shovel of the kind used for sweeping and shook it lightly above her head, allowing the grain to fall slowly for the chaff to blow away. The winnowed grain was swept into a large heap in the center of the threshing floor, usually by women.

All this time the landlord and his friends and children had been standing or sitting by, watching to see how good the crop would be and to make sure that none was stolen. Sometimes two landlords' servants threshed side by side on the same large threshing floor. Also present were the village servants – the carpenter, blacksmith, washerman, barber, village temple priest, Paṟayar scavenger, and the Paḷḷar watchman of the area. The leading Paḷḷar measured the grain, and the landlord had his Non-Brahman servant give their shares to each of the village servants.

After all payments had been made to the harvest laborers and the village servants, the remaining paddy was bagged and Non-Brahman servants carried it, or drove it on paddy wagons, to their landlord's grain bins in his home. If the hour was late, the paddy was left on the threshing floor. It was covered and tied with straw and a design in cow dung and water made on it. If a thief came in the night, the design would be disturbed. The paddy would then be remeasured and the Paḷḷar watchman required to make good the loss.

*Pōraḍi*, or "beating the straw," the second threshing, took place on the day after threshing by hand. About half a dozen Non-Brahman or Paḷḷar servant men spread the straw on the threshing floor and drove oxen over it in a circle for several hours. The straw was removed and stacked in the master's yard for fodder, and the grain winnowed and bagged. Old people and widows among the servants were allowed to remove the final remnants of bruised grain and chaff.

### *The Sambā Crop*

*Sambā* paddy, the main crop of the year, was grown between Āvaṉi and Māsi. Ten varieties, requiring from 120 to 190 days from sowing to harvest, were used in Kumbapeṭṭai. The rice was preferred to *kuruvai*, being of finer quality. *Kuruvai* paddy was usually exported to other areas of India, but people kept as much *sambā* as possible for their own use.

In fields where only one crop was grown, a 150-, 180-, or even 200-day variety of *sambā* was grown in the seed beds in Āḍi or Āvani and reaped in Thai or Māsi. Kumbapeṭṭai had thirty acres of such fields in Kīla Vaḷi. These fields were low lying and sometimes flooded in Aippasi or Karthikai and so were not used for *kuruvai* but were highly fertile for *sambā*.

Where two crops were grown, *sambā* was sown in the seed beds in Āvaṉi or Purattāsi and reaped in Thai, Māsi, or even early Panguni. The fields growing two paddy crops were reploughed quickly three times after the *kuruvai* harvest to be ready for transplanting in Karthikai.

The second crop was sometimes called *thālaḍi* (from *thāl*, meaning "stem" or "stubble"). In the *kuruvai* harvest most of the stem was left as stubble in the field, for the fields were under water in this season: The stalks were then ploughed in as valuable fertilizer and the second crop transplanted among them. In the *thālaḍi* harvest the fields were dry and long stems were cut with the paddy, both to facilitate the subsequent gram harvest and to provide straw for cattle fodder.

*Sambā* and *thālaḍi* cultivation differed from *kuruvai* in requiring only three ploughings instead of four. Only one *kalam* of seed instead of one-and-a-half *kalams* need be sown in order to transplant seedlings to one acre of ploughed land. The seedlings were transplanted thirty-five to forty days after sowing instead of eighteen to twenty-seven days, and the growing season was longer. In other respects the two crops were virtually identical. No ceremonies marked the first ploughing or transplanting of the *sambā* crop.

Heavy rain usually fell in Aippasi and Karthikai, sometimes causing flooding, which endangered a late *kuruvai* crop or washed out the *sambā* seedlings. On November 30, 1952, a cyclone flooded the fields, largely destroying the *sambā* crop. It blew down large numbers of coconut trees, destroyed Ādi Drāviḍa dwellings and grain stocks, ripped the roofs off many other houses, and shattered cow sheds. In Kumbapeṭṭai one middle-aged Kōṉār cultivator was killed by falling rafters on the day after the cyclone when he went to release the cattle trapped in his cow shed. Mr. C. Rājagopālachāri, then the Congress Party Chief Minister of Madras State, toured the district. The government provided minimum relief in the form of grain supplies and funds for new huts for the destitute.

The Public Works Department removed the fallen trees from roads and public property while local laborers cleared their masters' lands. It was several weeks before the debris was removed and buildings repaired, and seven years before new trees could be grown. Another cyclone wreaked similar damage in 1961 and a still worse one in 1977.

### *Deepāvaḷi*

On the fourteenth day after the full moon in Aippasi, the festival of Deepāvaḷi came to lighten the dark days. Although less celebrated than in north India, together with Pongal this festival was the most significant for gifts among relatives and between masters and servants. Deepāvaḷi celebrated the killing of the demon Nāgasuran by Lord Krishna, an incarnation of Lord Vishnū and the favorite god of love. It represented the triumph of good over evil and light over darkness, and had connotations similar to Halloween in North America and November 5 in England. In Kumbapeṭṭai, the heads of independent households gave new clothing to their families, and landlords to their Non-Brahman and Paḷḷar servants, to all the village servants, and to the Paḷḷar watchmen of their fields. If a marriage had occurred during the year, the bride's father feasted his daughter and son-in-law and presented them with new clothes. Among Non-Brahmans and Ādi Drāviḍas, if a woman had died during the year, each of her sons having an independent household brought a new *sāri*, placed it before a picture or small idol of one of the household gods, and offered incense and other objects before it. Women of the house wept and recalled the past, after which the son gave the *sāri* to his wife, perhaps transferring to her the female headship of the household. After dark on Deepāvaḷi, every family who could afford it decorated their house with tiny oil lamps and set off firecrackers for their own and their children's entertainment.

### *Pongal*

At the beginning of Thai came Pongal, Tamiḷ Nāḍu's greatest three-day agricultural festival. Before British rule it celebrated the end, or near end, of the *sambā* harvest, then grown as a single crop in most of Thanjāvūr. With the expansion of double cropping, the festival fell before the *sambā* harvest took place in mid-Thai and Māsi. It continued to be celebrated as a festival of the sun and rain, new grain, and cattle.

On the morning of the last day of Mārgari, called Bōhi Pāndikai (Indira's Festival), landowners who could afford it placed offerings of sugar cane, saffron, ginger plants, flowers, cooked rice and curries, a jaggery sweet meat called *sakkara pongal*, and a sweet gruel (*pāyasam*) of rice or millet, before pictures or small figurines of the gods in their living rooms. The Brahman household head made a *poojai* with the help of the household priest; Non-Brahmans simply prostrated themselves before the deity. The family then ate the food as their lunch. The offerings were to Indira, the head of all the Vēdic gods and the deity of thunderstorms, who commands Varuṇa, the god of wind and rain.

On Pongal day itself, the first of Thai, Non-Brahmans and Ādi Drāviḍas placed similar offerings together with a little new rice in their homes at midday. The men went out and worshipped the sun, facing upwards with hands together, before reentering to eat their meal. Brahmans performed a *poojai* before the offerings as on the previous day, often sitting on a flat roof or in a courtyard in order to see and offer prostrations to the sun. After this sun worship, each family ate their main meal of the year. On both days Brahmans paid their household priest As. 4, a chunk of sugar cane, spiced gram cakes called *vaḍai, sakkaṛa pongal*, and bananas. On Pongal day laborers came to their masters' homes in the morning. Brahmans gave their servants sugar cane, bananas and any uncooked foods. Non-Brahman landlords in other villages fed their servants in the backyards of their homes. Ideally everyone in the village ate *sakkaṛa pongal* on Pongal day.

During Pongal day each woman and girl tied a saffron seedling around the neck of a cooking vessel, Brahmans and Non-Brahmans around brass vessels and Ādi Drāviḍas around mud pots. Saffron signified marriage, and cooking vessels, a woman's status; it is probable that this ritual act was intended to symbolize the married state and to ward off widowhood.

In Thanjāvūr the day after Pongal was even more important than Pongal proper. This day, called Māṭṭu Pongal, or "Bullock Pongal," marked the worship of cattle. *Paṇṇaiyāḷs* bathed their landlords' cattle in the early morning, painted their horns in gay colors, garlanded them with flowers, and adorned them with yellow saffron powder and red *kungumam*. Tenant cultivators washed and decorated their own cattle and prostrated themselves before them in worship and thanksgiving for the harvest. In the Brahman street the household priest visited each home and instructed the owner to offer *poojai* to his milch cows with bananas, *sakkara pongal*, cooked rice, *pāyasam*, flowers, incense, and a camphor flame. The household priest made two saffron *lingams* representing Vināyakar and offered these objects first to Vināyakar and then to the cows. The food was then fed to the animals. Tenants gave their cows cooked rice, *sakkara pongal*, and bananas in the evening. *Paṇṇaiyāḷs* and Non-Brahman servants came again to their masters' houses and received As. 8 per man and woman.

The elderly women of the *agrahāram* put a saffron mark from top to bottom of the forehead of each Brahman girl. The girls carried saffron leaves, cooked rice yellowed with saffron, jaggery sweets, and gram cakes to the Appū Iyer bathing pool and gave them to the crows. They then bathed in the pool and came home. The offerings were said to be connected with marriage. Crows are somewhat mysterious, ancestral symbols that are fed during ceremonies to the forefathers. Perhaps on this day they were propitiated so that the girls might obtain husbands with whom they would live long. Non-Brahmans and Ādi Drāviḍas did not perform the ceremony, probably because husbands were easier to obtain among them and widowhood was less dreaded.

Māṭṭu Pongal was one of the auspicious days on which all Non-Brahmans and Ādi Drāviḍas who could afford it ate meat. Other such days were Āḍi Flood, a special *poojai* in Thai month for Non-Brahmans and Ādi Drāviḍas to

Ūriḍeichiyamman and Kāḷiyamman, the last day of the village festival, and Deepāvaḷi. Non-Brahmans ate meat on the sixteenth day after a death when the pollution of death had been ceremonially removed and the dead spirit propitiated after the annual sacrifice to the lineage god, and on occasions when special guests arrived. Meat might also be eaten on other, ordinary days, except that some Non-Brahmans avoided it as a vow during Purattāsi. Meat was obtained from sacrificial goats or chickens, or bought from butchers in Āriyūr.

In the evening of Māṭṭu Pongal, the idols of Lord Rāma and Seetha were brought out of the Vishnū temple and taken in procession down the Brahman street. As the gods emerged, the Brahman temple trustee drove out an ox belonging to the temple into the street. Each Brahman family in turn then drove all their cattle into the street as the deities reached their homes. A tremendous concourse took place with much laughter, mooing, and shouting as the cattle and deities were driven down the street. When they reached the bottom of the *agrahāram* about 8:00 P.M., the Paṟayar drummers drummed loudly first in Akkāchāvaḍy, then Vēṭṭāmbāḍi, Aḍichēri, and finally on Barber Street. As the drummers arrived, the Non-Brahmans, too, drove out their decorated cattle in turn. Finally, around 2:00 to 3:00 A.M., each of the Paḷḷar streets drove out any cattle they possessed through their own streets.

While the cattle drives were in progress, each man who owned a bull might tie up to Rs. 25 in a cloth and fasten it to the bull's horns, challenging any adventurous youth to remove it. In 1952 Kumbapeṭṭai had sixteen bulls, all of them seemingly very dangerous. Occasionally a daring Non-Brahman or Ādi Drāviḍa fought the bull and obtained the prize. Sometimes someone was gored; other times the bull escaped and roamed the fields all night, returning the next morning with the prize still attached to its horns. Fights often broke out in the fear and excitement of this night, on which the Non-Brahmans and Ādi Drāviḍas were, in any case, drunk. Literary sources indicate that in ancient Tamiḷ Nāḍu men fought bulls to obtain trophies before being allowed to marry the girl of their choice. Marriages were all arranged by elders in 1952, but young men liked to try their prowess in front of the unmarried girls and the neighbors.

The rivalry between the Non-Brahmans and Ādi Drāviḍas, always latent, was especially apt to break out at Māṭṭu Pongal. I was told that in 1950, Kumbapeṭṭai's Dēvendra Paḷḷars left the celebration immediately after the Brahman cattle drive had ended at 7:00 P.M., went to their own streets, and drove out their beasts without waiting for the Non-Brahman events. The reason, the Brahmans suggested, was that Paḷḷars had more cattle to drive because several of them had become tenants in the previous decade; with this rise in status they had also become "uppish." The next day the Non-Brahman street headman complained to the Brahmans. The Brahman *panchāyat* president and other elders summoned the Paḷḷar headmen of all four sections of south Kumbapeṭṭai to the village temple courtyard, the site for meting out justice. There the president condemned the Paḷḷars for their rebelliousness and fined each street Rs. 25 for the temple funds.

Pongal was the last great festival of the year involving the whole village. In

Thai, black and green gram and horse gram seeds were sown broadcast by men among the growing *sambā* paddy ten days before the harvest. Black and green gram were used in curries and to make savory cakes such as *vaḍai, idlies, dōshai,* and *appalam*, and a sweet called *jangiri*. Horse gram was used for cattle. Grams provided one of Thanjāvūr's main sources of protein. The grams were harvested in Panguni after the *sambā* harvest, mainly by women. Sometimes gram crops, millet, and *dhāl* were grown instead in the dry fields between the *sambā* harvest and *kuruvai* transplanting. A green manure plant, *kolinji,* was also sometimes grown in this period and ploughed in before *kuruvai*. *Kuthakai* tenants grew these dry intercrops without help from Paḷḷars and gave half of all their edible dry crops to the landlord.

For several weeks after the *sambā* harvest, duck farmers from Tiruchirappalli arrived with thousands of ducks to feed them on worms and grubs in the paddy fields. Because this visitation was considered somewhat of a nuisance, each Thanjāvūr village charged about Rs. 100 from the duck owners, which they gave to the village temple fund. The ducks remained until the end of Panguni, when the flow of the water was turned off at the Mēttur dam and most of the rivers and streams dried up.

Some landlords who normally cultivated with *paṇṇaiyāḷs* would lease out some fields on either *kuthakai* or *vāram* to a favorite Non-Brahman or Paḷḷar servant for the dry crops only, taking a fixed rent in the first case and half the crop in the second. *Pōraḍi* was sometimes leased out on *pōr-kuthakai*. In this lease the landlord took all the straw plus three to six *marakkāḷs* per *māh* of the paddy threshed from straw during *sambā* and nine to twelve *marakkāḷs* in *kuruvai*. The *kuruvai* weight was higher because the paddy was often wet and more of it clung to the straw, affording a yield of three *kalams* per *māh* instead of about one *kalam* as in *sambā pōradi*. Transplanting, finally, was sometimes "leased out" although the "lease" in this case was actually a global payment for services rendered. A landowner with too much land to oversee personally might pay one *kalam* of paddy per *māh* to a favorite *paṇṇaiyāḷ* and ask him to oversee and pay for the transplanting.

### Paddy Yields

Although I shall discuss crop sharing and wages in Chapter 12, it is necessary to say something here about crop yields in Kumbapeṭṭai and Thanjāvūr up to the early 1950s.

From the figures available, it appears that Thanjāvūr's average paddy yield per acre (or per hectare) per year did not change much between the early 1770s and the early 1950s. Table 11.2 shows the average paddy yields per *irrigated* acre and hectare per year for selected years between 1773–4 and 1952–3. These figures are not an accurate estimate of the actual paddy yield per "paddy acre," for some dry, unirrigated land was sown to paddy, while a small amount of irrigated land was used for sugar cane and other crops. Nevertheless, the figures are close enough to the actuality to give a definite idea of the range of paddy productivity in the period.

Table 11.2. *Paddy yields per net irrigated acre and hectare, Thanjāvūr district, selected years, 1773–4 to 1952–3*

| Year | Metric tons per acre per year | Metric tons per hectare per year |
|---|---|---|
| 1773–4 | 0.49 | 1.22 |
| 1776–7 | 0.52 | 1.31 |
| 1793–4 | 0.75 | 1.87 |
| 1800–1 | 0.58 | 1.44 |
| 1802–3 | 0.39 | 0.98 |
| 1833–4 | 0.74 | 1.84 |
| 1852–3 | 0.69 | 1.72 |
| 1875–6 | 0.64 | 1.58 |
| 1950–1 | 0.67 | 1.66 |
| 1951–2 | 0.76 | 1.87 |
| 1952–3 | 0.73 | 1.80 |

*Note:* This table is derived from Table 1.2.

Table 11.3. *Paddy yields per gross acre and hectare of paddy cultivation, 1875–6 to 1952–3*

| Year | Metric tons per gross acre | Metric tons per gross hectare |
|---|---|---|
| 1875 | 0.64 | 1.58 |
| 1950–1 | 0.61 | 1.51 |
| 1951–2 | 0.69 | 1.70 |
| 1952–3 | 0.64 | 1.59 |

*Note:* This table is derived from Tables 1.1 and 1.2. The terms "gross acre" and "gross hectare" refer to crop acres and crop hectares counted separately for each sowing.

Leaving aside the famine years of 1773–4 and 1802–3, the yield fluctuated between 0.52 metric tons per acre and 0.76 tons. It is probable that it had averaged more than 0.60 tons per acre before 1770, for yields throughout the 1770s and 1780s were notoriously poor because of the devastation caused by the Nizam's and Haidar's invasions.

Table 11.3 gives paddy yields per gross acre and per gross hectare *actually sown* to paddy, including both dry and irrigated areas, in 1875–6 and again in the early 1950s, the only dates for which these figures are available before 1953. They suggest that although the yield was rather low in 1950–1 because of drought, it improved somewhat in 1951–3. The belief of farmers, both in Kumbapeṭṭai and in Kirippūr, that average paddy yields had declined during the twentieth century, does not seem to be borne out by the available data for the district as a whole. Neither, however, had there been a noticeable improvement in yields per gross acre throughout British rule. Rather, the district's massive increase in paddy production had come about as a result of expansion of the net acreage sown to paddy (see Table 1.1). To a lesser extent it had also resulted from an increase in double paddy cropping, which was reported to amount to 10.27 percent of the total paddy area by 1951–2 (Tables 1.1 and 1.2).

Being on the "breast" of the Kāvēri, Kumbapeṭṭai normally had higher paddy yields than the district as a whole. Ninety-three percent of its wet paddy land was potentially double crop land in 1951–2, although not all of the available land was actually sown to crops in any given year. Unfortunately, I lack accurate figures for the actual acreage sown and the average overall yield for 1951–2. I can only report that the yield was regarded as a poor one both in Kumbapeṭṭai and Kirippūr. In a very good year in Kumbapeṭṭai – such as the village had not seen for at least five years – an appropriate average yield was considered to be fifteen to sixteen *kalams* per *māh* in *kuruvai* and twenty *kalams* in *sambā*. To these figures we must add the approximate harvest payments to village servants and harvest laborers, for Thanjāvūr's farmers calculated their yield *after* these workers had been paid. Theoretically, this means that the actual *kuruvai* yield in a very good year would be about seventeen to eighteen *kalams* per *māh*, or 1.4 to 1.5 metric tons per acre (3.5 to 3.8 tons per hectare) in *kuruvai*, and twenty-two *kalams* per māh, or 1.9 tons per acre (4.6 tons per hectare) in *sambā*.

In 1951–2, however, most farmers obtained a gross crop of only about fourteen *kalams* per *māh* in *kuruvai* and ten *kalams* in *sambā*, or 1.2 tons per acre (2.7 tons per hectare) in *kuruvai* and only 0.8 tons per acre (1.9 tons per hectare) in the *sambā* crop. As might be expected, these figures average out to a little higher than those for the district as a whole. Unfortunately I lack data either for the village or the district from 1875–6 to 1950–1, so I cannot say whether Kumbapeṭṭai farmers' idea of a very good year was often, or ever, realized in practice. All we can say is that Thanjāvūr's average yield per crop acre was much the same at the beginning, the middle, and the end of British rule and that it was roughly the same in the early 1950s, but that Kumbapeṭṭai's farmers had, at least occasionally, reaped about twice the average in some fields in years that were probably exceptional.

# 12 Economics and Class Structure: The Petty Bourgeoisie

By "economics" I refer to economic relations, especially to socioeconomic classes and their relations of production. In daily life economic relations and activities are interwoven with relations of power and authority and with the prescriptions of religion, especially of caste. I shall separate these themes for convenience, dealing with economic relations in this and the following two chapters.

In these chapters, "Kumbapeṭṭai" refers to the old *grāmam* plus Akkāchāvaḍy, Vēṭṭāmbāḍi, and the east side of Barber Street. I have omitted Sheṭṭiyūr and Veḷiyūr because they had little to do with the main village's social life. When I list the land holdings of Kumbapeṭṭai's people I do, however, list their total holdings whether inside or outside the *grāmam*.

## The Landlords

The distribution of the total land holdings by size and caste group among Kumbapeṭṭai's landowners and among those hailing from Kumbapeṭṭai who had left the village is given in Table 12.1. I have omitted owners born outside the village because the total extent of their holdings, in Kumbapeṭṭai and other villages, is not known to me in every case. I will, however, mention some prominent absentee owners in the course of my account.

The Non-Brahmans owned very little land and the Paḷḷars only one acre. Much of the land of these two groups was dry land, less valuable than the wet land, which was monopolized by the Brahmans. Most of the Non-Brahman lots were in Vēṭṭāmbāḍi and Akkāchāvaḍy. Of the Non-Brahmans, only two Nāyakkars and three Kōṉārs owned more than two acres, including either a little paddy land or valuable coconut gardens. Although they leased in more land and sometimes employed other people, we will regard these five men as middle peasants within the larger class of independent commodity producers and traders. Unlike the Brahmans, they and their families did most of their own cultivation. They were not called *mirāsdārs*, but *payirchelavukkārars* (cultivators). The rest of the Non-Brahman owners, and the two Paḷḷars, owned only a little land usually attached to their houses, and either traded, leased in more land, or worked as laborers.

The resident Brahmans who owned less than two acres were all widows, two of whom lived together and pooled their incomes, and one of whom lived alone

Table 12.1. *Distribution of total landownership among owners hailing from Kumbapeṭṭai, by caste group, 1952*

| | Present | | | Absent | | |
|---|---|---|---|---|---|---|
| | Brahman | Non-Brahman | Paḷḷar | Brahman | Non-Brahman | Paḷḷar |
| 20 + acres | 3 | — | — | 1 | — | — |
| 15–19.9 acres | 3 | — | — | 2 | — | — |
| 10–14.9 acres | 1 | — | — | 2 | — | — |
| 5–9.9 acres | 9 | — | — | 4 | — | — |
| 2–4.9 acres | 8 | 5 | — | 15 | — | — |
| 1–1.9 acres | 3 | 3 | — | 9 | — | — |
| Under 1 acre | — | 21 | 2 | 11 | 2 | — |
| Total | 27 | 29 | 2 | 44 | 2 | — |

on her rents. Although poor, because they were rentiers rather than working people and because of their family connections, I would place them in the lowest rank of the petty bourgeoisie.

Of the twenty-four Brahman *mirāsdārs* owning more than two acres, two were widows whose land was managed by a kinsman. The other twenty-two were men who had sources of income apart from their own land. Fourteen leased in paddy land on *uḷ-kuthakai*, or noncultivating tenures, from absent kinsmen, varying in amounts from two to fifty-two acres. Those owning more lands leased in more, for they were regarded as reliable managers. (''Money makes money,'' as the Brahmans often said). For this land they paid about 40 percent of the gross crop in rent, earning about 20 percent to 30 percent profit. Leasing in others' land also gave them control over a larger work force, which they could use freely for odd jobs such as cart driving or cattle grazing.

Fourteen Brahman landowners had supplementary work or pensions. Two carried on paddy trade. Two were trained as priests (*sāstrigals*) for the life-crisis ceremonies of the Brahmans; one of these men was also a cattle broker. One Brahman was the postmaster, one the village clerk, one the village headman, and one a grocery shopkeeper. Two were schoolteachers, one in the *agrahāram* and one elsewhere. Two had retired from government service on pensions. One was a religious devotee and healer who made small sums by attending the sick. One was trustee of the temple lands and one, the *panchāyat* president. The latter two men received no salaries but were suspected of appropriating amounts from the public money they handled. Two men, one of them mentally ill, received remittances from absent kin. Altogether, the Brahman landowners earned between about Rs. 1,200 and Rs. 10,000 per year, all being noticeably better off than all but five of the Non-Brahman agriculturists. Significantly, the village headman and the *panchāyat* president both owned more than fifteen acres and also managed others' land. It was, of course, because of their relative wealth that they were able to hold village offices; they had used their incomes and influence to bribe government servants or voters. Both in turn were able to use their offices to augment their incomes and power.

Some of the Brahman households contained two men (father and son, a man and his brother's son, or brothers) both engaged in managing cultivation. Altogether, thirty-two Brahman men were primarily rentier landlords or rich farmers engaging hired labor. Sixteen of these men leased out all their land to cultivating tenants. Twelve men did all their cultivation through *paṇṇaiyāls* and coolies. Four men cultivated mainly through laborers but also leased out some land, mostly land they had already leased in on *uḷ-kuthakai* from absent kinsmen. In general, able-bodied Brahmans were expected to manage their own cultivation with laborers, this being a somewhat more economical method. Men leased out their land when they were old and lacked a son at home, or were absent, ill, or regularly employed elsewhere. The same man might, however, give some land on *kuthakai* one year and cultivate with laborers the next, depending on his other pursuits or on whether he wanted to favor a servant by leasing him a plot.

Because they did not themselves engage in cultivation, I shall classify these thirty-two men as landlords. However, we should also regard them as at least in transition toward becoming a subcategory of the class of petty bourgeoisie because all Kumbapeṭṭai's landlords were really engaged in private small farm businesses and were regularly employing some two to ten members of the semiproletariat. First, the production relations into which these men entered with their laborers were all contractual; landlords could, and often did, change their tenants or *paṇṇaiyāls* after one or several years. Second, even the rentiers had to manage their own enterprises to some extent – select tenants each year, examine the harvest, grant concessions if the crop was poor, sell off part of their crops in profitable seasons, and calculate profits and losses. Almost all the rentiers also had low-grade salary work or other small businesses. Most of them kept cattle and hired cowherds to tend them. These men dealt constantly in money and markets. They bought and sold land in order to meet debts or make profits, traded in livestock, and, even in the case of the rentiers, purchased inputs such as cow cake and fertilizer. It seems that they were primarily small businessmen, although their roles did retain a strong flavor of the old prebendal life of the professional religiosi.

One absent Brahman landlord owned sixty-seven acres in and near Kumbapeṭṭai, managed by a cultivator of the Potter caste. This landlord's family managed a business in milk and foodstuffs in Thanjāvūr. He himself had a relatively well-paying government appointment as a tax officer in Madurai and was also a moneylender. Another young Brahman landlord living in Kaṇḍipeṭṭai owned forty acres there and in Kumbapeṭṭai and was a moneylender. The lifestyles, education, and solvency of these men set them apart from the villagers; they should perhaps be regarded as in the lower ranks of the bourgeoisie. So should an absent Veḷḷāḷar widow who owned seventy acres in Veḷiyūr, managed by her son-in-law, and some five Muslim and Cheṭṭiar traders of Āriyūr, each worth more than Rs. 200,000, and each owning a few acres in Kumbapeṭṭai. These owners drew surplus value from a number of sources and from several towns or villages.

Kumbapeṭṭai's three resident families who owned more than twenty acres were on a somewhat lower level; their incomes were lower and their enterprises and servants localized. I would place them in the upper ranks of the petty bourgeoisie. One, an elderly widow with one absent, adopted son, owned twenty-one acres and had her land managed by her brother and another kinsman. She lived comfortably from her rents, and maintained the water pandal where I lived as a charity. Another Brahman, aged fifty-three, owned thirty acres, all of which he had recently leased out on *kuthakai* as he was "growing older." This man owned his land jointly with a patrilineal extended family of twenty-five members, mostly absent – the largest joint family of Kumbapeṭṭai. Two of his brothers being dead, he spent much on the maintenance and education of the younger members who lived in Madras. This Brahman was relatively prosperous and solvent but owned little capital.

The third Brahman was the *panchāyat* president, an ambitious man of forty-six who had increased his holdings from two to twenty acres through diligence and, some said, sharp practice. The president shared his land jointly with a younger brother in a family of six members. Between them they managed fifty-two acres on *uḷ-kuthakai* in addition to their own. These lands included some of those of the elderly widow and of the young, absent landlord in Kaṇḍipeṭṭai. Their total estate was thus the largest in the village. The president exercised more power than any other man, including the village headman, and commanded the largest numbers of laborers. His house was neat, well painted, and prosperous. His women folk owned several silk *sāris* and considerable gold jeweḷery and bought Tamiḷ novels and magazines. He lent out small sums at an interest of 33 percent per annum to tenants and laborers. On the other hand, like most people with ten to twenty acres, he owed Rs. 5,000 to richer landlords and merchants outside the village and worried about how to pay it.

### *Cultivation*

Kumbapeṭṭai's landlords knew a great deal about every detail of cultivation. The twenty Brahmans who hired *paṇṇaiyāḷs* or coolies took a particularly close interest in every operation. In each agricultural season one could see Paḷḷars or Non-Brahmans toiling in the fields, the men stripped naked except for a narrow loin cloth, the women in old, looped up *sāris* with bare arms and legs. Standing on bunds beside the paddy fields or sitting on rope beds, benches, or chairs under shady trees, would be several Brahmans wearing white shawls and long white lower cloths. During the sowing, first ploughing, transplanting, and harvest periods, the landlords would stand at intervals each near his own field, prompting and supervising. At these seasons they often eyed each other suspiciously and sometimes quarreled over the distribution of irrigation water or over cattle that wandered and grazed among others' crops. During the threshing, they would gather at the threshing floor in groups of two or three, watching their own and each others' laborers, chatting, chewing betel, and joking, the tension between them past now that their crops were in.

It was essential that the landlord or his agent or noncultivating tenant be in the fields for the first days each of ploughing, sowing, channel digging, and transplanting, and throughout the harvest and threshing. If he grew two crops a year, the landlord had to be in the fields at least thirty days a year, but most were there much more often to supervise their laborers' work. Rentier landlords usually came to the fields only on harvest days to examine the crop, make concessions in the rent if it was very poor, and otherwise make sure that their full rent in paddy was measured out and carried to their store bins. Absent landlords who leased directly to cultivating tenants came home to supervise the harvest and claim their rents in paddy.

### *Leasing of Land*

The Brahmans, absent and present, altogether owned, or managed for their temples, about 342 out of 574 acres of wet land in greater Kumbapeṭṭai, plus about forty acres in nearby villages. One hundred seventy-three acres, or 46.5 percent of this land, was given on *kuthakai* to Non-Brahman or Ādi Drāviḍa cultivating tenants in 1952, 199 acres, or 53.5 percent, being cultivated by *paṇṇaiyāḷs* and coolies. One hundred sixty-three acres, or 43.8 percent of the total Brahman land was held on *uḷ-kuthakai* or preferential, noncultivating tenures by resident Brahmans from absent relatives, some of this land being re-leased to cultivating tenants and some of it cultivated by laborers. Of the land that the Brahmans leased to cultivating tenants, 131 acres were leased to Non-Brahmans, including some in Sheṭṭiyūr, Māniyūr, and Nallūr, and forty-two acres to Ādi Drāviḍas. In greater Kumbapeṭṭai as a whole, about 253 acres, or 44 percent of the total wet land, including that owned by absentee owners, was leased to cultivating tenants. Among the residents of Kumbapeṭṭai proper, Non-Brahman tenants leased roughly eighty-five acres and Ādi Drāviḍas another eighty-five.

### *Means of Production*

In 1952 land in Kumbapeṭṭai sold for Rs. 2,400 to Rs. 4,500 per acre depending on its quality. Dry land without nut- or fruit-bearing trees was the least valuable, then single-crop paddy land, with double-crop paddy land being the most valuable. When tree-bearing dry land was sold, each fully yielding coconut tree was worth about Rs. 100 in addition to the value of the land.

The landlords' productive property included cattle as well as land. In 1952 every house in the *agrahāram* had a milch cow or a she-buffalo; the richer landlords had four or five. Cows' milk was preferred to buffalo milk and was especially used in coffee, but buffalo milk was regarded as more nutritious. Each landlord or tenant needed at least one pair of bullocks or male buffalo for every *kāṇi* (1.33 acres) of land to be cultivated. Landlords owning more than fifteen acres of land had a total of twenty to twenty-five cattle, including cows, in their cowsheds; others, fewer, according to their means. Bullocks were used for ploughing, straw threshing, and drawing carts to transport goods or people; buffalo for ploughing, threshing, and drawing goods' carts. Being wilder than cattle, buffalo were considered somewhat unsafe for passenger carts. Cows lived about fifteen years and gave milk for ten; a good cow gave eighteen cups *(sērs)* of milk per day. A milk cow or a she-buffalo sold for Rs. 350 to Rs. 1,000, depending on age and quality; a bullock for Rs. 135 to Rs. 800, and a male buffalo for Rs. 75 to Rs. 400. In 1952, Kumbapeṭṭai's cattle were all hump-backed local animals, mostly emaciated and poor. English cattle were known and prized, but an English cow cost up to Rs. 2,000, a bullock up to Rs. 1,500, and Kumbapeṭṭai's landlords could not afford them.

In spite of the Brahmanical ban on killing cattle, the Brahmans sometimes sold old bullocks to Paṟayars, who ate the meat and sold the hides to a tanning mill in Āriyūr. Old buffalo were sold to peasants of Tirumadikkuṉṉam near Tiruvārūr, where a famous festival to Ayyanār required cattle sacrifices. Cows, the most sacred animals, were never killed. Most cattle died natural deaths and were eaten by the Paṟayars.

In 1952 twenty houses in the *agrahāram* owned passenger carts, each worth Rs. 200 to Rs. 500. Landlords who cultivated their own land with laborers also owned one or two carts for transporting paddy and other goods.

### *Houses*

Although sparsely furnished by European standards, the Kumbapeṭṭai landlords' houses had a degree of comfort. Each usually possessed two or three deck chairs and upright wooden armchairs, one or two wooden benches and a table or desk, one or more beds made of rope with wooden frames, an *almirah*, or wardrobe containing vessels and other oddments, and a small cupboard for the household idols. Each landlord's house had one or more wooden grain bins (*pathāyams*) about six feet wide, four feet broad, and nine feet tall. A large wooden swing with iron chains, or *oonchal*, hung in the living room and was essential for marriage ceremonies. On the walls were several framed photographs and colored pictures of deities. Every house possessed a number of grass mats for women to sit or lie on, and mattresses for men to sleep on. Each house had a variety of brass and bell-metal vessels for drinking, holding food, and carrying water, in addition to clay pots and aluminum or iron cooking vessels. Cutlery and crockery were rare, for people ate with their hands from food served on banana leaves. Kitchen fires set in rough clay hearths burned firewood, coconut shells, and cakes of cow dung. Sweeping was done with besoms and dust pans made of rushes.

Every house had a sacred brass household lamp and several religious books, usually translations of Sanskrit *purāṇas*. Other common household and personal items included kerosene lanterns, electric torches, fountain pens, and wooden dolls, slates, and notebooks for children. Most landlords carried a wooden or metal box containing betel leaves, arecanuts, quick lime and tobacco for chewing.

### *Incomes and Consumption*

Although vegetarians, the Brahmans ate a greater variety of foods than the Non-Brahman tenants and Ādi Drāviḍa laborers. In the previous thirty years, cold rice for breakfast had given place to coffee made with milk, and steamed cakes or fried pancakes with chutney. Lunch and dinner included plentiful boiled white rice, a main dish of dhāl or other lentils, two or three vegetable curries, lime and mango pickles, pepper water, buttermilk, curds, and a banana. On special occasions such as marriages, up to fifteen or twenty different curries might be served, with fried gram biscuits (*appaḷam*), sweet spicy pudding of rice or millets (*pāyasam*), jaggery sweets, and other delicacies. Tumblers of hot milky coffee, sometimes with sweet or savory cakes, were often served as snacks two or three times a day. By religious law, the Brahmans were strictly forbidden meat, fish, eggs, or alcohol. A few Brahman men, however, had eaten eggs or meat in Thanjāvūr, and at least two in the *agrahāram* secretly drank alcohol in the homes of Non-Brahmans.

Clothing for Brahman men consisted of a white cotton lower cloth, tied at the waist like a skirt, and a "second cloth" or shawl over the shoulders for warmth or to wipe away perspiration. Older men had a longer lower cloth drawn through their legs and tied with five knots, and wore their hair in buns at the back, with the front shaved in a half-moon shape. Young men wore European-style "crops." To go to town or on special occasions, men added white cotton shirts, second cloths with gold threads, and if they could afford them, leather sandals, a gold chain around their necks, and a wrist watch. Women ordinarily wore short-sleeved blouses, or *chōlis*, under a nine-yard cotton *sāri*. This was tied at the waist and drawn between the legs and across the chest, with a flap over one shoulder. Handwoven silk *sāris* that cost Rs. 60 to Rs. 500 were worn for marriages and ceremonial occasions. When they had spare funds to invest, men adorned their wives and daughters with heavy gold necklaces, bangles, silver anklets, and small ear and nose studs of gold and precious stones. These valuables served as the family's bank account and in the more prosperous houses might be worth up to Rs. 20,000. They were pawned or sold to pay debts or to meet unusual expenses. Women in poorer homes had to be content with many glass bangles, tiny earrings, a single, plain gold chain, or simply with the gold *tāli*, or marriage pendant, hung around the neck on a string.

Widows dressed solely in white *sāris*, had their heads shaved, and removed all ornaments. A widow's life was expected to be – and usually was – a life of penance for the death of her husband, of prayer for his soul, and of extreme abstinence from all sensual and worldly pleasures. Widows usually ate only one full meal a day and abstained from tasty foods such as onions, which were believed to excite the passions.

Families were evaluated financially in terms of the land they owned and the amount they paid in dowry and marriage expenses for their daughters. Marriage expenses included lavish feasting, gifts of clothing or valuables to prominent affines, the services of a group of musicians, and a taxi to transport the bridegroom. The dowry necessarily required silk and cotton clothing for the bride, considerable gold jewelry, and brass vessels; the bridegroom's family might also demand in the contract a gift of one or more acres of land to the bride or even a cash sum to be paid outright to the bridegroom. When marriages took place between cross-cousins, a man and his sister's daughter, or other close relatives, the dowry of jewels and vessels could he limited and no special gifts to the bridegroom would be demanded. The dowry had, however, greatly increased in the previous twenty years with the increase of marriages to strangers or to more distant kin of similar socioeconomic rank. In Kumbapeṭṭai in 1952, the total cost to the bride's father of a Brahman marriage, including dowry and wedding expenses, ran from about Rs. 1,000 to Rs. 12,000. It therefore usually equaled, or even exceeded, the amount a son could expect to inherit on his father's death.

Landlord families often fluctuated markedly in wealth between generations or even within one generation. The reasons for loss of wealth might be a large number of daughters to dower, or of sons who divided the property after the father's death; extravagance in purchases of consumer goods; prolonged illness requiring treatment by doctors or faith healers; or dissipation of wealth by one or more men in the family on prostitutes, a concubine, drink, or gambling on horses or at cards. By contrast, families in which there were only one or two sons; members were diligent and frugal; or absent members with well-paying jobs helped to fund the family and to invest in land at home, prospered more than the average. In general, more of Kumbapeṭṭai's families had declined in wealth in the previous generation than had prospered. Out of thirty-five resident Brahman families in 1952, fifteen owned markedly less property than their forebears did thirty years previously, eight had increased their wealth, and twelve stayed roughly the same. One Brahman, the head of a large joint family, had hanged himself in 1943 after losing fifteen acres and piling up debts. Although the Brahmans usually blamed such catastrophes on dissolute living, my impression was that several of them had begun to drink or gamble after already losing large sums in unavoidable ways. Overall, the Brahmans had been impoverished during British rule as a result of population growth coupled with the economic stagnation of the country and their role as small farm managers in an exploitative colonial economy. Personal tragedies were variations on this more general theme.

The landlords survived, and even achieved small comforts, by severely exploiting the semiproletariat, their cultivating tenants and laborers. When landlords gave double-crop paddy land on *kuthakai* to cultivators in Kumbapeṭṭai, they normally demanded between thirty-six and forty-eight *kalams* of paddy in rent per acre per year, depending on the quality of the land. Thirty-six *kalams* per acre were demanded in the far southeast of the village where flooding was a constant danger. Forty-five to forty-eight *kalams* were demanded in the north-

Table 12.2. *Landlord's average cultivation costs per acre of wet land growing two paddy crops, Kumbapeṭṭai, 1951–2*

| (*Kalams*) | *Kuruvai* (*kalams*) | *Sambā* |
|---|---|---|
| Seed | 1–6 | 1–0 |
| Manure | 2–6 | 2–6 |
| 1/3 annual wages of one *paṇṇaiyal* family | 9–2 | 9–2 |
| Transplanting (extra labor), 10 women coolies @ ½ *marakkaḷ* a day | 5 | 5 |
| Harvest wages @ 3 *marakkāḷs* a day, 10 extra people | 2–6 | 2–6 |
| Village servants (Blacksmith, Carpenter, Washerman, Poosari, Watchman, Barber, and Scavenger) | 2–6 | 2–6 |
| Total | 18–7 | 18–1 |

*Note:* Although manure and wages might be paid for at least partly in cash, and wages partly in clothing and other perquisites, I have translated all amounts into paddy at the going rates. The measures in this table and others to come are in *kalams* and *marakkāḷs*, there being 12 *marakkāḷs* to a *kalam*. I have calculated the *paṇṇaiyal* family's total annual wages at the rather high figure of 55 *kalams* per year.

west of the village, forty-five in Taliyapath and parts of Tekke Vaḷi, and forty-two to forty-five in Shānavaḷi, the least fertile area. Small concessions were made in the rent in seasons of flood or drought.

Lands that were cultivated with *paṇṇaiyāḷs* and coolies could expect to reap an even greater profit in a good or normal year. "Self-cultivating" landlords usually engaged one *paṇṇaiyāḷ* couple and their mature children for every three to four acres they owned, and hired extra, casual coolie labor for transplanting and harvesting. The landlord's expenses for one acre for each of the two crops, calculated in terms of paddy, were roughly as shown in Table 12.2.

In a moderate year with a yield of eighty-one to ninety *kalams* per annual acre, the landlord would realize about forty-four to fifty-three *kalams*. In a good year with a yield of ninety to 108 *kalams*, he would realize fifty-three to seventy-one *kalams*, much more than from *kuthakai*. In a bad year with a yield of forty-eight to sixty *kalams*, as happened to several landlords in 1951–2, he would in theory receive only eleven to twenty-three *kalams*. If, however, the yields were really poor and the landlord was hard pressed for both cash and paddy, he would lower the payments to his *paṇṇaiyāḷs* or delay paying them as long as possible. Even so, landlords who engaged in "self-cultivation" took the risk of losing money on particular crops. Those owning only a few acres were apt to lose more per acre because they could afford less manure, less weeding, less careful irrigation, and sometimes even less ploughing. Landlords with fifteen or twenty acres could use more of their own *paṇṇaiyāḷs* and fewer casual coolies per acre for planting and harvesting, thus reducing the cost of labor.

### *Rationing and Black Market Trade*

Since 1944 the landlords' profits had been somewhat curtailed by the government's system of rationing. Previously, as I have mentioned, some landlords and some Non-Brahman brokers drove carts of paddy south to Pudukkoṭṭai, where it would fetch twice the price that prevailed in Thanjāvūr. In 1952, landlords were legally obliged to sell their surplus paddy at the government price of Rs. 9 to Rs. 12 (depending on quality) per bag of two *kalams* or twenty-four *marakkāḷs*. The landlord or tenant was allowed to keep nine *marakkāḷs* per adult and six per child per month for each member of his own family, and to hold back paddy at the rate of five *kalams* per acre per crop to pay the wages of the village servants and his *paṇṇaiyāḷs* and to provide his seed. Permits for these amounts were supplied by the village *karṇam*. This allowance provided adult landlords with about one pound of husked rice per day, an ample amount for people who were not doing manual work, but not enough for a manual laborer who had little other food. It was, however, twice the eight ounce rice ration available in the ration stores to persons without private paddy stocks.

The landlords' paddy was sold to the mill in Āriyūr, which was British made and had been installed in 1927. The mill was owned by a Muslim businessman who had previously worked as an agent for a British firm in Ceylon. Licensed brokers living in Kumbapeṭṭai – one Brahman and three Non-Brahmans – transported the paddy in carts for a rate of Re. 1 per bag paid by the mill owner. The landlord had his own family's paddy hulled at the mill for the same price of Re. 1 per bag, and the rice returned to him. For the whole of his surplus paddy the landlord theoretically received the controlled price of Rs. 9 to Rs. 12 per bag. The miller hulled it and sold the rice to the government for Rs. 30 per bag, one bag of paddy being half the volume and 66 percent of the weight of paddy.

In fact, of course, considerable black market trade went on in both rice and paddy. Landlords sometimes bribed the *karṇam* to overlook extra supplies of paddy in their stores, and sold these privately, bribing the broker too if he had to transport the paddy. Alternatively, the landlord, a broker, or a private purchaser of paddy could have extra paddy above his ration permit hulled for double the normal hulling rate, and consume or sell the rice. Throughout the year, black market paddy was sold fairly openly in Āriyūr stores side by side with ration paddy in the ration shops. By about six weeks after each harvest, the black market price had risen to Rs. 18 per bag; in Vaigāsi to Puraṭṭāsi it was Rs. 24. The richer landlords and merchants could afford to hoard surplus paddy until they could sell at an optimum price, whereas the poorer ones ate their paddy or sold it immediately after the harvest in order to pay the land revenue. In the same season landlords owning more than about fifteen acres could often sell seed paddy for Rs. 30 a bag to needy landlords and tenants who had been obliged to eat their stock.

The richer landlords could thus make many profits over and above those normally accruing from owning more land, by engaging *paṇṇaiyāḷs* instead of coolies, by selling paddy on the black market, and by moneylending. Probably all the Brahmans with more than ten acres had Rs. 1,000 to Rs. 2,000 out on loans to their tenants, *paṇṇaiyāḷs*, and needier neighbors in the *agrahāram*, for which they drew anything from 6 percent to 33 percent interest. At the same time, probably all except the two richest landlord families owed Rs. 5,000 to Rs. 10,000 to bigger landlords or to merchants in Āriyūr and Thanjāvūr.

### *Collective Undertakings*

In Chapter 11 we saw that the Brahman landlords remained collectively responsible for organizing certain economic activities such as the digging out of channels and the date on which the *kuruvai* ploughing should begin. The Brahmans were jointly responsible for several other undertakings having an economic aspect, although most of their undertakings were primarily connected with religion. Every three or five years, the heads of households met to elect a trustee to manage the land belonging to the Siva and Vishnū temples or to consult the ongoing trustee about the temple finances. It was the trustee's duty to lease out the temple lands, obtain and sell the paddy rents from the tenants, and pay the Kurukkal and Bhaṭṭachār priests their monthly stipends in money. If the trustee ran into debt or defaulted too much on temple funds, he was removed and a new trustee was appointed.

The festivals of the Siva and Vishnū temples were financed not by the Brahmans collectively but by the five dominant lineages. Eight main festivals of one or other of these temples, in which the Brahmans were deeply interested, took place every year. Those celebrated in the Vishnū temple were the New Year, or Varusha Pirappu, on Chittrai 1; Uriyēḍi, or Srī Krishna Jayanti, the birthday of Lord Krishna, in late Āvaṇi; and Srī Rāma Navami, the birthday of Lord Rāma, in Panguni. The main festivals in the Siva temple were Kaṇḍa Shasti, celebrating the killing of the demon Soorapadman by Lord Subramania, in Aippasi; Kārthikai Pourṇami, the full moon night in Karthikai, involving a large bonfire; Panguni Utthiram, followed immediately at the end of Panguni by Vaḷḷi Kalyāṇam or the marriage of Subramania with Vaḷḷi; and Siva Rātri (the Night of Siva) in early Māsi. The special offerings for each festival, the wooden chariots or palanquins to bear the idols, the hired musicians, the fireworks and materials for bonfires, the special payments to the temple priests, and any food cooked and distributed to the attending Brahmans, were financed in turn by groups of patrilineal kin (*dāyādis* or *pangāḷis*), drawn from major branches of the four lineages, with the wealthier members usually contributing the most. Whenever possible, absent Brahmans responsible for a festival came home to celebrate it. If this was not possible they sent money to their closest patrilineal kin.

It seems appropriate that the Brahmans' own temple festivals should have been managed by groups of closely related patrilineal kinsmen, for these festivals, with their rich Puranic mythology and imagery, dealt primarily with themes and problems within the Brahman patrilocal family. The dramatic rites of these colorful festivals appeared to provide both a ritual acting out of forbidden Oedipal fantasies engendered in the family, and also a restatement of familial morality.

The Brahmans, however, were collectively responsible as a community for the finances and most of the celebrations of the village temple of Ūriḍeichiyamman, the nerve center of Kumbapeṭṭai's religious life. Unlike the Sanskrit deities, Ūriḍeichiyamman was concerned with the harsh forces of man and nature that could bring blessings or curses on all villagers regardless of their caste. We have seen that she and her godlings controlled health and epidemics and were responsible for female, animal, and crop fertility. In addition, Ūriḍeichiyamman guarded the village against marauding outsiders, protected its moral laws, and was concerned with the maintenance of right relations among the castes. This being so, it is perhaps significant that the funds expended on the annual festival and on other occasions in this temple were obtained either from offenders against village law or from outsiders who had economic relations with the village. Fines, extracted in cash or kind by the Brahman elders from lower-caste offenders against village laws, formed the major part of the funds. Another source came from the revenue department of the government. On the main roadside on government property were a number of coconut trees planted by the District Board. Once a year, the revenue officer arrived to auction the nuts to the villager. Each year, a few of the Brahmans agreed in advance to buy the nuts for a very low price. When the officer had left, the nuts were re-auctioned to the whole village and the profit given to the temple fund. A third source of funds came from farmers of Tiruchirappalli as fees for grazing their ducks. Finally, the Brahmans annually auctioned the fish in the Appū Iyer and Neṭṭi Kuṭṭai bathing pools either to local laborers or professional fishermen from outside the village. The profits from these sales, too, were devoted to the temple funds. These funds, called *pothu paṇam*, or common money, were held and expended by the hereditary Brahman trustee of the village temple. They were used to keep the temple in good repair and to celebrate festivals. The *panchāyat* president, however, had a large say in the collection and disposal of these funds, and tended to view the temple as his personal bailiwick, much to the annoyance of his rivals. Being the most powerful man in the village with the most followers, it was he who led the trials and fining of village dissidents, organized auctions, and leased fishing rights.

### *Revenue*

Although it had declined since the 1920s, the landlords' largest single cash expense was still the land revenue, or *kist*, collected by the village headman and *karṇam* shortly after the *sambā* harvest. The total revenue for Kumbapeṭṭai revenue village (which excluded Vēṭṭāmbāḍi, Akkāchāvaḍy, and east Barber Street but included Veḷiyūr and Sheṭṭiyūr) was Rs. 12,000 per year for 100 *vēlis* (667 acres) of taxable land. Double-crop paddy land was charged Rs. 13 to Rs.

17 per acre; single-crop paddy land, Rs. 11 to Rs. 14. Dry land was Rs. 8 per acre. The backyards of the older houses were tax free as *nattam* (village sites), but taxes were levied on bamboos and coconuts growing in them. An extra tax or cess of 21.5 percent of the land revenue was levied partly to pay for the irrigation works and partly on behalf of the local *panchāyat* board. The board also received part of the charge on documents registering sales of land and cattle. Altogether, the *panchāyat* board had an annual budget of Rs. 2,000 for its work of attending to minor road repairs and drinking water.

Assuming that the landlord received forty-five *kalams* of paddy per acre per year (the average *kuthakai* rent), his land tax and cess amounted to about 8 percent of his paddy income, or perhaps 7 percent of his total agricultural income.

### *Trade and Indebtedness*

Another part of the landlord's surplus went to pay the profits of merchants, especially of the big companies, often British, that owned and traded in plantation products or manufactures, whether in India or internationally. The most common expenses were for coffee, which cost Rs. 40 per month in many homes; sugar; kerosene; arecanuts and tobacco to chew with betel leaves; matches; garden and field tools made in England; knives and spoons; cotton clothing for the landlords' own and his servants' families; and train transport to absent relatives or to pilgrimage centers. In the richer families other "foreign" items had appeared such as kerosene lamps, electric torches, wrist watches, fountain pens, toilet soap, newspapers and magazines, talcum powder, toothpaste, ovaltine, oranges, and various patent medicines. Locally produced items that were bought for cash included gingelly and coconut oil for cooking, old-fashioned household and temple lamps, jaggery, lime fruits, ground nuts, beedies or country cigars, gold, silver, brass and bell-metal ware, handwoven silk *sāris*, flower garlands, fireworks, hair oil, perfume, saffron, and various spices. The two village stores sold beedies (country cigars), chillies, grams, saffron, vegetables, vegetable oil, and matches; the other products were bought in Āriyūr or Thanjāvūr. Although limited in scope, these purchases were evidently too costly for the average landlord's budget. Of the thirty-six Brahman houses, all formerly landowners, nine had lost their lands to traders or money lenders, nine had sold part of their holdings, and although eight had increased their holdings, all but two were perpetually in debt.

### The Other Petty Bourgeois

Two Brahman families of 1952 may be counted in the petty bourgeoisie although they owned no land. One was a widow whose two sons were clerks for business companies in Madras and Bombay and sent remittances to her.

The other was the family of Kurukkals or Saivite temple priests. The father and three sons in this family conducted the services in the Siva and Vināyakar temples of Kumbapeṭṭai, Sheṭṭiyūr, Veḷiyūr, N̄aṭṭār, and Āriyūr. The Kumbapeṭṭai and Sheṭṭiyūr temples were within their traditional jurisdiction of village servants; the rest were modern, contractual appointments. The father received a salary of Rs. 750 a year from the Madras government's Hindū Religious Endowments Board for the temple in Āriyūr. Stipends from the other, smaller temples were paid by local trustees of the temples' properties; Rs. 400 from Kumbapeṭṭai and Sheṭṭiyūr, Rs. 134 from Nāṭṭār, and Rs. 250 from Veḷiyūr. I have placed this family in the petty bourgeoisie because, like most of the Brahmans who had recently left Kumbapeṭṭai for the cities, they earned annual cash salaries for nonmanual work. In fact, however, they were a mixture of petty bourgeoisie, traditional village servants, and semiproletariat. The fact that they worked in a caste occupation in a traditional area of service made them resemble village servants, but unlike traditional village servants they earned cash salaries instead of paddy and derived most of their income from contractual appointments. Their low income of Rs. 1,534 per year for a family of eight members put them near the bottom of the petty bourgeoisie. On the other hand, they were learned in Sanskrit as well as Tamiḷ. Appropriately, the subcaste of Kurukkals ranked ambiguously in relation to the "regular" Smārtha Brahmans whose temples they served. As priests, they were thought to rank higher than other Brahmans in some respects, and were often reminded not to spoil their religious purity by sitting and chewing betel and arecanuts in Non-Brahman homes. On the other hand, as servants and poorer people they were patronized. It was said that in some ways Kurukkals were lower than other Smārtha Brahmans because some in their caste worked as household priests for Non-Brahmans – an occupation held by the Telugu Brahman in Kumbapeṭṭai. This stand-off regarding rank resulted in the Kurukkals' neither receiving food from nor giving it to the Brahacharaṇam Brahmans, the village's dominant community. When the Kurukkals celebrated a marriage or other auspicious occasions, they hired a Brahacharaṇam to cook for his caste men.

Having no power nor any great authority, this family's members seemed gentler and more modest than most of the Brahmans. The oldest resident son in particular was friendly and courteous to all the villagers, respecting those in authority and treating the poor with kindness. He was affectionately called "Kurukkali Iyer" and was liked by all. Incidentally, this family was one of only two Brahman households where it was said that the men had never beaten their wives.

### *Petty Bourgeois Characteristics*

All of the petty bourgeoisie resided on the Brahman street. Here we may consider some of the characteristics of social life and economic attitudes that seem to have been related to the petty bourgeois status of most Brahmans.

One common attitude was that it was permissible, or almost permissible, to cheat or bribe the government. This attitude seemed to derive from the fact that most Brahmans were either landlords to whom government appeared chiefly in the form of corruptible tax collectors and law enforcement agencies, or else were themselves low-paid government servants, some of whom were given large sums to handle or were otherwise exposed to opportunities for corruption. More generally, corruption is probably rife in most state capitalist societies where the government intervenes at many points in the economy but where private profit is the main economic incentive.

Ways of cheating the government included auctioning its coconuts for much less than their real value; selling black market paddy; bribing the *karṇam* or village headman to increase one's paddy permit, overlook illegal paddy stocks, or assess one's land for tax at lower value; bribing the police or the courts in criminal cases; bribing officials to have one's favorite candidate appointed as village headman, to obtain a government post, or have an erring relative reinstated to an appointment. During my stay two absent Brahmans were dismissed from government service for "misappropriating" several thousand rupees of government money, and returned to the village to live from their lands. Similar cases had occurred in the recent past. In 1952 the village headman himself "misappropriated" Rs. 1,600 of the annual revenue. It was rumored that he had spent it on the local prostitutes and on other recreations in Thanjāvūr. On the day the revenue was due, he had to be rescued from his plight by the money and influence of his older brother and another absent relative, both government servants. All such goings on raised little more than an eyebrow in the *agrahāram*.

Within the street, one felt that almost every family was engaged in a perpetual struggle for private profits, power, prestige, or at the lower end, survival. Competition, along with envy of others' success, were dominant motifs and made visiting the *agrahāram* an uneasy and sometimes painful experience.

At the same time, most of the Brahmans were close kin, and despite acrimonious quarrels, factional disputes, and personal rivalry, the community as a whole had considerable internal solidarity. This desirable quality was often referred to as *grāma oṯṯrumai* ("village unity"); in fact, it meant *agrahāram* unity against outsiders and the lower castes. It was necessary in order to run the village, organize the irrigation work and the temple festivals, protect the reputations of its members in the eyes of outsiders, and above all maintain dominance over the semiproletariat. The need for minimal cooperation within the *agrahāram* was probably responsible for various "leveling" institutions that periodically spread wealth somewhat more evenly throughout the Brahman community. Lineage members, rich and poor, cooperated in funding temple festivals, while the whole *agrahāram* cooperated in funding the Ūriḍeichiyamman festival. Considerable wealth was spent at marriages on feasting the whole *agrahāram*. After the feasting, rich and poor of other lineages had to contribute money to the bride's family according to their means during the final blessings of the wedding ceremonies. Above all, private theft within the community was considered despicable, and seldom happened.

### *Petty Bourgeois Women*

The women of this class did considerably more manual work than the men, who could often be seen playing cards or reciting prayers as early as 10:00 A.M. Thirty-seven percent of Brahman homes contained more than one married

A Brahman daughter-in-law makes the rice-flour pattern outside the door of her conjugal home.

or widowed woman. In these homes, it was the youngest daughter-in-law's task to rise at dawn, start the kitchen fire, and make a fresh pattern, or *kōḷam*, of colored rice powders outside the front door of her home. Women shared the work of cooking, preserving food, caring for children, and washing clothes in the channel or from well-water in the inner courtyard.

From about the age of ten, girls learned these tasks from their mothers in preparation for marriage. Visiting married daughters, however, had a position of honor and authority. They could command their younger brothers' wives but did little work themselves. In general, the daughter-in-law's life was laborious and onerous, lightened only by attendance at festivals and occasional visits home. As she grew older and her children reached maturity, she acquired more prestige.

The husband and mother-in-law, who in many cases had behaved harshly toward her in her youth, might eventually become her grateful dependents. Widowhood brought sorrow, seclusion, and a degree of ignominy, but it might also bring authority in the family, or, if there were no sons, financial independence.

Since the 1920s most Brahman families had had women of their Non-Brahman servants' houses to help with the housework. Previously Non-Brahmans were not allowed to enter a Brahman house, and Non-Brahman as well as Ādi Drāviḍa women were partly engaged in cultivation. Population growth and surplus female labor may have brought about this change; in any case it lightened the Brahman woman's load. In most homes the *vēlaikkāri* swept the floors, spread cow dung and water on them once a week, put fresh cow dung down each time on the place where people had sat to eat, and removed the dishes and washed them in the channel or bathing pool. *Vēlaikkāris* were not allowed to enter the kitchen, but they could tend the children, carry water and fuel, and wash the clothes. Non-Brahman male servants sometimes washed the clothes of their Brahman masters. In both cases a Brahman man or women had to rerinse the garments in fresh water and hang them to dry without touching another peon in order to restore their ritual purity.

Women of both Brahman and Non-Brahman castes were secluded and did no work during menstruation and birth pollution. At these times Brahman women occupied a small room adjacent to but not communicating with the kitchen, or else walked or sat in the backyard of the house. Small children were allowed to play with them, for children were exempt from pollution, and women in pollution might of course nurse their infants. Above all, they were forbidden to touch other adults and were prohibited from entering the kitchen, approaching the food of others, or taking part in ceremonies of the house or the temple. If a married couple lived alone, the husband might do the cooking or another person might bring food to both of them.

In 1952 no Brahman women living in Kumbapeṭṭai worked outside the home, although several had attended high school. The only proper roles for women were as wives, mothers, and housekeepers for the husband's family. Some women, however, carried on small private businesses. Before paddy rationing began in 1944, a few Brahman women who had received money from their fathers, had saved it, or had inherited it from their husbands, independently loaned it to Brahman or Non-Brahman brokers. The broker bought and transported paddy to Pudukkoṭṭai, sold it, and repaid the creditor the principal plus 5 percent interest within a week. In 1952 the more affluent Brahman women sometimes made loans at interest to other Brahmans or to Non-Brahman servants. Women, especially widows, sometimes kept cows of their own and sold the milk to families whose cows were not milking. Some Brahman widows knew herbal remedies for common ailments and tended women and children, sometimes in return for payments. Groups of Brahman women, like groups of men, sometimes ran chit funds. Members of the group would meet and contribute equal sums once a month on new moon day evening, and then draw lots as to the order in which one of them would enjoy the whole sum each month.

In spite of their general dominance of and frequent harshness toward their wives, men were lenient about these transactions, allowing women, especially middle-aged women, some financial autonomy. Many women received gifts of money from their families at Deepavāḷi or Pongal and used these as their principal. Usually, husbands either did not know or pretended not to know of their business ventures. If a Brahman ran short of money, his wife might occasionally lend him some, pretending that she had borrowed it from a neighbor.

In a few homes where a man was ill or incompetent, his wife or a widowed daughter took over the management of his estate. Very occasionally, a wife might even get rid of an erring husband and manage her own affairs. One Brahman woman born in Kumbapeṭṭai had a small son who had inherited land from her father as she had no brother. Her husband, who came from a village five miles away, squandered his own property and part of his son's, after which the wife returned to live in her dead father's house and barred the husband from her home. The husband filed a suit for management of the son's property. The court judged that the husband was the rightful guardian of the property until the boy came of age. Meanwhile the wife had given the land on lease to local Non-Brahman tenants. When the husband tried to take possession and change the tenants, Kumbapeṭṭai Brahmans protected the wife's claim and forbade local tenants from accepting a lease from the husband – an example of ''village unity.'' Some months later, the husband came to Kumbapeṭṭai seeking a reconciliation. As was customary on the part of in-laws from another village, he first approached Brahman leaders to ask their help. Having decided to give him another chance, four leading Brahmans brought him into his wife's house and locked the front door, hoping for a reunion. The wife, however, took up a stick and the husband fled through the back door, never to return. The husband became an insurance agent in Thanjāvūr and the wife continued to manage her son's property until he came of age.

# 13 Independent Commodity Producers and Traders

The class of independent commodity producers and traders was only slightly more prosperous than the semiproletariat and was hard to separate from it. Included in this class are individuals and families who owned some capital goods in addition to the tools of their trade and who ran small businesses using mainly the labor of their immediate family or relatives. The owners themselves were also workers, or had been workers until they reached old age. In 1952 this class comprised five households of owner cultivators, or middle peasants, three of paddy traders, two of grocery shopkeepers, three Poosāri households that made regalia for temple festivals and ran tea shops, the Brahman restaurant owner, and the Telugu Brahman priest for Non-Brahman life-crisis rites. All except two of these families were Non-Brahmans. Altogether there were fifteen men and sixteen women in this group.

## The Middle Peasants

The middle peasants owned from two to five acres of land including wet paddy lands or coconut gardens. They comprised three Kōṉār families who had formerly earned money through the paddy trade between Thanjāvūr and Pudukkoṭṭai, and two Tamiḷ Nāyakkar brothers who had formerly owned toddy shops and who probably still carried on a little illicit trade in liquor. The Kōṉārs came from families who had once been slaves of the Brahmans and had maintained close relations with them, leasing in an average of 7.3 acres of additional land per household from the Brahmans on *kuthakai*. The middle peasant households contained five men and six women workers in 1952, in addition to two students over fifteen who occasionally helped their fathers.

These families were more prosperous and independent than the ordinary *kuthakai* tenants. The Nāyakkars and the Kōṉār headman lived in tile-roofed houses, smaller versions of those of the Brahmans. Each family owned several oxen, cows, goats, and a bullock cart. The leading Kōṉār peasant could afford to maintain two wives. His first wife having died, he had married his second wife and her younger sister; he was the only polygynist in the village, although another of the Kōṉār middle peasants had formerly had two wives. The leading Kōṉār, who was killed in the cyclone of November 1952, was recognized as the chief elder (*nāṭṭāṇmai*) of the Kōṉārs and held an important office as *swāmiyāḷi*, or oracle of the godling Karuppuswāmy in the Ūriḍeichiyamman temple. At the annual festival he became possessed by the god and spoke to the people about whether he was satisfied with their offerings and sacrifices, admonishing them to propitiate him properly and protect the village laws. During the festival, while in a state of possession (*aruḷ*), he would drink blood from the neck of a decapitated rooster, a feat the villagers thought would have been quite impossible if the deity had not entered into him. It was the *swāmiyāḷi* whom the *panchāyat* president had persuaded to pay for a special ceremony in the village temple on New Year's Day.

The Nāyakkar headman was also respected as the custodian of the shrine built by his father to honor the *sannyāsi* who had helped him to recover his lost property. This man lived in a tile-roofed house above the shrine, to which his father had donated an acre of land with 150 coconut trees. Once a year in Āḍi, he performed a special offering to the dead *swāmi*, hired a Brahman cook, and fed about 700 Non-Brahman *sannyāsis*. Meetings of the Non-Brahman street headmen were usually held in this shrine or in the yard of the Ūriḍeichiyamman temple.

In general the middle peasants were among the elected headmen (*nāṭṭāṇmaikkārs*) of their streets and held respected positions in the village. The elder Nāyakkar brother was also the headman of all the families of his caste in Kumbapeṭṭai, Periyūr, and two other nearby villages.

The middle peasants' wives and unmarried daughters worked only occasionally in the fields, being considered too "respectable" for heavy labor. They did housework, cooked, tended the children, milked the goats, and carried cooked food to their menfolk working in the fields. Some sons of the middle peasants and the independent traders attended high school in Āriyūr. They, too, considered themselves above heavy labor, although their brothers, who had only attended the elementary school, worked hard in the fields. Part of the middle peasants' cultivation was done by patrilineal, affinal, and matrilateral relatives of the owner who were in less fortunate circumstances. One Kōṉār middle peasant had allowed a family of Kōṉār refugees from the drought in Rāmanāthapuram to settle at the back of his house and to work for him for three years until they were ready to go home again. The father of the Nāyakkar brothers had brought an indigent young Potter from Ṭhanjāvūr to live in Kumbapeṭṭai. He, too, worked for several years as a laborer and eventually married a Potter girl at his master's expense. Four middle peasants and one tenant had Paḷḷar coolies who worked for them fairly regularly. For the most part, however, the middle peasants had agreements with less fortunate kin and neighbors who provided labor for somewhat less than the going rates in return for loans of seed, carts, oxen, gifts of cooked food, and other favors. At the peak seasons of transplanting and harvest, the middle peasants hired Paḷḷar casual coolies to supplement their regular labor, paying them the going rates.

Although more prosperous than the ordinary tenants, the middle peasants lived very modestly and were sometimes in distress. The cash values of their incomes, after paying the land tax, usually varied from about Rs. 1,000 to Rs. 3,000 a year depending on the weather. The leading Kōṉār made no profits at all on his paddy crops in 1951–2. In late 1952 his cattle were injured in the cyclone and he was killed trying to rescue them. He left only two acres of paddy land, a garden, 100 bags of paddy, Rs. 1,500 worth of bullocks, buffalo, and cows, and Rs. 1,000 in debts. Because he had no children, the property after the debts were paid was divided equally between his wives. Fifteen bags of paddy were sold to a Kaḷḷar paddy merchant for Rs. 200, but Rs. 157 of this sum was spent on providing a troupe of Paṟayar pipers and drummers, a decorated palanquin, and a photographer for the funeral, and on gifts of As. 4 each to Paḷḷars and Paṟayars who served the family most often. The *panchāyat* president arranged the paddy sale and divided the property between the widows, and many Brahmans paid visits of condolence. All the Non-Brahman and Ādi Drāviḍa men in the village followed the body in procession to the cremation ground.

**The Independent Entrepreneurs**

These villagers included six men engaged mainly in the paddy trade and secondly in *kuthakai* farming. Four were Kaḷḷars and two Kōṉārs. They lived in three Kaḷḷar and one Kōṉār households, in which there were also four women workers. Four men and four women of the Poosāri caste also fell into this class; they were patrilineally related and lived in three households. The men were involved in temple *poojais*, making dolls and palanquins for temples, and, together with the women, maintaining two small tea shops, a coffee shop, and a grocery shop. There were two Nāyakkar grocery shopkeepers with their wives, younger brothers of the Nāyakkar middle peasants, from Vēṭṭāmbāḍi. One of these brothers had his store on the main roadside in Kumbapeṭṭai; the other traveled daily to Āriyūr. Finally, this class contained the Brahman owner of the vegetarian restaurant on the main roadside, and the Telugu Brahman household priest who lived in the *agrahāram*. The wives of these men, like the Nāyakkar women, did only household work.

The Telugu priest fell somewhat uneasily in this group. On the one hand, as well as being a Brahman, he was an English-speaking literate man who knew some Sanskrit, so that his social status was generally higher than that of the Non-Brahmans. On the other hand, unlike the other entrepreneurs he had no material capital in land or shops. His role was somewhat similar to that of a village servant, for he worked in a hereditary profession, mainly within a designated group of villages. Nonetheless, the priest resembled the other independent entrepreneurs in that his literacy and knowledge of Sanskrit life-crisis rites served him as a kind of capital and allowed him to carry on a "business" among the Non-Brahman clientele. Unlike the other village servants, the *purōhit* was paid solely in money and foodstuffs rather than partly in paddy from the threshing floor, and he was seen more as an authority than a servant. His income of about Rs. 1,200 a year resembled those of the middle peasants and independent tradesmen rather than those of most of the landlords on the one hand or the tenant cultivators on the other. His work was also partly of his own making. Some Non-Brahmans did not employ him, preferring to call *gurūs* from their

Kumbapeṭṭai: ox cart for transport of produce.

own or other Non-Brahman castes. The *purōhit*'s livelihood therefore depended on persuading Non-Brahman families that his Sanskrit *mantras* were appropriate and effective in propitiating the dead, blessing children, or sealing marriage vows.

Both Brahman families in this group differed from the Non-Brahmans in having no land of their own. The *purōhit* had never owned any land, while the Brahman restaurant owners's father had sold his land. Both Brahman families were regarded as of low social rank by the other Brahmans and as in some sense not "proper" Brahmans. The priest was of a lower subcaste than the Brahacharaṇams to begin with, and his ritual services for Non-Brahmans made him seem lowly in the other Brahmans' eyes. The restaurant owner, too, served Non-Brahmans as well as Brahmans in a menial capacity, and lived on the main roadside among Non-Brahmans rather than in the *agrahāram*.

Perhaps partly as a cause of their lower-class status and partly as a result, both families had members who behaved in ways that were unacceptable to the other Brahmans. We have already seen how the *purōhit*, in a fit of anger, tore off his sacred thread, and how he ploughed the land like a Non-Brahman. The father of the restaurant owner, a former police constable, became an alcoholic after losing a leg in a railway accident. He carried on loud, brawling quarrels with his Brahman neighbors in Nallūr, sold all his land, and eventually went to live with an Ādi Drāviḍa woman in a hut outside the village. When prohibition came he quieted down and returned to live with his wife before her death. In 1952 he lived partly from the earnings of his son, the restaurant owner, and partly by traveling ticketless by rail on pilgrimages and begging in distant temples. Both his sons borrowed money and became restaurant owners who associated mainly with Non-Brahmans. The women of the family had difficulty finding husbands because of their poverty and the household head's "immorality." One was married "down" at the age of eleven to a Telugū Brahman boy of fifteen whose family paid bridewealth for her instead of receiving dowry. This girl was taken by her husband's family to Āndhra Dēsa, where she pined and died within four months. Two other women of the family were married as second wives, one to a man whose first wife had died, and the other to a husband whose first wife had proved infertile. When these women married, the total expenses of their weddings, *sāris*, and imitation jewelery were only Rs. 200, similar to the weddings of the poorer Non-Brahmans, and much less than was usual for a Brahman marriage. The elder son of the restaurant owner attended high school and had a brilliant scholastic record. Two Non-Brahman boys of his own economic class, also in high school, were his closest friends.

The Poosāris had production relations that were transitional between those of precapitalist labor servants and petty commodity producers. Three households – two brothers' families and that of their father's brother's sons – jointly shared the service of the village temple and the minor village godlings, the eldest man being in charge of these operations. Two of the families lived on land bequeathed to the temple as *grāma samudāyam*, or joint village land, by the Brahmans. They were heavily dependent on the Brahmans with respect to their house sites and village service, and were liable to be evicted if they did not obey their masters. The third family lived on a private site on the east side of Barber Street. For their temple service the Poosāris collectively received the usual village servant's payments of paddy from the threshing floor – a total of about forty-five bags worth about Rs. 540 at the ration price and about Rs. 1,080 at the highest black market price. To earn it, the Poosāris conducted daily offerings and special festivals with goat sacrifices to the village goddess and the minor godlings. They also maintained a flower garden, owned by the Brahmans, to supply flowers for offerings and garlands in all the village temples.

In addition, all three Poosāri households worked in a workshop belonging to the eldest Poosāri in which they made clay and cloth dolls and palanquins for hire or sale for temple festivals. This trade was plied partly in Kumbapeṭṭai, but mainly in Thanjāvūr and other towns having famous temples. On one occasion the head Poosāri's son had even traveled by train to provide dolls for a festival in Bombay. Finally, the three families separately ran two small tea shops, a grocery store, and a coffee shop for passersby on the main roadside. The head Poosāri's mother owned the coffee chop independently and made rice-flour cakes for breakfast for Non-Brahman workmen. This woman's earnings were probably about Rs. 30 per month. In addition, she owned Rs. 1,000 capital, which she loaned to Ādi Drāviḍas at two *kalams* of paddy interest for Rs. 100 (about 18 percent per annum). The grocery shop and one small teashop, both outside the temple, were run by the head Poosāri's younger brother, and a second tiny shack in Akkāchāvaḍy by the head's father's brother's son. Each of these operations probably made about Rs. 50 to Rs. 70 per month. Altogether, the three families earned respectively about Rs. 1,500, Rs. 1,400, and Rs. 1,000 per year.

The occupational separation I have made between the Non-Brahman traders and the middle peasants is somewhat artificial, for the middle peasants did occasional brokerage of cattle and paddy, while the traders also owned a little land and leased more on *kuthakai*. The traders' incomes, including their crops and their black market earnings, ranged from about Rs. 1,000 to Rs. 3,000 per year. Three of them – a Nāyakkar and two Kaḷḷars – lived in tile-roofed houses and had oxen, cows, and carts. Like the middle peasants, women of the trading families worked mainly in their homes, occasionally in their families' fields, but never for the landlords. The paddy traders, like the middle peasants, employed their unmarried sons and poorer relatives as cart drivers and fieldhands. One of them had a resident servant, a Nāḍār bachelor from Madurai who was somewhat retarded and who worked for food and clothing. Like the middle peasants, the traders were recognized leaders in their streets.

I have already explained how the paddy traders transported the landlords' paddy to the Āriyūr mill for hulling and brought back the permitted quantity of rice, making Re. 1 per bag on each transaction. In addition they bought surplus paddy from the landlords outright on the black market and sold it illegally to the mill or to other black market merchants in Āriyūr. In February 1952, the *sambā* harvest season, the traders bought black market paddy from the landlords at Rs. 13–8 instead of Rs. 9 to Rs. 12 and sold it for Rs. 14–8. (The measures Rs. 13–8 and Rs. 14–8 and other like measures that follow are in rupees and annas, there being sixteen annas to a rupee.) By August, the purchasing price from richer landlords who had stocks had risen to Rs. 20 per bag, while the sale price of black market paddy in Āriyūr stores to the poorer villages was Rs. 24 per bag, or about Rs. 50 per bag of husked rice. In February 1952, Kumbapeṭṭai's Brahman landlords sold a total of about 1,000 bags of paddy from their 342 acres of land, probably keeping about 5,000 bags to pay their servants, to sell later on the black market, or to have hulled for their own consumption. In the *kuruvai* season the sales were much higher because most of the *kuruvai* paddy was sold as an export crop.

The grocery shopkeepers' and the restaurant owners' earnings were probably less than those of the most successful paddy traders. The restaurant served an average of about thirty customers a day for vegetarian meals at As. 8 each for coffee and light snacks at As. 4. Its profits were about Rs. 1,500 a year, as were those of the Nāyakkar grocery shop. The Nāyakkar grocery shopkeepers, however, like the Nāyakkar middle peasants, probably made more money by selling illicit liquor. Toddy and arrack being forbidden, a favorite drink was called Madurai *kashāyam*, or "potion from Madurai." Its chief ingredient was said to be French polish. Another drink similar to arrack was made from orange juice, margosa tree bark, bananas and the juice of the shrub *vēḷai maram*, boiled together and condensed. In 1952 this substance cost Rs. 5 a bottle and was sometimes available in Kumbapeṭṭai.

The Brahmans had an interesting belief about the traders and those in similar occupations. They believed that if a man made money through cattle brokerage; trading paddy, milk, or buttermilk; in the restaurant or hotel business; as a temple trustee; or as a household priest for Non-Brahmans, this money would leave his family within a generation because it was made in immoral ways. Cattle brokerage was thought to be immoral because the broker sometimes hid the faults of the animal from the buyer and raised the price. Milk sellers put water in the milk. Paddy traders stole paddy from the landlords, saying they had measured less than they really had. Hotels mixed powder in their coffee. *Purōhits* sometimes pretended to say *mantras* they did not really know in order to get money from ignorant Non-Brahmans. Temple trustees often stole money or paddy from the deities; hence the saying, *Siva sothu kuḷam nāsham*, or "the property of Siva will destroy a family." Instances were not wanting of people in these occupations who had lost all, had died accidentally, or had committed suicide. These beliefs seemed to reflect the landlords' envy of and contempt for those who made money in occupations other than landowning, especially in market trade, and thus rivaled the landlords' traditional dominance. They also showed the landlords' efforts to comfort themselves with the thought that such people came to naught, and their understandable resentment at being cheated by traders and temple managers. Some Brahmans repeated these beliefs rather ruefully because they themselves, or their ancestors, had made money in these ways. The beliefs were at the same time part of an effort to explain why so many people in this peripheral economy did indeed experience bankruptcy and ruin.

# 14 The Semiproletariat

The semiproletariat consisted of those who did manual labor for one or more masters and who surrendered their surplus product either as rent or as surplus value to their employers. I have included in this class the village servants who had no substantial source of livelihood other than their hereditary work. Like the tenant farmers and agricultural laborers, the village servants carried on their work for the village in return for little more than subsistence payments. Their level of living was similar to that of the tenant cultivators and agricultural laborers. They associated closely with these groups, and if they became too numerous, some took up tenant farming or agricultural labor for a livelihood.

The semiproletariat had two clearly defined strata, one of which was seen as, and was usually in fact, slightly more prosperous than the other. The upper layer consisted of those who owned most or all of their own tools of production and carried on the major part of their work without supervision by a master. It included the *kuthakai* tenants and most of the village servants. The lower layer consisted of those who owned few or no tools or equipment, who worked mainly under supervision, or who could provide only what Tanjoreans called "body help" to their masters. It included the agricultural laborers together with two groups of village servants, the Paṟayar scavengers, and the Paḷḷar watchmen of the paddy fields. Also in this group were a small number of nonagricultural manual wage workers, either for private employers or for the government.

The upper layer of the semiproletariat was usually thought of as being Non-Brahman, and the lower layer as Ādi Drāviḍa. In the early twentieth century these correspondences were probably fairly accurate. In 1952, however, only twenty-four out of fifty-nine, or 41 percent of the Non-Brahman agriculturalists, including three middle peasants and six paddy traders, actually held *kuthakai* tenures, while thirty-six out of ninety-three Ādi Drāviḍas, or thirty-nine percent had some, although usually smaller amounts, of land on *kuthakai*.

This development of tenant farming among the Paḷḷars had resulted mainly from the purchase and leasing of lands by Non-Brahmans and Muslims outside the village, and from the leasing out of absent Brahmans' lands. Altogether, only fifty-four percent of Kumbapettai's Ādi Drāviḍa laborers and tenants were under the direction of resident Brahmans in 1952, whereas, sixty-three percent of the Non-Brahmans were under the Brahmans' direction.

The two layers of the semiproletariat were not neatly separated by 1952. Twenty out of 145 Non-Brahman and Ādi Drāviḍa male tenants and laborers worked regularly both as agricultural laborers (coolies or *paṇṇaiyāḷs*) and *kuthakai* tenants, two of them being Non-Brahmans and eighteen, Ādi Drāviḍas. These men spanned the two layers, although they were mainly laborers. Again, most of the regular tenant farmers worked occasionally as laborers, although they were mainly tenants. Similarly, the Paṟayar scavengers and the Paḷḷar watchmen did not fit neatly into the low stratum. Although most of their work of scavenging and guarding cremation grounds was purely "body help," the Paṟayars also owned their own drums and trumpets, which they played at Non-Brahman funerals, and in general their work as village servants was largely unsupervised. So was that of the Paḷḷar watchmen. The watchmen, however, owned no tools or other equipment. Neither the watchmen nor the scavengers spent their whole lives in these tasks. The landlords selected the watchmen from among the Paḷḷar laborers and they could be dismissed and returned to ordinary agricultural labor at any time. The Paṟayars were agricultural laborers as well as scavengers.

In spite of these complexities, I shall treat the two strata separately, because they did represent definite income and status groups.

## Workers Owning Most of their Own Equipment and Largely Managing their Own Labor

### *The Tenant Farmers or Poor Peasants*

Kumbapeṭṭai had thirteen Non-Brahman men distributed in eight households, and eighteen Pallars in eighteen households, who were engaged almost solely in *kuthakai* cultivation, although they occasionally did extra jobs for their landlords or hired themselves out as coolies to eke out a livelihood. Three of the Non-Brahman households were Kaḷḷars, one Telugu Nāyakkar, one Nāḍār, one Potter, and two Kōṉārs. In addition three Non-Brahman middle peasants and three paddy traders, in five households, held *kuthakai* land amounting to an average of 9.5 acres per household as well as their own lands. Two Non-Brahman and eighteen Pallar households whose members were mainly laborers also held small plots of *kuthakai* amounting to about one acre each or less. I have placed the middle peasants and paddy traders in the class of independent commodity producers and traders, and the laborers-cum-tenants, among the agricultural laborers.

The Non-Brahman "pure" tenant cultivators, or poor peasants, averaged 5.6 acres per household. Their holdings ranged from 2 to 13.3 acres, the household with the largest holding having two unmarried sons as workers in addition to the household head. The eighteen Paḷḷar tenant farmers averaged only 3.8 acres per household. The Paḷḷar tenants were therefore poorer than the Non-Brahmans, although there was overlap between the two groups' incomes. The average leased holding per household among the "pure" tenants and the middle peasants of all castes was 5.34 acres; among the "pure" tenants or poor peasants only, it was 4.35 acres. Among the "pure" tenants, the middle peasants and traders who leased land, and the laborers who leased land, the average leased holding per household was 3.3 acres.

Tenant cultivators paid a fixed rent of fourteen to sixteen *kalams* of paddy per *māh*, or forty-two to forty-eight *kalams* per acre per year for the land they leased. Most tenants paid forty-five *kalams* per acre per year, twenty-five for the *kuruvai* crop and twenty for *sambā*. In the landlords' idea of a "good year," with 100 to 108 *kalams* per acre from two crops, these rents would amount to only about 40 percent to 45 percent of the total annual yield. In fact, however, as we have seen, Kumbapeṭṭai's fields produced an average of only about sixty *kalams* per acre in 1951–52 and for several years previously because of drought, while some fields produced as little as forty-eight *kalams* from the two crops. In addition, the tenant had to pay the costs of his seed and manure, the village servants' crop shares, and extra labor for transplanting and harvest. These expenses amounted to a total value of about 15.7 *kalams* of paddy for the two crops, apart from all the labor of the tenant's own family. The cultivator was allowed to keep about thirty to forty bundles of straw per year to feed his oxen, paying only six bundles to the landlord, so he had little or no expense for feeding his animals. He had, however, to buy or breed them and to purchase his plough and other implements, an average total cost of about one *kalam* of paddy per year. With a rent of forty-eight *kalams* and expenses of seventeen *kalams* per acre per year, in a good year a cultivator might obtain a maximum of forty-six *kalams* per acre, or 43 percent of his yield. In a more moderate and normal year, with a gross yield of eighty-one to ninety *kalams* (thirty-six to forty in *kuruvai* and forty-five to fifty in *sambā*) he would retain sixteen to twenty-five *kalams* per acre, or 20 percent to 27 percent, after his rent and all of his expenses were paid. In a bad year such as 1951–2, several tenants lost money and paddy on their crops in the course of the year. Landlords granted concessions in the rent for a very poor harvest, but most did so only if the yield after paying the extra harvest laborers and the village servants was actually less than the rent. In a bad year, therefore, the tenant went into debt at the end of the year whether or not concessions were made.

The landlords' theory was that losses in a bad year could be made up in a good year. In fact, rents were so high that good years did not compensate for bad. Most tenants perpetually owed Rs. 300 to Rs. 1,000 to their own or some other landlord at 12 percent to 33 percent per annum, so that even in good years a large part of their earnings went to repay debts and interest.

Occasionally, a landlord would persuade a tenant to lease a field on *vāram* ("share"). In this case the tenant's expenses were the same as in *kuthakai*, but the landlord took a flat four-fifths of the crop after the village servants and harvest laborers had been paid. Tenants refused, however, to take the poorer fields in Shānavaḷi on *vāram* leases, as the one-fifth share was never worth their labor in these fields. Dry crops such as millets and grams were always divided equally between the tenant and the landlord, with the tenant providing the seed. These crops provided both parties a much needed supplement to their diet and a few rupees profit from sales.

In spite of their harsh conditions, most tenants in moderately good years were slightly better off than the agricultural laborers. With an average of 5.6 acres, a Non-Brahman family might sometimes make a profit of about ninety to 100 *kalams*, or forty-five to fifty bags of paddy per year, in addition to their green and black gram crops and any coconuts and vegetables their backyards yielded – a total monetary value of about Rs. 540 to Rs. 600 per year. If they failed to clear this amount they were likely to borrow in order to maintain a certain level of consumption slightly above that of the agricultural laborers. In an exceptionally good year they would repay all or part of their debt.

There was variation in the tenants' incomes depending on their holdings, so that the more fortunate tenants resembled the middle peasants in their living standards, while the poor tenants were little better off than the laborers, and might become regular laborers in an unlucky year. One man of the Potter caste, for example, who had given up his village servant's work in favor of cultivation, leased ten acres of paddy land from an absent Brahman landlord, owned one acre of dry land, and in addition managed fifty-seven more acres in Nallūr from the same Brahman, which he distributed among several Nallūr tenants. In 1951–2 this man cleared only fifty *kalams*, worth Rs. 300 at the controlled price, after his rent was paid, in addition to black and green gram, dhāl, chillies and vegetables from his own dry land. Even this tenant had to go into debt, because his household normally used seventy-two *kalams* plus Rs. 460 per year. In a moderately good year, however, he might clear 250 *kalams*, or Rs. 1,500 a year.

Similarly, among the Paḷḷar tenants, two middle-aged brothers jointly leased nineteen acres belonging to absent Brahmans. The older brother owned one acre of dry land and Rs. 2,000 worth of bullocks, cows, and goats. Another fortunate Paḷḷar leased ten acres from an elderly Brahman in the village. These men lived in larger and roomier houses than the other Paḷḷars, each with three rooms, a verandah, and a wooden door. Two of their sons were the only Paḷḷar boys to attend high school. These men used their other children and one of the wives' sisters, her husband, and her children as laborers, and so were able to farm economically.

At the other extreme, a Nāyakkar widowed mother and son with only two acres in *kuthakai* and a garden would usually clear less than sixty *kalams*, or about Rs. 360 worth of crops in a normal year. Most of the Paḷḷar tenants were in a similar situation.

Each tenant farming household usually owned at least one pair of working oxen, one or two cows, a paddy wagon, and two or three goats. Some tenants who were poorly off hired carts or oxen for a fee. The houses of the Non-Brahman tenants were poorer than those of the middle peasants, with thatched roofs and with only one or two small rooms in addition to a kitchen and verandah. Paḷḷar tenants' houses were on the whole smaller than the Non-Brahmans' but of better quality than the laborers' shacks, having a small raised verandah, a room in which one could stand upright, and a tiny kitchen at the back. Like the middle peasants, the tenants stored their paddy in the main room in large circular clay vessels, called *kuḍirs*, four to six feet tall. A tenant house was likely to contain a bench, perhaps a wooden chair, a wooden front door with a lock, one or two suitcases containing clothing and small bits of jewelry, two or three grass mats, a few iron and clay pots, and in the kitchen, a number of clay storage vessels suspended from the roof on ropes in order to avoid the ever-present rats, cockroaches, and ants. Whereas middle peasants might own a deck chair, a table, a little gold jewelry, one or two white shirts for the men, and one or two silk *sāris* for the women, few of the tenants owned such items. At best, in addition to her gold marriage *tāli*, a woman of the tenant class might own ear or nose studs and a marriage *sāri* woven from a mixture of silk and cotton, costing about Rs. 60. A marriage in the Non-Brahman middle peasant class cost the bridegroom's family about Rs. 800 to Rs. 1,000; in the tenant class it cost about Rs. 200 to Rs. 500.

Like the middle peasants, women in the ''pure'' tenant class mostly refrained from work in the landlords' homes and fields. Tenant women, however, worked hard in their husbands' leased fields in addition to doing their own housework, cooking, and tending their children. In 1952 the eight Non-Brahman tenant women helped with the paddy sowing, weeding, and black gram and paddy harvest, but did not usually do transplanting, the most arduous of feminine agricultural tasks. The twenty-one Paḷḷar tenant women performed all agricultural tasks, including transplanting. The Non-Brahmans' cultivation expenses were higher than the Paḷḷars' because they paid Paḷḷar coolies for transplanting and in part, for threshing. The Paḷḷars exchanged labor with each other at the peak seasons and so had almost no labor costs apart from the work they did themselves.

In 1951–2 the Communist movement had not arrived in Kumbapeṭṭai, although the landlords greatly feared it. Kumbapeṭṭai's tenants and laborers had no labor union and had not waged any united struggles to have their rents reduced or their wages raised. The landlords knew, however, that new legislation to lower rents and given fixity of tenure to the tenant might be in the offing. For that reason they gave no tenancy documents to their tenants as had sometimes been done in the past. Instead they obtained promissory notes from them to pay a stipulated amount in paddy or its equivalent in cash by the end of the year.

On August 23, 1952, in response to repeated Communist agitations in east Thanjāvūr, the Madras government passed the Tanjore Tenants' and Paṇṇaiyāls' (Protection) Ordinance. This ordinance stipulated that cultivating tenants should pay no more than three-fifths of the gross crop as rent in a given year. The tenant was to meet all the expenses of cultivation including manure, while the landlord was to pay the land revenue. The tenant was to retain the bulk of the straw. Landlord and tenant together were to execute a document guaranteeing the tenant occupancy for five years provided that he paid the rent and did not destroy or sublet the land. Conciliation officers were appointed to settle disputes between landlords and their tenants or laborers. The ordinance applied only to estates of more than 6.7 acres (one *vēli*) of wet land in one village.

Kumbapeṭṭai's landlords took no immediate notice of this ordinance and because their tenants were mostly illiterate, none of them pressed for documentary tenures in 1953–4. In any case, in a good year with a yield of twenty-five *kalams* per *māh* Kumbapeṭṭai's *kuthakai* tenants were already paying only three-fifths (fifteen *kalams*) of the crop as rent, and in addition were receiving half their manure from the landlord. The cyclone of November 1952, however, damaged the *sambā* crop, and in February–March 1953, disputes over tenants' crop shares and laborers' wages were common throughout the district. Although I was living at that time in Kirippūr, I heard from friends that Communist organizers had arrived and had organized Kumbapeṭṭai's Paḷḷars into a labor union with other Ādi Drāviḍas in four neighboring villages. In the harvest of February 1953, when the crop was poor, the Ādi Drāviḍa members of this union went on strike in order to compel all the landlords, regardless of the size of their holdings, to grant their tenants concessions amounting to two-fifths of the crop and to pay their harvest laborers wages only slightly less than those stipulated in the ordinance. When I went back to Kumbapeṭṭai on a visit in March 1953, the landlords had given in at least temporarily, and the red flag was flying in south Kumbapeṭṭai's Paḷḷar streets. The Non-Brahman tenants and laborers had not formally joined the union, but some of them were giving it their support and were benefiting from its militancy. The "trouble" subsided soon after I left Thanjāvūr in April 1953, but Kumbapeṭṭai's landlords knew that they might eventually have to make permanent concessions to their tenants.

### *The Non-Brahman Village Servants*

In 1952 Kumbapeṭṭai had six groups of village servants (*grāma thōṛiḷāḷikaḷ*) whose socioeconomic status roughly paralleled that of the tenant farmers. They were the laundryworkers, barbers, potters, carpenters, blacksmiths, and goldsmiths. Their economic relations with their patrons were transitional between precapitalist labor service and capitalist commodity production.

The laundryworkers, barbers, carpenters, and blacksmiths, like the village temple priests, were paid mainly in paddy at traditional village rates. When paddy was being threshed during either the *kuruvai* or the *sambā* harvest, the headmen of each of these groups came to the threshing floor with a sack. Before the threshing, each man received a gratuity of one hand bundle (*kōṭṭu*) of unthreshed paddy stalks for each area of 1.33 acres to be threshed. This area, comprising four *māhs* of land, was called a *kāṇi*, and the amount given, "one bundle per *kāṇi*." A bundle of unthreshed paddy produced about half to one *paḍi* (Madras measure) of grain, one *paḍi* being half a *marakkāḷ* and weighing roughly 2.65 pounds, worth As. 4 at the ration price. As their main harvest payments, each servant group traditionally received six *marakkāḷs* of grain (about thirty-two pounds worth Rs. 3) at each harvest for every plough and pair of bullocks owned by the farmer. Landlords paid the servants directly from land they had cultivated by laborers; *kuthakai* tenants in theory paid them at the same rate for the land they leased. The six *marakkāḷs* were paid at each of the two harvests when two crops were grown, and so amounted to twelve *marakkāḷs*, or one *kalam* per plough per year. Because a farmer needed roughly one pair of working oxen for each *vēli* (6.67 acres) he cultivated, the grain measure really amounted to six *marakkāḷs* per harvest for each *vēli* harvested. Because the relevant area of Kumbapeṭṭai *grāmam* contained roughly 53 *vēlis* (354 acres) of wet land, only five *vēlis* of which was single crop, each of these village servant families obtained in theory about 805 *marakkāḷs* per year from the threshing floors, or roughly sixty-seven *kalams* (33.5 bags).

These payments were derived from the time when the village land was owned jointly by the Brahmans, and when village servants and harvest laborers were paid before the crop was divided between the king, the landlords, and any tenant cultivators. In 1952 the theory of payments still obtained but the practice had been modified. Landlords and tenants with holdings of one *kāṇi* or more still paid roughly one bundle per *kāṇi* to each servant group. Middle and poor peasants with holdings of about four to seven acres paid a flat rate of one *kalam* per year each to the barber and washerman, but not to the other servants. Instead they paid the carpenter, blacksmith, and goldsmith in small amounts of paddy or cash for each job of work. Carpenters, for example, received six *marakkāḷs* for each plough they made. These villagers also paid the village priest small sums when they made special offerings in the temple to ward off sickness or in thanksgiving after childbirth or recovery from illness. If they cultivated through laborers, however, landlords with more than about four acres still paid about six *marakkāḷs* each of paddy per *vēli* per harvest on the threshing floor to the carpenter, blacksmith, Poosāri, and washerman.

The carpenters' regular work included making ploughs, yokes for bullock carts, and sticks to goad the oxen while driving the cart; the blacksmith's, making iron pestles and mortars for use in the kitchen, iron parts for ploughs and other agricultural implements, and fixing a pin in the stick to goad the oxen. For other work connected with houses, carts, and so on, these specialists were paid separately at the rate of Rs. 2–8 per day.

Because there were two patrilineally related Barber houses, they had divided their Kumbapeṭṭai clientele in two halves. Each barber was paid six *marakkāḷs* per year for each man, boy, or widow whom he shaved and whose hair he cut regularly. Landless people paid the Barber As. 2 per shave and As. 3 to As. 4 per haircut.

The village servants received other payments at festivals. The Brahmans jointly gave each group four *kalams* of paddy at the village temple festival in return for their contribution of one goat each to be sacrificed by the village priest. At Deepāvali and Pongal, each landlord and tenant paid each servant As. 2 to As. 4 – a total of about Rs. 10. For Deepavāḷi the landlords jointly provided a man's clothing (but not a woman's), worth about Rs. 10 to each of their village servants.

Table 14.1. *Traditional annual payments of carpenters, blacksmith, village priests, and laundry workers, Kumbapeṭṭai, 1952*

| | Kalams of paddy | Rs. or Re. value of other payments |
|---|---|---|
| 6 *marakkāḷs* per *vēli* harvested (5 *vēlis* of single-crop paddy and 48 *vēlis* of double-crop paddy) | 50–6 | — |
| 1 *paḍi* (½ *marakkāḷ*) plus straw per *kāṇi* harvested (approx 505 *kāṇis*) | 15–9 | — |
| Brahmans' gift at village festival | 4–0 | — |
| Share of crops on 1 *māh* paddy land (approx.) | 4–0 | — |
| Brahmans' gift of clothing at Deepāvaḷi | — | 10–0 |
| Deepāvaḷi and Pongal gifts, As. 8 cash from 87 farmers | — | 43–8 |
| Cooked food at 3 festivals | 6 | — |
| Total | 74–9 | 53–8 |

On the day after the festivals of Pongal, Deepāvaḷi, and Ādi Flood, landlords and tenants served cooked food to any village servant who cared to come for it. The servants sat and ate in the Non-Brahman houses, but carried away their food, or its equivalent in raw rice and legumes, from the Brahman houses. Furthermore, these village servants collectively shared one *māh* of rent-free paddy land set aside for them by the Brahmans, from which each of them might obtain up to about five *kalams* a year.

The barber, washerman, and village priest received other gifts on special occasions. At a Brahman or Non-Brahman marriage, the hosts gave Rs. 1 plus a lower cloth to the barber for shaving the bridegroom. At a birth, and also after a first menstruation, the washerwoman was given Rs. 1 to Rs. 3 for washing the soiled cloths. When a cow calved or a woman safely delivered a child, Brahmans and Non-Brahmans gave one *marakkāḷ* of paddy and an iron pestle and mortar to the village priest.

Just as the Poosāris made dolls and palanquins outside their designated area, the other village servants worked at their trades for cash in Thanjāvūr whenever they were able to do so. The barbers, carpenters, and blacksmiths picked up odd jobs there. The laundry workers had acquired a few regular customers in the town.

I was unable to estimate the precise amounts actually received by the village servants in cash and kind in 1951 and 1952. They seemed, however, to be similar to what they had supposedly received traditionally. The traditional payments that were common to the carpenters, blacksmiths, village priests, and washmen approximated those shown in Table 14.1.

Kumbapeṭṭai: the village blacksmith.

If we include additional, special perquisites, together with earnings in the town, we may estimate each village servant's total income from his trade at about ninety *kalams* per year, worth Rs. 540 at ration prices. This was roughly the income of a tenant farmer with 5.6 acres in a fairly good year, or of a Non-Brahman *vēlaikkāran* who had one or two children working. The two Barber households' incomes seemed to be about the same as those of the other Non-Brahman village servants, given the fact that each of them served roughly half the Brahman and Non-Brahman households in the village but received six *marakkāḷs* per year from each individual they served.

My impression of the amounts of the Non-Brahman village servants' payments in *mirāsi* villages is borne out by the fact that in former *iṉam* villages such as Nāṭṭār, each village servant household was traditionally granted a service tenure of one *kāṇi* of tax-free land (1.33 acres) instead of harvest payments. In a good year this would provide each of them with a gross yield of 100 *kalams*, or about seventy-five or eighty *kalams* after their cultivation expenses were paid. This amount was similar to the Kumbapeṭṭai village servant's total payments from the harvests, the village festival, and his share of one *māh* of paddy land.

In 1952, Kumbapeṭṭai had one house of Goldsmiths and two of Potters who carried on more or less traditional work. One of the Potter households made pots on the wheel; the other specialized in whitewashing houses and temples and in

Kumbapeṭṭai: the village carpenters.

plumbing and cement repairs. The Potters enjoyed the right to work in both Kumbapeṭṭai and Māniyūr. The Goldsmiths, who arrived from Tiruchirappalli during 1952, had no traditional village right. Kumbapeṭṭai's Brahmans and Non-Brahmans formerly employed the Māniyūr Goldsmiths, but at market rates. A few Brahmans and Non-Brahmans gave work to the new Goldsmith, paying him in cash for each transaction. Similarly, in 1952 the Potters received their payments in paddy and cash for each job of work. As far as I could estimate, the Potters were roughly on the same economic level as the tenant farmers and the other Non-Brahman village servants. As a refugee, the Goldsmith was living very poorly from hand to mouth.

The village Potter had a special responsibility as a Poosari in the Paḷḷars' shrine of the goddess Kāḷiyamman. He also made offerings to the Paḷḷars' boundary deities on the border of Kumbapeṭṭai and Nallūr. The Potter offered flowers, water, bananas, coconuts, incense, and a camphor flame to Kāḷiyamman every evening and sacrificed goats to her after the village festival. He was paid four *kalams* of paddy after each harvest by the Paḷḷars for these services – about one *marakkāḷ* per house per year. When a Paḷḷar woman or cow had a safe delivery, the Paḷḷar family paid the Potter one *marakkāḷ* of paddy and one grindstone as an offering of thanks to their deities.

Kumbapeṭṭai had one other Non-Brahman household whose members somewhat resembled village servants: the Kūtthāḍis, or village prostitutes, who lived just within the boundary of Veḷiyūr. The men of this caste traditionally ran puppet shows and played cymbals at village temple festivals. The women danced before village deities. Kumbapeṭṭai's Brahmans customarily summoned Kūtthāḍis from Kanḍipeṭṭai to dance at the festival of Ūriḍeichiyamman; the Veḷiyūr Kūtthāḍis no longer knew the art. The grandfather of the oldest woman had come to Veḷiyūr in the 1890s as manager of the absent Veḷḷāḷars' estate. In 1952 the men of this family were dead and the household was a bilateral joint family composed of four female prostitutes, a boy, and a small girl. Although poor, this house and its inmates were the neatest and cleanest in the village, its women members wearing pretty *sāris*, cosmetics, and many glass bangles. For ten years, the leading woman had been the concubine of a Kumbapeṭṭai Brahman elder whose wife had leprosy. The Brahman, who was twenty-six years older than the woman, gave his mistress forty gold sovereigns, several silk *sāris* worth Rs. 1,000 each, and beds, mattresses, and other furniture for her home. He also leased three acres of paddy land for a rent of only half the crop to her father. After having two daughters by her, he cursed her and cast her off when he discovered her infidelity with another man. She later developed venereal disease, which the villagers believed resulted from the Brahman's curse. After this association ended the woman became a village prostitute like the other members of her family.

The Kūtthāḍi women were often visited by several of the Brahmans and occasionally, by Non-Brahmans who could afford their services. Women of the *agrahāram* treated them with contempt and would not allow them inside their street. Non-Brahman women, many of whom were themselves the occasional mistresses of Brahmans, behaved with greater leniency toward them and joked with their children. In general it was accepted that they were plying the trade of their caste, even though this trade was sinful and could bring divine punishment on the families of the men who patronized them. The women were paid in cash at each visit and pooled their earnings. Although I did not discover their income, they lived on a par with the more prosperous tenants. In addition to their prostitution, the women received a small allowance from their Veḷḷāḷar landlords for sweeping the Siva Temple in Veḷiyūr and lighting the lamp each evening.

## The Laborers

### *The Agricultural Laborers*

In 1952 Kumbapeṭṭai had a total of 112 male and eighty-eight female agricultural laborers over the age of fourteen. Thirty-six of the men and five of the women were Non-Brahmans; seventy-six of the men and eighty-three of the women, Paḷḷars from Kumbapeṭṭai's five streets of that caste.

Although all very poor, the agricultural laborers were differentiated in three main respects. First, they were divided between landless laborers on the one hand and, on the other hand, people who had been given a small amount of land, usually less than two acres, on *kuthakai* tenure, but who worked mainly as laborers. Second, they were divided into *paṇṇaiyāḷs*, or attached debt laborers, regular coolies who worked mainly for one employer, and casual coolies who worked by the day for anyone who would hire them. Third, Non-Brahmans of all castes were differentiated from Ādi Drāviḍas. Non-Brahmans tended to do lighter work than Ādi Drāviḍas, they were paid more, and in the case of *paṇṇaiyāḷs* they were paid by the month instead of by the day. The distinction between Non-Brahmans and Ādi Drāviḍas, however, broke down in the case of the casual coolies.

For the most part, men and women living in the same household belonged to the same category. Table 14.2 shows these categories with respect to both men and women among the Non-Brahmans; Table 14.3, among the Paḷḷars.

These tables show that a surprisingly large number of Paḷḷars compared to Non-Brahmans were coolies who also leased in a little land. These Paḷḷars, like the "pure" Paḷḷar tenants, were mainly families who had been fortunate enough to obtain leases of fields belonging to absentee landlords. These landlords were mostly Non-Brahmans from outside the village. In the past few years, however, some land of absent and even of one or two resident Brahmans had also been leased to Paḷḷars, who were generally regarded as more skilled and economical than Non-Brahmans in paddy cultivation.

Most of the Paḷḷar laborers who had leased in a little land did casual coolie work rather than being *paṇṇaiyāḷs*. One reason was that, because their landlords were absent, most of them had no regular master in the village. Laborers who had *kuthakai* land also usually preferred coolie to *paṇṇaiyāḷ* work because the latter was the more time consuming and involved a semiservile relationship of debt. Finally, the landlords on the whole preferred *paṇṇaiyāḷs* or regular coolies who had no *kuthakai* land, because they were likely to be more reliable. One liberal young Brahman, however, employed two Paḷḷar couples as regular coolies who were also his lessees.

Twenty-one other Paḷḷars and sixteen Non-Brahmans were also casual coolies, but without land to lease. These men, and an even larger number of women, were the most marginal and insecure of the laborers. Except at the peak seasons of transplanting (women) and harvest (both sexes) they were surplus people

Table 14.2. *Non-Brahman agricultural laborers, Kumbapeṭṭai, 1952*

| | Attached laborers (*Vēlaikkārars*) | | Regular coolies | | Casual coolies | | Total | |
|---|---|---|---|---|---|---|---|---|
| | M | F | M | F | M | F | M | F |
| With some leased land | 1 | — | — | — | 1 | — | 2 | — |
| Landless except for house site | 18 | — | — | — | 16 | 5 | 34 | 5 |
| Total | 19 | — | — | — | 17 | 5 | 36 | 5 |

Table 14.3. *Paḷḷar agricultural laborers, Kumbapeṭṭai, 1952*

| | Attached laborers (*Paṇṇaiyāḷs*) | | Regular coolies | | Casual coolies | | Total | |
|---|---|---|---|---|---|---|---|---|
| | M | F | M | F | M | F | M | F |
| With some leased land | 1 | 1 | 2 | 2 | 15 | 15 | 18 | 18 |
| Landless except for house site | 21 | 24 | 15 | 6 | 22 | 35 | 58 | 65 |
| Total | 22 | 25 | 17 | 8 | 37 | 50 | 76 | 83 |

whom the village did not really need. Ideally, they should have been employed for nine months of each year in craft or factory work, but Thanjāvūr's economy was not so structured to be able to engage them.

Table 14.2 shows only a small number of Non-Brahman women agricultural workers because most women of the Non-Braham servant families worked in their masters' homes in the *agrahāram*. In all, twenty-three Non-Brahman women not shown in Table 14.2 worked in this capacity. The five Non-Brahman coolie women who did agricultural work came from very poor families of casual coolies who had no regular masters. Some of the women who worked in the *agrahāram* occasionally helped out with light agricultural work.

The category of "regular coolies" was created in 1952 as an adaptation to the Māyuram Agreement of October 28, 1948, and the Tanjore Tenants' and Paṇṇaiyāḷs' Ordinance of August 1952. As I have mentioned earlier, these ordinances raised the wages of *paṇṇaiyāḷs* on estates having more than 6.67 acres of wet land in one village. To circumvent them, Kumbapeṭṭai's bigger landlords dismissed their *paṇṇaiyāḷs* and rehired them as daily coolies to whom the law did not apply. Although the daily wages of coolies were higher than the old wages of *paṇṇaiyāḷs*, they totaled less in a year than the new payments for *paṇṇaiyāḷs* prescribed by ordinance, for coolies received no perquisites such as clothing or gifts at marriages and funerals. Some *mirāsdārs* kept on their old *paṇṇaiyāḷs* as regular workers throughout most of the year, and slightly raised their wages. They sometimes made loans to them, gave them small gifts at festivals, and paid them the usual harvest wages in paddy. At the same time, they called them coolies and omitted the customary gifts of clothing and marriage and funeral donations. I have classed such laborers as "regular coolies." Landlords and *uḷ-kuthakai* tenants managing estates of less than 6.67 acres in Kumbapeṭṭai, and several others who thought that they would not be contested, engaged *paṇṇaiyāḷs* in the traditional manner. The Non-Brahman middle peasants and tenants hired only casual coolies, relying mainly on family labor, although six Paḷḷars worked fairly often for the same Non-Brahman masters.

Caste rank was crucial in differentiating the Non-Brahman *vēlaikkārars*' from the Pallar *paṇṇaiyāḷs*' work. Non-Brahman *paṇṇaiyāḷs* or *vēlaikkārars* milked the cows of their masters, drove paddy and passenger carts, and did the garden work. They ran errands, shopped, and sometimes tended small boys in the Brahman home. Often, they supervised the Paḷḷar *paṇṇaiyāḷs*, summoned extra coolies to work at peak seasons, and paid out daily wages. Non-Brahman *vēlaikkārars* did some ploughing and sowing, and occasionally picked up the seedlings from the seed beds before transplanting or drove the cattle for *pōraḍi*, but they seldom did the heavy work of harvesting the paddy or threshing it by beating. *Vēlaikkārars* were sometimes employed in fencing or in simple repairs to their master's house or cattle shed.

Among both Non-Brahman and Paḷḷar *paṇṇaiyāḷs*, old men, or boys of about six to fourteen, were often employed in grazing and washing the oxen. Small girls were occasionally engaged to graze cattle at the same rates as boys, but girls more often took care of their younger siblings before puberty. After puberty, a Non-Brahman girl was secluded in her home until marriage, when she took up the regular work of a *vēlaikkāran*'s wife.

Non-Brahman women in *vēlaikkārar* families did domestic work in the Brahman home. They swept the floors, washed dishes in the canal or the Kīla Kuṭṭai bathing pool, laundered clothing, and cared for the small children. Occasionally, they and their husbands might harvest black or green gram or other dry crops or help in sowing the paddy seed. Two Non-Brahman women cleaned the Brahman temples of Siva and Vishnū, apart from the inner shrines and the kitchens, which only the priests might enter.

In 1952, *vēlaikkārars* in Kumbapeṭṭai were paid four *kalams* of paddy per month for what was in theory full-time work; their womenfolk, one *kalam* for part-time housework in the morning and the late afternoon. Some men received three *kalams* of paddy and Rs. 6 (the ration price of one *kalam*) in cash. *Vēlaikkārars* were paid separately one *marakkāḷ* and As. 2 per day if they helped with the sowing or picked seedlings for transplanting, and As. 2 if they climbed a coconut tree to pluck the nuts. Some *vēlaikkārars* cared for some of their masters' cattle in their own byres to minimize the risk of cattle epidemics, and some grazed large herds in the fields in summer for a fee.

At Deepavāḷi, *vēlaikkārars'* masters provided clothing for each adult man and woman worth about Rs. 10 per person. Either cooked foods or the materials for cooking were supplied at Pongal, Māṭṭu Pongal, Ādi 18, and Deepavāḷi, and at a marriage in the master's house. Small change was also given at these festivals and at First Ploughing and First Sowing. The expenses of births, marriages, and deaths were paid for by the *vēlaikkāraṉ*'s master. For a marriage the master provided a gold *tāli*, or marriage pendant, worth half a sovereign, and either loaned or gave the bridegroom Rs. 200 to Rs. 300 for the wedding clothes and feasting. When a birth occurred, the master gave a *marakkāḷ* of raw rice to the family and a container of castor oil for the mother. The *vēlaikkāraṉ* and his wife received new clothes and a few rupees at a death in either their own family or their master's. Some *vēlaikkārars* received loans of up to about Rs. 70 at New Year or in an emergency, which they paid back in paddy from their monthly wages at the rate of one *kalam* (valued at Rs. 6) per month. Boys over the age of about twelve who regularly grazed the cattle were paid one *kalam* a month; smaller boys, two to six *marakkāḷs* according to age. Because their pay was monthly instead of daily and because they did not do regular work in the fields, *vēlaikkārars* were presumed to be unaffected by the Tanjore Tenants' and Paṇṇaiyals' Act. No change was therefore made in their wages in 1952.

Table 14.4 summarizes the estimated annual wages of a *vēlaikkāraṉ* and his wife. If the family had one working child aged twelve, the annual income might be valued at about eighty-seven *kalams*, roughly the same as a village servant. In a year of bad weather, the *vēlaikkārar* family might earn more than that of a small tenant farmer, but in moderate or good years, most tenants were better off. Most of the *vēlaikkārars* owned goats and chickens and eked out their livelihood with meat and milk. The masters provided them with small gardens behind their houses and with mud, thatch, and timber for building their dwellings.

Most of Kumbapeṭṭai's *vēlaikkārars* were of the Kōṉār caste, the village's traditional dairymen and former Non-Brahman serfs. Three, however, were of the former inland fishing caste of Ambalakkārars, one was a part-time Kaḷḷar paddy trader, and one, a Tamil Nāyakkar, or former palm wine toddy tapper.

The homes of *vēlaikkārars* tended to be slightly poorer than those of the tenant farmers. Most consisted of only one small room with a loft for personal belongings, a tiny verandah, and a kitchen. All were thatched. The floors were of beaten earth washed over with cow dung and water to provide a smooth, clean surface and to keep out worms. A few *vēlaikkārars'* huts were no better than the shacks of the Paḷḷar laborers, having no verandah, no windows, only one room (in which one could not stand upright), and a three-foot high doorway hung with a sack. The *vēlaikkārar* family's belongings were usually restricted to a few clothes slung on a clothes line, a metal suitcase containing bits of jewelry and other finery, perhaps a single religious picture, one or two mats, a tiny oil

Table 14.4. *Estimated annual wages of Non-Brahman attached laborer and his wife, Kumbapeṭṭai, 1952*

| | Kalams of paddy | Rs. or Re. value of other payments |
|---|---|---|
| Man's annual paddy wage @ 4 *kalams* per month | 48–0 | — |
| Woman's annual paddy wage @ 1 *kalam* per month | 12–0 | — |
| Clothing for man and wife at Deepāvaḷi | | 20–0 |
| Food and gifts at festivals | 0–6 | 5–0 |
| Annual average of gifts for births, marriages, and funerals | | 20–0 |
| Miscellaneous payments for agricultural work | 5–0 | 25–0 |
| Total | 65–6 | 90–0 |

lamp, a few agricultural tools, a comb and sometimes a tiny mirror, one or two bell-metal vessels, and some clay and iron pots.

Kumbapeṭṭai's Paḷḷar *paṇṇaiyāḷs* did all the tasks connected with paddy cultivation and irrigation, in addition to sowing and harvesting legume crops. The men ploughed, scattered seed, picked up seedlings from the seed beds for transplanting, managed the flow of irrigation water from channels to fields, harvested the paddy crops with sickles, transported it on their heads to the threshing floor, threshed it by beating, and later carried out the second threshing with bullocks. The women covered the seed with ash after sowing, transplanted the young seedlings, weeded the fields, harvested the green and black gram crops, harvested paddy alongside the men, and helped with the threshing. Boys under fourteen grazed and washed the cattle, being paid the same amount as Non-Brahman boys. Girls, too, sometimes grazed the cattle for a fee, but small girls usually tended younger children, gathered cow dung for their own and their masters' fuel, and helped with their families' cooking. Paḷḷar girls were not secluded after puberty or during menstruation. From about the age of thirteen or fourteen they did women's work and were paid as adults. At fifteen or sixteen they usually married men aged seventeen to twenty.

*Paṇṇaiyāḷs*, like Non-Brahman *vēlaikkārars*, were usually hired in nuclear family units. The official unit was spoken of as a *jōthi*, or pair. Normally it was a man and his wife, but occasionally it comprised a widowed mother and her unmarried son, or a widower father and his divorced or widowed daughter. Usually, it was understood that children over the age of about six could be called to work if their masters needed them and that they would be paid at the customary rates for children of various ages. Only one Paḷḷar boy, aged nine, attended an elementary school for Harijan children two-and-a-half miles away; two older Paḷḷar youths whose father was a fairly prosperous tenant were in high

Table 14.5. *Estimated annual payments for Paḷḷar attached laborer* (Paṇṇaiyāl) *and wife, Kumbapeṭṭai, 1952*

| | Kalams of paddy | Rs. or Re. value of other payments |
|---|---|---|
| Man's wages @ 3/4 *marakkāḷ* + As. 4, 222 days a year | 13–10½ | 55–8 |
| Woman's wages @ 3/8 *marakkāḷ*, 180 days | 5–7½ | — |
| Harvest wages for couple, 60 days @ 2 *marakkāḷs* per day | 10–0 | — |
| *Kaḷavaḍi* or bounty in 2 harvests @ 5 *kalams* per harvest | 10–0 | — |
| 1 *marakkāḷ* per pair per *māh* at each harvest | 4–0 | — |
| 1 *kalam* stones and paddy gleaned after *pōraḍi* threshing, per *kaṇi*, shared by all workers | 3–0 | — |
| Gifts at First Ploughing | 1 | 0–4 |
| Gifts at Seed Scattering | ¼ | 0–8 |
| Gifts at First Transplanting | ½ | 1–0 |
| Gifts at Āḍi 18 | 1 | 8 |
| Gifts at Pongal and Māṭṭu Pongal | 1 | 1–0 |
| Gifts at First Paddy Cutting ("New Rice") | 2 | 4 |
| Clothing at Deepāvaḷi for couple | — | 20–0 |
| Average annual gifts for births, marriages, and funerals | ¼ | 10–0 |
| Total | 47–0 | 89–0 |

school in Āriyūr. Already in 1952, however, a few landlords with small estates employed only a single *paṇṇaiyāḷ*, or regular coolie man, engaging casual coolies for the rest of their operations. Some families kept widows in their employment after their husbands had died. Some old men and women over the age of sixty were kept as *paṇṇaiyāḷs* to tend oxen at children's wages. Others were dismissed and if they were still able to work, picked up odd jobs as casual coolies.

The annual wages of the Paḷḷar *paṇṇaiyāḷs* were less than those of Non-Brahman *vēlaikkarārs*. The customary payments were mainly divided into two portions: a lower rate of wages paid by the regular master and by all others who employed the *paṇṇaiyāḷs* on nonharvest days, and a higher rate paid during the two harvest seasons for about sixty days a year. In addition there were a number of complicated perquisites given at festivals and at the harvest seasons. Table 14.5 summarizes the various customary payments for a couple in 1951–2. These payments are based on my estimate that *paṇṇaiyāḷ* men worked a total of about 282 days a year, and women about 240 days including the harvest seasons.

Table 14.6. *Estimated annual wages of Paḷḷar attached laborer* (Paṇṇaiyāḷ) *and wife, Kumbapeṭṭai, 1952*

| | Kalams of paddy | Rs. or Re. value of other payments |
|---|---|---|
| Man's wages @ 3/4 *marakkāḷ* + As. 4, 282 days | 17–7½ | 70–8 |
| Woman's wages @ ½ *marakkāḷ*, 240 days | 10–0 | — |
| *Kaḷavaḍi* or bounty, 2 harvests | 16–0 | — |
| Gifts at festivals and life crises as in Table 14.4 | 6 | 33–8 |
| Total | 44–1½ | 104–0 |

In fact, not all *paṇṇaiyāḷ* families received this amount in full. In some cases where the landlord's estate was small, *paṇṇaiyāḷ* men worked only seven months, or about 210 days a year, and women only about 140 days. Their annual wages would then amount to the value of 43.36 *kalams* plus clothing and other perquisites. The payments given in Table 14.5 assume that the *paṇṇaiyāḷ* man would have nonagricultural work such as fencing, channel digging, raising vegetables, plucking tree fruits and nuts, grazing cattle, and gathering cow dung and wood for fuel during the slack months of Chittrai and Vaigāsi, Āvaṉi, Kārthikai, and Mārgari; but in fact, these jobs were few on the smaller estates. In addition, *paṇṇaiyāḷs* usually borrowed about Rs. 60 in cash on New Year's Day and returned it in paddy in the following *sambā* harvest. In April to October, however, Rs. 60 might buy only five *kalams* of paddy on the black market, whereas in the harvest season it was worth 10 *kalams*, so that the laborer might lose five *kalams* a year in repaying his debt. Although I have no complete individual records of debts and of the number of days worked in a year, I estimated that few *paṇṇaiyāḷ* couples received the total of 56–10 *kalams*' worth of paddy and cash in a year, leaving aside the wages of their children, and that some received as little as forty-five *kalams*' worth. (The measure "56–10 *kalams*" and other like measures that follow are in *kalams* and *marakkāḷs*, there being twelve *marakkāḷs* to a *kalam*.)

Two alternative, customary methods of harvest payment of *paṇṇaiyāḷs* existed in Kumbapeṭṭai in 1952. Some landlords paid their men servants seventy-five percent of a *marakkāḷ* plus As. 4 per day and their women fifty percent of a *marakkāḷ* throughout the year, but at harvest time gave each couple a harvest bonus (*kaḷasam* or *kaḷavaḍi*) of eight *kalams*. In this case the extra payments during the harvest process were omitted except for the "New Rice" gift. The annual wage was then as in Table 14.6, a total value of about 55–8 *kalams*.

Yet another mode of payment involved paying the regular wage for all except the harvest seasons, but instead of harvest wages, giving all the harvest workers collectively one-thirteenth of the total amount they had harvested. Other harvest payments were then omitted. This method, called *virunthukooḷi*, or "guest wages," was naturally more popular among the laborers when the harvest was good, but more popular among the landlords when the harvest was poor. Some landlords consistently paid on the share method regardless of the crop, whereas others never used it. Others waited until the crop was on the threshing floor and then decided whether to pay harvest wages or to divide the crop. As a result, acrimonious disputes sometimes broke out between the workers and the landlords, but in 1952 in Kumbapeṭṭai, the landlords' will prevailed. In a moderately good year with fourteen *kalams* yield per *māh*, if a couple harvested the equivalent of twelve *māhs* of land per harvest, they would obtain about 310 *marakkāls* in harvest payments in a year, or 25.83 *kalams* – roughly the same as by the method recorded in Table 14.5.

Kumbapettai's landlords had formerly allotted half a *māh* of wet paddy land to each *paṇṇaiyāḷ* couple as a tax-free service tenure. In a moderately good year, this land might yield them twelve *kalams* of paddy. In 1952 almost all landlords had stopped allotting *paṭṭakkāḷ*, the poorer ones because they could not afford it, and the richer because they were engaging regular coolies instead of *paṇṇaiyāḷs*. When *paṇṇaiyāḷs* were engaged, the annual *kaḷavaḍi* of five *kalams* per harvest was paid instead of *paṭṭakkāḷ* (see Table 14.5).

Although no landlords in Kumbapeṭṭai paid their *paṇṇaiyāḷs* at these rates, it is of interest to record the statutory wages of *paṇṇaiyāḷs* according to the Madras government regulations of 1951–3. Under the Māyuram Agreement of October 28, 1948, after the Communist agriculturists' strike in east Thanjāvūr, landlords owning more than 6.67 acres of wet land or twenty acres of dry land in one village were required to pay a *paṇṇaiyāḷ* couple as shown in Table 14.7, assuming the same number of days worked as in the previous tables.

Under the Tanjore Tenants' and Pannaiyals' Ordinance of August 1952, *paṇṇaiyāḷs* might in theory choose whether to be paid under the Māyuram Agreement or under the terms of the new ordinance. The wages described in 1952 ordinance are given in Table 14.8.

Instead of paying these amounts, most of Kumbapeṭṭai's fifteen landlords who owned more than 6.67 acres in one village had dismissed their *paṇṇaiyāḷs* in 1949 and officially rehired them as daily coolies or as workers engaged for a particular task such as transplanting, harvesting, and so on. In fact, as we have seen, most of these workers were actually regular coolies who did the work of *paṇṇaiyāḷs* throughout the working year, but who were not called *paṇṇaiyāḷs* and were paid somewhat higher than the daily rates for *paṇṇaiyāḷs*. In 1952 the rates for regular coolies were in theory one *marakkāḷ* plus As. 2 or As. 4 per day per man and three-quarters of a *marakkāḷ* per day per woman during all the seasons except harvest. Harvest payments were either on the share method at one-thirteenth of the gross produce divided among the workers, or at the rate of three *marakkāḷs* per day per person for both men and women. No clothing and

Table 14.7. *Payments of* Paṇṇaiyāl *couple for one year, Māyuram Agreement, 1948*

| | Kalams of paddy | Rs. or Re. value of other payments |
|---|---|---|
| Man's wages @ 1 *marakkāḷ* for 222 days | 18–8 | — |
| Woman's wages @ ¾ *marakkāḷ,* for 180 days | 11–3 | — |
| Harvest payments of 1/7 share of total paddy harvested and threshed by couple, @ 12 *māhs* per couple | 41–2 (estimate)[a] | — |
| Other perquisites at festivals and life-crises according to custom | 6 | 33–8 |
| Total | 71–7 | 33–8 |

[a]In a good year, this might rise to about 51½ *kalams*, affording a total annual income of 82–1 *kalams*, plus Rs. 33–8 in cash or other gifts.

Table 14.8. *Payments of* Paṇṇaiyāl *couple for one year, Tanjore Tenants' and Paṇṇaiyals' Ordinance, August 1952*

| | Kalams of paddy | Rs. or Re. value of other payments |
|---|---|---|
| Man's wages @ 2 *marakkāḷs* per day, 282 days | 47–0 | — |
| Woman's wages @ 1 *marakkāḷ,* per day, 240 days | 20–0 | — |
| Crop share of ½ *marakkāḷ* per *kalam* of gross paddy harvested and threshed | 12–0 (estimate)[a] | — |
| Other perquisites at festivals and life crises according to custom | 6 | 33–8 |
| Total | 79–6 | 33–8 |

[a]In a good year, this might rise to 15 *kalams*, affording a total annual income of 82½ *kalams*, plus Rs. 33–8. In a good year the payments under the Māyuram Agreement (Table 14.6) and the Tanjore Tenants' and Paṇṇaiyāḷs' Ordinance would thus be virtually equal, but in a bad year the laborer would earn more under the terms of the ordinance.

Table 14.9. *Annual payments of Paḷḷar regular coolie married couple, Kumbapeṭṭai, 1952*

| | Kalams of paddy | Rs. or Re. value of other payments |
|---|---|---|
| Man's wages 222 days @ 1 *marakkāḷ*, plus As. 3 | 18–6 | 41–10 |
| Woman's wages, 180 days @ ¾ *marakkāḷ* | 11–3 | — |
| Harvest wages, 60 days @ 6 *marakkāḷs* per pair per day | 30–0 | — |
| Total | 59–6 | 41–10 |

no extra gifts were given at festivals, marriages, or funerals. Using the latter method, the annual wages of a married pair of regular coolies were optimally as in Table 14.9, that is, a total value of about 64–2 *kalams* per year.

In fact, however, regular coolies were sometimes paid entirely in cash instead of paddy, and at rates less than those shown in Table 14.9. Men, for example, received only As. 12 per day for digging out the channels in July, the equivalent of one *marakkāḷ* of paddy at the black market price in that month. Women often received only As. 3 to As. 4 per day for transplanting (worth three-eighths to a one-half *marakkāḷ* at ration prices, but less at black market prices). The reason was that because many more women turned up for work than were summoned, the landlord shared out the official wages of those he had actually summoned. Again, one landlord regularly paid his women coolies only one-half a *marakkāḷ* instead of three-quarters, plus As. 1 per day. Altogether, it is probable that few regular coolies earned more than did *paṇṇaiyāḷs*.

Casual coolies who had no regular masters but were merely hired by the day were paid mainly in cash, with different rates prevailing in different seasons and for varying types of work. At harvest time both men and women were paid in either paddy or cash at the rate of three *marakkāḷs* or Rs. 1–8 per day. Assuming that the man worked about 270 days and the woman 240 days, their schedule and payments were as given in Table 14.10.

This amount is hard to convert into *kalams* of paddy because the price of black market paddy varied during the year. Coolies were obliged to buy at least some of their paddy on the black market, for the ration was only eight ounces per day per adult, but both men and women needed between about twenty-six and thirty-two ounces of husked rice per day according to their size and work. We shall be fairly accurate if we assume that paddy cost the coolie Rs. 6 per *kalam* during half the year and Rs. 12 during the other half. At this rate, the optimal annual income of a couple as given in Table 14.10 would be worth about fifty-four *kalams* per year.

Like the regular coolies, casual coolies actually often received lower than the standard wages. Men were in fact sometimes paid only As. 12 for digging

Table 14.10. *Seasonal payments of casual coolie married couple for one year, Kumbapeṭṭai, 1952*

| | Rs. or Re. value of other payments |
|---|---|
| *April to September* | |
| Man's wages, 75 days @ Re. 1 (cutting bunds, digging channels, carting manure) | 75–0 |
| Man's wages, 75 days @ Re. 1–4 (ploughing, leveling, sowing, and removing seedlings) | 93–12 |
| Woman's wages, 120 days @ As. 6 (sowing, transplanting, and weeding) | 45–0 |
| *October* | |
| *Kuruvai* harvest, 30 days @ Re. 1–8 per day each for man and woman | 90–0 |
| *November to January* | |
| Man's wages, 60 days @ Re. 1–4 (ploughing, leveling, and removing seedlings) | 75–0 |
| Woman's wages, 48 days @ As. 6 (transplanting, weeding) | 18–0 |
| *February to March* | |
| *Sambā* harvest, 30 days @ Re. 1–8 each for man and woman | 90–0 |
| *March* | |
| Gram harvest, woman's wages, 12 days @ As. 2½ | 1–14 |
| Total | 488–10 |

channels and Rs. 1–2 for ploughing and leveling, and women As. 4 for weeding. If too many women arrived for transplanting, each might receive only As. 3 to As. 4 for half a day's hard labor.

Young men often preferred coolie to *paṇṇaiyāḷ* work, especially if it was combined with *kuthakai* farming, for if they were strong and diligent they could be fairly confident of working at least six months of the year and sometimes up to 270 days. For middle-aged and older men and women, however, casual labor provided bare subsistence. They could be certain of work only during the two months of the harvest, and in the case of women, in the transplanting seasons. Such couples probably earned little more than Rs. 333 or about thirty-seven *kalams* per year. They were especially hard pressed because they received no gratuities at festivals or life-crises rites, had to buy their own clothing, and could offer no security for loans. Although they lived rent free on house sites owned by the landlords, they had to provide the materials for their own huts, which cost about Rs. 40 to Rs. 50. Their children could not be sure of obtaining work because the parents had no regular master to whom they could appeal.

In 1952 the Paḷḷars told me that an adult male Paḷḷar required 1.25 *sinna paḍis* of husked rice per day, and a woman one *sinna paḍi* as basic food in order to live without hunger.[1] Ideally, children aged six to ten ate on average half a *sinna paḍi*. Husked rice amounted to half the volume (66 percent of the weight) of paddy. A couple with two growing children would thus need about 1.63 *marakkāḷs* of paddy per day as food, or 49.4 *kalams* per year. Even sparing nothing for supplementary food, clothing, or shelter, it is easy to see that a couple earning only the equivalent of thirty-seven *kalams* per year would be severely short of food for themselves and their children. The two children might with luck earn an additional six to twelve *kalams* as bullock boys, but the family would still be hard pressed and could not be sure of this amount in any given year. In fact, casual coolies and many *paṇṇaiyāḷs* and regular coolies reported that they ate only one meal instead of two per day during the months of Chittrai, Vaigāsi, Āni, Āḍi, Āvani, Karthikai, and Mārgaṛi, when work was scarce. In these months the laborers often caught and ate field or house rats, or after the water came, fish or minnows and small crabs in the irrigation channels. Some of the least fortunate casual laborers, especially old women, dug for roots in the village's wasteland. A few Paḷḷar women had sexual relations with Non-Brahman men for money, usually for As. 4 to Rs. 2 per time. During Chittrai and Vaigāsi thefts of paddy, gram, and coconuts from landlords' and middle peasants' houses and yards were common. Such forms of "hunting and gathering" in the interstices of the economy were essential to the casual laborers' existence, and were also often practiced by the *paṇṇaiyāḷs*, for without *kuthakai* land or gardens of their own, agricultural laborers were unable to keep goats or chickens.

In spite of their deep poverty, the semiproletarians were said to be slightly better off than they had been before prohibition was instituted in 1947. It was said that in those days, a Paḷḷar laborer often spent two out of three *marakkāḷs* of his paddy payments in the harvest season on toddy, relying on his one *marakkāḷ*, plus his wife's wages, for food for the family. Many of the Non-Brahman tenants and laborers, too, were often drunk. Both the landlords and the laboring men opposed prohibition: the laborers because it provided an escape from their toil and misery, and the landlords because they were afraid of the laborers' becoming "too rich" and disobeying them. But women of the tenant and laboring families, very few of whom ever drank toddy, were thankful for prohibition because it gave them and their children a little more food to eat. Some laborers occasionally bought illicit alcohol at Rs. 5 a bottle, and two went to jail for short periods during my stay, but the majority drank tea with milk and jaggery from the tea shops.

The homes and lifestyles of the *paṇṇaiyāḷs* and coolies reflected their poverty. Most of their houses were small thatched shacks about five feet high with a single room, a tiny raised platform as a front verandah, and a space under the eaves behind the house for cooking. These minute hovels lacked windows and had only a sack hanging in the doorway to ensure privacy. They contained little except a few cooking vessels, a few rags of clothing, and the ubiquitous rats. Among *paṇṇaiyāḷs* the expenses of birth, marriage and death were similar to but slightly more modest than those of the *vēlaikkārars*, being paid by the family's master. The Paḷḷar *paṇṇaiyāḷ*'s marriage usually cost Rs. 100 or less. About Rs. 60 was spent on, or received as, clothing. In addition, the landlord provided the gold *tāli* worth one-quarter of a sovereign.

The majority of the casual coolies were Paḷḷars, but sixteen men and five women among the Non-Brahmans were also casual coolies without land. The men included five Kaḷḷars, two Nāyakkars, two Nāḍārs, one Poosāri, one Ambalakkārar, and six Kōṉārs. The Non-Brahman coolies were thus not selected by caste, but were simply men who could not find work as *vēlaikkārars* or tenant farmers and who had no specialized skills or capital to start a business. One of the Nāḍārs and the Poosāri were recent refugees from the drought in Rāmanāthapuram where they had been farmers. The five Non-Brahman women coolies included three local Kaḷḷars and two Paḍaiyācchi women refugees from Rāmanāthapuram.

Unlike the *vēlaikkārars* and their wives, Non-Brahman casual coolies mostly did the same work as the Paḷḷars and were paid at the same rate. Altogether, ten Non-Brahman households were composed entirely of coolies who were as poor as the Paḷḷar laborers.

It is clear that *paṇṇaiyāḷs* and even coolies were still paid largely in kind in 1952, although supplementary cash payments were gradually replacing the old gifts of clothing and housing and even part of the customary payments of grain. On the whole, the Ādi Drāviḍas' purchases on the market were mainly confined to coconut or gingelly oil for cooking, *iluppeṇṇey*, or wild olive oil, black and green gram, betel and arecanuts for chewing, and for men, tea bought in teashops. After the *sambā* harvest, each Paḷḷar street sold a little of its members' surplus paddy through the Kaḷḷar traders to buy goats and other materials for the festival of Kāḷiyamman, their caste goddess.

Among the Paḷḷar agricultural laborers were seven families whose men worked full or part time in specialized tasks. Five of them were the village's watchmen (*kāvalkkārars*) of the paddy fields. They were selected from time to time by the Brahman landlords and paid as village servants. Each family lived in an outlying hut on a threshing floor in one of the main blocks of paddy fields. The watchman's work included protecting the crops from marauding animals, setting up scarecrows and beating a tocsin to keep away birds, seeing that the irrigation water flowed regularly to the fields, and protecting paddy and straw on the threshing floor from thieves. If a theft occurred, he had to make it good from his earnings.

Each watchman guarded about ten *vēlis*, or 66.7 acres of paddy land and was paid from that area. Each received as a gratuity two hand bundles or one *marakkāḷ* of unthreshed paddy for every *kāṇi* (1.33 acres) cultivated and threshed in his area. This fee was called *puthukuruṇi* ("new *kuruṇi*" or "new marakkāḷ"), being given on the first day of harvest. On the following day when the straw was rethreshed with bullocks, the watchman received one *marakkāḷ* per *kāṇi* threshed, called *pōra* (straw) *marakkāḷ*. This was a special fee for

Table 14.11. *Paddy payments per harvest to Paḷḷar watchman, Kumbapeṭṭai, 1952, on ten* vēlis *of land*

| | Kalams |
|---|---|
| "New *marakkāḷs*" @ 1 *marakkāḷ* per *kāṇi* (1.33 acres) | 4–2 |
| "Straw" *marakkāḷs* @ 1 *marakkāḷ* per *kāṇi* | 4–2 |
| 6 *marakkāḷs* per 106 *kalams* threshed, @ 15 *kalams* per *māh* | 14–2 |
| Total | 22–6 |

guarding the straw overnight. As his main payment the watchman received six *marakkāḷs* out of every 106 *kalams* threshed *in toto*. If the harvest was good and 300 *kalams* per *vēli* were threshed, the watchman's main payment came to about 170 *marakkāḷs* for ten *vēlis* in each harvest. His total payment for one harvest would then be 270 *marakkāḷs*, or 22.5 *kalams* (see Table 14.11).

If the land was all double cropped, the watchman at this rate would make forty-five *kalams* per year, the usual amount of paddy (minus cash) received by a *paṇṇaiyāḷ* couple. If, however, the harvest was poor (as in 1951–2) and each crop yielded only about nine *kalams* per *māh*, the watchman's annual take would amount to only 404 *marakkāḷs*, or 33.6 *kalams* per year. His wife, however, would earn more as a coolie. Watchmen received clothing and gifts at festivals, contributed jointly by the landlords. In general, the post brought about the same as, or a slightly higher income than, that of a *pannaiyāḷ*. It required less arduous manual labor but was honored for its heavy responsibility.

Although he lived outside the village in Māniyūr, the Paṟayar scavenger (*veṭṭiyaṉ*) should be mentioned as the last of the village servants. The scavenger removed dead cattle from the village after the Kōṉārs had lifted them out of the landlords' cowshed. The family cut open each animal and if it did not contain worms they ate the meat or sold it to other Paṟayars. The hides were sold to a tannery in Āriyūr owned by the same Muslim who owned the rice mill. The scavenger and his male relatives drummed and played pipes at Non-Brahman funerals and guarded cremation grounds. The *veṭṭiyaṉ* received one bundle or one-half a *marakkāḷ* per *kāni* of new paddy on the threshing floor, plus one *marakkāḷ* per plough (or *vēli*) at each harvest. His annual payments from Kumbapeṭṭai *grāmam's* 354 acres (fifty-three *vēlis*) of paddy land came to about 245 *marakkāḷs*, or 20.4 *kalams* per annum. Because the scavenger worked in Māniyūr as well, his threshing floor payments might be roughly double that amount, plus a few annas earned at a Non-Brahman funeral and any income his wife earned as a coolie. The scavenger, unlike the watchman, did not receive gifts from landlords at festivals. In all, the Paṟayar scavenger earned roughly the same amount per year as a Paḷḷar *paṇṇaiyāḷ,* whereas the higher-ranking, Non-Brahman village servants earned roughly the same as a Non-Brahman tenant.

Kumbapeṭṭai's Paḷḷars had two other families of part-time specialists. One was their barber, or Pariyāri, who lived on Upper Paḷḷar Street. He cut the hair of Paḷḷar men and boys, shaved them, and had some rudimentary knowledge of herbal medicines. His wife was the Paḷḷars' midwife. The barber worked in both Kumbapeṭṭai and Māniyūr and was paid in paddy after the two harvests; occasionally, he and his family worked as agricultural coolies. The Pariyāri belonged to a separate, slightly lower subcaste of Paḷḷars and married only in other Pariyāri families of the region.

The Paḷḷars had formerly had another low-ranking servant family, of Vaṉṉārs, or Washermen. Like the Non-Brahman Vaṉṉār in relation to Brahmans and Non-Brahmans, this family washed ritually polluted cloths after funerals, menstruation, and childbirth. The family had run away five years previously, taking with them all the Paḷḷar clothing they could assemble. Since that date the Paḷḷars had cheerfully washed their own polluted clothes.

The last family of Paḷḷar specialists was that of a *vādyar,* or teacher, who came to Kumbapeṭṭai in 1948 from Būdalūr, about twenty miles away. He had been brought up there by his mother's brother, also a teacher. He had patrilineal kin in Kumbapeṭṭai and was the only literate adult in the Paḷḷar streets. Unlike the other Paḷḷars, who were cropped, he wore his hair in a bun like the older Brahmans and Non-Brahmans. He possessed an old harmonium bought in Thanjāvūr for Rs. 60, and ten manuscript books of songs and Tamiḷ religious plays. These were Non-Brahman compositions that combined Sanskrit themes and heroes with local myths. The favorite plays concerned the smallpox goddess Māriyamman, the goddess Meenakshi of the great temple at Madurai, *Vaḷḷi Tirumanam* or the marriage of Subramania and Vaḷḷi, *Kōlan-Kaṇṇaki* from the *Silappadikkāram*, and the marriage of Arjuṉaṉ, hero of the *Mahābhārata*, with Alli, a queen of Madurai. At the time of my visit the teacher had several men of Upper Paḷḷar Street as reading and singing pupils and was teaching the drama *Alli-Arjuṉaṉ* to the men and boys of Long Paḷḷar Street. The whole street attended nightly rehearsals in a shed they had built for the performances. The two streets where he worked paid the teacher collectively in paddy after the harvest. A resident *guru* was clearly an innovation for these laborers; it was moving to see their eagerness to acquire literacy and knowledge, develop skills in drama and singing, and transcend their daily routines. The Paḷḷars could not afford to support the teacher fully, however, and he and his wife worked as coolies when they could.

### *The Nonagricultural Laborers*

Four men and twenty-six women did manual wage work in occupations other than agriculture. One couple were Koravars who had been settled by the government as road sweepers in Kumbapeṭṭai in 1947. The wife earned Rs. 18 a month for sweeping in Kumbapeṭṭai; the husband, Rs. 40 as a roadsweeper in Thanjāvūr. The couple had previously been gypsies who wandered about,

Non-Brahman domestic servant washing dishes in Akkāchāvaḍy tank.

singing, dancing, basketmaking, begging, and thieving. Whether justifiably or not, the husband was often in jail on charges of theft and I saw very little of him during my visit.

Two other nonagricultural manual workers were Marathas (called Raos) whose family had once served the *chattram* when it belonged to the Thanjāvūr palace. One of these men was the village *talayāri*, or assistant to the village headman and the *karṉam*, earning Rs. 18 a month. In his spare time he worked as a casual coolie. The other Maratha worked in a small Muslim cigar factory in Āriyūr. He earned Rs. 18 a month, while his wife earned Rs. 6 as a household worker in the *agrahāram*.

A fourth nonagricultural worker was the Muslim watchman of the broken down *chattram* opposite Akkāchāvaḏy. This man and his family occupied a small house built into one wing of the *chattram*. The Muslim's main task was to guard the fish in the tank from local marauders and to have the tank fished once a year by fish merchants from Thanjāvūr on behalf of his master. In the three summer months the Muslim owner hired an old, local Kōṉār woman for Rs. 5 a month to give drinking water to passersby as a charity – a relic of the *chattram's* munificence in the days of the Mahārājas.

One nonagricultural woman worker was a servant in the Brahman restaurant. She and her husband, of the Poosāri caste, had arrived from Rāmanāthapuram in the drought of 1948; the husband was a coolie.

### The Mendicants

In 1952 Kumbapeṭṭai had three elderly Brahmans who had lost their lands and lived mainly from religious charity. One was the one-legged, former police constable, father of the restaurant owner. This old man and another Brahman lived mainly by traveling on trains without tickets to temple festivals, where they ate and slept in *chattrams*, or charitable houses provided by the faithful for Brahmans as an act of merit, and begged small change from pilgrims. The third Brahman lived mainly by attending the last day of mourning after the funerals of wealthy Non-Brahmans and receiving food, clothing, a cow, a bed, or other gifts given to Brahmans by the mourners in order to expiate the sins of the departed. These modes of livelihood were all considered appropriate to the Brahman caste, for Brahmans, however indigent, were not traditionally expected to take up manual work. Charity to Brahmans had, moreover, been a way of obtaining salvation for two-and-a-half millennia. At the same time, other Brahmans found these occupations socially degrading and were inclined to believe that the gifts transferred the donor's sins to the recipients. That Kumbapeṭṭai's Brahmans should be forced to such expedients was seen as punishment for their own sins, and as symptomatic of the decline of the community.

### The Class Structure

Table 14.12 summarizes the class affiliations of men over age fifteen in Kumbapeṭṭai in 1952, separating those mainly dependent on agriculture from those not so dependent.

Table 14.12 reflects a largely poverty-stricken community. Although 83.3 percent of the men depended mainly on agriculture, only forty-two men, or 18.9 percent of the total, owned enough land for their livelihood and only sixty-six men, or 29.7 percent, owned any land at all. Fifty-three percent of the village men were propertyless laborers working under supervision and earning bare subsistence. Almost 73 percent of the village men were either semiproletarians or paupers. The very large number of agricultural laborers – 50.4 percent of the total villagers – reflected a high degree of underemployment. Twenty-two, or 10 percent of the village men, were casual coolies employed mainly at peak seasons

Table 14.12. *Class affiliations of men over fifteen in Kumbapeṭṭai, showing agriculturalists and nonagriculturalists, 1952*

| Class | Agricultural | Nonagricultural | Total |
|---|---|---|---|
| Petty bourgeois | 35 | 5 | 40 |
| Independent family entrepreneurs | 7 | 13 | 20 |
| Semiproletarians | — | — | — |
| Tenants and village servants under little supervision | 31 | 10 | 41 |
| Laborers with leased land | 20 | — | 20 |
| Landless laborers | 92 | 6 | 98 |
| Mendicants | — | 3 | 3 |
| Total | 185 | 17 | 222 |

*Note:* Students have been placed in the classes of their fathers.

and living usually on the edge of starvation. An even larger number of women were in this situation, thirty-five, or 14.7 percent of the total women, being casual coolies with the most precarious employment.

Although the data are imperfect, it seems probable that Kumbapeṭṭai's people were, on average, roughly as poor if not poorer in 1952 as in 1827, while their class structure had become more polarized. In 1827, thirty-three out of ninety households, or 36.6 percent, owned land, and 33.3 percent owned enough to live on. It is true that 56.6 percent of the households were *āḍimai āḷukaḷ* in one or another form of slavery; it is not clear whether any of them were also cultivating tenants. Their proportion was, however, considerably smaller than that of the semiproletarians in 1952. In 1827, the top 25 percent of the owners owned roughly 60 percent of the village land, and roughly 37 percent of the village households were landed. In 1952, however, the top 25 percent of owners living in the village owned 76 percent of the land owned by residents, while nearly three-quarters of the households were landless and were reduced to barest subsistence.

# 15 Village Politics: Religion, Caste, and Class

By "politics" I shall refer to the distribution of power and authority within groups larger than the family.

We have seen that members of the petty bourgeoisie were able to maintain their standard of living and pay their taxes only by severely exploiting the semiproletariat and, to a lesser extent, the middle peasants. The main political problems of the petty bourgeoisie were, therefore, how to maintain order among themselves and how to prevent or suppress rebellion by the lower classes. Those of the middle peasants and the semiproletariat were how to maintain order among themselves and how to carry on the struggle for survival, or, if possible, for betterment of their conditions.

The landlords' chief sources of control were religious beliefs and activities. As late as 1952, the religious moment dominated the political and economic moments in village social life. It is therefore necessary to refer to the religious system as it affected the political structure, although a full analysis of religious institutions cannot be undertaken here.

In Brahmanical thought, the whole social order was divinely ordained and sanctioned, its component units being seen as castes and groups of castes. As is well known, the four *varṉas* were symbolically represented as issuing from the head, arms, thighs, and feet of the creator. The castes were seen as proliferating from the *varṉas*, each divinely required to carry out its *dharma*, or caste duty.

The individual soul, or *ātmā*, was believed to pass through many lives, or *jenmas*, being capable of rebirth as an animal or in one of the castes of humans. The lowest form of rebirth was thought to be the pig, the highest, the cow, and the second highest, the Brahman. Among humans the lowest rebirth was that of the Paṟayar with the Paḷḷar slightly above him.

By performing his or her *dharma* well in this life, an individual might ensure that his or her soul was reborn in a higher caste. The ultimate goal of these efforts was the release (*mōksam*) of the soul from rebirth and its eternal union with the divine soul (*paramātma*). For castes below Brahmans and Kshattriyas, *dharma* consisted chiefly of faithful service to those above them; for Kshattriyas, of righteous government. For Brahmans, *dharma* lay mainly in avoidance of the cardinal sins, and in the performance of numerous religious ceremonies pertaining to the caste, the household, or the individual. Brahmanical *dharma* also involved the progressive control, through fasting, sexual abstinence, and other austerities, of all sensual desires.

A Brahman man's life was divided into five phases, or *āshramas*: childhood, adolescence (*brahmachāryam*), the young married state (*grahastham*), middle age (*vāṉaprasaṉam*), and old age (*sannyāsam*). In his irresponsibility, a child was compared with a Sūdra. He was not truly a Brahman, had no recognized social personality, and acquired the obligations of a Brahman only at initiation into *brahmachāryam* (*upanayaṉam*), when he was given the sacred thread. During *brahmachāryam*, from about the age of twelve to marriage at about age twenty to twenty-five, a Brahman was required to learn the Sanskrit texts and rites of his castes, obey his elders, and strictly control his bodily desires and functions. In the *grahastham* period, a man governed his household and the village under the guidance of the elders and enjoyed children, property, and sexual life. At about the age of fifty to fifty-five he was expected to begin to forsake bodily pleasures and worldly activities. He was to devote more time to ceremonies and the spiritual life, and ideally engage regularly in fasting and meditation. The Sanskrit term for this period, *vāṉaprasaṉam*, meant "life in the forest." A few middle-aged Brahmans in the neighborhood did in fact live in small huts outside their villages tended by their wives. They engaged in ceremonies, instructed disciples in the spiritual life, and abstained from sexual relations. None of Kumbapeṭṭai's Brahmans lived outside the village, but four middle-aged men lived lives of austerity and religious devotion within their homes.

*Sannyāsam* began at about age sixty-five to seventy and was ideally a period of total devotion to the divine. In theory, a man of this age should give up his family life and worldly goods and wander forth as a religious mendicant, owning only a yellow robe, a staff, and a begging bowl. As we have seen, three of Kumbapeṭṭai's older Brahmans did, at least part time, live similarly to religious mendicants. These men were not much respected for they had previously led very worldly lives and had had no property to surrender. Three other Brahmans, however, had completely discarded family life and left the village at various ages as ascetics. They were regarded by some people as "true *sannyāsis*." So, too, was the holy man who had earlier visited Kumbapeṭṭai and died there in 1936. True *sannyāsam*, which could in fact be begun at any age, was considered the highest path to ending rebirths and to attaining *sammādi*, or union with the divine.

*Sannyāsis* could come from any caste, for the *sannyāsi* discarded his caste membership along with his property, *dharma*, and family connections. In practice, most *sannyāsis* were Brahmans or Veḷḷāḷars.

The Brahmans' belief in *dharma* and in *karma*, the lot or fate that befell a man as a result of actions in this or a past existence, was buttressed by a further belief in inherited characteristics that justified the inequalities of the caste system. The Brahmans held that each caste had physical, intellectual, and spiritual powers suited to hereditary tasks. In general, Ādi Drāviḍas were thought to be intellectually inferior to Non-Brahmans, and Non-Brahmans to Brahmans. For this reason it was seen as improper and even ungodly for Ādi Drāviḍas to read or write, and it was traditionally forbidden for both Ādi Drāviḍa and Non-Brahman castes even to hear the recitation of the Vēdas.

The Brahmans recognized that they followed their religious prescriptions poorly; many were negligent of some of their fasts and ceremonies, and some indulged themselves with prostitutes or even alcohol. Nevertheless, religion was probably the ultimate concern of all the Brahman men and women and a very prominent one in the lives of the Non-Brahmans and Ādi Drāviḍas. True to their theory, it was Brahman men in *grahasthāshramam*, aged about twenty-two to fifty, who organized the affairs of the street and governed the lower castes. Those with more than about ten acres of land were especially prominent for they had more tenants, laborers, debtors, and other dependents.

In everyday life, the Brahmans maintained order in the village by insisting on the ritual ranking of castes. Ideally, each caste and each endogamous subcaste had a recognized place above or below each other group. The widest social distance was observed between the Brahman, Non-Brahman, and Ādi Drāviḍa categories; they were clearly segregated residentially and socially. Within each category, members were the ones most concerned about the rank of the particular castes and subcastes. Ādi Drāviḍas did not concern themselves with relative ranking among the Brahmans or the Non-Brahmans, being aware only that all Brahmans ranked above all Non-Brahmans, and both above themselves. Non-Brahmans were not concerned with ranking among the subcastes of Brahmans or Paḷḷars, and were only aware that Paḷḷars outranked Paṟayars. Even the Brahmans were little concerned with details of rank among subcastes within the Non-Brahman and Ādi Drāviḍa castes. When, however, caste or subcaste rank was a matter of public recognition, as in the village festival, the Brahmans were the ultimate authorities.

In Brahman theory, the castes and major subcastes found in Kumbapeṭṭai ranked as listed in Table 8.1. Subcastes have been indicated only when the caste had more than one subcaste represented in the village.

Referring to Table 8.1, among the Brahmans, the Kurukkals and Telugu Brahmans were generally thought to rank below the Brahacharaṉams because they served other villagers rather than being village governors. The Ayyangārs were admitted to rank above the Smārtha Brahmans because of their greater strictness in eating habits.

The Veḷḷālars were generally considered the highest of the Non-Brahman castes in villages throughout Tamiḷ Nāḍu. Together with the Brahmans, they had governed villages since Chōḷa times. The Marathas ranked high because they had been attendants upon the conquering Maratha royalty; the Agambaḍiyars, relatively high because they had supposedly been indoor servants of royals since ancient times. The Kaḷḷars' rank was high because Kaḷḷars were peasants who governed their own villages in much of southern Thanjāvūr. On the other hand, Kaḷḷars were considered low in some respects because some had been highwaymen and cattle thieves, and because they were originally a semitribal hill people in Madurai. The Paḍaiyācchis ranked below the Kaḷḷars because they were mostly tenant farmers and some in South Ārcot were thought to have once been slaves.

The Muslims were anomalous, being of an alien religion. Some Brahmans placed them outside the system altogether, yet in certain contexts they were part of the village society. They were generally viewed vaguely as being somewhere in the middle of the Non-Brahman group. Their customs of divorce and widow marriage placed them a little below the high-caste Hindūs, and it was known that they ate beef in their own communities, although not when they lived among Hindūs. On the other hand, there was no evidence that their ancestors had been slaves.

The Kōṉārs ranked relatively low among the Non-Brahmans, for they had been slaves of the Brahmans and still had a semiserflike relationship with them. Although they held a prestigious social position as priests in the Non-Brahman community, the Poosāris' "real" religious rank was regarded as low because they belonged to the somewhat despised caste of Āndis, formerly itinerant puppet players and acrobats.

The Potters and the Smiths posed a problem of rank in Kumbapeṭṭai as in Tamiḷ Nāḍu generally. In the eyes of both Brahmans and other Non-Brahmans, they ranked below the castes of middle peasants and tenants because they served these castes as manual workers. Their ritual value was also seen as less than that of the Poosāris, who had the religious vocation of temple priests. The artisan castes themselves, however, claimed to be Vaishyas, wore the sacred thread, and regarded themselves as immediately below the Brahmans. Until recently, the anomaly had been bypassed by both the artisans and the other Non-Brahmans refusing each others' food.

Most of the castes designated "Polluting Non-Brahmans" (*teeṇḍā jātimār*) were traditionally regarded as definitely below the other Non-Brahmans because of certain qualities of their occupations. The Tōṛuvar and Tamiḷ Nāyakkars and Nāḍārs ranked low because they manufactured toddy and arrack. These were believed to be polluting because they excited the senses. As former fishermen, the Ambalakkārars had taken life: Pollution attached to all flesh and to those who killed, handled, or processed it. The Vaṇṇārs ranked low because they washed the polluted cloths of menstruation, death, and childbirth; the Ambaṭṭārs, because they cut hair and nails, polluting refuse of the body. The Kūtthāḍis ranked especially low because they lived from illicit carnal relations. As far as I am aware, the Koravars had no specially polluting occupations. They were merely despised as gypsies of irregular customs, half outside the system of castes in the villages.

The very low rank of the Paḷḷars derived from the fact that for centuries the whole caste had been slaves who performed the heaviest manual work of the higher castes. Their status was therefore low even though their occupation of agriculture was relatively pure from a ritual point of view. The Paṟayars (not present in Kumbapeṭṭai) ranked still lower because they tended cremation grounds, removed dead cattle, and ate beef, an act strictly forbidden to all caste Hindūs above the Panchamas.

It must be emphasized that when villagers stated that one caste was higher or lower than another they referred to ritual or religious rank, whether or not this coincided with wealth or authority. Ritual rank inhered in castes by virtue of birth and had connotations of worth. Wealth and power, by contrast, in modern times inhered in individuals, and had connotations only of magnitude. A rich or powerful man was a "big" man; a poor and powerless person a "small" man, but a high caste might be referred to as a "good" caste, and a low caste, a "bad" one.

As discussed in Chapter 2, the ranking of castes was expressed in terms of the belief in ritual purity (*maḍi*) and pollution (*teeṭṭam*). These concepts applied not only to castes; they ran throughout the philosophy of the Hindūs, particularly that of the Brahmans. Ultimately, this philosophy appears to involve an opposition between those objects, experiences, and impulses that are regarded as spiritual and that aid union with the divine, and those that are regarded as bodily and that hinder such union. In the latter category fall all aggressive and libidinal impulses, the body itself, especially when robbed of life and soul, the whole of the material world in its economic aspect, and all activities that might chain man to the material world and prevent spiritual growth leading to release from rebirth. In this context Dumont has an important point when he argues that pollution especially occurs when there is an eruption of the organic into the supraorganic or cultural realm, as in the emission of blood, feces, urine, semen, nose drippings, intestinal gas, breath, or the decay and odor of death.[1] The realm of the spiritual, by contrast, is that of the soul itself, divorced from sensual and material motives, and all ritual acts or acts of abstention designed to raise man above his organic self.

Ostensibly, castes received their rank chiefly on the basis of the ritual quality of their traditional occupations. The differentiation and ranking of the major occupational groups (priests and scholars, kings, landlords, soldiers, traders, tenants, artisans, menials, and slaves) was not peculiar to the Hindū system but arose in almost any precapitalist state. Ritual rank, in the traditional system, merely sanctioned these broad social gradations resulting from the division of wealth and political power, with the proviso that the Brahmans, the religious codifiers of the system, ranked above all other groups. Within these major categories, some occupations – butchering, fishing, palm wine manufacturing, disposal of dead bodies, and prostitution – were branded especially impure because of the beliefs already noted. Yet other occupations appear to have been actually created and set apart as especially polluting *because* of the religious beliefs, as a means of ensuring that the higher castes would be exempt from acts that would endanger their salvation. Segregation of the tasks of barbers, launderers of polluted cloths, guards of cremation grounds, and removers of dead cattle, for example, scarcely had economic justification in a society with as simple a technology as that of India.

Given these criteria, the precise ranking of particular castes involved arbitrary decisions and rationalizations on the part of those in authority in particular regions. The authorities, moreover, tolerated and even encouraged certain ambiguities and competition for rank among some of the castes, especially those in the middle of the hierarchy. Barbers and Washermen, for example, perennially disputed for rank and were usually treated equally by the castes above them. In Kumbapeṭṭai, in spite of the rank order described, the mutual ranking of Marathas, Kaḷḷars, Kōṉārs, Paḍaiyācchis, and Agambaḍiyars was not really clear, all being middle peasants, tenant farmers, traders, or laborers who shared the same streets. I have already referred to the major discrepancy over the ranking of the artisans. These ambiguities were able to continue because the performance of the annual temple festival, the main rank-confirming occasion, did not clarify the rankings. It was to the advantage of the Brahmans to allow such bickerings to continue, for they decreased the solidarity of the lower orders.

The main rules of intercourse among the castes have been referred to in Chapter 2. In Kumbapeṭṭai, because the Brahmans largely retained the administrative control over the village, and because wealth, power, and ritual rank were not grossly discrepant, the traditional rules were fairly strictly observed.

With the exception of Barbers and Midwives, people were prohibited from touching or even approaching anyone in a category higher than their own. Non-Brahmans might approach up to about three feet away from Brahmans, but Ādi Drāviḍas normally remained beyond a distance of at least three yards. "Clean" Non-Brahmans might enter the houses but not the kitchens of the Brahmans; "polluting" Non-Brahmans, the street but not the home. Ādi Drāviḍas were forbidden to enter the Brahman street; they approached Brahman houses from the backyards and stood beyond the cowsheds. Brahman men were permitted to enter the homes and kitchens of Non-Brahmans but, for fear of their own pollution, might not enter the houses of "polluting" Non-Brahmans or the streets of Ādi Drāviḍas. When a Brahman went to the Ādi Drāviḍa street to settle a civil dispute he called the parties to the open space before the Kāḷiyamman shrine, or discussed household matters on the sites behind the Paḷḷar houses. It was believed that if a Brahman did enter a street of Ādi Drāviḍas, the whole street would fall prey to disease or financial ruin. Because of this, Ādi Drāviḍas theoretically had the right to drive a Brahman from their street. No such opportunity had, however, occurred. Ādi Drāviḍas were permitted to enter the streets but not the homes of Non-Brahmans. Non-Brahmans, in turn, might enter the streets of Paḷḷars but would not pollute themselves by entering Paḷḷar homes.

Brahman women lived within their own streets and entered the main road only to catch the bus or to attend the village temple with male relatives. They would have considered it polluting as well as immodest to enter a Non-Brahman home, and had never seen the streets of the Ādi Drāviḍas of south Kumbapeṭṭai. Women were in general required to be more punctilious than men with respect to ritual pollution.

The strictness of these rules was brought home to me on my first day in the village. A group of Paḷḷar women stopped by my house in Akkāchāvaḍy in the evening on their way home from work. I invited them in and gave them betel and arecanuts, which I knew was a recognized form of hospitality. The next day my cook, a Malabāri, brought the news from my landlady, a Brahman widow, that by inviting the Paḷḷars I had polluted my house and my cook. He had then polluted her well, from which he had gone to draw water. In order to purify the well, it would be necessary to pour into it *panchagavyam*, a mixture of the five products of the sacred cow – milk, butter, curds, dung, and urine – with appropriate Sanskrit texts. If I wanted to stay in the house, I must not entertain the "ADs." That evening, a small deputation of Brahman male elders arrived and tactfully confirmed her judgement. For some weeks, the Brahmans strongly opposed my visits to the Paḷḷar streets, assuring me that they could summon the Paḷḷars at any time to give me information. When I persuaded them that it was essential to my work for me to see Paḷḷars in their own streets, they at last relented on condition that I take a plunge bath in the irrigation channel before entering the main part of the village, or, in the dry season, bathe in my bathroom before entering my home. I did this and, living on the middle ground of a Non-Brahman street, I was able to associate fairly freely with all three main blocks of castes. Doing so, however, created social, ethical, and emotional problems that I was never able to solve.

Each caste might in theory distribute cooked food to all below it. In fact, each Brahman family fed its own Non-Brahman tenants and servants at marriages in the yard behind its house, and gave cooked food to be eaten at home to the Non-Brahman servants and specialist castes at major festivals. Brahmans did not demean themselves by serving cooked food to Paḷḷars, but gave them raw rice and other materials at festivals and life-crisis rites. At their own marriages and funerals, the middle peasants and better-off Non-Brahman tenants gave the remains of food in their yards to Paḷḷars who had often worked for them.

In the modern Non-Brahman tea shops, tea and coffee were served to all Non-Brahmans regardless of caste. Paḷḷars were served with separate glasses across a counter behind the tea shops as in the toddy shops of old. In the Brahman restaurant vegetarian food was served to Brahmans and Non-Brahmans in separate halves of the room, divided by a curtain; Ādi Drāviḍas were not admitted. Brahmans refused to drink tea and coffee, which were "cooked," from the shops of Non-Brahmans but would call for bottled soda drinks from these shops as they were uncooked. In recent years, some Brahman men had begun to drink coffee at the marriages of "clean" Non-Brahmans in a separate booth built in front of the verandah. After a good deal of debate, several Brahmans rather nervously drank coffee in my house, although others refused it.

Sexual relations, like marriage, were in theory prohibited between the castes. In fact, many Brahman men frequently had sexual relations with Non-Brahman women in the women's homes, sometimes in return for a small gift to the woman or her husband. This was especially common on the part of landlords with the wives of their tenants or servants. Although these liaisons were described by the Brahmans as love matches, it would have been hard for the tenant and laboring women (or their husbands) to refuse their landlords. About a generation ago,

Brahman men were said to have deflowered women of the Non-Brahman servants' families on the wedding night before their husbands went to them.

Relations between Brahman men and Ādi Drāviḍa women occurred less often and aroused strong condemnation. As late as the 1920s, a Brahman of Kumbapeṭṭai was expelled from the *agrahāram* with his whole household for sleeping with a Paḷḷar woman. The family moved to Nāgapaṭṭaṇam, but retained land and tenants in Kumbapeṭṭai in 1952. At that date, at least two village Brahmans were said "secretly" to have sexual relations with Paḷḷar women in empty houses of the *agrahāram*. Because they were rich and powerful, the other Brahmans did not bring this to public notice, but they strongly condemned it in private. Extramarital relations between "clean" Non-Brahmans were extremely common, and those between "clean" Non-Brahman men and "polluting" Non-Brahman women were overlooked unless they led to quarrels. Relations between Non-Brahman men and Paḷḷar women were punished with fines by the street assemblies of both. Relations between a man of lower and a woman of higher caste category, especially a Brahman, were the most reprehensible. On the few occasions in recent years when they had occurred, they had usually been punished by flogging or lynching.

Disobedience of the rules of rank, as well as a range of other crimes and any form of rebellion against the landlords and against Brahman supremacy, were regarded as sins (*pāpangal*, singular *pāpam*). If not punished promptly by the village authorities, they invoked the wrath of the village goddess. She might then bring disease, financial loss, crop blight, cattle epidemics, drought, flood, or other disasters on the families concerned, on a street, or on the village at large. It was for this reason that major hearings to establish wrong doing on the part of Non-Brahmans and Ādi Drāviḍas against the village laws were held in the courtyard of the Ūriḍeichiyamman temple, and fines or harsher punishments meted out there. After the punishment a culprit was forced to swear before the deity that he would not repeat his sin. If he did repeat it, it was believed that he might suffer disaster or even death.

In 1952 the ritual rank order of the castes in Kumbapeṭṭai was not entirely coterminous with the class hierarchy. Table 15.1 shows the class affiliations of the adult men and women in the various castes. In the Table, I have omitted endogamous subcastes, listing only the castes. Women have been included in the classes of their nearest male relatives unless they had independent work outside the home. The village's one female and six male high school students over the age of fifteen have been placed in the classes of their nuclear families. So have a small number of old people who owned no property but were incapable of work.

In Table 15.1 the main anomalies are that three Brahman families had sunk to being virtual beggars, while twenty Paḷḷar households had become small tenant farmers. The anomaly is not as great as it appears, for as we have seen, mendicancy was an established way of life for some older Brahmans and it is possible that these families received about Rs. 500 per year; they also owned their own houses and gardens. Moreover, most of the Paḷḷars' leased holdings

Table 15.1. *Class affiliations of men and women over age fifteen by caste, Kumbapeṭṭai, 1952*

| Caste | Petty bourgeois | | Independent entrepreneurs | | Semiproletarians: Tenants & village servants | | Semiproletarians: Supervised laborers | | Mendicants | |
|---|---|---|---|---|---|---|---|---|---|---|
| | M | F | M | F | M | F | M | F | M | F |
| *Brahman* | 40 | 50 | 2 | 2 | — | — | — | — | 3 | 3 |
| *Non-Brahman* | | | | | | | | | | |
| Veḷḷālar | — | — | — | — | — | — | — | 1 | — | — |
| Maratha | — | — | — | — | — | — | 2 | 2 | — | — |
| Agambaḍiyar | — | — | — | — | — | — | 5 | 5 | — | — |
| Kaḷḷar | — | — | 4 | 3 | 3 | 2 | 5 | 3 | — | — |
| Paḍaiyācchi | — | — | — | — | — | — | 1 | 2 | — | — |
| Muslim | — | — | — | — | 1 | 1 | 0 | 0 | — | — |
| Kōṉār | — | — | 5 | 5 | 1 | 3 | 17 | 15 | — | — |
| Poosāri | — | — | 4 | 3 | — | — | 1 | 1 | — | — |
| Kusavar | — | — | — | — | 6 | 4 | — | — | — | — |
| Kammālar | — | — | — | — | 3 | 3 | — | — | — | — |
| Tōṛuva Nāyakkar | — | — | — | — | 1 | 1 | — | — | — | — |
| Tamiḻ Nāyakkar | — | — | 5 | 5 | — | — | 4 | 3 | — | — |
| Nāḍār | — | — | — | — | 1 | 1 | 1 | 1 | — | — |
| Ambalakkārar | — | — | — | — | — | — | 5 | 5 | — | — |
| Vaṇṇār | — | — | — | — | 2 | 1 | — | — | — | — |
| Ambaṭṭār | — | — | — | — | 3 | 4 | — | — | — | — |
| Kūtthāḍi | — | — | — | — | — | 4 | — | — | — | — |
| Koravar | — | — | — | — | — | — | 1 | 1 | — | — |
| *Ādi Drāvida* | | | | | | | | | | |
| Paḷḷar | — | — | — | — | 20 | 21 | 76 | 83 | — | — |
| Total | 40 | 50 | 20 | 18 | 41 | 45 | 118 | 122 | 3 | 3 |

*Note:* Housewives and students have been placed in the classes of their husbands or fathers.

were small. Even so, this anomaly did not exist in 1827 and was probably not present in 1898. The table also shows the further anomaly that the representatives of the three highest Non-Brahman castes had all become wage laborers, whereas they would traditionally have been landlords or peasants. Table 15.1 also reflects the fact that whereas 21 percent of the Paḷḷars had become "pure" tenants slightly above the general run of the Paḷḷar laborers, 67 percent of the Non-Brahman trading and agricultural castes were laborers rather than "pure" tenants or middle peasants. This discrepancy, too, is not as great as it appears because Non-Brahman laborers generally earned more than Paḷḷars, and Non-Brahman tenants usually had larger holdings than Paḷḷars. It does, however, show that while some Paḷḷars had benefited from the modern availability of absentee owners' land for tenant farming, a considerable number of Non-Brahmans, as well as Paḷḷars, had sunk to the marginal group of casual coolies.

Even so, Table 15.1 shows a high degree of correspondence between caste rank and socioeconomic class, with all the petty bourgeois within the Brahman group, and 64 percent of the laboring stratum within the Paḷḷar caste. The village servants had largely maintained their traditional position in the upper, unsupervised ranks of the laborers. It was, of course, because caste ranking was so closely consistent with the class structure that the Brahmans were able to administer the village through the traditional rules of caste.

The caste hierarchy was evidently still more closely consistent with class relations in the pre-British and early British period. Indeed, we may say that the castes of 1952 represented the production categories of pre-British times, with the proviso that each village contained a number of similar castes because of migration during the colonial and postcolonial periods. Thus in Kumbapeṭṭai, Vēḷḷālars, Agambaḍiyars, Kaḷḷars, Paḍaiyācchis, and Muslims had all arrived in the last century to do work similar to the Kōṉārs, and Tōṛuvar Nāyakkars and Nāḍārs had arrived to replicate work done by the Tamil Nāyakkars. In 1952 all of these former regional and production categories survived as separate, endogamous status groups, each with its own legends, history, and partial association with traditional occupations.

Table 8.1 shows that although Kumbapeṭṭai contained representatives of twenty separate castes, these broke down into twenty-nine endogamous subcastes. In addition to the subcastes of the Brahmans and Paḷḷars, there were two subcastes among the Agambaḍiyars and two among the Poosāris. This situation had arisen because two "foreign" households of Agambaḍiyars and one of Poosāris, as well as the Vēḷḷāḷar widow and her children, arrived during my stay as refugees from the drought in Pudukkoṭṭai. Because they were newcomers I did not obtain the names of their subcastes.

Traditionally, equal interdining as well as marriage occurred only among the members of the subcaste, all of whom could ideally trace relations with one another. The endogamous subcastes of most of the original microcastes present in Kumbapeṭṭai appear to have once been confined to villages in the north of the modern Thanjāvūr *tālūk*, slightly east into Tiruchirappalli, and slightly west into Pāpanāsam, all within about twenty miles of the village. It seems probable that this area was once a province of the kingdom. With the modern movement of families and groups of families, however, the villagers' subcastes tended to be scattered in different regions.

Most of the Maṟainād Brahacharaṇam Brahmans' kin came from the old region, as did the Dēvendra Paḷḷars. With the movement into urban work, however, the Brahmans also had kin in many of the major cities of south India and in Calcutta, Bombay, and Delhi. The Vaḍama Brahmans, the Ayyangārs, and the Tekkaṭṭi Paḷḷars had most of their kin east of Kumbakōṇam; the Kurukkals in many places as far east as Nāgapaṭṭaṇam *tālūk*. The Kaḷḷars', Kōnārs', Nāyakkars', and Ambalakkārars' groups extended south into Paṭṭukoṭṭai and Pudukkoṭṭai and west into Tiruchirappalli, and that of the Agambaḍiyars to Arantāngi and Tirutturaipoondi, up to seventy miles away. The fact that some of their close kin tended to live in different villages and sometimes in different *tālūks* or districts contributed to the villagers' feeling that their microcastes were of different "kinds."

In a few cases, the boundaries between regional endogamous subcastes of the same larger caste were gradually being broken down. In Kumbapeṭṭai, one Brahacharaṇam woman had recently married a Vaḍama of Sīrkāḷi. One Barber had kin in Malabar, and the Smiths stated that they might now marry into any family of their caste in the Tamiḷ country north of Madurai. This infringement of the older endogamous boundaries, however, did not occur between the several microcastes within the village.

As is well known, castes higher and lower in the hierarchy tended to have characteristically different customs related to the extent to which the Sanskritic and Brahmanical ideology had been adopted by the various castes. In Kumbapeṭṭai as elsewhere, the chief diacriticals of the Brahmans were vegetarianism, the ban on divorce or widow remarriage, cremation rather than burial of the dead, the use of Sanskrit prayers in household and temple ceremonies, the practice by which individual men might seek merit as ascetics or *sannyāsis*, and the prohibition of animal sacrifice except under special conditions in the performance of Sanskrit *yāgams*. Apart from the performance of *yāgams*, these customs also prevailed among Thanjāvūr's small groups of Kshattriyas and in the higher subcastes of Veḷḷāḷars.

Among the Ādi Drāviḍas, at the other extreme, there were few or no Sanskrit prayers, divorce and widow marriage were freely practiced, animal sacrifice was common, men did not become ascetics, and meat, including rats, was eaten whenever it was available. The Tekkaṭṭi Paḷḷars buried their dead instead of cremating them, and the Paṟayars (and, one suspected, some of the Paḷḷars) ate carrion beef.

In Kumbapeṭṭai, the Non-Brahman castes came between the Brahmans and the Ādi Drāviḍas in these and other customs. All strictly banned the eating of beef, refrained from eating rats, and ate vegetarian food at marriage and funeral feasts. Sanskrit prayers were used on their behalf by the Brahman *purōhit* at certain life-crisis rites and by the Kurukkal on special occasions in the village temple, but were not used by Poosāris, nor by the other Non-Brahmans in most of their household ceremonies. The adult dead were cremated, but small children were usually buried to avoid expense. Goats were sacrificed at special festivals in the village temple, and chickens in occasional ceremonies to lineage godlings located in the backyards of certain homes. Among the Nāyakkars, Nāḍārs, Koravars, Washermen, Barbers, and Kūtthāḍis, divorce and the marriage of divorcees or widows were permitted but were rare. In the other Non-Brahman castes, divorce and widow marriage were in theory forbidden. In fact, a wife might be sent back to her natal kin for a serious offense, and in some castes, rejected wives and widows were sent away to remarry in other subcastes of their caste in Madurai or Rāmanāthapuram where the remarriage of women was practiced. In Kumbapeṭṭai, moreover, Non-Brahman widows occasionally lived with men of their caste as concubines, and their children were considered legitimate. In marriage as in life-crisis rites, the middle- and lower-ranking Non-Brahmans of this area seemed to have adopted Brahman customs in the fairly recent past, but not to have adopted them very thoroughly.

It is clear that religious beliefs and caste divisions helped the Brahmans govern the village and keep down the lower classes by providing a rationale for the class structure. The beliefs in *karma*, *dharma*, and inherited characteristics justified the Brahmans' dominance. The proliferation of subcastes and the rules of ritual pollution kept the lower orders fragmented and maintained social distance among them and between them and the Brahmans. The marked social distance among the three main categories kept the Non-Brahmans and Ādi Drāviḍas from uniting against their exploiters, instituted competition and hostility between them, and placed both at a safe social distance from the Brahmans. The etiquette of servility in speech and behavior that was enforced on the lower castes from childhood contributed to the Brahmans' supremacy. The sanctioning of the whole scheme by belief in the vengeful powers of the village goddess instilled fear into the villagers. The singling out of certain small groups among the Non-Brahmans and Ādi Drāviḍas (Washermen, Barbers, Prostitutes, Scavengers) as especially polluting gave the majority some sense of superiority, even while they, too, were subjected to gross forms of discrimination and repression.

During the colonial period, as we saw in Chapter 2, a number of reform movements had gone on among the lower castes of Tamiḻ Nāḍu in an effort to raise the rank of particular castes of subcastes or to remove specific disabilities. An early pattern of mobility, which continued from pre-British times, was for a small in-marrying group to split off from the parent caste, change its occupation, reform its customs, and attempt to "pass" as a subcaste of some higher caste. I have already mentioned how groups of Kaḷḷars, Maṟavars, and Agambaḍiyars often turned into Veḷḷāḷars, usurping the caste title "Piḷḷai." It is probable that the meat-eating Oothanāth Veḷḷāḷars of Sheṭṭiyur once came from one of these lower castes. The Agambaḍiyars of Māniyūr and Kumbapeṭṭai had taken the title "Piḷḷai" in the twentieth century although they were still known as Agambaḍiyars.

In 1952, the Tōṛuvar and Tamiḷ Nāyakkars were trying to establish themselves as of similar rank to the "clean" peasant castes. Having gained a little wealth through the licensed toddy trade, they had been obliged to give up the trade because of prohibition. In 1952 they argued that their caste had not originally been tappers but had been obliged to take up the work temporarily because of poverty. Their caste title, Nāyakkar, probably assumed during the last fifty years, was traditionally a title borne by "clean" peasant and military castes of Telugu origin. Their claim to "clean" status was not publicly rejected, for they were wealthier than most of the Non-Brahmans, made gifts to the temple and small loans to poorer villagers, and controlled Vēṭṭāmbāḍi Street. On the other hand, the Nāḍārs and Ambalakkārars, who were poor and inconsequential, were still viewed as of lower rank.

Since about 1890, as I have mentioned in Chapter 2, a larger scale type of reform movement had begun among some of the castes, although it was not much in evidence in Kumbapeṭṭai. Such movements resulted from the breakdown of service obligations, and illustrated a growing unwillingness on the part of all the castes to accept low rank in the modern society. The modern pattern of mobility was for many endogamous groups of the same caste, over a wide area, to adopt a new, high-sounding name and challenge the claims to rank of the castes above them. The Smiths of Kumbapeṭṭai, for example, had until recently belonged to a movement of the Smith caste called Vishva-Karmalar extending over Thanjāvūr and South Ārcot districts. It was organized toward the end of the nineteenth century by an ascetic of the caste. This man traveled about, encouraging the Smiths to become vegetarians, abandon widow marriage, and refuse food from all except Brahmans. He was maintained by donations, extracted fines from offenders against the rules, and encouraged their local communities to ostracize them. The Paḍaiyācchis, Paḷḷis, Vaṉṉiyars, and related castes of Thanjāvūr and South Ārcot had been influenced by a powerful movement, the Vaṉṉiya Kula Kshattriyas, or "Kshattriyas of the Fire Race." Organized in the 1870s, this movement propagated the theory that the Vaṉṉiyars were once Kshattriyas, reduced to servitude by Veḷḷāḷar invaders. Like the Smith movement, it encouraged widow celibacy and vegetarianism in imitation of the Brahmans.

In the past twenty years, however, these efforts to raise the rank of castes or subcastes through "Sanskritization" had been challenged by the Drāviḍa Kazhakam and the Communist movement. Unlike the nineteenth-century movements, both of these bodies denied the existence of God and the legitimacy of the caste system in any form. In 1952 these movements had only peripheral influence in Kumbapeṭṭai, but some of the younger Non-Brahmans, especially the high school students, approved of the Drāviḍa Kazhakam, and some of the Paḷḷars, of the Communists.

In the privacy of their streets, the Non-Brahmans and Paḷḷars selectively approved certain features of the religious and caste ideology of the Brahmans, but challenged others. As might be expected, most people supported those claims that gave them advantages, but rejected those that demeaned them. Except for about a half dozen supporters of the Drāviḍa Kazhakam, the Non-Brahmans supported the caste system to the extent of believing that marriages should not occur between castes and that Ādi Drāviḍas should observe the traditional rules of social distance in relation to higher castes. Most families accepted the validity of Brahman priests and Sanskrit prayers, and gave reverence to the village goddess and to the gods of their own lineages. On the other hand, the Non-Brahmans often mimicked the Brahmans' excessive religiosity and sometimes said that all of them were a little mad. Brahman *sannyāsis* were especially thought to be lightheaded, or to be rascals who duped ordinary folk for a livelihood. Nonetheless, Non-Brahman ascetics and religious leaders were revered by most people and were fed annually in the Nāyakkars' lineage shrine. In anger against particular repressive or aggressive actions by the Brahmans, some individuals sometimes cried out that Brahmans, or *mirāsdārs*, were "evil." All the Non-Brahmans with whom I discussed the matter thought that land should be more evenly distributed, so that Non-Brahmans shared its control with the Brahmans.

Like the Non-Brahmans, the Paḷḷars were ambivalent about the claims of the higher castes. Once when I asked a Paḷḷar woman for some of her gruel to taste, she refused me saying it was a sin for I was not an Ādi Drāviḍa. Most Paḷḷars agreed that the Paṟayars were lower than they were, and that to marry or eat with them would be sinful. The Dēvendra Paḷḷars held the same view of the Tekkaṭṭi Paḷḷars, whom they saw as their inferiors because they buried the dead and came originally from southern regions. On the other hand, the Paḷḷars thought it wrong that they were not admitted into the Brahman street or into the houses of the Non-Brahmans, and often said that most of the higher-caste people, especially the *mirāsdārs*, were "cruel."

Although they were careful to observe their own ceremonies to their goddess Kāḷiyamman and to take part in the village festivals, the Paḷḷars were ignorant or skeptical of most of the beliefs that the Brahmans spent much time discussing. One day while sitting in Middle Paḷḷar Street I asked a group of older Paḷḷars their views about death, duty, destiny, and the rebirth of the soul. Where did they think the soul went after death? One old man nudged another and said "She wants to know where we go when we die!" The whole group then collapsed in merriment. Wiping his eyes, the old man replied, "Mother, *we* don't know! Do you know? Have you been there?" I said, "No, but the Brahmans say that if people do their duty well in this life, their souls will be born next time in a higher caste." "Brahmans say!" scoffed another elder, "Brahmans say anything! Their heads go round and round!" An old woman then said that she had heard, and believed, that a soul is born seven times in various bodies – as a pig, rat, or a person of any caste – and then leaves the earth forever. I asked her whether she thought that one's virtue in this life determined one's birth in the next, and she answered abruptly, "No." Another woman thought that we go to heaven (*swargam*) or hell (*naragam*) according to our sins and virtues during our human lives. A young man intervened, saying that he did not believe in life after death at all. "The soul is like breath; it simply goes out of the body – whoosh." Others thought that only the souls of those who died violently hung about the living, haunting them as ghosts or demons, which they burlesqued with laughter. Whatever they may have believed in the past, the Thanjāvūr Ādi Drāviḍas who discussed it with me all denied the orthodox Hindū theory, so reassuring to high-caste landlords, that the performance of duty in a past life determines one's wealth and caste status in this one.

# 16 Village Politics: The Street Assembly

In 1951 the corporate groups of village politics were, in the main, the territorial groups of the village and its component streets. Some separate political activity went on within each regional endogamous subcaste, encompassing many villages. This activity was chiefly concerned with boycotting people who disobeyed the group's rules of religious purity. The subcaste, however, both within the village and within the endogamous group as a whole, was mainly a loose network of interfamilial relations of kinship and affinity.

The men of each street settled a number of disputes among themselves without resort to any other authority. Women were excluded from these settlements and from judgments connected with the village at large. Because women were regarded as legal minors under the guardianship of their fathers or their husbands, it was thought proper for these men to chastise them privately by scolding or beating them if they did wrong. Quarrels among women were disregarded by the street assemblies unless they led to disputes among men.

The Paḷḷar streets were the most tightly organized, the Non-Brahman less so, and the Brahman least of all. This puzzled me at first, especially because the Brahmans administered the village in addition to their own streets. One reason may have been that the Brahman leaders often imposed collective punishment on the Paḷḷar streets for individual offenses, and sometimes did this in relation to the older Non-Brahman streets of Aḍichēri and Barber Street. This practice fostered discipline in those streets so that all might avoid the Brahmans' wrath. In addition, as small bourgeois with their separate holdings and often with separate urban connections, the Brahmans were more individualistic than the lower castes, who were accustomed to group labor and submission to authority.

## The Brahman Street

In the early nineteenth century when the village was still a commune, the Brahmans periodically selected five *panchāyattārs*, or group leaders, probably from the five lineages, to organize the affairs of their caste and of the village. The formal institution of *panchāyattārs*, however, died out in the late nineteenth century, probably when land became the property of individual landlords.

Traditionally, the Brahmans had no indigenous headman. Although rank by age and generation was marked among them, especially within the lineage, the microcaste as a whole would not submit to a single official. The adage "*Pārppārkku mooppu illai*" ("Brahmans have no headman, or betters") summed up this sense of joint supremacy over all other beings.

In 1952 although the village headman and the *panchāyat* board and president had certain statutory powers over the village at large, neither of them could exercise authority directly over their kinsmen and affines, the other Brahmans, in the way that they could over the lower castes. The headman must, of course, collect the land revenue, and he was obliged to summon the police in case of serious assault, murder, or suicide. In practice, however, the headman and his assistant, the *karṇam*, tended to be open to manipulation through bribes or threats by the bigger landlords over such matters as field boundaries or the revenue classifications of particular plots. Similarly as far as possible the headman represented cases of violence and death to the police in such a way that court verdicts would reflect the collective wish of the landlords. The headman was especially open to pressures from men of his own lineage, on whom he relied for support in village factional disputes. Covertly he might carry out actions or influence the authorities against rival lineages, but in doing so, a wise headman would be careful not to alienate them to the extent that they could have him deposed.

The headman and *panchāyat* president were thus mediators rather than merely government representatives in their relations between the government and their peers and kinsmen, the Brahmans. In this process the richer landlords used many networks of private influence within and outside the village in order to gain their ends, and if possible to score off their opponents.

The main sources of disputes among the Brahmans were (*a*) political offices (the village headship and the *panchāyat* presidency), (*b*) property and its enjoyment (irrigation water, field boundaries, debts, inheritance, dowry, marauding animals, cattle sales, the distribution of income in joint families, and so on), (*c*) threats to prestige such as insults, failure to pay due deference to personal rank, differences over precedence at ceremonies, or sexual interference with a wife or mistress, and (*d*) occasionally, disputes between tenants or *paṇṇaiyāḷs* in which the landlords of each became involved.

Almost any two men in the *agrahāram* could become involved in a dispute. Quarrels seemed to be most common (*a*) between brothers over property management or inheritance, (*b*) between close affines over dowry or the property of women, or (*c*) between influential landlords over field boundaries, irrigation water, or a number of other issues.

In the first two instances, and in quarrels between any two Brahmans of little wealth and influence, the disputants might appeal to one of the wealthier Brahman leaders to arbitrate their case. Until his death in the mid-1940s, the most prominent Brahman arbitrator had been a landlord of Kaṇḍipeṭṭai owning about forty acres there and in Kumbapeṭṭai – the father of the young absentee landlord mentioned in Chapter 12. This man had also often been summoned to settle disputes or mete out punishments in the lower castes. In 1952, Kumbapeṭṭai had no single popular arbitrator. Most of the older men had been absent from the village for many years in urban work and took little interest in its affairs. The young and middle-aged men of property were too involved in mutual competition, and were perhaps too similar in wealth, for any one of them to command general respect among the majority. In some disputes, a group of such influential men did occasionally get together to remonstrate with the parties, although they had no binding authority. Occasionally such disputes between close relatives or between "small" men of the *agrahāram* ended in court cases. More often, they dragged on desultorily, the participants engaging in covert backbiting, vows of silence, and fantasies of secret revenge. Such enmities tended to be forgotten when larger disputes between wider groups commanded the attention of the villagers.

Disputes between men of different branches of the same patrilineage, like those between brothers, also tended to be arbitrated, to drag on, or to be forgotten in wider conflicts. Such disputes did not mobilize whole segments within the lineage.

The disputes that rocked the village were those between relatively wealthy landlords of different exogamous patrilineages (*kooṭṭams* or *kuḷams*) and clans (*gōtrams*) of the dominant Brahacharaṇam Smārtha Brahman subcaste. Thirty-one households of this subcaste were present in 1951. Twenty-five were distributed among three patrilineages, respectively of the Shadamarashana, Kaundiniya, and Bāradwāj clans. Only two belonged to the fourth clan traditionally present (Āttreya), two more to a fairly recently arrived clan, Haritha, and one, a widow born in Kumbapeṭṭai, to her husband's clan, the Kausippa *gōtram*.

Of the three main clans, Shadamarashana claimed eleven resident households and was collectively the wealthiest and most powerful. Kaundiniya had seven resident households and Bāradwāj, eight. Kaundiniya, however, was more influential than Bāradwāj for it contained four resident families with substantial property. Bāradwāj had only two significant landlord families living in the village. Although one of them was the biggest landlord in Kumbapeṭṭai, he was a rentier and a retiring, older man who interested himself more in the affairs of his kin in Madras than in the village. The biggest village disputes were fought between the Shadamarashana and the Kaundiniya clans, each of whom recruited its close affines in other clans. Moreover, if a dispute arose between a man of one of these clans and a man of one of the smaller clans, the other main clan was apt to leap into the fray in defense of the smaller party.

Two major disputes had arisen between the two main clans in the past few years. One took place in 1948 when the last village headman died. His son Naṭarājaṉ, a youth of nineteen in the Kaundiniya clan, temporarily took over the duties and later officially applied for the post. So did Srinivāsa Iyer, his "cousin-brother" aged thirty from the Kaundiniya lineage, and Pranadāthikar Iyer, an ambitious man of Shadamarashana, aged forty-three. Before the appointment was made, someone, it was suspected Pranadāthikar Iyer, wrote a letter to the revenue divisional officer complaining that Naṭarājaṉ was too young for the post, and Srinivāsa Iyer, a person who drank alcohol and who could not keep order in the village. The revenue divisional officer appointed Pranadāthikar Iyer. Naṭarājan̲ appealed to the district collector on the grounds that he was educated, spoke English, and was the son of the previous incumbent, but the collector turned him down. Pranadāthikar Iyer unwisely boasted in the village that no matter what Naṭarājan̲, Srīnivasan̲, or other Kaundiniya people did, they could not overthrow him. The Kaundiniya stalwarts then collected Rs. 7,000 from their clan and affines – Rs. 5,000 of it from Naṭarājan̲'s eldest brother, a Public Works Department supervisor in Tirunelvēli – to dislodge Pranadāthikar Iyer. Through a clan sister's husband who was an advocate of Madurai, Naṭarājan̲ hired a Madras lawyer and appealed above the collector to the Board of Revenue in Madras. The board summoned the two contestants with their pleaders and relatives to Madras to hear the case. After several clandestine trunk calls had been made by other relatives and their professional connections to board members in Madras, the board set aside the collector's appointment and selected Naṭarājan̲. He remained as village headman in 1952.

Having wasted Rs. 2,000 on Pranadāthikar Iyer's case, the Shadamarashana side took their losses with ill grace. When the first *panchāyat* elections took place in Kumbapeṭṭai in 1950, they marshaled all possible voting members in their large lineage and among their servants, and elected a slate composed of four Brahmans and one Sheṭṭiyūr Veḷḷāḷar, with Pranadāthikar Iyer as its president.

Between them, the two enemies thus shared formal authority in the village by 1952. By that time they had again begun to play cards in the same group together, but were still not on speaking terms. The *panchāyat* president was the more powerful, for he owned more property than Naṭarājan̲, had a larger and wealthier lineage with many lower-caste followers, and possessed a more forceful and cunning personality. Naṭarājan̲ proved too immature to handle his family's estate and his office. Having sold considerable land to meet his debts, and having absconded twice with the village revenue, he was deposed in 1954 and Srinivāsa Iyer (his father's brother's son) was appointed in his place.

This case was remarkable in that indigent villagers managed to collect and spend Rs. 9,000 in a dispute over a village office worth an annual salary of Rs. 252. This large expenditure occurred, it seems, for several reasons. One was that absent as well as resident Brahmans had a stake in the outcome, for a new headman who was an enemy might have their lands reclassified at a higher revenue rate or might tamper with their boundaries. The village headman had other powers out of all proportion to his meager salary. In addition to collecting the revenue (and possible bribes accruing to that function) he had the legal right to settle civil disputes over sums up to Rs. 50. Only the lower castes normally appealed to his jurisdiction, but the right carried with it the possibility of fines and bribes. The village headman also had some ability to influence the police for or against disputants in cases involving violence. In general, his office carried great prestige, although in 1952 it was beginning to be overshadowed by that of the *panchāyat* president. For all these reasons the villagers, absent and present, had been willing to "go for broke" to prosecute their feud.

Another major dispute had occurred in 1939. Pranadāthikār Iyer of Shadamarashana clan and Subramania Iyer, a man of the much smaller Āttreya clan segment but the son of the then village headman, leased adjacent fields on *uḷ-kuthakai* from older men of their respective lineages. Pranadāthikar was then aged about thirty-three; Subramania about forty. Subramania Iyer, a somewhat arrogant man, repeatedly had his bullocks driven through a new channel made by Pranadāthikar on the edge of his field, and spoiled his cultivation. One day Pranadāthikar Iyer complained with abusive words. Subramania Iyer gave him blows and knocked him into a ditch. This was an outrageous act between Brahmans, who are supposed to observe nonviolence toward one another. A commotion arose and a concourse of Brahmans, Non-Brahmans, and Ādi Drāviḍas, some with sticks, came running to the threshing ground where the incident had occurred. Temporarily, neutral Brahmans separated the disputants. This was about 3:00 P.M.

Later that afternoon, Pranadāthikar Iyer's elder and landlord gave him Rs. 1,000 to pay his servants to beat up Subramania's party. The two sides prepared for a fray. The entire Shadamarashana clan joined on one side, whereas most of the men in Kaundiniya and Bāradwāj clans aligned with Subramania Iyer and the Āttreya clan, whose members were related as affines to several of them. Three fairly prominent older men remained neutral – one in Kaundiniya, one in Bāradwāj, and one in Haritha, a small clan segment with only two households. On Pranadāthikar Iyer's side were the Paḷḷars of Long Paḷḷar Street and the First Section of Upper Paḷḷar Street; on Subramania Iyer's those of the Lower Section of Upper Paḷḷar Street and of Middle and Lower Streets. Subramania Iyer paid a number of Paṟayars from Periyūr to come and fight on his side. By this time each side had spent about Rs. 400 in money and toddy payments to their followers. Kumbapeṭṭai's Non-Brahmans, however, all chose to "keep quiet" and not to fight, afraid, it was said, that the Brahmans might later unite and blame them. By 7:00 P.M. the two sides had assembled with heavy staffs, one side near the village goddess temple and one near the Akkāchāvaḍy tank.

Meanwhile, one of the neutral men of Bāradwāj clan, who was Kumbapeṭṭai's richest Brahman, had rushed to Kaṇḍipeṭṭai to bring the wealthy landlord and village headman, Sundarēsa Iyer, who was also in Bāradwāj. As the two sides were approaching, this landlord galloped up the road in a bullock cart, dismounted, seized the two disputants and ordered them to his empty house in the *agrahāram*. Because he was an old man, and because other Brahmans joined in, they felt unable to refuse. The elder was also an "indirect elder sister's husband" of Pranadāthikar Iyer, a respected relative who ought to be obeyed by him.

In his house this elder heard the details and blamed Pranadāthikar Iyer for starting the quarrel with vulgar words. It seems likely that he took this stance because, as his sister's husband, he had influence over Pranadāthikar Iyer, whereas blaming Subramania Iyer would have brought him into conflict with a fellow village headman. Sundarēsa Iyer commanded Pranadāthikar to prostrate himself before the Kumbapeṭṭai village headman, the father of Subramania Iyer.

This man then ordered his son to fall before the Brahman elder, and the quarrel was ended. Kaundiniya people said that from that date, Pranadāthikar Iyer kept quiet in the village and watched Subramania Iyer "like a snake watching a mongoose." In 1946, however, Subramania Iyer hanged himself in despair over his debts and over a village scandal. Pranadāthikar Iyer then emerged, and being a fairly wealthy Brahman with a large clan following, slowly advanced his struggle to dominate the village.

Brahmans told me that there had been earlier occasions when Paḷḷars and even Non-Brahman servants had actually fought battles with staffs on behalf of warring landlords, or on behalf of whole adjacent villages in quarrels between their landlords. The latter were most likely to occur over boundary or irrigation disputes or on the last day of the village temple festival, when men of nearby villages came to watch the spectacle and disputes might arise over ritual precedence. In such battles Brahmans themselves did not fight, but bands of Non-Brahmans and Paḷḷar laborers of the two villages were assembled by their landlords and fought on the boundary. In other cases quarrels arose, sometimes concerning adultery, between individuals of different villages from the lower castes. Paḷḷars fought their own battles, and Non-Brahmans and some Paḷḷars, those of the Non-Brahams. Four such intervillage battles were reported over the last twenty years, the last having taken place five years before my arrival. Intervillage battles tended to draw the members of each village together in temporary harmony. In general, it was considered wrong to spread scandal about one's own village in other villages and necessary to protect the village's reputation against outsiders' detractions.

It was clear, therefore, that there was a segmentary tendency in the landlords' disputes. Quarrels among brothers tended to be swallowed up in those between wider segments of the same lineage, and these, in interlineage disputes, whereas disputes between lineages of one village gave place to those between adjacent villages. In each of these types of disputes, especially those between lineages or between villages, the retainers of the appropriate segment might be mobilized to fight. In these disputes, close affines might be temporarily drawn in as supporters, but affines might also be enemies, while some affines with ties to both sides were eventually likely to act as arbitrators. The most effective arbitrators were rich and elderly men who could claim affinal links with both sides.

In prosecuting their feuds, Brahmans stressed that these ought not to override the landlords' ability to govern the lower castes, whether within each village or in a larger region. This imperative was, indeed, the strongest force making for truce if not peace in the *agrahāram*. During my stay, for example, Pranadāthikar Iyer and Srinivāsa Iyer were inveterate enemies. Both were householders of young to middle age owning eighteen to twenty acres, leasing in much land from absent Brahmans, and commanding large followings. The younger man's envy and dislike of the *panchāyat* president was so great that under normal circumstances it was impossible to imagine their making common cause. Both men grumbled at the way each treated his servants. Pranadāthikar Iyer claimed that

Srinivāsa Iyer's "soft" and comradely attitude to Ādi Drāviḍas would bring the village to ruin. Srinivāsa Iyer blamed Pranadāthikar Iyer's alleged meanness and cruelty. Yet in fact, when major class struggles erupted, the two united to suppress the lower castes.

Even so, the *agrahāram* and the village were scarcely well organized in 1952. The absence of a definite group of elected *panchāyattars* to organize the channel digging, the flow of irrigation water, the agricultural and temple festivals, and the settlement of major disputes, meant that these functions tended to be carried out hastily at the last minute, or not at all. When they were done, it was usually on the initiative of the *panchāyat* president, but the *agrahāram* did not yet recognize his authority to organize these tasks, and the modern statutory *panchāyat* for public works had not yet replaced the old *panchāyattars*.

As I have mentioned, in 1952, for the first time in living memory, the village festival did not take place. The reasons given by the Brahmans were that too many Brahmans were absent in urban work, too many quarrels were going on in the *agrahāram*, and the Brahmans were losing their powers to command the lower castes. The fact that several older Brahmans had spent their adult lives away from the village and returned as pensioners with little knowledge of its affairs was also relevant.

## The Non-Brahman Streets

The Kōn̲ārs had once had their own organization within their micro-caste. All Kōn̲ārs were kin or affines; they comprised five small, shallow, exogamous patrilineages (*kuḷams*) plus a few separate affinally attached households. Until about 1880, the Kōn̲ārs were localized in Aḍichēri. They did not intermarry or interdine equally with households of other castes.

In those days the Kōn̲ārs had a headman (*talaivan̲*). He was at first appointed by the Brahmans; later, the position became hereditary in one patrilineage. A link between the Brahman administrators and their Kōn̲ār servants, the headman summoned the Kōn̲ārs for collective work such as grazing cattle in the summer season. He also called Kōn̲ār offenders against village laws to the village temple courtyard to be tried and punished by the Brahmans.

The Kōn̲ārs conducted their street affairs through an assembly of the male heads of households. The assembly met each new moon night in the courtyard of the village temple and discussed current disputes over theft, debt, assault, adultery, slander, or infringement of the rules of caste. Emergency assemblies took place when grave disputes occurred. The headman led the assembly and pronounced the judgments, but their ratification required the consent of the whole group. Small offenses were punished by fines. The Kōn̲ārs used this money to celebrate their own festival to Ūriḍeichiyamman, who was their caste deity as well as the village goddess. In theory, serious offenders were punished by expulsion from the village with the Brahmans' consent, although no such case was reported. If disputants were not satisfied by the assembly's decision they might take their case for arbitration by their own Brahman landlords. In addition to their monthly assemblies, all the Kōṉār men met in the temple courtyard after marriages or funerals for special offerings and gift exchanges.

The village servants formerly lived together on the west side of Barber Street. Each household belonged to a caste group of related small patrilineages extending over six or eight adjacent villages. A male assembly in each of these groups settled marital disputes, upheld the laws of the caste, and prevented any outsiders from settling in their area of service. In the Maratha and the early British periods, the village servants appear to have come under some kind of protection from the government, whose officer supervised their harvest payments on the village's threshing floors. During the colonial period, the specialists lost any such protection and, like the other Non-Brahmans and Adi Drāviḍas, became mere tenants whom the landlords could evict at will. As we have seen, the landlords did evict the village's Barber family in the 1920s. By 1952 with mobility, increase in numbers, departures to the towns, and the landlords' powers of eviction, the specialist groups had virtually lost their functions of settling disputes and fixing areas of service. In Kumbapeṭṭai the village servants were directly administered by the Brahman landlords. Until shortly before my arrival, they had submitted any disputes they had with other Non-Brahman castes for Brahmanical judgment.

We have seen that since the 1860s representatives of many other castes of Non-Brahmans had arrived in the village. The Kaḷḷars comprised one patrilineage of eight households together with one house of affines. All Kaḷḷars lived in Akkāchāvaḍy. For many years they settled their own disputes and worshipped their lineage deity (*kuḷa daivom*) in a shrine in one of their gardens. So did the Tamiḻ Nāyakkars, who comprised one patrilineage with two attached houses of affines, most of them in Vēṭṭāmbāḍi. In 1952 the Nāyakkars retained a wider caste organization in Kumbapeṭṭai and three neighboring villages to settle marital or other disputes. The oldest man of the Kumbapeṭṭai lineage was its headman.

As families of many new Non-Brahman castes and some old ones bought house sites in Akkāchāvady and Vēṭṭāmbāḍi, on the main roadside, and on the east side of Barber Street, some wider form of Non-Brahman organization became necessary. About twenty years before my arrival, the Non-Brahmans had combined, irrespective of caste, to form four organizations in their four main settlements: Barber Street, Akkāchāvaḍy, Aḍichēri, including new houses on the main roadside, and Old and New Vēṭṭāmbāḍi. These modern street organizations were no longer based on caste, but carried out most of the functions of the old caste assemblies.

The married men of each Non-Brahman street annually elected or confirmed two headmen (*nāttāṇmaikkār*). The change to two headmen per street was a response to the need for multicaste representation: If only one were chosen it was feared that he might favor his own caste. All the headmen were middle aged to old and were middle peasants or better-off tenants. Akkāchāvaḍy had as headmen an old Kōṉār tenant and the leading Kaḷḷar trader. Vēṭṭāmbāḍi had the Tōṟuvar

Nāyakkar household head and the oldest and richest man in the Tamiḷ Nāyakkar lineage. Aḍichēri had the leading Kōṉār middle peasant and the leader of the potter caste, who was the most prosperous of the village's tenants. Only Barber Street had two Kōṉār headmen, one of them a middle peasant and one, a tenant. The headmen's offices were no longer hereditary, and the Brahmans, who no longer held complete control over the Non-Brahmans, had no power to depose them. Each headman served for several years until he died, resigned, or was deposed by the Non-Brahmans for inefficiency.

The street assemblies jointly conducted a Non-Brahman festival (formerly the Kōṉārs' private festival) to the village goddess in Thai. The festival was financed from cash fines paid to the headmen by disputants, from cesses on the sale of paddy and stock in the Non-Brahman streets, and from a general cash levy. Each new moon night the eight headmen met with any other interested men in the Nāyakkars' shrine dedicated to the dead *swāmi* who had aided their forebear. They first offered chickpeas before a photograph of the *swāmi*, then ate the peas, and then held their meeting to settle any outstanding street disputes. The headmen had the right to levy fines from offenders against the public peace, usually amounting to Rs. 4 to Rs. 10. Most disputes concerned theft, debt, adultery, slander, boundaries, or irrigation water. No attempt was made to administer the religious laws of the castes, and unless they led to physical violence or to complaints by an offended husband, cases of adultery between people of different caste went unpunished. Small disputes within the street were settled privately by street members with their headmen as the leading spokesmen. Large brawls or fights between people of the same or different streets required an immediate assembly from all the streets.

The modern street assembly had taken over another function of the old caste assembly: the witnessing of marriages. Formerly, among Non-Brahmans and Ādi Drāviḍas, the bride's and bridegroom's headmen witnessed an exchange of gifts at the final arrangement (*nischayadāṭṭam*, or "making certain") of a marriage and noted the numbers and amounts of vessels, cash, stock, clothing, and other items promised by the bridegroom's family to the bride's. If these amounts were not forthcoming or if a divorce took place, the headmen and household heads of both communities enforced the necessary payment or the return of the goods. In 1952 in Kumbapeṭṭai, although each caste and subcaste was still endogamous, the headmen of the multicaste street acted as witnesses of these marriage transactions.

Other barriers had also been broken down among the Non-Brahman castes. Except for the lower-ranking Barbers, Laundryworkers, and Koravars, the Non-Brahmans dined together at marriages and at the termination of funerals. Non-Brahman people of different castes who were born into the village called each other by kinship terms appropriate to patrilineal kin, and women married into the village called members of other castes by terms appropriate to their husbands' patrilineal kin. These kinship usages had a certain logic because marriage was forbidden both within the patrilineage and with members of other castes.

Among the Non-Brahmans and Ādi Drāviḍas, the lineage was a weaker entity than among the Brahmans. As far as I know, no disputes in recent times had mobilized whole lineages against other lineages among the Kōṉārs, while the other Non-Brahman groups were so small that each was dominated by a single lineage. Perhaps in the past Non-Brahman and Ādi Drāviḍa lineages were sometimes mobilized against others of the same order, but I think that the lineages of tenants and laborers had always been less forceful than those of the landlords. The landlords' lineages formerly had functions of land distribution and ceremonial duties, and were independent of higher local authorities, whereas the tenant and slave lineages had no such functions. Instead, in the lower classes, each nuclear family household was subordinated to one landlord, and the street at large, to the landlords collectively. Disputes among the Non-Brahmans and Ādi Drāviḍas in Kumbapeṭṭai therefore tended to take place between individual households or else between whole streets or whole microcastes.

Elsewhere, however, in villages dominated by rich Kaḷḷar peasants, the main disputes were between lineages or local segments of named dispersed clans (*vagappus*). Among the Non-Brahmans, the Veḷḷāḷars, the upper-caste Naidūs, and the Kaḷḷars all possessed named, dispersed patrilineal exogamous clans in addition to localized lineages. Among the lower-ranking Non-Brahmans and the Ādi Drāviḍas there were no dispersed clans, and lineages had no proper names.

We have seen that several important changes had occurred in the Non-Brahman community. The microcaste was no longer a localized, administrative and commensal unit, and had virtually ceased to perform exclusive religious ceremonies. These functions had been retained by the street, but it had become a multicaste community. In addition, all the streets had combined for important purposes as a Non-Brahman entity. Whereas, formerly, their Brahman masters had formed a final court of appeal for disputants and had forcibly intervened in disputes *between* the Non-Brahman castes, disputants among the tenants and laborers were now being encouraged by the traders and middle peasants to abide by the judgments of their own elected headmen and not to appeal to the landlords.

These pressures were strongest in Akkāchāvaḍy and Old Vēṭṭāmbāḍi, the newer streets where the majority of the families owned their own gardens and did not fear eviction. Shortly before I left Kumbapeṭṭai, a test case occurred in these streets. During a card game, a quarrel arose between a Kaḷḷar of Akkāchāvaḍy and four Tamiḷ Nāyakkar and Ambalakkārar boys of Vēṭṭāmbāḍi. The dispute spread until all the Kaḷḷars opposed all the Tamiḷ Nāyakkars and fishermen, and fighting ensued. A few Brahmans pressed for intervention, but the majority nervously held back, knowing that they had no sanctions to settle such a major quarrel in the two "upstart" streets. Eventually, the Tōṛuvar Nāyakkar headman of Vēṭṭāmbāḍi, who was of a different but similar caste to the Tamiḷ Nāyakkars, called a public Non-Brahman assembly and effected a compromise. When they heard of the settlement, the Brahmans felt that their powers in the village had been seriously undermined. Shortly after this incident they decided that they could not conduct the village festival. The *agrahāram* was too disunited, and the lower castes, they felt, were too rebellious to take part without a major brawl. One Brahman mentioned this dispute as evidence that the Brahmans had lost their power to organize the village.

Although these changes appeared, and were seen, as rearrangements among castes, they actually reflected a process of class struggle. They had grown out of the arrival or emergence in Kumbapeṭṭai of a new class of independent commodity producers and traders, most of whom owned house sites on new land in Akkāchāvaḍy and Vēṭṭambāḍi independently of the traditional landlords. At the same time, the bonds between the landlords and their former slaves and village servants had been loosened by the sale of some house plots to tenants, the absence of many landlords, the rise and fall of individual landlords' fortunes, and the short-term, contractual character of modern tenures and *vēlaikkārar* relationships. The new values of the anti-Brahman Drāviḍa Kazhakam and the anti-landlord Communist movement had also played a part in strengthening these Non-Brahman peasants' and traders' resistance against the traditional caste and class hierarchies.

## The Ādi Drāviḍa Streets

The Dēvendra Paḷḷars were a community divided into four streets. Apart from one family of Christians and one of Barbers, they formed a single microcaste composed of seven exogamous patrilineages distributed in forty-seven households, together with thirty households of affines and cognates who had arrived more recently from other villages. The Tekkaṭṭi Paḷḷars of Long Street formed an independent community consisting of two patrilineages distributed in ten houses, and two households of their affines. The two subcastes led largely separate social lives and did not interdine. Although they themselves denied it, the Tekkaṭṭi Paḷḷars were generally considered lower than the Dēvendra Paḷḷars.

The Dēvendra Paḷḷars were united by the worship of their goddess, Kāḷiyamman, whose shrine stood at the west end of the First Section of Upper Paḷḷar Street near the village boundary. It consisted of a small shelter built on a platform under a sacred tree, with iron gates that were kept locked except during offerings. Inside the shṛine was a brass statuette (*vigraham*) of the cholera goddess, and a phallic-shaped stone (*moolam*) representing the godling Karakam, said to be Kāḷiyamman's consort and guardian. The Paḷḷars collectively contributed Rs. 15 a month for lamp oil and *poojai* items for daily offerings by the village potter, Rs. 400 a year for their annual festival, held immediately after that of the village goddess, and eight *kalams* of paddy a year as payment for the potter priest. The expenses of the temple were met partly by fines collected from offenders against the community's laws, partly by cesses on the sale of paddy to Kaḷḷar traders, and partly by general levies. In addition, the Paḷḷars paid the Brahman Rs. 24 per year for the fishing lease of three bathing pools located ṇear their streets. This sum went to help finance the village goddess temple.

The Tekkaṭṭi Paḷḷars, more recent comers to the village, had no caste shrine of their own. Instead they presented goats for sacrifice to the village goddess immediately after the Non-Brahman festival in Thai. All the Paḷḷar streets had roles in the annual village temple festival, where they presented sacrificial goats after the other streets had done so.

Each Paḷḷar street had three male functionaries: a *nāṭṭāṇmai*, or headman, who led street assemblies; a *mooppādi*, or temple official, who helped administer the Kāḷiyamman temple and represented his street in the village temple festival; and an *ōḍumpiḷḷai* (literally "running child"), or messenger, who collected funds for the caste shrine, carried messages about deaths, births, marriages, and other events between villages, and summoned people to special street assemblies.

The Paḷḷar *nāṭṭāṇmaikkar* had formerly been hereditary, but for the past few years the Brahmans had allowed the Paḷḷars to elect their own, younger headmen. These headmen's appointments, however, had to be ratified by the landlords, who reserved the right to depose them. Leading Brahmans had in fact deposed one headman in 1947, after a drunken brawl in which he had been heard to ask whether anyone could tell him what use Brahmans were to the village.

The Paḷḷar headman formed a link between each street and the landlords. He called street members for collective tasks, such as channel digging or transplanting; summoned offenders for judgment by the Brahmans in the village temple yard; represented Paḷḷar grievances to the landlords, and presided over the monthly new moon meetings of the street. These assemblies dealt with such matters as debt, theft, marital disputes, divorce suits, quarrels over inheritance, and cases of assault or slander. Like the Non-Brahman street headmen, Paḷḷar headmen witnessed marriages and divorces between people of different streets or different villages. In the Dēvendra Paḷḷar *chēri* (settlement), the headmen and assemblies of all four streets combined to judge disputes between members of different streets.

In a serious dispute the Paḷḷars sometimes expelled the culprits from the village with the consent of their landlords. One such case happened during my visit. A man named Paṭṭāṇi had two younger sisters who brought their husbands to work in Kumbapeṭṭai, where there were paddy fields to be leased. One of the husbands, Kathiravēl, had been secretly distilling liquor. After a major incident in which several of the street's drinkers were arrested, he went home for a time to his village to escape the police. While he was gone his wife slept with Perumāl, her sister's husband. When Kathiravēl returned and asked her to go with him to his village, she refused. Kathiravēl became angry and dragged her by the hair, whereupon Perumāl ran and beat him with a stick. Enraged, and perhaps aware of the adultery, Kathiravēl drew a knife to stab him. Street men intervened, and the two were shut up in their houses for the night. Next morning the headman and the *mooppādi* called a meeting of all the streets, which decided to expel both couples. The headmen approached the Brahman landlords of both, who saw the seriousness of the case and decided to let them go. One landlord forgave Perumāl a debt of Rs. 30 in order to release him. Both couples were sent back to their home villages with their wives.

The Paḷḷars showed an almost fanatical passion for equality, sharing, and mutual surveillance within the street and the microcaste. Indeed, I found the equal and comradely style of life in the Paḷḷar streets a relief from the ritualism and hierarchy of the *agrahāram*, although its lack of privacy was sometimes disconcerting. The Paḷḷars' egalitarianism seemed to result in part from the fact that after about the age of fourteen, each boy and girl was employed as an adult by the Brahmans. Couples married when the girl was about thirteen to fourteen and the man sixteen to eighteen, whereas in modern times, Brahman and Non-Brahman men had married at the age of twenty to twenty-five and women at about sixteen to eighteen. Paḷḷar women and children received wages that were separate from those of their husbands and fathers. Although smaller than the wages of men, these payments tended to form a higher proportion of the family's income than those earned by Non-Brahman women and children, who either worked shorter hours or stayed at home. Brahmans ideally had patrilocal grandfamilies in which married sons were subordinated to their fathers and women to their husbands throughout the lives of these relatives. Non-Brahman married couples usually lived for two or three years in the parental home before building separate dwellings. Paḷḷar couples left the parental home almost immediately after the marriage. As the head of a separate dwelling, each married man of the street had equal rights with the rest. Paḷḷar women exercised almost equal authority with their husbands in the family and had the right of divorce and remarriage, even though women played no formal role in street assemblies. Inside their street – which the Brahmans might not enter – Paḷḷar men behaved somewhat like a large group of rivalrous but equivalent brothers. To be listened to, the headman had to express the will of the majority. In everyday life, order was maintained by the constant interference of the street in the lives of its members, privacy and individual choice being reduced to a minimum.

This intervention by the street and its headman repeatedly surprised me. When, for example, brothers divided their property, the headman and assembly witnessed the distribution of every pot and pan. If a kinsman or affine from elsewhere visited the village, he went first to the headman and only later to his relatives' hut. If surplus paddy was sold, it had to be sold through the headman and *mooppādi* and a toll exacted for the Kāliyamman shrine. Before prohibition, Paḷḷars, unlike Non-Brahmans, did not drink singly at the Nāyakkars' toddy shop. Instead they assembled in a queue behind the shop, delivered equal amounts of paddy to their street headmen, and received back an equal number of bottles per man. After a divorce, the men of the whole street (or of both streets if two were involved) drank together in the same manner to ratify their agreement and to terminate any ill will. Until recent years when some of the Paḷḷars had become tenant farmers and obtained slightly higher, private earnings, and when coolie labor had become prevalent, equality of payments and privileges for all *paṇṇaiyāḷs* (as, no doubt, for all former slaves) had been general. Even in 1952, I found that a gift to an individual Paḷḷar was refused unless it could be divided equally among all members of the street.

Toward the end of my stay, an incident occurred that illustrated the extent of the Paḷḷar street's control over individual lives. I have already mentioned the Paḷḷar *vādyar* who was teaching a play to the men and boys of Long Paḷḷar Street. The parts were cast among the young men and boys, and the whole street met nightly to watch and criticize the rehearsals. After two months, it was clear that the boy taking the part of Queen Alli had still not learned his part and was too shy to act: The teacher's sarcasm and his elders' promptings had reduced him to misery. At last he stayed at home, refusing to leave his hut for the rehearsal shed. After a week of fruitless persuasion, the headman called a street assembly, which decided to ostracize the boy's family. For a fortnight, no one spoke to them, entered their house, or showed awareness of their existence. Just as I left the village, I heard that the boy had given in and had returned to practice his part.

The high degree of equality, social discipline, and solidarity in Paḷḷar life seemed to result from their position in the structures of class and caste. I have mentioned that all Paḷḷars had once been *paṇṇaiyāḷs* (and formerly, slaves) who received equal payments from their masters. Linked with this was the fact that the work unit was either a married couple with their unmarried children or else a large gang of men or women, often the members of one or more streets, engaged in transplanting, harvesting, or channel digging. The five streets themselves were probably once attached to Kumbapeṭṭai's five Brahman lineages, for in 1952 each lineage still retained a number of servants in one street. The Paḷḷars were therefore long accustomed to working under strict discipline either in equal elementary families or in work gangs drawn from the street, and this organization carried over into their social life.

In 1952 the Brahman landlords continued in many contexts to treat the Paḷḷar streets as collectivities, not only with reference to communal labor, but also to punishments for "crimes." Individual offenses against the privileges of the higher castes were often punished by heavy fines levied on the street as a whole or by beatings inflicted randomly. As a result, there was a constant watchfulness and mutual discipline within the Paḷḷar streets. The headman was especially instrumental in reminding his street mates of the wages of sin, for he was held especially responsible by the landlords for the street's behavior.

Finally, the Ādi Drāviḍas were rejected and kept at a distance by all the castes above them. This forced them to fall back on each other for support and companionship, and may have contributed to the high value they placed on equality and order within their community. At the same time, the fact that the Non-Brahmans seldom entered their street and that the Brahmans were forbidden to do so, allowed them to relax there and engage in comradely behavior, far away from the concerns for hierarchy and precedence that permeated the main village and especially the *agrahāram*.

# 17 Class Struggle and Village Power Structure

## The Settlement of Civil Disputes

When men of the lower classes could not reach agreement through their own assemblies, it was common for them to take their grievances to the landlords. In 1952 the Paḷḷars did this more frequently than the Non-Brahmans for reasons given earlier, but some Non-Brahmans still approached the landlords with their disputes. Disputants might go to their own landlords, who would jointly effect a compromise, or to the *panchāyat* president or the village headman.

Several of these voluntary referrals of disputes occurred during my visit, and earlier cases were reported. Soon after I arrived, the *panchāyat* president settled a dispute over vegetable marrows among some of his Paḷḷar servants. Two Paḷḷar brothers, Karuppaṉ and Vēlaṉ, had brought their divorced sister Tulassi back to live near them in Kumbapeṭṭai and, with the landlord's consent, had settled her on a house site next to their own. Tulassi grew some marrows on a patch of garden behind her house. Some of the plants strayed into the next door patch of her second brother, Vēlaṉ, whose wife plucked ten marrows without her knowledge. Tulassi quarreled with her, and told Karuppaṉ that although she was willing to give marrows to him, she would not give them to Vēlaṉ or his wife. The brothers then quarreled and fought. Karuppaṉ's wife summoned her landlord, the *panchāyat* president, being afraid that the brothers might kill each other. The president came to the site and examined the gardens from the backs of the houses. Then he called the whole street before the Kāḷiyamman shrine and elicited the facts.

It turned out that Tulassi had a grievance against Vēlaṉ because he had not contributed to the marriage expenses of her daughter as a mother's brother should. Moreover, another sister's daughter had just matured, and Vēlaṉ had shown no signs of contributing the appropriate bangles, hair oil, and *sāri* for the first menstruation ceremony, so that the whole expense of the mother's brother would again fall on Karuppaṉ. The president decided that as a divorcee from another village, Tulassi had no categorical right to a garden at all, but only to house space, so he redivided the three plots into two between the brothers. At the same time he judged that Vēlaṉ must pay the expenses due from his niece's marriage, and must immediately pay over the gifts for his second sister's daughter's puberty ceremonies. If he did not do so, the president threatened to take back his whole share of the garden and give it to Tulassi. With this rather arbitrary judgment, the quarrel subsided.

In a second case, a Kaḷḷar tenant of Akkāchavaḍy one night grazed his cattle in the blackgram field of his Kōṉār neighbor. The Kōṉār took the case to their common Brahman landlord, who lectured the Kaḷḷar, fined him, and threatened to evict him if the offense was repeated.

In recent years, if the parties to a dispute had been village servants or tenants of the landlords from outside the village, the offended person had sometimes gone to the village headman, who under government law had the right to judge cases involving not more than Rs. 50. In one case in 1947, a Poosāri man who was impotent allowed his wife to have relations with a Kōṉār tenant farmer on condition the Kōṉār paid him for the privilege. On one occasion the Kōṉār took advantage of the arrangement and then refused to pay. The Poosāri knocked him over the head with a staff. Knowing that the Poosāri would not care to admit the full story, the Kōṉār charged him with assault before the village headman. The village headman lectured both of them and fined the Poosāri.

Occasionally, individual Brahmans intervened informally along with Non-Brahmans in Non-Brahman peasants' quarrels. During the *sambā* season of 1951–2, the Tamiḷ and the Tōṛuvar Nāyakkar headmen of Vēṭṭāmbāḍi cultivated nearby fields. The Tamiḷ Nāyakkar headman gave the Paḷḷar watchman a bribe of Re. 1 to supply water generously to his field in the night. He did so, and the Tōṛuvar Nāyakkar's field was left dry. Next day the Tōṛuvar Nāyakkar questioned the watchman, who admitted his error. The Tōṛuvar Nāyakkar met his adversary outside the Vēṭṭāmbāḍi teashop. "I am a tree without branches, a childless man!" he cried, "Come and I will kill you!" The Tamiḷ Nāyakkar shouted, "I am a sick man! But come, and I will fight you!" The two exchanged blows and the Tamiḷ Nāyakkar's brothers ran to help him. While a general brawl with occasional blows was going on, Srīnivāsa Iyer, who often consorted with Non-Brahmans, arrived with the Kōṉār headman of Barber Street and the Kaḷḷar Headman of Akkāchāvaḍy. Together they separated the fighters, told them to quiet down, and sent them home with laughter.

## The Punishment of Crimes

The landlords' central role in village politics was to operate as a kind of court when people of lower caste committed offenses regarded as both sins against the village goddess and crimes against village laws. In serious cases all the landlords, led by the wealthiest and most powerful, might take action. In such cases, the village headman, *panchāyat* president, or a group of Brahmans, would send the Paṟayar *veṭṭiyaṉ* to summon the wrongdoers and their street mates to the courtyard of the village temple, especially if the offenders came from the so-called *kaṭṭupāḍ* (slave, or tied) streets of Aḍichēri or the Paḷḷar streets.

It seemed clear from the accounts of the villagers that such cases had been more common, and the punishments harsher, before the 1940s when more of the wealthier Brahmans lived in the village and when the teachings of the Congress and Communist Parties about civil rights for Harijans had not yet reached the village. Even so, several cases occurred shortly before or during my visit. I will describe some of the cases that were reported to me in order to illustrate the kinds of offenses that occurred, the relations involved, and the punishments.

### *Case 1*

It was reported that in about 1910 the Brahman village headman, a landlord of Kaṇḍipeṭṭai who owned sixty acres there and in Kumbapeṭṭai, went to pay Rs. 500 revenue in Thanjāvūr, but found the revenue officer absent. Returning, he was set upon and robbed by about forty Paḷḷars of Kaḷḷūr. Next day, with the consent of the landlords of Kaḷḷūr, Brahmans of Kumbapeṭṭai and Kaṇḍipeṭṭai brought 400 Paḷḷar men, women, and children from Kaḷḷūr, tied them to 400 coconut trees, and flogged them. All the Paḷḷar streets of Kaḷḷūr were then fined Rs. 2,000 for the Ūriḍeichiyamman temple.

The Brahman landlord who told me this story remarked, "Today such cases can't be conducted." It may be that the incident gained in the telling, although it was corroborated by other Brahmans. It was the only case I heard of in which Ādi Drāviḍa women and children as well as men had been flogged by the landlords. Tying culprits to coconut trees, and punishing many for the offenses of a few, were common as late as 1952.

### *Case 2*

In 1930 a junior Poosāri village priest and a Barber one night visited the house of an Agambaḍiyar widow of doubtful reputation. A prominent Potter tenant farmer and two Kōṉār middle peasants saw them enter. As a joke, they bribed a Paḷḷar, Paṭṭāni, to beat both of them later when they left the house. The Paḷḷar did so and then ran away. Meanwhile, a Tamiḷ Nāyakkar had come along and heard the story; when the Paḷḷar inflicted the blows he shouted, "Beat them, Paṭṭāṇi!" Next day the Poosāri's father reported the beating to Sundarēsa Iyer, the village headman of Kaṇḍipeṭṭai, who owned the largest estate in Kumbapeṭṭai and possessed a house in its *agrahāram*. The Poosāri wept loudly before him, begging him to intervene.

Sundarēsa Iyer came to Kumbapeṭṭai, summoned the Paṟayar village servants from Māniyūr, and made them bind Paṭṭāni to a coconut tree. After giving him sixty blows with a cane, Sundarēsa Iyer forced him to drink a vessel (it was said, "half a gallon") of human dung mixed in water brought by the Paṟayar at his request. Sundarēsa Iyer then fined the Paḷḷar Rs. 25. The Potter and both Kōṉārs were also bound to trees and flogged by several other Brahmans, who cried, "You rascals! Why did you dare to touch a public man?" They were then forced to drink bottles of cow dung mixed in water. Both were fined Rs. 100. Sundarēsa Iyer himself refrained from beating one of the Kōṉārs, because this man's Brahman landlord had earlier pleaded with him not to beat his tenant and had promised him Rs. 500 if he would abstain. Finally, the Brahman headman gave two blows each to the Poosāri and the Barber and lectured them on the loss of dignity suffered by village servants who engaged in sexual offenses. The case lasted from 7:00 A.M. to 7:00 P.M., with all the Brahmans refraining from eating until it was ended. Although he had aided and abetted the Potter and the Kōn̲ārs, the Nāyakkar was let off because, it was said, "he was a solvent man."

This case was the only one I heard of in which a culprit was forced to consume human dung. The punishment was so revolting to the villagers that it seems likely it would be inflicted only for a very serious offense against caste morality, and only on an Ādi Drāviḍa. Forcing an offender to drink cow dung and water, however, was a common punishment for both Non-Brahman and Ādi Drāviḍa servants.

The case illustrates several facets of village law and practice. Three grades of offense were apparently involved: the village priest and the barber visiting an Agambaḍiyar widow; the Potter and the Kōn̲ārs ordering an attack on them; and the Paḷḷar making the assault. The first offense was evidently considered mild by the Brahmans, even though strictly speaking the woman was of higher caste than the men involved. Had their action not led to a brawl they would probably not have been punished, for the Brahmans paid little attention to irregular sexual relations among the Non-Brahman castes.

The second offense was seen as much worse because, as the Brahmans explained, it was wrong for ordinary Non-Brahmans to attack village servants (*pothu manithar*, or public men), who had a specially protected status. The attack on a village priest was seen as particularly reprehensible, as was the act of engaging an Ādi Drāviḍa to beat a Non-Brahman. The Paḷḷar's offense was "worst" of all because it breached the rules of submissive conduct on the part of Ādi Drāviḍas. The Paḷḷar therefore received the worst punishment in village eyes, although, as he was a poor person, his fine was the smallest one.

An interesting feature was that the Kōn̲ārs were both quite prominent middle peasants who later became headmen of their streets. They were, however, still tenants of the Brahmans, and for that reason the Brahmans were able to wreak vengeance on them. Moreover, their ancestors had been slaves of the Brahmans, and most of their relatives were tenants, or *vēlaikkārars*. The Potter was in a similar position. Although a prosperous tenant he leased his lands from Brahmans and was dependent on them.

It is significant that the Brahman landlord of one of the Kōn̲ārs tried to have him released from punishment, even (allegedly) to the point of offering a bribe to the village headman. (It was not clear from the report whether the bribe was accepted; probably not, but the headman refrained from offending a fellow Brahman). Efforts to save their own tenants and servants from punishment by others were in fact common among the landlords, and quarrels sometimes arose if a landlord tried to punish another's servant without the full consent of all the landlords. The reason seems to have been that the masters often became fond of their own servants, and also of course that they depended on them for good performance. Paṭṭāṇi's Brahman master, however, even though he was the richest landlord living in Kumbapeṭṭai and a man of mild manmers, usually kind to his servants, did nothing to save the Paḷḷar because his offense was considered so serious that the whole *agrahāram* demanded his punishment.

The Nāyakkar was exempt from punishment although he had urged on Paṭṭāṇi. The reason, no doubt, was that he owned his own coconut gardens and house site in Vēṭṭāmbāḍi, did not lease land from the Brahmans, and had a powerful protector in the rich Nāḍār landlord and toddy shop owner for whom he worked in Nāṭṭār. The case illustrates the fact that although the offenses and the punishments were phrased in caste terms by the Brahmans, they were also a form of class struggle. The landlords took their vengeance in full on upstart middle peasants and a laborer for quite mild acts that were undertaken in fun, because they were seen to threaten the landlords' conceptions of social order and their supremacy. Although of low caste, the Nāyakkar was exempt because he was not a servant of the landlords and because they could not rely on his own, "modern" capitalist employer, also of low caste, to ratify his punishment.

### *Case 3*

In 1932 the Kōṉār cowherd of an elderly bedridden Brahman landlord began to have sexual relations secretly with the Brahman's wife, a girl of eighteen who had married him after his first two wives had died. The Kōṉār would enter the back of the house from the cowshed in the late afternoon at milking time. Although the other Brahmans suspected something, they did nothing until one day the Kōṉār youth left the house by his master's front door and walked down the Brahman street. This route was forbidden to Non-Brahmans at that time. Both Brahmans and Non-Brahmans reported to me that a Brahman of the next house and his son caught the Kōṉār, beat him with sticks, and then hustled him into an empty house in the *agrahāram*. There, they castrated and killed him. The body was found a few hours later hanging from the rafters of this house. The village headman felt obliged to summon the police because the death had been violent. It was said that the Non-Brahman district constable reacted with horror and asked fearfully, "Oh, Pārppār, have you killed this man?" The village headman silenced him with a bribe of Rs. 300, collected from the Brahman street. A death certificate was issued, and a report drafted to the effect that the cowherd, harassed by debts, had hanged himself in despair. His brothers, lessees of the Brahmans, were said to have been thankful to escape wthout eviction.

Case 3 shows that occasionally, Brahman "justice" descended to spontaneous lynching. The offense of a Non-Brahman man having sexual relations with a Brahman woman was, however, so grave that the village headman and the whole *agrahāram* apparently supported the murder. As late as 1952, the young and middle-aged Brahmans who told me of the case seemed sure that the penalty was justified and the act of bribing the constable merely a way of ensuring that village justice did not miscarry. Certainly, the proverbial unity of the *agrahāram* in cases involving scandal and outside interference played a role. So, probably, did the fact that the Brahmans had never forgiven the British government for causing imprisonment and the death penalty to be extended equally to all castes. Although I am uncertain how murderers were punished in pre-British times, it seems likely that landlords had the right of life and death over their own slaves, and that the death penalty was inflicted if a man of lower caste had sexual relations with a woman of much higher caste. It is certain that Brahmans were exempt from imprisonment and from the death penalty and that fines were the worst punishment imposed on them. In their own eyes, therefore, the Brahmans were correctly fulfilling traditional laws. That such an incident could occur after 130 years of colonial rule illustrates the traditional character of socioeconomic relations in the 1930s.

***Case 4***

One day in 1943 the wife of the Brahman *karṇam* went to urinate in her backyard. As she approached the channel to wash her legs, she saw a Periyūr Paṟayar Christian schoolteacher watching her some yards away in the field across the channel. This man was then said to have urinated before her. Her husband reported the offense to Kumbapeṭṭai's village headman, who approached the Veḷḷāḷar village headman of Periyūr. The Paṟayar was bound and brought to Kumbapeṭṭai, tied to a tree, severely beaten with hands and sticks by "the whole *agrahāram*," and fined Rs. 150 for the Ūriḍeichiyamman temple.

Case 4, similar to Case 3, was a classic instance of the Brahmans' rage when a man of the lowest caste dared to make an apparently sexual approach to one of their women. Perhaps it also reflected their hatred of an "upstart" Paṟayar who had managed to become educated, and of a Christian who would dare to insult a Hindū woman. The case illustrates the operation of traditional "justice" across village boundaries; it was customary for the landlords of one village to hand over offenders to the village where the offense had occurred. In this instance the Brahmans could trust the high-caste Periyūr Veḷḷāḷars to ratify their judgment.

***Case 5***

As I have mentioned, according to tradition, Brahman landlords should be the first to carry out the First Ploughing ceremony, followed by Non-Brahman middle peasants and tenants, and finally Adi Drāviḍa tenants. In 1944, the three Kōṉār and the Nāyakkar middle peasants, the most prosperous potter tenant, and two other Kōṉār tenants did their own First Ploughing in the early morning before the Brahmans had reached their fields. The Brahman landlords were angry, and the village headman summoned Sundarēsa Iyer, the wealthy village headman and landlord of Kaṇḍipeṭṭai. He arrived at 7:00 P.M. and called all the Brahmans and Non-Brahmans to the village temple. As was customary, the Brahmans sat near the verandah of the temple while the Non-Brahmans stood further away at the back of the courtyard. Sundarēsa Iyer roundly abused all the culprits in turn and fined each of them Rs. 10 for the temple funds. A Kōṉār tenant was said to have cried, "Ayyo! I have no money!" Pranadāthikar Iyer gave him two blows with a cane. He shouted, "I don't care about your blows! I have no money!'' The landlords forced him to borrow from other tenants, and he paid.

This case reflects the significance of ceremonial relations in maintaining the village's power structure, and the sense of threat experienced by the Brahmans when their rules were disobeyed. The Non-Brahmans' rebellion represented a mild form of class struggle against the landlords by the rising middle peasants and the more prosperous tenants, who were trying to throw off the Brahmans' control. The petty bourgeoisie realized that such actions would undermine their control over all the lower orders, and tried to quash the peasants' bid for autonomy. In doing so, as in many other cases, they took care to summon their relative, the Kaṇḍipeṭṭai village headman, because he owned the largest landholding in Kumbapeṭṭai.

I have already mentioned that in 1950, a much ''worse'' case arose in which Ādi Drāviḍa tenants drove out their cattle before the Non-Brahmans on Māṭṭu Pongal Day. In that instance, each Paḷḷar street was fined Rs. 25. The two cases illustrate the loosening of the landlords' control of the middle and poor peasants in the 1940s and early 1950s, and their efforts to reassert it. The case of the Paḷḷars, however, shows that although the Non-Brahman middle peasants and tenants wanted to escape from the village hierarchy, they were not ready to see the Paḷḷars do likewise.

***Case 6***

In 1943 Subramania Iyer, whose father was then the village headman, ran short of seed for his *kuruvai* sowing. He went to the leading Kōṉār middle peasant, Pečhimuttu, who was known to have seed, and asked him to lend him four bags that were standing in his yard. The Kōṉār said he was sorry, but he needed the seed for his own fields. The Brahman went away, and two evenings later Pečhimuttu put his bags into the nearby channel to germinate before the next day's sowing. During the night, Subramania Iyer arrived with three Paḷḷars, who dragged the bags quietly through the water to the back of the *agrahāram* and put them in the landlord's yard. When he came to collect the bags at 3:00 A.M., Pečhimuttu shouted aloud that his seed was gone. A crowd of Non-Brahmans collected and searched the area. At last Pečhimuttu came to the back of Subramania Iyer's house and saw his bags. When the Brahman appeared he said humbly, ''Alas, *swāmi*, forgive me for not giving you the bags.'' The Brahman replied haughtily, ''What, Iḍaiyaṉ! These are my own bags! I took them to the channel last night and brought them back this morning.'' The Kōṉār embraced his knees and asked for pardon. Subramania Iyer ''took pity on him,'' laughed, and sent back the paddy, but fined him Rs. 25 for his ''insolence.'' The fine was worth slightly more than the cash value of the bags, but it gave the Kōṉār less trouble for seed paddy was very scarce. In all seriousness, the Brahman who told me of this incident ended his story by saying, ''In those days there was never any theft in Kumbapeṭṭai; Subramania Iyer wandered everywhere to check on things at night.''

This incident, reported to me as a "case" of village justice, shows that as late as the 1940s, some Brahmans held the traditional view that Non-Brahmans and Ādi Drāviḍas whose ancestors had been slaves had no right to private property, but must put their all at the service of the landlords whenever it was required. Subramania Iyer had the added advantage that his father was village headman, so that it was unlikely that anyone would rebuke him. Although individual Brahmans did not normally "fine" lower-caste men who were not their own tenants, in this case the village headman's power gave his son the ability to extract a fine.

***Case 7***

In 1949 a Kōṉār and an Agambaḍiyar, both *vēlaikkārars*, formed the habit of visiting a Paḍaiyācchi wife in Aḍichēri while her husband was away from home doing coolie work in nearby villages. After about five or six months of these visits, an Ambalakkārar coolie visited the woman one night. The Kōṉār and the Agambaḍiyar saw him enter. When he came out about 10:00 P.M., they bound him to a tree and beat him on the chest with sticks. It was explained that although they were not jealous of each other, being friends of similar peasant caste, they were furious with the Ambalakkārar because they had not invited him to join in their pleasure and because his caste was lower than the woman's or their own. The Ambalakkārar's cries were heard in Vēṭṭāmbāḍi. His father and the Nāyakkar headman of Vēṭṭāmbāḍi rushed to the scene; so did three Kōṉārs from Aḍichēri. The Kōṉār and the Agambaḍiyar released the Ambalakkārar and explained his offense. The Nāyakkar headman, unaware of the Ambalakkārar's injuries and angered that a low-caste man of his street should be involved in a village brawl, gave him further blows. The Ambalakkārar then fell dead.

When the Nāyakkar headman called the Brahman village headman, he was afraid to hide the case from the police, and the Kōṉār, Agambaḍiyar, and Nāyakkar were arrested for murder. Before the trial, the Brahmans collected Rs. 700 in the *agrahāram* and Vēṭṭāmbāḍi, and bribed the police to release the Nāyakkar and summon him merely as a witness. They then hired a Brahman lawyer to defend the Kōṉār and the Agambaḍiyar, who were released after a verdict of accidental death.

In discussing this case, the Brahmans argued that the Ambalakkārar deserved to die. As a man of a lower, polluting caste, he had committed a crime by sleeping with a Paḍaiyācchi woman, although it was not one of which the Brahmans would normally have taken cognizance. Mild jail sentences were in order for the Kōṉār and the Agambaḍiyar, but the Nāyakkar headman (although traditionally of a lower caste than the assailants, but higher than the murdered man) was blameless. As a headman, he had merely tried to preserve order in his street.

The case illustrated the fact that in spite of their extreme harshness with Non-Brahmans who offended them, the Brahmans were concerned to protect their servants from others and were prepared to spend money to save them from what they saw as an unjust fate. Although an "upstart" whom many Brahmans resented, the Nāyakkar headman had friends and supporters among the less orthodox Brahmans who drank toddy from his shop. Finally, the *mirāsdārs* as usual were concerned to keep government interference out of their village's affairs, or, failing that, to manipulate it to serve their more traditional ideas of justice.

***Case 8***

Shortly before I arrived in 1951 an incident occurred in one of the Poosāri family's teashops on the main roadside. The shop had been built on a plot belonging to an absent Brahman whose lands were managed by Seethā Rāma Iyer, a Brahman of a village four miles away. One day Rāmalinga Iyer, the younger brother of Subramania Iyer who hanged himself in 1946, was waiting for the bus near the village temple. Two Non-Brahman shopkeepers of Āriyūr who were passing stopped to talk to him. He sent a servant, without money, to bring two bottles of orange crush from the teashop. The Poosāri husband was absent. Knowing that the Brahman would never pay, his wife said, "No crush here." When the servant reported this, Rāmalinga Iyer became angry, and in the evening he sent for Seethā Rāma Iyer to come to Kumbapeṭṭai. He, too, was angry and went to report the offense to the village headman, who called a meeting in the *agrahāram*. Together with the *panchāyat* president, the village headman, Rāmalinga Iyer, Seethā Rāma Iyer, Srīnivāsa Iyer and another Brahman went to the teashop, ordered the Poosāri out, and began to smash bottles and glasses on the floor. Seethā Rāma Iyer, the landlord, ordered some Non-Brahman servants to open the roof and destroy the building. The Poosāri owner and his elder brother, the village priest, prostrated themselves before the Brahmans and begged forgiveness. The *panchāyat* president then stopped the destruction and fined them Rs. 25 for the temple funds. As the Brahman who told me this story commented, "Now that lady stands up if any Brahman passes by."

This outrageous incident, like Case 6, indicated that at heart, many of the Brahmans still regarded the Non-Brahmans (and, of course, the Paḷḷars) of the old *grāmam* area as similar to slaves. It is significant that until shortly before the abolition of slavery, slaves were not permitted to own property; everything in the village belonged to the landlords. Whether openly or secretly, many Brahmans felt that this situation ought to be preserved as far as possible. It is clear that they regarded the Poosāris, as village servants, as the bondsmen of the *agrahāram* collectively and resented their effort to run a "capitalist" business in the village, especially on Brahman land. The incident showed that in the landlords' (and the village officers') eyes, the lower-caste villagers, at least those of the old *grāmam* area, had no rights to cash transactions or profits except at their masters' pleasure. Although the Poosāri wife's action was seemingly so innocent, it was seen as threatening enough to bring together the *panchāyat* president and his two old enemies, the village headman and Srīnivāsa Iyer, in a common act of vengeance.

***Case 9***

During the first week of my stay in 1951 a Kumbapeṭṭai Paḷḷar *paṇṇaiyaḷ*, Noṇḍipayaḷ, was accused of stealing a brass vessel, valued at Rs. 6, from a Kaḷḷar landowners' street in a village six miles away. He was said to have run to the Paḷḷar street of that village, where he tried to sell the vessel for Rs. 4, saying he had paid Rs. 7. A woman offered him Rs. 2. While they were debating, Kaḷḷars arrived to inquire. They took back the vessel, seized the culprit, and bound his hands behind his back. Some of the Kaḷḷars began to beat him, but others stopped them and asked who the man's landlord was. He said that he worked for the *panchāyat* president of Kumbapeṭṭai. (In fact, he had worked for him the previous year, but was currently working for an Agambaḍiyar of Māniyūr. Perhaps he still thought of himself as the president's rightful servant because the rest of his family worked for him).

The Non-Brahmans decided that to punish Noṇḍipayaḷ themselves would offend the Kumbapeṭṭai president's prestige. Two Paḷḷars of the village were therefore ordered to march him, bound, to Kumbapeṭṭai. A Kaḷḷar accompanied them with a letter explaining the case. The *panchāyat* president, Pranadāthikar Iyer, sent a servant to summon all the Paḷḷar men and women of Upper Street to the village temple courtyard. It turned out that the accused was the son-in-law of Tulassi, whose affair of the vegetable marrows, described earlier, had been settled two days before. Noṇḍipayaḷ's relatives prostrated themselves before the president, pleading that they were very poor. He demanded a fine of Rs. 10. Within an hour, they brought Rs. 5 from their street and a silver bangle to be pledged the next day for Rs. 5. The president gave Noṇḍipayaḷ ten blows with a cane and forced him to drink a pint of cow dung in water "to purify him and to teach him a lesson." The man gagged and refused, but was forced to drink. The president then placed a white cloth on the ground before the deity and compelled Noṇḍipayaḷ to prostrate himself before it and promise not to thieve again. The case ended at midnight.

This case again illustrates the fact that when an offense occurred in another village, the landowning castes of both villages took action to punish the accused. It seems probable, however, that punishment was usually carried out by the higher or more prestigious landlords involved. In Case 4, the Periyūr Paṟayar was punished in Kumbapeṭṭai for an offense committed there, but in Case 9, the offender was marched back to his home village.

Tulassi's case and Case 9 both illustrate the Ādi Drāviḍas' subservience to and dependence on the landlords in 1951. Although revolting punishments were inflicted on them for small offenses, they continued to take many disputes voluntarily for settlement by the same landlords. It must be mentioned, however, that the government court's penalty for this theft might have been six months in jail and a fine of Rs. 25. The *panchāyat* president probably spoke correctly when he said that the Paḷḷars preferred a lighter and swifter punishment.

***Case 10***

At times the landlords did elect to use the police to carry out their task of repression. I was told that shortly before I arrived in 1951, the Paḷḷars of Kumbapeṭṭai had jointly bought a stock of French polish in a collective rebellion against prohibition. Large fires were built one night and huge pots of water, tree bark, French polish, lime fruits, and coconut flowers were boiled for several hours. All five streets were said to have been totally drunk and incapable of work for the next three days. When the bout subsided, the village headman called the police to the Paḷḷar streets to make select arrests. The whole Paḷḷar population was then marched to the temple yard, harangued by the leading landlords, and fined Rs. 200.

***Case 11***

During my visit a coolie boy of fifteen of the Ambalakkārar caste stole twelve coconuts from the yard of a small Brahman landlord's house during the dry season of 1952 when food was scarce. The Brahman's son, a schoolteacher, caught him and took him to the village headman. He wrote a report and sent the boy to the police station four miles away under the escort of the village *veṭṭi*. The police put him in a cell and came to Kumbapeṭṭai to make enquiries. Meanwhile, the boy's parents prostrated themselves before the schoolteacher and begged forgiveness. He asked the police to release the boy without a fine or a hearing, and this was done.

This case shows that some of the younger and more educated Brahmans objected to the traditional procedures of village "justice" and preferred to follow governmentally sanctioned procedures. In 1952 the village headman was a young man and an enemy of the *panchāyat* president. The latter was the main pillar of the traditional village court, who strongly objected to calling the police on any occasion. The village headman complied with the schoolteacher's wishes, and the latter was eventually soft-hearted enough to drop the charge in a season of acute food shortage. The fact that the boy's family were coolies without a landlord of their own may have influenced the way this case was conducted.

***Case 12***

At other times the village headman was willing to use the police to prosecute his personal vendettas. After the *sambā* harvest of 1952 he fell foul of one of Akkāchāvaḍy's young Kaḷḷar traders, who refused to transport some black market paddy for him on what he regarded as a dangerous mission. The headman then had the trader arrested for previous black market dealings. He was found guilty and spent six weeks in jail. The case illustrates the power of the village headman over the lower classes, and shows one of the reasons why they feared him and why leading Brahmans competed for the position.

The village headman was, in fact, the village's spokesman to the police and most of the outside authorities, and they were likely to avoid trouble by accepting his word. The Kaḷḷar trader was unlikely to have won the case because he could not afford a lawyer. He was also unlikely to reveal the full facts in court, for he would probably not have been believed, and doing so might have brought further harm to his family. Case 12 does, however, illustrate the weakness of the landlords' direct power over the traders of Akkāchāvaḍy. The headman could not punish the young trader in the ways that he might have punished a traditional servant of the *agrahāram*, so he used a subterfuge and brought in the police. Giving reports of wrongdoing to the police in order to score off an enemy was, in fact, a tactic sometimes used among the Brahmans themselves.

### Case 13

One night during the hunger season of 1952 the gate of the village temple was broken open. It was thought that thieves were trying to steal gold ornaments from the idol, for this had happened in some other villages. The Poosāri, who lived next door, awoke to the commotion and drove off the marauder without recognizing him. The next day the village headman came to investigate. Seeing a Koravar (village sweeper) boy loitering by the gate, he asked him what he had been doing the previous night. The boy said that he was at the cinema in Thanjāvūr, eight miles away. Perhaps annoyed that a low-caste boy should be able to attend the cinema, the headman had him bound to a tree, flogged him, and left him to stand all day as an example to the village. Several Brahmans privately showed uneasiness over this incident, but when I raised it in the Brahman Street it was quickly hushed up. The headman had been harsh, it was said, and the incident was hard on the boy, but no punishment was too great for an attack on the deity. Presumably, the landlords thought that such a punishment could scarcely be misplaced because Koravars were traditionally gypsies and many of these were said to have been thieves.

This incident shows that although the Koravars had been sent to the village by the government as road sweepers, and were government servants, the landlords treated them similarly to, if not more harshly than, the village Paḷḷars in view of their poverty, low caste, and reputation for theft. As a single household of low caste without kin in the neighborhood, the Koravars were ideal scapegoats. The father was in jail for theft during most of my visit. I never discovered whether or not he was guilty.

### Case 14

During my stay a poor Brahman who was sometimes mentally ill borrowed money from a Kōṉār *vēlaikkāraṟ* and tenant of Akkāchāvaḍy. When the Kōṉār asked for the money at the stipulated time, the Brahman refused. The Kōṉār grew angry and hit him on the head with a stick. The Brahman's neighbors reported the matter to the *panchāyat* president, who managed land leased by the Kōṉār. He fined the Kōṉār Rs. 100 and forced him to drink cow dung. Nothing was done about the debt during my stay.

The incident again reflects the fact that the landlords did not grant their laborers rights to property and fair dealings in financial matters, and also that even if a poor, weak-minded Brahman was assaulted by a servant of the village, revenge was swift. At the same time, the Kōṉār servant did assault the Brahman, an act that I was told would have been unthinkable on the part of a servant of the *agrahāram* a few years earlier. The Non-Brahmans, especially in Akkāchāvaḍy and Vēṭṭāmbāḍi, were beginning to expect to be treated "like men," as they sometimes said, even though they knew that they might suffer if they rebelled.

For several months I was under the impression that there were no limits to the landlords' powers over their laborers, and that the lower castes had no redress against landlord oppression and exploitation. Gradually, however, I realized that this was not always the case. Until recently, it seemed likely that the whole village acknowledged a common body of law defining the rights and obligations of the castes, which Brahmans as well as others were expected to observe. Brahmans, for example, were forbidden to enter the Ādi Drāviḍa streets, and this gave the lowest castes a certain degree of privacy. Similarly, as late as the 1920s, if a Brahman had sexual relations with an Ādi Drāviḍa woman he and his whole household were driven out of the *agrahāram*. This allowed the Ādi Drāviḍas a kind of dignity; as a consequence, they were well known to be morally more "correct" than all the other castes.

In recent times, the Brahmans had failed to curb Brahman offenders against the rules of caste. In 1952, for example, sexual relations with Non-Brahman women were extremely common although they were forbidden in theory, and occasionally, relations with Paḷḷathis occurred. If, however, a Brahman offended the kinsmen of his mistress, he could not rely on the *agrahāram* to protect him against their anger. In 1944, Subramania Iyer, the "haughty" Brahman's son of the then village headman, had an affair with a Kōṉār woman of a middle peasant family. Her brothers caught him one night in their house. In fury, they tied him to a cartwheel, beat him, and then drove both culprits out of the village. Although he was the village headman, the Brahman's father did nothing beyond evicting the Kōṉārs from land they had leased from him. Perhaps he was already weary of his son's general misbehavior. Indeed, it was said that when Subramania Iyer's honor had been lost in this public fashion, both his father and younger brothers refused to help, saying, "Go! Get away from here!" The Brahman abandoned his mistress in Coimbatore, where she was discovered destitute a year later and brought home by her brothers. Subramania Iyer eventually returned home, but he never recovered his bravado, and in 1946 he hanged himself, it was said in despair over his many debts.

Because supernatural sanctions were believed to uphold the laws of the village, Brahmans, like the lower castes, were sometimes afraid to infringe them. Brahmans, for example, believed that if they drank alcohol or slept with prostitutes they might be visited by Ūriḍeichiyamman in the form of a small girl, and might fall ill, unconscious, or even dead. It cannot be said that this belief had any noticeable effect on village morals in 1952, but it may have deterred some people from sexually exploiting their servants' wives. Similarly, the ghosts of murdered people and suicides were believed to haunt the village and cause those who passed near them, or those responsible for their deaths, to fall ill with a kind of trembling called "frightened disease."

A subordinate who could not gain justice by other means might occasionally appeal to a deity to aid him. One who believed himself wronged by a senior member of the family, a landlord, or some other authority, might, as a last resort, stand before the village temple and cast up sand over his head, praying, "Oh Goddess! My stomach is overflowing! Avenge me." Brahmans as much as lower caste people feared the Goddess's vengeance in the form of disease or financial ruin. It was said that if they knew that they had done wrong, they would sometimes make restitution.

There was also, of course, the fact that the landlords could not afford to exploit their servants without limits, for they needed them to work and preferably, to work hard. A landlord might need faithful servants to fight on his behalf against other landlords. Furthermore, most landlords liked to pride themselves that their servants were really very fond of them and that they were good masters. As everywhere in India, the landlord-servant relation was likened to that between father and children, and was ideally supposed to be as loyal and affectionate. Indeed, landlords who might behave cruelly in some contexts gave their servants gifts or favors in other situations. Some, of course, were more generous than others. Srīnivāsa Iyer, for example, habitually "moved freely" with his own servants, although he could be harsh with others. He paid generously for his servants' marriages, leased land to them, and even helped two *paṇṇaiyāḷs* buy some dry land of their own. These servants seemed, indeed, to be fond of him; one of them gave him a cow out of gratitude.

I noticed several other acts of generosity from landlords to their servants during my stay. The village's wealthiest Brahman widow, for example, sent pepper water and rice flour cakes to her Kaḷḷar tenant's house when his wife was ill. An absentee Brahman came home specially from Madras when his former tenant, aged eighty, died, and gave Rs. 100 toward the funeral expenses.

I was surprised to find that even tenants and servants who had been flogged or otherwise abused could continue to maintain friendly relations with the landlords as a class, accept favors from them, and view them with gratitude. One of the Kōn̲ār middle peasants in Case 2, who was flogged for ordering an attack on the village priest, was an instance. A few years later, when he was fifty-six, he wanted to marry a third wife as his first wife had died and his second had proved infertile. Rāmalinga Iyer in Case 8, who was currently friendly with him because of some dealings in the cattle trade, went to great lengths to help him to remarry. When a girl of sixteen from Kaḷḷūr was found those parents seemed willing, he invited them to Kumbapeṭṭai and fed them for a week in his house. Villagers laughed in telling me how the girl's mother had asked him doubtfully, "How old is Lakshmana Kōn̲ār?" "He's 42!" was the stout reply. "He looks nearer sixty to me," the mother objected. "If the Iyer is willing, don't open your mouth," said the father. On the engagement day the Brahman had the bridegroom shaved, scented, and dressed in new clothes at his expense, and lent him four gold rings for the occasion. He hired a bus and took the Kōṉār with a large party of Non-Brahmans to witness the contract in Kaḷḷūr. During the negotiations, however, the bride's side demanded an acre of land to be settled on the girl in case her co-wife mistreated her. Lakshmana was unwilling, so the marriage came to naught.

It must be mentioned that some landlords in Kumbapeṭṭai did not take part in proceedings against "erring" laborers of the kind recounted in Cases 1 to 14, either because they did not approve of them or because they kept aloof from village affairs. Chandrasēkhara Iyer, for example, was a leper who for years had kept a Maratha woman in Akkāchāvaḍy as his concubine. In his sixties, he tended to be disrespected for his long association with this woman, and retired from village affairs. So did Bālasubramania Iyer, a man of seventy-five who had earlier had a Kūtthāḍi concubine and whose eldest son had died. He became a recluse in early middle age, lived in a separate house from his family, and devoted himself to reading and meditation. Krishnaswāmi Iyer, a man in his fifties and a village temple trustee, took no part in trying cases or punishing servants. He so feared criticism that he walked with his head down so that no Brahman need speak to him and no Non-Brahman need stand up when he went by.

Swaminātha Iyer, aged fifty-three, the richest Brahman in the village, had never beaten or abused his servants, and often pleaded with others for lenience. In his youth he had had a Paḷḷar mistress with whom he was said to be deeply in love. He stopped the affair when his wife discovered it and berated him, but he was always unusually kind to the Paḷḷars. One day two bags of rare seed paddy worth Rs. 40 were stolen from his yard. "Why don't you investigate it?" asked another Brahman. "Why should I?" he replied. "Some suffering man has taken it, who needs it more than I." This Brahman was a congressman who had earlier been a disciple of Kumbapeṭṭai's *sannyāsi* and who tried to follow the ideals of Gāndhi. Each Deepāvāḷi he spent Rs. 700 on clothing for his tenants and servants. At marriages he made generous gifts to them. He made loans without interest, and was often seen giving food to Ādi Drāviḍas from the back door of his house. Even among the wealthier and more powerful landlords, therefore, there were some who did not believe in traditional forms of repression but who used their wealth in efforts to help the poor.

The smaller landlords with less than five acres also played only minor parts, while the landless Brahmans had no role in governing the village. This suggests that the cases I have described were perhaps primarily forms of class struggle and not solely "village administration through caste," as I once described them,[1] even though caste rules were often invoked by the landlords when trying their tenants and laborers. Essentially, in 1952 the village was governed by six Brahmans aged between twenty-two and forty-six, who owned, or whose fathers owned, between eight and twenty acres.

### Overt Class Struggle

Although mostly subservient, in unusual situations villagers sometimes rose up and smote their oppressors. Such assaults might be made individually or in groups. They were most likely to occur during crises or on the part of low-caste men who were not the personal servants of those who oppressed them. About 1917, for example, a Nāḍār from Salem district was tapping toddy for a wealthy Nāḍār toddy shop owner and landlord who lived in Nāṭṭār. One day this man came to tap toddy in the coconut gardens of Kumbapeṭṭai's Brahmans. Unaware, or uncaring, of the village rules regarding alcohol and lower-caste distance pollution, he carried two pots of toddy down the *agrahāram* at midday. A middle-aged Brahman shouted angrily, calling him "rascal" and "bloody fellow." The Nāḍār went off quickly, but returned in the evening to tap more toddy behind the *agrahāram*. Carrying a stick, the Brahman went and found him at the top of a coconut tree. He called to him to come down and take a beating. The Nāḍār descended, but when the Brahman ran to beat him, he attacked him and cut off his hand with his tapping knife. The Brahman died a few days later. The Nāḍār was tried for manslaughter, but it was said that his Nāḍār master "bribed the judge." The case was dismissed for lack of witnesses.

The largest local case of rebellion, directed against both Brahmans and the British government, occurred at Veerasingampeṭ, not far from Kumbapeṭṭai, in 1936. For many years, Non-Brahman and Ādi Drāviḍa devotees for many miles around had had the custom of putting thick pins through their tongues and hooks or small spears through their flesh at the time of the festival of the Veerasingampeṭ village goddess, Māriyammaṉ, in fulfilment of religious vows. The British government passed on order forbidding the use of such forms of self-torture at religious festivals. The people of Kalyānapuram near Veerasingampeṭ disobeyed the order and began to insert hooks in their flesh in the temple yard. Police attempted to prevent them from entering the temple. One Brahman constable, well known for his cruel behavior to the lower castes, mocked the devotees and hit a Kaḷḷar with his *lathi*. A Paḷḷar worshipper then hit the policeman with his fist; the constable shot him dead. At this, a crowd of several hundred Paḷḷars gathered and beat the constable to death, shouting, "How many people have you beaten like this? Why did you do so?"

After the assassination, the submagistrate, a Brahman, ordered the police to shoot into the crowd. They did this, but without bullets, except in the case of one gun that killed another Paḷḷar. The crowd then pushed the submagistrate into the center of the temple and knifed him; he died later in the Thanjāvūr hospital. That evening 200 Reserve Police drove all the devotees from the temple, removed the bodies, and arrested some thirty Kaḷḷars and Paḷḷars. After lengthy cases, three were deported to the Andaman Islands for life imprisonment. Police patrolled the village for a year, and the festival was banned for the next five years.

These incidents, and indeed Cases 1 to 14, were all examples of class struggle, although of an unorganized character. In all except the last case, independent enterpreneurs or semiproletarians in some way challenged the local hierarchy and thus, directly or indirectly, the exploitation and dominance of the landlords. In each case, the landlords retaliated with fury in attempts to restore their power.

### Constraints on Lower-class Struggles

Although there were certain limits to the landlords' repression and exploitation, there were also, of course, severe limits to the lower classes' ability and willingness to struggle against it. This was illustrated in an incident just before the general elections of 1952. Akkāchāvaḍy's leading Kaḷḷar paddy trader visited the *panchāyat* president to arrange a paddy sale. While keeping him waiting in the street beyond his verandah, the president continued a blustering conversation with two other Brahmans in which he complained that the Non-Brahmans and Paḷḷars were nowadays "all bloody rascals and Communists" and that it was folly to give them the popular vote. Soon after, the trader, a street headman, called a meeting of the Non-Brahman streets in the Ūriḍeichiyamman temple yard. He proposed that they should send a delegation to the president asking him why he spoke thus and demanding that he stop abusing the Non-Brahman and Ādi Drāviḍa castes.

In a revealing debate, other Non-Brahmans gave reasons against this action and, in general, against annoying the landlords. One pointed out that the traders needed the landlords to sell paddy and make profits; another, that the tenants needed them to get land to lease, and a third, that although they were often the most cruel, the richer landlords could command the most followers among the Paḷḷars. The meeting broke up without any direct action being taken.

### Class Struggle and Political Parties

This meeting may, however, have influenced voting in the village. Although the ballot was secret and accurate information was not available, I was told that practically all the Brahmans voted for the Congress Party. Several would have preferred the Hindū Mahāsabha, but thought the Mahāsabha candidate would lose and that the Congress, although theoretically anticaste and in favor of land reforms, was the next best alternative. The younger Kurukkal declared himself a socialist, but because there was no Socialist Party candidate, he, too, voted for the Congress Party.

"Long" Paḷḷar Street was said to have voted for the Congress Party as a result of bribes and instructions from the *panchāyat* president, who, together with a few others of his lineage, employed most of the street. It was rumored, however, that most people in the Non-Brahman and Dēvendra Paḷḷar Streets had voted for the Communist candidate in the national Parliamentary elections and for a candidate supported by the Communists and the DK in the elections to the Madras Assembly. (The latter candidate won, while a Congress candidate won the Parliamentary seat). These reports of Kumbapeṭṭai's voting accurately reflect the extent of enlightenment and disaffection against the landlords among the lower castes in 1952.

Although many of Kumbapeṭṭai's Paḷḷars probably voted for the Communists, in 1952 they had a very limited knowledge of the wider world and especially of international affairs, for they had not been exposed to Communist lectures and teachings. I was surprised, for example, to find that in Thanjāvūr generally, the Ādi Drāviḍas showed little or no antagonism to the British. Many older people, both in Kumbapeṭṭai and in Kirippūr, recalled British rule with nostalgia because they associated it with cheap imports of rice from Burma. Some in Kumbapeṭṭai thought that the monsoon had failed for five years because the British had left. Some older people thought that a Communist government in India would mean the return of white (Russian) rulers similar to the British. One old man, when I told him the British were not Communists, asked me, "But is not Russia in London?" Many village Non-Brahmans, as well as Paḷḷars, thought that America was part of England, and only a few youthful sophisticates were aware of the Cold War between the United States and the Soviet Union.

Because of such ignorance, the landlords mocked Ādi Drāviḍas as blockheads and asserted that they were led astray by political leaders, especially Communists. In their own village, however, where their experience lay, the Ādi Drāviḍas readily grasped the political realities. They sensed that no party supported by the landlords – as the Congress generally was in Thanjāvūr – could bring them real economic or legal improvements. Furthermore, the landlords to some extent brought about the electoral results themselves because they habitually called "Communist" any person who wanted to abolish caste discrimination, chat with Paḷḷars in teashops, raise the wages of laborers, or see equal civil rights extended to all citizens. Because they passionately desired these things, the Paḷḷars concluded that the Communists were good people.

In 1952, therefore, the lower classes of Kumbapeṭṭai voted for the Communists or the DK almost instinctively out of opposition to the landlords. By 1953, however, the Communist Party had sent cadres to the neighborhood and, as I have noted, organized the Ādi Drāviḍas and some Non-Brahmans in a harvest strike for higher wages and crop shares. The period of my visit (1951–2) was therefore one in which the lower classes were ready for organization from without against the landlords but had not yet experienced it.

**The Decline of Brahman Dominance**

In other ways it seemed clear that the landords of Kumbapeṭṭai were gradually losing their dominance in 1951–2. Several Brahmans complained that Akkāchāvaḍy and Vēṭṭāmbādi, the two "upstart" streets, were now "hopeless," and that even the Paḷḷars had become "loose" because many Brahmans were absent, no one collected rents from the gardens belonging to them on which Paḷḷars lived, the Paḷḷars' numbers had increased, and many of them had no masters.

Other events showed the Brahmans' loosening grip on the village. One of these had occurred just before I arrived. A young Nāyakkar grocery shopkeeper who had earlier attended high school fell in love with a Brahman girl from the *agrahāram,* the daughter of the village schoolmaster. After school days were ended the couple continued their love affair, for the girl's mother was dead and her father was a lame man who seldom moved about. After some time other Brahmans noticed that they were meeting in the cowshed behind the house. The *agrahāram* lacked sanctions to punish the Nāyakkar, for he occupied an independent house site and owned coconut gardens and a business. Instead, they urged the girl's father to have her married immediately. A marriage was duly arranged with a young Brahman government servant from another village who worked in Delhi. When the Brahman arrived for the engagement ceremony the Nāyakkar, mad with jealousy, was said to have waylaid him on the roadside and to have shouted, "Don't think you can marry Kalyāni! She is *my* wife – I married her long ago." The Kumbapeṭṭai Brahmans who were with the bridegroom hustled him away and told him that the Nāyakkar was the village idiot. The marriage was accomplished and the couple left for Delhi. One morning, however, the bridegroom received a letter from the Nāyakkar telling him about the earlier affair. In silence, he handed it to his wife. A few minutes later, the husband left for work, and the wife hanged herself.

In Kumbapeṭṭai, the Brahmans mourned that this tragedy could never have happened if low-caste people were kept in their place, away from high schools, and if the joint family still flourished among the Brahmans. As an interesting sequel, the Nāyakkar soon after divorced his own wife, even though she had an infant son. When I asked a Brahman friend why this had happened, he told me the husband was furious on discovering that he, the Brahman, had had relations with the wife before her marriage while on drinking sprees to distant villages with the Nāyakkar's father, and had actually visited her after marriage, "while *he* was in the *agrahāram*." "So you are really all alike," I commented. "No! That and this were quite different!" was his reply.

The teashops and coffeeshop on the main roadside were special sources of modern ferment, for they attracted bus passengers from the towns and were hotbeds of dissension. In May 1952, another incident occurred that stunned the *agrahāram*. A Kaḷḷar from Periyūr ran up a bill at the Brahman restaurant and was one day asked to pay. When he refused, promising to pay later, the Brahman slapped his face. The Kaḷḷar at once cracked the Brahman's head open with his staff and walked coolly out of the village. Streaming with blood, the Brahman was rushed by bullock cart to the Thanjāvūr hospital, and came home vowing to file a suit against his aggressor. He did not do so, however, for he was too poor to risk losing the costs. When I asked them why an intervillage fight did not ensue, the Brahmans replied gloomily that there was no longer any unity in Kumbapeṭṭai. Landless, the offended Brahman had no tenants or *paṇṇaiyāḷs* to fight on his behalf. If a battle was organized, a few Kōṉārs and Paḷḷars who served the *agrahāram* might fight for the Brahman, but the odds were that the Kaḷḷar traders and their own Paḷḷar coolies might join the enemy side, glad to defend their caste fellows and score off their rivals, the Brahmans. This event contributed to the Brahmans' decision not to hold the village festival.

## Conclusions

In 1951–2, Kumbapeṭṭai was still a largely traditional village. The village was dominated by a group of Brahman landlords and petty bourgeoisie who formed 16 percent of the population and owned and managed 60 percent of the land. The majority of the villagers were extremely poor and downtrodden semiproletarians, 73 percent of the people. Among them, 18 percent were slightly better-off tenant farmers, and the remainder, or 54 percent of the villagers, agricultural or other manual laborers. A thin stratum of middle peasants and independent traders (9 percent) divided the petty bourgeoisie from the semiproletarians. Paddy was by far the main village crop, about one-third of it being grown for subsistence and the rest for sale to urban or to export-crop producing regions of India.

The village landlowners survived and achieved a small margin of profit by severely exploiting their tenants and laborers. Although mostly poor and themselves oppressed by moneylenders and merchants, they supported the status quo and India's ruling class of big bourgeoisie and big landlords. Political divisions among the village landlords took the form of disagreements over whether to support the modern, capitalist-oriented Congress Party, or the revanchist, more "feudally" oriented Hindū Mahāsabha. Despite their poverty, it was scarcely to be expected that the landowners would support the region's radical parties, for the Communists preached land reform and the DK, anti-Brahmanism. The landlords' everyday experience was one of trying to keep down their own tenants and laborers in the lower castes.

The village world was a religious one in which the class structure was largely coterminous with socioreligious blocks of castes. The existence of castes facilitated the landlords' repression, for the numerous endogamous, ranked subgroups divided the lower orders. Mainly through belief in the divine ordination of the castes, the class structure was sanctioned by religion. The village goddess and her temple formed the central focus for landlord dominance through a traditional village judicial system and for affirming the ranking of castes through the ceremonies of the annual festival. The goddess was believed to bring natural misfortunes as punishment for rebellion against the laws of caste, and thus of class. Although they did not wholly accept all these beliefs, the semiproletarians were cowed by them and they gave the assurance of divine right to the landlords.

Constant, low-level class struggle by the middle peasants and the semiproletarians went on in the form of thefts, rebellion against the ritual hierarchy, attempts to establish sexual equality with the upper class, and above all, attempts at economic and judicial emancipation. These were all met by physical violence as well as by fines and systematic humiliations. The landlords' powers to inflict this oppression rested ultimately on their ownership of private property and on the armed might of the state that upheld it. When necessary, these small village landlords used their ties – often kinship ties – to the police, lawyers, and a variety of government servants to uphold their dominance. At the same time, class struggle was abated by cross-cutting loyalties to the village in its opposition to other villages, by the kinship involvement of each microcaste in its own wider endogamous subcaste, and by small segmentary disputes within each class between lineages or streets.

For at least 100 years, however, the class structure had been increasingly disturbed and the traditional landlords had been very gradually losing their dominance. Among the causes of this change were the legal abolition of slavery; bankruptcies among the landlords; the growing power, wealth, and absentee landownership of urban merchants; the departure of many Brahmans to urban salary work; the growth of tenant farming; the emergence of a thin layer of local traders and middle peasants; the loss of hereditary ties between laborers and their erstwhile masters; and the marginalization of coolie workers. More recently, the anticaste propaganda of the Drāviḍa Kazhakam and the class struggles waged elsewhere in the district by the Communists had affected Kumbapeṭṭai. Underlying all these "causes" was the district's increasing involvement in the market as part of the world capitalist periphery. These strains in the class structure were manifested in disputes that the landlords could no longer settle, a gradual loosening of caste restrictions, and even direct attacks upon landlords themselves. In 1952 Communist organizing in this unsettled village seemed around the corner. It began after the destruction and hardship wrought by the cyclone, in 1953.

# PART III: KIRIPPŪR

# 18 East Thanjāvūr

In 1951 East Thanjāvūr comprised the *tālūks* of Sīrkāḷi, Māyuram, Naṉṉilam, Maṉṉārguḍi, Nāgapaṭṭaṇam, and Tirutturaipūṇḍi; West Thanjāvūr, those of Kumbakōṇam, Pāpaṉāsam, Thanjāvūr, Paṭṭukkoṭṭai, and Arantāngi.

From its inception in the 1930s until the present, the Communist movement in the countryside has been far more prominent in East Thanjāvūr than in the west. In 1951, Nāgapaṭṭaṇam *tālūk* was the center of the movement, with Naṉṉilam and northern Maṉṉārguḍi the next most prominent areas, and Sīrkāḷi, Māyuram, and northern Turuttaraipūṇḍi peripheral regions. These areas comprised the eastern region of the old delta. The movement was much weaker in the western part of the old delta (Kumbakōṇam, Pāpaṉāsam, and the northern part of Thanjāvūr *tālūk*) and almost nonexistent in the dry and new delta areas of south Thanjāvūr, south Maṉṉārguḍi, Paṭṭukkoṭṭai, and Arantāngi, and in the southern salt swamp of Tirutturaipūṇḍi.

Historical circumstances and local leadership had played a role in this development. Communist organizing among poor tenants and agricultural laborers began with conferences in 1938 at Kīlvelur and Nāgapaṭṭaṇam, and the movement remained strongest in that area subsequently. Nevertheless, the success of Communist organizing in the villages of East Thanjāvūr undoubtedly was influenced by ecological and socioeconomic factors.

In a valuable article, André Béteille has argued that the Communist movement in Thanjāvūr has been strongest in areas where the landless or near-landless agricultural workforce is most numerous and most homogeneous with respect to both caste and class.[1] Citing figures from the 1961 census, Béteille shows that agricultural laborers generally formed a higher percentage of the rural agricultural workforce in the eastern *tālūks,* and that Harijans (Ādi Drāviḍas) formed a higher percentage of the agricultural laborers there than in the west and southwest. Tables 18.1 and 18.2 reproduce these figures, but divide the *tālūks* into eastern, western, and southwest regions. Table 18.3 presents similar information for 1951, providing figures for the total population dependent on agriculture and agricultural labor, and for the percentage of Harijans in the total rural population in each *tālūk*.

These tables may be compared with Tables 5.10, 5.13, and 5.24, which present the percentages of Harijans (Scheduled Castes) and agricultural labor-

Table 18.1. *Agricultural laborers in the rural agricultural workforce in the* tālūks *of Thanjāvūr district, 1961*

| *Tālūk* | Total workers in agriculture | Agricultural laborers | % of agricultural labor in total agricultural workforce |
|---|---|---|---|
| *Eastern region of old delta* | | | |
| Nāgapaṭṭanam | 61,534 | 42,828 | 69.59 |
| Naṉṉilam | 80,225 | 53,414 | 66.58 |
| Sīrkāḻi | 49,104 | 29,758 | 60.60 |
| Māyuram | 86,110 | 51,369 | 59.66 |
| Tirutturaipūṇḍi | 85,825 | 43,808 | 51.04 |
| Maṉṉarguḍi | 81,053 | 39,057 | 48.19 |
| Subtotal | 443,851 | 260,234 | 58.63 |
| *Western region of old delta* | | | |
| Pāpaṉāsam | 63,869 | 36,089 | 56.50 |
| Kumbakōṇam | 64,740 | 34,379 | 53.13 |
| Thanjāvūr | 78,261 | 34,823 | 44.49 |
| Subtotal | 206,870 | 105,291 | 50.90 |
| *Southwestern region of new delta and uplands* | | | |
| Paṭṭukkoṭṭai | 107,570 | 35,953 | 33.42 |
| Orathanāḍ | 86,247 | 19,718 | 22.86 |
| Arantāngi | 63,164 | 7,839 | 12.41 |
| Subtotal | 256,981 | 63,510 | 24.71 |
| District total | 907,702 | 429,035 | 47.27 |

*Source: Census of India, 1961, District Census Handbook, Thanjāvūr,* Vol. 1, Table BIII, Part B.

ers in the *total* population and/or the total workforce in 1951, 1961, and 1971.

It is clear from these tables that agricultural laborers were indeed more prominent in the eastern than the western *tālūks* in all three decades, and that Harijans were more prominent among the agricultural laborers. Furthermore, agricultural laborers and Harijans were least prominent in the southwestern *tālūks*.

The tables would be still more revealing if they separated the predominantly dry areas and the new delta regions from the old delta regions in Thanjāvūr and

Table 18.2. *Percentage of Harijans among rural agricultural laborers in the* tālūks *of Thanjāvūr district, 1961*

| *Tālūk* | Agricultural laborers: In rural population | Agricultural laborers: Among Harijans | Percentage of Harijans among agricultural laborers |
|---|---|---|---|
| *Eastern region of old delta* | | | |
| Nāgapaṭṭanam | 42,828 | 35,263 | 82.34 |
| Sīrkāḷi | 29,758 | 21,800 | 73.26 |
| Nannilam | 53,414 | 37,195 | 69.64 |
| Tirutturaipūṇḍi | 43,808 | 30,197 | 68.93 |
| Māyuram | 51,369 | 34,601 | 67.29 |
| Mannarguḍi | 39,057 | 25,499 | 65.29 |
| Subtotal | 260,234 | 184,555 | 70.91 |
| *Western region of old delta* | | | |
| Kumbakōṇam | 34,379 | 21,947 | 63.84 |
| Pāpanāsam | 36,089 | 23,106 | 64.03 |
| Thanjāvūr | 34,823 | 17,649 | 50.58 |
| Subtotal | 105,291 | 62,702 | 59.55 |
| *Southwestern region of new delta and uplands* | | | |
| Orathanāḍ | 19,718 | 6,720 | 34.08 |
| Arantāngi | 7,839 | 2,155 | 27.49 |
| Paṭṭukkoṭṭai | 35,953 | 9,771 | 27.18 |
| Subtotal | 63,510 | 18,646 | 29.36 |
| District total | 429,035 | 265,903 | 61.98 |

*Source: Census of India, 1961, District Census Handbook, Thanjāvūr,* Vol. 1, Part B.

Mannārguḍi *tālūks*, and if they separated the southern, mainly scrub area and salt swamp of Tirutturaipūṇḍi from the northern, mainly irrigated region. In short, part of Thanjāvūr and Mannārguḍi should fall in the southwest region, whereas southern Tirutturaipūṇḍi should be separately considered. As they stand, however, the tables are revealing.

I agree with Béteille that the prominence of agricultural laborers and Harijans is probably the central factor contributing to the strength of the Communist movement in East Thanjāvūr. Although the movement has espoused the cause of

Table 18.3. *Percentage of agricultural labor population in the total agriculturally dependent population, and of Harijans in the total rural population, in the* tālūks *of Thanjāvūr district, 1951*

| *Tālūk* | Agriculturally dependent population (1) | Agriculture labor population (2) | % of (2) in (1) | % of Harijans in total rural population |
|---|---|---|---|---|
| *Eastern region of old delta* | | | | |
| Nāgapaṭṭanam | 143,846 | 74,092 | 51.87 | 33.82 |
| Nannilam | 184,209 | 85,201 | 46.25 | 30.52 |
| Sīrkāḷi | 115,667 | 47,546 | 41.11 | 37.81 |
| Māyuram | 214,071 | 83,423 | 38.97 | 28.51 |
| Mannarguḍi | 188,061 | 70,542 | 37.50 | 28.55 |
| Tirutturaipūṇḍi | 195,429 | 65,123 | 33.32 | 30.74 |
| Subtotal | 1,041,283 | 425,909 | 40.90 | 31.11 |
| *Western region of old delta* | | | | |
| Pāpanāsam | 161,287 | 67,851 | 42.07 | 25.56 |
| Kumbakōṇam | 184,601 | 71,185 | 38.56 | 22.76 |
| Thanjāvūr | 243,965 | 75,847 | 31.10 | 22.83 |
| Subtotal | 598,753 | 214,883 | 36.44 | 25.54 |
| *Southwestern region of new delta and uplands* | | | | |
| Paṭṭukkoṭṭai | 341,538 | 65,557 | 19.19 | 14.21 |
| Arantāngi | 116,330 | 11,040 | 9.49 | 12.52 |
| Subtotal | 457,877 | 76,597 | 16.73 | 13.76 |
| District total | 2,088,913 | 717,389 | 34.34 | 25.35 |

*Source: Census of India, 1951, District Census Handbook, Thanjāvūr,* Vol. 1, p. 27.

tenant cultivators and small owners as well as agricultural laborers and has tried to attract supporters from every caste and religious group, its main following in Thanjāvūr has always been drawn from Harijan agricultural laborers.

To a considerable extent, the distribution of agricultural laborers and Harijans is explained by my hypothesis in Chapter 5. Both tend to be more prominent in areas of more widespread irrigation and more extensive paddy cultivation. Tables 5.10, 5.11, and 5.12 confirm these hypotheses, showing strong and

Table 18.4. *Percentage of net irrigated land in total geographical area in western, eastern, and southern regions and percentages of agricultural laborers and Harijans in the agricultural population and the total rural population, Thanjāvūr district, 1951*

| Region | Total area (Acres) (1) | Net irrigated area (Acres) (2) | (2) as % of (1) | Agricultural labor in agricultural population | Harijans in rural population |
|---|---|---|---|---|---|
| *Eastern old delta* (Sīrkāli, Māyuram, Nāgapaṭṭanam, Naṉṉilam, and Maṉṉarguḍi) | 822,720 | 580,693 | 70.58 | 40.94 | 31.19 |
| *Western old delta* (Kumbakōṇam, Pāpaṉāsam, and Thanjāvūr) | 550,976 | 325,829 | 59.13 | 36.44 | 23.54 |
| *Southern region* (Paṭṭukkoṭṭai, Arantāngi, and Tirutturaipūṇḍi) | 1,018,880 | 250,509 | 24.59 | 21.69 | 18.81 |

*Source: Census of India, 1951. District Census Handbook,* Thanjāvūr, Vol. 1.

significant correlations for 1951 between the percentages of net irrigated land and gross paddy land in the total geographical area on the one hand, and of agricultural laborers and Harijans in the total population on the other hand.

Table 5.10 especially differentiates the southwest *tālūks* of Paṭṭukkoṭṭai and Arantāngi from all the *tālūks* of the old delta, both west and east. In 1951 these *tālūks*, together with south Thanjāvūr and south Maṉṉārguḍi, were partly irrigated from the Grand Anicut and Vadavar Canals (the new delta), completed in 1934, and partly irrigated from the Grand Anicut and Vadavar Canals (the new delta), completed in 1934, and partly from tanks and wells, but productivity was lower than in the old delta and gardens and scrub still covered large areas. Table 5.10 further shows that the rainfall in Paṭṭukkoṭṭai, Thanjāvūr and Arantāngi *tālūks* was lower than in the old delta *tālūks*, making tank and well irrigation difficult.

Table 18.4 highlights these contrasts, showing the areas and percentages of net irrigated land to total geographical area in the eastern, western, and southern regions in 1951, together with the percentages of agricultural laborers in the agricultural workforce and Harijans in the rural population. In Table 18.4 Tirutturaipūṇḍi has been placed in the southern region along with Paṭṭukkoṭṭai

Table 18.5. *Gross paddy acreages as percentage of total geographical areas in eastern, western, and southern regions, Thanjāvūr district, 1951*

| Region | Total area (Acres) (1) | Gross paddy acreage (2) | (2) as % of (1) |
|---|---|---|---|
| Eastern old delta[a] | 822,720 | 588,400 | 71.52 |
| Western old delta[b] | 550,976 | 369,300 | 67.70 |
| Southern region[c] | 1,018,880 | 389,200 | 38.20 |

[a]Sīrkāli, Māyuram, Nāgapaṭṭanam, Naṉṉilam, and Maṉṉārguḍi
[b]Kumbakōṇam, Pāpaṉāsam, and Thanjāvūr
[c]Paṭṭukkoṭṭai, Arantāngi, and Tirutturaipūṇḍi
*Source: Census of India, 1951. District Census Handbook,* Thanjāvūr, Vol. 1.

and Arantāngi, for most of the *tālūk* was scrub or salt swamp, and a substantial part of the population was not engaged in agriculture.

Unfortunately, figures for net as distinct from gross paddy cultivation are not available for either 1951 or 1961, so that we cannot compare the net paddy areas as percentages of the total geographical areas for the three regions. If we could, we would probably have a result very similar to that for irrigation in Table 18.4, because the great bulk of the irrigated area in Thanjāvūr was used for paddy. Table 18.5 shows that if we take the *gross* paddy areas for 1951 (that is, the total acreage cultivated in the course of a year, doubling the acreages under double cropping) as percentages of the total geographical areas, the southwest region again lags behind with 38.2 percent, the eastern old delta tops the list with 71.52 percent, and the western old delta falls slightly behind it with 67.7 percent. This is so even though, in 1951, double cropping of paddy was far more prevalent in Kumbakōṇam, Papaṉāsam, and north Thanjāvūr than in the eastern delta.

Table 18.6 further confirms the predominance of paddy cultivation in the eastern old delta in 1951, giving the gross paddy acreage as a percentage of the gross acreage for all field crops (orchard crops are omitted, the figures being unavailable). In Table 18.6, Tirutturaipūṇḍi has been included with the eastern delta *tālūks,* because the salt swamp is not relevant to this measurement. (The field acreage lies largely in the northern half of the *tālūk*, where Communist support was already prevalent among the laborers in 1951). Here again, the eastern region tops the list with 91.87 percent; indeed, Nāgapaṭṭaṇam, Maṉṉārguḍi, and Tirutturaipūṇḍi actually had 97.23 percent, 96.99 percent and 97.80 percent respectively of their gross field acreages under paddy.

The southwest region, however, also had a higher percentage of its gross field acreage under paddy than did the western old delta. This was undoubtedly because as much as 86.9 percent of the southwest region's gross field acreage

Table 18.6. *Gross paddy acreages as percentage of gross field crop acreage in eastern, western, and southern regions, Thanjāvūr district, 1951*

| Region | Gross sown acres (1) | Gross paddy acreage (2) | (2) as % of (1) |
|---|---|---|---|
| Eastern old delta[a] | 800,000 | 735,000 | 91.87 |
| Western old delta[b] | 476,200 | 372,500 | 78.22 |
| Southern new delta and uplands[c] | 295,956 | 242,600 | 81.97 |

[a]Sīrkāli, Māyuram, Mannārguḍi, Nāgapaṭṭanam, Nannilam, and Tirutturaipūṇḍi
[b]Kumbakōṇam, Pāpanāsam, and Thanjāvūr
[c]Paṭṭukkoṭṭai and Arantāngi

was irrigated in 1951 as a result of the development of the Grand Anicut and Vadavar Canals in 1934. Because the rainfall was low and the irrigation in most places inadequate for more than one crop per year, most farmers evidently preferred to grow a single, long duration crop of paddy rather than to diversify their crops. The possibility of exporting surplus paddy to obtain cash for revenue and other payments was also an incentive.

In 1931, however, before the new delta was developed, the southwest region had only 20.41 percent of its gross field acreage irrigated from tanks and wells, and only 21.33 percent of it under paddy. Although the wet paddy acreage increased so dramatically between 1931 and 1951, agricultural laborers and their dependents increased more slowly, and in 1951 were still only 16.72 percent of the total agricultural population (Table 18.3). By 1961, however, agricultural laborers were 24.71 percent of the total agricultural workforce in this region, and by 1971, they were 38.33 percent (see Tables 5.13 and 5.16). The fact that the small size of the agricultural labor force did not "fit" the high percentages of irrigated and paddy land in the gross field acreage in the southwest region in 1951 was thus evidently because of the recency of wet paddy cultivation in that region. In the old delta, by contrast, the eastern region, with its higher percentages of irrigation and paddy in the gross field acreage, had a higher concentration of agricultural laborers in 1951 than did the western region, as was hypothesized in Chapter 5.

Even so, the eastern region of the old delta has a generally lower productivity and lower value of crops per acre than the western old delta region, contrary to my hypothesis in Chapter 5. The reason was that the western region lay inland, at a slightly higher elevation on the "breast" of the Kāvēri. It had the most fertile alluvial soils, received channel water about three weeks earlier in June and July than the coastal area, continued to receive water two or three weeks later, in February and March, and had better drainage. Especially near the coast, the eastern region, or "tail end" of the delta had clayey or sandy soils, was poorly drained, and was often waterlogged. In years such as 1952, cyclonic winds and rain from the northeast monsoon in November devastated the coast and caused the sea to flow inland, destroying the *sambā* seedlings. In any case, where it was grown, the *kuruvai* crop, which had to be transplanted as late as August because of the later arrival of the channel water, was often spoiled by rain during the harvest in October and November. On the other hand, the fact that channel water became scarce by early February meant that the *sambā* harvest might suffer from lack of moisture, and made intercrops such as black and green *gram* in March and April a risky business. It was probably mainly because of the shorter growing season that a higher proportion of East Thanjāvūr's gross field acreage was under paddy than was the case in the western old delta. Given the heavy rainfall in October and December and the deltaic channels, it was possible to irrigate almost the whole field acreage, but given the longer dry season from early February to August, it was difficult and often unprofitable to grow subsidiary crops, or, in most fields, to grow more than one paddy crop.

A further reason for the almost exclusive concentration on paddy in the eastern delta may have been that during the nineteenth and early twentieth centuries paddy was largely exported by sea from this region to Ceylon and Malaya. Steamers collected it at Nāgapaṭṭaṇam and small boats sailed from every tiny port. In 1951, considerable quantities of paddy were still being exported in local craft to Ceylon and to other regions of India, although Nāgapaṭṭaṇam was no longer a major port.

Thus, although my hypothesis that more extensive irrigation and paddy cultivation tend to produce higher productivity and a higher value per acre applies to Tamiḷ Nāḍu as a whole, it does not hold in the comparison of the western and eastern old delta of Thanjāvūr for special, local reasons.

At the same time, the greater extent of irrigation and paddy cultivation in the eastern old delta *was* accompanied by higher percentages of agricultural laborers and Harijans, as I predicted in Chapter 5. One reason for this may have been that irrigation and paddy cultivation were traditionally the special work of agricultural slaves, so that these were more numerous where paddy cultivation was found almost exclusively.

A further reason may lie in the dislocation of the population during and after the Mysorean invasion of 1781–4. The invasion chiefly devastated the northwestern *tālūks* of Thanjāvūr, Kumbakōṇam, and Papaṉāsam. Twelve thousand Paṟayars and Paḷḷars were deported, and many more thousands fled or were killed. After the invasion and the reconquest, as we have seen, the Maratha government brought in several thousand Non-Brahman *porakuḍis* from other districts. Although some Ādi Drāviḍa slaves returned, they remained much fewer in 1799 than they had been in 1781. It is probable that the smaller proportion of Harijans in northwest than in East Thanjāvūr results at least partly from Haidar Āli's visitation.

The relative proportions of tenants and landowners, as well as of agricultural laborers, may have been relevant to the success of the Communist movement. Table 18.7 gives the numbers and percentages of landowners, tenants, and agricultural laborers and their respective dependents in the total agricultural population in 1951. Table 18.8 gives the numbers and percentages of the three categories in the actual agricultural workforce in 1961. In 1951, the southwest region had a very high percentage of landowners (mainly peasant cultivators), and low percentages both of tenants and laborers, a situation least conducive to agrarian class conflict. The western old delta region had a lower percentage of owners, but fairly even percentages of tenants and laborers. The situation here is not entirely clear because we do not know what proportions of the tenants were noncultivating and/or relatively prosperous, and what proportion was poor cultivators. Even so, both figures and observations suggest that the semiproletariat in the western delta was relatively evenly divided among tenant cultivators and laborers. The eastern delta region had the smallest percentage of owners and a more uneven balance between tenants and laborers. This was especially true in Nāgapaṭṭaṇam, the center of the Communist movement, where tenants formed only 11 percent of the agricultural workforce and laborers, 52 percent.

In 1961 the situation in the eastern region was still more conducive to class struggle, with only 21 percent of the agricultural workforce represented by landowners, only 21 percent by tenants, and 58 percent by laborers (Table 18.8). In both decades, therefore, a large class of laborers faced a small class of owners, with relatively few tenants as intermediaries; this structure had become still more polarized by 1971. In the other two regions the percentages of laborers had increased by 1961, especially in the western delta, but the percentage of tenants had also increased in the southwest and had remained roughly stationary in the western delta.

It is true that by 1961 the situation in the western delta was apparently conducive to class struggle, with 51 percent of the agricultural workforce represented by laborers. This was even more true by 1971, when the agricultural laborers reached 62 percent, as against 67 percent in the eastern region and about 38 percent in the southwest (see Table 5.16). A problem therefore arises as to why the Communist movement has not been more successful in the western delta in the 1960s and 1970s. This problem will be discussed in a subsequent volume; clearly, something more than class percentages is at issue. Nevertheless, the *relative* strength of the three strata in the three regions remained most favorable to class struggle in the eastern delta throughout the period.

A further factor, mentioned by both Béteille and K. C. Alexander,[2] is that large private estates have traditionally been more prevalent in East Thanjāvūr than in the western delta or the southwest; so have estates (often large) held as trusts by temples, monasteries, or charitable establishments.

Table 18.9 gives some indication of the greater prevalence of large private estates in East Thanjāvūr by quoting figures for the numbers of owners owning more than 7.5 "standard acres" in each region in 1969. The "standard acre" measure is an effort to evaluate different qualities of land for the purposes of land

Table 18.7. *Landowners, tenants, and agricultural laborers and their dependents as percentages of the total agricultural population in the* tālūks *of eastern, western and southwest regions, Thanjāvūr district, 1951*

| *Tālūk* | Total agricultural population (1) | Landowners (2) | (2) as % of (1) | Tenants (3) | (3) as % of (1) | Agricultural labor (4) | (4) as % of (1) |
|---|---|---|---|---|---|---|---|
| *Eastern old delta* | | | | | | | |
| Nāgapaṭṭaṇam | 143,846 | 54,003 | 37.81 | 15,751 | 11.03 | 74,092 | 51.87 |
| Nannilam | 184,209 | 57,996 | 31.48 | 41,012 | 22.26 | 85,201 | 46.25 |
| Sīrkāli | 115,667 | 28,837 | 24.93 | 39,284 | 33.96 | 47,546 | 41.11 |
| Māyuram | 214,071 | 62,344 | 29.12 | 68,304 | 31.91 | 83,423 | 38.97 |
| Mannārguḍi | 188,061 | 80,599 | 42.86 | 36,938 | 19.64 | 70,524 | 37.50 |
| Tirutturaipūṇḍi | 195,429 | 95,657 | 48.95 | 34,649 | 17.73 | 65,123 | 33.32 |
| Subtotal | 1,041,283 | 379,436 | 36.44 | 235,938 | 22.66 | 425,909 | 40.90 |
| *Western old delta* | | | | | | | |
| Pāpanāsam | 161,287 | 48,517 | 30.08 | 44,919 | 27.85 | 67,851 | 42.07 |
| Kumbakōṇam | 184,601 | 49,837 | 27.00 | 63,579 | 34.44 | 71,185 | 38.56 |
| Thanjāvūr | 243,865 | 128,635 | 52.75 | 39,383 | 30.62 | 75,847 | 31.10 |
| Subtotal | 589,753 | 226,989 | 38.49 | 147,881 | 25.08 | 214,883 | 36.44 |
| *Southwest new delta and uplands* | | | | | | | |
| Paṭṭukkoṭṭai | 341,538 | 241,760 | 70.79 | 34,221 | 10.02 | 65,557 | 19.19 |
| Arantāngi | 116,339 | 59,776 | 51.38 | 45,523 | 39.13 | 11,040 | 9.49 |
| Subtotal | 457,877 | 301,536 | 65.85 | 79,744 | 17.42 | 76,597 | 16.73 |
| District total | 2,088,913 | 907,961 | 43.47 | 463,563 | 22.19 | 717,389 | 34.34 |

*Source: Census of India, 1951. District Census Handbook, Thanjāvūr,* Vol. 1, p. 27.

Table 18.8. *Landowners, tenants, and agricultural laborers as percentages of the agricultural workforce in the* tālūks *of Thanjāvūr district, 1961*

| *Tālūk* | Total agricultural workforce (1) | Landowners (2) | (2) as % of (1) | Tenants (3) | (3) as % of (1) | Agricultural labor (4) | (4) as % of (1) |
|---|---|---|---|---|---|---|---|
| *Eastern old delta* | | | | | | | |
| Nāgapaṭṭaṇam | 63,615 | 10,140 | 15.94 | 9,402 | 14.78 | 44,073 | 69.28 |
| Nan̲n̲ilam | 82,389 | 14,703 | 17.85 | 12,820 | 15.56 | 54,866 | 66.59 |
| Sīrkāli | 52,501 | 9,912 | 18.88 | 10,694 | 20.37 | 31,895 | 60.75 |
| Māyuram | 88,540 | 17,712 | 20.00 | 18,177 | 20.53 | 52,651 | 59.47 |
| Man̲n̲ārguḍi | 84,324 | 22,112 | 26.22 | 21,309 | 25.27 | 40,903 | 48.51 |
| Tirutturaipūṇḍi | 87,009 | 21,833 | 24.26 | 22,907 | 25.45 | 42,269 | 50.29 |
| Subtotal | 458,378 | 96,412 | 21.03 | 95,309 | 20.79 | 266,657 | 58.18 |
| *Western old delta* | | | | | | | |
| Pāpan̲āsam | 66,736 | 14,449 | 21.65 | 14,588 | 21.86 | 37,699 | 54.59 |
| Kumbakōṇam | 68,461 | 15,890 | 23.21 | 16,266 | 23.76 | 36,305 | 53.03 |
| Thanjāvūr | 84,198 | 22,628 | 26.87 | 23,761 | 28.22 | 37,809 | 44.90 |
| Subtotal | 219,395 | 52,967 | 24.14 | 54,615 | 24.89 | 111,813 | 50.97 |
| *Southwest new delta and uplands* | | | | | | | |
| Paṭṭukkoṭṭai | 109,618 | 34,349 | 31.34 | 38,498 | 35.12 | 36,771 | 33.54 |
| Orathanāḍ | 86,433 | 59,869 | 69.27 | 6,785 | 7.85 | 19,779 | 22.88 |
| Arantāngi | 63,719 | 34,354 | 59.92 | 21,410 | 33.60 | 7,955 | 12.48 |
| Subtotal | 259,770 | 128,572 | 49.50 | 66,693 | 25.67 | 64,505 | 24.83 |
| District total | 937,543 | 277,951 | 29.65 | 216,617 | 23.10 | 442,975 | 47.25 |

*Source: Census of India, 1961. District Census Handbook, Thanjāvūr,* Vol. 1, Part B, Table BIII.

Table 18.9. *Land holdings assessed under the agricultural income tax act in the three regions, Thanjāvūr district, 1969*

| Region | 7.5 to 12 standard acres | 12 to 20 standard acres | Above 20 standard acres |
|---|---|---|---|
| Eastern (including Tirutturaipūṇḍi) | 4,150 | 3,989 | 3,542 |
| Western delta | 2,848 | 1,407 | 1,180 |
| Southwest | 864 | 693 | 348 |
| Total | 7,498 | 6,089 | 4,980 |

*Source:* S. Ganapatia Pillai. *Report of the Commission of Enquiry on the Agrarian Labour Problems of East Thanjāvūr District, Government of Tamiḷ Nāḍu, Madras, 1969.* Quoted in K. C. Alexander, *Agrarian Tension in Thanjāvūr,* Hyderabad: National Institute of Community Development, 1975, p. 12.

reform and of agricultural income tax; 7.5 "standard acres" represent modest comfort. Table 18.9 shows that holdings of 7.5 to 12 "standard acres" were much more prevalent in East Thanjāvūr than in the western delta and southwest region, which together comprise a roughly comparable area. Furthermore, the disparity between the eastern and western regions is greater in the case of estates of twelve to twenty "standard acres," and much greater in the case of estates of over twenty acres. The fact that the southwest region with its low productivity had the fewest of these estates reflects the much weaker stratification of that region. What is not shown in Table 18.9 is that East Thanjāvūr also had a larger number of estates of several hundred, or even several thousand acres, some of which survived the Land Ceiling Acts of the 1960s and 1970s with relatively little depletion.

Table 18.10 gives figures for the numbers of temple, monastic, or charitable estates (public trusts) in the three regions in 1969. Again, the eastern region far surpasses the western, and the western delta, the southwest region. Both large private estates and public trusts often employed large numbers of agricultural laborers, who were drawn together in a common fate and could be fairly easily organized by the Communists. Such estates dramatized the extremes of wealth and poverty, especially in East Thanjāvūr.

A final economic factor is that my own research suggests a traditionally lower level of living for agricultural laborers in East than in West Thanjāvūr and greater relative deprivation during the 1940s. As we saw in Chapter 14, married couples among the *paṇṇaiyāḷs* and regular coolies in Kumbapeṭṭai earned between about forty-three and fifty-five *kalams* a year in 1951; this also seemed true of neighboring villages. In Nāgapaṭṭaṇam *tālūk,* by contrast, *paṇṇaiyāḷ* and coolie couples seldom earned more than forty to forty-five *kalams* and sometimes as

Table 18.10. *Lands held by public trusts in the three regions, Thanjāvūr district, 1969*

| Region | Trusts | Extent of land (Acres) |
|---|---|---|
| Eastern (including Tirutturaipūṇḍi) | 2,862 | 132,631.65 |
| Western delta | 697 | 36,843.20 |
| Southwest | 125 | 28,795.74 |
| Total | 3,666 | 198,270.59 |

*Source: Report of the Special Deputy Collector, Public Trusts, Thanjāvūr, 1969, Government of Tamiḷ Nāḍu, Madras,* pp. 4–5. Quoted in K. C. Alexander, *Agrarian Tension in Thanjāvūr,* p. 13.

little as thirty. The circumstances of laborers also seemed to have deteriorated more sharply in the eastern than the western delta during World War II and in the drought years of 1946–51. Communist organizers acknowledged that the strike of 1948 and the agitations leading to the Tanjore Tenants' and Paṇṇaiyāḷs' Act were influenced by hardship among the tenants and laborers resulting from drought. Its effects were especially marked in East Thanjāvūr because channel water was less plentiful there than in the western delta and arrived for a shorter period each year.

Aside from these economic and caste factors, I was struck by a different outlook among the people of East Thanjāvūr by comparison with those of the western old delta, both in 1951 and in 1976. It seemed that caste restrictions were less stringent, religious beliefs less confining, and Brahmans less wealthy and powerful in the East than in the western old delta.

The sense of greater freedom and secularism may have been even stronger in the southwest region, where Brahmans formed only 1.92 percent of the population, but I did not stay there long enough to find out. In East Thanjāvūr, *given* the polarization of classes, it seemed to me that the less orthodox atmosphere was conducive to radical organizing.

To some extent, this difference may have been a result rather than a cause of Communist initiatives, for the movement was already powerful by 1951. A more secular worldview seemed, however, to be widespread among the non-Communists and the upper-caste people of East Thanjāvūr, as well as among the Harijan laborers.

East Thanjāvūr's history is probably relevant to this difference. European trading companies settled in the east coast ports from 1612, and Arabs, Chinese, Southeast Asians, and other nationalities had long been resident there. The larger numbers of Muslims and Christians in the coastal area reflect the greater foreign influence. The European companies were early given control of groups of villages round their ports. In the 1760s, Tuljāji Mahārāja gave the British East India Company 277 villages near the port of Nāgore near Nāgapaṭṭaṇam; Kirippūr was probably among them. The company reorganized the estates under its private control and introduced commercial farming earlier than was common in other regions. Nāgapaṭṭaṇam port passed into British control in 1781. After the conquest, it was the district capital and the center of British influence until 1845; the collector then moved to Tranquēbār until 1861, and then to Thanjāvūr.

Above all, the nineteenth and twentieth centuries saw the emigration overseas of much larger numbers from the east coast *tālūks* than from the western old delta as indentured laborers and, later, as traders or free laborers. Every village of East Thanjāvūr has long had a number of returned migrants among the lower-ranking Non-Brahmans and the Harijans, with a wider experience of the world and much less regard for caste customs than is customary in West Thanjāvūr. It is probable that by 1951, commercial agriculture had upset traditional landownership among the castes more drastically in East than in West Thanjāvūr. Although none of these influences produced Communism, they gave the eastern delta a more cosmopolitan worldview and a greater openness to social change, as well as indirectly helping to polarize its class structure.

# 19 The Village

In describing Kirippūr, my second village, I shall omit much of the detail that was presented for Kumbapeṭṭai. My chief aim is to highlight similarities and differences between the two villages and the relationships among the differences. I shall also give some account of how the Communist movement had taken hold and was operating in this East Thanjāvūr village in 1952.

Kirrippūr lay in Nāgapaṭṭaṇam *tālūk*, two miles south of the Thanjāvūr-Nāgapaṭṭaṇam road and railway and a few miles from both Nāgapaṭṭaṇam and Tiruvārūr towns (see Maps 2 and 6). A cart road led east out of the village to join the main paved road and bus route south to Tirutturaipūṇḍi, and a tiny portion of the main road passed through the village at its southeast corner. Villages to the north and west of Kirippūr were accessible only by narrow raised footpaths across the paddy fields. On the south side, the village was bounded by the River Kaduvaiyār, a branch of the Ōḍumbōkkiyar and ultimately of the Vettār and the Kāvēri. For much of the year the river was too deep and swift for villagers to cross except by the main road bridge (see Map 6).

Kiruppūr was an *ūr*, or "Non-Brahman village" in contrast to Kumbapeṭṭai, which was a *grāmam*, or "Brahman village." Unlike Kumbapeṭṭai, Kirippūr's revenue village and socioeconomic community were coterminous and occupied a continuous area. In 1952, Kirippūr had not yet been organized as a *panchāyat* and had only the traditional village officers – the village headman, the accountant, and their assistants.

The villages surrounding Kirippūr were also for the most part dominated by Non-Brahmans; in Nāgapaṭṭaṇam *tālūk* as a whole only 5 percent of the people were Brahmans, the area being remote from the mainstream of the Kāvēri. South of Kirippūr across the river lay Tekkūr, a market town of about 4,000, controlled mainly by Veḷḷāḷars and Cheṭṭiars. Varying subcastes of Veḷḷāḷars held most of the land and power in the villages of Allur to the west, Patallūr to the northeast, and Vaḍakkūr to the east. Rānamangalam to the southeast had once been owned by Smārtha Brahmans of the Vāttimāḷ subcaste, but by 1952 it had passed partly to Kōṉārs and other middle-ranking castes. To the northwest lay Kuttaṉṉūr, a village owned mainly by Muslims (titled Maraikkars) and by Naidūs of Telugu origin.

Kirippūr's productivity was much lower than Kumbapeṭṭai's. In October 1952, Kirippūr had a total acreage of 652 and a population of 809, whereas Kumbapeṭṭai revenue village had 664 acres and a population of 820. Yet

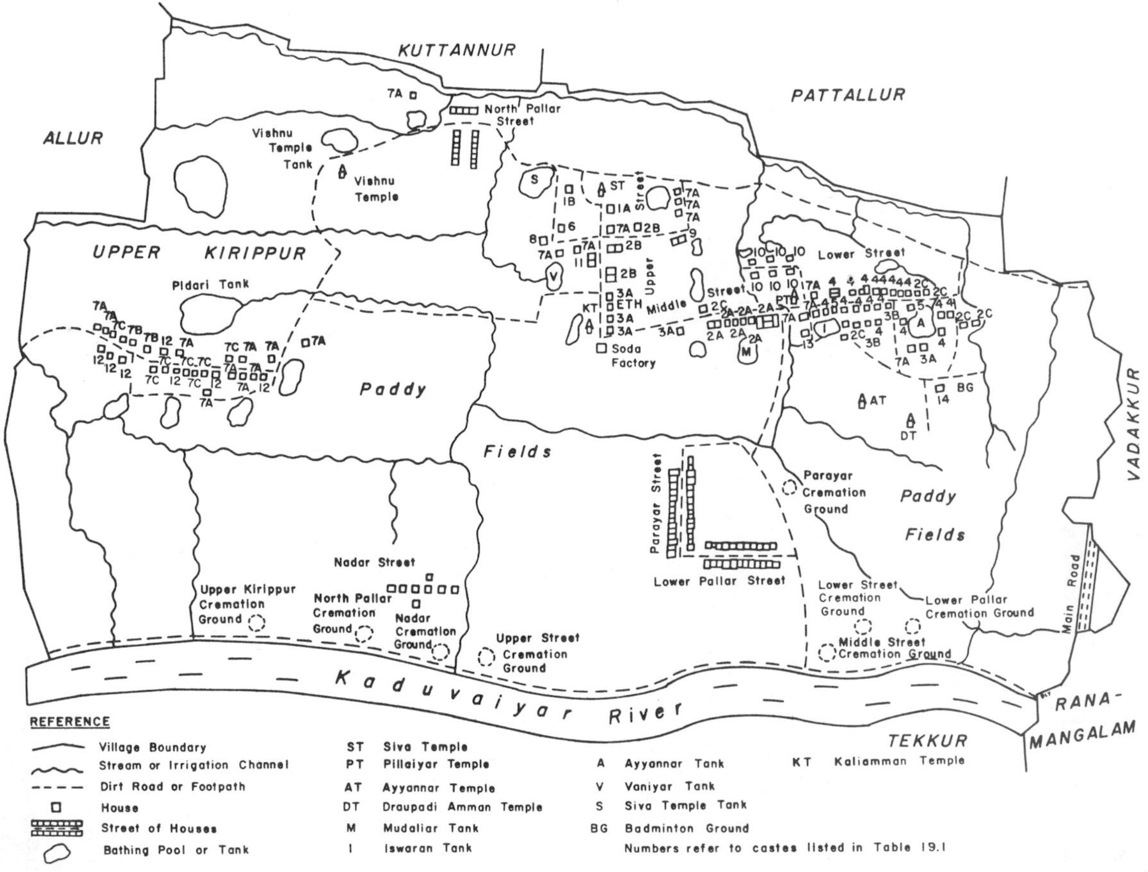


Map 6. Kirippūr village, 1952.

Kumbapeṭṭai paid about Rs. 12,000 a year as government revenue whereas Kirippūr paid approximately Rs. 4,000. This difference stemmed partly from the fact that whereas 90.5 percent of Kumbapeṭṭai revenue village's total area was cultivated for dry or wet field crops, only 77.2 percent of Kirippūr's was under field crops, the rest being house sites, orchards, channels, tanks, or scrub. Again, 91.3 percent of Kumbapeṭṭai's field area grew wet paddy, compared with 83.5 percent in Kirippūr. Most important, 94.2 percent of Kumbapeṭṭai's wet land grew two paddy crops in a year. By contrast, none of Kirippūr's wet land was registered as double cropped, although about 10 percent of it actually grew two crops in favorable years. Similarly, whereas grams were grown almost universally as "intercrops" in Kumbapeṭṭai, they were grown only sporadically in Kirippūr because the channel water stopped flowing about three weeks earlier. Finally, Kirippūr's soil was of a poorer quality than Kumbapeṭṭai's and its climate less clement. Being on the "breast" of the Kāvēri, Kumbapeṭṭai's rich alluvium gave a yield of forty-five to fifty-five *kalams* (1.3 to 1.5 metric tons) of paddy per crop acre in a favorable year. Located near the tail end of the delta, Kirippūr's soil was more clayey, and because the village was low lying it was more often water logged. In a good year the maximum yields were about thirty to forty-two *kalams* per crop acre (0.8 to 1.2 tons). During drought many fields might yield only 0.4 tons per crop acre. In a flood year, the Kaduvaiyār overflowed in November and December, the *sambā* seedlings might be washed away, and the crop almost totally destroyed. As a result, Kirippūr's wet fields sold on average for Rs. 1,500 per acre in 1952, whereas those in Kumbapeṭṭai sold for Rs. 2,400 to Rs. 4,500 per acre depending on quality.

Kirippūr did have more garden crops than Kumbapeṭṭai. The villagers produced coconuts, bananas, wild olive, gingelly, margosa and castor oils, a variety of vegetables, and in a few gardens, coffee, oranges, and lime fruits. Many peasants traded coconuts and banana leaves in Tiruvārūr, and a few by train as far as Madras.[1] Because of the greater extent of common land and scrub, Kirippūr had more goats and perhaps more cows than Kumbapeṭṭai. Goat's milk, cow's milk, and curds were traded, mainly by widows, in Kōvūr, a market village on the railway two miles north. Even so, Kirippūr's average farm production, whether calculated in cash or calories, was lower than Kumbapeṭṭai's.

The castes and subcastes of Kirippūr are listed in rough order of ritual rank in Table 19.1, the numbers corresponding to the houses on Map 6. As in Kumbapeṭṭai, most people in Kirippūr lived on a few adjacent streets (marked Upper, Middle, and Lower Streets on Map 6), with Ādi Drāviḍa colonies of former slaves to the south and north of the village proper. Kirippūr had its own Paṟayar street in addition to the two Paḷḷar streets, whereas Kumbapeṭṭai drew its Paṟayar servants from Māniyūr. In Kirippūr, a Non-Brahman "side-hamlet" called Upper Kirippūr lay about half a mile west of the main village, resembling Sheṭṭiyūr in its size and location. But whereas Sheṭṭiyūr's socioeconomic life had become almost totally separate from that of Kumbapeṭṭai proper, Upper Kirippūr's Non-Brahman tenants and owner cultivators had lived there longer and maintained closer ties with the rest of the village. The latter was sometimes referred to as Lower Kirippūr.

A comparison of Map 6 with Table 19.1 shows that, as in Kumbapeṭṭai, the chief landlord subcaste near the top of the hierarchy (the Toṇḍaimaṇḍalam Veḷḷāḷars), the Ādi Drāviḍas at the bottom, and the low-ranking Nāḍār toddy tappers, were segregated in their respective streets. In both villages, middle-ranking Non-Brahman castes, although largely separated into streets, were sufficiently close in rank to have intermingled to some extent. Altogether, Kirippūr had eight main streets or settlements in 1952 – Upper Kirippūr, Upper, Middle, and Lower streets in Lower Kirippūr, the Nāḍārs' Riverside Street, the Paṟayar Street, and the Northern and Lower Paḷḷar Streets. As was usual, their locations and composition partly reflected history and partly ongoing social relations.

Kirippūr's history is less well known than Kumbapeṭṭai's. No land records are available for 1827, and it may be that the village was not a separate entity at that date. In 1952 the village's main *grāma dēvatai* temple, dedicated to Draupadi Ammaṉ, was thought to be about 100 years old. Before that date, Kirippūr's people were fewer and had taken part in the annual village temple festival in Allūr. It is therefore possible that Kirippūr was once a hamlet of Allūr.

In 1952 the villagers thought that about 200 years earlier, most of Kirippūr's land and also the southern portion of Pattallūr (called Vēṭṭāmbāḍi) was owned by a family of Vāttimāḷ Smartha Brahmans related to those of Rānamangalam. A few landlord households of this subcaste occupied Upper Street, built the Siva and Vishnū temples, and continued to provide the village headman in the late nineteenth century. Branches of this Brahman family living in Rānamangalam still owned 10.3 percent of the village land in 1897 and 5.7 percent in 1952, but the last household had left Kirippūr about 1890. From this early period, there remained in Upper Street one Kurukkal Brahman household who served the Siva temple, and five patrilineally related houses of a Seiva Veḷḷāḷar subcaste[2] whose ancestors had been rich peasants owning some land and leasing more from the Brahmans. By 1952 the Seiva Veḷḷāḷar households were impoverished and owned less than one acre among them; only a large broken down joint-family house betokened their former prosperity. The Kurukkals continued to serve the Siva temple in Upper Street and the Piḷḷaiyār or Vināyakar temple in Middle Street and were paid from the temple lands.

The forebears of most of Kirippūr's Ādi Drāviḍas had been slaves of the Brahmans and Veḷḷāḷars. The Paṟayar Street and Lower Paḷḷar Street dated from the earliest known period, although the forebears of North Paḷḷar Street had arrived from Pattallūr, probably since 1890. Also of ancient vintage were the Carpenters, Goldsmiths, and Blacksmiths who lived in a separate side street near Lower Street; the Laundryworkers of Lower Street; the Nāḍār toddy tappers who rented coconut gardens by the riverside; and the Paḍaiyācchi peasants of Upper Kirippūr.

The Paḍaiyācchi peasants of Upper Kirippūr were believed to have been *vāram* tenants, perhaps even *aḍimai ālukaḷ*, of the original Brahmans. The Paḍaiyācchis of Lower Kirippūr had come later from Pattallūr; they were consid-

Table 19.1. *The castes and subcastes of Kirippūr, 1952*

| Major group | Caste | Subcaste | Traditional occupation | Households | People |
|---|---|---|---|---|---|
| *Brahman* | 1. *Brahman* | A. Bhaṭṭachār (Ayyangār) | Vaishnavite temple priest | 1 | 5 |
| | | B. *Kurukkal* | Saivite temple priest | 1 | 8 |
| *Non-Brahman* | 2. *Veḷḷālar* | A. Toṇḍaimaṇḍalam Mudaliar | Landlord, military officer | 10 | 33 |
| | | B. ''*Seiva*'' | Rich peasant | 5 | 24 |
| | | C. Chōḷiya | Rich peasant | 6 | 51 |
| | 3. Naidū | A. Kavarai | Builder | 5 | 30 |
| | | B. Poosāri | Village temple priest | 2 | 5 |
| | 4. *Kaikkiḷar (Sengunda Mudaliar)* | | Weaver | 24 | 103 |
| | 5. Agambaḍiyar | | Palace servant, peasant | 1 | 5 |
| | 6. Kaḷḷar | | Peasant, cattle thief | 1 | 6 |
| | 7. *Vaṉṉiya Kula Kshattriya* | A. *Paḍaiyācchi* (2 subgroups) | Peasant | 20 | 89 |
| | | B. Vaṉṉiyar | Peasant | 3 | 11 |
| | | C. Poṟayar | Peasant | 7 | 34 |
| | 8. Muslim | | Trader | 1 | 3 |
| | 9. Kōṉār | | Cowherd | 2 | 6 |
| | 10. *Kammāḷar* | | Goldsmith, carpenter, blacksmith | 6 | 23 |
| | 11. Vāṇiyar | | Oil monger | 2 | 11 |
| | 12. *Nāḍar* | (2 subcastes) | Toddy tapper | 15 | 66 |
| | 13. *Vaṉṉār* | | Laundry worker | 1 | 6 |
| | 14. Oṭṭar | | Road maker, ditch digger | 1 | 2 |
| *Ādi* | 15. *Paḷḷar* | | Agricultural laborer | 41 | 167 |
| *Drāviḍa* | 16. *Paṟayar* | | Agricultural laborer, scavenger | 31 | 121 |
| | | Total | | 186 | 809 |

*Note:* Numbers refer to households on Map 6. Castes and subcastes believed to have been present from the founding of the village are in italics.

ered lower than those of Upper Kirippūr. The Va<u>nn</u>iyars and Po<u>r</u>ayars arrived respectively in the 1890s and early 1900s, the former from near Nāgōre and the latter from Tirutturaipūṇḍi. They ranked locally below the Paḍaiyācchis, but shared their hamlet and lived in close association with them. All the Paḍaiyācchis, Va<u>nn</u>iyars, and Po<u>r</u>ayars regarded themselves as Va<u>nn</u>iya Kuḷa Kshattriyas, but the four groups did not intermarry. The Po<u>r</u>ayars and Va<u>nn</u>iyars of Upper Kirippūr and the Paḍaiyācchis of Lower Kirippūr received food at life-crisis rites from the Upper Kirippūr Paḍaiyācchis. Otherwise, the four subcastes drank only coffee in each others' homes.

In 1952 Kirippūr had twenty-four households of Sengunda, or Kaikkiḷar (colloquially called Kekkliyar) Mudaliars, a somewhat low-ranking caste of spinners and weavers. One patrilineal group had been there from time immemorial, weaving white and colored cotton cloths for the villagers. Other households of affines had joined the original weavers in the late nineteenth and twentieth centuries, so that by 1952 this caste dominated Lower Street. Most of the families were small owner or tenant cultivators as well as artisans; the women spun and the men wove in their spare time. The Sengunda Mudaliars and the Va<u>nn</u>iya Kuḷa Kshattriyas disputed for rank and did not interdine.

The Toṇḍaimaṇḍalam Veḷḷāḷars of Middle Street were the highest ranking subcaste below the Brahmans. In 1952 the members of all their ten households were small landlords; as a group, they possessed 10.5 percent of the village land. Although by no means wealthy, their average income, landownership, education, and power were higher than those of any other group in Kirippūr. In 1897 they had owned 40.2 percent of the village land and in earlier decades perhaps more. Six of their households formed a patrilineal group of the Mēlnāḍ (up country) subcaste; at the east end of the street four households of the slightly lower-ranking Kīlnāḍ (low country) subcaste formed another group. By 1952 the two subcastes interdined and, in Kirippūr as elsewhere, had recently begun to intermarry.

The Toṇḍaimaṇḍalam Veḷḷāḷars (titled Mudaliars) outranked other Veḷḷāḷar subcastes in Thanjāvūr. They were traditionally landlords, warriors, and officials of the state class. Like the Kāraikkāṭṭ Veḷḷāḷars, they were vegetarians and some of their kinship usages resembled those of the Brahmans. They originally migrated to Thanjāvūr from Kānchipuram in Toṇḍaimaṇḍalam in Chingleput district, the heartland of the ancient Pallava kingdom. It was thought that they had arrived in the fifteenth century in the wake of the Vijayanagar conquerors. In 1952 they were especially prominent around Tiruvārūr, such great landlords as the Mudaliars of Vāḍapādimangalam and the Bāvas of Kulikkarai belonging to this subcaste. Some of the most prominent Toṇḍaimaṇḍalam Veḷḷāḷar houses were appointed as *pattakdārs* (revenue collectors with military powers) after the Mysorean invasion in the 1780s and increased their wealth by this means. One such house of the Kīlnāḍ subcaste lived in Tekkūr and was related to the Kirippūr Mudaliars. Kirippūr's old people thought that the Toṇḍaimaṇḍalam Mudaliars had come to the village about 150 to 200 years previously and acquired land through purchase or through gift by a king. It is possible that they were appointed by the Mahārāja and perhaps the East India Company after the Mysorean invasion in the mid-1780s as *pattakdārs* or as relatives and allies of the Tekkūr *pattakdārs* and that they were given, or usurped, land by this means. As late as 1976, the castes present earlier in the village regarded the Toṇḍaimaṇḍalam Mudaliars as in some sense interlopers with less claim to their land than the original Brahmans and the Seiva Veḷḷāḷars. In 1952, however, the leading Toṇḍaimaṇḍalam Mudaliar had already been village headman for the past twelve years, the post having previously been occupied by a Seiva Veḷḷāḷar and earlier, by Brahmans.

About 1860 the Toṇḍaimaṇḍalam Mudaliars had the Piḷḷaiyar stone shrine built at the east end of their street. This temple became the shrine of the Mudaliars, its ceremonies being carried out by the Kurukkal. By 1952, however, the people of Upper and Lower Streets also worshipped there on special occasions, and helped the impoverished Mudaliars with its upkeep.

When they came to Kirippūr the Toṇḍaimaṇḍalam Mudaliars brought with them a family of Chōḷiya (meat-eating) Veḷḷāḷar peasants and servants. Their descendants lived in Middle Street across the road from the Mudaliars. Another Chōḷiya Veḷḷāḷar peasant family, unrelated to the first and of a different subcaste, had come to Kirippūr in the 1870s and had branched into three households in Lower Street by 1952. A third, unrelated family of Chōḷiya Veḷḷāḷars arrived about 1880. These three groups did not intermarry in Kirippūr but they interdined and one or two marriages had occurred between them in other villages. An Agambaḍiyar peasant family had arrived about 1930; they, too, had settled in Lower Street.

About 1857 a family of stonemasons and brickbuilders came to Kirippūr from Nāgapaṭṭaṇam, perhaps to build houses for the growing numbers of landlords in Middle Street. This family belonged to the middle-ranking Kavarai Naidū caste of builders, traders, and peasants of Telugu origin. The family expanded and brought affines to live near them, acquired land, and in 1952 comprised five households.

About 1890 a family of Vaishnavite Brahman priests of the Bhaṭṭachār subcaste were invited to Kirippūr to make offerings in the Vishnū temple. About 1930, this family's only son became the village accountant. The family gave up temple service and in 1952 called themselves Ayyangārs, refusing to admit that they were Bhaṭṭachārs of slightly lower rank. The accountant lived with his family in Upper Street in a house rented from the village headman.

The Vāṇiyars (oilmongers) of Upper Street were more recent comers. About 1925 the father of the two brother households had arrived from a village two miles away.

Five families of other castes had come to Kirippūr shortly before 1952. The Muslim who lived off Upper Street was brought from a nearby village by the leading landlords in 1942 to serve full time as watchman of the paddy fields, the Ādi Drāviḍa watchmen having proved unsatisfactory with the rise of the Communist movement. Like the Kumbapeṭṭai Muslims, the family dressed as Non-

Brahmans and were treated good humoredly by the other castes. The Kaḷḷar had been installed as an agent in 1950 by Kirippūr's biggest absentee landlord (called Manjūr Mudaliar) to manage his land and oversee and pay his laborers. Two Kōn̲ār families of sisters, east of Upper Street, who had arrived within the previous year, were refugees from the drought in Rāmanāthapuram. The Oṭṭars, on the village border south of Lower Street, were roadmakers who had squatted in the village in the past few months and eked out a living as construction workers in Tekkūr. They were strangers to the other villagers, who knew their caste but did not know their names.

Kirippūr had a number of *grāma dēvatai* shrines. The chief village temple south of Lower Street was dedicated to Draupadi Amman̲ and had formerly had a notable festival in Panguni-Chittrai. This temple was thought to have been built about a century earlier by Kirippūr's original Veḷḷāḷars.

Other *grāma dēvatai* shrines, believed ancient in the village, existed for Ayyanār south of Lower Street, for Kāḷiyamman southwest of Upper Street, and for Manmathan and Piḍāri in Upper Kirippūr. Whereas Draupadi Amman̲ was considered responsible for the general welfare, Ayyanār specialized in the health and sickness of cattle, Kāḷiyamman in cholera, Piḍāri in women's and other diseases, and Manmathan in rain and drought. In 1952 the Naidū *poosāri* propitiated Draupadi Amman̲ and Kāḷiyamman, and a second *poosāri* from a nearby village, the other godlings. The Kāliyamman shrine, which was regarded as the special deity of the Ādi Drāviḍas, was rebuilt from a village collection in 1946; the Piḍāri shrine, by the village headman in the 1930s. But although the Draupadi Amman̲ temple and its festival were the most popular, especially for the people of Upper and Lower Street, Kirippūr had no central village temple managed by the landlords and attended by all the castes such as existed in the Ūriḍeicchiyamman temple of Kumbapeṭṭai.

Perhaps because it was near the coast, and lacked a single clearly dominant caste of landlords, Kirippūr had a more fluid migration pattern than Kumbapeṭṭai. Apart from those mentioned, three households of Por̲ayars, five of Paḍaiyacchis, five of Sengunda Mudaliars, two of Par̲ayars, and five of Paḷḷars had come to the village singly in the last twenty years from other villages of Nāgapaṭṭaṇam or Tirutturaipūṇḍi *tālūks*. Some came to join distant relatives, others alone; all were in search of work.

Kirippūr's pattern of emigration also differed from Kumbapeṭṭai's. In the latter village, as we have seen, the main emigrants were Brahmans seeking white-collar work. Kirippūr's Toṇḍaimaṇḍalam Mudaliars were less educated than the Brahmans. Only four men had temporarily left the village, one as a schoolteacher, one in the Revenue Department in Madurai, one as a landlord's agent, and one as a manager of a temple estate. Again in contrast to Kumbapeṭṭai, however, as many as thirteen middle- or low-ranking Non-Brahman men who were still living, and nine Ādi Drāviḍas had left the village temporarily for work in other areas, while six Non-Brahmans had moved permanently to mill, agricultural, or artisan jobs. Of the temporary migrants, all the Ādi Drāviḍas had gone as coolies to rubber plantations in Penang or to dock work in Rangoon or Singapore. Four Sengunda Mudaliars and one Paṟayar were also in Burma or Malaya as plantation workers or traders. Of the remaining Non-Brahman migrants, five Naidūs had white collar jobs in Thanjāvūr or neighboring districts. A toddy tapper and a carpenter were plying their traditional trades nearby, and a Vaṉṉiyar was in the army in northern India. Exactly half of Kirippūr's temporary migrants, therefore, were in Burma or Malaya.

A larger number had left the village for these areas in earlier decades. This was especially true during the depression of the 1930s, when Sengunda Mudaliars, in particular, lost most of their weaving work because of the slump in handwoven goods. In 1952, one Paṟayar and seventeen Non-Brahmans, chiefly Sengunda Mudaliars, Paḍaiyācchis, Chōḻiya Veḷḷāḷars, Nāḍārs, and Kammālars lived in Kirippūr but had worked previously in Burma or Malaya. There, they had occupied various jobs, some but not all of them caste related – rubber estate coolie, postman, painter, native doctor, palmist, shopkeeper, goldsmith, and laundryworker. Five of the Non-Brahmans, and one Paṟayar plantation worker had walked from Rangoon to India before the Japanese advance of 1942 and had then returned by train; others had fled from Malaya. The period spent abroad varied from six months to forty-eight years, the average being fourteen years. Among the Ādi Drāviḍas a larger number had died abroad than had returned; this, however, was not true of the Non-Brahmans. Similar migrations had occurred in earlier generations back to about 1850, with a larger proportion of the earlier migrants being indentured laborers.

Most of the migrants, especially the Ādi Drāvidas, returned home destitute. A few brought or sent savings, which they or their families used to buy land or to build a better house. One successful Chōḻiya Veḷḷālar who traded to Singapore had built a fine tile-roofed dwelling in Lower Street called "Malaya House," and bought several acres of land. He lived mainly in Nāgapaṭṭaṇam, where he owned a bakery, but rented his house to other Veḷḷāḷars and considered Kirippūr his home.

The migrants' long absences affected kinship and social life in the village. None had taken along wives from Kirippūr, although all were married when they left. Three had brought back Tamiḻ women born in Malaya as their second wives, but these women were ill received and after a short time two returned to Malaya with their husbands. The Non-Brahman migrants, most of whom were literate, communicated with their kin by letter or telegraph, but the Ādi Drāviḍas did not. Several Ādi Drāviḍa women in Kirippūr had husbands who had been absent for three to thirty years, with no news of their whereabouts other than that they had "gone on a ship." Most of the Non-Brahman traders came on leave about every five years, when they usually begat children. Women whose husbands were away often had sexual relations with other men, sometimes for money. If they became pregnant, they procured abortions.

In general, migrant labor had the merits of providing a substantial proportion of underemployed men with a livelihood and allowing a few families of low rank

Table 19.2. *Proportions of village land owned by the main caste groups, present and absent, Kirippūr, 1897 and 1952*

| | 1897 | | 1952 | |
|---|---|---|---|---|
| | Acres | % of total | Acres | % of total |
| *Present* | | | | |
| 1. Brahmans | 11.32 | 2.3 | 6.50 | 1.3 |
| 2. Temples | 10.34 | 2.1 | 12.85 | 2.5 |
| 3. Toṇḍaimaṇḍalam Veḷḷāḷars | 200.78 | 40.8 | 54.45 | 10.6 |
| 4. Other Non-Brahmans | 156.00 | 31.7 | 206.47 | 40.2 |
| 5. Ādi Drāviḍas | — | — | 3.16 | 0.6 |
| Subtotal | 378.44 | 76.9 | 283.43 | 55.2 |
| *Absent* | | | | |
| 1. Brahmans | 51.18 | 10.4 | 21.56 | 4.2 |
| 2. Temples | — | — | — | — |
| 3. Toṇḍaimaṇḍalam Veḷḷāḷars | — | — | — | — |
| 4. Other Non-Brahmans | — | — | 152.81 | 29.8 |
| 5. Ādi Drāviḍas | — | — | — | — |
| 6. Muslims | 62.50 | 12.7 | 52.82 | 10.2 |
| 7. Christians | — | — | 3.07 | 0.6 |
| Subtotal | 113.68 | 23.1 | 230.26 | 44.8 |
| Total | 492.12 | 100.0 | 513.69 | 100.0 |

to acquire land and greater prosperity at the expense of others of high caste. It widened the horizons of villagers, and tended to reduce the more ritualistic observances of caste rank among those who had been abroad and among their children. On the debit side it added very little wealth to the village as a whole, and tended to increase the economic insecurity and the sexual degradation of women.

The land records of 1897 and 1952 shed further light on Kirippūr's recent history. Table 19.2 shows the percentages of the village land owned by the main caste groups at these two dates. I have separated the Toṇḍaimaṇḍalam Mudaliars from the other Non-Brahman castes because they were traditionally aristocrats of the state class. Table 19.2 reflects the fact that as in Kumbapeṭṭai, the "ruling class" (in this case Brahmans and the more recent Toṇḍaimaṇḍalam Mudaliars) had lost considerable land to Muslim traders (in this case of Nāgōre and Nāgapaṭṭaṇam) during the nineteenth century, the latter having made profits through the sale of British manufactures and through the colonial trade with Burma, Ceylon, Malaya, and Singapore. By 1897 the old ruling group of Brahmans had left the village for Rānamangalam. The Toṇḍaimaṇḍalam Mudaliars owned the greatest amount of land and largely governed the village. At that date most of the Paḍaiyācchis and Nāḍārs were their *kuthakai* tenants and the Ādi

Drāviḍas their *paṇṇaiyāḷs*. The Seiva Veḷḷāḷars, however, still owned twenty-three acres, and the Kavarai Naidūs, Kaikkiḷar Mudaliars, and Paḍaiyācchis had bought or retained considerable amounts.

Although the details are unclear, it seems probable that these latter castes had all gained land directly or indirectly as a result of the colonial export trade in paddy and in handwoven cloths to Malaya. The few Paḍaiyācchis who owned land were said to have bought it out of savings from *kuthakai* cultivation and from paddy husking for the export trade. In the second half of the nineteenth century before rice mills were instituted, traders who dealt with British export firms delivered paddy to inland villages to be pounded by hand, so that the rice could be exported. Apparently, three Paḍaiyācchi families were able to buy land out of their savings from such work in the nineteenth century and to augment it in the twentieth. Similarly, half a dozen Sengunda Mudaliar families acquired land through the trade in cotton piece goods to Malaya. Some of them, and some Chōḷiya Veḷḷāḷars, increased their holdings in the twentieth century as a result of various kinds of trade or jobs in Southeast Asia. Finally, although they did not go abroad, the Kavarai Naidūs appear to have profited from constructing new buildings in the Nāgapaṭṭaṇam area, especially for Muslim and Hindū traders. A few in this caste, too, invested in land in Kirippūr in the late nineteenth century. Instead of going abroad or trading, however, Kirippūr's Naidūs aimed for education and white-collar jobs. Although some succeeded in their aims, the caste as a whole, like the Toṇḍaimaṇḍalam Mudaliar landlords, lost wealth and land in the depression of the 1930s, so that their position in 1952 was poorer than in 1897.

Between 1897 and 1952 the greatest losses were experienced by the Toṇḍaimaṇḍalam Mudaliar landlords. All of them sold land in the depression when paddy prices were low but manufactures remained costly. Apart from a few lower-ranking Non-Brahman migrant traders and rich peasants of Kirippūr, the main gains were by Cheṭṭiar shopkeepers of Nāgapaṭṭanam, to whom the landlords became indebted, and by a single wealthy Sengunda Mudaliar family from Manjūr, a village five miles away. This family made money in the early twentieth century by buying cotton from the mills of Erode, Salem, Coimbatore, and Madurai, and selling it to local weavers. They then invested in a weaving mill and in retail stores in several parts of south India. By 1952, the weaving mill had been sold but the family owned more than 100 acres of land and a rice mill. Ninety acres of this land, the largest estate in Kirippūr, had been bought in the 1930s from the village headman, who had become heavily indebted to these prosperous industrialists and traders.

These losses of the 1930s chiefly accounted for the growth of absentee landownership in Kirippūr between 1897 and 1952. A comparison with Table 10.1 shows that very similar proportions of the village land in Kumbapeṭṭai and in Kirippūr had been sold by the traditional aristocrats to cover debts to middle ranking Non-Brahman and Muslim traders and industrialists, both before 1897 and between 1897 and 1952.

We may close this chapter by considering general social relations and the "feel" of life of Kirippūr. Although more of the men had supplementary, nonagricultural work, the village as a whole was probably poorer than Kumbapeṭṭai. Yet it seemed to me a happier village. Although about 57 percent of the people lived at bare subsistence level, there was a greater sense of equality, love of life, and freedom than in Kumbapeṭṭai.

In part this may have been due to the small numbers and relative powerlessness of the Brahmans. Lacking a Brahman caste of landlords to elaborate and enforce ritual rank and purity, the people were less concerned about these matters. People of different castes did not interdine or intermarry and the Non-Brahman castes sometimes bickered over rank, but Non-Brahman men visited freely in each others' homes and touch and distance pollution were not observed among them. Ādi Drāviḍas were not permitted to enter Non-Brahman homes, but they walked freely in the streets and wore shirts when they could afford them.

More significant was the absence of any single dominant caste of landlords. Among the residents, land was divided into small fractions among most of the Non-Brahman castes. Although Toṇḍaimaṇḍalam Mudaliars officially managed the village and the Sanskritic temples, they were too poor to dominate its political and social life. The two wealthiest men in the village – a Naidū owner of a soda factory and a Paḍaiyācchi rich peasant – were "upstarts" of relatively low rank with little authority beyond their work places. Lacking a dominant caste, Kirippūr was in many respects a field of social relations rather than a corporate community, with each street living its social life in relative independence but with interpersonal visiting and transactions among the streets.

As we shall see in Chapter 20, the middle- and low-ranking Non-Brahmans were on average more prosperous in Kirippūr than in Kumbapeṭṭai. A greater proportion of them owned their own land or enterprises and almost all of them, their house sites. Although there were very poor people among them, their security gave the middle castes a degree of equality and freedom with each other and with the former aristocrats not found in Kumbapeṭṭai. As a result, there was less watchfulness, more laughter, and more comradeship in the middle-caste streets of Kirippūr.

Being more prosperous, the middle castes were also more literate. Probably all the Non-Brahman men, and a few women, could read and write. Almost all the Non-Brahman children attended the village elementary school on Upper Street. Kirippūr boasted a Naidū master of arts and a Nāḍar bachelor of arts, achievements unthinkable among the Non-Brahmans of Kumbapeṭṭai. Both were unemployed, but were seeking government appointments and received them soon after I left the village. Together with youths of the Toṇḍaimaṇḍalam Mudaliar, Kaikkiḷar and Chōḷiya Veḷḷāḷar castes, the Naidū MA organized a badminton club south of Lower Street to which all Non-Brahmans were welcome – a form of recreation hard to imagine in the more somber and authoritarian atmosphere of Kumbapeṭṭai.

Such comradeship among the Non-Brahman castes was also seen in a chit fund run from Lower Street. Organized by a Chōḷiya Veḷḷāḷar, the members included Toṇḍaimaṇḍalam Mudaliars, Kammāḷars, Kaikkiḷar Mudaliars, Naidūs, and Paḍaiyācchis. They met on new moon nights, paid Rs. 10 each per month, and drew lots to withdraw the whole amount in turn. In Kumbapeṭṭai chit funds were run only among the Brahmans.

Although poverty stricken, segregated, exploited, and discriminated against, Kirippūr's Ādi Drāviḍas had greater freedom than those of Kumbapeṭṭai. The Communist movement, to be discussed in Chapter 22, was relevant. By organizing, agitating, and publicizing, it had ended such degrading punishments as forcing "offenders" to drink cow dung. A few landlords and rich peasants in Kirippūr occasionally struck their laborers with a cane in anger, but the village recognized that the days of tying men to coconut trees and flogging them were ended. The absence of a single dominant caste of landlords contributed to the laborers' freedom, for no group had the unity or power to judge and punish their "misdoings" forcefully or to control their social life. Ādi Drāviḍa youths went freely to the cinema, for example. Migrant labor had also to some extent improved the Ādi Drāviḍas' social image, for those with foreign experiences were more cosmopolitan and knowledgeable than many other villagers. Although the group as a whole was almost propertyless, one Paḷḷar whose brother had brought money from Malaya owned three acres and a tile-roofed house and was respected. None of the Ādi Drāviḍa children attended school, for they were needed in the fields. In Lower Paḷḷar Street, however, the parents of fifteen boys paid a Paḷḷar school teacher from Tekkūr Rs. 7–8 a month to teach them from 6:00 to 9:00 P.M. each evening.

Kirippūr had a more secular atmosphere than Kumbapeṭṭai. Festivals and special *poojais* of the Siva and Vishnū temples were financed very modestly in turn by the Mudaliar landlords, the Kurukkals, and leading rich peasants of the other Non-Brahman castes. As was usual, the Brahmans and the high-caste, noncultivating landlords were most interested and most learned in religious matters. Agricultural festivals were celebrated separately by each household or each street, but those of the village deities had not been performed for the last four years, ostensibly because of drought and poverty. Both the DK and the Communist Party had to some extent undermined religious sentiments. Several men in each Non-Brahman caste supported the DK and a few professed to be atheists. Some went so far as to dispense with ancestral ceremonies, although all employed a Brahman priest from Tekkūr to conduct their marriages and funerals. The Ādi Drāviḍas were solidly for the Communist Party. True, they hired a Non-Brahman priest (*pandāram*) for their marriages. Many of them also made individual offerings to Kāḷiyamman after a birth or in times of sickness, but some did not. When I asked a youth from North Paḷḷar Street whether his group had any deity, he replied firmly, "Here we do not have any god. All that went five years ago. Now we are Communists." Many villagers of all castes attended the annual festivals of the Tiruvārūr temple, the Nagōre mosque, and the Vēlankanni church to see the spectacles. Some Kaikkiḷars and Veḷḷāḷars of Lower Street went on annual pilgrimages to the Subramania temple at Paḷni in the Western Ghats. For most men under forty, however, the films shown in a cinema tent in Tekkūr held greater attraction than temple festivals.

In other ways Kirippūr gave the impression of being a more "modern" and a more Western-influenced village than Kumbapeṭṭai. A dozen or more men had worked for British employers in Nāgapaṭṭaṇam, Malaya, or Burma and were familiar with their customs. So were a few Mudaliar boys who attended the Methodist high school in a nearby village. A few Paḷḷars and Non-Brahmans smuggled whiskey, brandy, fountain pens, wrist watches, cuff links, and other small consumer goods from Kāraikkal and sold them in Kirippūr or nearby villages; one Paḷḷar spent six weeks in jail for this offense during my stay. Many Non-Brahman men used condoms bought in Nāgapaṭṭaṇam, especially in their dealings with prostitutes. On the other hand, many women seemed ignorant of the world beyond the village and were curious about European habits. Many asked me, for example, whether it was true that Europeans bathed their babies in whiskey immediately after birth to make them white. At first I thought this was a joke, but the question was repeated so often throughout East Thanjāvūr that I began to wonder whether some, at least, were serious. Women of all castes in both villages were naturally curious about women's customs in sex and childbirth. Several women walked the distance of one or two villages to ask me whether English women menstruated and if so, how they dealt with their periods.

The lives of women in the various classes seemed similar to those of Kumbapeṭṭai, but in some cases slightly more independent. Some Non-Brahman women had the advantages of birth control and of having their babies delivered in the Nāgapaṭṭaṇam hospital or by a modern midwife from Tekkūr. Except, however, for a few Toṇḍaimaṇḍalam Mudaliar girls, almost all women suffered from illiteracy, male dominance, poor health care, poverty, grinding toil, and narrow experience. Among the Non-Brahmans, as in Kumbapeṭṭai, girls were secluded in the house between puberty and marriage. Except among Ādi Drāviḍas, women stayed out of the kitchen and did not touch others during their menstrual periods. They were not, however, shut in a separate room nor kept out of doors as among the Brahmans. A number of Non-Brahman widows and wives whose husbands were abroad lived in direst poverty. Four were prostitutes and three (and three village men) were known to have venereal disease. Two retired prostitutes had died of venereal disease on consecutive days six months before I arrived. Men occasionally beat their wives in Kirippūr as in Kumbapeṭṭai, and were jealous of their sexuality. Yet many women showed resilience and daring, and a surprisingly large number of married women carried on illicit affairs out of love rather than for money or from compulsion. In contrast to Kumbapeṭṭai, most landlords lacked the power to exploit women of the lower castes sexually, for most Non-Brahman tenants owned their own house sites and could change their landlords, while Ādi Drāviḍas had the protection and the censure of their Communist assembly. Sexual offenses did occur occasionally. One man had raped his stepdaughter – the only case of rape known to me in Thanjāvūr villages. When he was discovered and ostracized, he committed suicide. In general, Kirippūr's women seemed less downtrodden than those of Kumbapeṭṭai. Old women in particular came and went freely and, although they had no part in formal assemblies, held greater influence in their communities.

# 20 Economy and Class Structure

## The Annual Round

The agricultural year in Kirippūr resembled that in Kumbapeṭṭai except that almost all operations occurred two to three weeks later because of the later arrival of the water, usually in late Āṉi or early Āḍi (early to mid-July). As in Kumbapeṭṭai, shepherds from Rāmanāthapuram grazed their sheep in the paddy fields in mid-April to mid-June.

The greatest difference from Kumbapeṭṭai was that only about 10 percent of the wet land grew two crops a year. On most of their land, the majority of farmers grew only a single *sambā* crop, which was sown in Āvaṉi and reaped in Thai or Māsi (see Table 11.1 for the seasons in Kumbapeṭṭai). A few farmers whose land lay on higher ground might grow a single *kuruvai* crop and dispense with *sambā* on at least part of their land. Those who grew two crops a year normally sowed and transplanted both sets of seeds together in Āḍi. The *kuruvai* crop, of short duration, was harvested in late Aippasi (early November). Long stalks were left in the field, so that the second crop, called *oṭṭadan*, could continue to grow and be harvested in Māsi. Separately sown *kuruvai* and *sambā* crops could not be grown in Kirippūr, for the *kuruvai* harvest came late and there was no time to replough the land before the *sambā* transplanting. On the other hand, Kumbapeṭṭai did not grow *oṭṭadan* because the crop required much water, which was available during the heavier, coastal rains of October and November in east Thanjāvūr.

Even *oṭṭadan* double cropping was considered too risky in low-lying land in Kirippūr, for the first crop might be ruined by flooding, while the *oṭṭadan* crop was usually in any case poorer than a single *sambā* crop. Farmers with higher land did, however, sometimes grow a single *kuruvai* crop and dispensed with *sambā*. In fields having enough water late in the year, gram crops were grown between Thai and Panguni, but these fields were fewer than in Kumbapeṭṭai. During the dry summer months a green manure crop, *koḷinji*, was usually grown and was later ploughed into the soil.

Kirippūr's single cropping meant that agricultural laborers worked fewer days per year than in Kumbapeṭṭai. Although I have no precise figures throughout the year for large numbers of workers, I estimated that *paṇṇaiyāḷ* and regular coolie men worked about 180 days a year and women about 110 to 140 days. Casual coolies could be certain of only about ninety days work a year, but might obtain more if they were known to be diligent. A few *paṇṇaiyāḷs* entrusted with fencing and garden work might work up to 200 days a year.

### The Class Structure

Table 20.1 shows the class memberships of Kirippūr men and women divided in terms of caste. It may be compared with Table 15.1, which gives the corresponding figures for Kumbapeṭṭai.

These tables, together with Table 20.2, which lists only the strata among the male agriculturalists, bear out my statement in Chapter 19 that Kirippūr was less hierarchical and its class structure less polarized than Kumbapeṭṭai's. The interesting point is that although it had lower productivity and was probably a poorer village in general, Kirippūr had a larger percentage of relatively prosperous people or at least of people living above barest subsistence. Thus, 22.6 percent of Kirippūr's men fell in the petty bourgeoisie as landlords, rich peasants hiring regular labor, or small entrepreneurs with hired hands, while only 18 percent fell in this class in Kumbapeṭṭai. Similarly, 19.9 percent in Kirippūr fell in the class of independent entrepreneurs composed of middle peasants with no regular hired labor, or independent family artisans or traders. Only 9.9 percent fell in this class in Kumbapeṭṭai. Correspondingly, in Kirippūr "only" 57.5 percent were semiproletarians, of whom "only" 48.7 percent were propertyless laborers working under supervision. In Kumbapeṭṭai, 71.6 percent were semiproletarians, 53.2 percent being laborers under supervision. A comparison of the figures for the agricultural strata in Table 20.2 gives the same general picture.

It seems to me that this contrast existed *because* Kirippūr had lower productivity from agriculture, as I have suggested in Chapters 5 and 18. Where the surplus from the land was less, fewer people were able to live as noncultivating landlords, and hence fewer were reduced to being mere tenants or laborers. Parodoxically therefore (and no doubt within limits) the poorer the village, the better off were the majority of its inhabitants.

The same conclusion is reached if we compare the percentages of people owning land in each village, and the size distributions of their holdings. The censuses reveal that in 1897, 13.4 percent of the total resident population of Kirippūr (including children) were registered as landowners, while 13.5 percent were so registered in 1952. In Kumbapeṭṭai, 8.4 percent of the total resident population were registered as landowners in 1897, and 8.8 percent in 1952. The concentration of landownership in both villages thus remained roughly stationary over the fifty-five-year period, but Kumbapeṭṭai had a lower percentage of owners than did Kirippūr. Similarly, in 1952, 60 percent of the households in Kirippūr owned a little land, if only a house site, whereas in Kumbapeṭṭai only 29 percent of the households owned any land. In 1952, 24 percent of the households owned more than one acre in Kirippūr, but only 18 percent in Kumbapeṭṭai.

Tables 20.3 and 20.4 respectively show the size distribution of land holdings among present and absent owners in Kirippūr in 1897 and 1952. They may be

Table 20.1. *Class affiliations of men and women over age fifteen, by caste, Kirippūr, 1952*

| Caste | Petty bourgeois | | Independent family entrepreneurs | | Tenants and servants under little supervision | | Laborers under supervision | | Total | |
|---|---|---|---|---|---|---|---|---|---|---|
| | M | F | M | F | M | F | M | F | M | F |
| *Brahman* | 4 | 3 | — | — | — | — | — | — | 4 | 3 |
| *Non-Brahman* | | | | | | | | | | |
| Toṇḍaimaṇḍalam Veḷḷāḷar | 15 | 8 | — | — | — | — | — | — | 15 | 8 |
| Seiva Veḷḷāḷar | — | — | 5 | 4 | 1 | 1 | 1 | 2 | 7 | 7 |
| Chōḷiya Veḷḷāḷar | 11 | 9 | 1 | 1 | 1 | 1 | — | — | 13 | 11 |
| Kavarai Naidū | 7 | 4 | 2 | 1 | — | — | 1 | 1 | 10 | 6 |
| Poosāri | — | — | 1 | 3 | 1 | — | — | — | 2 | 3 |
| Sengunda Mudaliar | 6 | 7 | 18 | 22 | — | — | 3 | 4 | 27 | 33 |
| Agambaḍiyar | — | — | — | — | 2 | 1 | — | — | 2 | 1 |
| Kaḷḷar | — | — | — | — | 1 | 1 | — | — | 1 | 1 |
| Paḍaiyācchi | 3 | 4 | 6 | 10 | 6 | 10 | 7 | 5 | 21 | 29 |
| Vanniyar | — | — | — | 2 | 1 | 1 | 1 | 1 | 2 | 4 |
| Porayar | — | — | — | — | 2 | 2 | 5 | 4 | 7 | 6 |
| Muslim | — | — | — | — | 1 | 1 | — | — | 1 | 1 |
| Kōnār | — | — | — | — | — | — | 1 | 2 | 1 | 2 |
| Kammāḷar | 3 | 2 | 3 | 5 | — | — | 1 | 1 | 7 | 8 |
| Vāṇiyar | — | — | 2 | 2 | — | — | — | — | 2 | 2 |
| Nāḍār | 2 | 2 | 4 | 6 | — | — | 10 | 15 | 16 | 23 |
| Vaṇṇār | — | — | 2 | 2 | — | — | — | — | 2 | 2 |
| Oṭṭar | — | — | — | — | — | — | 1 | 1 | 1 | 1 |
| *Ādi Drāviḍa* | | | | | | | | | | |
| Paḷḷar | — | — | 1 | 1 | 3 | 3 | 40 | 40 | 44 | 44 |
| Parayar | — | — | — | — | — | — | 40 | 34 | 40 | 34 |
| Total | 51 | 39 | 45 | 59 | 19 | 21 | 111 | 109 | 226 | 228 |

*Note:* Women and students have been placed in the classes of their husbands and fathers.

Table 20.2. *Male agricultural strata by major caste groups in Kumbapeṭṭai and Kirippūr, 1952*

| *Kirippūr* | High caste[a] | Other Non-Brahman | Ādi Drāviḍa | Total |
|---|---|---|---|---|
| Landlords | 17 | 2 | — | 19 |
| Rich peasants | — | 29 | — | 29 |
| Middle peasants | — | 24 | 1 | 25 |
| Tenant cultivators | — | 14 | 3 | 17 |
| Farm overseer | — | 1 | — | |
| Village watchman | — | 1 (Muslim) | — | 1 |
| Laborers with leased land | — | — | 3 | 3 |
| Landless laborers | | | | |
| (a) Vēlaikkārars | — | 7 | — | 7 |
| (b) Paṇṇaiyāḷs | — | — | 49 | 49 |
| (c) Regular coolies | — | 3 | 9 | 12 |
| (d) Casual coolies | — | 5 | 19 | 24 |
| Total | 17 | 86 | 84 | 187 |

| *Kumbapeṭṭai* | Brahman | Non-Brahman | Ādi Drāviḍa | Total |
|---|---|---|---|---|
| Landlords | 35 | — | — | 35 |
| Middle peasants | — | 7 | — | 7 |
| Tenant cultivators | — | 13 | 18 | 31 |
| Laborers with leased land | — | 2 | 18 | 20 |
| Landless Laborers | | | | |
| (a) Vēlaikkārars | — | 18 | — | 18 |
| (b) Paṇṇaiyāḷs | — | — | 21 | 21 |
| (c) Regular coolies | — | — | 15 | 15 |
| (d) Casual coolies | — | 16 | 22 | 38 |
| Total | 35 | 56 | 94 | 185 |

[a]Brahman and Toṇḍaimaṇḍalam Veḷḷaḷar

compared with Tables 10.2 and 12.1, which present similar data for Kumbapeṭṭai. These tables reveal that Kumbapeṭṭai had higher percentages of owners with substantial holdings of more than five acres between 1897 and 1952, even though the land was more fertile in Kumbapeṭṭai than in Kirippūr. The top 25 percent of Kirippūr's resident owners owned 71 percent of the land owned by residents in 1897, and 73 percent in 1952. In Kumbapeṭṭai the top 25 percent of resident landowners owned 62 percent of the land owned by residents in 1897, and 76 percent in 1952. The *centralization* of landownership among residents had

Table 20.3. *Distribution of landed estates by size among present and absent owners by caste group, Kirippūr, 1897*

| | Present | | | Absent | | | |
|---|---|---|---|---|---|---|---|
| Size of estate (acres) | High caste[a] | Other Non-Brahman | Ādi Drāviḍa | High[a] caste | Other Non-Brahman | Ādi Drāviḍa | Muslim and Christian |
| 20+ | 3 | — | — | 1 | — | — | — |
| 15–19.99 | 1 | — | — | — | — | — | 1 |
| 10–14.99 | 3 | 1 | — | — | — | — | — |
| 5–9.99 | 2 | 5 | — | — | — | — | 3 |
| 2–4.99 | 6 | 15 | — | 1 | — | — | 5 |
| 1–1.99 | 4 | 17 | — | 1 | 1 | — | 1 |
| Under 1 | 6 | 30 | — | 1 | — | — | 1 |
| Total | 25 | 68 | — | 4 | 1 | — | 11 |

[a]Brahman and Toṇḍaimaṇḍalam Veḷḷāḷar

Table 20.4. *Distribution of landed estates by size among present and absent owners by caste group, Kirippūr, 1952*

| | Present | | | Absent | | | |
|---|---|---|---|---|---|---|---|
| Size of estate (acres) | High caste | Other Non-Brahman | Ādi Drāviḍa | High[a] caste | Other Non-Brahman | Ādi Drāviḍa | Muslim and Christian |
| 20+ | — | 1 | — | — | 1 | — | — |
| 15–19.99 | 1 | — | — | — | — | — | — |
| 10–14.99 | 1 | 2 | — | 1 | — | — | 2 |
| 5–9.99 | 2 | 5 | — | 1 | 3 | — | 1 |
| 2–4.99 | 3 | 11 | 1 | 1 | 6 | 1 | 5 |
| 1–1.99 | 1 | 16 | — | 1 | 5 | — | 2 |
| Under 1 | 2 | 40 | 24 | 1 | 17 | — | 2 |
| Total | 10 | 75 | 25 | 5 | 32 | 1 | 12 |

[a]Toṇḍaimaṇḍalam Veḷḷāḷar and Brahman.

therefore somewhat increased in both villages, but it had increased more in Kumbapeṭṭai, and was somewhat greater in Kumbapeṭṭai than in Kirippūr in 1952. Landownership among the residents was thus both more concentrated and slightly more centralized in Kumbapeṭṭai than in Kirippūr.

Somewhat different results, however, are obtained if we calculate the centralization of ownership among owners both absent and present. In Kirippūr, the top 25 percent of all owners owned 68 percent of the total land in 1896 and 69 percent in 1952. In Kumbapeṭṭai revenue village (as distinct from the *grāmam* proper) the top 25 percent owned 62 percent of the total land in 1896 and 69 percent in 1976. Centralization had thus increased more among the total owners in Kumbapeṭṭai, although it was not more marked than in Kirippūr in 1952.

Although landownership conferred a degree of security, one of the effects of the greater number of landowners in Kirippūr was a worse situation regarding the fragmentation of holdings. Thus, 66, or 60 percent of the landowners living in Kirippūr owned less than one acre, while only 23, or 40 percent owned less than one acre in Kumbapeṭṭai. Eighty-three, or 75 percent of Kirippūr's resident owners owned less than two acres, but only 29, or 50 percent in Kumbapeṭṭai. Among the total owners both absent and present, 35 percent in Kirippūr owned less than one acre in 1897 and 57 percent less than two acres. In 1952, however, 53 percent owned less than one acre and 69 percent less than two acres. In Kumbapeṭṭai, by contrast, 21 percent owned less than one acre in 1896, and 34 percent less than two acres. Twenty-five percent in Kumbapeṭṭai owned less than one acre in 1952, and 43 percent less than 2 acres. The fragmentation of holdings was thus proceeding apace in both villages, but was more marked in Kirippūr.

### The Division of Labor

Probably because of its low agricultural productivity, Kirippūr had less specialization than did Kumbapeṭṭai. A larger proportion of Kirippūr's workers depended both on agriculture inside the village and on crafts or other work for people outside the village in order to obtain their livelihood. Such people added to the total wealth of the village and to some extent compensated for its low agricultural productivity.

The most prominent of the landlords who earned money from outside the village were a Naidū owner of a "soda," or lemonade-bottling plant in Upper Street, and a Toṇḍaimaṇḍalam Mudaliar and a Veḷḷāḷar who jointly owned a small rice mill on the border of Kirippūr and Vaḍakkūr. In the lower ranks, twenty-three of the Kaikkiḷar Mudaliars combined weaving and spinning with agriculture. The weavers were divided into (*a*) those who owned their own looms, had shares in a weavers' marketing cooperative three miles away, and also employed other laborers, (*b*) those who owned their own looms but could not afford to belong to the cooperative and merely made purchases from and sales to it, and (*c*) those who could not afford looms or shares but simply worked as coolies for better-off weavers. These strata tended to coincide respectively with (*a*) the rich peasants who hired laborers, (*b*) the middle peasants who did most of their own labor, and (*c*) the tenant farmers within the weavers' caste. In Table 20.1 I have placed these categories respectively in the petty bourgeoisie, the family entrepreneurs, and the semiproletariat, and in Table 20.2 in their respective peasant strata. These weavers worked about half of their time in their trade and the other half in agricultural pursuits. Six weavers, however, were not agriculturalists, and they are listed among the nonagriculturalists (Table 20.6).

Other craftsmen who sold their wares or services outside the village but also worked land within it were the Goldsmiths, who were also rich peasants hiring laborers, and the Laundryworkers and Oilmongers who were also middle peasants cultivating mainly with family labor. In general, 187 out of 226 village men, or 82.7 percent were landlords, cultivators, or agricultural laborers, compared with 83.8 percent in Kumbapeṭṭai, but thirty-three of these men combined agriculture with business or crafts. In Kumbapeṭṭai, only seven out of 186 agriculturalists or landlords had supplementary work that drew income from outside the village, although, as in Kirippūr, several others, such as paddy traders and Brahman household priests, obtained cash by rendering services to their fellow villagers.

### The Nonagriculturalists

Tables 20.5 and 20.6 lists the male nonagriculturalists in Kumbapeṭṭai and Kirippūr respectively in terms of class strata and specific occupations. I have omitted from these tables men who gained at least half their living from agriculture. Two main differences between the villages may be noted. The first is that Kirippūr had a higher percentage of regularly supervised workers living entirely from cash wages, that is, 44 percent of the total nonagriculturalists as against 11 percent in Kumbapeṭṭai. The reason for this simply was that Kirippūr had more industries close at land – a small mechanized rice mill and a hand-bottling soda plant inside the village itself, and two other rice mills in Tekkūr and Pattallūr. More of Kirippūr's men also had need of nonagricultural wage work, because of the village's lower productivity from agriculture.

The second difference is that Kirippūr had more independent entrepreneurs than Kumbapeṭṭai: 46 percent as opposed to 36 percent, and no "unsupervised workers" among the nonagriculturalists. My classification may seem arbitrary when it is noted that the village servants are placed among the "unsupervised workers" in Kumbapeṭṭai and among the "independent entrepreneurs" in Kirippūr. I have made this distinction, however, because Kirippūr's artisans were really private entrepreneurs working very largely or entirely for cash payments for each job of work. They owned their own house-and-work-sites, were independent of the village landlords regarding their social behavior and working hours, and either sold some of their wares or did considerable work in other villages.

The weavers, for example, belonged to a weavers' cooperative in a village three miles away, begun eight years earlier under the government's cooperative movement. The cooperative bought raw cotton from Madras via Kumbakōṇam and marketed the woven goods. The builders worked entirely for cash and entirely outside the village, as did one of the carpenters. The shopkeepers, the village doctor, and the veterinarians were involved in cash transactions with whomever summoned them. The village temple priest did receive a cash salary from collections on Upper and Lower Streets, but he was not in a servile relationship as was the village priest in relation to the landlords of Kumbapeṭṭai,

Table 20.5. *Male nonagricultural occupational strata in Kumbapeṭṭai, by caste group, 1952*

| | Brahman | Non-Brahman | Ādi Drāviḍa | Total |
|---|---|---|---|---|
| *Petty bourgeois* | | | | |
| Temple priests | 4 | — | — | 4 |
| Grocery shopkeeper (landed) | 1 | — | — | 1 |
| *Independent entrepreneurs* | | | | |
| Paddy traders | — | 7 | — | 7 |
| Village temple priests, teashop keepers | — | 4 | — | 4 |
| Restaurant owner | 1 | — | — | 1 |
| Household priest | 1 | — | — | 1 |
| *Unsupervised workers* | | | | |
| Laundryworkers | — | 2 | — | 2 |
| Barbers | — | 3 | — | 3 |
| Potters | — | 4 | — | 4 |
| Carpenter | — | 1 | — | 1 |
| Blacksmith | — | 1 | — | 1 |
| Goldsmith | — | 1 | — | 1 |
| *Supervised workers* | | | | |
| Road sweeper | — | 1 | — | 1 |
| Village policeman | — | 1 | — | 1 |
| Cigar factory worker | — | 1 | — | 1 |
| *Chattram* watchman | — | 1 (Muslim) | — | 1 |
| *Mendicants* | 3 | — | — | 3 |
| Total | 10 | 27 | — | 37 |

and he was also an independent weaver. In short, capitalist relations had developed more fully among the nonagriculturalists of Kirippūr than of Kumbapeṭṭai, and these villagers were also more involved in transactions within a wider neighborhood.

Some of Kirippūr's former village servants were more prosperous than those of Kumbapeṭṭai. This was certainly true of the Goldsmiths, Oilmongers, Laundryworkers, and several of the weavers, who owned land in addition to their craft and who are therefore not listed in Table 20.6. It was also true of some of the landless artisans, such as the leading carpenter and the builders. These men earned the equivalent of about 190 *kalams* of paddy per year, as opposed to about ninety *kalams* among most of the village servants of Kumbapeṭṭai. The weavers, blacksmith, village doctor, veterinarians, and the second carpenter, however, earned the equivalent of only about fifty to ninety *kalams* a year and so were as

Table 20.6. *Male nonagricultural occupational strata in Kirippūr by major caste group, 1952*

| | High caste[a] | Other Non-Brahman | Ādi Drāviḍa | Total |
|---|---|---|---|---|
| *Petty bourgeois* | | | | |
| Village accountant | 1 | — | — | 1 |
| Schoolteachers | 1 | 1 | — | 2 |
| Pensioned government servant | — | 1 | — | 1 |
| *Independent entrepreneurs* | | | | |
| Weavers | — | 4 | — | 4 |
| Carpenters | — | 2 | — | 2 |
| Blacksmith | — | 1 | — | 1 |
| Builder and tilemakers | — | 2 | — | 2 |
| Village doctor | — | 1 | — | 1 |
| Village temple priest (also weaver) | — | 1 | — | 1 |
| Veterinarians and dairy farmers | — | 2 | — | 2 |
| Shopkeepers | — | 5 | — | 5 |
| *Supervised workers* | | | | |
| Coolie weaver | — | 1 | — | 1 |
| Coolie brickmaker | — | 1 | — | 1 |
| Village policeman | — | 1 | — | 1 |
| Rice mill workers | — | 6 | — | 6 |
| Soda factory workers | — | 6 | — | 6 |
| Village messenger | — | 1 | — | 1 |
| Carpenter's apprentice | — | 1 | — | 1 |
| Total | 2 | 37 | — | 39 |

[a]Brahman and Toṇḍaimaṇḍalam Veḷḷāḷar

poor as, although more independent than, their counterparts in Kumbapeṭṭai. In general, among the nonagriculturalists as among the agriculturalists, Kirippūr had a larger proportion of people living above subsistence level.

### The Landowners

Kirippūr had no landlords in the sense of people who leased out their land to others, for the landowners were able-bodied men employed solely or mainly in agriculture. All the village's tenants leased from absentee landlords. Kirippūr did, however, have nineteen men of aristocratic caste who did no personal cultivation, but simply managed laborers. I have classified these men as "landlords" in Table 20.2. The village also had twenty-nine rich peasants of other Non-Brahman castes who worked themselves but regularly hired laborers, and twenty-five middle peasants, including one Paḷḷar, who hired a few laborers only at peak seasons.

Kirippūr had a somewhat different method of distributing irrigation water and digging out the channels than did Kumbapeṭṭai. The village's wet land was divided into eight portions, or *karaivaris* of eight *vēlis* (about 53.33 acres) each. Each portion was under the management of a *karaivarikkār*. In 1952, Kirippūr's *karaivarikkārs* were five Toṇḍaimaṇḍalam Mudaliars including the village headman, one Chōḷiya Veḷḷāḷar, and the Manjūr Sengunda Mudaliar landlord owning ninety acres, whose agent managed two *karaivaris*. These men had been chosen at a meeting of the owners ten years previously, and would continue until any of them resigned or were removed.

Each *karaivarikkār* had the responsibility of calling the *paṇṇaiyāḷs* of the owners in his portion to dig out the irrigation channels before the water arrived. The *paṇṇaiyāḷs* were then paid separately by their masters. The *karaivarikkār* also settled any disputes regarding irrigation water within his portion, and met with other *karaivarikkārs* to settle disputes between owners in different portions. When irrigation water was scarce, each *karaivari* had the right to three hours of irrigation water per twenty-four-hour period. It was the *karaivarikkārs*' duty to see that these periods were observed, and to appoint *paṇṇaiyāḷs* to open and close the channels.

The *karaivarikkārs* evidently derived from the period of the joint village when the lands of each *karaivari* (also called *karai* in some villages) were periodically redistributed to different owners. The post was honorary, but carried with it respect and the privilege of ordering laborers about. In Kirippūr the *karaivarikkārs* were selected partly on the basis of size of holdings and partly of hereditary privilege. The Manjūr landlord, although of lower caste, managed two *karaivaris* because he owned the equivalent of two of them. One of the Toṇḍaimaṇḍalam Mudaliars owned no land at all in Kirippūr, although he owned two acres elsewhere, while another one owned only one *māh* although he leased in nineteen acres on *uḷ-kuthakai* from absentees. These men were chosen because their lineage and households had "always" had this right. The single Chōḷiya Veḷḷāḷar *karaivarikkār* owned 3.5 acres and leased 6.66 acres more. This was a smaller estate than those of the two richest men in the village, a Paḍaiyācchi rich peasant with twenty acres and the Naidū soda factory owner, who owned 13.5. These men were not chosen because they were of lower caste than the Veḷḷāḷar, were less favored by the Toṇḍaimaṇḍalam Mudaliars, and lacked the personalities to push themselves forward into public offices.

A further common interest of the landlowners was a village credit society managed by the village headman. Run from a bank in Kumbakōṇam, it had been in the village for about twenty-five years. Landowners with six acres of land were permitted to borrow Rs. 1,000 at 6 percent interest; those with less land, less. The interest had to be paid annually and the whole sum returned within three years. Usually, the sum was returned through a loan from a local moneylender; the borrower might then take back his loan from the credit society after fifteen days and start another three-year period. Although the credit society obviously removed surplus from the villagers, it was much preferable to private loans at 12 percent interest. As in Kumbapeṭṭai, many landlords took these loans too, and in turn gave loans to their *paṇṇaiyāḷs* at considerably higher interest.

It is hard to estimate the cultivation expenses and profits of landowners in Kirippūr in 1952–3, because (*a*) most wages were raised in September 1952, and (*b*) the cyclone of November 1952 disrupted cultivation and made the *sambā* crop of January and February 1953 extremely poor. Table 20.7 shows the actual yield and cultivation expenses of the village headman on one acre of wet land, which was sown only with *kuruvai* in 1952. It may be compared with the expenses cited for Kumbapeṭṭai in Table 12.2. The Kirippūr expenses per crop were lower than in Kumbapeṭṭai because manure (paddy chaff, cow dung, ashes and oil-seed husks) was provided entirely from the farm, and because the total agricultural labor costs were only 9–5 *kalams* instead of 11–1 *kalams* as in Kumbapeṭṭai, even though twice as much seed was used in Kirippūr as in Kumbapaṭṭai. In addition, the Kirippūr landlord paid only seven *marakkāḷs* instead of 2–6 *kalams* to village servants, for Kirippūr's village servants received most of their pay in cash for each job of work. The Kirippūr expenses were also low, however, because the yield was very low, being only 21–7 *kalams* gross output, or eighteen *kalams* after the harvest payments were made. Table 20.8 shows what the same landlord's expenses per acre would have been had he had a relatively good yield (for Kirippūr) of thirty-six *kalams* after the harvest expenses were paid. In this case the harvest expenses are closer to those for Kumbapeṭṭai, where a good yield would have been about forty-five *kalams* per acre after harvest expenses were paid. In Table 20.8 the Kirippūr landlord would obtain 21–11 *kalams* per acre per crop, whereas the Kumbapeṭṭai landlord whose yield was good would receive 26–5 *kalams*. In general, labor costs, inputs, payments to village servants, yields, government revenue, and profits were all higher in Kumbapeṭṭai than in Kirippūr. When, moreover, we consider that most Kumbapeṭṭai landlords grew two crops per year, it is clear that Kirippūr's farmers were, on average, poorer per acre of land owned, even in spite of some profits from dry lands. Whereas a landlord with ten acres of wet land and one acre of dry land might expect to make an income of about Rs. 2,500 to Rs. 3,000 per year in Kumbapeṭṭai in a normal year, he would make only about Rs. 1,400 to Rs. 1,500 in Kirippūr.

This difference showed up in the lifestyles of Kirippūr's landowners. In general the more prosperous landlords had fewer consumer goods, fewer silk *sāris* and gold ornaments, and less well-painted houses, than in Kumbapeṭṭai. In Kirippūr, moreover, all the traditional landlords had lost wealth in the preceding two decades, while the village as a whole, like Kumbapeṭṭai, was poorer than in 1897 because of land sales to outsiders. On the other hand, because land and wealth were spread somewhat more evently in Kirippūr, a larger proportion of

Table 20.7. *Landlord's cultivation costs per acre of wet land growing only* kuruvai *crop, with yield of six* kalams *per* māh *after harvest costs, Kirippūr, 1952*

| | Kalams |
|---|---|
| Seed | 3–0 |
| Manure (provided from the farm) | — |
| Nonharvest labor costs | 4–6 |
| Harvest labor costs @ 1/7 gross yield | 3–6 |
| Payments to village servants (2 *poosāris,* 1 washerman, 1 barber from Tekkur, 1 carpenter, 1 Muslim watchman, and 1 Parayar scavenger @ 1 marakkal each | 0–7 |
| Total | 11–1 |

*Note:* The landlord's yield on this crop was only 21–7 *kalams,* or 6 *kalams* per *māh* after the harvest payments were made. The profit was therefore only 10–6 *kalams* per acre.

Table 20.8. *Landlord's hypothetical cultivation costs per acre of wet land growing only 1 crop, with yield of 12* kalams *per* māh *after harvest payments, Kirippūr, 1952*

| | Kalams |
|---|---|
| Seed | 3–0 |
| Manure | — |
| Nonharvest labor costs | 4–6 |
| Harvest labor costs @ 1/7 gross yield | 6–0 |
| Payments to village servants as in Table 20.7 | 0–7 |
| Total | 14–1 |

*Note:* Because the landlord's yield on this crop would be 42–7 *kalams,* or 36 *kalams* after the harvest payments were made, his profit would be 28–6 *kalams.*

households had a modest degree of comfort. To take one example, only forty-two out of 193 houses, or 21.8 percent in Kumbapeṭṭai had tile roofs, whereas forty-seven out of 184, or 25.5 percent had tile roofs in Kirippūr.

### The Tenants

Kirippūr had slightly less land under *kuthakai* than Kumbapeṭṭai and no *vāram* tenures at all. Forty-one percent of the wet land was under cultivating tenants in 1952, as distinct from 44 percent in Kumbapeṭṭai. There were, however, only seventeen "pure" tenants, or poor peasants, in Kirippūr as against thirty-one in Kumbapeṭṭai. Only three laborers in Kirippūr also held small plots of *kuthakai* land, as against twenty in Kumbapeṭṭai. Much of Kirippūr's *kuthakai* land was leased in by twelve middle peasants living in five households, or by nine rich peasants living in five households, all with their own holdings, whereas only six middle peasants or traders leased in land in Kumbapeṭṭai. The average leased holding of a cultivating tenant household (whether rich or middle peasant, "pure" tenant, or laborer) was 6.6 acres in Kirippūr, 3.3 acres in Kumbapeṭṭai. The average leased holding of a "pure" tenant was 4.9 acres in Kirippūr, and 4.4 acres in Kumbapeṭṭai. Table 20.2 presents the differences in the numbers of cultivating tenants as part of a larger picture of agricultural strata in the two villages.

The leasing in of more land by rich and middle peasants in Kirippūr resulted from the fact that Kirippūr *had* more of these cultivators than did Kumbapeṭṭai. Kumbapeṭṭai had no rich peasant cultivators who regularly hired laborers, and had a much smaller number of middle peasants than did Kirippūr, so that landlords who wished to lease to cultivators had to choose mainly "pure" tenants or part-time laborers. Kirippūr's landlords (mainly absentee) preferred when possible to lease to credit-worthy rich or middle peasants rather than to poor tenants or laborers.

Considering the yields, the rents of cultivating tenants were high in Kirippūr. Most tenants paid five to eight *kalams* per *māh*, or fifteen to twenty-four per acre per annum for land from which they seldom received more than eight to twelve *kalams* per *māh*, and often only five to eight. In the *sambā* harvest of 1953, after the cyclone, landlords inspected the fields and, through the mediation of the village headman, lowered the rent to about five *kalams* per *māh*. Several tenants, however, threshed only two to four *kalams* per *māh* and had to go still further into debt in order to pay their rents. Because the tenants were not involved in the Communist movement and had no solidarity, they did not insist on the terms of the Tanjore Tenants' and Paṇṇaiyals' Act, which required the tenant to pay no more than three-fifths of the crop. None of them, in fact, seemed aware of these provisions.

Kirippūr had only twenty acres under noncultivating *uḷ-kuthakai* leases, held by two Toṇḍaimaṇḍalam Mudaliars, whereas in Kumbapeṭṭai fourteen noncultivating landlords held 163 acres on *uḷ-kuthakai*, chiefly from absent Brahmans. The differences in the amounts and numbers of *uḷ-kuthakai* tenures occurred because in Kumbapeṭṭai a large number of Brahman landlords were absentees who leased land on noncultivating tenures to their kinsmen, whereas very few of the Toṇḍaimaṇḍalam Mudaliars – the noncultivating landlord caste – were absent in Kirippūr.

### The Agricultural Laborers

Kirippūr had seven Non-Brahman men who were *vēlaikkārars* in 1952. As in Kumbapeṭṭai, the men tended cattle, gardened, and did some

Table 20.9. *Annual payments of* paṇṇaiyāḷ *couple before the Māyuram agreement of 1948, Kirippūr*

| | Marakkāḷs | Rs. |
|---|---|---|
| Man's wages, 140 nonharvest days at ½ *marakkāḷ* per day | 70 | — |
| Woman's wages, 80 nonharvest days at ⅜ *marakkāḷ* per day | 30 | — |
| Couple's harvest wages, 40 days at ¾ *marakkāḷ* per day | 30 | — |
| Harvest bonusses, ½ *marakkāḷ* cutting pay + 1 *marakkāḷ* threshing pay per 13½ *marakkāḷs* threshed, @ 12 *māhs* per couple, 15 *kalams* per *māh* per year | 240 | — |
| *Paṭṭakkāḷ* of 50 *kuris* @ 12 *kalams* per *māh* | 72 | — |
| Deepāvaḷi clothing | — | 20 |
| Average annual gifts at life crises | — | 10 |
| Gifts at agricultural festivals | 6 | |
| Total | 448 | 30 |

*Note:* With paddy at Rs. 9 per *kalam,* this equals the equivalent of 40–8 *kalams* per year. If, however, only 12 *kalams* per *māh* per year were harvested, the total annual earnings would equal only 36–8 per year.

cultivation of paddy. Their wives were housemaids who also did occasional agricultural work. The payments of two couples were roughly the same as in Kumbapeṭṭai: four *kalams* of paddy per month per man and one *kalam* per woman, together with clothing and gifts at festivals. Five men were employed by the Manjūr landlord. These men received four *kalams* and Rs. 4 per month, but no additional gifts. Their wives received the usual one *kalam* as housemaids in local homes. The annual incomes of these couples were therefore virtually the same as those of the old-fashioned *vēlaikkārars*, but the method of payment was more similar to capitalist wages.

Because of the lesser number of days worked per year, the annual agricultural wages of *paṇṇaiyāḷs* and coolies tended to be lower in Kirippūr than in Kumbapeṭṭai. Table 20.9 gives an estimate of the average annual earnings of a *paṇṇaiyaḷ* married couple before the Māyuram Agreement of 1948, calculating the man's days of work at 180 and the woman's at 120. Although rather generous for Kirippūr's conditions, the total amount was only 37–4 *kalams* plus about Rs. 30 in goods, or the equivalent of a total of about 40–8 *kalams*. Table 20.10 gives an estimate of the average earnings of *paṇṇaiyāḷ* married pairs engaged by small holders in Kirippūr in 1952, four years after the Māyuram Agreement of 1948 and during the year that the Tanjore Tenants' and Paṇṇaiyāḷs' Ordinance was passed. Table 20.11 estimates the earnings of a couple engaged by bigger landlords with holdings of more than 6.66 standard acres in one village. It will be seen that these earnings were actually slightly lower than those paid by small holders who continued to give clothing, *paṭṭakkāḷ*, and other perquisites. The Manjūr landlord, who owned ninety acres, actually paid his male *paṇṇaiyāḷs* Re.1 and

Table 20.10. *Modified annual payments by small holders to* paṇṇaiyāḷ *couple after Māyuram Agreement, Kirippūr, 1952*

| | Marakkāḷs | Rs. |
|---|---|---|
| Man's wages, 140 days @ ¾ *marakkāḷ* + As.1 or As.2 | 105 | 8.75 or 17.50 |
| Woman's wages, 80 nonharvest days @ ½ *marakkāḷ* | 40 | — |
| Couple's harvest wages as in Table 20.9 | 30 | — |
| Harvest bonusses, as in Table 20.9 | 240 | — |
| *Paṭṭakkāḷ* as in Table 20.9 | 72 | — |
| Deepāvaḷi clothing | — | 20 |
| Average gifts at life crises and agricultural festivals | 6 | 30 |
| Total | 493 | 58.75 or 67.5 |

*Note:* With paddy at Rs. 9 per *kalam,* this equals the equivalent of 47–4 or 48–7 *kalams* per year. If, however, the yield was only 12 *kalams* per *māh,* the annual income would equal only 43–4 or 44–7 *kalams* per year.

Table 20.11. *Modified payments by large holders to* paṇṇaiyāḷ *couple per year, Kirippūr, 1952*

| | Marakkāḷs | Rs |
|---|---|---|
| Man's wages, 140 nonharvest days @ 1 *marakkāḷ* + As. 4 per day | 140 | 35 |
| Woman's wages, @ ¾ *marakkāḷ*, 80 nonharvest days | 60 | — |
| Harvest bonus of 1/7 crop harvested, @ 12 *māhs* per couple, 15 *kalams* per *māh* | 308.57 | — |
| Total | 508.57 | 35 |

*Note:* With paddy at Rs. 9 per *kalam,* this equals the equivalent of 46–3 *kalams* per year. If, however, only 12 *kalams* per *māh* were harvested, the annual income would equal only 40–2 *kalams* per year.

the women As. 12 per day in some seasons other than harvest, as he preferred to sell most of his paddy crop. I have classified these laborers as "regular coolies" in Tables 20.2 and 20.13. At the usual black market price of Rs. 24 per bag, their payments equaled the amounts paid to their *paṇṇaiyāḷs* in paddy by most of the bigger landlords. Table 20.12, finally, estimates the earnings that *should* have been paid to a *paṇṇaiyāḷ* married couple in Kirippūr under the Māyuram Agreement, the method under which Kirippūr's bigger landowners all purported to pay their laborers.

It will be seen that the bigger landlords in fact paid the wages stipulated in the

Table 20.12. *Hypothetical payments due to paṇṇaiyāḷ couple per year under Māyuram Agreement, Kirippūr, 1952*

| | Marakkāḷs | Rs. |
|---|---|---|
| Man's wages, 140 nonharvest days @ 1 *marakkāḷ* per day | 140 | — |
| Woman's wages, 80 nonharvest days @ ¾ *marakkāḷ* per day | 60 | — |
| Harvest bonus, 1/7 crop, @ 12 *māhs* per couple, 15 *kalams* per *māh* | 308.57 | — |
| *Paṭṭakkāḷ* of 50 *kuris* @ 12 *kalams* per *māh* | 72 | — |
| Deepāvaḷi clothing | — | 20 |
| Average annual gifts at life crises and agricultural festivals as in Table 20.9 | 6 | 10 |
| Total | 586.57 | 30 |

*Note:* With paddy at Rs. 9 per *kalam,* this would be the equivalent of 52–2 *kalams* per year. If, however, the harvest yield was only 12 *kalams* per *māh,* the annual payments would equal only 47–9 *kalams* per year.

Māyuram Agreement, but contravened it by refusing to give the traditional clothing, gifts at life crises and festivals, and plot of paddy land. In 1952, the small holders (who were not legally bound by the Māyuram Agreement) struck a balance by slightly increasing the daily wages while continuing to give customary gifts and *paṭṭakkāḷ* plots. During the harvest of February 1953 after the cyclone, however, the Ādi Drāviḍas' Communist Union pressed the small holders to pay one-seventh of the crop as harvest wages, the amount stipulated in the Māyuram Agreement, even though that agreement actually applied only to landlords owning more than 6.66 standard acres. At that point, some of the small holders, too, took away their workers' *paṭṭakkāḷ,* saying that they could not afford both *paṭṭakkāḷ* and increased wages. Having lost their *paṭṭakkāḷ*, the workers of such peasants earned about 36–3 *kalams* plus about Rs. 38 to Rs. 48, or the equivalent of forty-two *kalams* for the year.

Kirippūr had twenty-four men and twenty-eight women who were casual coolies (see Table 20.2). Five men and thirteen women were Non-Brahmans; the rest, Ādi Drāviḍas. In theory, casual coolies were paid a flat rate of Re. 1 per day per man and As. 12 per woman for all tasks, including harvest. With 180 days' work per man and 120 per woman, this meant an annual income of Rs. 270 per couple. With paddy at its legal price of Rs. 6 per *kalam* this sum supposedly bought the equivalent of forty-five *kalams* a year, but with paddy at its actual, average black market price of Rs. 9 per *kalam* a couple would receive only about thirty *kalams*. With a food requirement of one *kalam* of paddy per adult per month, it is clear that the casual coolies were woefully poor and sometimes hungry. Young coolies who worked more days received, however, somewhat more per year, while older coolies who received less had no children to feed. Three casual coolies, moreover, leased a little land in addition to their daily labor. In general, Kirippūr had fewer destitute casual coolies than did Kumbapeṭṭai (see Table 20.1). Roughly the same proportion of Kirippūr's agriculturalists, however, were landless laborers in general, namely 49.2 percent as against 49.7 percent in Kumbapeṭṭai.

It is clear that although the Communist movement had arisen in Kirippūr in 1948, in 1952 it had not managed to raise the wages of laborers to the amount stipulated by law. Indeed, Kirippūr's wages had risen no more than Kumbapeṭṭai's since the Māyuram Agreement of 1948, and its annual wages remained somewhat lower than those in Kumbapeṭṭai. The main reason was that productivity was lower in Kirippūr. Even the wealthiest landlords, however, failed to pay all of the stipulated payments. Among the bigger owners, the Manjūr landlord, with his ninety acres, had only twelve regular laborers in Kirippūr, whom he hired officially as coolies who were not covered by the legislation. During the harvest and transplanting seasons, he brought extra laborers by truck from Manjūr and paid them even lower wages as casual coolies. Although several Communist meetings were held concerning wages during my stay, the laborers did not succeed in compelling the bigger landlords to pay both the full wages under the Māyuram Agreement and also the customary perquisities in gifts, clothing, and *paṭṭakkāḷ*, such as were required by law. In the economic sphere, the net effect of the Communists' agitation had been to turn the laborers' payments into something approaching capitalist wages and to increase somewhat the annual payments, while unintentionally abolishing the landlords' "feudal" dues to the laborers.

The Communists' efforts, however, must not be underestimated. Had they not organized in East Thanjāvūr, it is probable that no legislation would have been passed at all, and that no increase in wages would have occurred in the district as a whole. As it was, an increase of about five or six *kalams* a year (14 percent of the former wage) was a great bonus to the laborers.

The Communist leaders had been in jail from the time of the strike of 1948 until late 1951. They were released with the beginning of universal franchise and formed a parliamentary party engaged mainly in electoral and trade union work. While the leaders were in jail, wages in East Thanjāvūr had dropped back to roughly what they had been before the strike of 1948. With the reemergence of the leaders, laborers' unions were revitalized and several strikes were held in East Thanjāvūr that contributed to the passing of the Tanjore Tenants' and Paṇṇaiyāḷs' Ordinance. Kirippūr's landlords had raised wages again to something approximating the Māyuram Agreement of 1948 (which the government had offered as an alternative to the Tenants' and Paṇṇaiyaḷs' Ordinance) in September 1952, just before I came to the village, and a month after the ordinance was passed.

### Women Workers

Table 20.13 shows the occupational strata of women in Kumbapeṭṭai in 1952, and Table 20.14 shows those of women in Kirippūr. In these tables, unlike tables 15.1 and 20.1, I have classified women in their own right and not in

Table 20.13. *Occupational strata of women by major caste groups, Kumbapeṭṭai, 1952*

| | Brahman | Non-Brahman | Ādi Drāviḍa | Total |
|---|---|---|---|---|
| *Agricultural* | | | | |
| Landlords | 6 | — | — | 6 |
| Tenant cultivators | — | 8 | 21 | 29 |
| Laborers | | | | |
| With leased land | — | — | 18 | 18 |
| Paṇṇaiyāḷs | — | — | 24 | 24 |
| Regular coolies | — | — | 6 | 6 |
| Casual coolies | — | 5 | 35 | 40 |
| Total agricultural | 6 | 13 | 104 | 123 |
| *Nonagricultural* | | | | |
| Housewives | 43 | 37 | — | 81 |
| Independent entrepreneurs (coffee or teashop or restaurant) | 1 | 2 | — | 3 |
| Unsupervised workers | | | | |
| Prostitutes | — | 4 | — | 4 |
| Laundryworkers | — | 2 | — | 2 |
| Midwife | — | 1 | — | 1 |
| Supervised workers | | | | |
| Servant in water pandal | — | 1 | — | 1 |
| Restaurant worker | — | 1 | — | 1 |
| Road sweeper | — | 1 | — | 1 |
| Housemaids | — | 23 | — | 23 |
| Total nonagricultural | 44 | 71 | — | 115 |
| Grand total | 50 | 84 | 104 | 238 |

the groups of their husbands. Thus, no middle peasants are found in these tables, for the women in those households were housewives rather than agricultural workers. "Housewives" are placed at the top of the nonagricultural list because women's abstention from work outside the home was seen as a sign both of status and greater income. In these tables, "housewives" refers to women who worked in the house and garden and who received no wages, although they might tend goats and chickens, grow vegetables, and preserve foods. "Landlords" refers to landowning widows who had some right of management of their own land and income, rather than to women whose land was managed by their husbands.

Comparing these tables, we reach conclusions similar to those reached in connection with male occupations and the total class structure. Kumbapeṭṭai's "upper class" was larger, but more of Kirippūr's women worked in relatively

Table 20.14. *Occupational strata of women by major caste groups, Kirippūr, 1952*

| | High caste[a] | Other Non-Brahman | Ādi Drāviḍa | Total |
|---|---|---|---|---|
| *Agricultural* | | | | |
| Landlords | — | 1 | — | 1 |
| Tenant cultivators | — | 17 | 4 | 21 |
| Laborers | | | | |
| With leased land | — | — | 3 | 3 |
| Paṇṇaiyāḷs | — | — | 47 | 47 |
| Regular coolies | — | 3 | 9 | 12 |
| Casual coolies | — | 13 | 15 | 28 |
| Total agricultural | — | 34 | 78 | 112 |
| *Nonagricultural* | | | | |
| Housewives | 11 | 62 | — | 67 |
| Independent entrepreneurs | | | | |
| Dairy and poultry farming and sales | — | 10 | — | 10 |
| Cookery for teashops | — | 1 | — | 1 |
| Shopkeepers | — | 3 | — | 3 |
| Spinners | — | 13 | — | 13 |
| Unsupervised workers | | | | |
| Spinners | — | 2 | — | 2 |
| Prostitutes | — | 4 | — | 4 |
| Laundryworkers | — | 2 | — | 2 |
| Supervised workers | | | | |
| Housemaids | — | 14 | — | 14 |
| Total nonagricultural | 11 | 105 | — | 116 |
| Grand total | 11 | 139 | 7 | 228 |

[a]Brahman and Toṇḍaimaṇḍalam Veḷḷāḷar

independent circumstances. Thus, landlords plus housewives were 36 percent of the women in Kumbapeṭṭai but only 30 percent in Kirippūr; more women in Kirippūr went out to work. The two villages' laboring groups were of virtually the same proportions; Kumbapeṭṭai's "supervised laborers" were 47.5 percent of the women; those of Kirippūr, 46.5 percent. In Kirippūr, however, 14.5 percent of the women were independent entrepreneurs or unsupervised workers, whereas only 4 percent fell in these strata in Kumbapeṭṭai.

As in the case of men, more of Kirippūr's women worked for cash sums from outside the village. The dairy and poultry farmers and the spinners (twenty-five women or 11 percent of the total) sold their wares in Tekkūr or other nearby, larger villages.

## The Cyclone

Because it was the most significant event of 1952–3, which pointed up certain features of village life and organization, some mention must be made of the cyclone that hit East Thanjāvūr on November 30, 1952. On December 2, I recorded in my field notes:

> The cyclone came about 10:00 A.M. on Sunday (the Kārthikai Full Moon Festival) and ended at 8:00 P.M. A tremendous wind swirled about the village; when I went out of doors for a minute about noon, it blew the breath from my nostrils and almost knocked me down.
>
> The initial loss was estimated at Rs. 30,000, Rs. 50,000, and Rs. 100,000 by different landlords. The Pa<u>ll</u>ar and Pa<u>r</u>ayar Streets were wiped out; the river overflowed and "drowned" the lower streets. All thatched houses in the village were practically destroyed. The Pi<u>ll</u>ayār temple was destroyed; many tiles were blown off the tile-roofed houses, leaving gaping holes through which rain has been sheeting down. About half the coconut trees and almost all the other trees were demolished. The Village Headman, who owns nine acres of dry land, has lost about 200 coconut trees; another Mudaliar, 30. The rice mill on the eastern boundary is temporarily out of action; families began to pound their own paddy yesterday.
>
> Natēsha Paḍaiyācchi of Upper Kirippūr died on his way home from the Tekkūr market with his vegetables. He was found sitting under the eaves of the Kāḷiyamman Temple by Dāsil, the *poosāri*, at 5:00 P.M. yesterday. The funeral was today but was attended by only about two dozen Paḍaiyācchi men and women, as the family is very poor and most people are busy rebuilding their homes. Few of the relatives could come because the roads are blocked with fallen trees and the buses and trains have stopped. The widow was totally hysterical, screaming and tearing her hair. When his brother garlanded the corpse before leaving the house, she tried to get inside the garland, shouting "One garland is enough for both of us!" As the bier was carried to the cremation ground she ran and flung herself on the ground after it. Some of this behavior is customary, but I have never seen quite such grief. Natēshan left one-and-one-third acres of land and a twelve-year-old daughter.
>
> The storm brought out certain social and psychological characteristics. First, there was a great deal of humour and laughter, especially among the young people and children. The barber's son arrived, broadly grinning, to tell me his house was "sitting down." Another man from Lower Street, when I asked today how his house was, said "Oh, I've lifted that up and carried it away."
>
> Those who believed in gods continue to do so, and those who didn't, don't. In spite of the chaos, a small version of the Karthikai festival was held in the Siva temple last evening, one day late. A big bonfire was lit before the temple and there were fireworks and bobbins of palmyra flowers surrounded by coconut husk, lit and swung round by the children. But few people attended, mainly the Toṇḍaimaṇḍalam Mudaliars who are responsible for the festival. Veḷḷi Guṇḍu ("Silver Bomb," my middle-aged Naidū neighbour, so called because he is very dark and stout) says festivals are useless and if there is a God, he must be totally unjust.

Despite the disaster and despite much generosity, caste observances and inter-caste hostilities have gone on as before. Bhoomā Dēvi ("Silver Bomb's" wife, and my next door neighbour) fed 8 or 10 destitute Paḷḷars last night outside the back of her house as well as her own cowboy, whom she feeds every day. She did it out of kindness, but today tells me she hates their Communist attitudes and doesn't like giving them anything nowadays. Both she and "Silver Bomb" are furious because I gave bed sheets to 30 Paḷḷars who arrived with their clothes blown off on the storm night, let them cook on my front verandah, and am sheltering them in my living room until their houses are built again. They daren't say much, however, as I pay rent which is needed by their kinsman, an absent Naidū. Even Vēlan and Navaneethan (high school boys) have let me down. They sneered at my "friends" and wouldn't take part in the firework display we put on last night in my inner courtyard. Only K., one of the younger Mudaliar landlords, has expressed pity for the Harijans whose huts were swept away, although all the landlords and peasants have allowed their *paṇṇaiyāḷs* to stay at home the first two days to re-build them. And K. and T. (two younger Mudaliars) went down to the Paḷḷar Street on the first evening to see what damage had been done.

The Paḷḷars are actually perfectly clean and polite, like everyone else here. They are grateful for the smallest favour and tidy up and sweep the floor each time they leave. Children are bonked lightly on the head if they misbehave, and are kept quite quiet. The men have promised to mend my roof and whitewash my house free of charge as soon as their huts are rebuilt.

There is a great deal of kindness by landowners to the villagers, but, of course, all within the limits of caste rules. The Mudaliars took their tenants and *vēlaikkārars* into the backs of their houses and fed them, but not the Paḷḷars and Paṟayars. The Ayyangārs took in two Paḍaiyācchi families; the Kurukkals another one. The V.H.M. is sheltering the two Kōṉār families and C. Patthar (the Goldsmith) took the Washermen, but no one offered a roof to the Harijans. K. Mudaliar did, however, give me rice for their evening meal, although his wife was unwilling – no doubt, she has to make sure there is enough for her family. In spite of the danger they were in when their house collapsed, the Washerman's family refused to take shelter with Sengunda Mudaliars, claiming they were of lower caste! They went reluctantly to the Goldsmiths' but won't eat there; they say they can receive food only from Toṇḍaimaṇḍalam Mudaliars and Brahmans. M., the Washerwoman, is very angry with me for lending cloths to the Harijans and says I must wash them myself when they return them. (In fact, M. relented and did wash them, but with many moans about her loss of purity.)

There is somewhat of a hope that a force mightier than them will save the villagers. Many people have been to ask if I will pay for rebuilding their houses, and people hope the government will supply rice and money. (This, in fact, was done about a week after the cyclone occurred.) Many have complained that the former British government would have cleaned things up more quickly, as it did, apparently, when a train was de-railed in the 1930s, but this may be mainly blarney. The Chief Minister does promise food and cash relief on the radio, and will shortly tour the district.

It surprises me that in all this mess and chaos people cling to ideas of

> "respectability." Although it was obvious that my cook was busy and no one else was there to help, neighbours objected strenuously when I began to clean up my house. Neelāvati (a Naidū neighbour) came to meet me as I went to draw water from her well, complaining in shocked tones that I had mud on my feet and sweat on my brow. As usual, almost no value is given to manual labour and practical competence; the landlords and rich peasants wait around amid the ruins until servants come to clear up for them. I think, too, that many are stunned and disheartened, for the repair work is being done slowly, without enthusiasm. "Silver Bomb" says many people are mad, or would like to go mad, this week, in order to forget their sorrows.
>
> There is no organization for relief or repairs at the village level and little cooperation. The V.H.M. has assumed responsibility only for his own repairs, and each landowner has arranged individually and haphazardly with his servants how the work will be done. Yet there is so much spontaneous friendliness and affection. Several times I have seen people pressing handfuls of cooked rice and salt into neighbours' hands in case they are hungry. Things seem to happen this way because the village is disunited in terms of land ownership. The family, the caste, and inter-household obligations across caste provide the networks in such a crisis.

By contrast, although the damage in Kumbapeṭṭai was less severe, there was greater unity and initiative at the village level. As leader of the Brahman landlords, the *panchāyat* president and his friends organized shelter, feeding of the poor, and a full village turnout for the funeral of the Kōṉār victim.

# 21 Village Politics: The Caste Hindūs

### The Settlement of Disputes

In 1952 the Brahmans and Non-Brahmans of Kirippūr had had no street headman for the past thirty years. Although I am unsure why, I believe that labor migration, the arrival of newcomers, economic disparities within each street, and the fact that many people earned money outside the village produced disunity. On Lower Street, two Sengunda Mudaliars did collect money for the Draupadi Ammaṉ temple, managed its two-thirds acre of land, and leased out fishing in the Ayyaṉār temple tank to Nāḍārs once a year to obtain more cash for the two Lower Street temples' expenses. They had, however, no authority to settle disputes or witness marriages.

The Toṇḍaimaṇḍalam Mudaliar street also had no regular group of elders to manage its affairs or to govern the lower castes, probably because its members lacked the power of landownership over the village at large. The two wealthiest men in the village – the Paḍaiyācchi rich peasant owning twenty acres and the Naidū soda factory owner – were too newly rich, uneducated, low in caste, and unassuming in personality to command much authority in the village or even in their streets.

The village headman did have the legal right to settle civil disputes involving not more than Rs. 50, and the obligation to call the police in case of crime. Coming from an old, high-caste family and owning fifteen acres of land in addition to being headman, he was also often called on by disputants to settle general kinds of "trouble" such as theft, adultery, or assault among Non-Brahmans of lower caste. At times, the headman called the police to ratify his judgment, or the police might be approached independently by the plaintiff if he was dissatisfied. A second middle-aged Toṇḍaimaṇḍalam Mudaliar, sometimes called "Law Point," prided himself on knowledge of the law and was sometimes approached to settle disputes. This man owned only one *māh* of land but held nineteen acres of *uḷ-kuthakai* and so had some command over tenants and laborers.

As it happened, the two most recent cases that had come before the two Toṇḍaimaṇḍalam Mudaliar elders both appeared to have involved gross miscarriages of justice. In the first case a Sengunda Mudaliar wife accused a neighbor of her caste of stealing her bangles from where they were hidden in a pot of rice. The family and neighbors brought the accused to the village headman, who called the police. The police kept the accused in the police station three miles away all night, threatening to beat her if she did not confess. Next day a Mudaliar relative and a Veḷḷāḷar rich peasant of Lower Street posted bail to get her out. When she returned, the accused "cast up sand" before the Draupadi Ammaṉ temple, swearing her innocence. The bangles turned up a month later in another place in the plaintiff's house. Since then, the two households had not spoken to one another.

In the second case, a group of Naidūs and Veḷḷāḷars of Upper Street had a long-standing grudge against Kaliya Perumāl, a young Sengunda Mudaliar of Lower Street who was well known for his rebellious attitudes and disregard of caste. Wanting to harm him, they were said to have paid a Paḷḷar girl to report to the village headman that he had used threats to coerce her into having sexual relations and had then given her money. The girl made a statement to "Law Point," who summoned both the young man's and the girl's relatives and then sent for the police. The police sent the girl home, took Kaliya Perumāl to the police station, and kept him until his family raised Rs. 100, half of it for themselves and half for "Law Point." Whether or not Kaliya Perumāl had actually slept with the girl, it was widely felt that he was unlikely to have forced her and that in any case, paying off the police and "Law Point" was venal and inappropriate.

In a case six years earlier, a young, unmarried Paḍaiyācchi tenant of Upper Kirippūr had an affair for about a year with the wife of another tenant of his caste. Eventually, the man's younger sister told her parents. The mother went to berate the son's mistress and was overheard by the girl's husband, who beat his wife severely. A crowd gathered and eventually brought the disputants to "Law Point." On hearing the facts, he ran and beat the youth several times with his shoes. The boy's father felt deeply insulted by this assault and went and "cast up sand" outside the Piḷḷayār temple. The youth himself became "half mad" over his disgrace in the village, and sat in his house for a year, often refusing food. At last he was taken to live in a relative's house in Chidambaram for a few months until he recovered and came home to work again. The two disputing households still did not speak to one another six years later.

It was said that because "justice" in Kirippūr was uncertain, for the previous year individuals with disputes had tried to avoid the landlords and the police and had resorted to other means. As in Kumbapeṭṭai, because the Drāviḍa Kazhakam claimed the allegiance of most middle- and lower-ranking Non-Brahmans, while the landlords supported the Congress Party, these lower-ranking Non-Brahmans aspired to greater independence.

In one recent case, a Paḍaiyācchi suspected a neighbor of stealing his wife's jewelry, worth Rs. 100, when she had placed it on her verandah before going to bathe. The accused denied the charge "on the heads of her children," a serious vow, which it was believed could kill them if she spoke untruly. The plaintiff consulted a magician in a nearby village, who confirmed that the accused was guilty. The plaintiff then wrote the accused's name and the circumstances on a paper and placed it before Ayyaṉār in his shrine. Supposedly, the accused would fall ill if she were guilty. Nothing, in fact, happened, but the two households maintained silence with each other throughout my stay.

In Kirippūr the biggest quarrels were not between landlords' lineages and their followers, as in Kumbapeṭṭai, but between whole caste groups or streets. The most serious fray had occurred in the 1920s. At that time the Paḍaiyācchis of Upper Street were still sufficiently lowly to drag the chariot of the god Subramania at the Soora Samhāram festival celebrated in the Siva temple. One year, the Paḍaiyācchis were late in assembling to drag the car. A Naidū bully, Gōvindan, abused them with vulgar words. A Paḍaiyācchi youth, Vairavan, replied using the second person singular: "Do you think I can carry the thing alone?" Gōvindan was furious, for the Paḍaiyācchis were "mere" tenants and *vēlaikkārars* whereas some Naidūs owned land, employed laborers, and considered themselves of superior caste rank. Gōvindan ran to punch Vairavan but was intercepted by another Paḍaiyācchi, Subbayyan. The two fought on the threshold of the temple. Finally the Paḍaiyācchis converged on Gōvindan and forced him to go home.

A few days later, Gōvindan gathered a group of Naidū stalwarts who beat up Subbayyan. When they heard of the assault, a great band of Paḍaiyācchi men and women rushed up Upper Street toward Gōvindan's house, shouting for vengeance. Gōvindan met them on his threshold with a staff and cracked open Vairavan's head; when he fell unconscious, the fight was over. The Paḍaiyācchis took Vairavan to hospital and filed a charge of assault against Gōvindan. He lost and had to pay a Rs. 300 fine, the alternative to six months in jail. This marked the beginning of Gōvindan's financial downfall. By the time I reached the village he had sold his land and gone to work as a bailiff on a large estate elsewhere, so that I was able to rent his house. Animosity was still rife between the Naidūs and the Paḍaiyācchis of Upper Street, who seldom exchanged more than essential information.

In this case, neither the Paḍaiyācchis nor the Naidūs had been settled long in Upper Street, which was the earlier home of Brahmans and Veḷḷāḷars and had perhaps once been an *agrahāram*. The Paḍaiyācchis were traditionally tenants and laborers, but their local landlords were becoming bankrupt while some members of their caste in Upper Kirippūr were acquiring wealth and land. They therefore resented the "upstart" bullying of the Naidūs, whose caste origins were not well known and were probably quite lowly.

In a case that occurred some months before I arrived, Kaliya Perumāl, the Sengunda Mudaliar of Lower Street mentioned earlier, rode a hired bicycle too quickly through Upper Street and knocked down a poverty-stricken Seiva Veḷḷāḷar boy, Sivasāmi, aged twelve, near the oilmonger's house. The boy's leg was injured; it was not clear how badly. His family bandaged the leg with splints and gave out that it was broken. The family appealed to their Naidū neighbors who had land and influence. The Veḷḷāḷars, Naidūs, and Vāṇiyars threatened to beat up Kaliya Perumāl, whereupon a crowd of weavers came flying from Lower

Street to his support and a loud quarrel took place. Finally, the Veḷḷāḷars took the case to "Law Point." This gentleman was already angry with Kaliya Perumāl for daring to ride a bicycle through Middle Street. He summoned the youth, who offered to take Sivasāmi to hospital and pay for treatment. This was refused; instead "Law Point" fined him Rs. 100, three-quarters of it as compensation to Sivasāmi and one-quarter for himself as judge. Sivasāmi was taken to his mother's brother's house in another village. He returned home hale after a month. It was six months later that the Naidūs and Veḷḷāḷars were said to have instigated the case of the Paḷḷar girl against Kaliya Perumāl. Although a rebel who rode a bicycle and "smoked cigarettes everywhere" regardless of people's rank, Kaliya Perumāl was too poor to withstand these onslaughts and simply paid his fine. The case illustrated a long-standing animosity between the Naidūs and Veḷḷāḷars of Upper Street and the Sengunda Mudaliars of Lower Street, whom the Naidūs regarded as "low" and "trashy." The Paḍaiyācchis of Upper Street took no part in this affray for they were at enmity with the Naidūs.

Disputes between Non-Brahman castes were common, it seemed, because Kirippūr was not a "traditional" village with a clearly defined caste hierarchy. About 60 percent of the people belonged to families who had arrived within the previous century. By the 1920s landownership was so distributed that none of the middle-ranking Non-Brahmans could claim authority or clarity of rank in relation to the rest. There was therefore constant competition and bickering among the largest groups (the Paḍaiyācchis, Naidūs, and Sengunda Mudaliars), ultimately for authority and status. Because they were landlords who had once been wealthy and because one of them held the village headmanship, the two leading Mēlnād Toṇḍaimaṇḍalam Mudaliars were convenient arbitrators, but even they lacked the power to intervene voluntarily.

### Political Parties

As in Kumbapeṭṭai, and as was usual in Thanjāvūr, the Congress Party drew its main support from the upper castes, the landlords, and the richest peasants. They included the Brahmans and almost all the Toṇḍaimaṇḍalam Mudaliars, the richest Naidū, Paḍaiyācchi and Chōḷiya Veḷḷāḷar landowners, and some of their high caste but poverty-stricken followers among the Seiva Veḷḷāḷars. The Laundryworkers, Oilmongers, Poosāris, and Smiths were also Congress supporters. As village servants with few caste members and relatively little property, they looked for protection to the landlords and were proverbially snobbish about their religious observances and "purity" in relation to villagers of lower caste than themselves. Support for the Congress Party was thus based primarily on class rather than caste membership, but caste was relevant in the case of some of the smaller client groups who looked to the landlords as their benefactors.

Congress supporters in Kirippūr showed a characteristic ambivalence toward social reforms such as land legislation and the betterment of Harijan conditions. One of the Toṇḍaimaṇḍalam Mudaliars, a man of about thirty-five, classically illustrated the Congress-supporting landlord's dilemmas. A member of the District Congress Committee, he spent considerable time in my house lecturing me on the Congress government's achievements regarding social reform. Correctly, he pointed out that the central government had forbidden caste discrimination by law as soon as it came to power in 1947. Since then, the state government claimed to have removed 124,619 Ādi Drāviḍas in Thanjāvūr from house sites owned by landlords and to have placed them in new streets on government land where they owned the produce of their gardens. In Kirippūr, indeed, Lower Paḷḷar Street had benefited from such action; by 1952 its members were living on former wasteland where each family cultivated about 0.02 acres of garden free of charge. Since 1949, 147 Harijan schools had been opened in the district, one of them in Tekkūr. Ten thousand children were reported to be studying and receiving free midday meals. By law, no government school might refuse access to Harijans, although many – including the one in Kirippūr – did. Any Harijan who could obtain a high school education was assured of a job in government service. Slowly and gradually, it was argued, the Harijans must be uplifted; in time, cottage industries might be started among them. My mentor also stressed that the Congress government had passed the Māyuram Agreement and the Tanjore Tenants' and Paṇṇāiyals' Act.

In fact, however, this Congressman did not encourage reform in his own village. He admitted that he had never entered the Harijan streets. He argued smilingly that if he did, the people would be so consternated to see a high-caste intruder that they would run away. During the harvest of February 1953, this small landlord was one of the few who refused to pay his Harijan laborers one-seventh instead of the traditional one-ninth of the harvest. The Communist Union had to reprimand and fine his *paṇṇaiyāḷs* for "scabbing" and force them to promise that they would never again work for less than the statutory wage. The landlord (who owned only two acres) could ill afford the extra payment, but his attitude helped cause the laborers to hate the Congress Party.

The DK in Kirippūr drew its support from most of the middle- and low-ranking Non-Brahmans and from a Kīlnād Toṇḍaimaṇḍalam Mudaliar man, aged twenty-seven. The latter was something of a village rebel whose parents had died young and who had been educated in a Nāgapaṭṭaṇam high school, where he knew several Christians and became unorthodox about caste. In his social life, this young man threw in his lot with the youth of Lower Street and some of the peasants of Upper Kirippūr. Along with them, he had voted for the DK in the recent elections, and was even sympathetic to the Communists. The leading lights of the DK were a Chōḷiya Veḷḷāḷar schoolteacher and some twenty rich or middle peasants of the Chōḷiya Veḷḷāḷar, Naidū, Paḍaiyācchi, Sengunda Mudaliar, and Nāḍār castes. Lower Street was considered to be the hotbed of the DK, but it seemed probable that most of the middle- and lower-ranking Non-Brahmans had voted for it.

It was interesting to see that the peasants of Upper Kirippūr, Upper Street, and Lower Street supported the DK even though their streets were rivals in village affairs. As in the case of the Congress supporters, class rather than caste was the determinant. Although there were exceptions, Congress followers were mainly landlords and their beneficiaries; DK supporters, mainly rich and middle peasants. The caste barrier between Ādi Drāviḍas and all other castes was, however, so great that open support for the Communists in this village was confined not only to landless laborers, but also to Harijans.

It is true that because the DK supported the local Communist candidate in 1952, the village's Congress supporters regarded the DK supporters as also vaguely "Communist" and therefore dangerous. Some did attend large Communist public meetings in Tiruvārūr and Nāgapaṭṭaṇam and had a certain admiration for N. Sivarāj and Manali Kandaswāmy, the Communist (and Non-Brahman) legislative assembly members for Nāgapaṭṭaṇam and Maṉṉārguḍi. Within the village, the DK men behaved somewhat more affably toward the Harijans than did the Congress supporters. Some in theory disbelieved in caste and religion and admitted that in a few years, there was no reason why Harijans should not take their place with other members of society. During the cyclone, the lone Toṇḍaimaṇḍalam Mudaliar DK supporter approved my sheltering Paḷḷars in my home and supplied them with rice. None of the DK members, however, received Ādi Drāviḍas in their own homes and none would enter the Ādi Drāviḍa streets. Some said that they would not mind doing so, but that it would cause too much fuss in the village. Most of the DK supporters, unlike the Congress voters, were not violently opposed to the Tanjore Tenants' and Pannaiyāls' Act and the Māyuram Agreement, because they owned less than 6.66 standard acres and were not strictly speaking affected by it. They did grumble when their own laborers demanded harvest pay approaching that stipulated in the act, but they paid up. Some DK supporters thought that Communism had made the Harijans too impudent, but anti-Communist labor attitudes had not hardened among them.

Kirippūr's Non-Brahman tenant cultivators and *vēlaikkārars* did not form conscious political blocks in the village. They were scattered among the several streets and had their closest ties with relatives of their own caste. Like their caste mates, most or all of them probably voted for the Drāviḍa Kazhakam (and thus incidentally for the Communists) but they had no liaison with the Ādi Drāviḍas' Communist labor union. Because they were either *vēlaikkārars* or casual coolies, the Non-Brahman laborers did not come under the Māyuram Agreement or the Tanjore Tenants' and Paṇṇaiyāḷs' Act and were paid at different rates from the Ādi Drāviḍa *paṇṇaiyāḷs*. Secretly, they may have admired the Ādi Drāviḍas' struggles, but I am afraid that I did not enquire into this. Because there was no laborers' strike during my stay in Kirippūr, I cannot say whether the Non-Brahman laborers would have "scabbed." In some villages, like the one in Kumbakōṇam *tālūk* studied by Sivertsen in 1957, Non-Brahman tenants and laborers such as Paḍaiyācchis and Paḷḷis did form a Communist Peasant Union that agitated both for higher wages and for lower agricultural rents, and themselves recruited the local Ādi Drāviḍas. During the agricultural strike of 1948, moreover, Non-Brahman tenants and laborers as well as Ādi Drāviḍas were widely involved in many parts of Thanjāvūr. In Kirippūr, however, Non-Brahmans had played little or no part in the struggles of 1948 and were not active in 1952–3. The same was true of the neighboring villages. Elsewhere in Naṉṉilam and Nāgapaṭṭaṇam *tālūks* I found that in 1952–3, Ādi Drāviḍas formed the main Communist force in most villages. In Kirippūr it might have been especially difficult for Non-Brahman tenant and laborers to join the Communists because every major caste had a number of rich and middle peasants who were their relatives, who lived on their street, and on whom they depended for friendship, loans, occasional employment, and help at life-crisis rites. In Kirippūr, the Non-Brahman streets were not, as a whole, poor and downtrodden enough to take the giant step of throwing in their lot with Ādi Drāviḍas and the Communists. In the balance of forces at that time, their poorest members would probably have lost more than they gained by doing so individually.

# 22 The Communist Movement

Kirippūr's Ādi Drāviḍas joined the Communist movement during the agitation of 1947–8. They told me that for about five years previously, wages had been very low and prices had risen. Struggles to raise wages were met with brutality in the neighborhood. In 1947 in a village six miles from Kirippūr, for example, a Naidū landlord owning a thousand acres seized a Harijan worker who led a party of Ādi Drāviḍas demanding higher rates of pay, and nailed his hand to a tree. The nail was removed some hours later and the man fled the district.

In 1947–8, as I have mentioned, a widespread *kisan* (peasant) movement was formed to demand higher wages for workers and bigger shares of the crop for tenants. Some branches of the movement were Gāndhian and reformist, appealing to the consciences of the landlords and of the government. Others – the majority in Nāgapaṭṭanam, Naṉṉilam, and Maṉṉārguḍi *tālūks* – were Communist, with some hope of turning the rural agitation into a revolutionary upsurge in many parts of India. In some villages of East Thanjāvūr in late 1947, armed bands of Ādi Drāviḍas attacked the houses and granaries of big landlords in order to distribute grain and other wealth to laborers. In Nāgapaṭṭaṇam *tālūk* the Communist Party dominated the six-week strike at harvest time in January–February 1948. In many villages Communists neutralized landlords and police and organized the harvesting of crops on behalf of small holders, tenants, and laborers. After the harvest was over, however, armed special police moved into the area, crushed the movement, and jailed the Communist leaders and thousands of their supporters.

Because there were no big landlords in their village, Kirippūr's Ādi Drāviḍas took no part in attacks on landlords' homes. In January 1948, however, they raised the red flag in their street and struck for higher wages during the *oṭṭadan* and *sambā* harvests. Perhaps because of the presence of many small-holding peasants who were related to the Non-Brahman tenants and laborers, Kirippūr's strike was less successful than in villages having big landlords, and the Ādi Drāviḍas were eventually forced back to work.

Shortly after the *sambā* harvest, police arrested a number of strikers in Pattallūr who had attacked landlords' granaries. They then drove to Kirippūr to enquire whether the landlords there had any complaints. The village headman summoned the leading Ādi Drāviḍa in order to impress on him the uselessness of further strikes. Thinking their headman would be arrested, men of the Ādi

Drāviḍa streets arrived with him in a body. The village headman became angry and ordered them to disperse. They refused, shouting that their lives were miserable anyway and that all of them should be taken to jail. Some climbed into the police trucks and made so much disturbance that thirty men were in fact arrested and driven some hundred miles to Trichinopoly jail, where they were imprisoned for fifty-two days. In Vaigāsi, the landowners needed men for ploughing and applied to the court. The workers were released to their former conditions of pay.

In 1952 the Ādi Drāviḍas looked back with pride and some amusement on the period spent in jail. They were housed four to a cell, but said that they were beaten with staffs only when they broke the mud vessels from which they were required to eat. They referred to the jail as *māmaṉār veeḍu* (father-in-law's house), for they said that there, one had no work and plenty to eat – but one did not feel quite at home. In jail they met Communist cadres and other Communist supporters, learned Communist songs, and came back resolved to continue their struggle for greater freedom and better living conditions.

In the villages round Kirippūr, occasional small-scale strikes over wages were conducted by Ādi Drāviḍa laborers during the next three years. Communist Party members were released from jail shortly before the elections of February 1952, which they entered as a parliamentary party with a program of economic and social reforms. With Drāviḍa Kazhakam support, two Communist members of the legislative assembly were elected in Nāgapaṭṭaṇam, one to a seat reserved for a Harijan member. A Communist member of the legislative assembly was also elected in Maṉṉārguḍi.

As in Kumbapeṭṭai, Kirippūr's Ādi Drāviḍa streets had flourishing assemblies of male household heads that witnessed marriages and settled disputes over theft, debt, assault, property, and marital conflict. Each street elected a headman, a messenger, and a treasurer. (On Lower Paḷḷar Street the treasurer was a literate schoolboy, who was able to write the accounts). Since the strike in 1948, Kirippūr's Ādi Drāviḍas had ceased taking their own disputes to the landlords and settled them themselves. A strong sense of unity and of a need for solidarity against the landowners had persisted among all the Ādi Drāviḍas.

Early in 1952 Communist cadres again visited the village and helped the Ādi Drāviḍa assemblies to reorganize themselves as part of a wider labor union. Whereas the assemblies had previously met separately on New Moon evenings on each street, the Ādi Drāviḍas now claimed and won the right of a public holiday on New Moon Day. Each month, the men of all three streets met in conclave for two to four hours on the wasteland under the trees south of Lower Paḷḷar Street or the threshing ground near North Paḷḷar Street. There they sat in a long horseshoe formation. At the top were their three street headmen and sometimes one or two visiting cadres from nearby villages. After any outstanding disputes within the streets had been dealt with, the leaders spoke to the group about the goals and tactics of struggle currently advocated by the Communist Party. In 1952–3, the main goals relevant to the Ādi Drāviḍas were to claim the full payment stipulated in the Māyuram Agreement, to work only an eight-hour day instead of at all hours as had previously been demanded by the landlords, and by united, nonviolent resistance to prevent any beating or other violence against individual laborers. As was usual in Thanjāvūr, the struggles to extract full payment became most intense during the harvest seasons. The harvests were especially significant because in those seasons about half the year's payments were made. During the harvest, moreover, workers had the power to coerce landlords by refusing to cut or thresh the crop when their labor was urgently needed.

Under the Māyuram Agreement and the Tanjore Tenants' and Paṇṇaiyāls Act, only landlords owning more than 6.66 standard acres in one village were required to pay the stipulated wages and harvest shares. In the *oṭṭadan* and *sambā* harvests of January–February 1952 after the cyclone, however, Kirippūr's union demanded the full one-seventh of the crop from all owners, big and small. Almost all of them complied, although, as I have noted, some succeeded in taking away their service plots of one-sixth of an acre (*paṭṭakkāḷ*) from the laborers to compensate for their losses.

Although the struggle for wages was intense, little violence and few confrontations occurred in East Thanjāvūr during the harvest of 1953. On the one hand, since 1951 the Communist policy has been one of peaceful action to bring about a gradual change toward socialism, with emphasis on electoral and trade union organizing. On the other hand, landlords appeared somewhat cowed by the strength of the agricultural union and by the election of Communist members to the legislative assembly.

Some confrontations, however, did occur. In Kirippūr in February 1953 a Sengunda Mudaliar small holder told his four *paṇṇaiyāḷs* that he would fire them at the end of the year in April because their work had been negligent. This was legally permitted, for under the new act only landlords owning more than one *vēli* were obliged to keep on their *paṇṇaiyāls* or resort to arbitration. Each of the four *paṇṇiyāḷs* had received a loan of about Rs. 75. To get back the loans, the farmer ordered them to cut the paddy of their *paṭṭakkāḷ* plots and deliver it to his house. (If the plots yielded ten *kalams* to the *māh*, each plot of half a *māh* would have yielded five *kalams*, or Rs. 60 at the going rate). The *paṇṇaiyāḷs* cut and threshed their paddy but then refused to deliver it to the farmer, complaining that they had been half starving since the cyclone and that yields were so poor, they could expect little from their harvest wages. The farmer summoned "Law Point" and the Mudaliar District Congress Committee member to the field. They agreed with his decision and began to berate the laborers. Meanwhile, however, a large crowd of Ādi Drāviḍas from Kirippūr and Kuttaṉṉūr arrived together with a Naidū Communist leader from Kīlvelur. A confrontation occurred in which the laborers and their leaders made it plain that they would remove the paddy, retain the loans, and refuse to allow any other laborers to work for the farmer if he fired his *paṇṇaiyāḷs*. At least temporarily, the landlord had to accept the decision and retired in discomfiture.

In some other cases the union was less successful. Laborers suffered losses and sometimes retaliated privately. A Veḷḷāḷar farmer from Lower Street owning 3.5 acres and leasing another 6.66 acres refused to allow his laborers to harvest their *paṭṭakkāḷ* plots, saying he was too short of paddy to maintain his large family and pay his workers the full one-seventh of the harvest. After his own fields were harvested, his relatives went to the *paṭṭakkāḷ* plots, cut the paddy, and delivered it to his shed. That night four *kalams* of paddy were stolen from the shed, it was thought by the *paṇṇaiyāḷs*. The village headman was called to inspect the scene but did not summon the police, fearing a commotion, and the thieves were not discovered.

In some villages near Kirippūr, more serious events occurred. In the village six miles away where a laborer's hand had been nailed in 1947, the landlord, a well-known bully owning 1,000 acres, failed to pay the wages stipulated in the act. A large crowd of Ādi Drāviḍas was said to have thronged to his house carrying the Communist flag. The landlord picked up a gun and threatened to shoot them; eventually they dispersed. A local Veḷḷāḷar Communist leader was later arrested and charged with inciting the incident.

In March 1953 as the harvest was ending, four stack fires occurred near Kirippūr, one in Kuttaṉṉūr and others in nearby villages. An extract from my notes of March 19 describes one of these fires and the uncertainty surrounding it.

> A large stack fire started about 4:00 P.M. in a village east of Kirippūr. Another was reported this morning from Kuttaṉṉūr, but was put out at once. Others took place yesterday at Vadugachēri (a large Naidū estate) and in a village beyond Rādhāmangalam.
>
> The straw belonged to a Kōṉār of Rānamangalam. He is said by some ADs to be "a big *mirāsdār*." Sōmū Patthar (a Goldsmith youth) says he owns about 10 acres and some *kuthakai*. It was not known who started the fire, but the Goldsmith and "companykkār" (the Naidū soda factory owner) said independently that it was bound to be Ādi Drāviḍa Communists, as part of the Kisan movement. If so, this seems highly unlikely to be official policy, for non-violence was strongly counselled in the Kirippūr union meeting a week ago. The estimated loss was about Rs. 1,000 in straw and paddy, as the straw had not yet been threshed by bullocks.
>
> A crowd of landlords, tenants, and Ādi Drāviḍas had collected by 5:00 P.M. Someone had gone by cycle to fetch the fire engine from Nāgapaṭṭaṇam. All stood at a distance except the ADs of the village who alone were fetching water, pulling away what straw they could from the flames, and throwing earth on the stacks. Ādi Drāviḍa women worked with the men, and some moaned a loud lament. In the midst of this, the owner's wife came and prostrated herself before the stack and then screamed loudly, "Who has done it? Who has done it?" She shrieked at some AD women whom she seemed to suspect and who screamed back indignant denials. Her husband meanwhile sat hopelessly on the path near the stack while a local middle-aged man stood near him and held forth on the losses he had sustained. After a while the woman's son-in-law came and led her away. A small group of Non-Brahman women gathered round her and started a sort of ceremonial wailing as at a funeral,

raising their hands in despair, beating their breasts, and reciting in a monotone. Not one Non-Harijan, however, helped to fight the fire.

Nobody at the scene suggested to me that this was Communist work. S. Mudaliar (a Kirippūr landlord) said lamely that someone might have dropped a country cigar. His cousin, the VHM's son, said going home that people thought a Harijan child had dropped a lighted match in play. The Kirippūr Ādi Drāviḍas appeared to know nothing of it. None of them came to the fire, and Kāḷi and Gōvindan (Kirippūr Paṟayars), who were buying oil in Tekkūr, professed ignorance. But as I walked across the fields alone two Ādi Drāviḍas from Kuttaṉṉūr caught up with me and acted somewhat suspiciously. Both asked me what people were saying and whom they blamed. When I suggested that it was a rotten trick, they smiled and kept silent, then asked me to "go along." I can't help doubting that four fires in two days were started by accident. I suspect either rightist agents throwing blame on the Communists, or Communist labourers acting against Party policy. It is hard to believe the Party would secretly engineer these events, so alienating to the small holders and tenants and, indeed, to most labourers.

Whereas some laborers took private vengeance against their landlords, other persons made attacks on Harijans. In Tekkūr, where a Harijan Labour School had been started by the government, a young Harijan teacher lived alone in a rented room. This was the man who taught Lower Paḷḷar Street boys in the evenings. One night during the harvest three khaki-clad figures, purporting to be police, robbed him of his salary of Rs. 60. They then tied him up in a teashop in Vaḍakkūr saying they suspected him of theft and were going to bring a police van from Kīlvelūr. The gang did not return and in the morning the man was released. Kirippūr's Ādi Drāviḍas believed he had been robbed by some landlord's agents because of his support of the Kisan movement, or conceivably, by police themselves.

Despite these incidents and the hardship following the cyclone, the mood of Kirippūr's Ādi Drāviḍas in 1953 was cheerful and relaxed. To convey its flavor, I give below an account of one Ādi Drāviḍa union meeting (*kooṭṭam*) from my notes of March 15.

The *kooṭṭam* was delayed today as it was Sunday and most men had gone to the Tekkūr market. North Street Paḷḷar men waited idly round Murugaṉ's verandah till mid-day; the meeting started gradually at 2:00 P.M. and went on until 5:30. Eventually, about 50 men and boys assembled under two big trees near Murugaṉ's house. Idumbaṉ, the North Street *nāṭṭāṇmai*, opened the meeting, most of the other street officials being absent. He was helped by the brother-in-law of Paṭṭū, the VHM's servant from Oriyūr who, though young, seemed well informed and respected. On the other side of Idumbaṉ sat another of the Street's "brothers-in-law" from Soṭṭālvaṇṇam. I think that the two visitors were Communist Party cadres, or at least Kisan leaders, as they assumed leadership roles and seemed versed in the Party's policies. These two both wore black shirts with red buttons, bought in Tekkūr. The group acknowledged that they indicated DK affiliations, but denied their significance. They laughed when I asked how Black Shirts (atheists) could support a

Ādi Drāvida union meeting, Kirippūr, March 15, 1953.

demand for money for the Kāḷiyamman temple, with which the meeting opened. The money was taken up by Rās, the Lower Street Paḷḷar priest, for a small offering next week to replace the old temple festival. (Rās also collects betel and aracanuts, bananas, etc., for periodic offerings to the goddess and kills the Ādi Drāviḍas' goats there, although the *poojai* is actually done by Dāsil, the Non-Brahman *poosāri*).

Mūthayyan̲, one of P. Mudaliar's (the District Congress Committee Member's) *paṇṇaiyaḷs* was first called and questioned by Idumban̲. Along with two other servants of P.M., he had agreed to receive the old wage of 1½ *marakkāḷs* per *kalam* for threshing, instead of two. He was called up before the *nāṭṭanmais* at the last meeting and fined Rs. 10; he paid 5 and owes 5. He said he could not pay yet because he had no other work and no money in his house; it was decided that he must pay next week. (Sedayan̲ said that if he didn't pay then he would be given another week, and so on.) P. Mudaliar's two other *paṇṇaiyāḷs* were then called and fined for the same offence.

Idumbaṉ and the two visitors then made speeches on how to conduct grievances against *mirāsdārs*. No Kirippūr man is to interfere in grievances in Tekkūr or other villages unless he is working there as a coolie and has his own complaints. He should then go to the Village Headman of that village (or of Kirippūr in a local dispute) and ask for justice. If the VHM will not help, he must ask the local Communist leaders to write to the Collector or other official. No one must resort to violence and no one must ever quarrel with another Ādi Drāviḍa. Much emphasis was placed on unity.

Thayyāṉ, the Paṟayar *nāṭṭāṇmai* and the oldest officer, then arrived about one hour late and came to sit in front. He was at once questioned by Idumbaṉ, by the Lower Street Messenger and by bystanders about why he was late. He made a flowery speech of excuses, the gist of which was that he had to go to the market. He agreed that the "village children" were correct to lecture him, and then took over the meeting. There was, however, no real authority in the meeting, and no set opening or ending; equality and informality were evident. Kāḷi (aged 25) and a friend also arrived quite late. The friend was called up for questioning but Kāḷi took a back seat near me and so escaped. Two other men from Pattallūr then arrived and were greeted with a joyful *namaskāram* above the head by Idumbaṉ. One was the elder brother of Chokkaṉ in Lower Street who has just gone to live in Pattallūr. The other was a "brother-in-law of the street," visiting his wife's father's house. Both sat at the back and chatted to those around them.

There were many other long speeches, but the only big case concerned Kunji and Nāgappaṉ, the *paṇṇaiyāḷs* of "Silver Bomb." Nāgappaṉ was summoned first and made a long statement with many gestures and rhetorical questions, accusing Kunji of agreeing to go threshing for "Silver Bomb" alone. This is forbidden; the rule is that all of a landlord's *paṇṇaiyāḷs* must thresh together, or none. (The question of equal pay for all the *paṇṇaiyāḷs*, whether or not they are summoned to work, is raised at many threshings.) Kunji, an older man with a top-knot, then made a speech in his own defence. Thayyāṉ made statements condemning him, and got into an argument with Vēlaṉ, who has just returned from jail for illicit trade in alcohol. Kunji was finally fined Rs. 5, and the meeting gradually broke up.

*Comments*. The men sat in a long horseshoe with Idumbaṉ, Thayyāṉ, and other leaders at the head. The Lower Paḷḷar Street headman and treasurer were absent; they had had to go to Nāgapaṭṭaṇam to arrange a marriage. The main business was conducted at the leaders' end, but other men called out freely, argued, walked about, and gave opinions. Fathers and sons all sat in the *kooṭṭam* and apart from the headman there were no seating arrangements according to age or precedence. Many trivial conversations were started, especially at our end. When the noise became too loud some outspoken person would shout for silence. Boys under about 18 offered no opinions. There were no women present apart from me, although in the morning one Paḷḷar told me they might come if they were interested. Clearly, they have never been invited. Any interruption, for example my taking a photograph, created immense disturbance, and order had to be restored by a messenger, who walked round good humouredly tapping people on the head with a cane.

There was no haranguing against the landlords in the course of the union meeting. Nor is there in ordinary conversation – the *paṇṇaiyāḷs* have never reviled their masters in my presence. The employers seem to be regarded as a blank force about whom the less said the better, to be handled through tactics that have been generally agreed upon. All present, even the officers, seem ready to submit to another opinion if it is forcefully expressed. As in ordinary assembly meetings in Kumbapeṭṭai, there is always emphasis on equality, unity, and submission to group policy. I felt no suspicion about my presence and no sense of secrecy, no fear that I might tell what I heard outside. This has been true since the Paḷḷars stayed in my house after the cyclone, and in fact, ever since I first entered their streets. Simply because I walk often in AD streets and have been inside their huts, everyone assumes I am a Communist.

There was a lot of joking in the meeting by young and old and much use of kinship terms, such as "uncle" and "younger brother." The *mirāsdārs* are referred to by their traditional title of *ayyā* ("father"), as in "Company *ayyā*" (the soda factory owner), "*mādi-veeḍu ayyā*" ("the owner with two storeys"), or "Nāgapaṭṭaṇam *ayyā*" for "Silver Bomb" (who came from there 30 years ago). The Village Headman is "*paṭṭāmani ayyā*" or "the father who gives the title-deeds." (Meetings like today's are "little *kooṭṭams*"; large rallies in Tiruvārūr or Nāgapaṭṭaṇam, "big *kooṭṭams*.") The main note of the meeting was jollity. The Oriyūr visitor proudly wound a huge white towel around his head as a turban. Mani stuck a book of cinema songs into his turban to have his photo taken and another man arranged his towel over his head like a tent, to everyone's amusement. Gōvindan̲ and Kāḷi threw small bits of bark at me to attract attention when they wanted to explain a point.

Apart from Thayyān̲, who is about 55, the officers are young men and young and middle-aged men spoke most. Murugan̲, aged 60, the village's one Paḷḷar middle peasant, used to be *nāṭṭānmai* six years ago, but gave it up because, as he said, he "couldn't be bothered." Today he sat on the edge of the meeting and left early. Another day, young men of his street hinted that he was old-fashioned; in North Street, only he was expected to know about religion. It may be that because he has three acres of land, he is seen as less trustworthy. Certainly, he is less likely to be interested in the union than those who are labourers. In Pattallūr in 1948 a disturbance arose because a Par̲ayar peasant who owned three-and-a-third acres refused to join the union. A Brahman landlord there told me that the ADs of several villages tried to sack his house and were arrested by the police, but I am not sure of this, for ADs have told me the arrests came because landlords' granaries were pillaged. At all events, small holders have no leadership in the union. In Kirippūr this is really concerned only with labourers – their pay, hours of work, and treatment.

The Ādi Drāviḍas seem to have no clear idea about the possibility of a Communist government for the country, and no hopes of anything beyond gradual reforms. They seem to worry little about untouchability and do not seem to care about mingling freely with the higher castes; they want more pay, better houses, wells and roads, schools, and the freedom to live their own life. Not surprisingly, they have very little idea of the structure of government. They call their Communist leaders "big men" and know that some of them

> are MLAs. They seem confident in the knowledge that they can call on Communist leaders from outside if things go wrong. But above all, they are confident of their own comradeship and unity.

I was interested to find that although the Ādi Drāviḍas had no qualms about my attending their political meetings, their elders objected to my sitting through meetings to deal with purely personal, especially sexual offenses on the part of members of their streets. Thus on March 25, 1953, I wrote the following account of another *kooṭṭam*.

> A special *kooṭṭam* was convened this morning to discuss outstanding cases of debts, and the case of a Paḷḷar, Gōvindan̠, who is said to have molested Māri's wife.
>
> The group met about 8:00 A.M. under the trees south of Lower Paḷḷar Street. About 40 Paḷḷar and Par̠ayar men and youths were present, together with some children. The three *nāttāṇmais* of the Par̠ayar, North Paḷḷar, and Lower Paḷḷar Streets sat in the curve of the horseshoe along with Ammāsi, the creditor, his son-in-law from Kuttan̠n̠ūr, who is visiting, and the messengers and treasurers of the three streets. A youth in this group, the Lower Street treasurer, wrote down in a book the amounts involved. The main body of men sat in two rows facing each other; the rest sat behind them or, haphazardly, on the ground sloping down from the path to the river.
>
> Ammāsi explained that he became a creditor because he had a little jewelry which he sold in the hard time after the cyclone in order to help the "children" of his street. His debtors were Sedayan̠ (two *marakkāḷs* of paddy), Appāsāmi (Rs. 3), Māri (one *marakkāḷ*), Kōn̠an̠ of the twisted face (Rs. 10, in three instalments), and Thōlan̠ (Rs. 4). Each was called in turn except Māri, who slipped away to his house; it was said that he would be summoned later.
>
> Ammāsi first recited his grievances in each case. Then came a long agrument between the chief adjudicators; then each culprit was called and told how much money he must pay, and when. Kāḷi whispered to me that not all the debtors stood up respectfully with their arms folded, as offenders should do. Sedayan̠ stood for a short time in this position, but Kōn̠an̠ stood with his hands on a branch above his head, and Appāsāmi didn't stand at all, except to bounce round on his neighbour Idumban̠ and accuse him of telling lies. Kōn̠an̠'s was the largest and most difficult case. He was finally told to bring all the money within 18 days (i.e. before the New Moon meeting), otherwise his house property would be seized. At first he promised reluctantly to bring the money "in a month"; then "in about 10 days," but he was mocked and made to fix a definite date.
>
> Some of the young men, (Kāḷi, Thōlan̠, Mūthayyan, Thoppalan̠, and others) at first came and sat near me on the bank. Kāḷi and Thōlan̠ had warmly invited me yesterday and Sedayan̠ came and fetched me this morning, although he must have known that his own case would be conducted. The older men, however, objected quietly to my presence, perhaps because the young men surrounded me and carried on private conversations, which is improper, but more probably, because Gōvindan̠'s *poṇmanāthi nyāyam* (woman's case) was to be conducted, and this was not permissible before a woman. After a while a messenger came up and motioned the young men with his cane

to sit down among their elders, while an older man asked aloud why I was there. After the debt cases were finished an awkward pause ensued followed by aimless conversation. At last the leaders took up Gōvindan̲'s case in low tones, with uneasy glances in my direction. Nāgan̲, aged about 30, then came up and asked me whether I would not like to go home, suggesting lamely that I might be wanting to sleep! There were half-hearted protests from the rest, and obvious relief when I got up to go. Kāḷi told me earlier that no Ādi Drāviḍa (nor, of course, higher caste) woman is ever in attendance at the *kooṭṭams*, although Thōlan̲ said that Māri's wife would be summoned today to answer the accusation of flirting with Gōvindan̲. The sum and substance of the charge seemed to be that Gōvindan̲ had "caught her hand" and she had not repulsed him. Kāḷi said that the woman would probably be reprimanded by the headman, and Gōvindan̲ made to pay a small fine to her husband.

This case illustrates the fact that although women were less subordinate to men among the Ādi Drāviḍas than in the other castes, they were firmly excluded from men's deliberations and were under the authority of their husbands and the street meeting with respect to their personal lives. The Communist movement, moreover, had apparently made no change in their position, even though women earned independent wages and took part in strikes.

In several other respects, however, the Communist movement had greatly changed the Ādi Drāviḍas' social lives. Whereas these were once confined to their own streets and their relatives in other villages, the movement had drawn the three streets into a single organization. In 1952 disputes could not be settled nor marriage agreements ratified without the presence of the assemblies and headmen of all the streets. Kirippūr's Ādi Drāviḍas in turn belonged to a wider union of twelve neighboring villages whose members came to each others' aid in times of crisis.

Interdining at marriages between the Paḷḷars and Par̲ayars had become customary, in spite of the higher rank of the Paḷḷars and the age-old antagonism between the two lowest castes. To accommodate the Paḷḷars' customs, the Par̲ayars had stopped eating carrion beef. In order to be worthy of being treated "like men" by the higher castes, both Paḷḷars and Par̲ayars claimed to have given up eating rats, small crabs, and minnows from the irrigation channels, even though these were their main sources of meat.

The aims of Kirippūr's Ādi Drāviḍa union were not entirely met in their relations with the landowners. The union did succeed in raising agricultural wages, even to the extent of forcing small holders to pay the newly instituted harvest shares. As we have seen, however, the landowners retaliated by taking away the Harijans' customary plots when they were able, and by refusing them the traditional gifts of clothing, food, and cash at marriages and festivals. Some farmers, moreover, managed to side-step the union and seriously undermine its efforts by using scab labor from outside the village. In the transplanting season of October 1952, a Nāḍār peasant owning 3.5 acres brought ten Christian Par̲ayar women by bus from Tirutturaipūṇḍi to work instead of the local coolies. These women, who did not belong to a union, worked for twelve hours for half a *marakkāḷ*, whereas local women were willing to work only eight hours for the same amount, and were receiving three-quarters of a *marakkāḷ* from the bigger landlords. More serious, the Manjūr landlord owning ninety acres brought some laborers from his own village to work at transplanting and harvest time for low cash wages instead of paying local coolies in paddy at the going rates. In 1952 the union was not strong enough to exclude such "outside" labor.

Despite these failures, the union had brought great gains to the laborers. The increase in wages, although small, meant the difference between semistarvation and reasonable subsistence. Wage struggles were especially vital in early 1953, for without them landlords and farmers might have withheld even barest rations from the laborers in the period of shortage and poor harvests after the cyclone.

Of equal importance were improvements in working hours and conditions. The eight-hour day, the public holiday on New Moon Day, and the stoppage of flogging and other degrading punishments greatly improved the workers' morale and dignity. Along with these rights came others, not measurable but much valued, such as the right to walk freely on the roads, to wear clothing as one pleased, to attend public rallies far away, to ride on buses, and to go to cinemas. Above all the workers had learned that struggle was possible and that with unity they might win a decent life. There is no wonder that, symbolizing all this, the red flag was their most prized possession.

# 23 Conclusion

Like most ethnographies, this book is primarily a descriptive account interspersed with theoretical insights. In my concluding chapter I draw together and expand upon the more general themes.

The political economy of pre-British Thanjāvūr seems to me to have approximated Marx's model of the Asiatic mode of production, and Darcy Ribeiro's of the Theocratic Irrigation State.[1] This type of state was perhaps the earliest to emerge in the world; variants of it may have existed in the pristine states of Egypt, Mesopotamia, northwest India, north China, Mesoamerica, and the Andes. Certainly it preceded such other types as the "privatistic" slave states exemplified by ancient Greece and Rome (Marx's Ancient Society), or the feudal systems that emerged in post-Roman Europe, Japan, and certain other regions, including (I would argue) Kēraḷa.

As Marx recognized, states of the Asiatic mode remained closer to primitive, prestate societies than did the "privatistic" archaic states, in that land was owned jointly by the monarch and the kinship-based village commune, rather than by individual households or members of the noble or peasant classes.

At the same time, I would argue that states of the so-called Asiatic mode did not constitute a general evolutionary stage between prestate society and Ancient or Feudal societies in the sense of representing a particular stage in the development of the productive forces and of energy appropriation that was necessarily surpassed in the Ancient or the Feudal state. Further, I would argue that societies of the Asiatic mode were not stagnant as Marx supposed, but instead that they were capable of great development in the productive forces, the division of labor, bureaucratization, commodity production, the size of cities, and the size of the maximal political unit. In these respects, at their height some states of the Asiatic mode were probably as "advanced" as the Ancient slave societies, and certainly as the largest of the Feudal states. States of the Asiatic mode seem therefore to have constituted a specific *type* of political economy within the general stage of the Archaic (preindustrial) state, rather than a general stage of state development. It seems probable, as Marx and many later writers have argued, that this type was most likely to endure in states whose heartlands were large, semiarid regions with large-scale and complex irrigation works managed by a central authority that necessarily shared control of the land with the village communities.[2]

The main features of the Asiatic mode of production were:

1. An absence or relative unimportance of private (that is, household or individual) property in land.

2. Land rent and land tax were therefore the same, being simply the "upper share" of the village product that was taken by the monarch or his representatives, the "lower share" being left to the local inhabitants.

3. The villages, or most villages, were communes based on kinship. In Thanjāvūr the simplest village comprised a kinship community of peasants who worked the land cooperatively, had collective possession of land, stock, and slaves, and paid land revenue jointly to the monarch's representatives. In more complex villages, portions of the land, stock, and slaves were redistributed every one to five years to separate households of the land-holding community, usually through the medium of their four or five patrilineal lineages.

4. As Marx noted, the village was "contaminated by distinctions of caste and by slavery."[3] Throughout most of the known pre-British period, however, and in most villages, these distinctions appear to have been communal rather than private. The slaves, like the village servants, were "owned" collectively by the village's dominant caste, and were overseen by government bureaucrats.

5. Again as Marx noted, the cities were *mainly* royal and military encampments.[4] They were largely provisioned from the surplus drawn from villages, especially the land revenue.

6. Commodities were derived mainly from the surplus product. Working villagers had very little access to commodities, which were mainly confined to urban merchants and artisans, the state class, and the state servants. Although there was barter between villages producing different crops, and also small periodic local fairs involving groups of villages, the working population of villages was not involved in a wider, interconnected system of markets. Moreover, much of the surplus product was itself redistributed directly to members of the state class and to the state servants without entering the market. As the surplus product grew, however, larger and larger proportions of it seem to have necessarily entered the market through the medium of traders.

7. In the case of Thanjāvūr, the question of whether classes existed in the Asiatic mode must be answered in the affirmative, even in the absence or near absence of private property in land. The main classes appear to have been the state class, the state servants, the commodity producers and merchants, the peasants, and the slaves.

8. As I have noted, there was apparently no private landowning nobility, although some of the government bureaucrats, the military, the priesthood, the monasteries, and the highest ranks of merchants were allotted the "upper share" of designated prebendal estates.

9. The king was in theory a despot, but he appears to have been despotic mainly within the state class. As Marx noted, the "village republics" as well as the temples, monasteries, and provincial assemblies had a large measure of local government.[5]

10. The villages were largely self-sufficient, especially their working populations of peasants, artisans, and slaves. They surrendered much to the state in land revenue and other taxes but traded little and received little from the state in return.

11. Thanjāvūr was a classic instance of large-scale, centrally coordinated irrigation works, which Marx regarded as common although not essential in the Asiatic mode. Concomitantly, the state undertook other public works such as roadbuilding, hospitals, and charities, and was responsible for building vast religious monuments.

12. Finally, Marx's "stagnation" theory seems to have been correct to the extent that the basic structure of villages was apparently very resilient. Thus it seems probable that the division of labor and form of organization among the village producers changed little between the first and the eighteenth centuries A.D. What did change was the size of the surplus, which apparently increased from about one-sixth of the gross product in the early centuries of the Chōḷa era to about half in the mid-eighteenth century. As the surplus increased, so did the size of cities, commodity production, and the division of labor within the state class and among the commodity producers.

Despite these classic characteristics, by the mid-eighteenth century Thanjāvūr had developed certain other features not strictly characteristic of the Asiatic mode, but tending toward a kind of "communal feudalization." Thus, a large number of *resident* bureaucrats and state servants, including kinship communities of Brahman priests and government servants, groups of temple managers, or single ministers or military officers, held prebendal estates and exercised local authority over peasants and other village workers. This process had begun in the Chōḷa period but seems to have much increased in the periods of Telugu and Maratha dominance.

Second, in some villages, these officers had usurped control of the "lower share" of land produce and had turned the peasants into communal serfs. The peasants in such villages became mere occupancy tenants without self-government, paying either labor rent or rent in kind to the local officials as well as the central government. Because the communal serfs (the ancestors of some of today's middle ranking Non-Brahmans) ranked above the lowest castes of agricultural slaves and had separate tasks and relations of production, this meant that there were in many villages at least two layers of serfdom and slavery in addition to the regular peasantry. Such a state of affairs was not clearly recognized by Marx, who wrote of the "general slavery of the Orient" and thought that over time, captured slaves became submerged in the generally servile population of peasants and artisans.[6]

Third, as we have seen, by the eighteenth century the surplus product was vast and commodity production correspondingly great. Already in early Chōḷa times, *sections* of the main cities were devoted to traders and artisans who dealt in foreign and inland markets,[7] so that cities were not solely royal, military, and religious encampments. Commodity production, already advanced under the merchant guilds in Chōḷa times, may have further expanded after the arrival of the Europeans. Individual merchants and usurers were sometimes wealthy and prominent, although still under state control.

Fourth, by the mid-eighteenth century there was apparently a tendency in some villages for shares of the village land to be divided more or less permanently among the households of land managers (whether peasant or bureaucratic), and for land shares to be unequal and heritable, and thus to begin to approximate private property in land. By 1805, 38 percent of the villages were reported to be under the *arudikkarai*, or "divided share" system; there had also been some sale of land shares to Muslim and Christian merchants. It is likely that the proportion of "divided share" villages was much less in the 1760s before the British conquest, but the process was already underway.

Finally, as Thanjāvūr came under the control of foreign dynasties, the powers of its indigenous Brahman state class seem to have declined somewhat. Especially under the Marathas, local government passed partly to secular, Non-Brahman nobles in charge of provincial forts with their complements of cavalry and artillery and with attached prebendal estates. Something more closely approaching feudal fief holding and military service seems therefore to have developed in parts of the former kingdom in the Telugu and Maratha periods.

These "deviations" from the Asiatic mode seem to have occurred for several reasons. One was that states of the Asiatic mode did apparently periodically undergo a kind of "communal feudalization," especially in border regions and when the central power was weakening. As an outpost of the Vijayanagar and Maratha empires, Thanjāvūr may have been typical in that respect.

Second, Thanjāvūr in the later centuries was reacting to and defending itself against the Muslim empires of north India. These empires, led initially by militarized formations of pastoral nomads, were apparently not strictly typical of the Asiatic mode in its classical phase, for they developed city life and commerce at the expense of irrigated agriculture, expanded commodity production into the local economies of villages, and allowed considerable development of private land holding by peasants.[8] Thanjāvūr may have been influenced in some of these respects by the Mōghul empire, especially in the late seventeenth and the eighteenth centuries.

Third, by the seventeenth and eighteenth centuries, European merchant capital was probably making inroads into Thanjāvūr's villages through the medium of agents among the native traders. This increasingly powerful influence may have been largely responsible for the gradual breakdown of the village commune and for the system of "divided shares."

In spite of these deviations, however, the Asiatic mode of production appears to have remained dominant in Thanjāvūr until the 1770s and the beginnings of the British conquest.

Between 1771 and 1860, as we have seen, the Asiatic mode was shattered by the British conquest and the district emerged as an agricultural hinterland within the world capitalist system and the British empire. In this period I would argue that most production relations became hybrid or transitional to capitalist relations. Some remained precapitalist, but generally changed from communal to private relations.

The change to a colonial agricultural hinterland occurred in four main stages. The period 1771 to 1799 saw wars of conquest, devastation, and depopulation, culminating in the British annexation of the former kingdom as a district of the Madras Presidency. The period 1800 to 1812 saw a brief revival of traditional craft exports, coupled with continuing heavy revenue exactions. From 1812 to 1845, Thanjāvūr's crafts and traditional exports were gradually destroyed by the policies of Britain's industrial bourgeoisie. There was a deep depression, while the district's surplus produce and accumulated treasures were depleted by the continuing heavy extraction of revenue. Later, from about 1845 to 1860, a rice export economy was built on the basis of improved irrigation, and migrant labor to British plantations began. In this period, too, there occurred a severe drain of Thanjāvūr's capital to the British government and private British firms, because most of the value of rice exports was collected as revenue, which was spent mainly outside the district, remitted to Britain, or used for warfare or repression. The value produced by migrant labor also went mainly to British firms owning plantations, yet the laborers were raised in Thanjāvūr and mainly fed on rice from their homeland. The period 1771 to 1860 was thus one of primitive accumulation on behalf of British industry and later, of British export crop plantations, mainly through the extraction of revenue and the eventual incorporation of Thanjāvūr as an adjunct of the British plantation economy.

During this period I would argue that most production relations became hybrid or semicapitalist, for the following reasons. First, the landlords who returned to Thanjāvūr after Haidar Āli's invasion of the 1780s, together with the newly installed *pattakdārs*, or tax farmers, were often individual landlords rather than members of joint village communes as heretofore. Second, the *porakuḍis*, or "outside tenants" who were brought in as sharecroppers, were tenants-at-will who could be evicted, rather than occupancy tenants like the former communal serfs and slaves. As Marx noted, such sharecropping, or *métayage*, was a form of labor relation transitional between precapitalist labor service or peasant farming on the one hand, and capitalist farming with wage labor on the other.[9] Third, in the early 1880s village servants were no longer assured of hereditary occupancy rights and crop shares, but became private servants of the landlords, potentially subject to eviction. Fourth, during the nineteenth century land itself was gradually transformed into capitalist property, that is, individual or family property that could be used for the owner's private purposes and could be freely sold in the market. By 1805, 38 percent of the villages were already under the "divided share" system, while 31 percent were still joint village communities, and 31 percent were each under some kind of individual tax farmer, manager, or owner. Fields were not finally registered as the private property of individuals until 1891, but individual owners became responsible for the payment of revenue from 1865. Toward mid-century, with the development of the rice-export economy, landlords came to resemble rural capitalists who sold half or more of their crops in the market. Some also became paddy merchants, or hired teams of laborers to husk paddy for the export trade.

During this period precapitalist relations did survive among the Ādi Drāviḍas in the form of agricultural slavery. In the early nineteenth century, however, many slaves ceased to be communally controlled by a village community of peasants or land managers and instead became the individual chattels of private landlords, subject to market sale. Slavery was gradually abolished between 1843 and 1861, and replaced by attached debt labor or free wage labor.

With the abolition of slavery, precapitalist servitude as a legally instituted form of extra-economic coercion came to an end, and was replaced by relationships based mainly on private economic coercion. It is true that such forms of extra-economic coercion as the flogging of agricultural laborers continued into the 1950s; in this respect precapitalist features remained. Such coercive relations, however, were probably little different from the forms of force and violence applied to wage laborers in the early stages of capitalism, as described by Marx.[10]

We have seen that the period 1860 to 1947 saw the flowering of Thanjāvūr's agricultural hinterland economy, with rice as a virtual monocrop employing some 77 percent of the workforce. I would argue that during this period Thanjāvūr was a colonial segment within the British empire, which as a whole was dominated by the capitalist mode of production.

As a colonial region, however, Thanjāvūr's actual production relations were mainly characterized by what Marx called the "formal" rather than the "real" subsumption of labor under capital.[11] Traditional, rather than modern industrial, technology was for the most part retained in such forms as the ox plough and the handloom, but new production relations were organized around it that were either actually those of wage labor or were similar in content and were no longer relations of precapitalist legal servitude. Through these production relations absolute surplus value was extracted for private profit, most immediately by local landlords and merchants, and less directly by British financial, trading, industrial, and plantation-owning companies.

The agrarian relations of this period fell into three main categories. The first comprised the *kuthakai* tenants, or fixed-rent tenants-at-will. The bigger ones became small rural capitalists marketing much of their produce and often owning land as well. The small ones were little different from annually engaged laborers, except that they had some temporary control over their means of production for part of the year. The second category was that of the *paṇṇaiyāḷ*, or laborer hired by the year, who was paid both in kind and cash, was usually indebted, and might differ from the true wage laborer in being given a tiny allotment for part of his subsistence. The third type was the casual laborer hired by the day and paid in rice or cash, the closest approximation to a wage worker. Casual laborers, as we have seen, increased in the twentieth century, especially after the end of labor migration in 1939. Perhaps a quarter of the workers in all fields were casual laborers by 1952.

During the "British century" Thanjāvūr did experience *some* gradual rise in the organic composition of capital in agriculture, in the form of new irrigation, double cropping, composting, and chemical fertilizers. Modern machinery was introduced in fields connected with the export trade – rice, oil and tanning mills, railroads, shipping, trucking, and buses. These sectors of the economy saw the development of what Marx called the "real" rather than the merely "formal" subsumption of labor under capital, the "specifically capitalist relations of production" involving the extraction of relative, as well as absolute, surplus value. The workers in these enterprises were true wage workers, paid in cash.

Although the real subsumption of labor under capital occurred in only limited sectors of the economy, I regard the mode of production as a whole as capitalist because land and other resources became private, marketable property; crops and other products were largely marketed; hired labor was predominant; and workers were largely separated from their means of production, for even when they were tenant farmers they were engaged only for short periods and could be evicted at will. Further capitalist features were that labor was no longer in political forms of bondage, but was mainly under economic coercion, and that Thanjāvūr formed part of a world division of labor, concentrating on the production of rice and labor for export. Finally, the state was a bourgeois state, dominated by the British bourgeoisie and, to a limited extent, by the colonial compradore bourgeoisie and by a nascent Indian industrial bourgeoisie.

The system was, however, distinctively *colonial* capitalist, in that the main accumulation of capital occurred in Britain as the metropolis, or in metropolitan outposts such as British plantations and industries abroad. Because of the drain of capital to Britain in such forms as salaries, profits, migrant labor, revenue, and debt repayments, Thanjāvūr, like India as a whole, largely failed to industrialize. Therefore, most production relations remained ones of only formal subsumption under capital. Again, although commodity production gradually became generalized, the Indian economy was largely disarticulated, being harnessed externally to British metropolitan needs. In this process the division of labor *inside* Thanjāvūr became greatly simplified by comparison with its condition under the native rulers, as the towns declined, crafts died out or were reduced, and the majority of the people were driven to work in rice production or export. Finally, Thanjāvūr underwent the extreme impoverishment characteristic of colonial capitalist regions, as the bulk of its surplus value was exported to the metropolitan center or its outposts.

Although I agree with Hamza Alavi's analysis of colonial, and especially Indian, economic processes, I cannot accept his separation of a "colonial mode of production" from the capitalist mode as a whole. The reason is, of course, that as Alavi insists, "the colonial mode *is a capitalist mode*";[12] it is also inextricably linked with and dominated by metropolitan capital. It does not seem reasonable to distinguish two separate capitalist modes, one colonial and one metropolitan – or even perhaps three, one "core," one "peripheral," and one "semi-peripheral," to use Wallerstein's terms.[13] It seems rather that we must admit that India did *not* develop along the same path as Britain, as Marx expected it to do, that it developed along a complementary and specifically colonial trajectory, yet that it developed within the (single) capitalist mode.

In exploring the modern political economy of Thanjāvūr, I have tried to place it in the context of ecological and demographic variation in Tamiḷ Nāḍu as a whole, and also among the *tālūks* of Thanjāvūr.

My statistical findings confirmed the hypotheses that both in Tamiḷ Nāḍu and in Thanjāvūr, higher rainfall tends to be accompanied by more intensive irrigation, more wet paddy cultivation, a higher population density, and in Tamiḷ Nāḍu, higher productivity and a greater money value of crops per acre. This last, however, is not always true in Thanjāvūr, where the north and center of the coastal region, although having relatively high rainfall, irrigation, and wet paddy, also suffer from poor drainage, salinity, and periodic cyclones and so tend to have lower productivity than the "breast" of the Kāvēri in the northwest and north center of the district.

Both in Tamiḷ Nāḍu and in Thanjāvūr, the areas of higher rainfall and irrigation tend to produce a social structure having more noncultivating landlords, agricultural laborers, Brahmans, Scheduled Caste members, and Scheduled Caste members who are agricultural laborers. On the whole these regions tend to have a lower workforce participation, a tendency that has increased in the 1960s and 1970s with the growth of unemployment. In Tamiḷ Nāḍu, these areas also tend to have higher proportions of cultivating tenants, but this correlation is not apparent in Thanjāvūr. Despite detailed local variations, I would argue that both in Tamiḷ Nāḍu and in Kēraḷa, the areas of high rainfall, density, irrigation, wet paddy, and high proportions of noncultivating landlords, Harijans, and agricultural laborers, are also ones in which class struggle is most pronounced between landowners and semiproletarians, and the Communist movement or some similar form of class struggle is most prominent in rural areas. By contrast, political struggles in the dryer areas have tended to see owner cultivators pitted against the state over such questions as crop procurement, debt relief, and the prices of grain.

With respect to Thanjāvūr, I agree with André Béteille that the spread of the Communist movement in the eastern region has been aided by the fact that the landless or near-landless agricultural workforce there tends to be more numerous and more homogeneous in terms of both caste and class. Most landless cultivators are agricultural laborers rather than tenants, and most landless laborers are Harijans. The class struggle therefore tends to be simpler in East Thanjāvūr, pitting low-caste laborers against middle- or upper-caste landowners and hirers of labor.

Other circumstances that have fostered the growth of class struggle and the Communist movement have been the greater prevalence of large estates in East Thanjāvūr, a lower level of living and greater relative deprivation among East Thanjāvūr laborers in the 1940s and 1950s, and I would argue, the fact that the coastal region has been more disturbed in modern times by the export trade, migrant labor, land sales to nontraditional owners, and greater European cultural influence. These circumstances to some extent broke through age-old, caste-based religious beliefs together with the economic and political dominance of the Brahmans and Veḷḷāḷars, and made the area more open to new ideas and forms of organization.

In Kumbapeṭṭai, an inland village in the northwest of the delta, despite the inroads of merchant and usurious capital, we found a relatively traditional structure with a high degree of caste/class congruence. Brahmans still owned 72 percent of the traditional village land, and more than 60 percent of that in the modern village area. All the landlords and petty bourgeoisie who dominated the village were Brahmans of the traditional landowning subcaste. Their leading members administered the lower castes of tenants, village servants, and agricultural laborers as far as possible in traditional ways. These involved heavy reliance on religious rules pertaining to the ranking of castes, and belief in religious sanctions (illness, crop blight, loss of wealth, or the deaths of humans and cattle) against infringement of caste rules. The village's unofficial judicial system, run by the Brahmans, was carried out under the auspices of the village goddess, and punishments such as flogging and the administration of cow dung to drink were meted out in the temple yard. In spite of such institutionalized forms of repression, low-level class struggle was endemic in the form of individual or small-group rebellions against the economic hierarchy or the politico-religious order, and occasionally even of strikes.

In contrast to most of Thanjāvūr *tālūk*, where the percentage of Ādi Drāviḍas in the total population was only 16.4 percent, Kumbapeṭṭai's population was 43 percent Ādi Drāviḍa.[14] Seventy-three percent of the villagers were semiproletarians or mendicants. One might therefore have expected a high degree of working-class organization against the Brahman petty bourgeoisie, and perhaps of Communist influence. The semiproletarians, however, were divided by subclass as well as by caste. Eighteen percent of the agriculturalists were tenant cultivators (poor peasants), while 10 percent out of the 54 percent of agricultural laborers also had some leased land. Differences of economic status and interest, as well as of caste, thus divided the semiproletariat. The fact that the Communist Party had done little work in this region was also relevant to the workers' lack of organization, although some organizing began soon after I left the village. In particular, the rivalry between the Non-Brahmans living within the village and the Ādi Drāviḍas who lived outside it kept them from organizing except on the most temporary basis.

This intercaste rivalry was not merely ideological or "superstructural"; it also had a material basis, even though it cross-cut the division between tenants and laborers. Thus, Non-Brahman tenants tended to be given larger and better plots than Ādi Drāviḍas; Non-Brahman attached laborers performed lighter work as gardeners, dairy workers, and domestic servants rather than as wet rice cultivators. The retention by the landlords of some kinds of hereditary distinctions among the workers thus contributed to their disunity, although these distinctions were being undermined by the fact that the Ādi Drāviḍas *were* being given land to lease, and that both among the Non-Brahmans and the Ādi Drāviḍas there was an increasing number of casual coolies doing undifferentiated kinds of agricultural work.

The main group conflicts in Kumbapeṭṭai were between the fairly recently arrived middle peasants and traders of Sheṭṭiyūr, Akkāchāvaḍy, and Veṭṭāmbāḍi belonging to castes not traditionally under the local Brahmans' dominance, and the Brahman petty bourgeoisie. These middle-ranking, independent commodity producers and traders could sometimes challenge the Brahmans' diktat, and were gradually undermining their control over the village at large.

In general, salient effects of Kumbapeṭṭai's encapsulation into the wider political economy and class structure of peripheral capitalism were as follows:

1. The village as a whole had been impoverished, and its class structure further polarized, between 1828 and 1952.

2. There had been some loss of Brahmanical supremacy as a result of the local landlords' indebtedness to Muslim and middle-ranking Hindū traders, who foreclosed on village lands, became absentee landlords, and themselves engaged some of the local tenants and laborers.

3. As noted earlier, Brahman land sales to "foreign," upstart middle peasants and traders who settled in the village after making money in the paddy or liquor trade, or by leasing wasteland on the outskirts of the village, further undermined the Brahmans' control.

4. Whereas the Brahmans had once been prebendaries of the state class whose local administration had been upheld by the Maratha kings, during British rule they became private landlords, some of whom were also petty bourgeois salary earners in towns elsewhere for part of their lives.

In 1952 the Brahmans also had relatives in the rural or urban bourgeoisie and the petty bourgeoisie of salary earners who were living temporarily or permanently away from the village. As petty bourgeois, the local Brahmans had thus come to form a tiny segment of the lower ranks of a class pyramid that extended throughout Tamiḷ Nāḍu, and even throughout India and overseas. Whereas they had formerly surrendered part of their surplus directly to the native rulers, they now surrendered surplus value in hidden ways to Indian or British finance capitalists, industrialists, and merchants, as well as to higher-ranking government bureaucrats who were paid from the land revenue. On the one hand, the local Brahmans had declined in socioeconomic status and political power as a result of these class developments. On the other hand, they still had relatives in the medium bourgeoisie (bigger landlords, tax collectors, lawyers, and others) on whom they could draw for occasional subsidies and, more important, for influence in upholding their local power.

5. The village's government-appointed or government-sanctioned leaders – the village headman and the *panchayat* president – were themselves prominent landlords who acted as the main intermediaries between the local petty bourgeois property owners and significant figures in the bourgeoisie and the government administration outside the village. In these roles they brought certain benefits to

the village, helped maintain the Brahman landowners' dominance and uphold the village hierarchy, and also enhanced their own power, prestige, and wealth. Examples of benefits to the village were the practice of cheating the government out of various revenues and, more recently, bringing development funds to the village through the *panchayat* system. The village hierarchy was maintained through such practices as bribing police investigators, obtaining lawyers for court cases, filing reports with the police, arresting offenders, and, in the case of village headman, settling small property disputes with government sanction. Personal aggrandizement was achieved, for example, through the power to classify others' lands for revenue, collect and levy local taxes for public works, and obtain loans and development funds.

In spite of their local powers, Kumbapeṭṭai's landlords were only modestly prosperous to very poor. The two or three richest village landlords earned only about twenty times the income of a landless laborer. More of the landlords earned only about ten times a laborer's income, and several, only three times. By contrast, the richest landlords and merchants in the district probably earned about 200 times the income of Kumbapeṭṭai's biggest landlord and about 4,000 times the income of a landless laborer.

Kumbapeṭṭai's landlords felt exploited by big merchants, by richer landlords who acted as moneylenders, and by government taxation. Their relative poverty and exploitation, however, did not lead to political radicalization. For the external figures who exploited them were on the whole distant and impersonal, whereas their day-to-day experience was one of themselves exploiting and suppressing rebellion among their tenants and laborers. Therefore, because they relied on these groups to oppose radical land reforms and to quell labor unrest, they supported the state's most conservative political parties. In Kumbapeṭṭai the Brahman landlords' favorite organization was the right wing, religion-oriented Hindū Mahāsabha, but in the elections they supported the Indian National Congress Party as the more powerful party and the one most likely to win.

As we have seen, however, Kumbapeṭṭai's landlords could not control the voting behavior of their local subordinates. Whereas the Indian National Congress Party was led by and chiefly represented the bigger all-India rural and urban bourgeoisie, the Drāviḍa Kazhakam represented Tamiḷ Nāḍu's medium and petty bourgeoisie of middle- or low-caste rank who were challenging the more traditional dominance of the Brahmans and Veḷḷāḷars and the upper ranks of the Naidūs. The Communist Party represented the industrial and craft workers, the poor peasants, and the agricultural laborers, especially among the Harijans. Although there was little organized campaigning in Kumbapeṭṭai, the parties' propaganda reached the village. The Brahman petty bourgeoisie appears to have voted solidly for the Congress Party, but probably 80 percent of the Non-Brahman and Ādi Drāviḍa middle peasants, traders, poor peasants, and laborers supported the joint DK/Communist candidate in the Madras assembly elections. The success of this candidate gave them greater confidence and leverage vis-à-vis the upper-caste landlords, although no immediate benefits.

In some respects, Kirippūr, although an East Thanjāvūr village near the coast, did not conform to the caste/class profile noted by Béteille, myself, and others as characteristic of East Thanjāvūr. Only 36 percent of the villagers were Ādi Drāviḍas as against 43 percent in Kumbapeṭṭai. Only 61 percent of the villagers were semiproletarians, compared with 73 percent in Kumbapeṭṭai, the rest being landlords, rich peasants, middle peasants, family traders or artisans, or petty bourgeois salary earners. Kirippūr had no big landlords living within the village. The Ādi Drāviḍas of Kirippūr were organized into a Communist labor union less because of particular features of their village than because they lived in an area characterized in general by Communist organizing, big landlord estates, and high proportions of Harijans and landless laborers.

Kirippūr did, however, conform to the East Thanjāvūr model in other major respects. Among the agriculturalists, only 9 percent were tenant cultivators, 52 percent being laborers and 49 percent, landless laborers. Kirippūr had fewer rentier landlords than Kumbapeṭṭai, most of its landowners being rich or middle peasants who hired at least some laborers. The village had a simpler class structure than Kumbapeṭṭai and was closer to a two-class system of owners versus laborers, in which conflicts over agricultural labor conditions and wages affected almost all the agriculturalists. Kirippūr was also a poorer village than Kumbapeṭṭai and its prosperity had apparently declined more during the 1940s. Its people suffered more severely as a result of the cyclone of November 1952.

Kirippūr's traditional aristocrats, the Brahmans and Veḷḷāḷars, had undergone a much greater decline than those of Kumbapeṭṭai. In 1952 they owned only 19 percent of the village land, the rest being owned by middle-ranking Non-Brahmans and absent Muslim traders. About 60 percent of the village's families had arrived within the previous century. Labor migration to Burma, Ceylon, and Malaya had introduced new, more secular values. Proximity to the coastal ports had brought a more thorough absorption of the village into the land and labor markets and the growth of new merchant and industrialist landlords. One absentee industrialist of middle-caste rank owned ninety acres in the village. The two biggest owners inside the village were also of middle rank and were not "traditional": One was of peasant background and one, a soda-factory owner. More of Kirippūr's people were employed or in some way received wealth from outside the village than was the case in Kumbapeṭṭai.

These conditions had undermined or broken the traditional bonds between landlords, tenants, village servants, and laborers, and had given the laborers a sense of having no one to turn to but each other. Caste rules were less strictly observed than in Kumbapeṭṭai, and village administration through caste had largely disappeared. Unlike Kumbapeṭṭai, Kirippūr had no central village goddess to whom all the castes paid deference and who sanctioned traditional moral laws.

As in Kumbapeṭṭai, the landlords and their immediate retainers among the village servant castes supported the Congress Party, and the middle ranking Non-Brahman peasants, artisans, and traders, supported the Drāviḍa Kazhakam.

The middle-ranking Non-Brahman castes, however, quarreled among themselves over rank and power in the village. These intercaste disputes among Naidūs, Paḍaiyācchis, and Sengunḍa Mudaliars, the largest Non-Brahman castes, formed the main horizontal conflicts in Kirippūr, whereas in Kumbapeṭṭai the main horizontal conflicts were between Brahman lineages of the traditional landlord subcaste.

The Communist Party had stepped into this situation in the 1940s with its capacity for organization, and with a vision of greater prosperity, future equality, and an end to the caste order. Although it had some appeal for the Non-Brahman poor peasants and laborers, its main success was among the Ādi Drāviḍas, whose caste assemblies it had adopted and organized into an agricultural labor union. In much of East Thanjāvūr, a six-week strike and partial insurrection in 1948 temporarily broke the landlords' power, but the movement was crushed by paramilitary forces and its Communist leaders jailed. With the coming of universal franchise in 1951, the party was permitted to reorganize itself as a constitutional body engaged mainly in parliamentary politics and labor union work. Our study has shown how the agricultural labor union was revived in Kirippūr in 1952–3 and was able to exact living wages for the laborers in a period of hardship following the cyclone of late 1952.

When I left Thanjāvūr in April 1953, I was deeply impressed by the achievements and potential of the Communist movement.[15] Looking back after twenty-six years, however, it seems to me that a flaw was already apparent in the union in Kirippūr and neighboring villages. This was the failure to enlist the firm support of small holders, cultivating tenants, and even laborers in the Non-Brahman castes. In 1953 the tag, "Paḷḷan-Paṟayaṉ Party" was already attached to the Communist Party in Thanjāvūr. Although the unions enrolled Non-Brahman tenants and laborers in some villages in the 1940s and 1950s, this did not appear common, and was to become still less common in the early 1970s.

It is easy to criticize a social movement, especially with hindsight, but hard to recommend alternatives. Perhaps the agricultural labor union was the best that could have developed at that date and in those circumstances. Over the long run, however, it is clear that parliamentarism and labor unions were no substitute for a revolutionary movement. In 1948 the goals of the Communist Party had been expropriation of all big property owners, nationalization of large industry, land to the tiller, and eventual cooperative farming. In 1953 these were still the ostensible goals but the emphases in the countryside had narrowed to moderate land reforms, fixity of tenures with lower rents, control of inflation and essential prices, expanded industrial employment, and increased wages for agricultural workers. In practice, the last became the chief concern because it was possible to implement it to some extent within the framework of a labor union. But this necessarily alienated the small holders and tenants, for they, too, were obliged to hire labor at peak seasons and could ill afford higher wages. Already in 1953, Kirippūr's laborers were pressing small holders to pay the statutory wages even though these were not yet required by law. With such a policy, or with *concen-*

*tration* on such a policy, the rift between small holders and laborers could only deepen.

The Communist wage policy probably also helped to perpetuate the formidable caste barrier between Ādi Drāviḍas and Non-Brahmans, a barrier too high for even the laborers among the Non-Brahmans to vault. With small holders and tenants forced onto the side of the landlords in the wage struggle, it was all too easy for the Non-Brahman laborers to side with their relatives and take on the role of scabs – a role they were to play increasingly in the later decades.

Already in 1953, moreover, we have seen that Communist policy was to curb the laborers' militance, persuade them to rely on constitutional channels for redressing grievances, and even confine them to strikes within their own villages. Over the next two decades, the stress on small increments in agricultural wages at the expense of wider revolutionary change was to deepen the rift between the Ādi Drāviḍas and other castes in the countryside, eventually to the Harijans' own detriment.

# Notes

### *Preface*

1 V. I. Lenin, "A Great Beginning," *Collected Works* 29. Progress Publishers: Moscow, 1965, p. 420.
2 A *panchāyat* is a modern administrative unit comprising one or more villages. Its president and board members are elected.
3 Ten of these were Brahmans, thirteen Non-Brahmans, and one Harijan.
4 Twelve of these were Brahmans, twenty-nine Non-Brahmans, and nine Harijans.
5 See, e.g., G. U. Pope, 1926, pp. 6–7.

### *1. The District*

1 *Census of India, 1951*, Volume 3, Part 1, p. 43.
2 *Techno-Economic Survey of Madras*, 1961, pp. 93, 99; *Madras in Maps and Pictures*, 1955, pp. 12–24; *Madras in Maps and Pictures* (Rev.), 1959, p. 51.
3 F. R. Hemingway, 1906, pp. 8–9; *District Census Handbook, Tanjore, 1951*, p. 3.
4 See *The Hindū*, Madras, December 1 to 23, 1952, for full accounts.
5 K. A. Nīlakanta Sāstri, 1955a, pp. 124–40; 1955b, pp. 63–100.
6 For the Maratha period, see especially K. P. Subramanian, 1928, and K. Rājayyan, 1965 and 1969.
7 The last Mahārāja left an heiress but no heir. For the dispute surrounding the abolition of the kingship, see W. Hickey, 1874.
8 *District Census Handbook, Tanjore, 1951*, pp. 18–19.
9 For details of the *panchāyat* system and its evolution, see B. S. Baliga, 1957, p. 301.
10 *Census of India, 1951*, Vol. 3, Part 1, pp. 104–5.
11 *District Census Handbook, Tanjore, 1951*, Annexure 1, p. 10. For accounts of the culture of the crops mentioned here, see V. T. Subbiah Mudaliar, 1960, pp. 4–303.
12 *Madras District Gazetteers, Tanjore*, Part 2, 1915, p. 20.
13 *Census of India, 1961*, Vol. 9, Part 1-A-(ii), p. 442.
14 B. S. Baliga, 1957, pp. 160–1.
15 *District Census Handbook, Tanjore, 1951*, p. 9; B. S. Baliga, 1957, pp. 188–200.
16 B. Naṭarājan, 1953, p. 15.
17 B. Naṭarājan, 1953, p. 202.
18 B. S. Baliga, 1957, p. 202.
19 *Census of India, 1951*, Vol. 3, Part 1, pp. 206–10.
20 For a summary account of major south Indian works in Tamiḷ and Sanskrit classical literature, see K. A. Nīlakanta Sāstri, 1955a, pp. 327–75.

### 2. *Castes and Religious Groups*

1 For earlier brief accounts of caste in Thanjāvūr, see K. Gough, 1955a, pp. 90–102; 1955b, pp. 36–52; 1962, pp. 11–60. See also especially D. Sivertsen, 1963, and A. Béteille, 1965.
2 See, e.g., such well-known works as J. H. Hutton, 1946; G. S. Ghurye, 1961; M. N. Srinivas, 1962 and 1966; L. Dumont, 1970; and D. G. Mandelbaum, 1972, 2 vols.
3 See, e.g., the Bhāratiya Itihāsa Samhiti, 1951, Vol. 1, pp. 249, 384–8, 449–52, 507–10; D. D. Kosambi, 1965, pp. 81, 86; G. S. Ghurye, 1961, pp. 42–73.
4 A. C. Mayer, 1970, pp. 4, 161, 170–1.
5 N. Yalman, 1967, pp. 206–7.
6 A. C. Mayer, 1970, pp. 4, 161, 171–2.
7 For more detailed accounts of the castes of Thanjāvūr, see T. V. Row, 1883, pp. 149–205; F. R. Hemingway, 1906, pp. 55–90; B. S. Baliga, 1957, pp. 124–57.
8 Smārtha Brahmans in Kumbapeṭṭai, some of whom had received biblical instruction in high school, likened the Advaita philosophy of Sankara to Jesus's statement, "I and my Father are one." Vishishta Advaitam was likened to the statement, "I am the vine, thou art the branches," and Dvaityam, in which the soul is separate from a transcendant deity, to "Pray to your Father which is in heaven."
9 The 1921 Census of India was the last occasion on which figures for caste and subcaste membership were collected in detail, although most castes were enumerated in 1931. For the Thanjāvūr figures, see *Madras District Gazetteers, Tanjore*, 1933, p. 19.

### 3. *The Agriculturalists*

1 The figures for 1951 in this and subsequent chapters are taken from the *Census of India, 1951*, Vol. 3, Part 1, or from the *District Census Handbook, Tanjore*, 1951.
2 *Census of India, 1961*, Vol. 9, Part 11-D. The nineteen wealthiest temples were those of Sīrkāḷi, Vaidīswarankōvil, Tiruvengād, Māyuram, Tirukkadaiyūr, Pāndanallūr, two at Tiruppaṉandhāḷ, Tiruvidaimaruthūr, Tirubhuvanam, Tiruppugalūr, Tiruchendāttankudi, Punnainallūr, Tiruvaiyāru, Tiruvārūr, Maṉṉārguḍi, Sikkal, Nāgapaṭṭaṇam, and Vēdāranyam.
3 For the conditions of *mirāsi* ownership at the beginning of British rule, see *Report of the Tanjore Commissioners of 1799*, and W. H. Bayley and W. Hudleston, eds., 1862. For the earlier history of land tenures in Thanjāvūr, see especially B. S. Baliga, 1957, pp. 15–94, 351–381; 1960, Vols. 1 and 2; F. R. Hemingway, 1906, pp. 167–94; T. V. Row, 1883, pp. 396–414, Appendix C, pp. viii–xli; K. N. Sāstri, 1955b, pp. 567–91; B. Stein, 1968, pp. 175–216; 1975, pp. 64–91; A. Appādorai, 1936; K. M. Gupta, 1933; A. Krishnaswāmi, 1964. For land tenures in the nineteenth century see, e.g., D. Kumār, 1965, pp. 22, 30, 86, *et passim*.
4 For the history of the *pattakdārs*, see especially T. V. Row, 1883, pp. 467–71; K. R. Subramanian, 1928, pp. 66–7, 91–2.
5 See D. A. Washbrook, 1976, pp. 185–9 for the fortunes of the great temple estates between 1861 and 1908.
6 B. S. Baliga, 1957, pp. 375–8.
7 Mao Tse-Tung, 1954, Vol. 1, p. 138; 1954, Vol. 3, p. 88.
8 T. V. Row, 1883, p. 204. Paddy is rice in the husk, and is also the name given to rice plants and seedlings. Transplanting of seedlings from a seedbed to a flooded field is

done by women when the seedlings are a few weeks old (see Chapter 11).

9 I. and D. Crook, 1979, p. 47. Mao Tse-Tung's fuller characterization runs: "The rich peasant as a rule possesses land. But there are some who possess only a part of the land they farm and rent the remainder. There are still others who possess no land at all and rent all the land they farm. The rich peasant as a rule possesses comparatively abundant means of production and liquid capital, engages in labour himself, but regularly relies upon rural exploitation for a major part of his income. The exploitation the rich peasant practises is chiefly that of hired labour (hiring long-term laborers). In addition, he may also let part of his land for exploitation by rent, lend money, or engage in commercial or industrial enterprises" (Mao Tse-Tung, 1954, Vol. 1, p. 139).

10 I. and D. Crook, 1979, p. 47. Mao Tse-Tung's characterization is: "In many cases the middle peasant possesses land. In some cases he possesses only part of the land he farms and rents the remainder. In other cases he possesses no land at all and rents all the land he farms. In all cases he has adequate implements of his own. The middle peasant relies wholly or mainly on his own labour as the source of his income. As a rule he does not exploit other people; in many cases he is even exploited by other people and has to pay a small amount of land rent and interest on loans. But the middle peasant as a rule does not sell his labour power. A section of the middle peasants (the well-to-do middle peasants) subjects other people to some slight exploitation, but this is not its regular or principle occupation." (1954, Vol. 1, p. 139).

11 "Poor peasants in general have to rent the land they farm. They suffer exploitation in the form of rent and interest, and they must occasionally hire themselves out. The selling of labour for limited periods is the basic feature distinguishing them from lower-middle peasants" (I. and D. Crook, 1979, p. 48). Mao Tse-Tung writes: "In some cases the poor peasant possesses a part of the land he farms and an incomplete set of implements; in other cases he possesses no land at all, but only an incomplete set of implements. As a rule the poor peasant has to rent land for cultivation and, exploited by others, has to pay land rent and interest on loans and hire out a small part of his labour" (Mao Tse-Tung, 1954, Vol. 1, p. 140).

12 "The worker (including the farm labourer) as a rule does not possess any land or implements, and only in some cases possesses a very small amount of land and a few implements. A worker makes his living wholly or mainly by selling his labour power" (Mao Tse-Tung, 1954, p. 140).

### 5. *Variations in Ecology, Demography, and Social Structure*

1 A somewhat similar statistical study of the interrelations among irrigation, paddy cultivation, population density, and the percentages of agricultural laborers, Scheduled Castes, and workers in the total population has been carried out by K. C. Alexander for the districts of Tamil Nāḍu using figures from the 1961 Census (K. C. Alexander, 1975a, pp. 664–72). My findings corroborate those of Dr. Alexander and expand the study to cover the 1951 and 1971 censuses, the *tālūks* of Thanjāvūr district, the percentages of tenants and Brahmans, the average size of land holdings, and the size distribution of land holdings. My own statistical calculations were made before Dr. Alexander's study appeared. My conclusions differ from Alexander's in that he attributes the preference for paddy cultivation and the rank ordering and

percentages of landowners and agricultural laborers to the values held by the people. By contrast, I attribute the preference for paddy cultivation to its higher caloric value per acre, and the extent of social stratification to the level of productivity from agriculture.

2 Wherever possible, figures were obtained from the *Censuses of India* for 1951, 1961, and 1971. The relevant volumes are the *Census of India, 1951*, Vol. 3, Part 1, the *District Census Handbook, Tanjore, 1951*, Vols. 1 and 2, the *Census of India, 1961*, Vol. 9, Part 1-A-(ii), the *District Census Handbook, Tanjore, 1961*, Vols. 1 and 2, and the *District Census Handbook, Thanjāvūr, 1971*, Vols. 1 and 2. Figures for Tamiḷ Nāḍu state for 1971 were obtained from the *Statistical Handbook of Tamiḷ Nāḍu, 1972*. Figures for the gross monetary value of output per acre in the districts of Tamiḷ Nāḍu were obtained from the *Techno-Economic Survey of Madras*, 1961, pp. 76, 94–5.

3 "Cultivating owners" or "owner cultivators" in the Census refers to all landowners who cultivate primarily with hired labor or with family labor. It therefore contains some noncultivating owners who use only hired labor, although in Tamiḷ Nāḍu as a whole, the majority of "owner cultivators" and their families probably did some cultivation themselves. "Landlords" in the 1951 census refers to landowners who subsisted mainly by leasing out their lands.

### *6. The Colonial Background and the Sources of Poverty*

1 Parts of this chapter have been published earlier in K. Gough, 1977 and 1978.

2 Marx's writings on this subject are mainly contained in a series of articles in the *New York Daily Tribune* in the 1850s, in *Pre-Capitalist Economic Formations* (1857–58), in the preface to *A Contribution to the Critique of Political Economy* (1859), in *Capital* (1867 to 1894), and in the *Ethnological Notebooks* (1880–2). For modern writings on the subject see especially R. Garaudy, ed., 1969; L. Krader, 1975; M. Sawer, 1977; F. Tökei, 1979; and U. Melotti, 1977.

3 D. Ribeiro, 1968, pp. 55–64; S. Amin, 1974, Vol. 1, pp. 140–1, 1976, pp. 14–15.

4 See, e.g., K. A. Nilakanta Sāstri, 1955a, pp. 191–6; 1955b, pp. 63–100, 445–545, 567–612. Burton Stein has argued that Sāstri and others greatly exaggerate the bureaucratization and centralization of the Chōḷa kingdom, and that it was in fact little more than a series of self-governing, irrigated nuclear areas separated by tribal forests and loosely linked by moral relations to a king as mediator (B. Stein, 1969, 1975). There is no doubt that the assemblies of groups of local communities held economic, revenue, judicial, and religious authority and that the empire contained relatively independent tribal regions. But there also seems little doubt that, at least in the Kāvēri delta, the central government had strong coercive powers and great resources. Thus, for example, the Chōḷa government organized the building of at least 150 large temples in Thanjāvūr district alone, including the vast and famous Brahadeeswara temple in Thanjāvūr city (*Census of India*, 1961, Vol. 9, Part 11-D, *passim*). The government surveyed and elaborately classified all cultivated land, charged a land revenue that was at times oppressive, supervised the collection of revenue in villages, audited the accounts of temples and seminaries, remitted taxes when the crops were poor, and imprisoned members of village assemblies if they failed to pay their dues. It had a regular court that settled disputes between the assemblies of different provinces (*nāḍus*) and punished high-ranking criminals. It built large irrigation works, notably

the Grand Anicut dam, and conscripted village slaves to build and repair them. The government had an army and navy and conquered, however briefly, lands as far south as Ceylon and Southeast Asia and as far north as the Ganges (K. M. Gupta, 1926, pp. 55–240). It is hard to imagine such a kingdom being governed by a ruler who was little more than a mediator. The problem of combining a strong central government with largely self-sufficient rural regions disappears if (as I think we must) we regard the temples, monasteries, and other holders of prebendal estates as branches of the government rather than as separate from and opposed to it.

5 K. M. Gupta, 1926, pp. 155–9.

6 Whether or not there was strictly speaking any private property in land is debatable. Sāstri states that there was, and that individual landowners could sell their land or transmit it from father to son (Sāstri, 1955b, p. 567). It is clear, however, that at least some, perhaps all, of the individual estates (*ēkabhōgam*) were really prebendal estates held by officials who were permitted only the "upper share" of the produce (the revenue) and who had under them joint village communities of peasants. Sāstri's account of the four types of land sales indicates that they were (*a*) sales of cultivators' common lands to pay arrears of revenue, (*b*) sales of the land (prebendal estates?) of officers condemned for treason, (*c*) sales of part of the common land of a village or other similar body, and (*d*) sales of land by Siva temples. These types do not suggest individual land sales; Sāstri notes that there was no free market in land (K. A. Nilakanta Sāstri, 1955b, pp. 601–2). As late as the nineteenth century, it was regarded as proper to sell shares in the village land only to persons of the same caste as the communal owners.

7 K. A. Nilakanta Sāstri, 1955a, p. 192.

8 C. P. V. Ayyar, 1916, pp. 80–97.

9 K. A. N. Sāstri, 1955b, pp. 592–613; M. D. Rājukumār, 1974; A. Appādorai, 1936, Vol. 1, pp. 338–442; Vol. 2, pp. 443–653.

10 This is assumed because the same mode of delegating ploughs and oxen to the sharecroppers and the communal slaves persisted in many villages well into the nineteenth century. It seems almost certain that, like most village institutions, it derived from Chōḷa times.

11 M. D. Rājukumār, 1974, quoted in J. P. Mencher, 1978, p. 32. Rājukumār also holds the view that the bondage and taxation of peasants and artisans, and their removal from control of their lands, increased toward the end of the Chōḷa period.

12 It is not known what the Kēraḷa states were like during the Chōḷa period (ninth to thirteenth centuries), but Kēraḷa was evidently divided into small feudallike principalities similar to those of the later period from at least the ninth century. See E. M. S. Namboodiripāḍ, 1967, pp. 14–60; K. M. Paṇikkār, 1960, pp. 1–323.

13 D. Ribeiro, 1968, p. 61; S. Amin, 1974, pp. 140–1.

14 For similarities and contrasts between these features and European feudalism, see, e.g., T. V. Mahālingam, 1952, pp. 88–90. For further details of the Vijayanagar system, see Burton Stein, 1969, pp. 188–96; T. V. Mahālingam, 1969; K. N. Sāstri, 1955a, pp. 153–300. For the Maratha period in Thanjāvūr, see especially K. R. Subramanian, 1928.

15 A. Sārada Rāju, 1941, pp. 164–8.

16 In 1805, in addition to 17,149 Brahman land managers, there were 43,442 managerial households of Non-Brahmans and Christians and 1,457 of Muslims. The Non-Brahmans would be mainly Veḷḷāḷar peasants and noncultivating managers, Naidū

aristocrats installed by the Vijayanagar conquerers, especially in East Thanjāvūr, or Kaḷḷars from Rāmanāthapuram and Madurai, found mainly in the southwest uplands. Christians, who today form only 3.7 percent of the population, were probably mainly merchants of Thanjāvūr town and the major ports. Muslims were mainly merchants in the ports and in a few inland trading centers (T. V. Row, 1883, p. 408).

17 See R. C. Dutt, 1963, Vol. 1, pp. 66–78, and R. Mukherjee, 1958, pp. 367–74, for accounts of this process and of the scandals surrounding the private fortunes extracted by servants of the company from the revenues of Thanjāvūr. A revenue of Rs. 8,100,000, plus Rs. 9,000,000 in special payments, was extracted in 1775, whereas the highest revenue previously collected had been Rs. 5,750,000 in 1761. £234,000 was claimed by Paul Benfield, a servant of the company who was a creditor of the Nawāb of Ārcot. Altogether, £2,520,000 were extracted in 1771–6 from the revenues of the Karnatak region of which Thanjāvūr formed part, in order to pay debts incurred by the Nawāb and other native princes to servants of the Company. See also W. Hickey, 1874, pp. 133–6; K. R. Subramanian, 1928, pp. 60–4; K. Rājayyan, 1965; 1969, pp. 61–71.

18 *Fourth Report of the Committee of Secrecy, 1782*, Appendix No. 22, quoted in R. C. Dutt, 1963, Vol. 1, pp. 71–72.

19 K. R. Subramanian, 1928, p. 65; F. R. Hemingway, 1906, pp. 50–51, 190; T. V. Row, 1883, pp. 45, 793–814. The *kalams* of Thanjāvūr, each of which weighs about 63.69 lbs., have been converted into metric tons of 2,205 lbs.

20 Writing in 1785, Colonel Fullarton of the British army reported of Thanjāvūr, "No spot on the globe is superior in production for the use of man," but added that since Haidar's invasion it was everywhere "marked with the distinguishing features of a desert" (A. S. Raju, 1941, p. 8).

21 T. V. Row, 1883, pp. 135–46, 481–3.

22 K. R. Subramanian, 1928, p. 92. The city may have been larger under the Chōḷas. The Great Temple alone employed 400 hetaerae and owned land in many villages, including some in Ceylon (K. N. Sāstri, 1955b, p. 653).

23 When the British took over the government in 1799 they allowed the Rāja his private estates, one-fifth of the revenue, and the administration of the Thanjāvūr fort. The Rāja patronized the arts and maintained a reduced retinue in Thanjāvūr town until 1855, when the direct male line died out. The British used this as a pretext to abolish the dynasty, and after this date Thanjāvūr town decreased in size. See W. Hickey, 1874, for the history of the royal family. For figures, see T. V. Row, 1883, pp. 118, 321; D. Kumar, 1965, pp. 120–1; *Census of India, 1951*, Vol. 3, Part 1, pp. 18, 44–5, 78.

24 The Abbé J. A. Dubois, 1947, pp. 94–5.

25 For details, see A. S. Rāju, 1941, pp. 146–82; R. S. Raghavaiyangar, 1892, pp. 9–10. Between 1814 and 1835, British exports of cotton goods to India increased from 1,000,000 yards valued at £26,000 to 51,000,000 yards valued at £400,000. Indian exports of cotton goods, amounting to 1-1/4 million pieces at 1.3 million in 1814 had fallen to 300,000 pieces valued at £100,000 in 1832, and to 63,000 pieces in 1834 (M. Barratt-Brown, 1970, p. 47).

26 A. S. Rāju, 1941, p. 67; T. V. Row, 1883, p. 518.

27 Imports to Madras as a whole fell from Rs. 7,000,000 in 1806 to Rs. 4,000,000 in 1840, and the export trade suffered similarly. Except for the years of acute famine, the Presidency's grain price index dropped from 100 in 1801–10 to fifty in 1843–4 (A. S. Rāju, 1941, pp. 200, 230).

28 Bayley and Hudleston, 1892, p. 104.
29 D. Kumar, 1965, p. 104.
30 A. S. Rāju, 1941, p. 282.
31 T. V. Row, 1883, p. 338; W. Hickey, 1874, p. 23.
32 Here and elsewhere, figures for exports and imports come from T. V. Row, 1883, F. R. Hemingway, 1906, or from the annual volumes of the Seaborne Trade and Navigation of the Madras Presidency, Customs House, Madras. To obtain the paddy equivalent of husked rice exports I have multiplied the husked rice tonnage by 1.515.
33 Similarly, Thanjāvūr's net exports of paddy by sea and rail reached 214,207 metric tons in the famine of 1887, which must have been at least half of its gross produce and probably more. This must have left the population (whose normal requirements would be about 436,000 tons) in acute distress. In other years of that decade between 114,000 and 178,000 tons approximately were exported, leaving only about 427,000 tons. If paddy was also going out by land, it is no wonder that the 1870s were a decade of famine.
34 *Report on the Settlement of the Land Revenue of the Provinces under the Madras Presidency for Fasly 1267 (1857–1858)*, Madras, 1860, pp. 243–4.
35 On kidnapping at Nāgapaṭṭaṇam, see H. Tinker, 1974, p. 128. For the figures cited, see D. Kumar, 1965, pp. 128–30.
36 F. R. Hemingway, 1906, pp. 176, 185.
37 *Madras Land Revenue Settlement Report, 1857–1858*, p. 241.
38 T. V. Row, 1883, pp. 296–7, 308–9, 390–2.
39 Proceedings of the Board of Revenue of the East India Company, June 23, 1800, quoted in A. S. Rāju, 1941, p. 260.
40 W. H. Bayley and W. Hudleston, 1862, p. 94.
41 K. Marx, *Capital*, Vol. 1, 1976, pp. 1019–38. Marx's distinction of the two modes of subordination of labor to capital (both of which he viewed as capitalist) are quoted, for example, by J. Banaji, 1978, p. 1376. Banaji here reaches similar conclusions regarding the Deccan peasantry of the late nineteenth century to those that I have reached regarding Thanjāvūr. For a description of the dissolution of precapitalist relations of production in manufacture and agriculture in India and China under the impact of merchants' capital in conjunction with British industrial capital, see also K. Marx, *Capital*, Vol. 2, 1967, pp. 323–37.
42 For a discussion of both communal and privately owned slaves in the nineteenth century, see B. Hjejle, 1967, pp. 80–1.
43 Slaves, working under the village managers or the peasant cultivators, cultivated 1,012 villages (21 percent), and sharecropping tenants, 1,898 (39 percent), while 1,923 villages (40 percent) were cultivated partly by tenants and partly by slaves. There were 62,048 households of land managers responsible for paying the land revenue or else receiving it on behalf of the government, and 47,312 cultivating tenants. Of the latter, 29,323 or 60 percent leased from Brahmans, whose religious rules forbade them to touch the plough. 18,989 tenants leased from Non-Brahman Hindūs, Christians, or Muslims. The number of slaves is not known, but many tenants as well as land managers used slaves (Bayley and Hudleston, 1862, p. 94).
44 W. H. Bayley and W. Hudleston, 1862, pp. 86–94, 380–2; A. S. Rāju, 1941, pp. 28–39, 78–9. Hjejle notes that (as in modern times) Paḷḷar and Paṟayar slaves might also be given land on lease, but that they paid a still higher rent than did the *porakuḍis*. The three types of tenants still existed in the 1950s. *Uḷ-kuḍis* were favored tenants, usually of the same caste as the *mirāsdār*, often Brahmans or Veḷḷāḷars. *Porakuḍis* or

*pora-kuthakaikkārar* were usually from middle-ranking Non-Brahman castes such as Paḍaiyācchis, Pallis, Vanniyars, Kallars, and Agambaḍiyars. In addition, Pallars and Parayars sometimes received land on *kuthakai* and sometimes paid higher rents than the middle-ranking Non-Brahman *kuthakai* tenants.

45 Quoted from contemporary sources in Arūn Bandopādhyāy, 1976.

46 In 1921 industrial export crops occupied 37.4 percent of Madras Presidency's cultivated acreage, and in 1941, 37.7 percent (S. Y. Krishnaswāmy, 1947, pp. 339–41).

47 Small quantities of textiles had continued to be exported even earlier via the French port of Karaikkal. They formed 1.7 percent of the value of Thanjāvūr's total exports in 1841–2, while textiles from Britain were 10 percent of imports. See "*Seaborne Trade and Navigation of the Madras Presidency," 1941–42*, pp. 120–1, 198–9, 313.

48 "Railway stores" formed 30 percent of the value of imports in 1871, in preparation for building the railway, but this was unusual. ("*Seaborne Trade and Navigation of the Madras Presidency," 1871–1872*).

49 In 1882, 67.14 percent of the Madras revenue was remitted to the Imperial Treasury of the Government of India; in 1897, 71.40 percent (*Report of the Committee Appointed by the Secretary of State for India on the Question of the Financial Relations between the Central and Provincial Governments of India*, Parliamentary Papers, 1920, Vol. VIV, quoted in D. A. Washbrook, 1976, p. 24.) Washbrook concludes that in 1870–1920, between 65 percent and 70 percent of the Madras revenue went to the Imperial Treasury.

In 1890–2, 58 percent of the Imperial Revenue was spent on debt service, military services, and the collection of revenue, and another 30 percent on the civil service and civil works. The rest (5 percent) was spent for irrigation, railways, post and telegraph, and famine relief. The amounts and proportions spent under these heads were almost identical in 1901–2. In 1911–12, 50 percent went on the first category, 46 percent on the second and 4 percent on the third, and in 1920–1, 68 percent on the first, 31 percent on the second, and less than 1 percent on the third. "Military services" were more than 60 percent of the Imperial Revenue throughout the 1920s and about 58 percent to 60 percent in the 1930s. Throughout the 1920s and 1930s, 60 percent to 70 percent of the *combined* imperial and provincial revenues were spent on debt service, military services, justice, police, and jails (V. Anstey, 1949, pp. 538–43).

50 T. V. Row, 1883, p. 386; G. Slater, ed., 1918, p. 82; P. J. Thomas and K. C. Rāmakrishnan, 1940, p. 426. The figure for 1947–53 is from my fieldwork enquiries.

51 *Census of India, 1951*, Vol. 3, Part 1, p. 49.

52 Figures come from the Censuses of India, Madras volumes, for the years 1881, 1891, 1901, 1911, 1921, 1931, and 1951, in the sections on emigration.

53 Madras city alone contained 47,198 Tanjoreans in 1961 (*Census of India, 1961*, Vol. 9, Part 1-A-(i), p. 108).

54 For which see H. Tinker, 1974, pp. 116–333.

55 Settlement Report for Tanjore, 1921, pp. 9–10, quoted by D. Kumar, 1965, p. 22.

56 T. V. Row, 1883, pp. 381, 476; D. Kumar, 1965, p. 221. The 1951 figures are from my fieldwork.

57 See, e.g., B. Hjejle, 1967, pp. 71–126. Word for word, the Abbé Dubois's account of the conditions of the Parayars in 1818 was true of the 1950s. See the Abbé J. Dubois, 1947, pp. 81–2.

58 At twenty-eight ounces of husked rice per day, considered desirable for an adult manual worker with little other food, this would feed about 2½ adults. Part of it,

however, was bartered for tea, palmwine, and chewing stuffs. For payments in 1871–92, see R. S. Raghavaiyangar, 1926, pp. 81, xliv–1; T. V. Row, 1883, p. 388. The higher figure of fifty to sixty *kalams* tended, and still tends, to be paid in the most fertile region of northwest Thanjāvūr; the lower figure of forty *kalams*, near the coast around Nāgapaṭṭaṇam.

59 T. V. Row, 1883, p. 663; *Census of India, 1951*, Vol. 3, Part 1, p. 97.

60 *Census of India, 1891*, Vol. 13, p. 217; *Census of India, 1951*, Vol. 3, Part 1, p. 208.

61 In the last century of British rule the two greatest famines affecting Thanjāvūr were those of 1877 and 1918. Both were accompanied by epidemics, the latter in particular by numerous deaths from influenza. The famine and epidemic, plus emigration, caused the population to decline between 1910 and 1920. The only other decade of British rule in which population decline occurred was 1851–61 (D. Kumar, 1965, pp. 120–1).

62 Figures are taken from the decennial censuses of the Madras Presidency.

63 P. J. Thomas and K. C. Ramakrishnan, 1940, pp. 421–2.

64 C. W. B. Zacharias, 1950, pp. 347, 350.

65 Actually, although he separated the peasant strata from the urban strata for the purposes of discussion, Mao Tse-Tung himself said that the middle and small landlords were "of a more or less capitalist complexion," that the rich peasants were "called the rural bourgeoisie," and that the petty bourgeoisie of intellectuals, small peasants, handicraftsmen and professionals had "a status somewhat like that of the middle peasants among the peasantry" (Mao Tse-Tung, 1954, Vol. 3, pp. 88–92). My classification is therefore similar to Mao's for China, but I have placed the rich peasants in the petty bourgeoisie and the middle peasants in a separate class along with other family entrepreneurs, as "simple commodity producers, service-vendors and traders." I have also included both the poor peasants (the cultivating tenants with no land of their own) and the agricultural laborers in the class of the semiproletariat, because both surrendered practically their whole surplus above subsistence needs to the landowners.

66 See especially A. G. Frank, 1967.

67 See especially I. Wallerstein, 1974a and 1974b.

68 See especially A. R. Desai, 1975, pp. 123–31 and 145–57.

69 See especially H. Alavi, 1975. In Note 1 of this article Alavi lists the main contributors to the debate over the mode of production in India over the past decade. For an early exchange, see K. Gough, 1968–9, pp. 526–44, and S. A. Shah and K. Gough, 1969, pp. 360–8.

70 Doug McEachern, 1976.

71 J. Banaji, 1978, where Banaji makes a break from his position in some earlier articles.

72 See especially G. Omvedt, 1975; Omvedt and Patankar, 1977.

73 Rudra, 1975 and 1978.

74 S. Amin, 1976, pp. 193–386.

75 As is recognized, for example, by Banaji, even though he polemicizes against Alavi's conception of a "colonial mode of production." See J. Banaji, 1975, 1978.

### *7. Political Parties*

1 For valuable works on the Congress Party in Tamil Nāḍu, see especially D. A. Washbrook, 1976, C. J. Baker, 1976, and D. Arnold, 1977. For the Congress Party in

Thanjāvūr, see especially B. S. Baliga, 1957, pp. 96–123.

2 In Kumbapeṭṭai at that date, only one Brahman family supported the Congress Party, the rest being pro-British or indifferent. The supporter was a cosmopolitan who had run restaurants in several railway stations of south India, read newspapers, and talked to travelers. He was also a follower of a local *sannyāsi* who influenced him in favor of Mahātma Gāndhi. This Brahman fed the marchers and organized a public meeting on the outskirts of Kumbapeṭṭai. The next day the police came to arrest him, but Brahman village solidarity protected him. The nationalist movement in Kumbapeṭṭai dated from this event.

3 B. S. Baliga, 1957, pp. 155–6.

4 For the election results as a whole in 1952, 1957, and 1962, see Chandidas et al., 1968.

5 For valuable works on the Drāvida Kazhakam, its origins and history, see especially R. L. Hardgrave, 1965, and M. Ram, 1968.

6 S. Harrison, 1960, p. 185.

7 R. L. Hardgrave, 1965, p. 42.

8 For the early period of the Dravidian nationalist movement see, in addition to the works cited, D. A. Washbrook, 1976, pp. 265–329; C. J. Baker, 1976, pp. 26–88, 237–44, 271–4, 305–12.

9 See, e.g., D. A. Washbrook, 1976, pp. 265–87, 294, *et seq.*

10 M. Ram, 1968, pp. 70–2.

11 The slogan had been introduced by the Dravidian Association twenty-eight years earlier (M. Ram, 1965, p. 81).

12 For information on events involving the Communists up to 1947, I am largely indebted to a Tamiḻ pamphlet, *The Communist Party in Thanjāvūr*, published by the Communist Party of India (Marxist) in 1974. My assistant, Srī M. Balū, did the translation.

13 See, e.g., M. Ram, 1969, pp. 1–42; G. D. Overstreet and M. Windmiller, 1959, pp. 271–4, 285–7.

14 For an account of the Thanjāvūr agriculturalists' strike by an American eyewitness, see J. F. Muehl, 1950, pp. 266–92.

15 J. F. Muehl, 1950, pp. 289–91.

### *9. Kumbapeṭṭai before 1855*

1 Although both are strictly speaking called *veṭṭiyan*, the government-appointed servant is usually referred to as *veṭṭi* to distinguish him from the lower-ranking Paṟayar *veṭṭiyan*.

### *10. Kumbapeṭṭai from 1855 to 1952*

1 For details, see B. Hjejle, 1967, pp. 97–103; D. Kumar, 1965, pp. 42–75; A. S. Rāju, 1941, pp. 274–6.

2 *Report of C. M. Lushington, Collector of Trichinopoly*, dated July 1, 1819, quoted in Hjejle, 1967, p. 83. About fifteen *kalams* were paid to the couple at harvest time, and about eleven to twelve *kalams* to the male laborer in other seasons. Hjejle's calculation that twenty-seven *kalams* = 9072 lbs. of paddy (rice in the husk) seems to be incorrect, for in Thanjāvūr and the neighboring part of Trichinopoly, one *kalam* = 63.69 lbs. Twenty-seven *kalams* would therefore equal about 1,720 lbs.

3 The caste of Paḷḷis, related to the Paḍaiyācchis, was also enslaved by Brahmans in some villages, apparently from early times. Paḷḷis ranked above Paḷḷars and Paṟayars and today are classified as Non-Brahmans, but like the Paḷḷars and Paṟayars they specialized in paddy cultivation. See Bayley and Hudleston, 1862, p. 19, from a memorandum of 1816.

### *11. The Annual Round*

1 A cent is one-hundredth of an acre.

### *14. The Semiproletariat*

1 Two *siṉṉa* (small) *paḍi*s = one *paḍi* or *periya* (big) *paḍi*, and 2 *paḍis* = 1 *marakkāḷ*.

### *15. Village Politics: Religion, Caste, and Class*

1 Dumont, 1966, p. 61 *passim*.

### *17. Class Struggle and Village Power Structure*

1 Gough, 1962, p. 47.

### *18. East Thanjāvūr*

1 A. Béteille, 1974, pp. 164–7.
2 K. C. Alexander, 1976, pp. 12–13.

### *19. The Village*

1 Because banana leaves are used almost universally as plates to eat from, they are in great demand in towns.
2 In Tamiḷ, "Seiva" or "Saivite" is often used to mean "vegetarian." "Seiva Veḷḷāḷars" are Veḷḷāḷars who do not eat meat, fish, or eggs. The term is not properly speaking the name of a traditional subcaste. Kirippūr's Seiva Veḷḷāḷars had been nonvegetarians until the twentieth century, and perhaps were formerly Chōḷiya Veḷḷāḷars. They evidently adopted the term "Seiva" along with vegetarianism in an effort to raise their rank.

### *23. Conclusion*

1 For more extended discussions of the modes of production in Thanjāvūr and Kēraḷa before British rule and during and since the colonial period, see Gough, 1979 and 1980.
2 See Gough, 1980; Melotti, 1977; Ribeiro, 1968.
3 Marx, "The British Rule in India" (1853), quoted in Avineri, 1969, p. 94; Tokei, 1979, p. 23.
4 Marx, 1858, quoted in Hobsbawm, 1965, p. 71.
5 Marx, "The British Rule in India" (1853), quoted in Avineri, 1969, pp. 88–95.
6 Marx, 1858, quoted in Hobsbawm, 1965, p. 91.

7 See, e.g., C. P. V. Ayyar, 1916, pp. 80–97.
8 As is noted in Irfan Habib, 1963, and Perry Anderson, 1974, pp. 496–520. Ribeiro separates the Sassanian, Byzantine, and Islamic empires from the theocratic irrigation states and designates them "Despotic Salvationist Empires" (Ribeiro 1968, pp. 74–9).
9 Marx, *Capital*, Vol. 3 (1894), 1967, pp. 803–13.
10 Marx, *Capital*, Vol. 1 (1867), 1976, for example pp. 353–67, 850–2.
11 Marx, *Capital*, Vol. 1 (1867), 1976, pp. 1019–38.
12 Alavi, 1965, p. 34.
13 Wallerstein, 1974a and 1974b.
14 Kumbapeṭṭai lay on the border of Thanjāvūr and Pāpaṉāsam *tālūks*. Pāpaṉāsam had 24.4 percent Ādi Drāviḍas in 1951. In all the *tālūks*, Ādi Drāviḍas were more prevalent in the countryside than in the towns.
15 See, e.g., Gough, 1973, an article written in 1954.

# Glossary

*ādhīnam*: Hindū seminary, monastery
Āḍi: July–August
Ādi Drāviḍa: "Original Dravidian," the lowest castes of Paḷḷars and Paṟayars, otherwise known as Scheduled or Exterior Castes or as Untouchables
*aḍimai*: Slavery
*aḍimai āḷ* (pl. *āḷukaḷ*): slave
Agambaḍiyar: A caste of peasants, formerly indoor servants of Rājas
*agrahāram*: Brahman street
Aippasi: October–November
*āḷvār*: Vaishnavite saint
Ambalakkārar: low-ranking caste of Non-Brahman cultivators and inland fishermen
Ambaṭṭār: Caste of barbers and midwives
Āndi: Caste of ballad singers and village temple priests
Āṉi: June–July
*aṉṉādāna*: Offering of rice to a deity or a Brahman
*apishēka*: Libation on an idol
*appaḷam*: Thin fried wafer biscuit
Arjuṉaṉ: Hero of the *Mahābhārata* epic
*arudikkarai*: Communal landownership by a village caste community with indefinite distribution of shares among households
*aruḷ*: State of possession by a deity
*āshram*: Hermitage
Ashtasahāsram: Subcaste of Smārtha Brahmans
*ātmā*: Soul
Āvaṉi: August–September
Ayyaṉār: A village god
Ayyangār: Title used by Vaishnavite Brahman men
Ayyar, Iyer: Title used by Smārtha (Saivite) Brahman men
Bhaṭṭachār: Subcaste of Brahman priests in Vaishnavite temples
Brahacharaṇam: Subcaste of Smārtha Brahmans
*brahmadeya*: Grant of land to Brahmans
Brahman: The highest Hindū *varṇa* or major subdivision, traditionally priests and scholars

*chattram*: Choultry or charitable building for feeding, housing, or supplying drinking water to travelers
*chēri*: A hamlet of the Ādi Drāviḍa castes
Cheṭṭiar: Group of trading castes
Chittrai: April–May
Chōḷa, Cōḷa: A dynasty of the Tamiḷ country centered in Thanjāvūr, c. 250 B.C. to sixth century A.D. and ninth to thirteenth centuries
*chōḷam*: A kind of millet
*chōli*: Woman's blouse
Chōḷiya, Chōṛiya of the Chōḷa country: A subcaste of the Veḷḷāḷar caste
*dāyādi*: Patrilineal kinsman
Deepāvaḷi: Festival of lights in November
*dēvatai*: God
*dharma*: Duty, especially pertaining to membership of a caste
Drāviḍa Kazhakam or Kaṛakam: South Indian nationalist party
Drāviḍa Muṉṉētra Kazhakam: Tamiḷ nationalist party, a split from the Drāviḍa Kazhakam
*garuḍa chāyaṉam*: Eagle-shaped stone platform commemorating a Vedic sacrifice
Ganēsh, Ganapati, also called Piḷḷaiyar or Vināyakar: God of good luck, the eldest son of Siva and Parvati
*grāmam*: Village dominated by Brahman landlords
*grāma samudāyam*: Village common land
Hindū Mahāsabha: A right-wing, religiously oriented nationalist movement based in north India
Iḍaiyar: Caste of herders
*iṉam*: A prebendal estate
*jajmāni*: A Hindū term referring to village service rights and obligations
*jāti*: Caste or kind
*jōthi*: Male and female pair
Kaikkiḷar: Caste of weavers, also known as Sengunda Mudaliars
*kalam*: A dry measure, usually of paddy, amounting to half a bag, and in the case of paddy weighing about 63.69 lbs. Equals twelve marakkāḷs.
*kaḷam*: Threshing floor
*kaḷasam, kaḷavaḍi*: Harvest bonus of paddy paid to a laborer, usually five kalams per couple
Kāḷi: A village goddess; the consort of Siva in terrible form
Kaḷḷar: Caste of cultivators and formerly, of highwaymen and cattle thieves
Kalthacchar: Stonemason
Kāmakshi: Village goddess
Kamma Naidūs: Aristocratic caste of landowners and former warriors of Telugu origin
Kammāḷar: The Smith caste, including carpenters, braziers, blacksmiths, goldsmiths, and stonemasons

*kaṇakku piḷḷai, karṇam*: Village record keeper, accountant
*kāṇi*: Land measure of about 1.33 acres. Four māhs
*kāṇiyācchi*: Landownership or management by a caste community within a village; same as mirāsi
Kaṉṉaḍa: A language of south India
Kaṉṉar: Brass workers
Kāraikkātt: A subcaste of the Veḷḷāḷar caste
Karaiyar: Caste of coastal fishermen
*karaiyiḍu*: Communal landownership by a village caste community with periodic redistribution of shares among the households
*karma*: Act, action, in this or a previous birth; fate resulting from such actions
*karṇam*: Village accountant and record keeper
Kārthikai: November–December
*kaṭṭu aḍimai*: "Tied" or individual slavery
kāvalkkāraṉ: Watchman
*khādi*: Handwoven cloth
*kīlvāram*: The lower share or local owners' share of the produce of land
Koḍikkal: A subcaste of the Veḷḷāḷar caste
*kōḷam*: Circular pattern in rice powder outside the threshold of a Brahman house
Koltacchar: Blacksmith
Kōṉār: Title of the Iḍaiyar caste of herders
Koṇḍaikkaṭṭi: A subcaste of the Veḷḷāḷar caste
*kooliyāḷ*: Wage worker, coolie
*kooṭṭam*: Literally "crowd." A lineage among Brahmans; an assembly of men among Ādi Drāviḍas
Koṟavar: Gypsy caste
*kōṭṭu*: Bunch of paddy stalks
Krishṇa: The god of love, an incarnation of Vishnū
Kshattriya: The second of the Hindū *varṇas* or major subdivisions, traditionally rulers and warriors
*kuḍimarāmatt*: Corvée labor for public works
*kuḍir*: Grain bin made of earthenware hoops
*kuḍiyan* (pl. kuḍiyānavar): Tenant
*kūja*: Water vessel
*kulam*: Clan or lineage
*kuḷam*: Bathing pool or tank
*kumbu*: A kind of millet
*kungumam*: Red powder used as cosmetic or for other purposes on auspicious occasions
*kuṛi*: Land measure of about one three-hundredth of an acre
Kurukkal: A subcaste of Brahman priests in Saivite temples
*kuruṇi*: Dry measure; a marakkāḷ
*kuruvai*: Rice crop harvested in October
Kusavar: Caste of potters

*kuthakai*: A fixed-rent tenure
*kuṭṭai*: Tank or bathing pool
Kūtthāḍi: Caste of puppet players, village temple dancers, and prostitutes
Labbai: A caste of Muslims
Lakshmi: Consort of the deity Vishnū; goddess of wealth
*lathi*: Staff used by police to beat demonstrators or rioters
*lingam*: Phallic symbol; emblem of Lord Siva
Lok Sabha: House of the People, the Indian parliament
*maḍi*: Ritual purity
*māh*: One-third of an acre
Malayālam: Language of southwest India
*maṇḍakapaḍi*: Right or obligation to organize a temple ceremony
*mantra*: Sanskrit text or prayer
*māṉyam*: Plot of land granted tax free in return for services, usually within one village
Maraikkar: A caste of Muslims
Maṛaināḍ: Subcaste of Brahacharaṇam Smārtha Brahmans
*marakkāḷ*: Dry measure, usually of paddy, about four liters; one-twelfth of a *kalam*
Maratha: Person descended from immigrants or conquerors from Maharashtra
Maṟavar: A caste of cultivators
Mārgaṛi: December–January
Māsi: February–March
Māṭṭu Pongal: A festival for cattle in January
Mēḷakkār: Caste of temple musicians, dancers, and courtesans
*mēlvāram*: The "upper share" or king's share of the produce of lands; land revenue
*mirāsdār*: Landlord
*mirāsi*: Landownership; formerly communal control of village lands
*mōksa*: Release of the soul from the cycle of rebirths
Mudaliar: "First ones"; title used by men of the Toṇḍaimaṇḍalam Veḷḷālar and Kaikkiḷar castes
Mūppaṉār: A caste of cultivators
*mutt, maḍam*: Monastery or place of meditation
Nāḍār: Caste of toddy tappers
*naḍavu*: Transplanting of paddy seedlings into flooded fields
*nāḍu*: Country or province
Naidū: Male title in several Telugu castes
Nalla Yēr Kaṭṭravadu or Nallēr: First Ploughing ceremony
*naragam*: Hell
*nattam*: Tax-free residential land
nāṯṯangāl: Seed bed or nursery
*nāṭṭānmai*: Headman of a Non-Brahman street
Nāṭṭukkoṭṭai Cheṭṭiars: A caste of traders and bankers
Nāyak: Title of former feudatories of the Vijayanagar empire

Nāyakkār (pl. of Nāyak): Title of certain Telugu castes of warriors, farmers, and toddy tappers
*nāyanār*: Saivite saint
*nischayadāṭṭam*: Marriage-engagement ceremony
Oṭṭar: Caste of ditchdiggers, road makers, and builders
Paḍaiyācchi: Caste of cultivators
*paḍi, periya paḍi*: Dry measure, about two liters or half a marakkāḷ
*paḍukai*: The fertile bank of an irrigation channel
Paḷḷar: A Harijan or "Untouchable" caste of agricultural laborers in rice fields
Paḷḷi: Cultivating caste closely related to Paḍaiyācchis
Pallava: Tamiḷ dynasty of Kānchipuram that flourished in the sixth to ninth centuries
*paṇakkār*: A rich or "money" man
Panchama: The fifth or lowest major subdivision of Hindū society, in Thanjāvūr equivalent to the Scheduled or "Untouchable" castes.
*panchāyat*: Group of five elders traditionally selected to govern a Brahman village. In modern times, an administrative unit comprising one or more villages, organized for public works
*panchāyattār*: One of five elders of the Brahman caste traditionally selected to govern a village
Paṇḍāram: Caste of village temple priests
*pandārasanidhi*: The head of a monastery
*pangāḷi*: Patrilineal kinsman or co-parcener of property
*pangu*: Share, especially of village communal land
Panguni: March–April
*paṇṇaiyāḷ* (fem. *paṇṇaiyācchi*): Farm laborer
*pora-kuḍiyāṉavar*: "Outside" tenants or cultivating tenants
*paramātma*: The Supreme Being or Soul
Paṟayar: The lowest Harijan caste of agricultural workers, scavengers, and village drummers
Pariyāri: Barber
Pārppār: Brahmans
*paṭṭā*: A deed of lease
*pattakdār*: A revenue farmer in the 1770s and 1780s
*paṭṭakkāl*: Laborer's service tenure of a small strip of land
*paṭṭāmaṇiyayyar*: Village headman and collector of revenue
Paṭṭanavar: Caste of coastal fishermen
Patthar: Goldsmith
Paṭṭunoolkkār: Caste of silk weavers, originally from Gujarat
*pāyasam*: Gruel or milk pudding
*payirchelavukkārar*: Farmer, cultivator
Piḍāri: A village goddess
Piḷḷai: Title used by men of the Veḷḷāḷar and Agambaḍiyar castes, literally "child"
Piḷḷaiyar: Ganapati, the eldest son of Siva and Parvati

Pongal: Festival to the sun in January
Poṉṉēri: A subcaste of the Veḷḷāḷar caste
poojai or poosai: An offering to a deity
Poosāri: Village temple priest
*pōraḍi*: "Beating Straw"; second threshing with bullocks
Poṟayar: Caste of cultivators closely related to Paḍaiyācchis
*pothu manithaṉ*: Public man, village servant
*pothu paṇam*: Village common fund
*prasādham*: Materials offered to a deity and afterwards distributed to the worshippers
*prāyaschittam*: Expiation
Pūndamalli: A subcaste of the Veḷḷāḷar caste
*purambōke*: Land owned by the government
*purāṇam*: A Sanskrit epic
Purattāsi: September–October
*purōhit*: Household priest for Non-Brahmans
*purushaṉ*: Man, husband
Rādha: Consort of the deity Krishṇa
*ragi*: A kind of millet
Rāma: Hero of the Sanskrit epic *Rāmayana* and an incarnation of Vishnū
Rāmānuja: Twelfth-century exponent of the Vishishta Advaita philosophy
*ryot*: An individual landowner
*ryotwāri*: Individual landownership
*sambā*: Rice crop harvested in February–March
*sāmbrāni*: Incense
*sammādi*: Attainment of union with the divine spirit
*sanchayaṉam*: Funeral ceremony for disposal of bones and ashes
Sankara, Sankarāchārya: Eighth-century expounder of Advaita philosophy
*sannyāsi*: Ascetic or holy man
*sāstri*: Brahman household priest for other Brahmans
*satyāgraha*: Nonviolent civil disobedience
Sembadavar: Caste of coastal fishermen
Sengundar or Sengunda Mudaliar: A caste of weavers, also called Kaikkiḷar
Shāstras: Sacred, post-Vēdic books of the Hindūs.
*shētti*: Section of a street; an annex to a village
Sīlpi: Caste of art-metal workers making idols
*siṉṉa paḍi*: "Small paḍi"; about one liter; a quarter of a marakkāḷ
Siva: The great deity of Saivite Hindūs, often spoken of as both creator and destroyer
Soorapadmaṉ: Giant or demon killed by Lord Subramania
Srī Krishṇa Jayanti: festival to celebrate the birthday of Lord Krishṇa
Sūdra: The fourth major subdivision of Hindū society, traditionally of manual workers
*swadēsamitraṉ*: Patriot

*swāmi*: Deity, Brahman
*swāmiyāḷi*: Oracle of a deity
*swargam*: Heaven
Tacchar: Carpenter, a branch of a Kammālar caste
*tahsildār*: Administrative head of a *tālūk*
*talayāri*: Village watchman and policeman appointed by the government to assist the village headman
*tāli*: Marriage pendant
*tālūk*: Administrative subdivision of a district
Tamiḷ, Tamiṛ: Language of southeast India
*tampaṭṭam*: A drum beaten by Paṟayars at funerals
*tandōrā*: A skin drum beaten by the village watchman
*taṉṉīr pandal*: Shed for distributing water to passersby
*teeṭṭam*: Ritual pollution
Tekkaṭṭi Paḷḷar: Southern Paḷḷars, a subcaste of Paḷḷars
Telugu: A language of south India
Tengalai: "Southerners," a subcaste of Vaishnavite Brahmans
Thai: January–February
Tombar: Caste of basket weavers
Toṇḍaimaṇḍalam Veḷḷāḷar: A subcaste of Veḷḷāḷars, originally from the area of Kānchipuram
*tōpe*: Garden
*tōṛiḷāḷikaḷ*: Servants or workers
*uḷ-kuthakai*: "Inside" tenure; an intermediary tenure of land
*upanayaṉam*: Initiation ceremony of Brahman boys
*ūr*: Village dominated by Non-Brahmans
Uriyēḍi: Festival of Lord Krishṇa
Uttira Kāṭṭēri: A bloodthirsty village goddess
Vaḍakalai: "Northerners"; a subcaste of Vaishnavite Brahmans
Vaḍama: Subcaste of Smārtha Brahmans
*vaguppu*: Dispersed clan of the Kaḷḷar caste
Vaigāsi: May–June
Vaishya: The third major subdivision (*varṇa*) of Hindū society, traditionally traders, artisans, and cultivators
Valaiyar: Caste of inland fishermen
vāṉaprasaṉam: Middle age; the third stage of adult life
Vāṇiyar: Caste of oilmongers
Vaṉṉār: Caste of laundryworkers
Vaṉṉiyar: A caste of cultivators
*varagu*: A kind of millet
*vāram*: A sharecropping tenure
*varāmdār*: Sharecropper
*varṇa*: Literally "color"; the name of the four major subdivisions of caste-Hindū society

Varusha Pirappu: New Year's Day
Vātthimāl: A subcaste of Smārtha Brahmans
Vēdas: The four most sacred books of the Brahmans
*vēlaikkāraṉ*: A Non-Brahman workman
*vēli*: Land measure of five *kanis* or six-and-two-thirds acres
*veḷiyāṭṭam*: Sport, play
Veḷḷāḷar: A high-ranking Non-Brahman caste, traditionally of landlords and cultivators
Veḷḷikaṉṉar: Caste of silversmiths
*veṭṭi*: A minor government servant appointed to assist the village headman
*veṭṭiyaṉ*: Village scavenger and tender of cremation grounds, of the Paṟayar caste
*vigraham*: Metal statue of a deity
Vijayanagar: A city and empire based in the Telugu-speaking region of south India, fourteenth to seventeenth centuries
Vishishta Advaitam: The Brahmanical philosophy that teaches that the soul is an appendage or branch of the Supreme Being
Vishnū: The supreme deity of Vaishnavite Hindus, often described as the Preserver
Vināyakar: Ganapati, the eldest son of Siva and Parvati
*virunthukooli*: Payment of laborers with a share of the harvest
*yāgam*: Vedic sacrifice
*zamindāri*: A type of landed estate

# Bibliography

### *Government Records*


*Fourth Report of the Committee of Secrecy*. Proceedings of the Board of Revenue of the East India Company, 1782. (India Office Library).

*Letter of Colonel Fullerton to the Court of Directors, January 7, 1785*. Proceedings of the Board of Revenue of the East India Company, 1785. (India Office Library).

*Report of Mr. Harris, Collector of Tanjore, June 23, 1800*. Proceedings of the Board of Revenue of the East India Company, 1800. (India Office Library).

*Report of C. M. Lushington, Collector of Trichinopoly, July 1, 1819*. Proceedings of the Board of Revenue of the East India Company, 1819. (India Office Library).

*Seaborne Trade and Navigation of the Madras Presidency*, Customs House, Madras, annual volumes, 1840 to 1930. (India Office Library).

*The Tanjore Settlement Register (Paimash Record) of 1827*, recorded in Tamiḻ in 1828. (Public Records Office, Thanjāvūr).

*The Tanjore Settlement Register of 1897*. Madras: Government Press, 1898. (Tamiḻ Nāḍu Archives, Madras).


### *Official Publications*

**1** Census of India


*Census of India, 1881. Madras*. Madras, 1882–3. Madras: Government Press, 1884.

*Census of India, 1891. Madras*. Volumes 13 to 15. Madras: Government Press, 1893.

*Census of India, 1901. Madras*. Volumes 25 to 26. Madras: Government Press, 1902.

*Census of India, 1911. Madras*. Volume 12. Madras: Government Press, 1912.

*Census of India, 1921. Madras*. Volume 13. Madras: Government Press, 1922.

*Census of India, 1931. Madras*. Volume 14. Madras: Government Press, 1933.

*Census of India, 1951. Madras and Coorg*. Volume 3. Madras: Government Press, 1953.

*Census of India, 1961. Madras*. Volume 9. Madras: Government Press, 1968.

*Census of India, 1961. District Census Handbooks. Tanjore*. Madras: Government Press, 1965.

*Census of India, 1971. Series 19. Tamiḻ Nāḍu*. Madras: Government Press, 1974.

*Census of India, 1971. District Census Handbooks. Thanjavur*. Volumes 1 and 2. Madras: Government Press, 1972.


**2** Madras District Manuals and Gazetteers


Baliga, B. S. *The Tanjore District Handbook*. Madras: Government Press, 1957.

Hemingway, F. R. *Madras District Gazetteers. Tanjore*. Part 1. Madras, 1906. Part 2. Madras: Government Press, 1915.

Krishnaswami Ayyar, K. N. *Statistical Appendix and Supplement to Tanjore Gazetteer of 1906*. Madras: Government Press, 1933.

Row, T. V. *A Manual of the District of Tanjore in the Madras Presidency*. Madras: Government Press, 1883.

3 Miscellaneous Government Publications

Bayley, W. H. and Hudleston, W., eds. *Papers in Mirasi Right. Selected from the Records of the Government and Published by Permission*. Madras, 1862. India Office Library.

Dutt, R. C. *The Economic History of India, Volume I. Under Early British Rule, 1757–1837*. Phalguna, 1884. Reprinted by the Ministry of Information and Broadcasting, Government of India. Delhi, 1963.

Krishnaswamy, S. Y. *Rural Problems in Madras*. Madras: Government Press, 1947.

*The Madras Estates (Abolition and Conversion into Ryotwari) Act, 1948*. Madras: Government Press, 1948.

*Madras in Maps and Pictures*. Director of Information and Publicity. Madras: Government Press, 1955.

*Madras in Maps and Pictures. (Rev.)*. Madras: Director of Information and Publicity. Government of Madras, 1959.

Natarajan, B. *Food and Agriculture in Madras State*. Madras: Government Press, 1953.

*Report of the Committee Appointed by the Secretary of State for India on the Question of the Financial Relations Between the Central and Provincial Governments of India*. Parliamentary Papers, 1920, Volume 14. (India Office Library.)

*Report of the Tanjore Commissioners of 1799*. Madras: Government Press, 1905. (Tamiḷ Nāḍu Archives, Madras.)

*Report on the Settlement of the Land Revenue of the Provinces under the Madras Presidency for Fasly 1267 (1857–58)*. Madras: Fort St. George Gazette Press, 1860. (India Office Library).

Slater, G. *Some South Indian Villages*. Madras: Government Press, 1918.

*Statistical Handbook of Tamil Nadu, 1972*. Madras: Department of Statistics, Government of Tamiḷ Nāḍu, 1973.

*The Tanjore Tenants' and Pannaiyals' Protection Act, 1952*. Act XIV of 1952. Madras: Government Press, 1952.

*Techno-Economic Survey of Madras. Economic Report. Report of the National Council of Applied Economic Research*. Madras: Department of Industries, Labour and Cooperation, Government of Madras, 1961.

### *Newspapers*

*The Hindū*, Madras, December 1 to 13, 1952

### *Books and Articles*

Alavi, H. "India and the Colonial Mode of Production." *Economic and Political Weekly* 10: (1975): 33–35.

Alexander, K. C. "Some Characteristics of the Agrarian Structure of Tamiḷ Nāḍu." *Economic and Political Weekly* 10: (1975a): 16.

*Agrarian Tension in Thanjavur*. Hyderabad: National Institute of Community Development, 1975b.

Amin, S. *Accumulation on a World Scale*. Vol. 1. New York: Monthly Review Press, 1974.

*Unequal Development*. New York: Monthly Review Press, 1976.

Anstey, V. *The Economic Development of India*. London: Longmans, 1949.

Arnold, D. *The Congress in Tamilnad. Nationalist Politics in South India, 1919–1937*. Columbia, Mo.: South Asia Books, 1977.

Appadorai, A. *Economic Conditions in Southern India, 1000–1500 A.D.* 2 Vols. Madras: University of Madras, 1936.

Baker, C. J. *The Politics of South India, 1920–1927*. Cambridge University Press, 1976.

Baliga, B. S. *Studies in Madras Administration*. 2 vols. Madras: Government of Madras, 1960.

Banaji, J. "India and the Colonial Mode of Production: Comment." *Economic and Political Weekly* 10: (1975): 49.

"Capitalist Domination and the Small Peasantry. Deccan Districts in the Late Nineteenth Century." *Economic and Political Weekly* 12: (1977): 33–4.

Bandopadhyay, A. "The Pattern of Protest and Reaction in Rural Tamiḻ Nāḍu: the Case of the Mirasdars in the Early Nineteenth Century." Unpublished article, Calcutta University, 1976.

Barratt-Brown, M. *After Imperialism*. London: Heinemann, 1970.

Béteille, A. *Caste, Class and Power. Changing Patterns of Stratification in a Tanjore Village*. Berkeley: University of California Press, 1965.

*Studies in Agrarian Social Structure*. Oxford University Press, 1974.

The Bharatiya Itihasa Samhiti. *History and Culture of the Indian People. Volume I. The Vedic Age*. London: Allen and Unwin, 1951.

Chandidas, R., Morehouse, W., Clark, L., and Fontera, R. *India Votes. A Source Book on the Indian Elections*. New York: Humanities Press, 1968.

*The Communist Party in Thanjāvūr*. Tamiḻ pamphlet published by the Communist Party of India (Marxist), Thanjāvūr, 1974.

Crook, I. and D. *Ten Mile Inn. Mass Movement in a Chinese Village*. New York: Pantheon, 1979.

Dubois, J. A. *Hindu Manners, Customs and Ceremonies*. 3rd ed. Translated from the author's later French manuscript and edited with notes, corrections, and biography by H. K. Beauchamp. Third edition. Oxford: Clarendon Press, 1947.

Dumont, L. *Homo Hierarchicus. The Caste System and its Implications*. Translated by Mark Sainsbury. London: Weidenfeld and Nicolson, 1970.

Frank, A. G. *Capitalism and Underdevelopment in Latin America*. New York: Monthly Review Press, 1967.

Garaudy, R., ed. *Sur le Mode de Production Asiatique*. Paris: Maspero, 1969.

Ghurye, G. S. *Caste, Class and Occupation*. Bombay: 1961.

Gough, K. "The Social Structure of a Tanjore Village." In *India's Villages*, ed. M. N. Srinivas. Calcutta: West Bengal Government Press, 1955a.

"The Social Structure of a Tanjore Village." In *Village India*, ed. M. Marriot, pp. 36–52. Chicago: University of Chicago Press, 1955b.

"Caste in a Tanjore Village." In *Aspects of Caste in South India, Ceylon, and North-West Pakistan*, ed. E. R. Leach, pp. 11–60. Cambridge Papers in Social Anthropology, No. 2. Cambridge University Press, 1962.

"Peasant Resistance and Revolt in South India." *Pacific Affairs* 41, (1968–9): 526–44. *Bulletin of Concerned Asian Scholars*, 8, (July–September 1976): 2–18.

"Class and Agrarian Change: Some Comments on Peasant Resistance and Revolution in India." *Pacific Affairs* 42: (1969): 363–8.

"Harijans in Thanjāvūr." In *Imperialism and Revolution in South Asia*, ed. K. Gough and H. Sharma, pp. 222–45. New York: Monthly Review Press, 1973.

"Colonial Economics in Southeast India." *Economic and Political Weekly* 12: (1977): 541–54.

"Agrarian Relations in Southeast India, 1950–76." *Review* 2 (1978): 25–53.

"Dravidian Kinship and Modes of Production." Iravati Karve Memorial Lecture, Tenth International Congress of Anthropological and Ethnological Sciences, in *Contributions to Indian Sociology (N.S.)* 13 (October 1979): 266–91.

"Modes of Production in Southern India." *Economic and Political Weekly* 15, Special Issue. (1980): 337–64.

Gupta, K. M. *The Land System of South India Between c. 800 and 1200 A.D.* Lahore: Punjab Sanskrit Book Depot, 1933. Earlier version available as a Ph.D. thesis, School of Oriental and African Studies, London, 1926.

Hardgrave, R. L. *The Dravidian Movement*. Bombay: Popular Prakashan, 1965.

Harrison, S. *India: the Most Dangerous Decades*. Princeton: Princeton University Press, 1960.

Hickey, W. *The Tanjore Mahratta Principality in Southern India*. Madras: 1874.

Hjejle, B. "Slavery and Agricultural Bondage in South India in the Nineteenth Century." *The Scandinavian Economic History Review* 15 (1967): 71–126.

Hutton, J. H. *Caste in India*. Cambridge University Press, 1946.

Kosambi, D. D. *Ancient India*. New York: Routledge, 1965.

Krader, L. *The Asiatic Mode of Production*. Assen: Van Gorcum, 1975.

Krishnaswamy, A. *The Tamil Country Under Vijayanagar*. Annamalai-nagar: Annamalai University, 1964.

Kumar, D. *Land and Caste in South India*. Cambridge University Press, 1965.

Lenin, V. I. "A Great Beginning." In *Collected Works* 29, p. 420. Moscow: Progress Publishers, 1965.

Mahalingam, T. V. *Economic Life in the Vijayanagar Empire*. Madras: University of Madras, 1952.

*Administration and Social Life Under Vijayanagar*. Madras: University of Madras, 1969.

Mandelbaum, D. *Society in India*. 2 vols. Berkeley: University of California Press, 1972.

Marx, K. *Precapitalist Economic Formations (1858)*. Translated by J. Cohen, with an introduction by E. Hobsbawm. New York: International Publishers, 1965.

Preface to "A Contribution to the Critique of Political Economy" (1859). In *Marx-Engels Selected Works*. Vol. 1. Moscow: Foreign Languages Publishing House, 1958.

*The Ethnological Notebooks (1880–1882)*. Transcribed and edited, with an introduction by L. Krader. Assen: Van Gorcum, 1974.

*Capital*. Vol. 1 (1867). New York: Penguin Books, 1978. Volumes 2 and 3 (1885 and 1894), edited by F. Engels. New York: International Publishers, 1967.

Mao Ze-dong (Mao Tse-tung). "How to Analyse the Classes in the Rural Areas" (1933). In *Selected Works*. Vol. 1. New York: International Publishers, 1954.

"The Chinese Revolution and the Chinese Communist Party" (1939). In *Selected Works*. Vol. 3. New York: International Publishers, 1954.

Mayer, A. C. *Caste and Kinship in Central India*. 4th ed. Berkeley: University of California Press, 1970.
McEachern, D. "The Mode of Production in India." *Journal of Contemporary Asia* 6 (1976).
Melotti, U. *Marx and the Third World*. Translated by Pat Ransford. London: Macmillan, 1977.
Mencher, Joan P. *Agriculture and Social Structure in Tamiḻ Nāḍu*. New Delhi: Allied Publishers Private, 1978.
Muehl, J. F. *Interview with India*. New York: John Day, 1960.
Mukherjee, R. *The Rise and Fall of the East India Company*. Berlin: Monthly Review Press, 1958. 2nd ed., New York: 1974.
Namboodiripad, E. M. S. *Kerala Yesterday, Today and Tomorrow*. Calcutta: National Book Agency, 1967.
Nilakanta Sastri, K. A. *Studies in Çōḻa History and Administration*. Madras: University of Madras, 1932.
*A History of South India from Prehistoric Times Until the Fall of Vijayanagar*. Oxford University Press, 1955a.
*The Çōḻas*. 2nd ed. Madras: University of Madras, 1955b.
Omvedt, Ġ. "India and the Colonial Mode of Production: Comment." *Economic and Political Weekly* 12 (1975): 53.
Omvedt, G. and Patankar, B. "The Bourgeois State in Post-Colonial Social Formations." *Economic and Political Weekly* 12 (1977).
Overstreet, G. D., and Windmiller, M. *Communism in India*. Berkeley: University of California Press, 1959.
Panikkar, K. M. *A History of Kerala, 1498–1801*. Annamalai-nagar: Annamalai University, 1960.
Pope, G. U. *Handbook of the Ordinary Dialect of the Tamil Language*. 7th ed. Oxford University Press, 1926.
Raghavaiyangar, R. S. *Memorandum on the Progress of the Madras Presidency Under the Last Forty Years of British Administration*. Madras: Government Press, 1892.
Rajayyan, K. *A History of British Diplomacy in Tanjore*. Madras: University of Madras, 1969.
"Mohammad Ali's Conquest of Tanjore and After." *Journal of the Saraswathi Mahal Library*, Thanjāvūr, 18 (1965).
Rajukumar, M. D. "Struggles for Rights During Later Chola Period." Translated from Tamiḻ by N. Ram. *Social Scientist* 18–19 (1974): 29–36.
Raju, A. S. *Economic Conditions in the Madras Presidency, 1800–1850*. Madras: Government Press, 1941.
Ram, M. *Hindi Against India: the Meaning of the DMK*. New Delhi: Rachna Prakashan, 1968.
*Indian Communism: Split Within a Split*. Delhi: Vikas Publications, 1969.
Ribeiro, D. *The Civilizational Process*. Translated, with an introduction by Betty Meggers. New York: Harper Torchbooks, 1968.
Rao, K. Venkoba. *Tamiḻ Nāḍu Land Reform Acts*. Madras: Madras Law Journal Office, 1975.
Rudra, A. "India and the Colonial Mode of Production: Comment." *Economic and Political Weekly* 10 (1975).

"Class Relations in Indian Agriculture." *Economic and Political Weekly* 13 (1978).
Sawer, M. *Marxism and the Question of the Asiatic Mode of Production.* The Hague: Martinus Nijhoff, 1977.
Shah, S. A. "Class and Agrarian Change: Some Comments on Peasant Resistance and Revolution in India." *Pacific Affairs* 42 (1969): 360–3.
Siverstsen, D. *When Caste Barriers Fall.* London and Stockholm: Allen and Unwin, 1963.
Srinivas, M. N. *Caste in Modern India and Other Essays.* New York: Asia Publishing House, 1962.
*Social Change in Modern India.* Berkeley: University of California Press, 1966.
Stein, B. "Integration of the Agrarian System of South India." In *Land Control and Structure in Indian History*, ed. R. E. Frykenberg, pp. 175–216: Madison: University of Wisconsin Press, 1969.
"The State and the Agrarian Order in Medieval South India: A Historiographical Critique. In *Essays on South India*, Hawaii: University of Hawaii, 1975.
Subbayya Mudaliar, V. T. *South Indian Field Crops.* Madras: Central Art Press, 1960.
Subramanian, K. R. *The Maratha Rajas of Tanjore.* Published by the author, 60, T. S. V. Koil Street, Mylapore, Madras: 1928.
Thomas, P. J., and Ramakrishnan, K. C. *Some South Indian Villages: A Resurvey.* Madras: University of Madras, 1940.
Tinker, H. *A New System of Slavery.* Oxford University Press, 1974.
Tökei, F. *Essays on the Asiatic Mode of Production.* Budapest: Akademiai Kiadu, 1979.
Wallerstein, I. "The Rise and Future Demise of the World Capitalist System: Concepts for Comparative Analysis." *Comparative Studies in Society and History* 16 (1974a): 387–415.
*The Modern World System. Capitalist Agriculture and the Origins of the European World Economy in the Sixteenth Century.* New York: Academic Press, 1974b.
Washbrook, D. A. *The Emergence of Provincial Politics. The Madras Presidency, 1870–1920.* Cambridge University Press, 1976.
Yalman, N. *Under the Bo Tree. Studies in Caste, Kinship and Marriage in Interior of Ceylon.* Berkeley: University of California Press, 1967.
Zacharias, C. W. B. *Madras Agriculture.* Madras University Economics Series, No. 6. Madras: 1950.

# Index

Ādi Drāviḍas, 19–20, 32–3; agricultural labor among, 131, 271; agricultural work differentiated from Non-Brahmans', 273, 276; alcohol consumption among, 197; behavioral characteristics of, 173; caste sanctions among, 317; characteristic customs of, 299; Communist movement among, 148, 396–406; Congress government actions on behalf of (as Harijans), 393; and Congress Party members, 394; disputes among, 314–17, 318–19, 404–5; distance pollution among, 294–5; Drāviḍa Kazhakam members' attitudes toward (as Harijans), 393; education among, 285, 290–1, 365; exclusion from high-caste streets, 216, 294–5; funeral customs of, 165; headmen among, 315–16; historical origins of, 146; labor migration among, 131, 193, 360–1; meat eating among, 13, 32, 230; percentages of (as Scheduled Castes), correlated with ecological and social variables, 68–94, 104, 414; political beliefs of, 334–5; 403–4; punishment of by Brahman landlords, 320–2, 327–8; segregation in ghettos of, 163–4; slavery among, in Chōḷa period, 109–10; under East India Company, 126, 174, 180–1, 412; in Nāyak and Maratha periods, 115–16; street assemblies of, 314–17, 397–8, 400–5; tenant farming among, 203; village deities among, 182, 314; village police among, 154–5; voting among, 141, 334, 394–5; women's position among, 316; women's work among, 46; *see also* Paḷḷars, Paṟayars
Ādi flood, 218, 225–6, 230
*aḍimai, see* slavery
administration, 7, 138
adoption, 209
advaita philosophy, 27
Agambaḍiyars, 177; becoming Veḷḷāḷars, 29; geographical distribution of, 18; occupations of, 30, 45, 184, 291; *porakuḍis* among, 155; ranked regional subcastes among, 22; tenants buying royal lands, 154
*agrahāram*, 28, 155–6, 159, 172, 249, 316, 317; Ādi Drāviḍas forbidden to enter, 216; common land of, 179–80, 207; destroyed by Haidar Āli, 174; disputes within, 220, 303–10; in 1827, 188–9; Non-Brahmans forbidden to wear long clothes and shoes in, 169; temples attached to, 159–60, 178
agricultural laborers, 46, 271–85, 379–83, 396–406, 412, 414; and Communist movement, 141, 147–8, 396–406, 414; incomes of, 132–3, 193–4, 204, 274–5, 276–82, 380–3; increase of during British rule, 132; percentages of, correlated with ecological and social variables, 36, 68–84, 97–8; production relations among, 50–5, 194–5, 271–85, 412; strikes among, 195, 396–8
Alavi, Hamza, 135, 136, 137, 413
Alexander, K. C., 347
Ambalakkārars, 31, 51, 161, 292
Ambaṭṭars, *see* barbers
Amin, Samir, 105, 113, 136
Āndis, 32, 162, 181, 292; *see also*

CAMBRIDGE STUDIES IN SOCIAL ANTHROPOLOGY
*General Editor:* Jack Goody

1 The Political Organisation of Unyamwezi R. G. ABRAHAMS
2 Buddhism and the Spirit Cults in North-East Thailand* S. J. TAMBIAH
3 Kalahari Village Politics: An African Democracy ADAM KUPER
4 The Rope of Moka: Big-Men and Ceremonial Exchange in Mount Hagen, New Guinea* ANDREW STRATHERN
5 The Majangir: Ecology and Society of a Southwest Ethiopian People JACK STAUDER
6 Buddhist Monk, Buddhist Layman: A Study of Urban Monastic Organisation in Central Thailand JANE BUNNAG
7 Contexts of Kinship: An Essay in the Family Sociology of the Gonja of Northern Ghana ESTHER N. GOODY
8 Marriage among a Matrilineal Elite: A Family Study of Ghanaian Senior Civil Servants CHRISTINE OPPONG
9 Elite Politics in Rural India: Political Stratification and Political Alliances in Western Maharashtra ANTHONY T. CARTER
10 Women and Property in Morocco: Their Changing Relation to the Process of Social Stratification in the Middle Atlas VANESSA MAHER
11 Rethinking Symbolism* DAN SPERBER, *Translated by Alice L. Morton*
12 Resources and Population: A Study of the Gurungs of Nepal ALAN MACFARLANE
13 Mediterranean Family Structures *Edited by* J. G. PERISTIANY
14 Spirits of Protest: Spirit-Mediums and the Articulation of Consensus among the Zezuru of Southern Rhodesia (Zimbabwe) PETER FRY
15 World Conqueror and World Renouncer: A Study of Buddhism and Polity in Thailand against a Historical Background* S. J. TAMBIAH
16 Outline of a Theory of Practice* PIERRE BOURDIEU, *Translated by Richard Nice*
17 Production and Reproduction: A Comparative Study of the Domestic Domain* JACK GOODY
18 Perspectives in Marxist Anthropology* MAURICE GODELIER, *Translated by Robert Brain*
19 The Fate of Shechem, or the Politics of Sex: Essays in the Anthropology of the Mediterranean JULIAN PITT-RIVERS
20 People of the Zongo: The Transformation of Ethnic Identities in Ghana ENID SCHILDKROUT
21 Casting out Anger: Religion among the Taita of Kenya GRACE HARRIS
22 Rituals of the Kandyan State H. L. SENEVIRATNE
23 Australian Kin Classification HAROLD W. SCHEFFLER
24 The Palm and the Pleiades: Initiation and Cosmology in Northwest Amazonia STEPHEN HUGH-JONES
25 Nomads of South Siberia: The Pastoral Economies of Tuva S. I. VAINSHTEIN

26 From the Milk River: Spatial and Temporal Processes in Northwest Amazonia CHRISTINE HUGH-JONES
27 Day of Shining Red: An Essay on Understanding Ritual GILBERT LEWIS
28 Hunters, Pastoralists and Ranchers: Reindeer Economies and their Transformations TIM INGOLD
29 The Wood-carvers of Hong Kong: Craft Production in the World Capitalist Periphery EUGENE COOPER
30 Minangkabau Social Formations: Indonesian Peasants and the World Economy JOEL S. KAHN
31 Patrons and Partisans: A Study of Two Southern Italian *Comuni* CAROLINE WHITE
32 Moslem Society ERNEST GELLNER
33 Why Marry Her? Society and Symbolic Structures LUC DE HEUSCH
34 Chinese Ritual and Politics EMILY MARTIN AHERN
35 Parenthood and Social Reproduction: Fostering and Occupational Roles in West Africa ESTHER N. GOODY
36 Dravidian Kinship THOMAS R. TRAUTMANN
37 The Anthropological Circle MARC AUGE, *Translated by Martin Thom*
38 Rural Society in Southeast India KATHLEEN GOUGH

---

*Published also as a paperback